NOMENCLATURE FOR WAVELENGTH

UNIT	ABBREVIATION	EQUIVALENT
metre	m	$10^0 m$
centimetre	cm	$10^{-2} m$
millimetre	mm	$10^{-3} m$
micrometre (micron)	μm	$10^{-6} m$
nanometre	nm	$10^{-9} m$
angstrom	Å	$10^{-10} m$

NOMENCLATURE FOR FREQUENCY

UNIT	ABBREVIATION	EQUIVALENT
hertz	Hz	1 cycle per sec
kilohertz	kHz	10^3 cycles per sec
megahertz	MHz	10^6 cycles per sec
gigahertz	GHz	10^9 cycles per sec

INTERPRETATION OF AERIAL PHOTOGRAPHS

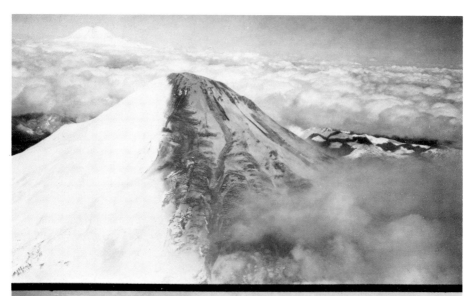

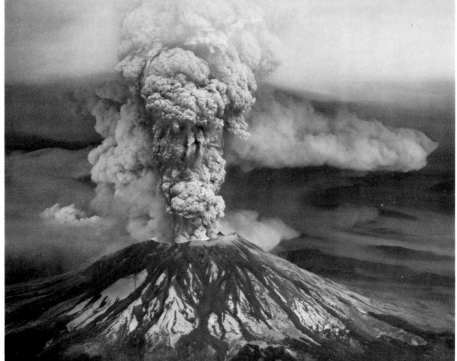

INTERPRETATION OF AERIAL PHOTOGRAPHS

Fourth Edition

Thomas Eugene Avery
Graydon Lennis Berlin

Burgess Publishing Company
Minneapolis, Minnesota

Development editor: Anne E. Heller
Assistant development editor: Charlene J. Brown
Copy editor: Greg Breining
Art coordinators: Judy Vicars, Melinda Radtke
Cover design: Editing, Design & Production, Inc.

Cover photograph: High-altitude infrared color photograph of San Francisco and vicinity at a scale of about 1:120,000. Courtesy EROS Data Center, U.S. Geological Survey.

Frontispiece: Top—Mount Saint Helens, Washington, 30 March 1980, looking north-northeast. Mount Rainier in distance. Distribution of dark ash resulted from wind control of plume drift. Left portion of cone is free of ash; right portion is largely covered. Snowstorms later covered these ash layers, which in turn were covered by new ash. Bottom—Mount Saint Helens on 18 May 1980. Catastrophic eruption began at 0832 PDT. The photograph was taken at approximately noon toward the northeast. The debris avalanche, explosive eruption, and associated mudflows and floods caused 63 deaths and billions of dollars of damage. Courtesy EROS Data Center, U.S. Geological Survey.

Copyright © 1985, 1977, 1968, 1962 by Thomas Eugene Avery and
   Graydon Lennis Berlin
Printed in the United States of America

Library of Congress Cataloging in Publication Data

Avery, Thomas Eugene.
   Interpretation of aerial photographs.

   Half t.p.: Interpretation of aerial photography.
   Includes bibliographies and index.
   1. Photographic interpretation. 2. Photography,
Aerial. I. Berlin, Graydon Lennis, 1943–
II. Title. III. Title: Interpretation of aerial
photography.
TR810.A9 1985   778.3′5   84-23249
ISBN 0-8087-0096-0

Burgess Publishing Company
7108 Ohms Lane
Minneapolis, MN 55435

J I H G F E D C B A

Contents

■ Preface

This book is concerned with remote sensing,[1] that is, with the detection, identification, and analysis of objects or features through the use of imaging devices (sensors) located at positions remote from the subjects of investigation. Remote sensing may be regarded as reconnaissance from a distance, and that distance may range from a few metres to thousands of kilometres. The sensors record electromagnetic radiation (EMR) that is reflected or emitted from these objects or features. The visible, infrared, and microwave regions of the electromagnetic spectrum have received primary attention in remote sensing. Particular emphasis is on the branch of remote sensing that is concerned with the acquisition and interpretation of aerial photographs obtained from the visible spectrum.

The fourth edition has been prepared with a coauthor—Graydon Lennis Berlin. It follows the same organizational structure as the previous edition. Emphasis is still on aerial photographic interpretation, but sections dealing with other remote sensors have been revised and updated. This edition also includes a new set of color plates, a number of new black-and-white illustrations, and an updated glossary.

Major changes have been made in Chapter 7, Nonphotographic Imaging Systems, and Chapter 8, Geographic Information Systems and Land-Use–Land-Cover Mapping. Chapter 15, Digital Image Processing, represents entirely new material that replaces the former chapter on military applications. Chapters 7 and 15 could compose the foundation for a second, more advanced course in remote sensing. All three of the above chapters provide the text with an added emphasis on geographic and geologic applications.

For many years, cameras, films, and photogrammetric equipment have been calibrated in metric units. Therefore, wherever feasible, the International System of Units (SI) is used for numerical examples in this book. (In accordance with SI practice, the American word *meter* is spelled *metre*). In some instances, tabular material is presented in both metric and English units; conversion tables are included on the inside back cover.

---

1. The mention of commercial companies and equipment manufacturers in this book does not imply any endorsement of those particular companies or their products; other suitable brands may be available.

With the International System of Units, there are seven base units and two supplementary units that encompass all measurement problems; all other SI units are *derived* from these fundamental units. For example, area is measured in square metres (or square kilometres), vehicle speeds in kilometres per hour, and density in kilograms per cubic metre.

Each metric unit is related to another by multiples or submultiples of 10. For instance, there are 10 millimetres (mm) in 1 centimetre (cm), 100 centimetres in 1 metre (m), and 1,000 metres in 1 kilometre (km). Another advantage of SI units is that multiples and submultiples of various quantities are *named* according to a system of numerical prefixes. Thus a *milli*metre is 1/1,000 of a metre, while a *kilo*metre is equal to 1,000 metres. The more common prefixes are listed in the following table.

Common Metric Prefixes		
Prefix	Symbol	Meaning
tera-	T	one trillion times
giga-	G	one billion times
mega-	M	one million times
kilo-	k	one thousand times
hecto-	h	one hundred times
deka-	da	ten times
deci-	d	one tenth of
centi-	c	one hundredth of
milli-	m	one thousandth of
micro-	μ	one millionth of
nano-	n	one billionth of
pico-	p	one trillionth of

As in the previous editions, many stereopairs have been purposely re-oriented (e.g., with south at the top of the page) to make shadows fall toward the observer and thereby aid stereovision.

Our objective has been to provide an interesting, readable introduction to photographic interpretation and remote sensing for all students, irrespective of their academic department or major field of study. Therefore, we hope that the text continues to be useful to geographers, geologists, foresters, range managers, civil engineers, archeologists, and others who have need for an elementary guide to remote sensing.

We wish to thank the following individuals for their technical contributions to the preparation of this edition:

Piet van Asch and Don Trask, New Zealand Aerial Mapping, Ltd.
Jessie K. Bixler, Goodyear Aerospace Corporation
Pat S. Chavez, Jr., David D. Greenlee, Charles M. Trautwein, and Richard E. Witmer, U.S. Geological Survey
George England, Daedalus Enterprises, Inc.
Douglas E. Grant, Texas A & M University

Beth A. Hall and Christopher T. Lee, Northern Arizona University
Laurens C. Hammock, Arizona State Museum
Thomas M. Holm and Thomas R. Loveland, Technicolor Government Services, Inc.
Kevin H. Horstman, Cities Service Company
Thomas R. Lyons, National Park Service
Robert D. Miles, Purdue University
Thomas Schafer and R. E. Kauffman, Abrams Aerial Survey Corporation
John J. Welsh, Eastman Kodak Company

Chapter 1

Photography, Films, and Filters

The process of image interpretation is highly dependent on the capacity of the mind to generalize. To learn to identify objects on aerial imagery, one needs to study known features on many photographs so that the characteristic clues of shape, size, tone, pattern, shadow, and texture become automatically associated with particular subjects. Eventually, mental processes permit the conscious abstraction of key features from known objects so that such information may be applied to the recognition of unknown objects.

HISTORY OF PHOTOGRAPHY

An understanding of the photographic process is essential for full comprehension of photogrammetry and aerial photo interpretation. The origin of photography has been traced back to 1839, when Louis J. M. Daguerre, of Paris, invented a positive-image process for making portraits. The daguerreotype method utilized metal film plates that had been light sensitized with a layer of silver iodide. The early-day camera was often no more than a light-tight box with a pinhole or a simple glass plate for the lens. After a picture was taken, the photographic plate was removed from the camera, exposed to fumes of mercury, and then heated to produce a direct-positive image. These positive images, of course, could not be duplicated.

A few years after Daguerre's technique had been developed, an Englishman, William H. Fox-Talbot, introduced the negative-positive process that continues in use today. The early 1840s also witnessed a reduction in camera exposure time from several minutes to a few seconds. This was made possible by the development of new lenses and the discovery of the superior light sensitivity of photographic plates coated with silver chloride and, later, silver bromide. For all practical purposes, the photographic techniques devised by Fox-Talbot remained basically unchanged for more than 100 years.

THE SIMPLE CAMERA

In design and function, a camera is not unlike the human eye. Each consists of an enclosed chamber with a lens at one end and a light-sensitive film (retina) at the other. The lens gathers light rays reflected from given objects and transmits them in an orderly fashion back to the light-sensitive area. A shutter assembly serves to regulate the amount and duration of light reaching the film when an exposure is made (Figure 1.1).

When a camera is focused at infinity, the distance from lens to film is known as the focal length, and the area in which the film is held flat during an exposure is referred to as the focal plane. Shutters may be positioned behind the lens, between elements of the lens, or in the focal plane immediately in front of the film. The focal plane shutter is analogous to a slitted curtain drawn across the area where the film is positioned. Intensity and length of exposure can be changed by variation of the width of the curtain slit and the tension of a spring-driven roller. Between-the-lens shutters are commonly characterized by a series of overlapping metal "leaves" that are rapidly opened and closed by an intricate gear chain (Figure 1.2). The diameter of the lens opening (effective aperture) can be varied by adjustment of a second set of thin, metal blades that compose the iris diaphragm.

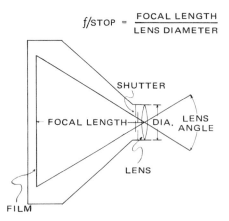

$$f/\text{STOP} = \frac{\text{FOCAL LENGTH}}{\text{LENS DIAMETER}}$$

Figure 1.1. Nomenclature of a simple camera.

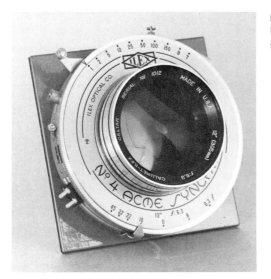

Figure 1.2. Camera lens with between-the-lens shutter. Note shutter-speed and f/stop settings. (Courtesy Calumet Manufacturing Co.)

RELATIVE APERTURES

The ratio of the camera focal length to the diameter of the lens opening is known as the *f/stop*, an expression used to designate the relative aperture setting or "speed" of a lens system. For example, a camera with a focal length of 40 mm and a lens diameter of 10 mm at full aperture would have an f/4 lens. If the aperture were 20 mm instead of 10 mm, the lens rating would be f/2; conversely, a 5-mm aperture with a 40-mm focal length would result in a lens rating of f/8. Thus the smaller the f/rating, the "faster" the lens, that is, the more light admitted through the lens opening.

While the focal length of a camera is normally fixed, the iris diaphragm can be used to regulate the effective aperture, with accompanying changes in f/stop values. When an f/4 lens is "stopped down" to f/8, it simply indicates that the effective *diameter* of the lens opening has been cut in half. More explicitly, the *area* of the lens opening is only one-fourth as large. Similarly, a lens setting of f/16 admits only one-fourth as much light as a setting of f/8 and only 1/16 as much as a setting of f/4.

A complete system of relative apertures begins at f/1, and multiplication of any aperture by 1.4 (i.e., the square root of 2) yields the succeeding smaller aperture. Thus, the sequence of full-stop increments would be f/1, f/1.4, f/2, f/2.8, f/4, f/5.6, f/8, f/11, f/16, f/22, f/32, f/45, f/64, f/90, f/128, f/180, f/256. Each lens opening in the series transmits one-half as much light as the preceding lens opening (e.g., f/5.6 transmits half as much light as f/4). Most lenses do not have a range of openings this great. Sometimes the largest opening for a lens is less than one full f/stop from the next marked lens opening. Examples are f/3.5, f/4.5, and f/6.3.

The more commonly used aperture settings and corresponding shutter-speed ratios are as follows:

Relative aperture or f/stop	Larger lens openings — — — — — Smaller lens openings										
	f/2	2.8	4	5.6	8	11	16	22	32	45	64
Index number for shutter speed	Faster speeds — — — — — — — — — Slower speeds										
	1	2	4	8	16	32	64	128	256	512	1,024

These relationships are well known to most camera enthusiasts. Simply stated, changes in aperture settings must be accompanied by adjustments of shutter speeds if a constant exposure is desired. For instance, a lens setting of 1/100 second at f/4 admits the same amount of light as a setting of 1/25 at f/8 or 1/400 at f/2. These paired relationships are the basis for light-value systems featured on many cameras; when the iris diaphragm is coupled with the shutter-speed selector, a change in either value results in an automatic adjustment of the other.

CAMERA VIEWING ANGLES

The angle of view encompassed by a camera lens is a function of the focal length and the diagonal measure of the film negative. When these two distances are approximately equal, the angle is roughly 45° to 50°, and the lens is referred to as *normal angle*. The distinction between normal and wide lens angles is somewhat arbitrary. For aerial cameras, lens angles of up to 75° are considered normal, those with angles of 75° to 100° are termed *wide angle*, and those that exceed 100° are designated *ultrawide*. As will be seen later, the choice of a proper camera focal length and lens angle is of prime importance in planning photographic surveys.

Lenses may vary from a single curved piece of glass to multielement, distortion-free designs that are little short of optical perfection. A thorough evaluation of camera lenses is beyond the scope of this volume, but it should be noted that lens quality is the major factor to be considered in the purchase or use of any camera.

PHOTOGRAPHIC FILM

Photographic film is ordinarily composed of a cellulose acetate or polyester base that has been coated on one side with a light-sensitive layer known as the *emulsion*. On the other side of the film base is the antihalation backing, a light-absorbing dye that prevents the formation of halos around bright images. A simplified film cross section of a black-and-white film is illustrated in Figure 1.3. The prime ingredient in the film emulsion is metallic silver, generally in

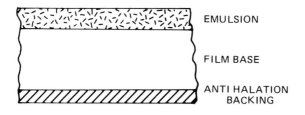

EMULSION

FILM BASE

ANTI HALATION
BACKING

Figure 1.3. Simplified cross section of photographic film, greatly enlarged.

the form of silver halide crystals suspended in a gelatin vehicle. During the split second when the camera shutter is open, light reaches the emulsion and a latent image of the scene viewed is recorded on the film. The image is made visible to the human eye by subsequent processes of film development and printing.

Emulsions for photographic films possess varying degrees of sensitivity to light waves, and knowledge of a particular film's "speed" is essential to obtaining a correct exposure. "Slow" films may require bright sunshine or artificial light for proper exposure, while "faster" films permit good pictures under minimal light conditions. A disadvantage of high-speed film, however, is that resultant negatives and prints are apt to be excessively grainy (i.e., coarsely textured).

In the United States, the American Standards Association rates each film emulsion on a relative scale of light sensitivity. The ASA exposure index, as it is called, provides a uniform classification system that can be applied easily under changing light intensities. Black-and-white films most commonly used have exposure ratings of 50 to 300, although extremes may range from around 8 to 1,000. The larger the ASA rating, the greater the sensitivity of the emulsion. Many black-and-white aerial films are rated at 80 to 200, and such speeds provide a reasonable latitude of exposure with a minimum of graininess. In West Germany and other European countries, film speeds are rated on a Deutsche Industry Norm (DIN) scale of sensitivity. Most camera exposure meters provide settings for either ASA or DIN film ratings. As noted in later sections, however, *aerial films* are not usually rated according to these sensitivity scales.

DEVELOPING AND PRINTING

When a roll of exposed film is removed from a camera, it must be protected from light, extremes of temperature, and humidity until it is processed. Briefly, the step-by-step darkroom procedure in the production of a film negative is as follows:

1. Developing: Immersion of film in a chemical solution to produce the photographic image recorded during exposure. Image highlights take the form of heavy metallic silver deposits; medium tones are characterized by

lighter silver deposits. Negative tones are the reverse of those on a positive print.

2. Short-stop: Immersion of film in dilute acetic acid to stop the developing reaction.
3. Fixing: Removal of unaffected silver salts from the emulsion.
4. Washing: Agitation in running water to remove all processing chemicals.
5. Drying: Hanging of film on clips and drying by natural air circulation or in special film-drying ovens.

Positive prints are produced by a series of steps similar to those followed in film development. A sheet of sensitized photographic paper is placed over the negative and "exposed" by light from underneath. The exposed paper is then subjected to a developing solution, followed by a short-stop bath, fixing, washing, and drying. If a hard, high-gloss photographic surface is desired, the print is dried on heated stainless steel rollers or platens, a process known as *ferrotyping*.

RESOLUTION AND SPECTRAL SENSITIVITY

Among the image characteristics contributing to the recognition of features on aerial photographs are qualities that are dependent on the type of photographic film selected, the type of filter used, and the season during which the exposure is made. Of special interest here are the factors of resolution and light sensitivity of the film.

Resolution, or *resolving power*, refers to the sharpness of detail afforded by the combination of film qualities and the camera lens system. In photographic terms, it is commonly expressed as the maximum number of lines per millimetre that can be resolved or seen as individual lines. Any magnification beyond that required to make the line-count for the resolution of the final print will only decrease the image quality and interpretation possibilities of the photographs.

The sensitivity of a film implies more than just its speed or exposure index. Of additional importance is the range of wavelengths to which the film is sensitive. For example, the portion of the electromagnetic spectrum visible to the human eye and most conventional color and black-and-white films includes the wavelength region of 0.4 to 0.7 μm, that is, the visible spectrum (Figure 1.4). However, film emulsions may be sensitized to a wider or narrower span of wavelengths. For instance, certain black-and-white films have a sensitivity range of 0.3 to 0.7 μm. This bandwidth includes the long wavelength ultraviolet region (0.3 to 0.4 μm). When a camera is equipped with a special quartz lens and ultraviolet transmit filter (e.g., Kodak Wratten 18-A Filter), only the invisible ultraviolet wavelengths are transmitted to the film *(ultraviolet photography)*. Most infrared black-and-white films are sensitive to the visible spectrum and the 0.7 to 0.9 μm near-infrared region of the electromagnetic spectrum. A special, two-color aerial film sensitized to only blue and green light is available for water-penetration photography.

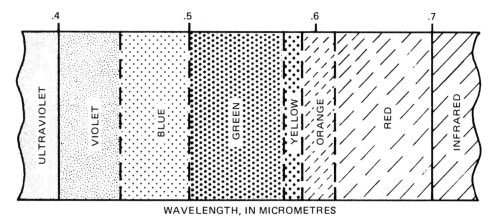

Figure 1.4. Schematic diagram of the visible spectrum. Color divisions are for illustrative purposes only; hues actually blend continuously from one wavelength to another.

It is apparent that the image quality or photographic tone is dependent on both the spectral reflectance of an object and the degree of film sensitivity to different wavelengths of reflected light. Thus, if it is desired to differentiate between various types of healthy vegetation, a knowledge of foliage reflectance characteristics under varying light conditions is essential (Figure 1.5). Photo interpreters are ordinarily limited to two basic types of black-and-white film (panchromatic and infrared) and two variants of color emulsions

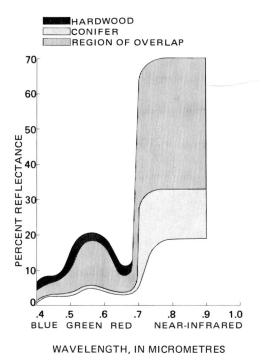

Figure 1.5. Generalized reflectance pattern from vegetation. (Courtesy P. A. Murtha and Canadian Forestry Service.)

(conventional color and infrared color—Plates 1–6. Nevertheless, when these films are correctly exposed through proper filters, a wide range of light sensitivity can be made available for producing desired tonal contrasts.

HAZE-CUTTING FILTERS FOR BLACK-AND-WHITE FILMS

Aerial films are usually exposed through haze-cutting filters placed in front of the camera lens. Such filters are essential, because small dust and moisture particles in the air scatter light rays, preventing distant images from registering on the film. Scattering of light rays also destroys fine detail on the photographs. The effect of haze increases with the height of the air column that must be penetrated; therefore, the effect of haze is significantly greater in high-altitude photography. Because of their short wavelengths, blue light rays are scattered to a much greater extent than green and red rays. A yellow or "minus-blue" filter reduces the effect of haze by absorbing the short rays and transmitting only the longer wavelengths to the film. Because haze-cutting filters remove part of the available light, longer film exposures are required. The ratio of the increased exposure to the normal exposure is known as the *filter factor*.

Table 1.1 includes several colors of filters that might be used for black-and-white photography. Filter factors will range from 1.5 to 4, depending on prevailing light and atmospheric conditions.

HAZE-CUTTING FILTERS FOR COLOR FILMS

Filters used with color films are different from those employed with black-and-white emulsions, because the radiation representing the visible spectrum must be transmitted by the filter to ensure that the film's color balance is not altered or destroyed. If excessively dense color filters are used, aerial color transparencies or prints may assume an overall hue similar to that of the filter.

Scattering of the short, invisible wavelengths of ultraviolet radiation increases the haze effect on color films by producing an overall bluish cast. This results because the film's blue-sensitive emulsion layer is especially sensitive to ultraviolet radiation. Thus, a haze-cutting filter (e.g., Kodak HF-3 Filter) is normally used with aerial color films to absorb ultraviolet radia-

TABLE 1.1. Filter Color Versus Colors of Light Absorbed

Filter Color	Colors of Light Absorbed
Medium yellow	Violet, most blue
Deep yellow	Violet, all blue
Blue	Red, some yellow, some green
Green	Red, some blue
Red	Violet, blue, and most green

tion. The use of such a filter effectively reduces excess bluishness caused by atmospheric haze without affecting the rendering of other colors. Because these haze-cutting filters are either colorless or very light yellow, they ordinarily have a filter factor of 1 (i.e., their density does not require exposure increases).

PANCHROMATIC FILM

The principal film used for aerial mapping and interpretation in Anglo-America is panchromatic, a black-and-white negative material having approximately the same range of sensitivity as that of the human eye. Standard-speed panchromatic film provides reasonably good tonal contrast, a wide exposure latitude, satisfactory resolution, and low graininess. *Pan* film, as it is called, has slightly higher than normal sensitivity to red light, thus permitting greater speed through haze filters (Figure 1.6).

Images on panchromatic photographs are rendered in varying shades of gray, with each tone comparable to the density of an object's color as seen by the human eye. Panchromatic film is superior for distinguishing objects of truly different colors, but its lack of high sensitivity to green light makes separation of vegetative types (e.g., tree species) difficult. A yellow haze filter is generally used for exposures on panchromatic film.

High-speed versions of standard panchromatic aerial films are also available (e.g., Kodak Tri-X Aerographic film), and these are intended for exposure under lesser light conditions. These films typically are about twice the speed of standard panchromatic aerial films. They are exposed through similar haze filters and, except for increased graininess, produce comparable tonal renditions.

INFRARED BLACK-AND-WHITE FILM

Infrared black-and-white film is primarily sensitive to the spectral region between 0.4 and 0.9 μm (Figure 1.6).[1] The film's infrared sensitivity is best described as *near infrared* because it uses only a narrow band (0.7 to 0.9 μm) of the total infrared spectrum. Nonetheless, this spectral range, about two-thirds the size of the visible spectrum, is capable of yielding important information that lies beyond the upper wavelength limits of human vision. Infrared black-and-white film is a negative material from which positive prints can be made with conventional darkroom equipment and photographic materials.

A wide range of filters can be used with infrared black-and-white film. If it is desired that only infrared radiation reflected from a ground scene be recorded, an infrared-transmitting, visually opaque filter is used to absorb the entire visible spectrum (e.g., Kodak Wratten Filters 89B, 88A, 87). Prints

1. Specially sensitized infrared films have an infrared range of 0.7 to 1.1 or 1.2 μm.

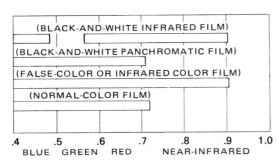

Figure 1.6. Approximate wavelength sensitivities of four common aerial films. (Courtesy P. A. Murtha and Canadian Forestry Service.)

resulting from this type of filtration are referred to as *true infrared* photographs. *Modified infrared* photographs result when infrared film is exposed through yellow, orange, or red filters because radiation from the longer wavelength portions of the visible spectrum is allowed to react with the film in addition to the near-infrared. Exposures with red filters usually increase contrast, especially among different types of vegetation. Infrared photographs usually have excellent haze penetration, because all of the filters recommended for use with this film reduce atmospheric scattering effects that occur in the ultraviolet and blue spectral regions.

When properly filtered, the gray tones on an infrared photograph result from the degree of near-infrared reflection of objects. Healthy broadleaf vegetation is recorded in light gray tones, because near-infrared radiation is strongly reflected from the cell walls of the mesophyll tissue of the leaves; the vegetation's green color is caused by green light being reflected from the pigment cells of chlorophyll, which are transparent to infrared radiation. Coniferous, or needle-leaf, vegetation tends to reflect less infrared radiation and consequently registers in darker tones. The characteristic vegetative tones rendered on this film make it especially valuable for delineating timber types (Figure 1.7).

Bodies of water absorb infrared radiation to a high degree and usually register quite dark on the film (unless they are heavily silt laden). This rendition is useful for determining the areal extent of river tributaries, tidal marshes, shorelines, and canals (Figure 1.7). However, this film cannot be used for underwater detections (e.g., reefs, shoals, channel obstructions) because of infrared absorption by water.

In some cases, the unusual tonal rendition of infrared photography blends light objects such as unpaved roads with light-toned vegetation. Furthermore, the dark (black) shadows on infrared prints can be a source of annoyance in the interpretation of ground detail; shadows are black because blue energy is absorbed by the lens filter.

Figure 1.7 illustrates comparative panchromatic and infrared photography of an area in Switzerland. Close inspection of these exposures confirms that neither film has a clear-cut superiority over the other. When a choice of the two emulsions is available, the selection will depend mainly on the objectives of interpretation.

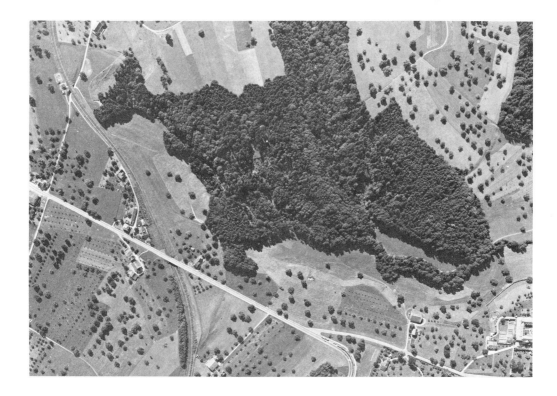

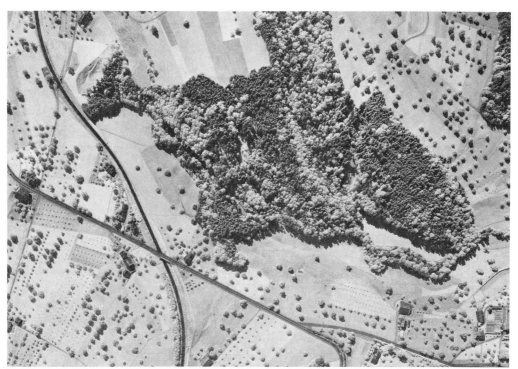

Figure 1.7. Panchromatic (top) and infrared photography of Goldach, Switzerland. Scale is about 1:7,700. (Courtesy Wild Heerbrugg Ltd.)

COLOR FILMS

Color films are of two basic types—color reversal (normal color and infrared color films) and color negative (normal color film only). Reversal films are processed to produce color-positive transparencies that are viewed with a source of white light (e.g., a light table). Color-negative films produce negatives from which positive prints are made (negative-to-positive sequence). Photographic prints have a lower resolution than positive transparencies do, but they offer versatility in the field. With a reversal film, color positive prints and duplicate transparencies (positive-to-positive sequence) are often made for frames of interest when the use does not require the maximum detail offered by the original transparencies. This is done because the original transparencies cannot be replaced if damaged or destroyed.

CONVENTIONAL COLOR-POSITIVE FILM

Conventional color-positive film is a reversal film of the subtractive type. The film's three emulsion layers are sensitive to the three primary colors of the visible spectrum: blue, green, and red (0.4 to 0.7 μm). When properly exposed and processed, positive transparencies provide a color rendition that closely approximates the original scene as viewed by the human eye (Plates 2, 4, and 6). For this reason, the film goes by various names—*normal color, conventional color*, and *natural color*.

Color film has a limited exposure latitude as compared with black-and-white emulsions, and it is preferably exposed under conditions of bright sunlight. Without the correct exposure and proper filtration, pictures are likely to be of poor quality. Today's color films have faster speeds, better definition, and less granularity than films of previous years.

With black-and-white films, contrasting gray tones and size and form provide the chief clues in object identification. Color film offers the two additional qualities of hue (color) and chroma (strength of color) as aids to interpreters. Photo interpreters usually find color films much easier to work with than black-and-white emulsions because the human eye can detect many more color variations than it can gray tones. There are many documented instances where the added dimension of color has improved interpretation reliability while reducing the amount of time required for photo analysis and inference.

Because the largest single cost in obtaining new aerial photography is that of aircraft operation, color photography is not much more expensive than black-and-white photography. Although film and processing costs are greater, these factors are not normally significant in terms of the total cost of a photographic survey.

Conventional color film is especially useful for identifying soil types, lithologies and surficial deposits, and various forms of polluted water. For clear water, it has good penetration qualities and is therefore valuable for detecting and delineating underwater features (e.g., reefs, shoals, channel obstructions). The film is best suited for low- to medium-altitude operations under conditions of low humidity.

INFRARED COLOR FILM

Infrared color is a tri-emulsion reversal film first developed during World War II. It was originally designed to emphasize differences in near-infrared reflection between live vegetation and various objects visually appearing to be healthy vegetation (e.g., objects painted with infrared-absorbing green paints to simulate the color of foliage). Because of this application, the film was originally known as *camouflage-detection film.*

This type of film differs from conventional color film in that its three separate emulsion layers are sensitive to green, red, and near-infrared radiation levels (0.5 to 0.9 μm). A yellow filter (e.g., Kodak Wratten 12 Filter) is always placed over the camera lens to absorb blue light to which the three emulsion layers are also sensitive. Such filtration ensures that the film possesses excellent haze-penetration capabilities, and sharp images are usually attainable from high altitudes.

Infrared color film produces the same dyes in its three emulsion layers that are formed in a normal color reversal film—yellow, magenta, and cyan—but each emulsion layer is sensitive to a different portion of the spectrum (Table 1.2). Consequently, when infrared color film is correctly exposed and processed as recommended, the resulting colors will be false for most natural features: dominant green reflectance reproduces as blue; dominant red reflectance reproduces as green; and dominant near-infrared reflectance reproduces as red. Numerous other colors will be formed depending upon the relative portions of green, red, and near-infrared radiation reflected by ground objects (Plates 1, 3, and 5). Because of these color shifts, infrared color film is sometimes referred to as *false-color film.*

Although infrared color film was originally developed for locating camouflaged military targets, it has proven very useful for a number of earth-science applications. For example, this film has become valuable for vegetation surveys aimed at species identification and the early detection of disease and insect outbreaks. Because of its ability to penetrate haze from high

TABLE 1.2. Dye Layer Sensitivities to Different Portions of the Spectrum for Color and Infrared Color Films

Dye Layer	Color Film	Infrared Color Film
Yellow (red + green)	Blue	Green
Magenta (red + blue)	Green	Red
Cyan (green + blue)	Red	Near infrared

altitudes, it has also become a valuable tool for mapping urban land use (see cover photograph).

Healthy vegetation, while appearing green on conventional color film, will appear in magenta or red hues on infrared color film because of the high near-infrared reflectance from the mesophyllic tissue of the leaves (Plates 1–5). Because healthy broadleaf trees have a higher infrared reflectivity than healthy needle-leaf trees, there are distinct differences between the colors of these tree groups as seen on infrared color film. In spring and summer, deciduous trees usually photograph in red hues, whereas conifers photograph reddish brown to bluish purple. There is a near similarity in visual color between deciduous and evergreen trees.

Infrared color film is valuable for detecting losses of plant vigor that may result from insect attacks, diseases, soil salinity, overfertilization, moisture stress, and other factors. When vegetation becomes stressed, some degree of collapse of the intercellular spaces within the mesophyll tissue will take place. Accompanying the collapse is a drop in near-infrared reflectance.

Stressed vegetation may first appear in darker or lighter shades of red. In some cases, plants under an early stress condition show up on this film before symptoms of decadence are visible on the ground or on conventional color photographs—an effect known as *previsual detection*. Advanced plant stress can appear in a variety of colors, including green, blue, cyan, and black. These colors indicate the vegetation has lost much of its ability to reflect near-infrared radiation.

Healthy foliage whose leaves have simply turned red or yellow in autumn still retain some of their infrared reflectivity. Red leaves will photograph yellow (equal reflectance in red and near-infrared), and yellow leaves register as white (equal reflectance in green, red, and near-infrared).

Because of its high absorption of near-infrared radiation, clear water, even if only a few centimetres deep, registers black on infrared color photographs; turbid (muddy) water usually has a blue or green signature. Damp ground shows up darker than dry ground because of infrared absorption by soil moisture. Shadows are dark on infrared color photos because the yellow lens filter absorbs blue scattered light.

COLOR-NEGATIVE FILM

A color-negative film is three emulsion layers deep and sensitized to the visible spectrum. The mandatory processing procedure with this film is a two-phase, negative-to-positive sequence. On the processed negative, a scene's geometry is reversed and colors are complements of the original colors. The image on a processed print incorporates a second reversal to a positive representation—the geometry and colors of the original ground scene are correctly reproduced.

A special type of color-negative film is Kodak's Aerocolor Negative Film, which forms the basis of the Kodak Aero-Neg Color System. By using processed negatives with several photographic techniques, the following products can be produced: color prints, black-and-white prints, color transparencies, black-and-white diapositives, and color diapositives. With such a system, the interpreter has the opportunity to select a variety of image forms from one aerial exposure.

MULTISPECTRAL PHOTOGRAPHY

From the preceding discussions of aerial films, it may be concluded that no single film serves all purposes. Instead, the varied tones or hues and patterns produced by different ranges of film sensitivity complement each other, and the maximum amount of information can be extracted only when several types of photography covering a given subject are interpreted in concert.

The technique of simultaneously obtaining aerial photographs of the same target from more than one spectral band is a form of *multispectral remote sensing* (see Chapter 7). Multispectral photography can be acquired by use of special multilens cameras (usually black-and-white film with different lens filters) or by mounting two or more cameras (each carrying a different film) in the same aircraft. Such photographic coverage presents the possibility of identifying features whose identifiable "signatures" lie beyond the limits of a particular spectral region. As an example, two vegetation types that are difficult to separate on a panchromatic photograph may be separable on a black-and-white infrared photograph (Figure 1.7).

AERIAL EXPOSURE INDEX

Because of the smaller range in subject luminance, atmospheric haze conditions, and other factors, the characteristics of aerial scenes differ considerably from those of ordinary ground views. As a result, the speed criterion used in the sensitometry of aerial films is different from the ASA or DIN ratings assigned to conventional roll and sheet films. The following definitions are quoted from the *Kodak Aerial Exposure Computer* (1970), published by Eastman Kodak Company, a manufacturer of aerial films:

> *Aerial exposure index* for black-and-white negative aerial films is defined as 1/2E, where E is the exposure (in meter-candle-seconds) at the point on the toe of the characteristic curve where the slope is equal to 0.6 of the measured gamma. *Aerial film speed* for black-and-white negative aerial films is defined as 3/2E, where E is the exposure (in meter-candle-seconds) at the point on the characteristic curve where the density is 0.3 above base plus fog density.

The two-dial Kodak Aerial Exposure Computer provides the aerial photographer with a quick and convenient means of determining the exposure parameters for Kodak black-and-white and color aerial films anywhere in the world. Of course, proper exposure will still depend, to some extent, on the aerial photographer's judgment of such factors as atmospheric haze conditions, amount of tolerable image motion, and selection of filters. For example, the photographer must remember to take the filter factor into account when determining the exposure setting for an aerial camera equipped with an antivignetting filter.

THE DEVELOPMENT OF PHOTOGRAMMETRY

Photogrammetry is defined as the science of obtaining reliable measurements of objects from their photographic images. The word *photogrammetry* is derived from three Greek roots meaning "light-writing-measurement." Odd as it may seem, aerial photographs and photogrammetric principles were employed in mapping and military reconnaissance before the Wright brothers' first historic flight in 1903. In the early 1850s Aimé Laussedat, a French army engineer, conducted a series of experiments with aerial photographs taken from kites and captive balloons. Although the work was later abandoned without notable success, Laussedat has often been referred to as the father of photogrammetry. During this same time period, a French photographer named Nader managed to obtain weak aerial images from the gondola of a balloon. His "flight altitude" was reported as 80 m above ground.

Captive-balloon photography (Figure 1.8) proved valuable during the American Civil War when General McClellan employed this innovation to make photomaps of Confederate positions in Virginia. From 1890 to 1910, new techniques in terrestrial photogrammetry were devised, and the U.S. Geological Survey used a panoramic camera for contour mapping in Alaska. In 1906 George R. Lawrence made some aerial "news" pictures of San Francisco stricken by earthquake and fire. Using a giant camera suspended from 17 kites, he exposed some of the largest negatives (about 48 by 122 cm) ever taken from an aerial platform.

By 1910 the airplane could fly at a speed of around 108 kph (58 kn), and the first aerial movies were taken from Wilbur Wright's aircraft by a Pathé news cameraman. However, it was World War I that brought together the airplane, improved films, and a real need for aerial photography and photo interpretation. Aerial reconnaissance is so much a part of today's national defense systems that it is difficult to believe that some military strategists opposed the concept at the start of World War I.

Before World War I many of the airphotos used in mapping were oblique views, that is, exposures made with the camera aimed at an angle to the vertical (Figure 1.9). In the ensuing years, however, emphasis was shifted toward greater use of stereoscopic coverage with vertical photography. In the early 1920s government agencies began to use aerial photography in map compilation, and several private survey firms were founded. Some of these pioneer corporations are still flourishing today.

The 1930s saw the formation of the Agricultural Adjustment Administration in the U.S. Department of Agriculture and the beginning of this agency's extensive photographic coverage of farmlands and rangelands. The Geo-

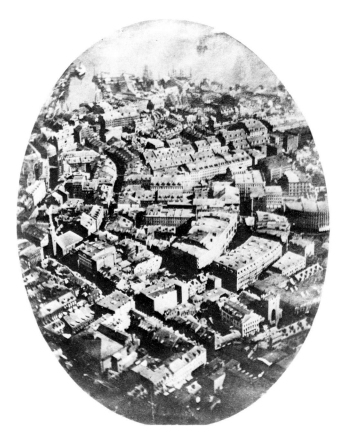

Figure 1.8. This 1859 picture of Boston Harbor, made by J. W. Black, was one of the first aerial photographs taken in the United States. The exposure was made from a captive balloon at an altitude of about 365 m. (Courtesy General Aniline and Film Corp.)

logical Survey began to rely more heavily on aerial photographs in topographical surveying, and the creation of the Tennessee Valley Authority gave new impetus to an expanding program of federal mapping. During this same period, the U.S. Forest Service demonstrated the feasibility of using airphotos for timber-type mapping on the national forests, and similar developments were taking place in other countries of the world.

THE DEVELOPMENT OF PHOTO INTERPRETATION

Photo interpretation may be defined as the identification of objects on airphotos and the determination of their meaning or significance. The art of photo interpretation was a little-known skill in America before 1939 and the advent of World War II. Within the following five or six years, however, countless military decisions were based on intelligence reports derived from aerial reconnaissance. After the war, many air-intelligence specialists converted their newfound knowledge of photographic interpretation into diverse civilian applications.

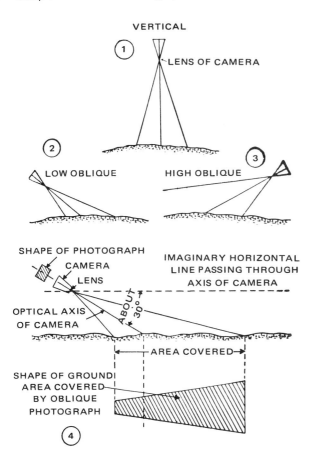

Figure 1.9. Orientation of an aerial camera for vertical and oblique photography. (Courtesy U.S. Department of the Army.)

During the past three decades, the nonmilitary uses of aerial photography have continued to multiply. Today, photo-interpretation techniques are used on such diverse projects as monitoring the changing water levels of lakes and reservoirs, assessing crop diseases, locating new highway routes, assessing real estate, and mapping archeological sites. In this same period, significant technical developments have been made in aerial cameras, optical systems, film emulsions, aircraft, and earth-orbiting satellites (Figures 1.10 and 1.11).

◼ TRAINING AND ADDITIONAL INFORMATION

Most colleges and universities, along with various government and professional organizations, offer courses in photogrammetry, photo interpretation, or remote sensing. In most instances, academic instruction is at the undergraduate level, and courses are commonly found in departments of geography, geology, forestry, and civil engineering.

On an international basis, one of the widely recognized seats of photogrammetric and airphoto interpretation is the International Institute for Aerial

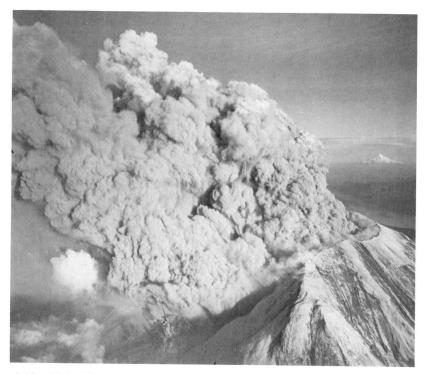

Figure 1.10.   High oblique aerial view (horizon included) of Mount Saint Helens, Washington. The view is to the southeast with Mount Hood in the distance. This exposure was taken on 18 March 1980. Compare with frontispiece. (Courtesy EROS Data Center, U.S. Geological Survey.)

Survey and Earth Sciences. Information on the various courses offered by the institute may be obtained at this address: International Institute of Aerial Survey and Earth Sciences, Boulevard 1945, P.O. Box 6, Enschede, The Netherlands. *Photogrammetria*, the official journal of the International Society of Photogrammetry, is edited and published under the auspices of the institute.

In the United States, the American Society of Photogrammetry is the lead organization devoted to photogrammetry and remote sensing. The society has published four valuable reference manuals: *Manual of photographic interpretation, Manual of color aerial photography, Manual of remote sensing*, and *Manual of photogrammetry*. In addition, the society publishes a monthly journal, *Photogrammetric Engineering and Remote Sensing*, and sponsors regularly scheduled remote-sensing symposia. Information regarding publications and conferences may be obtained at this address: American Society of Photogrammetry, 210 Little Falls Street, Falls Church, VA 22042.

In Canada a national program in remote sensing is coordinated by the Canada Centre for Remote Sensing in cooperation with other agencies of the national government, provincial remote-sensing centers, industries, and

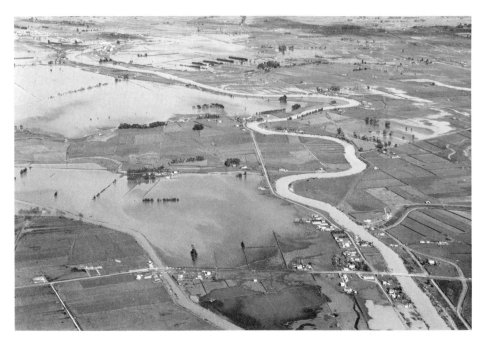

Figure 1.11.   Low oblique aerial view (horizon not shown) of a flooded area near Whakatane, New Zealand. (Courtesy Aero Surveys [New Zealand], Ltd.)

universities. These groups periodically sponsor special international symposia on remote sensing.

The *Canadian Journal of Remote Sensing* began publication in 1975. Information regarding subscriptions may be addressed to the Canadian Aeronautics and Space Institute, Saxe Building, 60–75 Sparks Street, Ottawa, Ont. K1P 5A5, CANADA.

The official journal of the Remote Sensing Society is the *International Journal of Remote Sensing.* It is published quarterly by Taylor and Francis, Ltd., 4 John Street, London WC1N 2ET, UNITED KINGDOM.

Remote Sensing of Environment, a multidisciplinary journal, is published six times a year by Elsevier Science Publishing Company, 52 Vanderbilt Avenue, New York, NY 10017.

PROBLEMS

1. Draw a series of circles that are scaled to represent several f/stops for a camera lens, for example, f/2, f/4, f/8, f/16, and f/32. Then assign a shutter speed to one lens setting and compute shutter speeds for all other f/stops.
2. List three or four commercially available films and their corresponding

ASA or DIN exposure ratings. What are the recommended shutter speeds and f/stops for these films under conditions of bright sunlight and strong shadows?

Name of Film	ASA or DIN Rating	Shutter Speed	f/Stop

3. Study a set of paired panchromatic and infrared black-and-white photographs. Make a list of features that can be recognized and compare the tonal differences of these features on the two photographs. Tabulate as follows:

Feature Identified	Panchromatic Tone	Infrared Tone	Preferred Film and Comments

4. Repeat the procedure outlined in the previous question for a set of paired color and infrared color photographs.

Feature Identified	Conventional Color	Infrared Color	Preferred Film and Comments

References

Avery, T. E. 1970. *Photo interpretation for land managers.* Eastman Kodak Co., Rochester, N.Y., Publication M-76, 26 pp., illus.

Colwell, Robert N., editor-in-chief. 1960. *Manual of photographic interpretation.* American Society of Photogrammetry, Falls Church, Va., 868 pp., illus.

———, editor-in-chief. 1983. *Manual of remote sensing.* 2nd ed. American Society of Photogrammetry, Falls Church, Va., 2,439 pp., illus.

Eastman Kodak Co. 1973. *Specifications and characteristics of Kodak aerial films.* Publication M-57, 4 pp. (periodically revised). Rochester, N.Y.

———. 1970. *Kodak aerial exposure computer.* Publication R-10, 6 pp. Rochester, N.Y.

———. 1969. *Optical formulas and their application.* Publication AA-26, 6 pp., illus. Rochester, N.Y.

Fritz, Norman L. 1974. Available color aerial photographic materials. *Photogrammetric Engineering* 40:1423–1425.

Jensen, John R. 1983. Educational image processing: an overview. *Photogrammetric Engineering and Remote Sensing* 49:1151–1157.

Jensen, John R., and Richard E. Dahlberg. 1983. Status and content of remote sensing education in the United States. *International Journal of Remote Sensing* 4: 235–245.

Land, Edwin H. 1959. Experiments in color vision. *Scientific American* reprint. W. H. Freeman and Co., San Francisco. 14 pp., illus.

Lillesand, Thomas M. 1982. Trends and issues in remote sensing education. *Photogrammetric Engineering and Remote Sensing* 48:287–293.

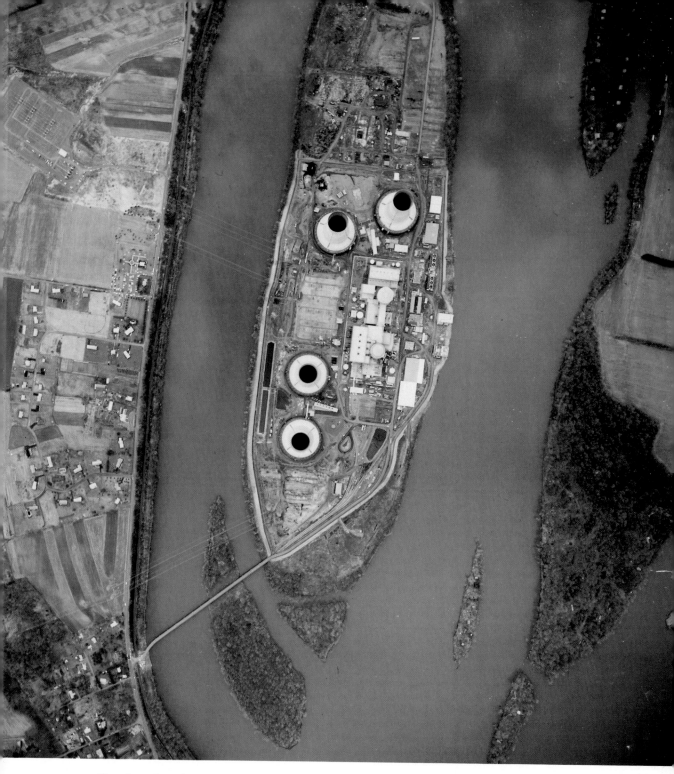

Plate 1. Infrared color photograph of nuclear power plant at Three-Mile Island on the Susquehanna River in Pennsylvania. Scale is about 1:10,700. (Courtesy Environmental Protection Agency.)

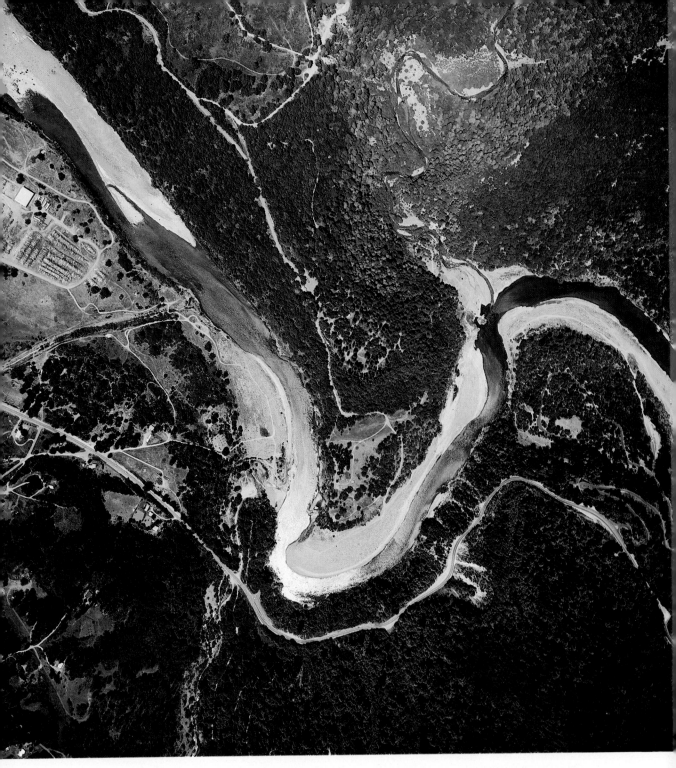

Plate 2. Normal color photograph of Trinity River and environs in northern California. Compare with infrared color photograph on facing page. (Courtesy National Aeronautics and Space Administration.)

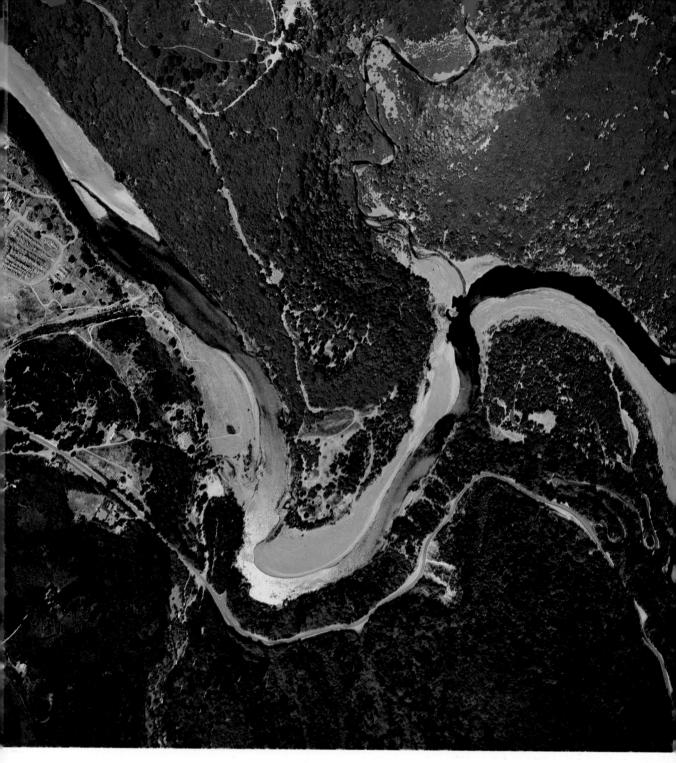

Plate 3. Infrared color photograph of Trinity River and environs in northern California. Compare with normal color photograph on facing page. (Courtesy National Aeronautics and Space Administration.)

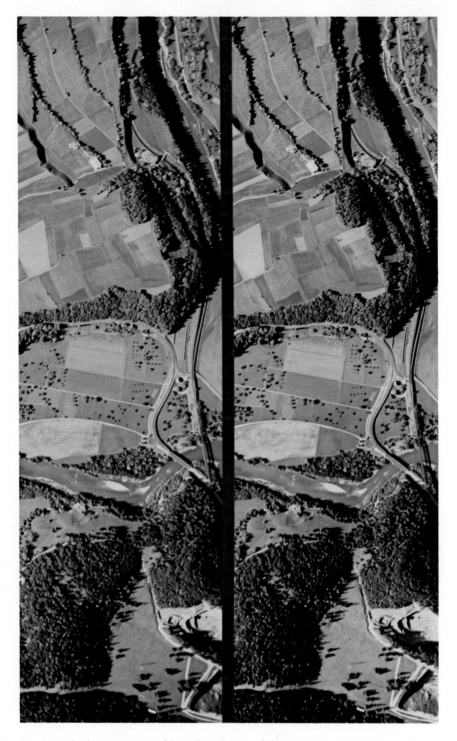

Plate 4. Normal color stereogram of Bonaduz, Canton of Grisons, Switzerland (taken in October). Scale is about 1:11,000. (Courtesy Wild Heerbrugg, Ltd.)

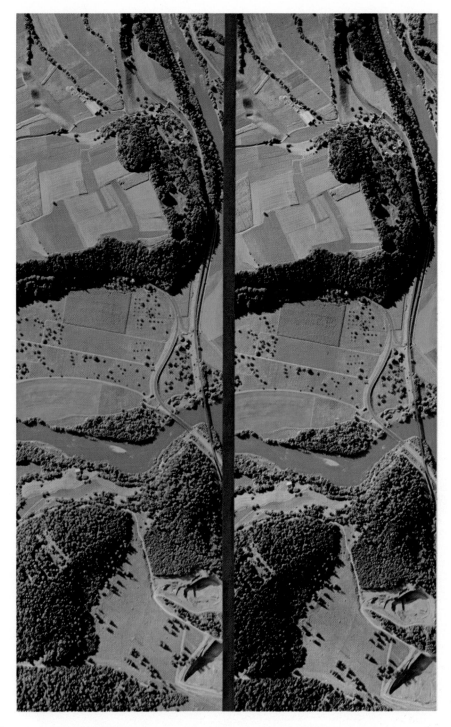

Plate 5. Infrared color stereogram of Bonaduz, Canton of Grisons, Switzerland (taken in September). Scale is about 1:11,000. (Courtesy Wild Heerbrugg, Ltd.)

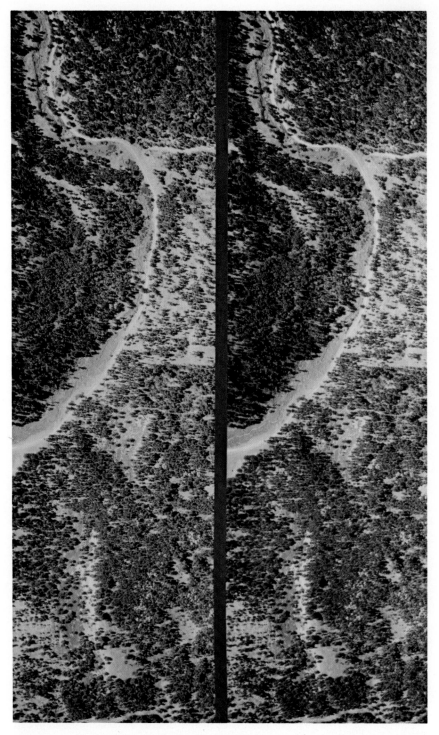

Plate 6. Normal color stereogram illustrating damage caused by mountain pine beetle on ponderosa pines in the Black Hills of South Dakota. Clumps of dead trees (brownish-yellow crowns) are clearly discernible. Scale is about 1:6,200. (Courtesy U.S. Forest Service.)

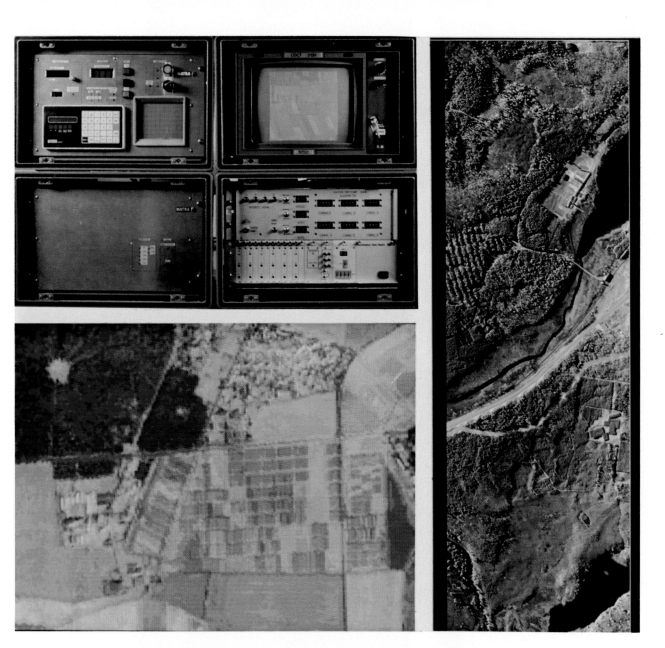

Plate 7. Upper left—Electronics unit, operator's console, and airborne quick-look visualization unit of the Matra Thematic Scanner. Lower left—False color image of an area near Grignon, France (Centre d' Experimentation) produced in flight by the Matra Thematic Scanner. The image incorporates three spectral channels: 0.48 to 0.57 μm (printed blue), 0.58 to 0.69 μm (printed green), and 10.5 to 12.5 μm (printed red). The data were obtained from an altitude of 1,800 m. (Courtesy B. Deffis and Jean Seligmann, Matra Optique, Bois-d Arcy, France.) Right—Pushbroom scanner false color image of an area near Petawawa, Ontario, produced by the Multispectral Electro-optical Imaging Scanner. The image incorporates three spectral channels (center wavelengths): 0.445 μm (printed blue), 0.59 μm (printed green), and 0.871 μm (printed red). The aircraft altitude was 1,750 m, the swath width was 1,265 m, and the ground resolution cell was 1.2 m. (Courtesy G. P. Jackson, MacDonald Dettwiler and Associates, Ltd., and the Canada Centre for Remote Sensing.)

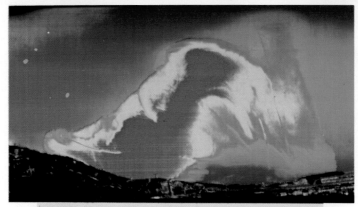

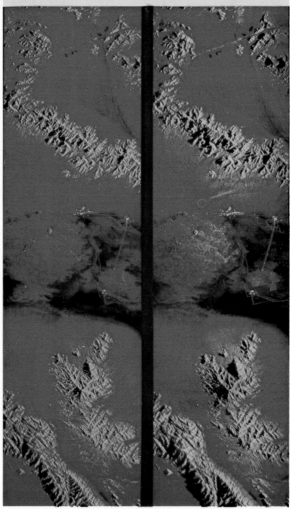

Plate 8. Top—Color-coded thermal infrared image (4.5 to 5.5 μm) of a thermal plume. The thermal data were collected in August 1970 at 0718 hours. Each 1°C temperature interval is depicted in one of six different colors: coolest is magenta, warmest is red. The image is produced by the Daedalus DIGICOLOR™ process (see Chapter 7). (Courtesy George England, Daedalus Enterprises, Inc., and the University of Wisconsin.) Bottom—Two-color X-band radar stereogram of the Amboy region, Mohave Desert, California. See Chapter 7. (Courtesy Goodyear Aerospace Corporation, Arizona Division, and Aero Service Division of Western Geophysical of America.)

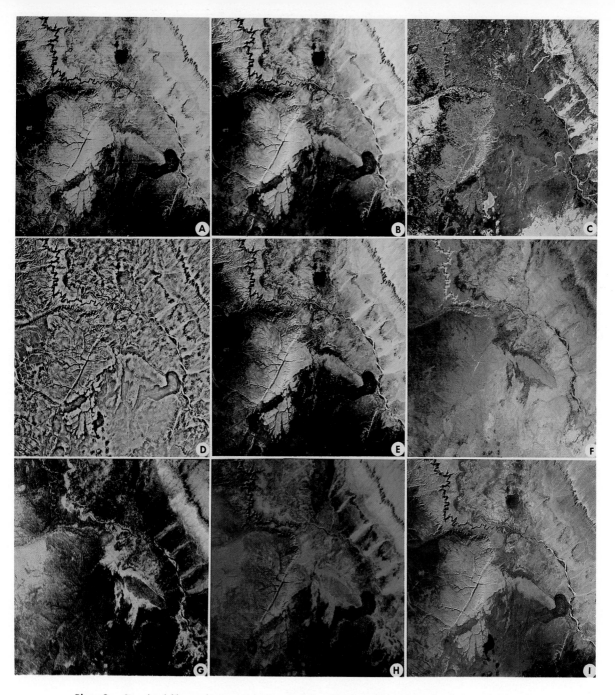

Plate 9. Standard film and computer-processed (i.e., image restoration and enhancement operations) Landsat-1 MSS color-composite images of a volcanic-sedimentary area in northern Arizona. The MSS data were collected 29 October 1973. (A) MSS 4,5,7 standard infrared color image (band 4 printed blue, band 5 printed green, band 7 printed red), (B) linear contrast stretched MSS 4,5,7 infrared color image, (C) sinusoidal contrast stretched MSS 4,5,7 false color image, (D) 31 × 31 high-pass filtered MSS 4,5,7 false color image, (E) edge-enhanced MSS 4,5,7 infrared color image, (F) triple-ratio false color image (4/5 printed blue, 5/6 printed green, 6/7 printed red), (G) triple-ratio false color image (5/4 printed blue, 6/4 printed green, 7/4 printed red), (H) hybrid-ratio false color image (5/4 printed blue, 5 printed green, 7/5 printed red), (I) simulated natural color image (band 3 printed blue, band 4 printed green, band 5 printed red). See Chapters 7 and 15. (Courtesy U.S. Geological Survey, Flagstaff, Arizona.)

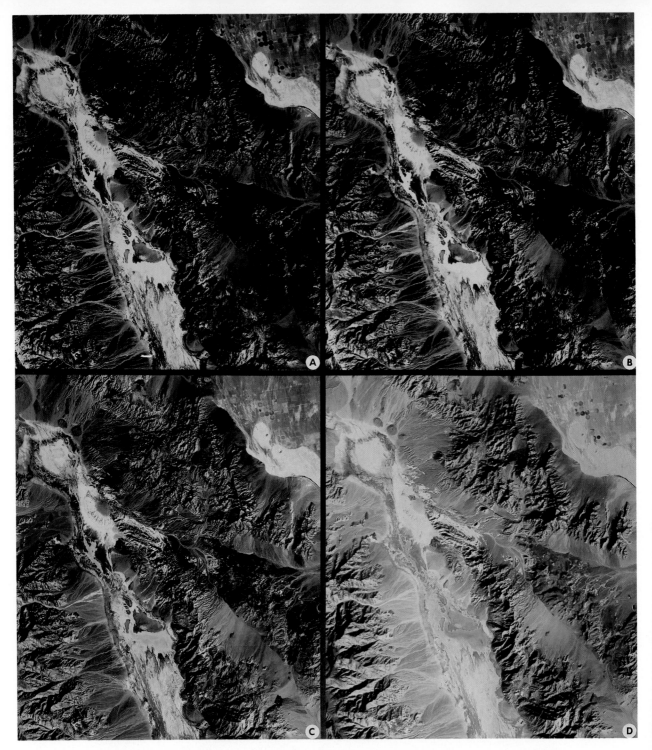

Plate 10. Landsat-4 TM color-composite images (computer processed) for Death Valley and vicinity. The TM data were collected 17 November 1982. (A) natural color image (band 1 printed blue, band 2 printed green, band 3 printed red), (B) infrared color image (band 2 printed blue, band 3 printed green, band 4 printed red), (C) false color image (band 1 printed blue, band 4 printed green, band 5 printed red), (D) false color image (band 1 printed blue, band 5 printed green, band 6 printed red). See Chapters 7 and 15. (Courtesy Pat S. Chavez, Jr., U.S. Geological Survey, Flagstaff, Arizona.)

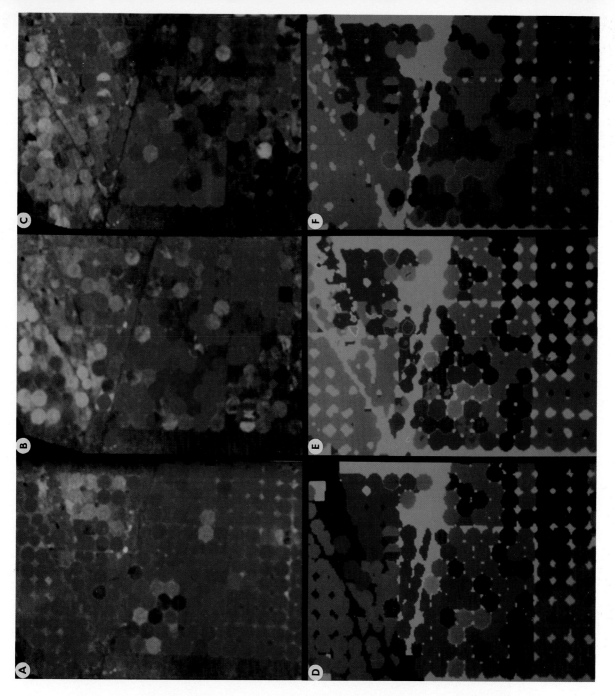

Plate 11. Crop type discrimination for an area near Clarke, Oregon, using a 12-band multi-temporal Landsat-2 MSS digital data set (three 4-band MSS scenes combined). (A) MSS 4,5,7 infrared color image acquired 3 June 1979, (B) MSS, 4,5,7 infrared color image acquired 18 July 1979, (C) MSS 4,5,7 infrared color image acquired 10 September 1979, (D) ground-reference data representing six major crops, (E) six-channel canonical transformed minimum distance to mean classification used for comparison to the ground-reference data, (F) maximum likelihood classification used for comparison to the ground-reference data. The color scheme for Images E and F is as follows: brown is wheat, red is alfalfa, green is potatoes, light blue is corn, dark blue is soybeans, and yellow is rangeland. See Chapter 15. (Courtesy Thomas M. Holm, Technicolor Government Services, Inc., EROS Data Center, Sioux Falls, South Dakota.)

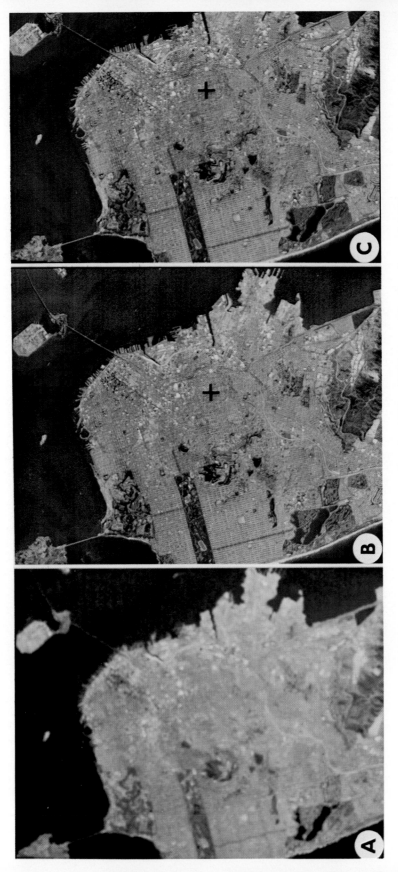

Plate 12. Separate and digitally merged Landsat MSS and RBV images of San Francisco and vicinity (partial frames). (A) MSS 4,5,7 infrared color image with a resolution of 79 m (acquired 3 September 1975), (B) RBV image with a resolution of 30 m (acquired 18 August 1978), (C) digital merging of images A and B, spectral resolution provided by the MSS component and spatial resolution by the RBV component. See Chapters 7 and 15. (Courtesy EROS Data Center, U.S. Geological Survey.)

Meyer, M., R. Harding, and J. Ulliman. 1981. Status of airphoto interpretation training in accredited U.S. forestry schools. *Journal of Forestry* 79:404–405.

Murtha, P. A. 1972. *A guide to air photo interpretation of forest damage in Canada.* Forest Management Institute, Canadian Forestry Service, Ottawa. Publication 1292, 62 pp., illus.

Nealey, L. David. 1977. Remote sensing/photogrammetry education in the United States and Canada. *Photogrammetric Engineering and Remote Sensing* 43: 259–284.

Slama, Chester C., editor-in-chief. 1981. *Manual of photogrammetry.* 4th ed. American Society of Photogrammetry, Falls Church, Va., 1,056 pp., illus.

Smith, John T. 1968. *Manual of color aerial photography.* American Society of Photogrammetry, Falls Church, Va., 550 pp., illus.

Streb, Jack M. 1969. Photography from the air—then and now. Kodak photo information book AE-87, Eastman Kodak Co., Rochester, N.Y., 72 pp., illus.

U.S. Department of the Army. 1969. *Lenses and the f/system.* U.S. Army Engineer School, Fort Belvoir, Va. Lesson file, pp. 1–9.

U.S. Department of Commerce. 1972. *The International System of Units (SI).* Government Printing Office, Washington, D.C. National Bureau of Standards, Special Publication 330, 42 pp.

■ Chapter 2

Orientation and Study of Aerial Photographs

■ THE INTERPRETER'S TASK

Because photo interpretation often involves a considerable amount of subjective judgment, it is commonly referred to as an art rather than an exact science. Actually, it is both. The interpreter must know how to use the scientific tools and methodology of the photogrammetric engineer; yet these objective findings must often be supplemented with deductive reasoning to supply a logical answer to the perennial question "What's going on here?"

The skilled interpreter must have a large store of information at hand to perform this exacting task adequately. He or she should have a sound general background in geography, geology, forestry, engineering, and other disciplines oriented toward the study of natural and cultural features. Complex features are rarely identified as a result of quick stereoscanning. Thus, the interpreter who knows which features to expect in a given locality, as well as those not likely to occur, can make a more positive identification in a shorter time.

Under certain circumstances the mental processes of deduction and association may permit "detection" of objects not actually visible on the photographs, for example, a buried pipeline or a camouflaged military airfield. The value of experience and imagination can hardly be over-emphasized, for the interpreter who does not recognize an unusual object when standing alongside it cannot be expected to identify a similar feature on

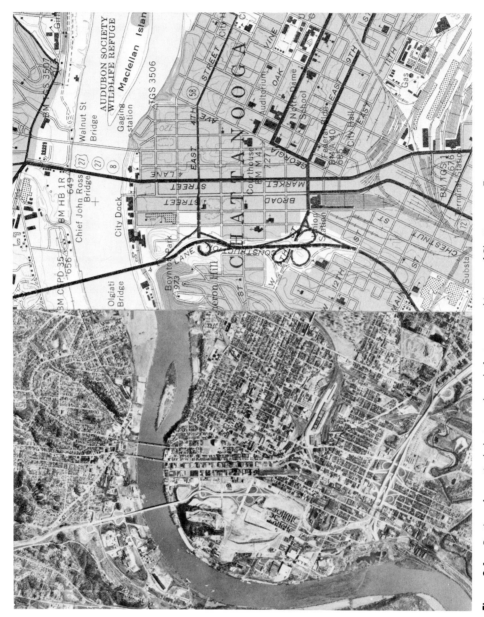

Figure 2.1.   Portion of a vertical photograph and of a topographic map of Chattanooga, Tennessee. Photo scale is about 1:48,000; map scale is 1:24,000. (Courtesy Tennessee Valley Authority.)

a small-scale print (Figure 2.1). There are situations in which photographic limitations or a lack of associated information preclude positive identification of objects. In such cases, the terms *probable* and *possible* are customarily used to qualify the interpreter's findings.

While the cartographer or photogrammetric engineer is normally interested only in up-to-date mapping photography, the interpreter's job can often be made easier when comparative coverage is available. Comparative or *sequential* coverage refers to two or more sets of imagery of the same area taken at different times. With favorable timing of photographic flights, changes in land use may be readily detected, and activities that might otherwise pass unnoticed may be readily identified.

PRINCIPLES OF OBJECT RECOGNITION

Most persons have little difficulty in recognizing features pictured on oblique photographs, for such views appear relatively "normal" to the human eye (Figures 1.10 and 1.11). On the other hand, a vertical or near-vertical view from an altitude of several thousand metres can be quite confusing, particularly for individuals who have never ridden in an airplane (Figure 2.2). An experienced aerial photo interpreter exercises *mental acuity* as well as *visual perception* and consciously or unconsciously must evaluate several factors in identifying features on vertical photographs. Prominent among these are the following:

Shape.   This characteristic alone may serve to identify some objects. Examples include a highway cloverleaf intersection, an airfield, or a football stadium.

Size.   Both relative and absolute sizes are important. Thus a superhighway will not be confused with a rural road, or a small residence with an apartment building. Size, of course, is a function of the photographic scale.

Photographic Tone and Color.   Objects of different color have different qualities of light reflectance and, therefore, register in varying shades or tones on a photograph. Obvious examples include quartz sand versus dark topsoil, cultivated versus fallow fields, or coniferous versus broad-leaved tree crowns.

Pattern.   If the spatial arrangement of trees in an orchard is compared with that of natural vegetation, a contrast in patterns will be evident. As another example, a pattern produced by contour plowing might reveal information on topography, type of soil, or the nature of the crop.

Shadow.   A truly vertical photograph of a tall smokestack or an isolated oil derrick might present a difficult identification problem, except for the characteristic shadows cast by these objects. By the same token, shadows may hinder the interpreter by obscuring ground detail.

Topographic Location.   Relative elevation, including drainage features, can be an important clue in predicting soil conditions or the probability of encountering a particular vegetative association. The natural occurrence of willow trees on floodplains or river sandbars supplies a good example.

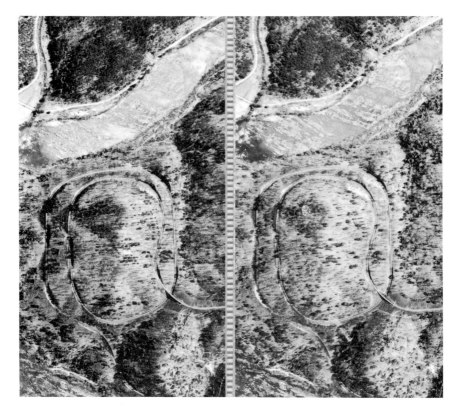

Figure 2.2.   This unusual loop was designed to reduce the grade for tracks of the L&N railroad in Polk County, Tennessee. Scale is about 1:15,840. What are the main clues for recognizing such features? (Courtesy Tennessee Valley Authority.)

Texture.   The degree of coarseness or smoothness exhibited by photo images can be a useful key to identification. Texture, just like object size, is directly correlated with photo scale. Contrast the texture of grass with that of a cornfield, or the texture of saplings with that of large, overmature trees.

CHECKLIST OF TYPICAL FEATURES

In the identification of unfamiliar features on vertical photographs, it has been found that the power of suggestion is often beneficial to beginning interpreters. Accordingly, the following checklist has been prepared to illustrate the kinds of features commonly encountered in the study of aerial photographs. The groupings according to ten general categories are somewhat arbitrary; therefore, a given feature might logically be assigned to more than one of the classifications shown (Figure 2.3).

Figure 2.3 Checklist of typical features encountered in the study of aerial photographs.

Forests and rangelands
_____ Coniferous forests
_____ Hardwood forests
_____ Mixed coniferous and hardwood forests
_____ Forest plantations
_____ Herbaceous rangeland
_____ Shrub and brush rangeland
_____ Mixed rangeland
_____ Tundra

Agricultural features
_____ Cultivated crops (e.g., corn)
_____ Contour plowing or terraced cropland
_____ Irrigated crops (specify type)
_____ Orchards (specify type)
_____ Vineyards
_____ Improved pastures
_____ Fences or hedgerows
_____ Barns or silos
_____ Baled hay or shocked wheat
_____ Livestock or wild game
_____ Greenhouses
_____ Nurseries
_____ Abandoned or fallow fields

Mining and excavation
_____ Strip mines (e.g., coal)
_____ Placer mines (e.g., gold)
_____ Open-pit mines (e.g., copper)
_____ Sand and gravel excavations
_____ Rock quarries
_____ Oil-drilling and development operations
_____ Channel-dredging operations
_____ Land-clearing operations

Water and natural shoreline features
_____ Shorelines and beaches
_____ Coastal bays and inlets
_____ Swamps or marshes
_____ Floodplains or deltas
_____ Permanent rivers or streams
_____ Inland lakes or ponds
_____ Sandbars or mud flats
_____ Lime sinks or potholes

Physiographic and geologic features
_____ Active glaciers
_____ Cirques or cliffs

_____ Eskers or drumlins
_____ Talus slopes and alluvial fans
_____ Gully erosion
_____ Sheet erosion
_____ Volcanic lava flows or cones
_____ Rock outcrops
_____ Hogbacks
_____ Anticlines and synclines
_____ Faults and dikes

Urban-residential patterns
_____ Apartment houses
_____ Mobile homes
_____ Garages
_____ Schools (specify type)
_____ Churches and cemeteries
_____ Parks or playgrounds
_____ Statues or monuments
_____ Civic or recreational centers
_____ Shopping centers
_____ Downtown business districts
_____ Gas stations
_____ Automobile dealerships
_____ Mobile home dealerships
_____ Motels or hotels
_____ Drive-in theaters
_____ Country clubs
_____ Swimming pools
_____ Golf courses
_____ Tennis courts
_____ Football fields
_____ Other athletic fields
_____ Race tracks
_____ Auto junkyards
_____ Prisons
_____ County rest homes
_____ Hospitals

Industrial and utility features
_____ Electrical power plants
_____ Electrical power substations
_____ Steel towers for electrical lines
_____ Cleared rights-of-way
_____ Buried pipelines
_____ Sewage disposal plants
_____ Water-purification plants
_____ Petroleum or chemical industries
_____ Petroleum-products–storage tanks
_____ Sawmills and lumber yards
_____ Pulp and paper mills

continued

_____ Furniture-manufacturing plants
_____ Automobile-manufacturing plants
_____ Steel or other metal industries
_____ Cement-block–manufacturing plants
_____ Ready-mixed–concrete plants
_____ Stockyards or meat-packing plants

Transportation and communication features

_____ Four-lane, divided highways
_____ Three-lane, paved highways
_____ Two-lane, paved highways
_____ Graded, nonsurfaced roads
_____ Woods roads or Jeep trails
_____ Traffic circles and interchanges
_____ Overpasses and underpasses
_____ Railroads
_____ Railroad terminals
_____ Bus terminals
_____ Trucking terminals
_____ Airports
_____ Radio or TV transmission towers
_____ Radar antennas
_____ Railroad coal-dumping spurs
_____ Boat docks and piers

Engineering structures

_____ Dams (describe type of material)
_____ Bridges (describe type of material)
_____ Road cuts and fills
_____ Levees
_____ Athletic stadiums
_____ Fire lookout towers
_____ Water tanks
_____ Canals or drainage ditches
_____ Reservoirs
_____ Ferry landings

Military and defense installations

_____ Post headquarters
_____ Barracks and residences
_____ Temporary encampments
_____ Ammunition dumps
_____ Rifle or artillery ranges
_____ Tanks
_____ Warships
_____ Shipyards and drydocks
_____ Missile test sites
_____ Operational missile bases
_____ Airfields and planes
_____ Radar installations

▓ PHOTO INTERPRETATION KEYS

A photo interpretation key is a set of guidelines used to assist interpreters in rapidly identifying photographic features. Keys are valuable as training aids for neophyte interpreters and as reference or refresher material for more experienced personnel. Depending on the method of presenting diagnostic features, photo interpretation keys may be grouped into two general classes—*selective keys* and *elimination keys*.

Selective keys are usually made up of typical illustrations and descriptions of objects in a given category. They are organized for comparative use; the interpreter merely selects the key example that most nearly coincides with the feature to be identified. By contrast, elimination keys require the user to follow a step-by-step procedure, working from the general to the specific. One of the more common forms of elimination keys is the dichotomous type. Here, the interpreter must continually select one of two contrasting alternatives until he or she progressively eliminates all but one item of the category—the one being sought.

When available, elimination keys are sometimes preferred to selective keys. On the other hand, elimination keys are more difficult to construct, and their use may result in erroneous identifications if the interpreter is forced to choose between two unfamiliar image characteristics. Studies have revealed no significant difference between results from the two types of keys as long as the material within each key is well organized.

The determination of the type of key and method of presentation to be used depends on (1) the number of objects or conditions to be recognized and (2) the variability normally encountered within each classification. As a general rule, keys are much more easily constructed and applied in identifications of man-made features than for natural vegetation and landforms. For reliable interpretation of natural features, training and field experience are often essential to ensure consistent results.

THREE-DIMENSIONAL PHOTOGRAPHY

In many instances, it is entirely feasible to use single, vertical photographs for the recognition or classification of specific features. The principal disadvantage of the technique, however, is that only two dimensions (length and width) of most objects can be perceived. This is the equivalent of using only one eye, an effect referred to as *monocular vision*. The all-important third dimension of depth perception is provided only when objects are viewed with *both eyes*. Here, the converging lines of sight from each eye are transmitted to the brain, and the result is *binocular* or *stereoscopic vision*.

One can quickly compare "one-eyed" vision to stereoscopic vision by viewing a distant object, first with a telescope and then with binoculars having equal magnification. There is also the "coin-on-a-table" trick. If one eye is covered and only the coin's *edge* is seen from the level of the tabletop, it becomes quite difficult to place a forefinger directly on top of the coin. When one has both eyes open, the difficulty vanishes.

While almost everyone possesses and automatically employs stereoscopic vision, there have been a number of fairly successful business enterprises based on the somewhat startling effects of exaggerated three-dimensional pictures. In the early 1900s the stereopticon or "periscope" was almost a standard fixture in American parlors. This instrument, shown in Figure 2.4, was used in viewing paired photographs that had been taken from slightly

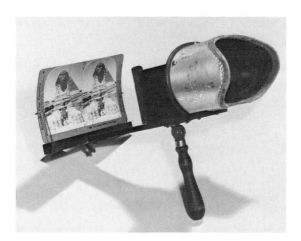

Figure 2.4. Old-fashioned parlor stereoscope. Note stereopair of the Sphinx. (Courtesy Keystone View Co.)

different camera positions. The stereopticon allowed each eye to see only one print, thus creating the illusion of depth for the viewer. A stereopair of the Rock of Gibraltar is shown in Figure 2.5. Although the corresponding images are rather widely separated, persons experienced in stereo viewing may be able to see this scene three-dimensionally without the aid of special instruments.

Three-dimensional motion pictures were popular for brief periods during the 1930s and again in the early 1950s. Two cameras were used to photograph each scene; both views were then projected on theater screens through polarized or red and blue-green lenses. Each patron was issued a pair of viewing spectacles to provide "fusion" of the projected images into a three-dimensional picture. Today, the emphasis on wider and wider movie projection screens is partially an attempt to create an illusion of depth without the necessity of two film projectors and special eyeglasses for the audience.

Stereophotography has also enjoyed periodic revivals of popularity among camera hobbyists. A few years ago, 35-mm stereo cameras with dual lens systems were marketed by several leading camera manufacturers (Figure 2.6). The decline of interest in three-dimensional color slides may be partially attributed to (1) the fact that hand viewers can be used by only one person at a time and (2) the fact that audience projection equipment is quite expensive by comparison with that required for conventional color slides.

When objects farther than 400 to 500 m away are viewed by unaided eyes, the special ability of depth perception is essentially lost. At such distances, lines of sight from each eye converge very little; in fact, they are nearly parallel when the eyes are focused on the horizon. If the human eye base

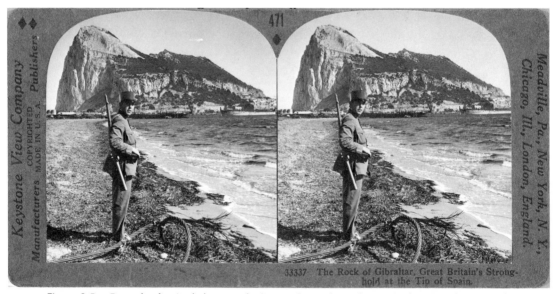

Figure 2.5. Example of paired photographs that produce a three-dimensional picture when viewed through a parlor stereoscope. View shows the Rock of Gibraltar at the southern tip of Spain. (Courtesy Keystone View Co.)

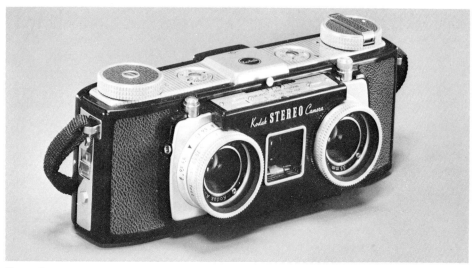

Figure 2.6.   Stereo camera for making three-dimensional color slides. (Courtesy Eastman Kodak Co.)

(interpupillary distance) were increased from the normal 60 to 66 mm, the perception of depth could be greatly increased. In a manner of speaking, this feat can be accomplished through aerial photography. From an airplane in level flight, overlapping camera exposures are made at intervals of several hundred metres. When any two successive prints are viewed through a simple stereoscope, each eye "occupies" one of the widely separated camera stations. This "stretching" of the human eye base results in a greatly exaggerated three-dimensional photograph for study and interpretation (Figures 2.7 and 2.8 and Plates 4, 5, and 6).

PHOTO-INTERPRETATION EQUIPMENT

Equipment essential to one interpreter may be of limited value to another, but anyone who uses aerial photographs regularly will probably find that this list closely approximates minimum needs:

Lens stereoscope, folding pocket type
Stereometer or parallax bar for measuring object heights
Engineer's scale, graduated to 0.5 mm or 0.02 in.
Drafting instruments, drawing ink, triangles, and protractor
Drop-bow pen and pencil set
Fountain pen for use with drawing ink
China-marking pencils or water-soluble inks
Tracing paper, vellum, drafting tape, and lens-cleaning tissue
Solvent and cotton swabs for cleaning photos
Needles for point-picking
Proportional dividers

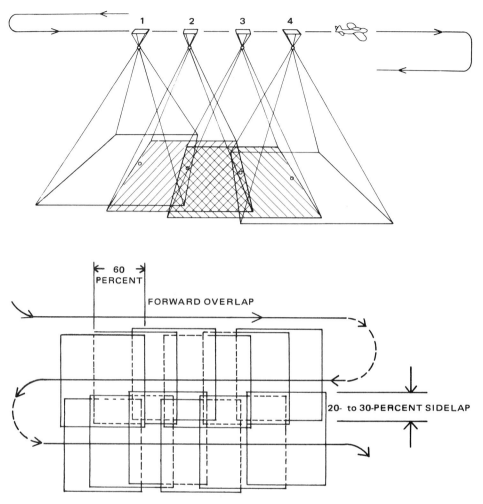

Figure 2.7.   Aerial camera stations are spaced to provide for a 60-percent forward overlap of aerial photographs along each flight line and a 20- to 30-percent sidelap for adjacent lines.

Magnetic or spring clipboard for holding stereopairs
Illuminated tracing table or fluorescent desk lamp
Dot grids or polar planimeter for area measurements

Several of the items listed may be improvised. One can build a good tracing table by installing several fluorescent tubes in a desk drawer and then covering the top with double-weight, frosted, or "flashed-opal" glass. To eliminate the need for fastening down stereopairs with drafting tape, an efficient holder can be made with a few ordinary magnets and a sheet of steel measuring about 30 by 40 cm. Individuals with extensive interpretation and mapping duties may find it desirable to acquire more specialized equipment, such as a mirror stereoscope, a vertical sketchmaster, a reflecting projector, or

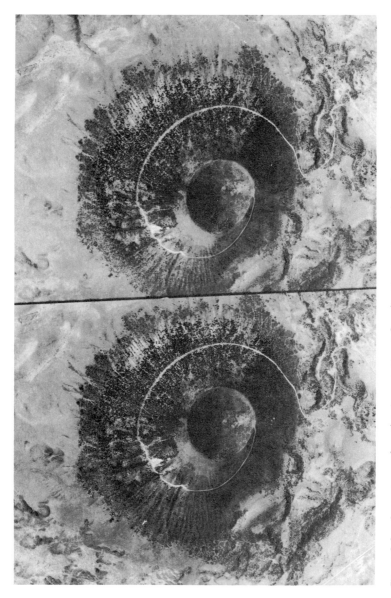

Figure 2.8. Stereogram of a volcanic cone, Mount Capulin, New Mexico. Scale is about 1:20,000. (Courtesy U.S. Department of Agriculture.)

stereoplotting devices. Functions of these items are detailed in sections that follow.

TYPES OF STEREOSCOPES

The function of a stereoscope is to deflect normally converging lines of sight so that each eye views a different photographic image. Parlor stereoscopes accomplished this by the placement of a thin prism before each eye. Ordinarily, no magnification was involved, but the result was a sharply defined, if occasionally distorted, three-dimensional picture.

Instruments used today for the three-dimensional study of aerial photographs are of three general types, namely, lens stereoscopes, mirror or reflecting stereoscopes, and zoom-type, magnifying stereoscopes. Lens stereoscopes utilize a pair of simple magnifying glasses to keep the eyes working independently and to keep their lines of sight approximately parallel. Photographs are viewed at a distance roughly equal to the focal length of the lenses, that is, the height of the instrument legs.

Most lens stereoscopes have a magnifying power of two to three diameters. They are inexpensive and relatively durable and can be quickly folded for field use or storage. The lens stereoscope pictured in Figure 2.9 has a fixed interpupillary distance of 65 mm and 2.8 × magnifying lenses; other suitable makes are available, and many have adjustable interpupillary settings. The primary drawback to lens stereoscopes is that only one-third to one-half of a standard print overlap can be studied stereoscopically at one time. However, the low cost and portability of such devices ensure their continued popularity among photo interpreters.

Reflecting stereoscopes provide a view of the entire overlap zone through a system of prisms or first-surface mirrors that effectively increase the interpupillary distance from about 65 mm to anywhere from 160 to 220 mm.

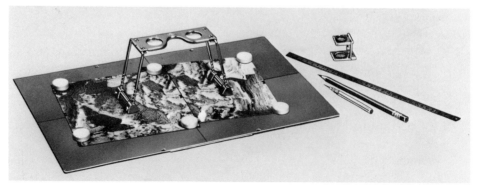

Figure 2.9. Pocket-sized lens stereoscope for viewing overlapping pairs of aerial photographs. Stereoscope and prints are held firmly to portable steel table by magnets. (Courtesy Carl Zeiss, Oberkochen.)

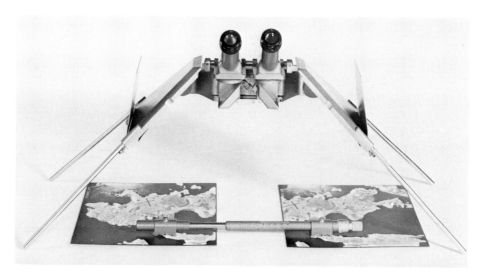

Figure 2.10.   Mirror stereoscope with inclined magnifying binoculars. Positioned on the photographs is a stereometer for measuring object heights. (Courtesy Wild Heerbrugg Instruments, Inc.)

Most basic models afford no magnification, but 3× to 8× binocular attachments are available as options. The greater the enlargement, however, the smaller the field of view. Reflecting stereoscopes, being rather specialized instruments, are produced in a variety of designs and price ranges. One type is illustrated in Figure 2.10.

Zoom magnifying stereoscopes are highly versatile, desk-type instruments that are normally intended for office interpretation (Figure 2.11). The asset of variable magnification can be paired with a capability for 360° optical image rotation of each optical system. This feature is ideal for studying uncut roll film where there is drift or crab in the line of flight (Figure 2.12).

Stereoscopic lenses, prisms, and other optics should be protected from dust or corrosion and should be cleaned only with optical lens cloth or tissue. Mirror stereoscopes, vertical sketchmasters, and other devices having first-surface mirrors also require delicate handling. Because these mirrors are silvered on the reflecting surface, they are easily corroded by fingerprints or perspiration. First-surface mirrors should be cleaned only in accordance with the manufacturer's instructions.

STEREO VIEWING WITHOUT INSTRUMENTS

Persons with normal vision and eyes of equal strength can often develop a facility for stereoscopic vision without the necessity of special aids or devices. With practice, some individuals can learn to keep lines of sight from each eye parallel and still bring images into focus. Stereoscopic fusion is aided by practice of the "sausage" exercise sketched in Figure 2.13. The eyes are

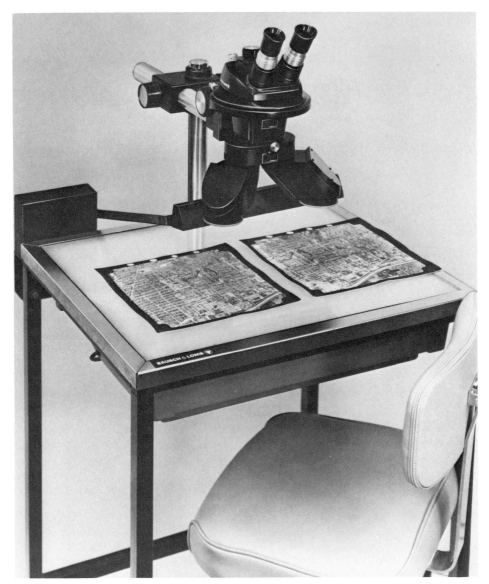

Figure 2.11. Zoom stereoscope with variable magnification ranging from 2.5× to 20×. The instrument is adapted for viewing of prints or transparencies of two sizes—13 by 13 cm or 23 by 23 cm. (Courtesy Bausch and Lomb, Inc.)

focused on a distant object as the forefingers are brought slowly into the line of vision. The farther apart the fingers when the "sausage" begins to form, the more nearly parallel are the lines of sight.

Another means of "forcing" each eye to see a different image is to place a card upright between left- and right-hand views of a stereopair such as that shown in Figure 2.8. In practice, most persons easily master the art of keeping the lines of sight parallel; the primary difficulty is that of maintaining this

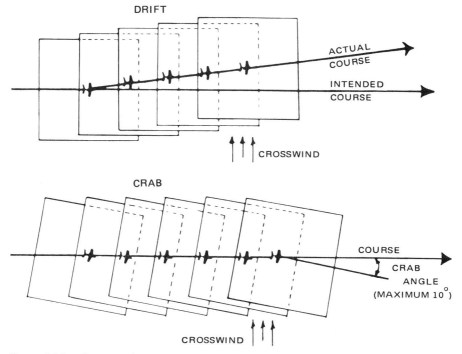

Figure 2.12.   If crosswinds are encountered during flight, the photographic airplane may be blown off course, causing an alignment defect known as *drift*. The pilot can avoid this by heading the airplane slightly into the wind. If the photographer does not adjust the camera to counteract this condition, a skewed or *crabbed* photograph results. Excessive drift or crab may reduce overlap to an undesirable level. (Courtesy U.S. Army Engineer School.)

condition while bringing the two different images into focus. In the case of the three-dimensional motion pictures discussed earlier, stereoscopic fusion was assisted by the use of polarized spectacles (*vectograph* principle), or by the viewing of images projected in complementary colors through eyeglasses having lenses of the opposite complementary colors (*anaglyph* principle). Stereoscopic prints based on these two concepts can be constructed for specialized illustrations, and instruments such as the Kelsh plotter utilize the anaglyph principle to create a three-dimensional model for contour mapping.

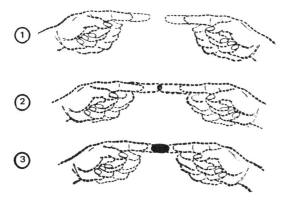

Figure 2.13.   The "sausage" exercise is a helpful technique for developing the facility of stereoscopic vision with unaided eyes. (Courtesy U.S. Department of the Army.)

PREPARING PHOTOGRAPHS FOR STEREO VIEWING

Photographic flights are planned so that prints will overlap about 60 percent of their width in the line of flight and 20 to 30 percent between flight strips. For effective stereo viewing, prints must be trimmed to the nominal size of 23 by 23 cm, preserving the four fiducial marks at the midpoints of each edge. Then the principal point (PP) or optical center of the photograph is located by alignment of opposite sets of fiducial marks with a straightedge. A light cross is drawn at the photo center and a fine needle hole picked at the intersection.

Next is the location of conjugate principal points (CPP) on each photograph (i.e., the points that correspond to principal points of adjacent photos). The lens stereoscope is adjusted to the proper interpupillary distance, and the first two photographs from a given flight line are arranged so that gross features overlap. Image shadows should be toward the observer; if they fall away from the viewer, there is a tendency to see relief in reverse. One photograph is clipped down, and the adjacent photograph is moved in the direction of the line of flight until corresponding images on each print are about 5.5 cm apart. The lens stereoscope is placed over the prints *parallel to the line of flight* so that the left-hand lens is over the left photograph and the right-hand lens is over the same image on the right-hand photograph. The area directly under each lens should then appear as a three-dimensional picture.

The movable photograph should next be fastened down. While viewing the three-dimensional picture, the observer places a needle on the unmarked print until it appears to fall precisely in the hole picked for the PP. This locates the CPP, although a monocular check should be made before the print is permanently marked. This procedure is repeated for all photographs; each will then have one PP and two CPPs, except that prints falling at the ends of the flight lines will have only one CPP. When all points have been verified, they should be marked with an inked circle.

Flight lines are located on each print by aligning the PPs and CPPs. The edges of the aligned circles should be connected with a finely inked line. Because of lateral shifting of the photographic aircraft in flight, a straight line will rarely pass through the PP and *both* CPPs on a given print. The photo base length for each stereo overlap is the average of the distance between the PP and CPP on one photograph and the corresponding distance on an overlapping print. This value should be measured to the nearest 0.5 mm and recorded on the back of each overlap. There will be two average base lengths for each print, that is, one for each set of overlapping flight lines.

ALIGNING PRINTS FOR STEREOSCOPIC STUDY

Stereoscopic study is beneficial to individuals having eyes of approximately equal strength and will not induce eyestrain or headaches if the photographs are aligned properly at all times. A print is selected and clipped down with

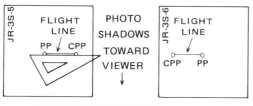

PRELIMINARY PHOTO ORIENTATION

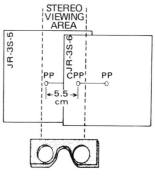

FINAL PHOTO ALIGNMENT

Figure 2.14. Method of aligning contact prints of 23 by 23 cm for viewing with a lens stereoscope. Principal points are denoted as PP; conjugate principal points are marked CPP.

shadows toward the viewer. The adjacent photograph is placed with its CPP about 5.5 cm from the corresponding PP on the first photograph. With flight lines superimposed, the second photograph is positioned and clipped down. The stereoscope is placed with its long axis parallel to the flight line and with the lenses over corresponding photo images. In this way, an overlapping strip 5.5 cm wide and 23 cm long can be viewed when the stereoscope is moved up and down the overlap area (Figure 2.14).

With the photos still clipped down, the prints can be flipped into reverse position with the opposite photo on top. This presents another area of the overlap for stereo viewing. In order to study the narrow strip between, one must curl the edge of one print upward or downward and move the stereoscope parallel to the flight line until the "hidden area" comes into view.

PROPER USE OF THE STEREOSCOPE

Beginning photo interpreters should be especially careful to cultivate proper stereoscopic viewing habits. Some of the more important rules to be observed are as follows:

1. Make certain that the photographs are properly aligned at all times, preferably with shadows falling toward the viewer.
2. Be careful to keep the eye base and the long axis of the stereoscope parallel to the flight line at all times.
3. Maintain an even, glare-free illumination on the prints or transparencies being studied and arrange for a comfortable sitting position.
4. Keep the stereoscope lenses clean, properly focused, and separated to the correct interpupillary distance. For most individuals, interpupillary distance is about 62 to 64 mm.
5. At the beginning, do not attempt to use the stereoscope more than 30 min out of any given 1-hr period.

SPECIAL PROBLEMS AFFECTING STEREOVISION

Interpreters who have difficulty in mastering the use of the stereoscope should be cognizant of the following factors that may affect stereovision:

1. A person's eyes may be of unequal strength. If one normally wears eyeglasses for reading and closeup work, one should also wear them when using the stereoscope.
2. Poor photographic illumination, misaligned prints, or uncomfortable viewing positions may result in eye fatigue.
3. Illness or severe emotional stress may create sensations of dizziness in one using a stereoscope.
4. An erroneous reversal of left and right prints will often cause a *pseudoscopic view* (i.e., topography will appear reversed). A similar view may be created if shadows fall away from the observer rather than toward the viewer as recommended.
5. Objects that change positions between exposures (i.e., automobiles, trains, boats) cannot be viewed stereoscopically.
6. In areas of steep topography, scale differences of adjacent photographs may make it difficult to obtain a three-dimensional image.
7. Dark shadows or clouds may prohibit stereoscopic study by obliterating detail on one photograph.
8. Individuals who have continued difficulties in using the stereoscope should not attempt to master the art of stereoscopic vision with unaided eyes.

CARE OF AERIAL PHOTOGRAPHS

In using and handling aerial photographs, one must exercise special care to protect the emulsion surface. Exposure to direct sunlight or excessive moisture should be avoided, and prints should not be marked on when damp. If drafting tape is to be removed, it should be pulled slowly toward the edge of the print; otherwise, the emulsion may be peeled off. As long as the surface is free from cracks, photographs may be cleaned with carbon tetrachloride or a damp sponge. Prints subjected to heat, even that produced by a desk lamp, have a tendency to curl. For this reason, aerial photographs should always be stored flat and under moderate pressure.

PROBLEMS

1. Position a lens stereoscope over the Zeiss stereoscopic vision test chart shown in Figure 2.15. Then rank the details within rings 1, 2, 3 and 6, 7, 8 in height order (highest = 1, second highest = 2, and so on). Answers are on page 48.

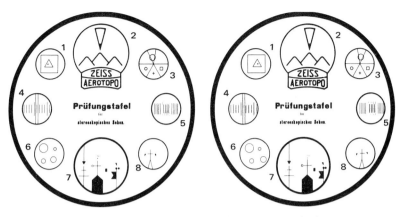

Figure 2.15.   Stereoscopic vision test chart. (Courtesy Carl Zeiss, Oberkochen.)

1. ( ) Triangle
   ( ) Square
   ( ) Point
   ( ) Marginal ring
2. ( ) Flanking mountains
   ( ) Marginal ring
   ( ) Spotting mark and central mountain
3. ( ) Square
   ( ) Cross
   ( ) Marginal ring
   ( ) Circle, lower left
   ( ) Circle, upper center
6. ( ) Circle, lower right
   ( ) Circle, upper left
   ( ) Circle, lower left
   ( ) Marginal ring
   ( ) Circle, upper right
7. ( ) Black circle
   ( ) Black triangle
   ( ) Flag with ball (black)
   ( ) Marginal ring
   ( ) Tower with cross and ring
   ( ) Black rectangle
   ( ) Double cross with arrowhead
8. ( ) Marginal ring
   ( ) Steeple and the two triangles

2. Position a lens stereoscope over the hidden word stereograms shown in Figure 2.16. What words appear in the three views? Answers are on page 48.

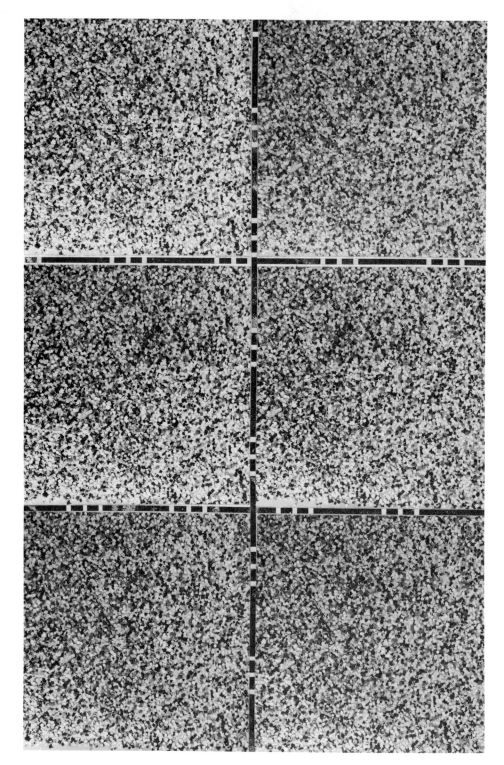

Figure 2.16. Hidden-word stereoscopic test developed by Sims and Hall (1956).

Top view _____

Middle view _____

Bottom view _____

3. Obtain four or more overlapping aerial photographs of your local area. At least two flight lines should be represented. Write your name on the back of each print. Following previous instructions, trim each print, locate principal points (PP) and conjugate principal points (CPP). Double-check to verify precise location; points picked incorrectly will appear to "float" or "sink" with respect to surrounding terrain. When available, a set of older prints should be used for practice in point-picking.

   With an ink pen, circle each PP and CPP. Ink flight lines and record average photo base length for each overlap as directed; you will use these values in Chapter 3 for computing object heights from parallax measurements.

   Arrange prints in mosaic fashion and observe direction of flight lines and orientation of shadows. If time of day is not shown, estimate the time of day (early morning, midday, late afternoon). Obtain the exact time and record on first and last prints in each flight line.

4. Record the following data for your own prints:
   a. Date(s) of photography _____
   b. Organization for which photos were originally flown _____
   c. Project symbol, film roll, and exposure numbers _____

   _____

   d. Film-filter combination used _____

   _____

   e. Approximate scale of photography _____
   f. Camera focal length (if shown on prints) _____
   g. Average ground elevation of local area _____ (above sea level)

5. Arrange prints in mosaic fashion and measure:
   a. Average forward overlap _____ percent
   b. Average sidelap _____ percent

6. Obtain a reliable map of the local area, such as a U.S. Geological Survey quadrangle sheet. With an engineer's scale and protractor, measure the following:
   a. Compass bearing of flight line 1 _____ °
   b. Compass bearing of flight line 2 _____ °
   c. Was the intended flight course north-south or east-west? _____

7. Check print alignment in each flight line. The combination of crab and drift

should not exceed 10 percent of the print width for any three consecutive photographs. Record as a percentage of print width affected:

Line 1 _____ percent   Line 2 _____ percent

8. Inspect all of your photographs closely and determine whether any of the following "defects" appear. Write print numbers opposite the applicable description.

Excessively long shadows _____

Shadows fuzzy due to overcast sky _____

Poor tonal contrast _____

Blurred print detail, especially in corners _____

Chemical streaks or stains _____

Emulsion scratches or cracks _____

Clouds or cloud shadows _____

Smoke or smog (industrial areas) _____

Excessive snow cover on ground _____

Floodwaters obscuring ground detail _____

Inadequate or incorrect print titling _____

Excessive forward overlap (more than 65 percent) _____

Deficient forward overlap (less than 50 percent) _____

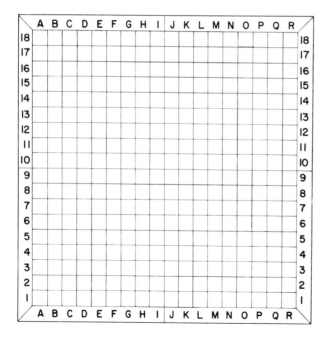

Figure 2.17. A point-designator grid for use as an overlay on contact prints of 23 by 23 cm. Small squares should be about 1 cm or 0.5 in. on a side.

Excessive sidelap (more than 45 percent) —————————

Deficient sidelap (less than 15 percent) —————————

Improper print alignment —————————————————

Tilted photographs (check ends of flight lines) ————————

9. On a 23-by-23-cm sheet of transparent cellulose acetate or heavy vellum, draft a point-designator grid such as that pictured in Figure 2.17. Set up your own prints for stereoscopic study with the point-designator grid carefully taped over the right-hand print so that grid midpoints are aligned with the four photo fiducial marks. Then refer to the checklist of typical features and write down (by grid location) as many items as you can identify. After the name of each feature, indicate a level of confidence for the identification (i.e., *confirmed*, *probable*, or *possible*). Tabulate information as follows:

Print number under grid ——————————   Locality ——————————

Grid Location	Feature Identified	Confidence Level

■ ANSWERS: ZEISS STEREOSCOPIC VISION TEST

1. (3) Triangle
   (2) Square
   (4) Point
   (1) Marginal ring
2. (2) Flanking mountains
   (1) Marginal ring
   (3) Spotting mark and
       central mountain
3. (4) Square
   (3) Cross
   (2) Marginal ring
   (1) Circle, lower left
   (5) Circle, upper center
6. (5) Circle, lower right

   (3) Circle, upper left
   (4) Circle, lower left
   (2) Marginal ring
   (1) Circle, upper right
7. (4) Black circle
   (3) Black triangle
   (5) Flag with ball (black)
   (1) Marginal ring
   (7) Tower with cross and ring
   (6) Black rectangle
   (2) Double cross with arrowhead
8. (1) Marginal ring
   (2) Steeple and the two triangles

■ ANSWERS: HIDDEN-WORD STEREOSCOPIC TEST

Top view: FATHER—SUN
Middle view: SOFT—SMOOT
Bottom view: FIR

References

American Optical Company. 1957. *A-O, H-R-R pseudoisochromatic plates.* 2nd ed. 15 pp. Buffalo, N.Y.

Hatch, C. R., and F. H. Kung. 1972. Computer-drawn stereograms. *Journal of Forestry* 70:489, illus.

Howard, John A. 1970. *Aerial photo-ecology.* Faber and Faber, London. 325 pp., illus.

Julesz, Bela. 1974. Cooperative phenomena in binocular depth perception. *American Scientist* 62:32–43, illus.

Moessner, Karl E. 1954. A simple test for stereoscopic perception. U.S. Forest Service, Central States Forest Experiment Station. Technical Paper 144, 14 pp., illus.

Seymour, Thomas D. 1957. The interpretation of unidentified information—a basic concept. *Photogrammetric Engineering* 23:115–121.

Sims, W. G., and Norman Hall. 1956. The testing of candidates for training as airphoto interpreters. Forestry and Timber Bureau, Commonwealth of Australia, Canberra. 12 pp., illus.

Wyllie, G. S., and F. B. Reeves. 1971. Stereograms as training aids. *Photogrammetric Engineering* 37:839–842, illus.

Chapter 3

Photo Scale and Stereoscopic Parallax

SCALE FROM FOCAL LENGTH AND ALTITUDE

As illustrated in Figure 3.1, the scale of a vertical aerial photograph is a function of the focal length of the camera lens and the height from which the exposure is made. The vertical aerial photograph presents a true record of angles, but measures of horizontal distance are subject to variation because of changes in ground elevations or flight altitudes. The nominal scale (e.g., 1:15,840) is representative only of the *datum*, an imaginary horizontal plane passing through a specified elevation above mean sea level (MSL). To make accurate measurements of distance, area, or height, it is necessary to determine, as nearly as possible, the *exact* photographic scale.

Cameras used for aerial photography may have focal lengths ranging from 50 to 610 mm (2 to 24 in.). The more commonly employed aerial cameras have focal lengths of 153, 210, or 305 mm (6, 8.25, or 12 in.). Knowledge of the focal length (F) and the altitude of the photographic aircraft above ground datum (H) makes it possible to determine the representative fraction (RF) or natural scale:

$$RF = \frac{F}{H} \qquad \textbf{Equation 3.1}$$

For example, with a camera focal length of 210 mm (0.21 m), a flight

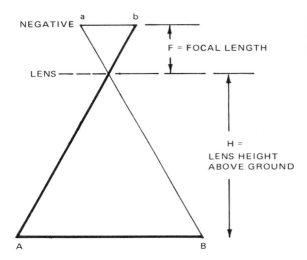

Figure 3.1. Relationship of focal length and height above ground to photo scale.

altitude of 2,500 m above MSL, and an average ground elevation of 400 m, the representative fraction would be computed as follows:

$$RF = \frac{0.21}{2,500 - 400} = \frac{0.21}{2,100} = \frac{1}{10,000} \text{ or } 1{:}10,000$$

It will be noted that the solution of this relationship requires that both numerator and denominator be *in the same units* (metres in this particular example). It is also emphasized that the computed scale of 1:10,000 will be precisely obtained *only* as long as the land surface is uniformly 400 m above sea level. If the elevation decreases, the photographic scales will be smaller; conversely, if higher topographic features are encountered, photo scales will be increased, because the land will have "moved closer" to the camera.

Aircraft flying heights are usually determined from altimeters that record barometric pressure and translate this information into height above sea level. The precision of such readings can vary considerably due to changes in air temperature and other factors. To improve on the accuracy of such instrumentation, Canada's National Research Council and Forest Management Institute have developed and tested a radar altimeter for use in low-altitude aerial photography.

The principal objective of the radar altimeter system is the precise measurement of aircraft-to-ground distance, irrespective of intervening vegetation. Over flat terrain, tests indicate that flying heights can be determined to within ±1 percent (probability level of 0.95) for altitudes of 240 to 1,100 m—the range desired for low-level photography. Over irregular terrain, the absolute error is about ±6 percent for the same altitudinal range.

SCALE FROM PHOTO-GROUND DISTANCES

While the preceding method of deriving photo scale is theoretically sound, it often happens that either camera focal length or the exact flight altitude is unknown to the interpreter. As a result, scale is more often calculated from the relationship between a photo measurement and a measured (or map-derived) ground distance:

$$\mathrm{RF} = \frac{\text{Photographic distance between two points (m)}}{\text{Ground distance between same points (m)}}$$ **Equation 3.2**

As an example, the distance between two road intersections might be measured on a vertical photograph as 60 mm, or 0.06 m. If the corresponding ground distance is measured as 1,584 m, the representative fraction would be computed as:

$$\mathrm{RF} = \frac{0.06}{1,584} = \frac{1}{26,400} \text{ or } 1{:}26{,}400$$

In the application of this technique, the two points selected for measurement should be diametrically opposed so that a line connecting them passes near the principal point (PP). If the points are also approximately equidistant from the PP, the effect of photographic tilt upon the scale determination will be minimized. To avoid the necessity of expensive ground surveys, terrain distances are often computed from reliable maps and substituted for measured ground distances in the foregoing relationship.

Scale approximations can also be made by use of objects or features of *known* ground dimensions, such as athletic fields, railway gauges, or aircraft wingspans. However, because the percentage of error increases as the measured distance decreases, very small objects are apt to produce sizable errors in such scale calculations.

In most instances, it is not essential to calculate the scale of every photograph in a flight line. Where the topography is relatively steep, measurements may be made on every third or fourth print; in flat terrain, even fewer checks are required.

Table 3.1 lists conversion factors for a wide range of photographic and map scales. Comparisons of identical photographic images at two different scales are shown in Figure 3.2

▓ IMAGE DISPLACEMENT ON AERIAL PHOTOS

On an accurate planimetric map, all features are depicted at their correct horizontal positions, and the observer thus has a truly vertical view of every detail shown. This standard cannot be met by aerial photographs, however, because of various sources of distortion or image displacement. Objects pictured on aerial photographs may fail to register in their correct plane positions because of (1) optical or photographic deficiencies, (2) tilting of the camera lens axis at the instant of exposure, or (3) variations in local relief.

The meaning of optical distortion is well understood by anyone who has gazed through the sharp curvature of a "wrap-around" auto windshield, or stared at his or her image in a doubly convex carnival mirror. When optical distortion is due to an inferior camera lens, the recorded images are displaced radially toward or away from the principal point of the photograph. Image

TABLE 3.1. Scale Conversions for Maps and Vertical Photographs

Representative Fraction (Scale)	Metres per Centimetre	Centimetres per Kilometre	Hectares per Square Centimetre	Feet per Inch	Inches per Mile	Acres per Square Inch
1:1,000	10	100.00	0.01	83.33	63.36	0.16
1:2,000	20	50.00	0.04	166.67	31.68	0.64
1:3,000	30	33.33	0.09	250.00	21.12	1.43
1:4,000	40	25.00	0.16	333.33	15.84	2.55
1:5,000	50	20.00	0.25	416.67	12.67	3.99
1:10,000	100	10.00	1.00	833.33	6.34	15.94
1:15,000	150	6.67	2.25	1,250.00	4.22	35.87
1:20,000	200	5.00	4.00	1,666.67	3.17	63.77
1:25,000	250	4.00	6.25	2,083.33	2.53	99.64
1:50,000	500	2.00	25.00	4,166.67	1.27	398.56
1:75,000	750	1.33	56.25	6,250.00	0.84	896.75
1:100,000	1,000	1.00	100.00	8,333.33	0.63	1,594.22
Method of calculation	$\dfrac{\text{RFD}^a}{100}$	$\dfrac{100,000}{\text{RFD}}$	$\dfrac{(\text{m/cm})^2}{10,000}$	$\dfrac{\text{RFD}}{12}$	$\dfrac{63,360}{\text{RFD}}$	$\dfrac{(\text{ft/in.})^2}{43,560}$

[a]RFD refers to the representative fraction denominator.

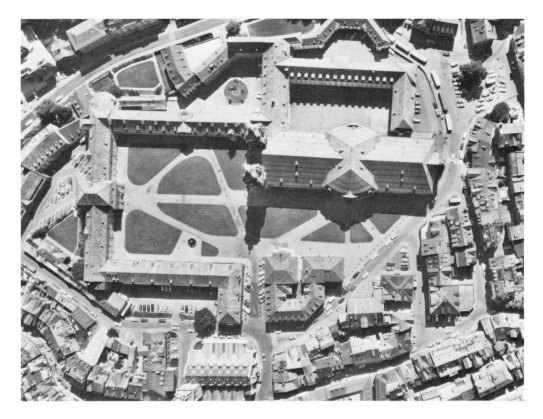

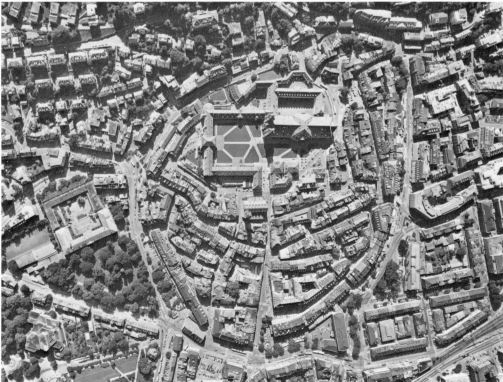

Figure 3.2. Comparison of photographic scales, Saint Gall, Switzerland. Top view is at a scale of about 1:2,000; the scale of the lower view is approximately 1:5,800. (Courtesy Wild Heerbrugg Ltd.)

distortions may also be induced by faulty shutters, film shrinkage, or failure of the film-flattening mechanism in the camera focal plane. Fortunately for the photo interpreter, such difficulties rarely occur. Modern camera systems in the hands of experienced flight crews have all but eliminated this source of image displacement.

A tilted photograph presents a slightly oblique view rather than a truly vertical record. Almost all aerial photographs are tilted to some degree, for the perfect aerial camera stabilizer has yet to be developed. The focus of tilt displacement is referred to as the *isocenter*, a point occurring at the "hinge" formed by the tilted negative and an imaginary horizontal plane. Images are displaced radially toward the isocenter on the upper side of a tilted photograph and radially outward or away from the isocenter on the lower side. Along the axis of tilt, there is no displacement relative to an equivalent untilted photograph. For these reasons, scale checks should make use of measurements between points located at the same elevation and on opposite sides of the print center. In this way, errors due to tilt (which may be present but not apparent) tend to be somewhat compensating.

The exact angle and direction of tilt are rarely known to the interpreter, and precise location of the isocenter is therefore a tedious process. Furthermore, the presence of small amounts of tilt often goes undetected. As only the central portions of most contact prints are used for interpretation, photographic tilt amounting to less than 2° or 3° can usually be ignored without serious consequences. In such cases, it is assumed that the isocenter coincides with the easily located principal point.

The most significant source of image displacement on aerial photographs is relief (i.e., differences in the relative elevations of objects pictured). Relief displacement is by no means limited to mountains and deep gorges; all objects that extend above or below a specified ground datum have their photographic images displaced to a greater or lesser extent. Skyscrapers, houses, automobiles, trees, grass, and even people are affected by this characteristic (Figure 3.3). An aerial photograph completely devoid of relief displacement is difficult to visualize. Perhaps the closest approximation would be a vertical photograph of a calm water surface (e.g., Lake Tahoe) or an unmarred landscape such as the Utah salt flats.

EFFECTS OF RELIEF DISPLACEMENT

The underlying cause of relief displacement can be traced to the perspective view "seen" by a camera lens pointed straight down toward the earth's surface. If a single exposure is precisely centered over a tall smokestack, the photographic image will appear merely as a doughnut-shaped ring, perhaps not unlike that of an open-topped cistern only a few metres high. There is little image displacement here, for this is the one point where the camera lens affords a truly vertical view. By contrast, suppose another smokestack occurs near the *edge* of the print. In this instance, the camera eye looks more at the *side* of the smokestack than "down the barrel." The recorded image thus

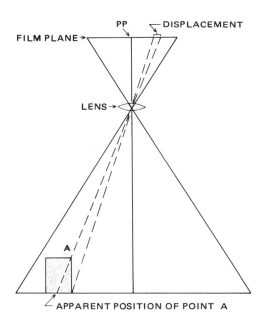

Figure 3.3. Schematic representation of relief displacement on a single, vertical photograph.

appears to lean radially *outward* from the center of the photograph. More specifically, displacement is radial from the *nadir*, a point that also coincides with the principal point on truly vertical photographs. It can be stated that objects projecting *above* a specified datum are displaced radially *outward* from the nadir, while those *below* the datum are displaced radially *inward* toward the nadir. Irrespective of the direction of displacement, a line drawn from the nadir through a displaced image will pass through the true horizontal position of the object.

An outstanding example of relief displacement is illustrated in Figure 3.4. In the left-hand view, the transmission line is almost directly under the camera lens. Therefore, relief displacement is minimized, and the right-of-way appears in its true ground configuration as a nearly straight line. In the right view, however, the transmission line was imaged near the edge of the photograph. As a result, the distance from the nadir, coupled with large topographic changes, has caused the right-of-way to be displaced into a nonlinear feature.

The meteoritic crater pictured in Figure 3.5 furnishes an example of relief displacement for images *below* ground datum. With an engineer's scale, it can be verified that corresponding images at the bottom of the crater are farther apart than those at the rim surface (ground datum). Thus the two images of the 175-m depression are displaced *toward* their respective nadirs (off the left and right print margins).

In summary, it may be concluded that the amount of relief displacement is directly correlated with the actual height (or depth) of an object and its distance from the nadir. Tall objects pictured near the edges of prints will exhibit maximum displacement. Displacement is affected also by the flight altitude and hence by the focal length of the camera used. At a given photo

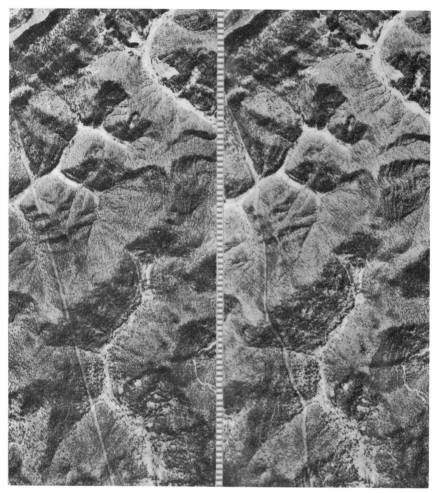

Figure 3.4. Stereogram illustrating the displacement of a transmission line due to relief. Location is Bell County, Kentucky; scale is about 1:36,000. (Courtesy Tennessee Valley Authority.)

scale, a 150-mm focal length will result in twice as much image displacement as a 300-mm focal length, because the former will be taken from one-half the altitude of the latter. While relief displacement constitutes a source of error in measuring horizontal distances on aerial photographs, it is this same characteristic that makes it possible to study overlapping prints stereoscopically. This point can be easily demonstrated with two prints made from the *same* negative; a three-dimensional view is unattainable due to a lack of relative image displacement.

Thus, the goal of the aerial surveyor is to make certain that there is sufficient image displacement to assure three-dimensional study and yet to avoid the excessive distortions that prevent stereoscopic fusion. Because the amount of relief itself cannot be controlled, this objective must be accomplished by manipulations in flight altitudes and camera focal lengths. When it is desired to increase the exaggeration of the third dimension, as in relatively flat terrain, a shorter focal length is commonly specified. Conversely, in extremely mountainous country, a longer lens might be used, because excessive displacement makes stereoscopic viewing uncomfortable.

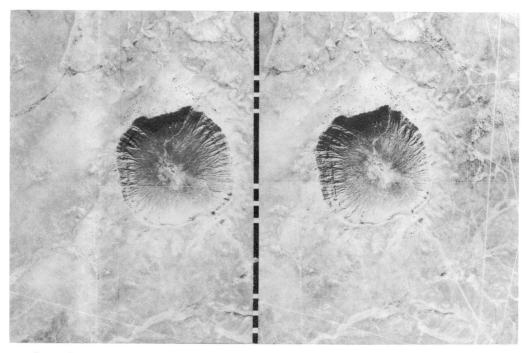

Figure 3.5.   Stereogram of Meteor Crater, Coconino County, Arizona. Scale is about 1:40,000. The crater is approximately 1,265 m across and 175 m deep. (Courtesy U.S. Department of Agriculture.)

▓ MEASURING HEIGHTS OF DISPLACED OBJECTS

The exaggerated displacement of tall objects pictured near the edges of large-scale, vertical photographs sometimes permits accurate measurement of object heights on single prints. This specialized technique of height evaluation is feasible provided that:

1. The principal point can be accepted as the *nadir* position.
2. The flight altitude above the base of the object can be precisely determined.
3. Both the top and base of the object are clearly visible.
4. The degree of image displacement is great enough to be *accurately* measured with available equipment (e.g., an engineer's scale).

When all of these conditions can be met, object heights may be determined by this relationship:

$$\text{Height of object (ho)} = \frac{d}{r} \, (\text{H})$$ **Equation 3.3**

where: d = Length of the displaced image
r = Radial distance from the nadir to the top of the displaced image
H = Aircraft flying height above the base of the object

Measurements of d and r must be *in the same units*; H is expressed in the units desired for the height of the object. For example, if it is assumed that the photograph in Figure 3.6 was taken from an altitude of 914 m, the tank heights might be computed as follows:

$$\text{Tank A: ho} = \frac{4.5 \, \text{mm}}{59.5 \, \text{mm}} \, (914) = 69 \, \text{m}$$

$$\text{Tank B: ho} = \frac{9.5 \, \text{mm}}{127 \, \text{mm}} \, (914) = 68 \, \text{m}$$

Thus both tanks are about the same height. The accuracy of height determinations by this technique is dependent upon vertical (nontilted) photographs, precise values for flying heights, and very careful measurement techniques. If any of these factors is open to question, resulting heights must be regarded as approximations only. In the calculation for tank B, for example, a measurement of 9.0 mm instead of 9.5 mm for the length of the displaced image would change the resulting object height from 68 m to only 65 m.

▓ STEREOSCOPIC PARALLAX

If a nearby object is observed alternately with the left eye and right eye, its location will appear to shift from one position to another. This apparent displacement, caused by a change in the point of observation, is known as parallax. Parallax is a normal characteristic of overlapping aerial photo-

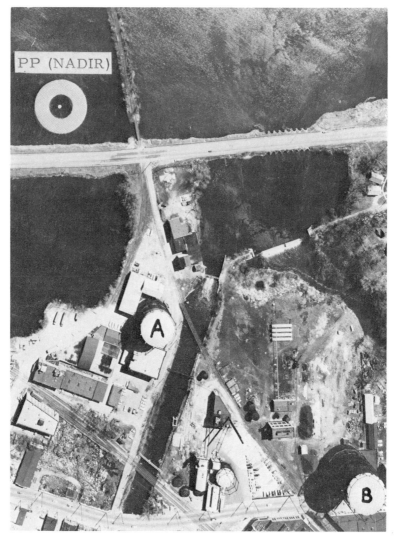

Figure 3.6. Industrial area, pictured at a scale of about 1:6,000. The tanks marked A and B are the same height; tank B shows more image displacement because it is farther from the nadir. (Courtesy Abrams Aerial Survey Corp.)

graphs, and it is the basis for three-dimensional viewing. The apparent elevation of an object is due to differences in its image displacement on adjacent prints.

Two measures of parallax must be obtained when object heights are being determined on stereoscopic pairs of photographs. *Absolute stereoscopic parallax* (x-parallax) is the sum of the distances of corresponding images from their respective nadirs. It is always measured *parallel* to the flight line. *Differential parallax* is merely the difference in the absolute stereoscopic parallax at the top and the base of the object being measured. The basic formula for determining object heights (ho) or differences in elevation from parallax measurements is:

$$(ho) = (H)\frac{dP}{P + dP}$$ **Equation 3.4**

where: H = Height of the aircraft above the ground datum
         P = Absolute stereoscopic parallax at the base of the object being measured
         dP = Differential parallax

The height of the aircraft (H) should be expressed in the units desired for the object height. This will usually be metres or feet. Once a precise photo scale has been ascertained, the flight altitude can be found by multiplication of the RF denominator by the camera focal length. Absolute stereoscopic parallax (P) and differential parallax (dP) must be *in the same units*. Ordinarily, these units will be millimetres and hundredths or inches and thousandths, depending on the calibration of the parallax device used for measurements. Because both metric and English instruments may be encountered, examples that follow illustrate both types of calculations.

▓ AVERAGE PHOTO BASE LENGTH

For reasons of convenience and ease of measurement, the average photo base length of a stereopair is commonly substituted as the absolute stereoscopic parallax (P) in the solution of Equation 3.4. This procedure produces reasonably accurate results if:

1. Photographic tilt is less than 3°.
2. Both negatives of the stereopair were exposed from the same flight altitude.
3. Both nadirs, or principal points, are at the same ground elevation.
4. The base of the object to be measured is at essentially the same elevation as that of the principal points.

Under these circumstances, y-parallax, or displacement at right angles to the flight line, is considered nonexistent. Furthermore, principal points can be substituted for nadir locations in measurements of absolute stereoscopic parallax.

Variations in the elevation of the two principal points of a stereopair will result in differing measurements of corresponding base lengths. In such instances, the use of the *average* photo base length supplies an estimate of the absolute stereoscopic parallax for an imaginary datum midway between the actual principal point elevations. A more serious situation is presented when the elevation at the base of the object being measured differs by more than 50 to 100 m from that of the principal points. Here, a new value should be calculated for absolute stereoscopic parallax:

1. Set up the stereopair for normal viewing. Flight lines should be super-

imposed and images separated about 5.5 cm. Both prints should be firmly fastened down to avoid movement.

2. Measure the distance between the two principal points to the nearest 0.5 mm.

3. Measure the distance (parallel to the flight line) between corresponding images on the two photographs at or near the base of the desired object. Subtract this distance from that obtained in step 2 to obtain the absolute stereoscopic parallax at the base of the object.

DIRECT MEASUREMENTS OF PARALLAX

Differential parallax (dP) is usually measured stereoscopically with a parallax wedge or parallax bar (stereometer) that incorporates the "floating-mark" principle. However, the *concept* of differential parallax can best be illustrated by direct scale measurement of heavily displaced images, and the stereopair of the Washington Monument (Figure 3.7) supplies an ideal example. The nominal photo scale of 1:4,800 is first corrected to an exact scale of 1:4,600 at the base of the monument. Because a 12-in. camera focal length was used, the flying height above ground (H) is 4,600 ft.

Average photo base length (P) for the stereopair is 4.40 in. Absolute stereoscopic parallax at the base and top of the monument is measured parallel to the line of flight with an engineer's scale; the difference (2.06 − 1.46 in.) is dP, the differential parallax of the displaced images. (Because the monument has the shape of an obelisk, measurements were made at the midpoint of the base and vertically above this position at the pyramidal top.) Substituting the foregoing values into Equation 3.4, we have:

$$ho = (4,600)\frac{0.60}{4.40 + 0.60} = 552\,ft$$

This is an unusually precise estimate, for the actual height of the monument is 555.5 ft (about 169 m). Had the nominal scale of photography (1:4,800) been used instead of the corrected scale, the height would have been computed as 576 ft, an error of 21 ft. Errors of similar magnitude would result from inaccurate parallax measurements. Thus, the necessity for precision can hardly be overemphasized.

A diagrammetric explanation of differential parallax is shown in Figure 3.8. If a flying height of 3,000 m and an average photo base length of 80.5 mm are assumed for this illustration, the tree height would be computed as:

$$ho = (3,000)\frac{0.52}{80.50 + 0.52} = 19.2\,m$$

FUNCTIONS OF STEREOMETERS

The interpreter must recognize that the degree of stereoscopic parallax encountered on small-scale (*high-altitude*) photography is often much less than that illustrated by Figures 3.7 and 3.8. Therefore, differential parallax is

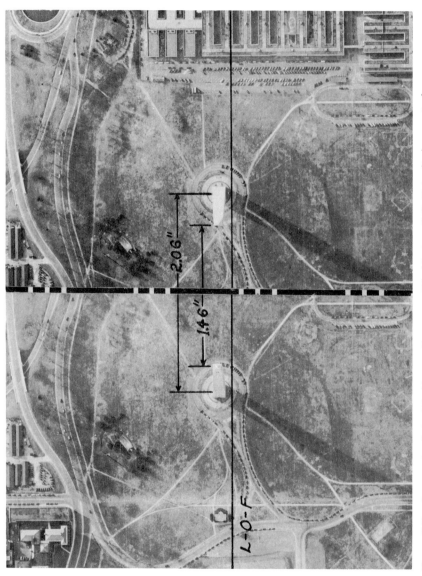

Figure 3.7. Stereopair of the Washington Monument, Washington, D.C. Note displacement of images parallel to line of flight (LOF) and measurements for determination of differential parallax. Scale is 1:4,600 at the base of the monument.

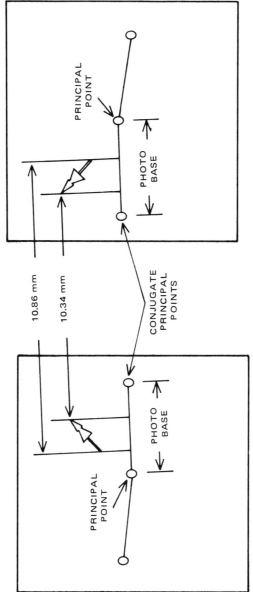

Figure 3.8. Direct measurement of differential parallax for a heavily displaced tree image. Note that base and height measurements are made exactly parallel to the photo base or line of flight. The differential parallax (dP) is 0.52 mm.

usually measured under the stereoscope with a parallax wedge or stereometer, because a precise determination by direct measurement is virtually impossible.

If a small dot is inked at precisely the same location on both prints of a stereopair, the two dots will merge into one when viewed through a stereoscope. Had one pair of dots been placed on level ground and another pair on top of a tree or building, each pair would merge into a single mark; the first pair would appear to lie at ground level, while the second pair (being slightly closer together) would appear to "float" in space at the elevation of the object on which the dots were inked. If the distance between each pair of corresponding dots can be precisely measured, the algebraic difference will be a measure of differential parallax. The function of a stereometer is to measure such changes in parallax that are too small to be determined by direct linear scaling.

■ THE PARALLAX WEDGE

An inexpensive device often used for measuring differential parallax is the parallax wedge. The basic design, usually printed on transparent film or glass, consists of two rows of dots or graduated lines beginning about 2.5 in. apart and converging to about 1.8 in. apart. Graduations on the wedge are calibrated for making parallax readings to the nearest 0.002 in.

In use, the parallax wedge is placed over the stereoscopic image with the converging lines perpendicular to the line of flight and then shifted until a single fused line of dots is seen sloping downward through the stereo model. If corresponding images are separated by exactly 2 in., a small portion of the wedge centered around the 2-in. separation of converging lines will fuse and appear as a single line. The line will appear to "split" above and below this section. Using the fused line of graduations, and counting the number of intervals between the point where a graduation appears to rest on the ground and the point where another graduation appears to "float" in the air at the same height as the top of the object, one then obtains the differential parallax.

In Figure 3.9, for example, the difference in parallax (dP) between the ground and the highest roof level of the building might be read as ten intervals on the wedge, or 0.020 in. Assuming a flight altitude (H) of 5,400 ft and a photo base length (P) of 1.850 in., one determines the building height as follows:

$$ho = (5,400)\frac{0.020}{1.850 + 0.020} = 58 \text{ ft}$$

■ THE PARALLAX BAR OR STEREOMETER

Many interpreters prefer the parallax bar to the wedge, because the floating dot is movable and thus easier to place on the ground and on the tops of objects. Stereometers of two different types are illustrated in Figures 3.10 and 3.11.

The typical parallax bar has two lenses attached to a metal frame that

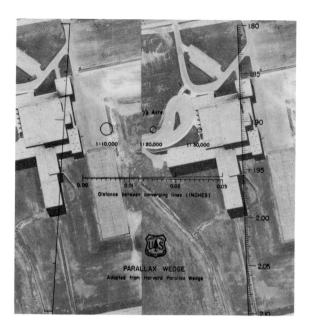

Figure 3.9. Parallax wedge correctly oriented over a stereogram of a large, flat-roofed building. Graduations on the right-hand side indicate the separation of the converging lines to the nearest 0.002 in.

houses a vernier and a graduated metric scale. The left lens contains the fixed reference dot; the dot on the right lens can be moved laterally by means of the vernier. The bar is placed over the stereoscopic image parallel to the line of flight. The right-hand dot is moved until it fuses with the reference dot and appears to rest on the ground, and the vernier reading is recorded to the nearest 0.01 mm. Then the vernier is turned until the fused dot appears to "float" at the elevation of the object being measured. A second vernier reading is taken, and the difference between the two readings is the differential parallax (dP). This value can be substituted in the parallax formula without

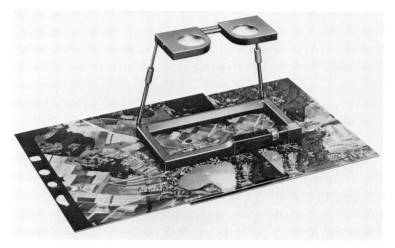

Figure 3.10. Lens stereoscope with attached stereometer. The knurled cylinder can be revolved to move the right-hand lens and create a floating dot. (Courtesy Carl Zeiss, Oberkochen.)

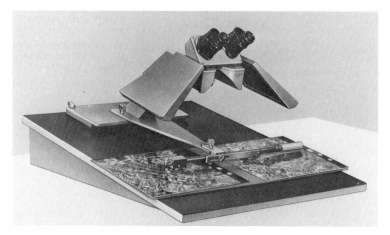

Figure 3.11.   Mirror stereoscope with inclined magnifying binoculars and an attached stereometer for measuring heights of objects. (Courtesy Carl Zeiss, Oberkochen.)

conversion if the absolute parallax (P) is also expressed in millimetres. Calculations are handled as in the metric example previously cited for Figure 3.8.

PRECISION OF HEIGHT DETERMINATIONS

Precision in measurement of object heights depends on a number of factors, not the least of which is the individual's ability to perceive stereoscopic parallax. It is also apparent that measurement precision will be improved when objects are clearly imaged on high-resolution, nontilted photographs of known scale, flight altitude, and photo base length.

TABLE 3.2. Precision of Height Measurements for Parallax Intervals of 0.05 mm

Average Photo Base (P), in Millimetres	Average Forward Overlap as a Percentage[a]	Flying Height (H) Above Ground, in Metres				
		500	1,000	2,000	5,000	10,000
		Object Heights, in Metres per 0.05 mm				
70	70	0.36	0.71	1.43	3.57	7.14
75	67	0.33	0.67	1.33	3.33	6.66
80	65	0.31	0.62	1.25	3.12	6.25
85	63	0.29	0.59	1.18	2.94	5.88
90	61	0.28	0.56	1.11	2.78	5.55
95	59	0.26	0.53	1.05	2.63	5.26
100	57	0.25	0.50	1.00	2.50	5.00
105	54	0.24	0.48	0.95	2.38	4.76
110	52	0.23	0.45	0.91	2.27	4.54

[a] Assumes photographs of 23 by 23 cm. Values for object heights were derived by solution of the parallax formula as presented elsewhere in this chapter.

Average Photo Base (P), in Inches	Average Forward Overlap as a Percentage[a]	Flying Height (H) Above Ground, in Feet				
		1,000	2,000	5,000	10,000	20,000
		Object Heights, in Feet per 0.002 in.				
2.7	70	0.74	1.5	3.7	7.4	14.8
2.9	68	0.69	1.4	3.4	6.9	13.8
3.1	66	0.64	1.3	3.2	6.4	12.9
3.3	63	0.61	1.2	3.0	6.1	12.1
3.5	61	0.57	1.1	2.8	5.7	11.4
3.7	59	0.54	1.1	2.7	5.4	10.8
3.9	57	0.51	1.0	2.6	5.1	10.2
4.1	54	0.49	1.0	2.4	4.9	9.8
4.3	52	0.46	0.9	2.3	4.6	9.3

TABLE 3.3. Precision of Height Measurements for Parallax Intervals of 0.002 in.

[a] Assumes photographs of 9 by 9 in. Values for object heights were derived by solution of the parallax formula as presented elsewhere in this chapter.

It is generally believed that skilled interpreters can detect and measure parallax differences of 0.05 mm (0.002 in.) when using the simple parallax devices discussed in this chapter. If these values are accepted as minimum measurement units, then the precision of height determinations will be solely dependent on the flying height of the aircraft and the average photo base length.

Provided stereoscopic fusion is not hampered by excessive image displacements, the precision of height measurements will improve as forward overlap and aircraft flying height are decreased (overlap should not be reduced to less than 50 percent, of course). This concept is illustrated by Tables 3.2 and 3.3, which were derived for various photo bases (i.e., overlaps) and flying heights by iterative solutions of the parallax formula. The tables are presented in both metric and English units for application with either stereometers or parallax wedges.

Interpreters should be conscious of the following points as a means of improving the precision of height measurements.

1. High-contrast (or color) exposures may improve object clarity and therefore make ground and top readings less tedious and more definitive.
2. Black-and-white positive transparencies used over a light table are greatly superior to ordinary prints for all types of measurements.
3. Individual interpreters often have much greater confidence (and ability) with a specific type of parallax-measuring device as compared to another type.
4. In rough terrain, the calculation of the exact scale and flying height for each overlap is desirable. For objects on high ridges or in deep ravines, it is better to compute new values for absolute stereoscopic parallax than to use the average photo base length.
5. Once a pair of photographs has been aligned for stereo viewing, they

should be fastened down to prevent movement. A slip of either exposure between readings at the base or top of an object will result in large errors.

6. To avoid single measurements of high variability, it is recommended that several parallax readings be made for each object and the results averaged. Rest periods are desirable between measurements of the same objects.

▓ PROBLEMS

1. Compute the scale for your own set of aerial photographs from ratios of several photo and ground distances. (Ground distances may be derived from reliable maps, from the lengths of known features, such as ground survey lines, or from direct field measurements.) Record below:

Description of Line	Ground Distance	Photo Distance	RF

Average Scale (RF)_____

2. Refer to Table 3.1 and convert your average scale to the following units:

_____m/cm or ft/in.

_____cm/km or in./mi

_____ha/cm² or acres/in.²

3. If the camera focal length is known, compute the flying height of the photographic aircraft above ground:

_____

Calculate the flying height above MSL:

_____

4. Measure the dimensions of several accessible features on your local photographs and convert to ground distances. Then check these distances

by direct ground measurement. Compare and explain possible reasons for differences.

Description of Feature	Photo-Derived Dimensions	Ground Check

5. Complete the following form for use in measuring heights on your own photographs. Determine the *exact* scale of your prints before computing flying height. Then solve the parallax formula to determine (a) the change in elevation per 0.01 mm of dP and (b) the change in elevation per 0.002 in. of dP.

Stereo Overlap Number	Height (H)		Average Photo Base Length (P)		Change in Height or Elevation	
	Metres	Feet	Millimetres	Inches	Per 0.01 mm dP	Per 0.002 in. dP

6. Locate several objects such as trees, buildings, or smokestacks within the overlap zones of your photographs. Select features that are not likely to have changed since your exposures were made. Measure their heights with a stereometer (floating-mark device) and record below. If feasible, check these heights by ground measurement for a comparison of results.

Stereo Overlap Number	Description of Object	dP	Photo Height	Ground Check	Difference (+ or −)

References

Avery, T. E. 1971. Two cameras for parallax height measurements. *Photogrammetric Engineering* 37:576.

———. 1978. Forester's guide to aerial photo interpretation. Government Printing Office, Washington, D.C. U.S. Department of Agriculture, Agriculture Handbook 308, 41 pp., illus.

Methley, B. D. F. 1970. Heights from parallax bar and computer. *Photogrammetric Record* 6 (35): 459–465.

Moessner, Karl E., and Grover A. Choate. 1966. Terrain slope estimation. *Photogrammetric Engineering* 32:67–75, illus.

Nielsen, U. 1974. Description and performance of the forestry radar altimeter. Forest Management Institute, Canadian Forestry Service, Ottawa. 17 pp., illus.

Schut, G. H., and M. C. van Wijk. 1965. The determination of tree heights from parallax measurements. *Canadian Surveyor* 19:415–427, illus.

■ Chapter 4

Stereograms, Shadow Heights, and Areas

■ AERIAL STEREOGRAMS

One of the best ways for an interpreter to build a file of reference material is to prepare sample stereograms for various classes of objects depicted on aerial photographs. Once a representative set of stereograms has been compiled, the interpreter can easily organize the material into a formalized selective or elimination key. Vertical, oblique, or ground photographs can be used for stereograms; in some cases, two or more views may be combined in the same illustration (Figure 4.1).

One can make stereograms by cutting out left-hand and right-hand views from overlapping photographs and mounting them in correct orientation on heavy card stock. Aerial stereograms are preferably prepared from single-weight, glossy prints. For maximum utility, all features in a given category (e.g., tree species, landforms, industries) should be pictured on prints of the same scale, made from the same film type and in the same season. When a set of stereogram cards have been indexed by subject and geographic region, they can be valuable for training purposes and for identifying similar features on subsequent aerial surveys.

The following step-by-step procedure has been found useful in the preparation of aerial stereograms from contact prints of 23 by 23 cm:

1. Determine the geographic locale of the prints from maps or photo index

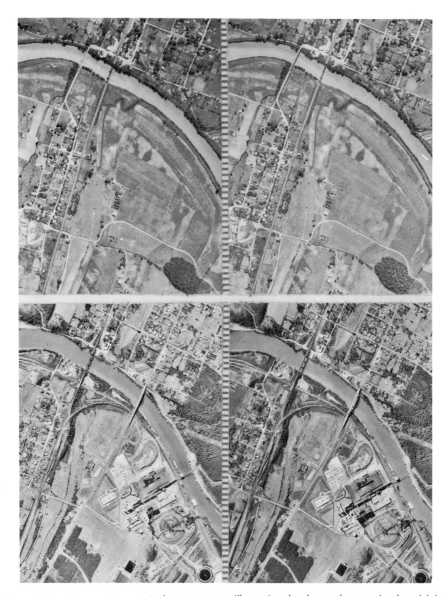

Figure 4.1. Comparative vertical stereograms illustrating land-use changes in the vicinity of Calhoun, Tennessee. The top view was made in 1937; the lower view was made in 1967. Scale is approximately 1:24,000. (Courtesy Tennessee Valley Authority.)

sheets; record all photographic data that might be lost after prints are trimmed. Then, clean all print surfaces thoroughly.

2. Locate principal points and conjugate principal points; pinpoint with fine needle holes.

3. Draw in flight lines for the overlapping pair; use a sharpened chinagraph pencil or a soft lead pencil so that the lines may be easily removed later. Measure and record the average photo base length.

4. Delineate the desired view within a space about 5.5 cm wide as measured along the flight line. Enclose this view with parallel lines drawn exactly at right angles to the flight line (Figure 4.2). Transfer the identical view to the overlapping print by using a stereoscope. Draw these lines with a hard pencil so as to indent the emulsion surface.

5. Orient prints with shadows falling toward observer; then mark the delineated portions to be cut as left (L) or right (R).

6. Recheck all items (steps 1 through 5). Be sure you have recorded the following data *before* cutting out views:
   a. Locality—county, state
   b. Project symbol, roll and exposure numbers
   c. Print scale
   d. Date and time of photography
   e. Average photo base length
   f. Camera focal length
   g. Agency responsible for photography, such as U.S. Department of Agriculture

7. Cut out the two views on a sharp paper cutter and align flight line (be sure to check left and right notations). Tape the two views about 1.5 to 2 mm apart by using a strip of transparent tape on the underside. Check stereoscopic fusion and alignment with a lens stereoscope.

8. Trim the stereopair in height to fit a standardized format such as a card reference file. Mount on card with rubber cement or gum arabic and record data from step 6 on the back of the card.

▨ GROUND STEREO CAMERAS

Ground stereophotography is most easily accomplished by means of a dual-lens stereo camera equipped with negative film. However, stereo cameras are produced by only a few manufacturers around the world. Those most recently

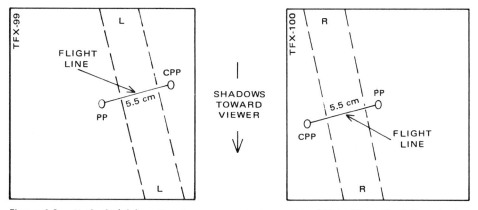

Figure 4.2. Method of delineating stereogram cutouts on prints of 23 by 23 cm. The 5.5-cm viewing width may be varied slightly, provided it does not exceed the observer's interpupillary distance.

marketed in North America have a 35-mm film format, while a model made in the U.S.S.R. uses number 120 (about 70-mm) roll film. Focal lengths of the paired lenses are usually about 30 to 40 mm for the 35-mm cameras and about 50 to 75 mm for the larger-format cameras.

A typical stereo camera has two lenses of identical focal length arranged on parallel axes and separated by an "average observer's" interocular distance (i.e., by about 65 mm). This arrangement is based on the theory that the ideal condition for orthostereoscopy requires a separation of camera lenses and stereo viewing lenses that is identical to the observer's interpupillary distance. If stereograms are made with the camera focused at infinity, the focal length of the stereoscopic viewing lenses should also be the same as the focal length of the camera lenses. All these conditions are seldom achieved, but slight departures are discernible only to the most critical observers.

▓ IMPROVISED STEREO CAMERAS

When stereo cameras are not available, one can make three-dimensional photographs by (1) mounting two identical cameras together on a plane table or level tripod and equipping them for simultaneous shutter release or (2) using a single camera to make two separate pictures from paired exposure stations.

In either case, it is essential that both photographs of a stereopair have the same base line; this condition is met only when the cameras are level in a lateral direction. If a camera is tilted laterally, each view might be trimmed separately so that vertical lines of the scene are vertical in the picture, but each then has a different base line. For this reason, cameras should be mounted in a frame or on a base that can be precisely leveled. Furthermore, the axes of the lenses must be exactly parallel; either convergence or divergence will introduce a distortion of parallax, resulting in difficult stereoscopic fusion or observer eyestrain or both.

Single-lens or twin-lens reflex cameras with a 70-mm film format are ideal for ground stereophotography, for the resulting overlap zone of 55 to 65 mm provides an optimum image separation for viewing with lens stereoscopes. The views in Figure 4.3 were made with two twin-lens reflex cameras mounted together on a common base and equipped with a dual cable release for the shutters. In these stereograms, an increase in the lens separation to about 15 cm for the upper view and about 30 cm for the lower view greatly exaggerated the three-dimensional effect.

▓ GROUND STEREOGRAMS FROM SINGLE CAMERAS

Ground stereograms can be made with a single camera when the scene being imaged remains stationary for the required interval between exposures (i.e., for several seconds). Objects in the overlap area that move between exposures (clouds, autos, windblown foliage) will *not* form satisfactory three-dimensional images, because their motion creates artificial parallax.

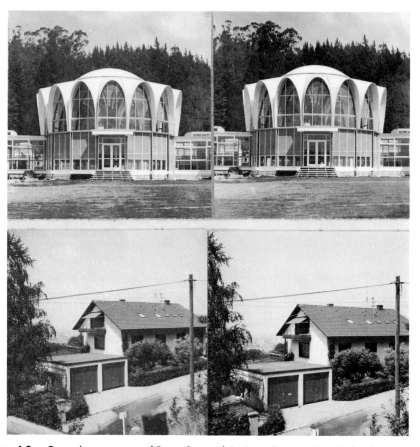

Figure 4.3.   Ground stereograms of Forest Research Institute, Rotorua, New Zealand (above), and a residence in Freiburg, West Germany (below). The views in each stereogram were made simultaneously with two Zeiss Super Ikonta cameras.

The basic geometry of overlapping views obtained with a single camera is illustrated by Figure 4.4. As previously outlined, care must be exercised to maintain a level, straight base line and absolute parallelism of lens axes. A level plane table thus provides an ideal camera platform. The addition of a box-type slide (for parallel movement of the camera between left and right exposures) and a graduated scale (for controlling the camera base length) completes the apparatus.

The three-dimensional effect (parallax) of a given scene will be heightened if the camera base length is increased (i.e., if the amount of overlap is decreased). For objects of limited relief, the recommended base is about 1/10 the distance to the foreground; with scenes of pronounced relief (e.g., landscapes), a base of about 1/20 of the distance to the foreground is likely to produce better results. For any given camera and subject, of course, the optimum base length is best obtained by experimentation.

As exposures are made, notes should be taken on whether left-hand or right-hand exposures were taken first on the film roll. The resulting pairs of

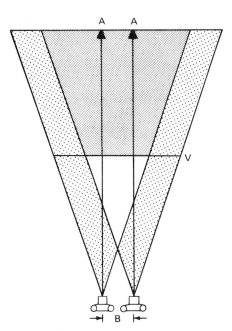

Figure 4.4. Overlap zone (dark shaded area) resulting from stereophotography with a single camera. Note parallel lens axes (A), camera base (B), and foreground area (V). (Adapted from a drawing by Carl Zeiss, Oberkochen.)

prints should be mounted so that images are correctly separated for the stereoscope being used. To avoid troublesome y-parallax (vertical parallax), the two views should also be aligned so that corresponding images are at an identical distance from the upper or lower edge of the card mount. Ground stereograms are especially useful for supplementing vertical (aerial) stereograms in photo interpretation keys and training exercises.

▨ SYSTEMATIC FILING OF STEREOGRAMS AND AERIAL IMAGERY

Organizations that accumulate large files of annotated stereograms may experience difficulty in locating reference illustrations on short notice. In many cases, the mounting of these stereograms on standard edge-punched cards provides a solution to the problem of filing, indexing, and relocating selected aerial views. Stereogram cards may be numerically coded according to subject matter, geographic region, scale, season, date of photography, type of film, or other classifications. Once coded and notched, all cards in a particular category can be retrieved through a simple system of mechanical sorting with a wire needle. Fifty to 100 cards can be handled per sort, and the system is well suited for stereogram files containing random mixtures of several hundred reference cards.

Stock cards may be purchased in several standard sizes from office supply houses. Various digital arrangements are available, and special "fields" or code groupings can be printed directly on the cards. A complete coding and indexing system is outlined by Avery (1967).

The most promising solution for the systematic filing and retrieval of aerial imagery appears to be miniaturization. It is technically feasible to copy 23-by-23-cm film frames onto microfilm or microfiche and still recover most of the image detail when the smaller frames are enlarged back to the original negative size. One approach is exemplified by the Recordak microfilm system developed some years ago (Figure 4.5). Although this particular format has not been widely adopted, various elements of such image storage and retrieval systems are used in many film libraries and repositories.

▓ SHADOW METHOD OF HEIGHT DETERMINATION

It has been previously shown that the heights of objects pictured on aerial photographs can be determined from image displacement on single prints or by measurement of parallax differences on stereopairs. Under rather specialized conditions, heights may also be computed from measurements of shadow lengths. First, objects must be vertical (i.e., perpendicular to the earth's surface); second, shadows must be cast from the true tips rather than from the sides of objects; and third, shadows must fall on open, level ground where they are undistorted and easily measured (Figure 4.6).

Because of the great distance between the sun and the earth, the rays of the sun are essentially parallel throughout the small area shown on a vertical aerial photograph. Thus, at any given moment the length of an object's shadow will be directly proportional to its height. Figure 4.7 illustrates the trigonometric relationship involved in determining object heights from shadow measurements. Angle a in this diagram is referred to as the angular elevation of the sun; the tangent of this angle multiplied by the shadow length (SL) provides a measure of object height (ho):

$$ho = SL \times \tan a \qquad \textbf{Equation 4.1}$$

Therefore, the basic problem is the determination of the true value of angle a. The sun's elevation cannot be measured directly, because it changes every hour of every day throughout the year. On the other hand, it may be easily computed if sharply defined objects of *known height* can be found on the photographs. For example, if a radio antenna known to be exactly 100 m tall casts a shadow 75 m long on level ground, the tangent of angle a can be found through transposition of Equation 4.1:

$$\tan a = \frac{ho}{SL} = \frac{100}{75} = 1.333 \qquad \textbf{Equation 4.2}$$

Other shadows can then be measured on the same stereopair and their lengths multiplied by 1.333 to give the heights of corresponding objects. For accurate results, shadows should be carefully measured to the nearest 0.1 mm or less. This can be done with special micrometer devices or magnifying monoculars.

Other things being equal, the precision of shadow-height measurements is highly dependent on the scale of photography; that is, precision improves with larger scales because of more accurate shadow measurements. An added

ROLL	FRAME	DATE	TOD	SCALE	COUNTY	STATE	
1	69	13 JAN. 67	1300	1:10M	—	D.C.	

THE ☰*RECORDAK*® AIR-PHOTO MICROFILM SYSTEM

with <u>NEW</u> *RECORDAK* DIRECT DUPLICATING FILM

introduced at
the ASP—ACSM Convention
Washington, D.C.

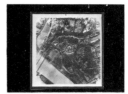

©Eastman Kodak Company / Business Systems Markets Division / Rochester, N.Y. 14650

☰*RECORDAK* MICRO-FILE ®MIL-D APERTURE CARD. MANUFACTURED IN U.S.A.   PAT PENDING

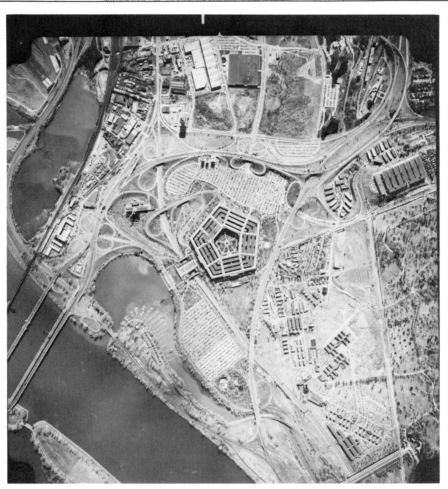

Figure 4.5. Airphoto microfilm system, with the smaller film frame incorporated into a standard, machine-sorted data card. The aerial photograph of the Pentagon in Washington, D.C., was produced directly from the microfilm. (Courtesy Eastman Kodak Co.)

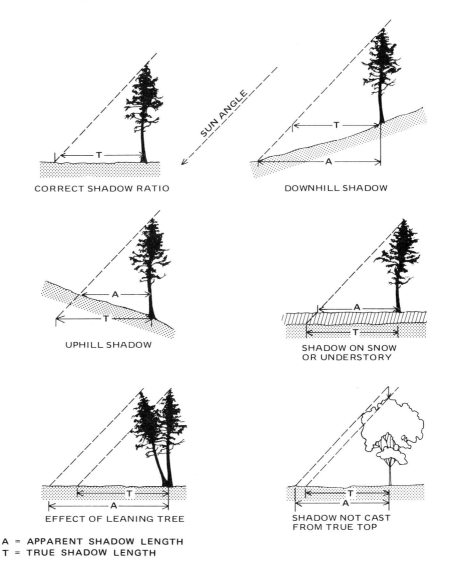

CORRECT SHADOW RATIO

DOWNHILL SHADOW

UPHILL SHADOW

SHADOW ON SNOW OR UNDERSTORY

EFFECT OF LEANING TREE

SHADOW NOT CAST FROM TRUE TOP

A = APPARENT SHADOW LENGTH
T = TRUE SHADOW LENGTH

Figure 4.6. Illustration of various factors affecting the length of shadows cast by trees or similar objects.

complication is that of determining the point from which the shadow is cast by a tall object. This problem is illustrated by a comparison of various types of shadows, as shown in Figure 4.8.

COMPUTING THE SUN'S ANGULAR ELEVATION

The foregoing technique of determining the angular elevation of the sun works well where the heights of one or two objects are known or can easily be checked. When this method of computation is not feasible, however, the sun's

HEIGHT = SHADOW X TAN *a*

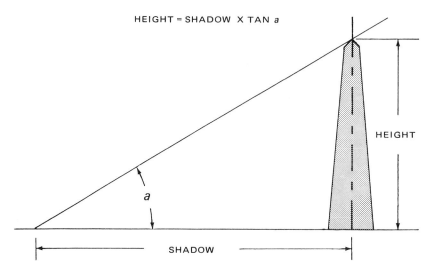

Figure 4.7.   Relationship of shadows and corresponding object heights.

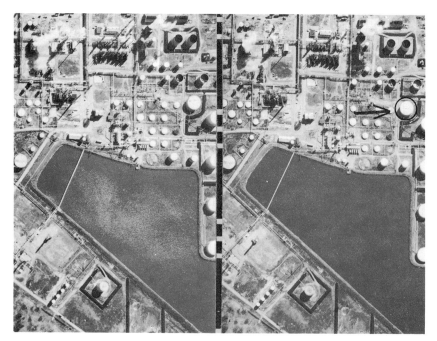

Figure 4.8.   Stereogram of an oil refinery in the midwestern United States. Scale is about 1:7,920. Compare shadows of cylindrical tanks to those cast by tall smokestacks.

elevation can be calculated by a more complex procedure requiring the use of special astronomical tables (i.e., a solar ephemeris). Such tables may be obtained from manufacturers of surveying equipment, from military installations, or from astronomical observatories.

Basic information needed is (1) month and day of photography, (2) time of photography (the nearest hour), (3) latitude and longitude of photography, and (4) exact scale of photography. The angular elevation of the sun (angle a in Figure 4.7) is determined from this equation:

$$\sin a = (\cos x)(\cos y)(\cos z) \pm (\sin x)(\sin y) \qquad \textbf{Equation 4.3}$$

where:

angle x = Sun's declination or latitude on the day of photography, corrected to Greenwich Mean Time (GMT) and read from a solar ephemeris
angle y = Latitude of photography
angle z = Hour angle, or the difference in longitude between the position of the sun and the locality of photography

The algebraic sign in Equation 4.3 is *plus* from March 21 through September 23 and *minus* from September 24 through March 20 in the Northern hemisphere; signs are reversed for the Southern Hemisphere. When the sine of angle a has been found, the angle itself is read from a table of trigonometric functions; then the tangent is determined for use in shadow-height conversions. To simplify solution of the equation, special computing forms have been developed by Johnson (1954). The technique is also detailed in the military *Image Interpretation Handbook* (1967).

For reliable height measurements, new values for angle a should be computed for each hour of the day, for each day of photography, and for significant changes in the geographic location of photography. Although most interpreters prefer to use the parallax method of height determination, the shadow technique furnishes a valuable alternative when stereopairs of photographs are not available.

OBJECT COUNTS

In certain photo interpretation activities, the ability to distinguish and count individual objects is of prime importance. Automobiles may be counted in traffic studies, trees in forest inventories, or ships and tanks in military operations. As a rule, man-made objects having some degree of uniformity (e.g., telephone poles) are more easily counted than natural features of the same size (e.g., trees in dense stands). The principal factors affecting counting accuracy are as follows:

Size and shape of objects
Scale and resolution of photography
Spatial arrangements of objects

Tonal or color contrasts between objects and associated backgrounds
Type of image material (e.g., transparencies versus prints)
Type of film emulsion (e.g., black-and-white versus color)
Use of stereopairs versus single frames for making counts

In Figure 4.9, for example, individual railroad ties and highway pavement cracks could be distinguished on the original prints of stereograms B and C. Where large numbers of objects are closely spaced, counts are commonly made on sample plots of predetermined size. Plot tallies are then expanded on the basis of the total area involved.

▥ COMPASS BEARINGS

Vertical and near-vertical photographs present reliable records of angles; therefore, compass bearings or azimuths may be measured directly on prints with a simple protractor (Figure 4.10). Flight lines usually run north-south or east-west, but the edges of prints are rarely oriented exactly with the cardinal directions. For this reason, a line of true direction must be established before bearings can be accurately measured. Such reference lines can be plotted from existing maps or located directly on the ground by determination of the bearing of any straight-line feature.

In Figure 4.11, the highway at the top of the print was established as a due north-south reference line. To determine the bearing of the buried pipeline (in direction of arrow), the included angle was measured with a protractor as 29°. Thus, the pipeline bears 29° east of due south. Expressed more conventionally, it has a bearing of S 29° E or an azimuth of $180° - 29° = 151°$.

A quick indication of compass direction on aerial photographs can also be obtained from imagery over airports. Runways are numbered according to their magnetic-compass direction (azimuth); the compass heading is determined to the nearest 10°, and the zero is dropped. Thus, in Figure 4.12, the runways have magnetic azimuths of approximately 160°, 220°, and 280°. At their opposite ends, these same runways would carry the numbers 34, 04, and 10, respectively. Where the local magnetic declination is known, lines of true compass direction may be approximated from runway numbers.

▥ AREA MEASUREMENTS

Areas and distances are preferably measured on reliable base maps when accuracy is essential. On the other hand, reasonably precise area estimates can be made directly on contact prints in regions of level to gently rolling topography. The reliability of such estimates is dependent on the precision with which photo scales and area conversion factors are determined. Where topographic changes exceed 100 m or so, large errors will be incurred unless new conversions are computed for each significant variation in land elevation. This point may be verified by an inspection of the area conversions previously

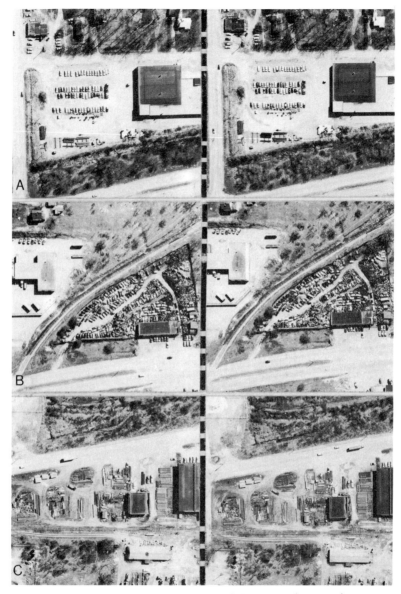

Figure 4.9. Three stereograms showing the effect of object size, shape, and arrangement on an interpreter's ability to count individual items. Automobiles in a parking lot are pictured at A, wrecked cars at B, and various stacks of structural materials at C. Scale is about 1:6,000. (Courtesy Abrams Aerial Survey Corp.)

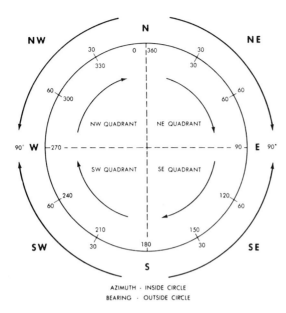

Figure 4.10. Relationship of compass bearings and azimuths. (Courtesy U.S. Department of the Army.)

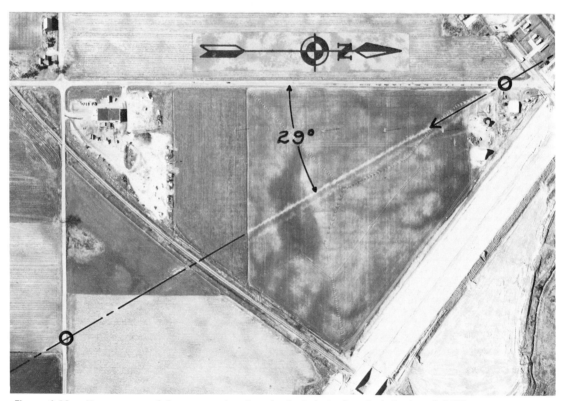

Figure 4.11. Measurement of the compass bearing of a buried pipeline. Scale is about 1:6,000. (Courtesy Abrams Aerial Survey Corp.)

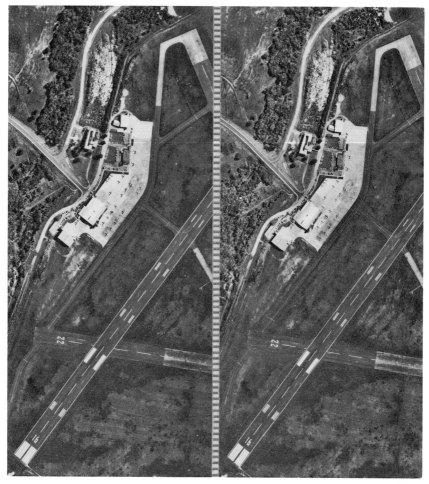

Figure 4.12.   Airport runways are numbered according to their magnetic-compass direction. Shown here are runways 16, 22, and 28. Photo scale is about 1:10,000. (Courtesy Texas Forest Service.)

listed in Table 3.1. The principal devices used for area measurement are dot grids, polar planimeters, and transects.

DOT GRIDS

Dot grids are transparent overlays with dots systematically arranged on a grid pattern (Figure 4.13). Thus, dot grids and graphical methods of area determination are based on the same principle; dots *representing* squares or rectangular areas are merely counted in lieu of the squares themselves. The principal gain enjoyed is that fractional squares along tract boundaries are less troublesome, for the nondimensional dot determines whether or not the

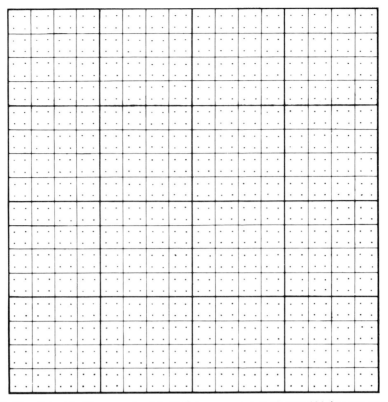

Figure 4.13.   Dot grid with approximately 10 dots per square centimetre (64 dots per square inch).

square is to be tallied. If an area is mapped at a scale of 100 m/cm, this is equivalent to 10,000 m^2/cm^2, or 1 ha/cm^2. Thus, on a grid having four dots per square centimetre, each dot will represent 0.25 ha. The simple conversion is represented by this relationship:

$$\frac{\text{Number of ha/cm}^2}{\text{Number of dots/cm}^2} = \text{ha/dot} \qquad \textbf{Equation 4.4}$$

The number of dots to be counted depends on the grid intensity, the map or photo scale, the size of area involved, and the desired precision. Grids in common use may have from 4 to more than 100 dots per square centimetre. For tracts of 500 to 1,000 ha, it is generally desirable to use a dot-sampling intensity that will result in a conversion of about 0.2 to 1.0 ha/dot.

Greater precision may be attained by derivation of an *average* dot count based on several random drops of a grid over the same area. Each unbiased drop of the systematic grid may be regarded as a simple random sample of one; thus ten random drops would provide $n - 1$, or nine, degrees of freedom for purposes of calculating the statistical precision of the area estimate.

PLANIMETERS

A planimeter is composed of three basic parts—a weighted polar arm of fixed length, a tracer arm hinged on the unweighted end of the polar arm, and a rolling wheel that rests on the map and to which is attached a vernier scale.

In use, the pointer of the instrument is run around the boundaries of an area in a *clockwise* direction; usually, the perimeter is traced two or three times for an average reading. From the vernier scale, the area in *square centimetres* (or other units) is read directly and converted to the desired area units on the basis of map or photo scale (Table 4.1). Prolonged use of the planimeter is tedious, and a steady hand is essential for tracing irregular boundaries.

It is often useful to check planimeter estimates of area by comparisons with dot-grid estimates, and vice versa. Relative accuracy of the two methods can be compared through the measurement of a few tracts of known area. Because individual preferences vary, it may also be informative to compare the *time* required for alternative estimation techniques. In the hands of skilled persons, dot grids and planimeters are generally regarded as devices of comparable precision.

TRANSECTS

The transect method is essentially a technique for *proportioning* a known area among various types of land classifications, such as forests, cultivated fields, and urban uses. A graduated scale is aligned on the photos so as to cross topography and drainage at right angles. The length of each type along the scale is recorded to the nearest desired unit, for example, 5 mm. The interpreter develops proportions by relating the total measure of a given classification to the total linear distance. For example, if ten equally spaced, parallel lines 15 units long are tallied on a given photograph, the total transect length is 150 units. If woodlands are intercepted for a total measure of 30 units, this particular type classification would be assigned an area equivalent to 30/150, or one-fifth of the total area. The transect method is simple and requires a minimum of equipment. For deriving area proportions on photo index sheets, special transparent overlays can be improvised for location of transect lines.

PROBLEMS

1. Prepare several aerial stereograms to illustrate a particular subject category or a variety of terrain features. The checklist presented here may be used to evaluate the quality of these stereograms.

TABLE 4.1. Conversions for Several Units of Area Measurement

Square Feet	Square Chains	Acres	Square Miles	Square Metres	Hectares	Square Kilometres
4,356	1	0.1	0.000156	404.687	0.040469	0.000405
43,560	10	1	0.0015625	4,064.87	0.404687	0.004047
27,878,400	6,400	640	1	2,589,998	258.9998	2.589998
107,638.7	24.7104	2.47104	0.003861	10,000	1	0.01
10,763,867	2,471.04	247.104	0.386101	1,000,000	100	1

Specifications Checklist	Stereogram Number			
	1	2	3	4
Subject properly centered				
Views properly cut out				
Left and right orientation correct				
Shadow orientation correct				
Image separation distance				
Vertical alignment (y-parallax)				
Quality of mounting				
Quality of lettering or inking				
Adequacy of title data				
Overall appearance and utility				

2. Devise and test your own camera system for making ground stereograms. Then obtain at least four ground stereograms to supplement existing aerial stereograms in your files. Explain how you determined the ideal ratio between camera base and distance to subject foreground.

3. Obtain several overlapping photographs of an accessible local area. By *ground measurement* of two or more tall objects whose shadows fall on level ground, compute an average value for the tangent of the angular elevation of the sun.

Description of Object	Object Height	Shadow Length	tan α

Average Value _____

4. Use the ratio derived from ground measurements in problem 3 to estimate the heights of several other objects from their shadow lengths.

5. Compute the angular elevation of the sun by the equation method outlined in this chapter. Compare the value derived for the tangent of angle a with that obtained from field measurements. Discuss advantages and disadvantages of the two methods of calculation for use in shadow-height determinations.

6. Using your own photographs, select several land parcels of irregular shape and determine their areas by using both a planimeter and an appropriate dot grid. Record results in the table below and compare differences obtained.

Description of Area	Area by Planimeter (Average of Three Readings)	Area by Dot Grid (Based on Three Random Drops)	Difference in Area

References

Anonymous. 1957. *The needle sort instruction manual.* Business Forms, West Hartford, Conn. 14 pp., illus.

Avery, T. E. 1967. All *sorts* of stereograms. *Photogrammetric Engineering* 33:1397–1401, illus.

Barrett, James P., and James S. Philbrook. 1970. Dot grid area estimates: precision by repeated trials. *Journal of Forestry* 68:149–151, illus.

Chester, G. S. 1965. A method of preparing an edge-punched card literature reference file. *Forestry Chronicle* 41(2):207–214, illus.

Cravat, Harland R., and Raymond Glaser. 1971. Color aerial stereograms of selected coastal areas of the United States. U.S. Department of Commerce, Government Printing Office, Washington, D.C. 93 pp., illus.

Johnson, Evert W. 1954. "Shadow-height" computations made easier. *Journal of Forestry* 52:438–442, illus.

Singh, R. S., and J. P. Scherz. 1974. A catalog system for remote-sensing data. *Photogrammetric Engineering* 40:709–720, illus.

U.S. Departments of the Army, the Navy, and the Air Force. 1967. *Image interpretation handbook,* vol. I. Government Printing Office, Washington, D.C., illus.

Chapter 5

Flight Planning

■ CONTRACT AERIAL PHOTOGRAPHY

Although many persons rely largely on existing aerial photographs for interpretation and mapping, such coverage may be unsuitable because of age, season, film-filter combination, or scale. As a result, there is considerable interest in the purchase of special-purpose photography contracted through aerial survey firms. However, even though a commercial firm may have the technical expertise to handle almost any type of photographic mission, the interpreter still may be responsible for defining project objectives, drawing up preliminary specifications or flight plans, estimating costs, and determining whether the finished product meets interpretation requirements.

In return for an investment that may amount to many thousands of dollars, the resource manager or land planner expects to receive high-quality photography that is uniquely suited to particular interpretation needs. To achieve this goal, the interpreter must define the exact project objectives, become familiar with photographic specifications and contracts, and negotiate only with reputable aerial survey companies. Without the interpreter's close attention to these considerations, special-purpose flights are unlikely to prove cost-effective.

Names and addresses of aerial survey companies can be obtained locally through consulting engineers, city managers, or interpretation specialists at various universities. Addresses and activities of many companies are also described annually in a yearbook issue of *Photogrammetric Engineering and Remote Sensing*. In choosing among several prospective companies, the purchaser is advised to request photographic samples from each; such image samples provide useful guides to the quality of work that may be expected.

Purchasers who feel unqualified to evaluate sample photography should retain the services of a special consultant to assist in drawing up photographic specifications, defining areas to be covered, and inspecting the completed imagery. All contract specifications and special requirements should be thoroughly discussed by buyer and contractor before actual flights. A few extra days of advance planning will sometimes alleviate the need for reflights and help prevent disputes arising from definitions of stereoscopic coverage, exposure quality, image contrast, or film-processing deficiencies. Aerial photographs that fail to supply the quantity and quality of information desired cannot be considered inexpensive by any standard.

FLIGHT ALTITUDES AND FOCAL LENGTHS

The range of photographic scales available is defined by the operating ceilings of available aircraft and the various camera focal lengths that are employed. For most nonmilitary photography, upper altitudinal limits might

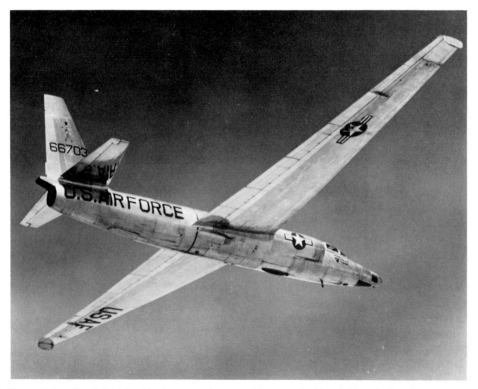

Figure 5.1.   The U-2 high-altitude research plane. (Courtesy Lockheed Aircraft Corp.)

TABLE 5.1. Common Focal Lengths of Mapping Cameras		
Camera Focal Length (Millimetres)	Maximum Angular Field (Degrees)	Ground Coverage at 1,000 m Above Ground (Square Kilometres)
85	125	7.32
153	93	2.27
210	75	1.20
305	56	0.57
610	30	0.14

be regarded as around 20,000 m (65,000 ft) above MSL, a level that can be achieved by such planes as the U-2 (Figure 5.1). For fixed-wing aircraft, the lower limit might be arbitrarily defined as around 300 m (1,000 ft) above ground, depending on topography, special hazards, and air safety regulations.

Aerial survey cameras are manufactured in a wide array of focal lengths and film formats. For example, in the standard 23-by-23-cm negative format, Zeiss mapping cameras are available with several focal lengths (Table 5.1).

If we now match the shortest focal length with the upper aircraft ceiling, and vice versa, the range of photographic scales available (allowing for terrain elevations of up to 3,000 m) might be computed with Equation 3.1 as follows:

$$RF = \frac{0.085}{20,000 - 3,000} = \frac{1}{200,000} \text{ or } 1{:}200{,}000$$

$$RF = \frac{0.610}{300} = \frac{1}{492} \text{ or } 1{:}500$$

In practice, the range of scales actually employed is usually somewhat less, namely, from about 1:1,000 to 1:125,000. Where simultaneous coverage at two different scales is desired, certain aircraft can be fitted with two or more aerial cameras (Figure 5.2).

AREA COVERAGE AND RELATIVE COSTS

Camera focal length is a critical contract specification because it determines the aircraft altitude that must be maintained for exposures of the desired scale to be obtained. Also, its direct effect on the image displacement of objects photographed controls the degree of three-dimensional exaggeration that the interpreter sees when viewing the exposures stereoscopically. Selecting an optimum scale–focal length combination is therefore an item of direct interest to the image interpreter.

It is generally desirable to specify the smallest photo scale that will meet the requirements of a given project; this approach not only tends to lower costs but also reduces the number of stereo models that must be handled by interpreters. When a photographic scale is doubled, as from 1:20,000 to 1:10,000,

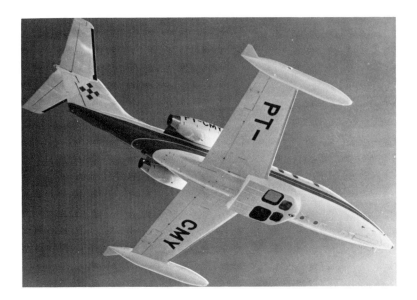

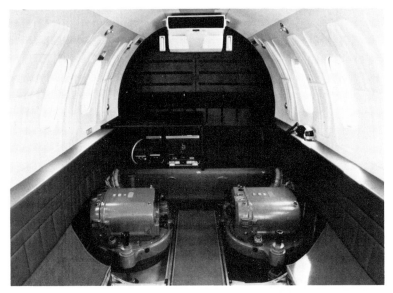

Figure 5.2. Dual-camera installation in a jet aircraft. (Courtesy Gates Learjet, Inc.)

approximately *four times* as many exposures will be required to cover the same area. Consequently, photographic scale and tract size are two of the principal factors affecting the cost of special aerial surveys.

Costs of contract aerial photography are also affected by such considerations as the required timing (season and sun angle) for flights, film-filter specifications, accessibility of the project area, prevailing weather conditions, and fluctuations in the business activities of aerial mapping companies.

Because any quotation must reflect a set of fixed conditions, it is not surprising that there have been few published accounts of photographic prices.

Table 5.2 lists the approximate number of exposures required for several photographic scales and tract sizes; it also includes relative cost indexes for black-and-white photography. Although these ratios are based on information from reputable aerial survey companies, they are merely averages that will not apply in all situations. It should be emphasized that the index numbers are relative values only and not actual prices. For example, the cost index value in the first cell of the table (25 km^2 at 1:5,000) is taken as unity (1.00) and all other cost estimates would be relative to this value. Average distances between airports and project areas are assumed; the prices for photographic coverage of small tracts may be influenced more by the cost of moving the plane and crew than by the actual flying time involved.

It is worthy of mention that commercial firms prefer to sell a complete package of photography, ground control, and finished planimetric or topographic maps instead of merely supplying aerial imagery. Furthermore, there is a trend toward negotiation of contracts and prices in lieu of the "lowest-bidder" approach.

TABLE 5.2. Approximate Number of Exposures Required and Relative Costs for Stereoscopic Coverage[a]

Size of Area (Square Kilometres)	Negative Scale: 23-by-23-cm Format			
	1:5,000	1:10,000	1:20,000	1:40,000
	Number of Exposures and Cost Index Values			
25	70	18	5	2
	1.00	0.85	0.80	0.70
50	139	36	9	3
	1.60	0.90	0.88	0.80
100	278	71	18	5
	2.60	1.00	0.90	0.83
500	1,389	353	89	23
	8.00	3.20	1.00	0.90
1,000	2,778	705	177	45
	19.50	7.50	2.90	1.30
5,000	13,889	3,522	881	221
	60.00	24.30	10.00	3.90
km²/photo	0.36	1.42	5.68	22.72

[a] Assumes an effective area of about 142 cm² per exposure. The first value represents the number of exposures required; for each flight line planned, four exposures should be added to the numbers indicated. The second number represents a relative cost index for two sets of black-and-white prints and one set of photo index sheets.

■ SEASON OF PHOTOGRAPHY

The optimum season for scheduling photographic flights depends on the nature of features to be identified or mapped, the film to be used, the number of days suitable for aerial photography within a given period, and the minimum sun angle or subject illumination required.

Because optimum weather conditions may not prevail during the season when photography is desired, it may be necessary to ascertain the average number of "photographic days" for a locality during each month of the year. A photographic day is defined as one with 10 percent cloud cover or less; this kind of information may be obtained from periodic reports issued by local weather services. Other factors being equal, aerial surveys are likely to be less expensive in areas where sunny, clear days predominate during the desired photographic season.

Another consideration in selecting the season for aerial photography is the project objective (i.e., the specific information to be extracted from the photographs). On the basis of generally divergent objectives, users of aerial photographs may be arbitrarily divided into two main groups—those engaged in topographic mapping, urban planning, or evaluation of terrain features and those primarily concerned with assessment of vegetation or management of wildland areas. The first group, typified by cartographers, civil engineers, and geologists, would be likely to schedule photography during seasons when tree foliage does not obscure the landscape. By contrast, persons in the second category tend to prefer photographs made during the growing season, when the vegetative cover is fully developed. This second group would include foresters, plant ecologists, and range managers.

For topographic mapping, photography is usually taken either in the spring or the fall, when deciduous foliage is absent and the ground is essentially free of snow. Only during these periods can terrain features be adequately distinguished and contours precisely delineated. As differences in vegetation are rarely of significance, mapping photographs are commonly made on panchromatic film. Similar coverage would be specified by geologists interested in stratigraphic mapping and by engineers concerned with proposed highway routes. Although summer photography may suffice in an emergency, dense canopies of foliage greatly inhibit the efficient evaluation of ground detail, thereby increasing costs.

Interpreters interested in vegetation analyses will ordinarily specify aerial photography made during the growing season, particularly when deciduous plants constitute an important component of the vegetative cover. When it is essential that deciduous trees, evergreens, and mixtures of the two groups be delineated, either infrared black-and-white or infrared color film is frequently specified. In regions where evergreen plants predominate, however, panchromatic film or conventional color film may be used with equal success.

Several research projects involving black-and-white photography of forest areas have indicated that the best timing for infrared coverage is from midspring to early summer—after all trees have produced some foliage but before maximum leaf pigmentation. Successful panchromatic photographs of timberlands can be made throughout the year, but in the northern United States and in Canada the best results have been obtained in late fall, just before deciduous species, such as aspen and tamarack, shed their leaves. For a brief period of perhaps two weeks' duration, foliage color differences will provide good photographic contrasts between most of the important timber species in this region.

TIME OF DAY

Time of day is an important contract specification, because the angle at which the sun strikes the earth's surface affects not only the quantity of light being reflected to the aerial camera but also the spectral quality of light. In clear weather, for example, solar illumination depends on latitude (it drops off as latitude increases), season of the year, and hours before or after local apparent noon. Because heavily vegetated lands are poor light reflectors, they usually should be photographed within 2 hr of local apparent noon. This is especially important when color films are exposed. It will be noted that solar altitude is one of the prime factors incorporated into the Kodak Aerial Exposure Computer (see Chapter 1).

A detrimental consequence of selecting the wrong combination of season and time of day is a phenomenon known as *hotspot* or *sunspot*. A loss of photographic detail results when a straight line from the sun through the camera lens intersects the terrain inside the area of photo coverage. At the center of the hotspot is a *no-shadow point* caused by the direct return of light rays to the camera lens; the effect is a washed-out (overexposed) circular area of perhaps 2 or 3 cm in diameter where detail is lost. Hotspot is most likely to occur with high sun angles, at lower latitudes, and with wide-angle camera lenses. After the season and latitude of photography have been determined, it is possible to calculate (and thus avoid) those midday hours when hotspots will occur.

As a general rule, photographic flights in the temperate zones of the world should be scheduled within 2 to 3 hr of local apparent noon, provided hotspots can be avoided. This timing assures maximum subject illumination and helps avoid the troublesome effect of long object shadows.

SUMMARY RECOMMENDATIONS

Table 5.3 has been prepared to supply a set of guidelines for aerial surveys. These generalized recommendations are based on published reports of varied photo interpretation projects. Therefore, they will sometimes reflect the types of coverage that were *available* rather than optimum specifications. Moreover, because individual project objectives will vary from one locality to another, other combinations of films, seasons, and scales may be equally suitable.

TABLE 5.3. Guidelines for Aerial Surveys[a]

Description of Task	Film Type	Season	Scale
Forest mapping: conifers	Pan	Fall, winter	1:12,000–1:20,000
Forest mapping: mixed stands	Infrared	Late spring, fall	1:10,000–1:12,000
Timber volume estimates	Pan or Infrared	Spring, fall	1:5,000–1:20,000
Location of property boundaries	Pan	Late fall, winter	1:10,000–1:25,000
Measurement of areas	Pan	Late fall, winter	All scales
Topographic mapping; highway surveys	Pan	Late fall, winter	1:5,000–1:10,000
Urban planning	Pan	Late fall, winter	1:5,000–1:10,000
Automobile traffic studies	Pan	All seasons	1:2,500–1:6,000
Surveys of wetlands or tidal regions	Infrared	All seasons—low tide	1:5,000–1:30,000
Archeological explorations	Infrared	Fall, winter	1:2,500–1:20,000
Identification of tree species	Color	Spring, summer	1:600–1:5,000
Assessment of insect damages	Infrared color	Spring, summer	1:600–1:5,000
Assessment of plant diseases	Infrared color	Spring, summer	1:1,000–1:8,000
Assessment of water resources and pollution	Multispectral	All seasons	1:5,000–1:8,000
Agricultural soil surveys	Color	Spring or fall, after plowing	1:4,000–1:8,000
Mapping of range vegetation	Color	Summer	1:600–1:2,500
Real-estate assessment	Color-negative	Late fall, winter	1:5,000–1:12,000
Assessment of industrial stockpile inventories	Color-negative	All seasons	1:1,000–1:5,000
Recreational surveys	Color-negative	Late fall, winter	1:5,000–1:12,000
Land-cover mapping	Color-negative	Spring, summer	1:20,000–1:100,000

[a] Adapted from Avery (1970).

The reader is reminded that simultaneous coverage with two or more films often provides superior results to those achieved with any single sensitized material. When the winter season is specified in the table, the absence of snow cover is presumed. And wherever the added cost can be justified, color photography may prove better than black-and-white.

▨ TECHNICAL SPECIFICATIONS FOR AERIAL PHOTOGRAPHY

When the decision to purchase new photography has been made, technical specifications are usually summarized in a formal contract. Such agreements assume a variety of forms, but most of the following items are covered to some degree. Readers interested in additional contract details should refer to sample specifications prepared by various state and federal agencies.

Business Arrangements. These include such items as the cost of the aerial survey, the posting of a performance bond, the assumption of risks and damages, a provision for periodic inspection of work, reflights, cancellation privileges, schedules for delivery and payments, and ownership and storage of negatives.

Area to Be Photographed. The area, which includes tract location, size, and boundaries, is ordinarily indicated on flight maps supplied by the purchaser.

Type of Photographic Film and Filter. Such items as film emulsion number, exposure rating, and dimensional stability of the film base may be specified.

Negative Scale. Maximum scale deviation normally allowed is ±5 percent.

The Aerial Camera. A certified calibration report may be required. Other camera specifications include size of negative format, method of flattening film during exposure, type of shutter, focal length, distortion characteristics of lens, and resolving power (Figures 5.3 and 5.4).

Position of Flight Lines. Lines should be parallel, oriented in correct compass direction, and within a stated distance from positions drawn on flight maps. Lines are usually run north-south or east-west, roughly parallel to the long dimension of the tract.

Overlap. Overlap is usually set at 55–65 percent (averaging 60 percent) along the line of flight and 15–45 percent (averaging 20–30 percent) between adjacent lines. At the ends of each flight line, two photo centers should fall outside the tract boundary.

Print Alignment. Crab or drift should not affect more than 10 percent of the print width for any three consecutive photographs.

Tilt. Tilt should not exceed 2–3° for a single exposure or average more than 1° for the entire project.

Time of Photography. Both season of year and time of day (or minimum sun angle) are usually specified.

Base Maps. If base maps or radial line plots are required, the responsibility for ground control (field surveying) should be established.

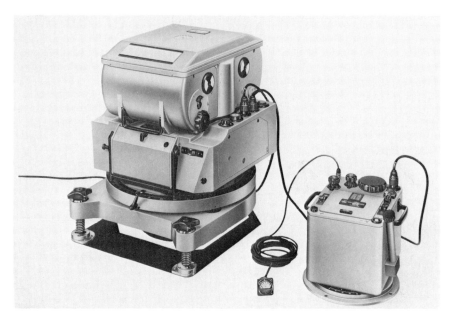

Figure 5.3. Zeiss RMK-A-15/23 aerial camera. Focal length is 15 cm, and negative size is 23 by 23 cm. (Courtesy Carl Zeiss, Oberkochen.)

Film Processing. Included here are procedures for developing and drying negatives, indexing and editing film rolls, and selecting the type of photographic paper (weight, finish, contrast) to be used.

Quality of Negatives and Prints. Negatives and prints should be free from stains, scratches, and blemishes that detract from the intended use.

Materials to Be Delivered. Two sets of contact prints (or transparencies)

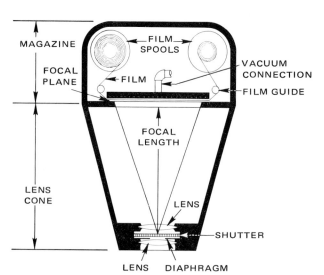

Figure 5.4. Simplified cross section of an aerial camera.

and one set of index sheets are usually supplied. A copy of the original flight log may also be requested. Additional items desired such as enlargements, mosaics, maps, or plan-and-profile sheets should be listed in detail.

INSPECTION OF CONTRACT PHOTOGRAPHY

Following completion of a photographic survey, it is customary for a representative of the purchaser to make a technical inspection of all prints, index sheets, and negatives. If the project was awarded to a reputable aerial survey firm at the beginning, the inspection and official acceptance of materials become a mere formality. In other instances, careful study may be required to determine whether the photography meets the standards set forth in the contract specifications.

Infrequent purchasers of aerial photography may have difficulty in evaluating the finished product, because the acceptance or rejection of photographic flights often requires checks of such items as film tilting, overlap, scale, and print quality. As a means of translating technical specifications into guides for the neophyte inspector, an itemized inspection checklist as designed by Avery and Meyer (1962) may prove useful.

As a rule, exposures should be dated in the upper left corner; project, roll, and exposure numbers should be shown in the upper right corner of each photograph. Nominal photo scale, as 1:15,000, and local standard time are ordinarily placed at the top of the first and last exposures in each flight line. The center of the photographic flight strip should be within a specified distance of the position plotted on original flight maps. Maximum deviation is usually set at 25 percent of the mean sidelap distance. The inspector should also check to make sure that the compass bearing of each flight line is within 5° of the specified direction and that adjacent lines are within 5° of parallel.

TILT AND SCALE CHECKS

As mentioned, photographic tilt should not exceed 2–3° for a single exposure or average more than 1° for an entire project. Tilt is most commonly encountered on prints near the ends of flight lines where exposures are made as the aircraft banks into a turn for the next strip. It is difficult to detect a small degree of tilt, but excessive amounts are quite evident on photographs of flat terrain having rectangular land subdivisions. In such instances, the oblique camera view results in an apparent convergence of grid patterns and parallel lines.

Because of the time required, photo scale checks are seldom made for individual exposures. Instead, ten or more overlapping prints or transparencies are selected from each flight line for a check of the average scale across an expanded geographic transect. After the exposures have been taped down in mosaic fashion, the distance between two points is carefully measured. Through computation of a simple ratio between the photo measurement and the corresponding distance on the flight map, average print scale can be quickly determined. After allowance is made for variations in local relief, this average should be within ± 5 percent of the specified scale.

ASSESSING PRINT QUALITY

Print quality is usually the most difficult item for an inspector to evaluate because of the lack of standards or criteria of comparison. The inspector must place heavy reliance on subjective judgment in deciding whether a given photographic defect constitutes a reasonable basis for rejection. Some of the photographic "defects" shown in Figure 5.5, for example, may be of minor importance for certain interpretation projects. Although the original exposures may be of high quality, carelessness in printing can produce photographs with poor contrast, stains, or blurred detail. For this reason, film negatives should be available for inspection over a light table. Special techniques in printing will often produce high-quality photographs even when negatives have poor density characteristics (Figure 5.6).

A SAMPLE FLIGHT PLAN

An aerial flight plan is simply a reliable map depicting the area to be photographed, the scale of photography desired, and the proposed location and altitude of flight lines. The final version may be prepared by an aerial survey firm, but it is usually to the purchaser's advantage to draw up a preliminary plan before the issuance of a photographic contract. Topographic quadrangle maps, ranging in scale from 1:24,000 to 1:250,000, are among the best maps available for the preparation of flight plans. In the United States and Canada these maps can be purchased at nominal cost from government agencies. The example that follows illustrates the various calculations involved in preparing a flight plan for an area of 20 km east-west by 30 km north-south, or 600 km^2. The basic information required is as follows:

Desired negative scale: 1:25,000 or 250 m/cm
Scale of base map: 1:50,000 or 500 m/cm
Average ground elevation above mean sea level: 500 m
Average forward overlap: 60 percent
Sidelap: To average approximately 30 percent
Negative format: 23 by 23 cm, or 5,750 by 5,750 m on the ground
Camera focal length: 153 mm or 0.153 m

FLIGHT MAP COMPUTATIONS

Items to be computed in preparing the flight plan are:

Flying Height Above Ground Datum: Height = focal length × scale denominator, or:

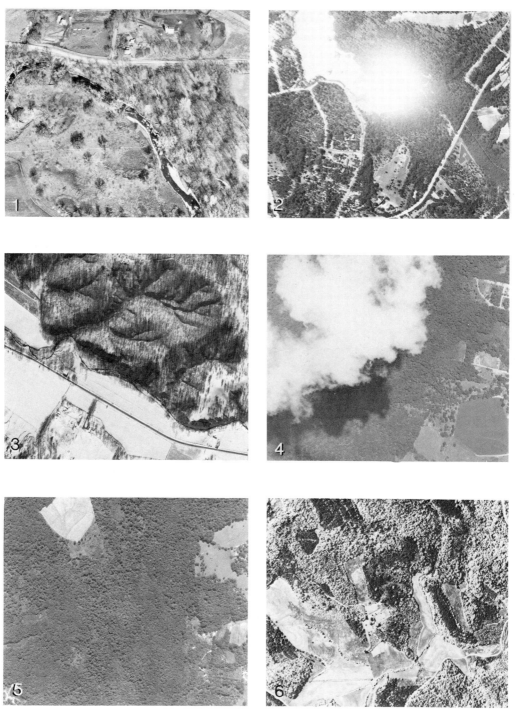

Figure 5.5. Illustration of several factors affecting image quality on aerial photographs: (1) tilted photograph (note oblique view), (2) hotspot or sunspot, (3) snow cover and long shadows, (4) clouds and cloud shadows, (5) insufficient print contrast, and (6) excessive print contrast.

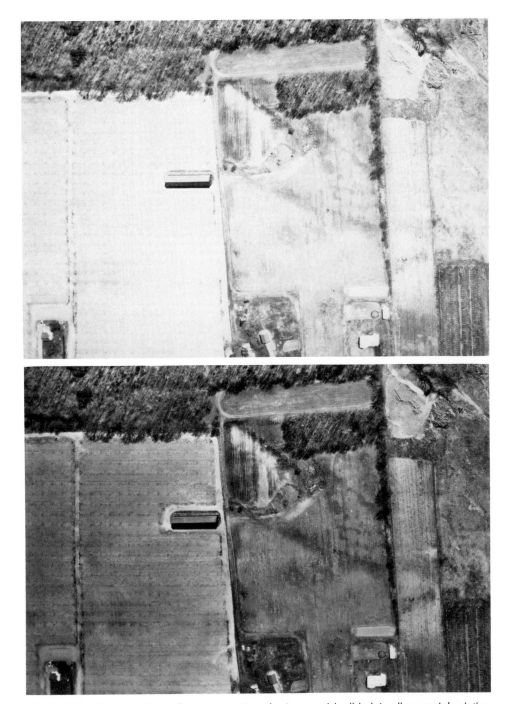

Figure 5.6. Photographic quality can sometimes be improved by "dodging," a special printing technique that results in greater resolution of fine details (see Glossary). These large-scale photos of a rural area, made from the same negative, illustrate the difference between an ordinary print (above) and a "dodged" print (below). (Courtesy Ronald C. Gibson, Log Etronics, Inc.)

$$H = 0.153 \text{ m} \times 25{,}000 = 3{,}825 \text{ m}$$

Flying Height Above Mean Sea Level:

$$3{,}825 + 500 = 4{,}325 \text{ m}$$

Direction of Flight Lines: North-south, following long dimension of tract.

Number of Flight Lines: Assuming an average sidelap of 30 percent, the lateral gain from one line to another is 70 percent of the negative format (on the ground) or $0.70 \times 5{,}750 = 4{,}025$ m between lines. The number of *intervals* between lines is found by division of the tract width (20 km or 20,000 m) by 4,025. The result is 4.97, or 5 *intervals* and 6 *flight lines.*

Actual (Adjusted) Ground Distance Between Flight Lines: Tract width (20,000 m) $\div$ 5 intervals = 4,000 m between lines.

Actual (Adjusted) Percentage of Sidelap:

$$\text{Sidelap percentage} = \frac{\text{Negative width (m)} - \text{Spacing (m)}}{\text{Negative width (m)}}(100)$$

$$\text{Sidelap percentage} = \frac{5{,}750 - 4{,}000}{5{,}750}(100) = 30.4 \text{ percent}$$

Map Distance Between Flight Lines (Map Scale is 500 m/cm):

$$\frac{1 \text{ cm}}{500 \text{ m}} = \frac{X \text{ cm}}{4{,}000 \text{ m}}; X = 8.00 \text{ cm between lines on map}$$

Ground Distance Between Exposures on Each Line: Assuming an average forward overlap of 60 percent, the spacing between successive exposures is 40 percent of the negative format (on the ground), or $0.40 \times 5{,}750 = 2{,}300$ m between exposures.

Map Distance Between Exposures on Each Line:

$$\frac{1 \text{ cm}}{500 \text{ m}} = \frac{X \text{ cm}}{2{,}300 \text{ m}}; X = 4.60 \text{ cm between exposure centers on map}$$

Number of Exposures on Each Line: Number of *intervals* between exposures is found by division of tract length (30 km or 30,000 m) by $2{,}300 = 13.04$ *intervals.* This will require 14 exposures *inside* the area, assuming that the first exposure is centered over one tract boundary. In addition, 2 extra exposures are commonly made at the ends of each flight line; thus, a total of 18 $(14 + 2 + 2)$ *exposures* would be taken on each flight line.

Total Number of Exposures Required to Cover Entire Tract: 6 lines $\times$ 18 exposures per line = 108 exposures.

The calculation procedures and interval-sidelap adjustments employed here (i.e., for direction and number of flight lines, actual ground distance between flight lines, and actual percentage of sidelap) will result in the two exterior flight lines' being centered precisely over the tract boundaries. Thus, there will be a safety factor to ensure boundary coverage because exposure locations are planned to overlap the boundaries by 50 percent.

▓ TAKING YOUR OWN PHOTOGRAPHS

If oblique or near-vertical photographs taken with small-format cameras are sufficient for supplementary coverage of project areas, the do-it-yourself approach provides an alternative for limited types of aerial surveys. High-wing monoplanes offer good side visibility and low stalling speeds; such aircraft can be rented (with pilot) at reasonable hourly rates. Under certain circumstances, it may be permissible to remove the aircraft door on the passenger's side to obtain even better visibility during flights.

For oblique exposures taken through aircraft windows, standard press cameras work quite well. When cameras must be exposed to the aircraft slipstream, however, rigidly designed lens systems should be used instead of those with folding bellows. Surplus military-reconnaissance cameras can sometimes be rented or purchased, but most scientists seem to prefer conventional 35-mm or 70-mm formats because films are readily available and inexpensive and cameras can be equipped with interchangeable lenses and motorized film drives. Furthermore, imagery in these two formats can be optically enlarged (e.g., for map revision and updating) by use of ordinary slide projectors.

Cameras with 35-mm or 70-mm formats will commonly have focal lengths ranging from about 50 to 100 mm. If we assume the use of such cameras in fixed-wing aircraft without oxygen equipment, the upper altitudinal limit would be about 3,000 m above mean sea level, and the lower limit about 300 m above ground. If we further assume that terrain elevations will not exceed 1,500 m, the range of negative scales available might be computed by the same procedure outlined earlier in this chapter:

$$RF = \frac{0.050}{3,000 - 1,500} = \frac{1}{30,000} \text{ or } 1{:}30,000$$

$$RF = \frac{0.100}{300} = \frac{1}{3,000} \text{ or } 1{:}3,000$$

This scale range (1:3,000 to 1:30,000) will be entirely adequate for most do-it-yourself aerial surveys.

▓ DEVISING A CAMERA MOUNT

Exposures made with hand-held cameras are satisfactory for oblique views and for spot coverage with a near-vertical camera orientation. However, if continuous strips of overlapping exposures are needed for stereoscopic study, a camera mount must be devised and constructed for best results. It is assumed here that most rented aircraft will *not* have camera ports or cargo hatches incorporated therein. Consequently most improvised camera mounts are designed to hold the photographic apparatus *outside* the airframe (Figure 5.7).

Hand-made camera mounts have been designed in many configurations,

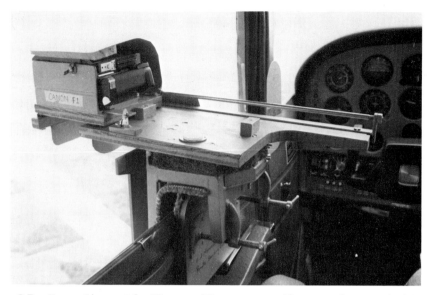

Figure 5.7. Meyer sidemount for 35-mm or 70-mm cameras. The mount clamps to the left door without an aircraft modification. (Courtesy Econ, Inc.)

since each must be adapted to a particular airframe and camera. To combine light weight with maximum platform stability, most camera mounts are constructed of plywood and aluminum; vibration problems are often minimized by the use of foam-rubber shock absorbers. Some of the more desirable attributes of improvised camera mounts are as follows:

1. Mount should be capable of attachment to a given airframe with no external modification of the aircraft.
2. Mount (or camera) should be equipped for in-flight leveling and flight-path orientation.
3. If the camera viewfinder cannot be used, a calibrated sighting tube should be devised to indicate the camera ground coverage at various heights above ground.
4. Mount should be constructed for maximum in-flight accessibility to the camera. This is essential for nonautomatic cameras, because it may be necessary to adjust aperture and shutter speeds, to wind film, and to change film cassettes in the air. A long cable release will generally solve the shutter-release problem.
5. If the camera mount is likely to affect aircraft flying attitude or performance, it may be necessary to obtain written approval for its use from federal or state aviation authorities. It will also be advisable to check on insurance rates for aircraft, camera, and crew if the plane is operated with the passenger door removed.

Two common problems with low-altitude, do-it-yourself photography are (1) the difficulty in determining exact altitude above ground for scale calculations and (2) poor camera stabilization, which may result in blurred or nonvertical imagery. In spite of these limitations, however, the technique is ideally suited for spot photographic coverage where low costs and exact timing of flights are chief factors of concern.

LOW-ALTITUDE HELICOPTER PHOTOGRAPHY

That helicopters are capable of horizontal flight at low airspeeds should make them particularly useful for taking large-scale airphotos of spot locations, such as mining operations, forest inventory plots, and urban centers. Sharp negatives are feasible at ordinary shutter speeds, and camera recycling time is not so critical as with faster-moving, conventional planes. The principal restriction is the high hourly cost of helicopter operation. Contract rates for helicopter and pilot are usually several times that charged for single-engine, fixed-wing aircraft.

Among technical difficulties peculiar to low-altitude helicopter photography are (1) limitations of weight and space for photographer and pilot, (2) severe airframe vibrations, and (3) difficulty of precise determination of altitudes above ground. Weight problems can be partially alleviated by use of lightweight cameras, and vibrations may be minimized if photographs are taken in horizontal flight rather than from a hovering position. However, exact flight altitudes (i.e., photo scales) pose the same problem as with rented, fixed-wing aircraft. Unless the use of a radar altimeter can be justified, there appears to be no simple solution to this problem.

In 1957 Avery devised a simple box mount for holding two identical 70-mm cameras and used the device to obtain helicopter stereograms from designated in-flight exposure stations. Camera lenses were separated by about 1 m, the maximum air base practical for the hand-held, manually operated device. Photographs made during this experiment were roughly comparable to those now obtained with 70-mm cameras from fixed-wing aircraft (Figure 5.8).

EXISTING PHOTOGRAPHY: COMMERCIAL SOURCES

A wide selection of photographic negatives are held by private aerial survey companies in the United States and Canada. In many instances, prints can be ordered directly from these companies after permission is obtained from the original purchaser. A large share of the available coverage has been obtained on panchromatic film with aerial cameras having 153-mm, distortion-free lenses. As a result, photographs are ideally suited for stereoscopic study because of fine image resolution and a high degree of three-dimensional exaggeration. Scales are usually 1:25,000 or larger for recent photography. In addition to contact prints and photo index sheets, most aerial mapping organizations will also sell reproductions of special atlas sheets or controlled mosaics. These items can be useful for pictorial displays and administrative planning.

Prints purchased from private companies may cost more than those from

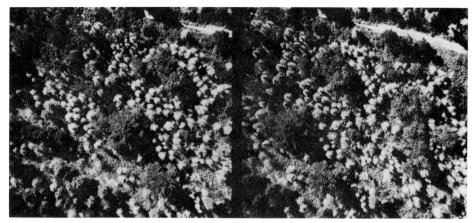

Figure 5.8. Sterogram illustrating dead balsam fir trees (white crowns) killed by the spruce budworm near Ely, Minnesota. Because of the forward overlap, corresponding images on these 70-mm exposures are separated by only about 45 mm. Scale is about 1:1,600. (Courtesy U.S. Forest Service Remote Sensing Project, Berkeley, California.)

public agencies, but they are often of higher quality and at larger scales—factors that may offset any price differential. Quotations and photo indexes can be obtained by direct inquiry to the appropriate company. Names and addresses of leading private aerial survey companies are available in current issues of *Photogrammetric Engineering and Remote Sensing*.

EXISTING PHOTOGRAPHY: UNITED STATES GOVERNMENT

During the past several decades, millions of aerial photographs of the United States have been produced by various federal agencies. Panchromatic film usually has been used, but there is a rapidly growing supply of normal color, infrared color, and infrared black-and-white photographs available for purchasing. The age of the photography dates from the early 1930s to the present; coverage for certain areas (e.g., urban, agricultural) may be available in several-year cycles. The most common film format is 23 by 23 cm.

The National Cartographic Information Center of the U.S. Geological Survey is the contact source for determining the availability of federal photography. A computerized indexing system, the Aerial Photography Summary Record System (APSRS), shows all holdings of cooperating federal agencies and directs the requestor to the agency that can furnish photo products for a particular area. Agencies cooperating in APSRS include the following:

> Agricultural Stabilization and Conservation Service
> Bureau of Land Management
> Department of Defense
> Library of Congress, Geography and Map Division

National Archives and Records Service
National Oceanic and Atmospheric Administration
Soil Conservation Service
Tennessee Valley Authority
U.S. Army Corps of Engineers
U.S. Bureau of Reclamation
U.S. Forest Service
U.S. Geological Survey

A pamphlet, *How to order photographs*, is available from the National Cartographic Information Center on request. Inquiries regarding photographs from these agencies should be made directly to the National Cartographic Information Center, U.S. Geological Survey, 507 National Center, Reston, VA 22092.

The following section describes the types and availability of photography held by several federal agencies.

The Aerial Photography Field Office is now the depository for photography obtained by the Agricultural Stabilization and Conservation Service, Forest Service, and Soil Conservation Service. The photography covers about 90 percent of the country. The bulk of the photography is panchromatic, but normal color, infrared color, and infrared black-and-white films have been obtained for several national forests. Common scales are 1:20,000 and 1:40,000, but recently the Soil Conservation Service has photographed many areas of the United States at scales ranging from 1:31,680 to 1:85,000. Photo index sheets (Figure 5.9) can be viewed at local or regional offices. Written inquiries may be addressed to the Aerial Photography Field Office, ASCS-USDA, 2222 West, 2300 South, P.O. Box 30010, Salt Lake City, UT 84125.

The EROS Data Center provides primary access to aerial photographs acquired by the U.S. Geological Survey and the National Aeronautics and Space Administration's (NASA) aircraft and manned spacecraft photography programs. U.S. Geological Survey photography currently exceeds 2 million frames, mostly panchromatic at a scale of 1:24,000. Since 1964 more than 1.3 million high-altitude photographs have been acquired by NASA. They cover about 80 percent of the country; many areas have been rephotographed. The most common photo scales are 1:60,000 and 1:120,000. Panchromatic, normal color, and infrared color photographs are generally available in a 23-by-23-cm format. Over 40,000 frames of manned-spacecraft photography are also filed at the EROS Data Center. A final category includes an incomplete collection (approximately 1 million frames) of aerial photographs acquired by various federal agencies at various scales and film types. For information, write to the EROS Data Center, User Services Section, U.S. Geological Survey, Sioux Falls, SD 57198.

The National Archives and Records Service is the archive for photography taken by the Agricultural Stabilization and Conservation Service, Soil Conservation Service, U.S. Bureau of Reclamation, and U.S. Geological Survey before World War II. The catalog *Aerial photographs in the National Archives* is available on request. For additional information, write to the

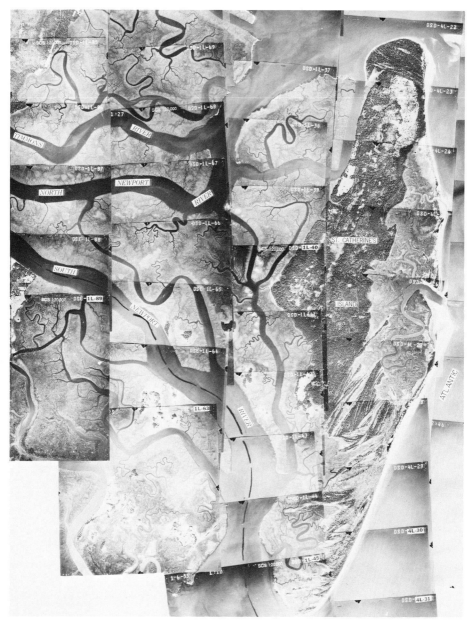

Figure 5.9. Portion of an aerial photo index sheet covering tidal marshes and Saint Catherines Island off the Georgia coast. (Courtesy U.S. Department of Agriculture.)

National Archives and Records Service, Cartographic Branch, General Services Administration, Washington, DC 20408.

NATIONAL HIGH-ALTITUDE PHOTOGRAPHY PROGRAM

The National High-Altitude Photography Program was established in 1978 to replace the similar programs of 14 federal agencies for acquiring aerial photographs. The objectives of the program are to (1) complete conterminous coverage of the United States and develop a national photographic data base by the end of 1986, (2) provide periodic updates of the data base, and (3) ensure that the photographs are available to any interested user. The program is managed by the U.S. Geological Survey.

Stereographic coverage is provided by panchromatic (1:80,000) and infrared color (1:58,000) vertical photographs. All photographs must meet certain standards (e.g., no cloud cover and a sun angle of 30° or more to reduce shadow effects). Inquiries regarding photo availability and ordering should be made to the User Services Section of the EROS Data Center.

EXISTING PHOTOGRAPHY: CANADIAN GOVERNMENT

The National Air Photo Library is the central storehouse for the Canadian government's air photography for coverage of the Yukon, Northwest Territories, Newfoundland, Labrador, Nova Scotia, Prince Edward Island, Manitoba, and Saskatchewan. Inquiries regarding this photography should be made directly to the National Air Photo Library, Surveys and Mapping Branch, Department of Energy, Mines, and Resources, 615 Booth Street, Ottawa, Ont. K1A OE 9, CANADA.

Photography obtained specifically for other provinces may be available through various agencies within those provinces. Written inquiries should include a map of the area involved, a statement regarding the proposed use of the photography, and specifications as to whether stereoscopic coverage is desired.

PROBLEMS

1. Assume you must plan a photographic mission for the area covered by a standard topographic map. Your instructor will supply basic data on photo scale desired, overlap, camera focal length, and so on. Compute the following values by the methods outlined in this chapter:

   a. Flying height above ground datum _____ 1500 + 1340

   Flying height above mean sea level _____ 2840'

   b. Direction of flight lines _____ E – W   90° , 270°

   Number of flight lines _____

    c. Ground distance between flight lines _____

    d. Actual percentage of sidelap _____

    e. Map distance between flight lines _____

    f. Ground distance between exposures on each line _____

    _____

    g. Map distance between exposures on each line _____

    _____

    h. Number of exposures on each line _____

    Total number of exposures _____

2. Use the foregoing data to convert the topographic map into a finished flight plan. Show location, direction, and altitude of all flight lines, positions of all exposure centers, actual percentage of sidelap, and so on. Add an appropriate title at the bottom of the map sheet.

3. Design and construct a simple camera mount for obtaining low-altitude, vertical exposures from a conventional, fixed-wing aircraft. Provide detailed drawings, specifications, and a bill of materials needed to build the complete apparatus. Then use the device to obtain aerial photographs of a designated area.

References

Applications Branch. 1978. Sources of remotely sensed data. In *Review of remote sensing terminology, systems, data, and analysis techniques*, EROS Data Center, Sioux Falls, S. Dak., Sec. III, pp. 1–10.

Avery, T. E. 1970. *Photo interpretation for land managers.* Eastman Kodak Co., Rochester, N.Y. Publication M-76, 26 pp., illus.

———. 1960. A checklist for airphoto inspections. *Photogrammetric Engineering* 26:81–84, illus.

———. 1958. Helicopter stereo-photography of forest plots. *Photogrammetric Engineering* 24:617–625, illus.

Avery, T. E., and Merle P. Meyer. 1962. *Contracting for forest aerial photography in the United States.* U.S. Forest Service, Lake States Forest Experiment Station. Station Paper 96, 37 pp., illus.

EROS Data Center. 1983. *The national high-altitude photography program.* U.S. Geological Survey, Sioux Falls, S.Dak., pamphlet, illus.

Howard, J. A., and Kosmer, H. 1967. Monocular mapping by microfilm. *Photogrammetric Engineering* 33:1299–1302, illus.

Lund, H. Gyde. 1969. Factors for computing photo coverage. *Photogrammetric Engineering* 35:61–63.

Paine, David P. 1981. *Aerial photography and image interpretation for resource management.* John Wiley & Sons, New York, 571 pp., illus.

Parker, Robert C., and Evert W. Johnson. 1970. Small-camera aerial photography: the K-20 system. *Journal of Forestry* 68:152–155, illus.

Ulliman, Joseph J. 1975. Cost of aerial photography. *Photogrammetric Engineering* 41:491–497.

U.S. Department of Agriculture. 1973. Aerial photography specifications. U.S. Department of Agricultural Stabilization and Conservation Service, Washington, D.C. 33 pp., with appendix, mimeographed (periodically revised).

Woodward, Louis A. 1970. Survey project planning. *Photogrammetric Engineering* 36:578–583, illus.

Zsilinszky, Victor G. 1970. Supplementary aerial photography with miniature cameras. *Photogrammetria* 25:27–38, illus.

Chapter 6

Planimetric and Topographic Mapping

PLANIMETRIC BASE MAPS

In areas of flat terrain where photographic scales can be precisely determined, direct print tracings may serve many useful purposes; nevertheless, such tracings cannot be technically referred to as true maps. Although the vertical aerial photograph presents a correct record of *angles*, constant changes in horizontal scale preclude accurate measurements of distance on simple overlays. The obvious alternative is to transfer photographic detail to reliable base maps of uniform scale. *Planimetric maps* are those that show the correct horizontal or plan position of natural and cultural features; maps that also show elevational differences (e.g., through contour lines) are termed *topographic maps*.

Construction of an original base map can be an expensive and time-consuming procedure. Therefore, existing maps should be used for the transfer of photographic detail wherever feasible. Topographic quadrangle sheets at a scale of 1:24,000 provide excellent, low-cost base maps. County maps, often available from state highway departments, may also serve as base maps when a high level of accuracy is not required. They may show township, range, and section lines in addition to geographic coordinates (longitude and latitude) to the nearest 5 min. County maps are usually printed at scales of about 1:100,000 to 1:125,000. Although compass bearings of section lines are not generally shown, such maps are much more reliable than oversimplified

115

plats showing idealized townships and sections oriented exactly with the cardinal directions.

Regardless of the base map selected, some enlargement or reduction is ordinarily required before print detail can be transferred, because differences between photographic and map scales must be reconciled. This may be accomplished optically by the use of special instruments to be described later or by the reconstruction of the map at the approximate scale of the contact prints. A pantograph may be used to aid the drafting.

GENERAL LAND OFFICE PLATS

General Land Office (GLO) plats provide another satisfactory means of compiling planimetric base maps. Most of the United States west of the Mississippi River and north of the Ohio River (as well as Alabama, Mississippi, and portions of Florida) was originally subdivided under the U.S. Public Land Survey (Figure 6.1). Township, range, and section lines are often visible on aerial photographs. If enough such lines and corners can be identified, GLO plats can be constructed as base maps from field notes available at state capitals or county surveyor's offices. The accuracy of this

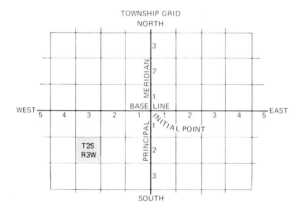

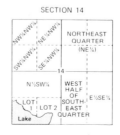

Figure 6.1. Subdivisions of the U.S. Public Land Survey.

method depends upon the number of grid lines and corners that can be pinpointed on the aerial photographs. The basic procedure is as follows:

A GLO plat showing sections, quarter-sections, and 40-acre parcels is drawn to the average photo scale from survey field notes. As many of the same lines and corners as possible are pinpointed on the aerial photographs, preferably arranged in a systematic framework throughout the project area. Ownership maps, county highway maps, and topographic quadrangle sheets may be helpful in the identification of such corners. Additional points may be needed. In such cases, the photographs must usually be taken into the field.

When photo interpretation has been completed, the annotated detail is transferred to the plat, one square of the grid being completed at a time. If the plat and photos are of the same scale, transfer can be speeded up by direct tracing over a light table; where scales differ, a proportionate grid system can be used. Photo detail is "forced" into corresponding squares on the base map.

MAP PROJECTIONS

A map projection is merely an orderly system of representing the earth's surface on a plane. Actually the approximately spherical form of the globe cannot be flattened into a map without the distortion of shapes or areal relationships. For small areas mapped at moderate scales (e.g., a small county), the curvature of the earth is so slight that distortion is negligible and often ignored. As larger areas (e.g., several counties or an entire state) are encompassed, however, distortion increases and it becomes impossible to represent a portion of the earth's surface precisely on a flat map sheet.

Historically, a large number of map projections have been devised, but only a relatively small number have enjoyed wide usage. There is no one projection that is best for all shapes and sizes of areas; all are designed for special purposes, and the value of a given projection depends on its specific use. Ideally a map projection provides a true representation of both shapes and areas, but, in practice, these two characteristics cannot be obtained on the same map. Projections that retain the true shapes of geographical units are referred to as *conformal;* those that provide correct area relationships are termed *equal-area* or *equivalent.* Other features of an ideal map projection include properties of true distance, true direction, and ease of plotting. Because no projection meets all of these requirements, three projections commonly used in the middle latitudes will be described: (1) Mercator, (2) Lambert conformal conic, and (3) polyconic. Descriptions are taken primarily from U.S. Army training manuals.

MERCATOR PROJECTION

This is a mathematically derived projection in which parallels and meridians are projected onto a cylinder tangent to the earth at the equator (Figure 6.2). When the cylinder is laid out flat, the meridians appear as

Characteristics	Mercator	Transverse Mercator	Oblique Mercator	Polyconic
Parallels	Parallel Straight Lines Unequally Spaced	Curves Concave Toward Nearest Pole	Sine Curves	Arcs of Non-Concentric Circles Equally Spaced on Mid-Meridian
Meridians	Parallel Straight Lines Equally Spaced	Complex Curves Concave Toward Central Meridian	Curved Lines	Mid-Meridian Straight Other Curved
Appearance of Grid	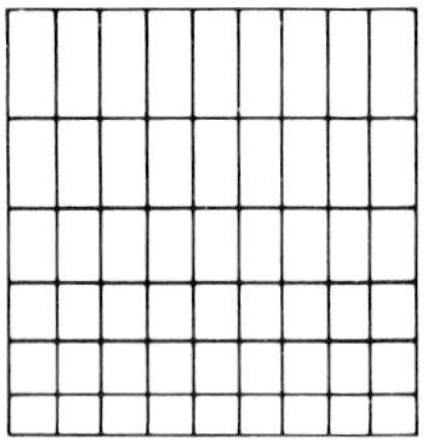	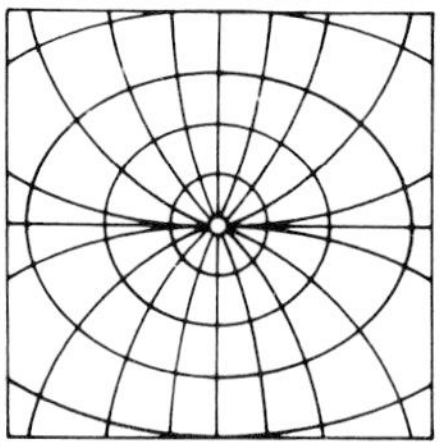	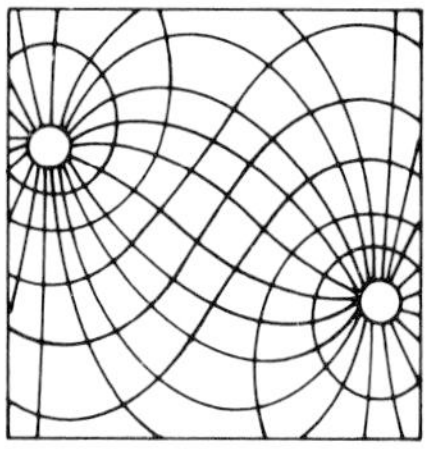	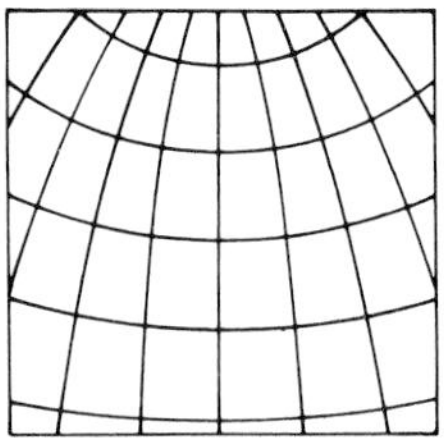
Great Circle	Curved Line (Except Equator and Meridians)	Curved Line	Straight Line Along Tangent Line	Approximated by Straight Line Near Mid-Meridian
Rhumb Line	Straight Line	Curved Line	Curved Line	Curved Line
Distance Scale	Mid-Latitude	Nearly Constant	Nearly Constant	Constant for Small Areas, Variable for Larger Areas
Graphic Illustration	Cylinder Tangent at Equator 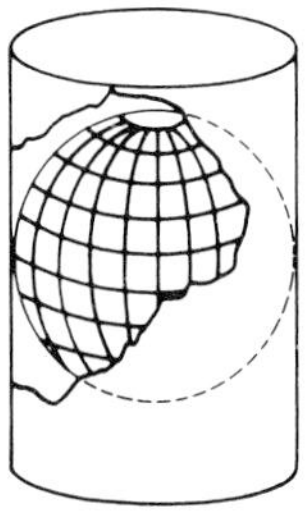	Cylinder Tangent Across Poles 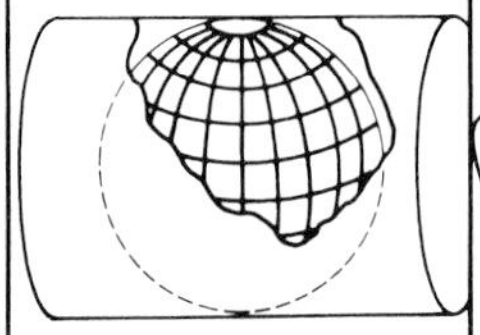	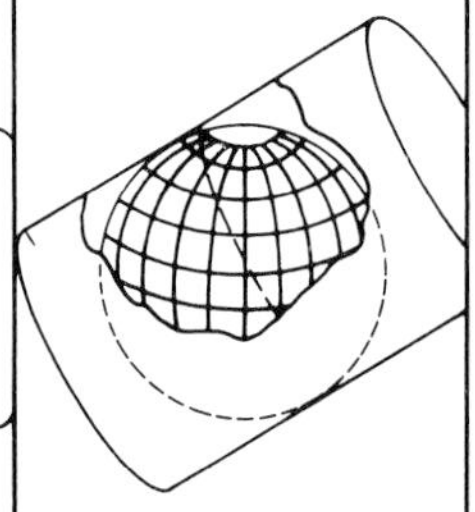	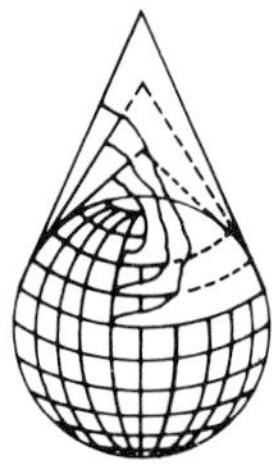
Origin of Projectors	Center of Sphere	Center of Sphere	Center of Sphere	Center of Sphere
Distortion of Shapes and Areas	Increases Away from Equator	Increases Away from Meridian of True Scale	Increases Away from Great Circle of True Scale	Increases Away from Mid-Meridian
Navigational Uses	Dead Reckoning and Celestial (Suitable for all Types)	Grid Navigation in Polar Areas	Strip Charts of Great Circle Paths	Ground Forces Maps
Conformality	Yes	Yes	Yes	Not Conformal but is Used as Such on Very Large Scale Maps

Figure 6.2. Characteristics of several map projections. (Courtesy U.S. Departments of the Army, the Navy, and the Air Force.)

Lambert Conformal	Polar Stereographic	Polar Gnomonic	Gnomonic	Azimuthal Equidistant
Arcs of Concentric Circles Nearly Equally Spaced	Concentric Circles Unequally Spaced	Concentric Circles Unequally Spaced	Conic Sections (Curved Lines)	Curved Lines
Straight Lines Converging at the Pole	Straight Lines Radiating from the Pole	Straight Lines Radiating from the Pole	Straight Lines	Curved Lines
Approximated by Straight Line	Approximated by Straight Line	Straight Line	Straight Line	Straight Lines Radiating from Center
Curved Line	Curved Line	Curved Line	Curved Line	Curved Line
Nearly Constant	Nearly Constant Except on Small Scale Charts	Variable	Variable	True at all Azimuths from Center Only
Secant Cone	Plane Tangent at Pole			No Geometric Application Can be Shown
Center of Sphere	Opposite Pole	Center of Sphere	Center of Sphere	Not Applicable
Very Little	Increases Away from Pole	Increases Away from Pole	Increases Away from Center of Projection	Increases Away from Center
Pilotage and Radio (Suitable for all Types)	Polar Navigation, All Types	Great Circle Navigation and Planning	Great Circle Navigation and Planning	Aeronautics, Radio Engineering and Celestial Maps
Yes	Yes	No	No	No

vertical, straight lines. Meridians are evenly spaced and true to scale at the equator or at the selected *standard parallel* of latitude. A standard parallel is any parallel along which linear measurements are the same as for a globe of equal scale. A meridian that has this property is called a *central meridian.* Lines of latitude are also straight and parallel, but they do not fall at their normally projected positions. Instead, they are mathematically spaced to produce the property of conformality or true shape.

For any *small area* (e.g., a 1° square), the relation of scale along meridians and parallels is the same as on the globe. Scale changes are slight in the midlatitudes, amounting to only about 3 percent at 30° north or south of the equator. However, because the meridians do not converge, areas in the higher latitudes are greatly enlarged (not distorted) when the equator is used as the standard parallel. Although relatively true shapes are maintained, the map scale is doubly exaggerated at 60° and exaggerated by six times at 80°. Thus, on a Mercator map of the world, Greenland appears larger than South America, although it is actually only about one-ninth as large. Polar regions are at infinity and hence cannot be shown on a Mercator projection.

The Mercator projection, devised around 1569 by a Dutch cartographer, is the oldest and probably the best-known projection in the world because of its continuous use for nautical charts. An outstanding feature of the Mercator is that all straight lines are *loxodromes* or *rhumb lines* (i.e., lines of true bearing or azimuth). Because parallels and meridians form a rectangular grid, it is easily plotted. The Mercator is widely used for navigational purposes in the midlatitudes, and it is the standard projection for Navy hydrographic and air-navigation charts.

▓ TRANSVERSE MERCATOR PROJECTION

The transverse Mercator projection is geometrically equivalent to a cylinder wrapped around the earth and tangent to it, along a meridian, with the origin of projection at the center of the earth. The cylinder is cut lengthwise, opened, and laid flat to produce the map. The projected longitude lines are almost straight and evenly spaced near the tangent meridian but become greatly distorted farther out.

With the transverse Mercator projection, most lines of latitude and longitude are curved lines. The quadrangles formed by the intersection of these curved parallels and meridians are of different sizes and shapes, complicating the location of points and the measurement of directions. To solve this problem, a rectangular grid system may be superimposed upon the projection. Such a grid (a series of straight lines intersecting at right angles) furnishes the map reader with a system of squares similar to the block system of most city streets. The dimensions and orientation of different types of grids vary, but these three properties are common to most grid systems, particularly those adopted by mapping and military agencies:

1. They are true rectangular grids.
2. They are superimposed on the geographic projection.
3. They permit *linear* and *angular* measurements.

UNIVERSAL TRANSVERSE MERCATOR GRID

The universal transverse Mercator grid (UTM grid) is designed for world use between 80° S latitude and 84° N latitude. As the name implies, it is superimposed over the transverse Mercator projection.

Starting at the 180° meridian of longitude and progressing east, the globe is divided into narrow zones, normally 6° of longitude in width, which are numbered 1 through 60. Each zone has as its east and west limits a meridian of longitude and one central meridian passing through the center of the grid zone (Figure 6.3). With the intersection of a central meridian and the equator as an origin or starting point, a location *could* be given by a listing of its linear distance north or south of the equator and east or west of the central meridian for the zone. This, however, would require the use of *north, south, east,* or *west* for identification of the direction of the distance or the use of plus or minus

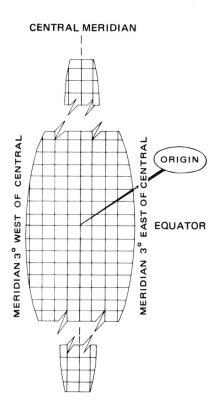

Figure 6.3.   A UTM grid zone. (Courtesy U.S. Department of the Army.)

values. This inconvenience has been eliminated by numerical values assigned to the origin which permit positive values for all points within a zone.

The value of 500,000 m is assigned to the central meridian to avoid negative numbers at the west edge of the zone. These readings are known as *false eastings* (Figure 6.4). The values increase from west to east. For north-south values, in the Northern Hemisphere, the equator is 0 m and the numbers increase toward the North Pole. In the Southern Hemisphere, the equator is 10,000,000 m and the numbers decrease toward the South Pole. These are known as *false northings*. The terms *false eastings* and *false northings* apply only to the original preparation of the grid system.

Each regularly spaced line that makes up the UTM grid on a map is labeled with its false easting or false northing value (showing its relation to the origin of the zone). The grid interval is usually 1,000 m for large-scale maps; 1,000 or 10,000 m for medium-scale maps; and 100,000 m for small-scale maps.

LAMBERT CONFORMAL CONIC PROJECTION

This projection, developed by a German mathematician, is derived by the projection of lines from the center of the globe onto a simple cone. The cone intersects the earth along two standard parallels of latitude, both of which are

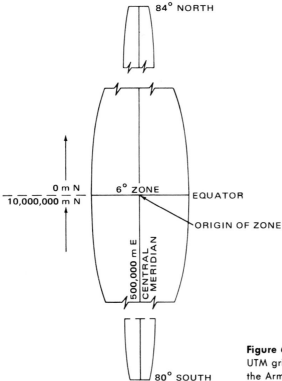

Figure 6.4. False easting and northing for a UTM grid zone. (Courtesy U.S. Department of the Army.)

on the same side of the equator. All meridians are converging straight lines that meet at a common point beyond the limits of the map. Parallels are concentric circles whose center is at the intersection point of the meridians. Parallels and meridians cross at right angles, an essential feature of conformality.

To minimize and distribute scale errors, the two standard parallels are chosen to enclose two-thirds of the north-south map area. Between these parallels, the scale will be too small, and beyond them, too large. If the north-south extent of maps is limited, however, maximum scale errors will rarely exceed 1 percent. Area exaggeration between and near the standard parallels is relatively slight; thus the projection provides good directional and shape relationships for areas having their long axes running in an east-west belt. The Lambert conformal conic is the most commonly used projection for sectional aeronautical charts of the United States.

POLYCONIC PROJECTION

Because of its suitability for large-scale maps of relatively small areas, the polyconic projection is ordinarily of interest to photo interpreters. It is derived by the projection of lines from the center of the earth onto a series of cones, each of which is tangent to a parallel of latitude. The central meridian of the area to be mapped is a straight line along which the linear scale is correct. Parallels are represented by arcs of circles that are not concentric but whose centers all lie in the extension of the central meridian. Distances between parallels along the central meridian are proportional to true distances on the earth's surface. Spacings between meridians are similarly proportioned. The projection is neither conformal nor equivalent, but both qualities are closely approximated for small areas.

For large areas, north-south distortion increases rapidly with increasing distance from the central meridian. Because of this, it is customary to limit the width of the projection and to use the central meridian of the area to be mapped as the central meridian of the projection. In short, the projection is best suited to areas whose long axes lie in a north-south direction. The polyconic projection has been used for topographic maps compiled by United States government agencies. Special tables have been computed that permit its use anywhere in the world.

RADIAL LINE TRIANGULATION

If acceptable planimetric maps cannot be compiled from the foregoing methods, the usual alternative is to construct a new map based on a *radial line plot.* A radial line plot is a photogrammetric triangulation procedure, usually controlled by ground surveys, by which the photo images are oriented and placed in proper relationship to one another. To a large degree, the field descriptions of available ground control points dictate the nature of the base map constructed. If control points are based on the U.S. Public Land Survey, a GLO plat would be constructed; if they are tied to a state coordinate system, the corresponding rectangular grid would be used; and if locations are described in terms of latitude and longitude, a suitable map projection would constitute the basic plotting framework.

On a vertical or near-vertical photograph, the principal point, isocenter, and nadir are assumed to occupy the same location. Thus a line drawn radially from the principal point to a given object will *pass through* the true location of the object. Expressed in another way, any displacement of photo images will occur along lines radiating from the center of the photograph. This concept is the basis for the construction of maps controlled by radial line plots.

The principle of radial line triangulation can be illustrated with any two overlapping prints. If a straight line is drawn from the principal point of each photo through images of the *same* object, the two lines will intersect at the correct position of the object when the prints are lapped in mosaic fashion with flight lines superimposed. By repetition of this procedure for several selected *wing points* on each photograph, the entire group of prints can be correctly oriented and tied to a base map. A wing point is any selected photo feature in the sidelap and overlap zone that can be easily pinpointed on all prints on which it appears.

It is presumed here that some of the wing points will also serve as ground control points. Ground control points are most effective when located around the perimeter of the project area (e.g., near the exterior boundaries). Even for small areas, a good radial line plot requires a minimum of one or two ground control points near each corner of the area being mapped, and most of these points should be common to at least three photographs.

Construction of a radial line plot for a small area (e.g., 25 to 50 km²) is normally accomplished by use of transparent paper templets. Larger radial line plots are preferably constructed by commercial mapping companies that are fully equipped for handling such work. In these instances, slotted templets may be used (Figures 6.5 and 6.6), or triangulation may be performed directly with first-order stereoplotting instruments.

CONSTRUCTING A RADIAL LINE PLOT

Because the use of transparent paper templets is the least expensive method of making a radial line plot for a small number of photographs, this procedure is outlined here. The same basic steps can be followed when slotted templets are available. At least six overlapping prints (three prints each in two adjacent flight lines) are needed. Principal points, conjugate principal points, and flight lines should be located and inked as described in earlier chapters.

1. Draw a suitable base map of the project area at the prescribed scale. All ground control points should be precisely plotted on the base map and marked with 5-mm diameter circles. Exact locations of control points

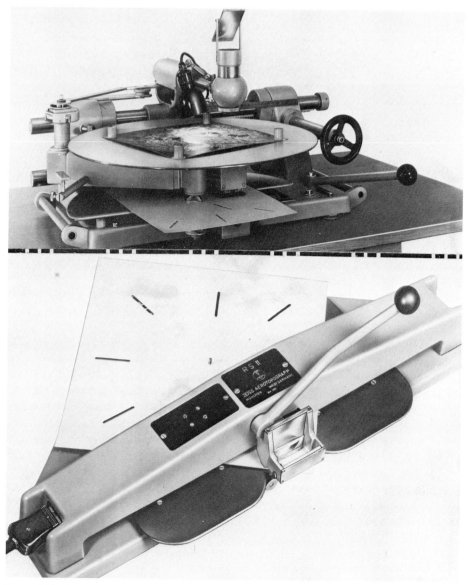

Figure 6.5. Two types of radial secators used for cutting slotted templets. (Courtesy Carl Zeiss, Oberkochen.)

may be obtained from ground surveys, GLO plats, or a network of known triangulation stations.

2. With a sharp china-marking pencil, outline the boundary of the project area on all photographs. Draw the line just *outside* the boundaries to avoid obscuring needed detail.

3. Pinpoint ground control points on all photographs and mark with 5-mm circles in colored ink (to contrast with PPs and CPPs). At least two, and

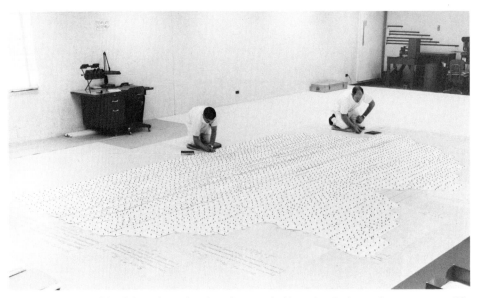

Figure 6.6. Assembly of slotted templets for a large radial line plot. Each templet represents a 23-by-23-cm aerial photograph. (Courtesy U.S. Department of Agriculture.)

preferably three, control points should be common to one pair of overlapping prints when the transparent templet method is used.

4. Locate wing points (well-defined features easily pinpointed on overlapping prints) near the middle of the sidelap zone and perpendicular to PPs and CPPs. If a control point has already been picked within 2 cm of a planned wing point, the wing point may be omitted. Except for the first and last photo in each flight line, all prints will have six wing points. These will be common to two, three, four, five, or six overlapping photographs. Mark with 5-mm-diameter inked circles—the same color and size as those used to designate PPs and CPPs.

5. Prepare 23-by-23-cm pieces of tracing paper for each photograph. Tape down each print over a light table with the transparent templet on top. Then, using a 4H pencil,
   a. Pinpoint all PPs, CPPs, control points, and wing points and trace the exact position of flight lines.
   b. Use a straightedge to align each wing and control point with the PP. Draw radial lines extending about 4 cm on both sides of wing and control points.
   c. Label each templet by writing the appropriate exposure number aside PPs and CPPs. Wing and control points should carry the same designation on all templets upon which they appear.

6. Tape down the base map over a large light table. Assembly of the radial line plot may begin with any transparent templet that includes three control points. (If the slotted method is used, a templet having one or two control points can be positioned first.) Shift templet over top of base map

until radial lines drawn through control points precisely intersect the same locations on the map. Fasten down with drafting tape.

7. The second templet positioned will be one in the same flight line that overlaps the first. With the common flight line superimposed, the templet is shifted back and forth *along the flight line* until radial lines representing control points pass through base-map positions (just as with the first templet). Intersections of radial lines from wing points will be obtained simultaneously. The second templet is then taped down.

8. Remaining templets in the first flight line are added in order of overlap position. When one flight line has been completed, assembly of the adjacent line should begin with the templet having the greatest amount of ground control, and so on. Radial lines from wing points, as well as those from control points, should precisely intersect at the same point. A wing point that appears on six photographs will thus be represented by a six-way "cross" of radial lines. In all instances, flight lines must be superimposed, and the templets may be shifted *only along the flight line* to yield intersections with radial lines from adjacent templets. The result will be an assembly similar to that shown in Figure 6.7.

9. When all templets have been correctly positioned and taped down, use a needle to punch through all PPs, CPPs, and wing point intersections. In this way, all points are located on the base map. Remove templets, mark all transferred points on the map with 5-mm-diameter penciled circles and label with appropriate designations as in step 5c.

10. The radial line plot is now complete. Photographic detail may be transferred to the base map with instruments described in the next section.

TRANSFERRING DETAIL FROM SINGLE PRINTS

Following completion of photo interpretation and preparation of a radial line plot, the next phase of map compilation is the transfer of photographic features to the base map. Although direct tracings may suffice under special circumstances, it is usually more efficient to use one of several photogrammetric devices designed for this purpose. The two types of instruments most commonly employed for transferring planimetric detail from single prints are camera lucidas and direct- or indirect-projection devices. Because these instruments do not provide for stereoscopic viewing, the desired features should be annotated on alternate prints before the transfer process. (If 23-by-23-cm photographs with 60 percent endlap and 30 percent sidelap are assumed, alternate prints will have effective, or nonoverlapping, areas of about 16 by 18 cm. Only one-half as many prints must be handled during the transfer process if annotations are confined to alternate photographs.)

One of the more common types of camera lucidas is the vertical sketchmaster pictured in Figure 6.8. This device employs a full-silvered and a semitransparent, or semisilvered, mirror to superimpose photo and map images. The annotated contact print is placed face up on the platform, directly under

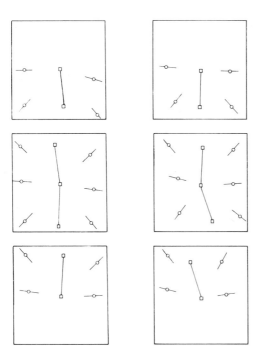

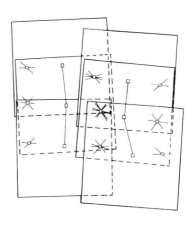

Figure 6.7. Diagram of paper templets (left) and assembly into a radial line plot (right).

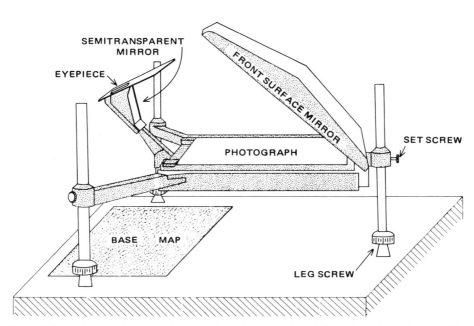

Figure 6.8. Schematic diagram of a vertical sketchmaster. A semisilvered eyepiece mirror enables the operator to view photograph and map simultaneously.

the large, full-silvered mirror. Photo images are reflected from the large mirror to the semisilvered mirror in the eyepiece housing. When the interpreter looks into the eyepiece, the semitransparent mirror provides a monocular view of the reflected photo image and the base map simultaneously.

For transfer of photographic detail to the radial line plot, the instrument can be raised or lowered by adjustment of the legs until both map and photograph appear at the same scale. Any combination of three common control or wing points is carefully matched; features that fall within the triangle thus formed are traced onto the base map. The instrument is then shifted and the legs readjusted until three more circles can be superimposed. Planimetric detail is thus transferred, one triangle at a time, until the base map is completed. Photo image displacement due to tilt or topography may result in slightly offset features (e.g., a highway) along common sides of triangles. Such discrepancies must be resolved by "hedging" locations until smooth, continuous lines are obtained.

Most sketchmasters provide for a relatively narrow range of scale changes; the type shown in Figure 6.8 has a scale range of about 0.7× to 1.5×, and the model pictured in Figure 6.9 accommodates changes of 0.4× to 2.8×. Base maps should therefore be drawn at the approximate photo scale when the sketchmaster is used for the transfer of detail.

Image-projection devices assume a wide variety of sizes and configurations; many are similar in operation to photographic enlargers. A contact print (or transparency) is placed near a light source and the photo image is reflected (or projected) onto a tracing surface such as a tabletop (Figure 6.10). These types

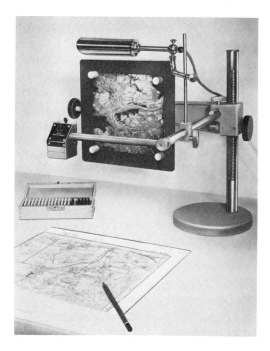

Figure 6.9. LUZ sketchmaster with aerial photograph held in position by magnets. This self-illuminated camera lucida operates on the same basic principle as the device pictured in Figure 6.8. (Courtesy Carl Zeiss, Oberkochen.)

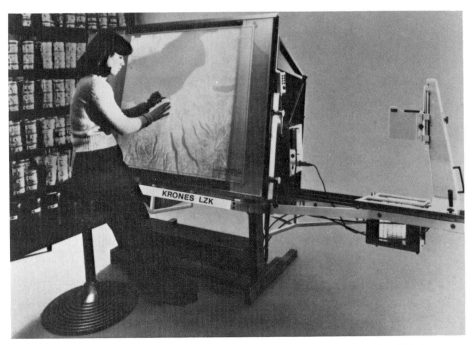

Figure 6.10. Krones LZK rear-projection device for use with transparent film. This instrument provides variable scale magnification up to 72X. (Courtesy Krones, Inc.)

of instruments offer a greater range of scale adjustments and more "elbow room" than vertical sketchmasters; however, they are somewhat less portable and must ordinarily be used in a semidarkened room.

Where aerial imagery is obtained on (or copied onto) 35-mm or 70-mm film frames, ordinary slide projectors provide ideal devices for enlarging and transferring image detail. Instead of projecting the image onto a screen or wall, a favored technique is to mount the projector underneath an ordinary table. The photographic image is projected onto a first-surface mirror inclined at 45° and then reflected upward to the underside of a translucent tracing glass mounted in the tabletop.

The system is simple and economical, because the mirror, mounting hardware, and translucent tracing top are the only specialized items of equipment to be purchased. The slide projector, being unmodified, can be removed and returned to routine use as desired.

GROUND CONTROL FOR TOPOGRAPHIC MAPS

At the turn of the century, the compilation of topographic maps was largely dependent on field surveys. Such maps now are produced by photogrammetric methods, and fieldwork is limited to obtaining a network of horizontal and vertical ground control required for accurate stereoplotting. Ground control points are carefully located positions that show longitude and latitude or elevation above mean sea level. Horizontal control is needed for correct scale, position, and orientation of the map to be maintained. For this purpose, the grid coordinates of many points within the area to be mapped must be determined by field surveys. Similarly, vertical control is needed for the correct location of contours. Therefore, elevations of many points must also be determined in the field.

Control points become the framework on which map detail is assembled. This framework determines the accuracy with which the positions and elevations of map features may be shown and makes it possible to join maps of abutting quadrangles without a break in the continuity of map detail. The control points are usually marked on the ground by metal tablets set in rock or masonry and are shown on maps by appropriate symbols. Some marks serve for both horizontal and vertical control.

COMPILATION OF TOPOGRAPHIC MAPS

Typical steps in the production of topographic quadrangles are as follows:

1. Vertical photography of the area to be mapped is obtained, usually on panchromatic film. Scale of photography is geared to the desired contour interval and the stereoplotting instrument to be used for map compilation.
2. Film is developed and a set of contact prints made for selection of ground control. Horizontal and vertical controls are established by field surveys, and control points are marked on contact prints.
3. Glass diapositives (usually 23 by 23 cm) are made from each film negative for use in stereoplotting instruments (Figure 6.11). The positive-image plates are oriented in the plotter so that they occupy the same relative positions in space as the original film negatives. Tie-ins to the base map or "manuscript" are established by use of ground control points. The resulting stereoscopic setup is referred to as a *stereo model.*
4. Contours, drainage, and culture are automatically traced onto the map manuscript by manipulation of a floating dot within the stereo model. When all detail has been transferred from a given stereo model, one diapositive is replaced, and an adjacent model is correctly oriented and tied into the manuscript by a process known as *bridging.*
5. The completed map manuscript is checked for errors and omissions. Detail is then traced onto a polyester film base by a technique known as *scribing* (Figure 6.12). Separate scribe sheets and negatives are made for each item to be lithographed or printed in a different tone on the finished map (Figure 6.13).

TOPOGRAPHIC MAPS FROM PAPER PRINTS

Photo interpreters concerned with topographic mapping are sometimes interested in plotting devices designed for use with paper prints rather than glass diapositives. Representative of this group of instruments is the Zeiss

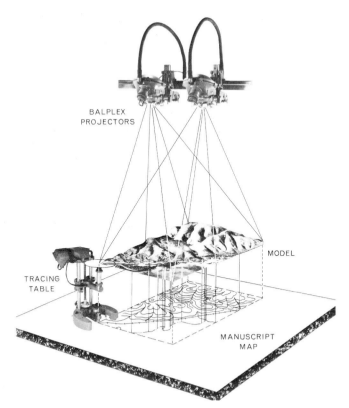

BALPLEX
PROJECTORS

MODEL

TRACING
TABLE

MANUSCRIPT
MAP

Figure 6.11. Schematic representation of a three-dimensional terrain model provided by stereoplotting instruments. (Courtesy TRB Associates, Inc.)

Stereotope, a compact stereoplotter built around a magnifying mirror stereoscope, stereometer (parallax bar), and tracing pantograph (Figure 6.14). The Stereotope is constructed primarily for making topographic maps at scales ranging from 1:25,000 to 1:100,000. With cameras commonly in use and currently obtainable flying heights, the recommended ratio of map scale to photo scale lies roughly between 0.7× and 1.6×.

In use, the floating-mark lenses remain stationary and centered in the field of view, while corrections for x- and y-parallax are made by moving the right-hand photo carriage. Although both photographs remain flat on the special carriages, allowance for tilt can be made by a mechanical computing device that corrects the parallax readings obtained for a given stereopair. The instrument is rugged, compact, and portable. If high-quality, vertical photographs are available on low-shrink papers, accuracy of results will be comparable to that shown in Figure 6.15.

The relative accuracy of various stereoscopic plotting instruments is usually expressed in terms of the precision with which contours can be reliably determined. The contour factor (usually termed *C-factor*) of a given plotter, multiplied by the desired contour interval, determines the maximum flight altitude that can be used for compilation of topographic maps of the accepted accuracy standard.

FORM LINES

Although precise topographic work should not be attempted without instruments specifically designed for drawing contours, approximate *form lines* can be sketched with a simple stereoscope and stereometer. Form lines are defined as relative contours that are drawn from visual observation to show the general configuration of terrain; thus they do not necessarily represent true elevations nor have a uniform contour interval.

If large-scale photographs of steep terrain are available, interpreters can often differentiate form lines having intervals of 10 to 20 m. Skilled interpreters may delineate these relative contours with only a stereoscope, but it is advantageous to measure several extremes of elevation with a stereometer or parallax bar.

AERIAL PHOTO MOSAICS

An aerial photo mosaic is an assembly of two or more aerial photographs that have been cut and matched together systematically to form a composite view of the area covered by the photographs. The mosaic gives the appearance

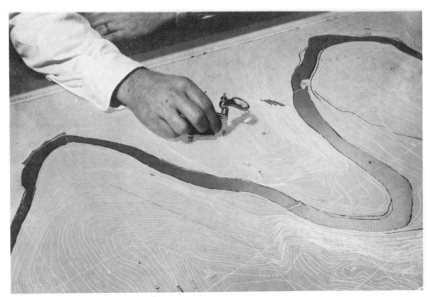

Figure 6.12. The technique of scribing has largely replaced conventional inked draftings in the preparation of finished maps. The polyester film base *(scribe-coat)* is dimensionally stable and provides lines of high uniformity and sharpness. Maps are reproduced photographically from the scribed manuscript. (Courtesy Abrams Aerial Survey Corp.)

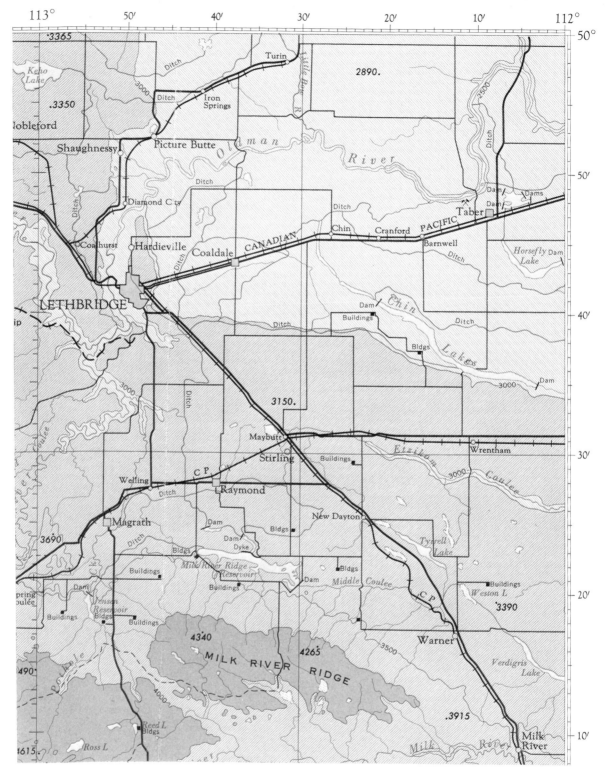

Figure 6.13. Portion of the Cranbrook-Lethbridge topographic quadrangle map. Elevations are in feet; map base is the transverse Mercator projection. Scale is 1:500,000. (Courtesy Canada Department of Mines and Technical Surveys.)

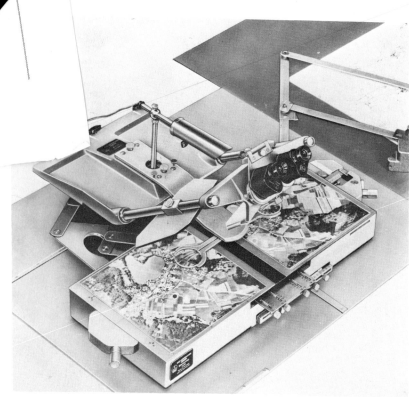

Figure 6.14.   Closeup view of the Stereotope showing movable photo carriages and floating-mark lenses. (Courtesy Carl Zeiss, Oberkochen.)

of a single photograph, producing a complete record of the area. Mosaics are particularly useful for terrain analysis and for studies of certain natural resources. Source areas for construction materials such as building stone, sand, gravel, and timber often can be determined through the study of mosaics.

Although several categories of mosaics are recognized, most of them can be conveniently grouped into two general classes: *controlled* and *uncontrolled*. A controlled mosaic is an assembly of rectified prints that are laid to ground control and supplemented by radial line triangulation. With the accuracy required of ratioed or rectified prints, all mismatches of detail are eliminated, and approximate measurements may be made directly on the mosaic. With an uncontrolled mosaic, photographic detail is matched without the aid of ground control. Only the central area of each photograph is used. Detail is matched with adjacent center areas, and the assembly is pasted to a stable base to form the mosaic. The scale of uncontrolled mosaics is not uniform, so measurements of distances and areas cannot be made on them.

Preparation of controlled mosaics is an expensive process involving highly trained technicians. It requires prints that match in terms of scale, tone, and

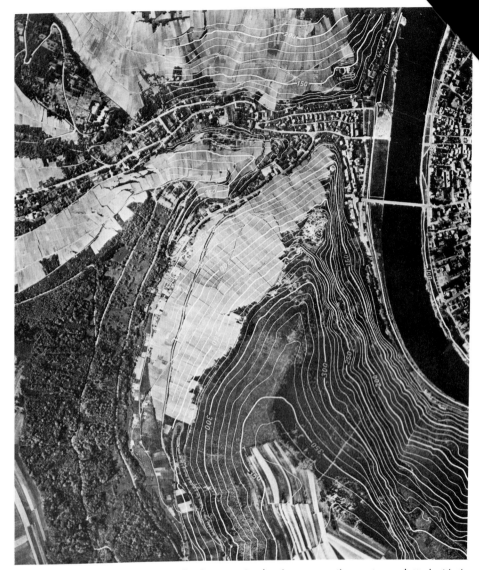

Figure 6.15. Vertical photograph of a German city showing perspective contours plotted with the Stereotope. Scale is approximately 1:10,000; contour interval is about 3 m (10 ft). (Courtesy Carl Zeiss, Oberkochen.)

freedom from tilt, and the edges of photographs must be bevel cut and sanded before an adhesive is applied to the backing. Therefore, the succeeding discussion is based on a simplified, do-it-yourself method of assembling uncontrolled mosaics, as described by Meyer (1962).

▒ PREPARING AN UNCONTROLLED MOSAIC

In the step-by-step procedure that follows, the use of single-weight, contact prints is presumed. Print edges are square cut (not beveled) for a butt-joint assembly. Supplies needed are a metal straightedge, a china-marking pencil, a sharp knife, rubber cement, drafting tape, photographs, and a hardboard base for mounting.

1. Photographs are first arranged in flight-line sequence as for the assembly of an ordinary index mosaic.
2. Starting with the middle flight line, photographic detail is matched in the *center* of each overlap area. As each overlapping print is matched, it should be taped down to prevent movement. Photos from adjacent strips are fitted together in a similar manner, priority being given to endlap detail, but also with sidelap detail matching as closely as possible. Close matches are important only in the centers of overlap areas.
3. After all photographs have been precisely lapped and taped down, *match lines* are drawn to delineate the usable or effective area of each print. Such lines are best drawn with a china-marking pencil and a straight-edge. Exact positions of match lines depend on photographic detail; lakes, roads, or square parcels of land should not be bisected if this can be avoided by slight shifting of match lines.
4. When all endlap and sidelap match lines have been drawn in their final positions, the mosaic is taped to a piece of plywood and made ready for cutting. Once cutting has begun, the mosaic must not be moved. Therefore, it is important that it be firmly attached to the cutting surface and that individual photos be fastened securely to one another. Cutting cleanly through several thicknesses of photos requires a sharp knife and considerable pressure. A knife with a stout handle and replaceable razorlike blade is recommended.
5. After they are cut, the effective areas of each print are retained, and each flight line is loosely taped together to keep the component sections in order. The final assembly, beginning with the middle flight line, is accomplished by cementing of the print sections to a sturdy hardboard backing. Although variations in print scale usually preclude perfect matches of detail, the more important cultural features usually can be closely matched if these photo sections are cemented first.

▒ ORTHOPHOTOGRAPHY

An *orthophotograph* is a continuous-tone photo image depicting terrain features in their true plan positions. In other words, geometric distortions and relief displacements are optically removed by an orthoprojection instrument that is connected to a stereoplotter. This specialized instrument scans the stereo model and rectifies the photographic image (bit by bit) along the scanning lines in one continuous operation.

The rectification of the perspective aerial photograph into an ortho-photograph permits the "corrected" imagery to be used as a planimetric map. Orthophotographs may be overprinted onto standard mapping sheets, with the resulting product being referred to as an *orthophotoquad*. Ortho-photoquads meet the same positional accuracy requirements that standard topographic maps do. With their abundance of detail not found on con-ventional line maps, they are useful interim map substitutes for unmapped areas and valuable complements to existing line maps.

PROBLEMS

1. Construct one of the map projections discussed in this chapter.

2. Design and demonstrate the use of an image-transfer system for use with single (nonstereo) photographs, for example, a slide projector and reflect-ing mirror apparatus.

3. Obtain a stereopair of contact prints illustrating pronounced topographic relief for use in form-line sketching.
   a. Lay off a 1-by-1-cm system of grid points within the overlap zone (mark only on one print).
   b. Determine the average photo base (P) and flying height (H) of the stereopair for use in obtaining parallax conversions.
   c. With a simple stereometer, find the lowest elevational plane within the overlap zone. If a lake or river is visible, the lowest water surface may be selected as the reference plane.
   d. Assuming the selected reference plane to be the equivalent of mean sea level (i.e., zero elevation), measure the elevation of each grid point. Record these values on an overlay traced from the marked photograph.
   e. Study the gridded area under the stereoscope and sketch in form lines or approximate contours by interpolation between points of known elevation. Supplement the grid points with added measurements, if necessary. Draw trial lines with a pencil so that changes and corrections can be made easily. If a third-order stereoplotting instrument such as the Stereotope is available, contours may be traced directly at a specified contour interval, and the grid points described here may be omitted.
   f. When discrepancies and irregularities have been resolved, draft a finished overlay of the contoured area. Label each form line with its approximate relative elevation. Add pertinent topographic symbols, scale, and legend.
   g. On a sheet of cross-section paper, draw a profile representing a transect across the area of greatest elevational change. Indicate the location of the profile line on both photograph and finished overlay.

References

Giroux, Mary J. 1966. *Maps: basic tools for national growth.* Department of Mines and Technical Surveys, Ottawa, Ont. 30 pp., illus.

Meyer, Dan. 1962. Mosaics you can make. *Photogrammetric Engineering* 28:167–171, illus.

———. 1962. A reflecting projector you can build. *Photogrammetric Engineering* 27:76–78, illus.

Sibert, Winston. 1972. Role of federal agencies in large-scale mapping. *Photogrammetric Engineering* 38:239–242.

U.S. Department of the Army. 1969. *Map grid systems.* U.S. Army Engineer School, Ft. Belvoir, Va. 50 pp., illus.

———. 1966. *Introduction to map projections.* U.S. Army Engineer School, Ft. Belvoir, Va. 57 pp., illus.

U.S. Department of the Interior. 1973. *Universal transverse Mercator grid.* Government Printing Office, Washington, D.C. Extract prepared by U.S. Geological Survey from Army Field Manual FM 21-26. 10 pp., illus.

———. 1972. *Topographic maps.* Government Printing Office, Washington, D.C. 20 pp., illus.

———. 1963. *Restoration of lost or obliterated corners and subdivision of sections.* Government Printing Office, Washington, D.C. 40 pp., illus.

Veign, James L., and Francis B. Reeves. 1973. A case for orthophoto mapping. *Photogrammetric Engineering* 39:1059–1063, illus.

Chapter 7

Nonphotographic Imaging Systems

■ TYPES OF NONPHOTOGRAPHIC IMAGING SYSTEMS

Nonphotographic imaging systems include *electro-optical sensors* and *imaging radar systems*. Because features are not photographed directly with either class of system, the term *image* is used to describe the picturelike presentation that is printed onto photographic film. Electro-optical sensors use radiation-sensitive detectors (e.g., photoemissive cells, semiconductors) that convert observed radiant-energy levels to proportional electrical signals that are then used to produce an image. The major types of electro-optical sensors are the vidicon camera, the multispectral scanner, the thermal infrared scanner, and the pushbroom scanner.

Radar systems produce images that represent the reflective characteristics of terrain objects to microwave energy. Imaging radars are *active*, providing their own radiation output as opposed to electro-optical sensors, which are normally *passive*, dependent upon natural sources of external energy such as solar radiation or thermal infrared emissions.

■ RADIATION AND SENSOR CAPABILITIES

A portion of the sun's electromagnetic radiation passes through the atmosphere, strikes the earth's surface, and interacts with soils, rocks, water, vegetation, and man-made objects. The nature of the interaction depends upon the wavelength, intensity, and polarization of the electromagnetic radiation and the physical and chemical properties of the solid, liquid, or gas with which the radiation is interacting. Three interactions are possible: (1) reflection, (2) transmission, and (3) absorption. This is expressed by the following relationship:

$$\rho + \tau + \alpha = 1 \qquad \textbf{Equation 7.1}$$

where: ρ = Decimal fraction reflected
τ = Decimal fraction transmitted
α = Decimal fraction absorbed

Most opaque materials transmit no radiation; hence $\tau = 0$ and $\rho + \alpha = 1$. Short-wave solar energy that is absorbed by opaque materials is then emitted as long-wave earth radiation.

Several nonphotographic imaging systems have been developed to detect radiation that is reflected or emitted (or both) from terrain features. Such sensors are capable of operating in one or several selectively defined regions of the electromagnetic spectrum—ultraviolet, visible, reflected infrared, thermal infrared, and microwave spectral ranges. Thermal infrared scanners and radar systems can function under both day and night conditions, and radar systems are additionally unaffected by weather conditions at a certain wavelength threshold. Each type of sensor reacts only to electromagnetic energy of specific wavelengths. For example, radar receivers are insensitive to visible light, and transmitted microwave energy cannot be detected by electro-optical sensor systems. Because of the uniqueness of thermal infrared radiation, its properties are discussed in the next section.

THE NATURE OF THERMAL INFRARED RADIATION

The total infrared portion of the electromagnetic spectrum lies between the visible and microwave regions (approximately 0.7 to 1,000 μm). The reflected infrared spectral band extends from about 0.7 to 3 μm. Because of atmospheric absorption effects, the spectrum bandpasses, or "windows," from 3 to 5 and from 8 to 14 μm are the most useful regions in the thermal infrared spectral region (Figure 7.1). There, under normal conditions, the atmosphere is quite transparent to thermal infrared radiation, and it escapes directly to space.

Thermal infrared energy results from atomic and molecular motions and is emitted by all substances having a temperature above absolute zero (-273 ° C). Therefore, all objects from animal life to vegetation and rocks are sources of thermal infrared radiation. Remote-sensing systems sensitive to wavelengths of radiation emitted from objects can be used both during daylight and darkness.

Thermal infrared remote sensing is concerned with measuring or displaying in image form the radiant energy emitted from terrain objects. With quantitative thermal infrared scanners, this type of energy can be used to determine an object's radiant or apparent temperature. On a standard

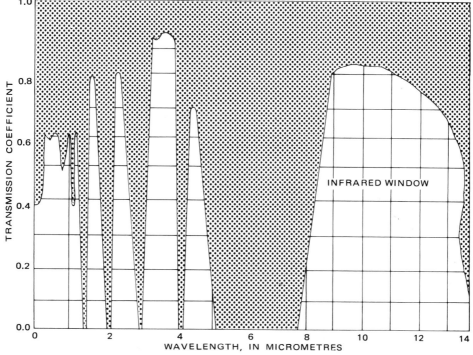

Figure 7.1.   Generalized transmission of electromagnetic radiation through the atmosphere. Actual transmission varies according to time of day, season, and locale. Most thermal infrared radiation is transmitted in the 3–5 and 8–14 μm atmospheric "windows." Detector elements have been designed to sense radiation in each of these spectral regions.

thermal infrared image, light tones indicate "warm" radiant temperatures, while darker tones represent "cooler" radiant temperatures (Figure 7.2).

It must be stressed that thermal infrared sensors cannot measure kinetic energy, which is the random motion of molecules. To determine kinetic or internal temperature, a measuring instrument (e.g., thermometer, thermistor) must be placed in physical contact with the object. The radiant temperature of an object is always less than its kinetic temperature because of a thermal property called *emissivity* (ε).

EMISSIVITY AND SURFACE TEMPERATURE

The total energy radiated by an object is primarily governed by its emissivity and surface temperature. Emissivity is a ratio expression of the energy radiated from an object at a given temperature (F_r) in relationship to the radiation emitted from a *blackbody* at the same temperature (F_b):

$$\epsilon = \frac{F_r}{F_b}$$

Equation 7.2

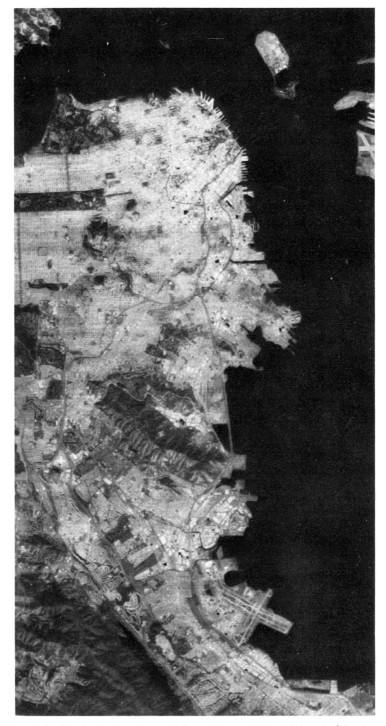

Figure 7.2. High-altitude, daytime thermal infrared image (8.5 to 13.0 μm) of San Francisco and vicinity (April 1980). The aircraft altitude was 20,000 m above ground level. Scale is about 1:110,000. Compare with cover photograph, Figure 7.15, and Plate 12. (Courtesy George England, Daedalus Enterprises, Inc. and NASA/Ames Research Center.)

A blackbody is a theoretical object that is both a perfect absorber and a perfect radiator or emitter; its emissivity is 1. All other bodies are less efficient absorbers and radiators, and their emissivities are always less than 1 (Table 7.1); these objects are termed *graybodies*. The closer emissivity is to 1, the more efficient the object is as an emitter. Conversely the closer ϵ is to zero, the more efficient the object is as a reflector. For example, a polished silver surface is an extremely poor absorber and radiator because its emissivity is 0.02; lampblack, by contrast, has an emissivity of 0.97 and is an excellent absorbing and emitting substance. Although emissivity is wavelength dependent, most natural objects have fairly high emissivities in the 8- to 14-μm wavelength region (Table 7.1).

Emissivity differences can influence apparent surface temperatures and, therefore, complicate the correlation between ground temperature and the resultant tones on a thermal infrared image. For example, an emissivity change of 1 to 2 percent has the same effect on radiant intensity in the 8- to 14-μm wavelength region as a temperature change of 1 °C (Fagerland et al., 1970).

The amount of energy and the wavelength distribution of energy emitted by a graybody is in accordance with the *modified Stefan-Boltzmann Law* and *Wien's Displacement Law*. Equation 7.3 describes the relationship between kinetic temperature (T) in degrees Kelvin (°K = °C+273) and emissivity (ϵ)

TABLE 7.1. Emissivities of Common Materials in the 8–14 μm Spectral Region[a]

Material	Emissivity (ϵ)
Water, pure	0.99
Ice	0.96
Snow	0.85
Concrete	0.97
Asphalt	0.96
Dolomite	0.96
Basalt	0.93
Granite	0.90
Dunite	0.89
Obsidian	0.86
Gooak fine silt loam, Oregon	0.98
Maury silt loam, Tennessee	0.95
Pullman loam, New Mexico	0.93
Jack pine twigs (green)	0.97
Mountain laurel (green)	0.92
Meadow fescue	0.88

[a]Adapted from Buettner and Kern (1965) and Dunning and Nicodemus (1965).

and its effect on total radiant emittance (W); σ equals the Stefan-Boltzmann constant (5.67×10^{12}) watt cm^{-2} ($^\circ$K)$^{-4}$:

$$W = \epsilon\, \sigma T^4 \qquad \text{\textbf{Equation 7.3}}$$

From Equation 7.3, one can observe that (1) features at the same temperature will have different emitted radiances if their emissivities differ, and (2) at a given emissivity, radiant emittance from an object is directly proportional to the fourth power of its temperature.

Wein's Displacement Law identifies the wavelength at which the maximum amount of energy is radiated (λ_{max}):

$$\lambda_{max} = \frac{W}{T} \qquad \text{\textbf{Equation 7.4}}$$

where: $W = 2{,}897\ \mu$m ($^\circ$K)
   $T = $ Temperature in degrees Kelvin

Note that as temperature increases, the wavelength where maximum energy is released (radiant power peak) shifts to progressively shorter wavelengths. Thus, the optimum thermal infrared spectral region for sensing hot targets, such as forest fires, geothermal activity, and volcanic activity is within the 3- to 5-μm atmospheric "window." The 8- to 14-μm region contains the peak energy emissions for most of the earth's passive features. Their ambient temperatures are in the neighborhood of 300 $^\circ$K, and by the use of Equation 7.4, it is demonstrated that the peak emissions occur in the vicinity of 9.7 μm. For this reason, most thermal infrared sensing is performed within the 8- to 14-μm atmospheric window (Figure 7.1).

Emissivity, a basic physical property dependent in part upon the surface finish of a graybody, can be considered constant for a given object in the 8- to 14-μm wavelength region. However, surface temperature variations of terrestrial targets are caused by many factors, including the following:

External (e.g., man-made) sources of heat
Convection currents in water bodies
Thermal conductivity of the object
Thermal capacity of the object
Size and shape of the object
Moisture content and the evaporation process
Convective cooling or heating by surface winds
Cooling by precipitation or condensation and subsequent evaporation
Topography and the recent history of incident radiation
Sky cover and its effect on radiation exchange
Elevation differences
Metabolism of plants

These factors can produce a complex field situation that is not amenable to quantitative analysis.

ATMOSPHERIC EFFECTS

The transmission characteristics of the intervening atmosphere must be considered for thermal infrared remote sensing, because certain aerosols can absorb and reradiate the energy emitted from a ground scene. The major absorbing aerosols in the lower atmosphere are water vapor and carbon dioxide. For terrestrial applications, thermal infrared scanners use detectors that operate in the two spectral bands corresponding to the transmission "windows" where the atmosphere is quite transparent to thermal infrared radiation under normal conditions (i.e., average amounts of water vapor and carbon dioxide) (Figure 7.1).

Emitted radiation can also be attenuated by suspended particulate matter in the lower atmosphere (e.g., dust, water droplets, ice crystals). For thermal infrared sensors operating from earth-resource satellites, the ozone layer in the upper atmosphere must be taken into account. Detector sensitivities are commonly narrowed with special filters to sense radiation in the spectral band from about 10.5 to 12.5 μm to avoid the attenuating effects of the ozone-absorption band.

ADVANTAGES OF NONPHOTOGRAPHIC IMAGING SYSTEMS

Even though they usually offer poorer resolution and are more complex (and hence more expensive), nonphotographic imaging systems offer several advantages over photographic cameras:

1. They are capable of operating in portions of the electromagnetic spectrum that are beyond the wavelength sensitivities of photographic emulsions.
2. Because the output signal is in electrical form, the data can be transmitted over radio links. This telemetry feature is essential for the use of un-manned spacecraft as data-collection platforms.
3. Certain systems employ some type of in-flight processor, enabling a ground scene to be viewed in image form in near real time.
4. The detection process is renewable because the detectors can be reused. This is in contrast to photographic systems where the film must serve as both the detector and storage medium.
5. Most detector elements have a wider dynamic range than photographic emulsions (i.e., they are better able to sense subtle changes in scene radiance).

Several categories of nonphotographic systems are reviewed in the next section.

▨ VIDICON CAMERA

A vidicon camera (similar to a television camera) covers about the same spectral region as a photographic camera, but it does not contain film. Rather, a latent image is temporarily stored on a photoconductive faceplate and is scanned by an internal electron beam. This process creates a series of electronic signals which, in a satellite environment, are telemetered to earth receiving stations, where they are used to produce visible images on photographic film or a television screen. Vidicon cameras are equipped with shutters to prevent image blur and to control exposure times. In addition, they can be designed to operate at very low light levels.

Vidicon cameras are important sensors in several meteorology satellites, providing timely images for weather forecasts and storm warnings and alerts. They also have been used successfully for imaging the moon and Mars. The Return Beam Vidicon (RBV) camera system on the earth-resources Landsat-3 satellite served as a successful high-resolution mapping device.

▨ ELECTRO-OPTICAL SCANNER

Rather than simultaneously viewing an entire ground scene, as does a photographic camera or vidicon camera, an electro-optical scanner, through its rotating or oscillating mirror, views a series of narrow ground strips at right angles to the line of flight. The forward motion of the aircraft or spacecraft causes new ground strips to be covered by successive scan lines, thus building up a two-dimensional record of reflectance or emittance information.

For a given altitude, the scanner mirror's *angular field of view* (AFOV), or *scan angle*, defines the length of each scan line or ground sweep. The scanner's *instantaneous field of view* (IFOV) determines how much ground area the sensor "sees" at any given instant in time; this ground area is called the *ground resolution cell* or the *ground resolution element* (Figure 7.3). A small IFOV is mandatory if there is an interest in spatial detail. The two major types of electro-optical scanners are the multispectral scanner and the thermal infrared scanner.

▨ MULTISPECTRAL SCANNER

A multispectral scanner is capable of operating simultaneously in the ultraviolet, visible, reflected infrared, and thermal infrared regions of the electromagnetic spectrum (Figure 7.4 and Table 7.2). The number of spectral channels can range from fewer than 10 to more than 20. The ability to operate throughout this broad spectral region presents the possibility of identifying objects or surfaces whose identifiable "signatures" lie beyond the limits of the

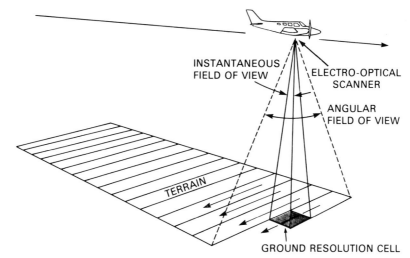

Figure 7.3. Basic operating configuration of an electro-optical scanner.

relatively narrow confines of the visible spectrum. In addition, positive black-and-white transparencies or video images of three discrete spectral bands can be used to produce color-composite images to take advantage of the eye's sensitivity to subtle color variations. Multispectral scanners are used routinely from both aircraft and satellites.

Figure 7.5 shows the essential components of an aircraft-based multi-spectral scanner. Operational features are as follows:

1. A rotating or oscillating mirror scans across the terrain at right angles to the flight path and collects reflected and emitted radiation line by line from the ground scene. (Satellite-mounted scanners usually collect multiple lines of ground data during each sweep of the mirror.)

2. Through a series of secondary mirrors, the radiation beam from each scan line is redirected to spectrum-separation devices (e.g., prisms, dichroic gratings) where the beam is then divided into a number of discrete bands or channels.

3. The scene radiation of each band is directed to and focused on very small detector elements that change the fluctuating radiation into an electrical (analog) signal that varies in intensity according to the strength of the radiation. Each detector is designed to have an optimum response over a specific portion of the electromagnetic spectrum. Detector elements sensitive to thermal infrared wavelengths must be cooled to very low temperatures (-200 °C and below) to suppress the noise of the electronic detector. In aircraft operations, this is accomplished by a liquid coolant such as liquid nitrogen. Satellite-based scanners make use of solid-cryogen, closed-cycle coolers, or passive-radiation-to-space methods.

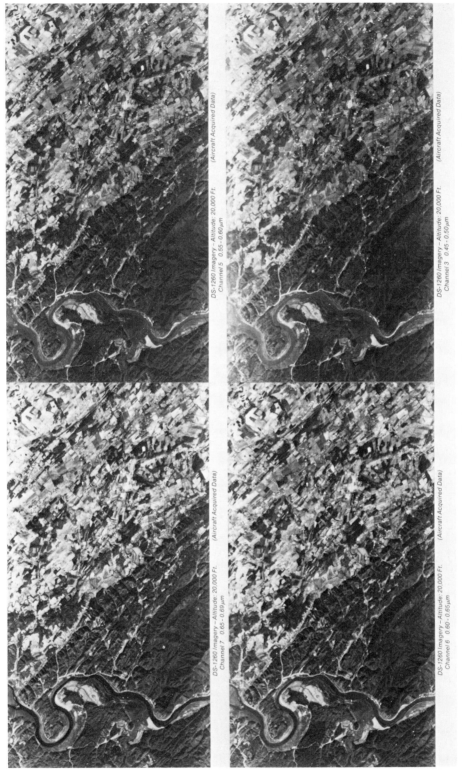

DS-1260 Imagery – Altitude: 20,000 Ft.   (Aircraft Acquired Data)
Channel 7   0.65 - 0.69 μm

DS-1260 Imagery – Altitude: 20,000 Ft.   (Aircraft Acquired Data)
Channel 5   0.55 - 0.60 μm

DS-1260 Imagery – Altitude: 20,000 Ft.   (Aircraft Acquired Data)
Channel 6   0.60 - 0.65 μm

DS-1260 Imagery – Altitude: 20,000 Ft.   (Aircraft Acquired Data)
Channel 3   0.45 - 0.50 μm

Figure 7.4.   Multispectral scanner images of a rural area near Knoxville, Tennessee. Each simultaneously acquired image represents a unique spectral view of the same ground scene. The multispectral data were obtained 10 December 1977 from an altitude of about 6,100 m above ground level. (Courtesy George England, Daedalus Enterprises, Inc.)

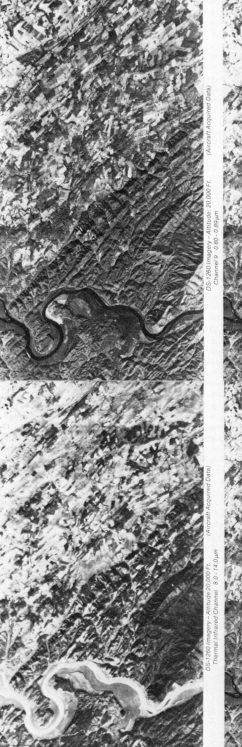

DS-1260 Imagery – Altitude: 20,000 Ft.   (Aircraft Acquired Data)
Thermal Infrared Channel 8.0 - 14.0μm

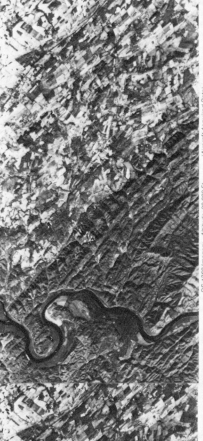

DS-1260 Imagery – Altitude: 20,000 Ft.   (Aircraft Acquired Data)
Channel 9 0.80 - 0.89μm

DS-1260 Imagery – Altitude: 20,000 Ft.   (Aircraft Acquired Data)
Channel 8 0.70 - 0.79μm

DS-1260 Imagery – Altitude: 20,000 Ft.   (Aircraft Acquired Data)
Channel 10 0.92 - 1.10μm

TABLE 7.2. Electro-optical Scanners Manufactured by Daedalus Enterprises, Inc.[a]

System, Primary Applications	Output	No. of Channels	Instantaneous Field of View (Milliradians)	Operating Wavelength (Micrometres)	Standard Data Recording Mode
AADS1220					
Terrain surveillance Forest-fire monitoring Search and rescue Animal census	Analog	2	1.0 or 1.7	3.0 – 5.5 8.5 –12.5	Analog magnetic tape or optional near-real-time hardcopy
AADS1220/MP					
Monitoring ship traffic Detection of open-sea dumping Detection of offshore oil spills Detection of harbor and coastal pollution Search and rescue	Analog	2	2.5 or 5.5	0.32– 0.38 8.50–12.50	Near-real-time hardcopy or optional analog magnetic tape
AADS1230					
Environmental monitoring Detection of energy loss Water quality analysis Volcanology Soil moisture studies Animal census	Analog	2	1.7 or 2.5	4.5 – 5.5 8.5 –12.5	Analog magnetic tape
AADS1260					
Land management Crop classification and inventory Mineral exploration Water-resource management Pollution studies	Digital	11	2.5 or 1.25	0.38– 0.42 0.42– 0.45 0.45– 0.50 0.50– 0.55 0.55– 0.60	High-density digital magnetic tape

AADS1268

Application	Output	Channels	Resolution	Spectral bands (µm)	Recording
Oil and mineral exploration	Digital	11	2.5 or 1.25	0.60– 0.65	High-density digital magnetic tape
Land management				0.65– 0.69	
Forest and crop classification and inventory				0.70– 0.79	
Water-resource management				0.80– 0.89	
Pollution studies				0.92– 1.10	
				8.50–12.50	

AADS1280

Application	Output	Channels	Resolution	Spectral bands (µm)	Recording
Agricultural surveys	Digital	5	0.54	0.42– 0.45	High-density digital magnetic tape
Forest and crop classification and inventory				0.45– 0.52	
				0.52– 0.60	
				0.60– 0.62	
				0.63– 0.69	
				0.69– 0.75	
				0.76– 0.90	
				0.91– 1.05	
				1.55– 1.75	
				2.08– 2.35	
				8.50–13.00	

AADS1285

Application	Output	Channels	Resolution	Spectral bands (µm)	Recording
Geologic mapping for discrimination of:	Digital	6	2.5	8.2 – 8.6	High-density digital magnetic tape
Silicate rocks				8.6 – 9.0	
Carbonate rocks				9.0 – 9.4	
Certain altered rock types				9.4 –10.2	
				10.2 –11.2	
				11.2 –12.2	

ᵃCourtesy George England, Daedalus Enterprises, Inc.

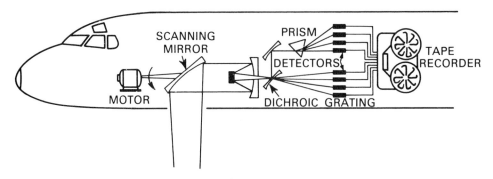

Figure 7.5. Major components of an airborne multispectral scanner. (Adapted from Landgrebe 1974.)

4. The electrical impulses from each detector are amplified and recorded on magnetic tape in analog or digital form for input to ground-based processing equipment. This type of storage provides for maximum versatility in data output because the tape signals can be processed to remove scanner distortions and accentuate information of special interest (see Chapter 15). In addition to a ground-based digital image-processing unit, the Matra Thematic Scanner system incorporates an on-board quick-look visualization unit (digital to video) that enables an analyst to view color images on a TV screen made from a selection of any three out of six channels (four visual and two thermal infrared). This unit enables one to have in-flight control over the recording process and to exploit the images in near real time (Plate 7). For an unmanned satellite system, the sensor signals are transmitted to ground receiver stations for processing.

THERMAL INFRARED SCANNER

A thermal infrared scanner functions in essentially the same manner as a multispectral scanner, but its operational sensitivity is restricted to one or both of the thermal infrared "windows" (*broadband thermal infrared*) or to multiple channels in the 8- to 14-μm wavelength region (*multispectral thermal infrared*) (Table 7.2). Broadband measurements (over wavelength intervals of 2 μm or greater) have a strong dependence on surface temperature in both the 3- to 5-μm and 8- to 14-μm regions.

Multispectral thermal infrared (constituent wavelength intervals of 1 μm or less) has important geologic applications. This is because narrow thermal bands contain important compositional information about silicate rocks, carbonate rocks, and certain altered rocks that cannot be found elsewhere in the electromagnetic spectrum. Diagnostic information in the multispectral data lies in emissivity variations as a function of wavelength (Kahle and Goetz 1983). Because the multispectral thermal infrared scanner was not developed until the early 1980s, it will be some time until narrowband thermal infrared sensing is fully evaluated for earth-science applications.

TYPES OF THERMAL INFRARED SCANNERS

Thermal infrared scanners can be either uncalibrated or calibrated. Gray tones on uncalibrated images show relative radiant temperatures of resolved ground objects rather than quantitative radiant temperatures. Uncalibrated images are well suited to qualitative analyses where the interest is in discriminating among different terrestrial objects. Calibrated images are desirable for certain environmental studies because they make it possible to obtain actual measurements of surface radiant temperatures. An example would be the monitoring of surface temperatures of water discharges from power plants.

Calibrated scanners are equipped with two internal temperature calibration sources (electrical heater elements)—a cold reference and a warm reference. These elements are mounted on either side of the scanner mirror's AFOV (Figure 7.6). For each scan line, the mirror views the first calibration element, scans the terrain, and then views the second calibration source. The resulting electrical signals are amplified by solid-state circuitry and sequentially recorded on magnetic tape. The reference standards provide a scale for determining the radiant temperature of any ground object resolved during the airborne survey; temperature accuracy is on the order of ±0.5 °C. The tape recorder is later played back in the laboratory to produce an image; each gray tone represents the same radiant temperature throughout the image (Sabins 1978).

With the Daedalus DIGICOLOR™ process, the analog tape record can also be "level sliced" into temperature ranges and displayed in a color-coded image (Plate 8). The basic slice divides the analog signal into six linear temperature increments and assigns an output color to each. The sequential thermal relationship from "warm" to "cool" is red, yellow, green, cyan, blue, and magenta; black is the base level. The temperature interval between each color is 1 °C in Plate 8.

ATA-RECORDING OPTIONS

Thermal infrared scanners introduced in the 1960s were usually configured with a film recording system, but more recent systems incorporate both photo emulsion and magnetic tape recording capabilities (Figure 7.6). The latter configuration is preferable because the photographic record provides imagery for immediate use, and the tape record can be later manipulated in a variety of ways to provide higher-quality images (Rinker 1975).

For direct film recording, the amplified detector signal modulates the intensity of a small light source (e.g., a glow tube or single-line cathode ray

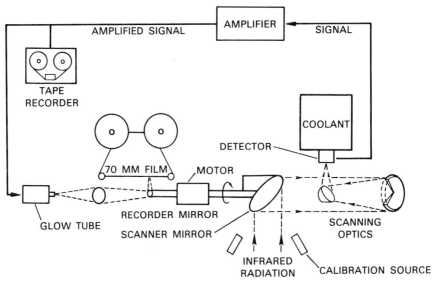

Figure 7.6.   Basic operating configuration of a calibrated thermal infrared scanner, incorporating film and magnetic tape recording components.

tube). The intensity-modulated spot of light is focused on the surface of a photographic film (70-mm roll film is a common form) and swept across the film line by line in synchronism with the speed of the rotating scanner mirror. The film moves across the exposure station at a rate proportional to the velocity and altitude of the aircraft, producing a continuous photographic record (Figure 7.6). Film density represents effective radiant temperature; dark tones depict "cool" temperatures, and light tones indicate "warm" radiant temperatures on a positive image (Figure 7.2).

Certain scanner systems have an in-flight film processor and printer that enable the analyst to see the results almost immediately. During the fighting of forest fires, paper images from such a system can be dropped to fire-fighting crews for immediate assessment.

RESOLUTION OF THERMAL INFRARED IMAGERY

Thermal infrared images have two resolutions—spatial and thermal. *Spatial* or *ground resolution* is determined by flight altitude and the IFOV of the detector element, which typically varies from 1.0 to 5.5 milliradians for thermal scanners (Table 7.2). Ground resolution at the nadir can be calculated from:

$$D = H\beta \qquad\qquad \textbf{Equation 7.5}$$

where: D = One side of the ground resolution cell in metres
H = Aircraft altitude above terrain in metres
β = IFOV in radians (1 milliradian = 10^{-3} radian)

For example, the ground or spatial resolution elements of two scanners having IFOVs of 1.7 and 5.5 milliradians and being operated from 2,000 m above the terrain would be 3.4 and 11.0 m, respectively. Because the sensor integrates its measurements over the full IFOV, objects having different temperatures will not be resolved when they occur within a single cell (Lillesand and Kiefer 1979). Even with a small IFOV, thermal imagery has relatively low spatial resolution as compared with conventional aerial photography.

Temperature or *thermal resolution* is the smallest distinguishable radiant temperature difference between an object and its background. For improved thermal resolution, a large IFOV is advantageous because a greater quantity of thermal infrared energy can be focused onto the detector element, thereby permitting more sensitive temperature measurements to be made (Lillesand and Kiefer 1979). The thermal resolution of declassified, state-of-the-art scanners is on the order of ± 0.1 °C.

From the previous discussion it is observed that an inverse relationship exists between spatial and thermal resolution and IFOV; the larger the IFOV, the greater the thermal sensitivity and the poorer the spatial resolution. Because water bodies usually offer backgrounds with relative uniform emissivity, they lend themselves better to the use of large IFOVs for a greater detection capability for small temperature variations. A small IFOV finds widest application when there is a need for spatial definition (Stingelin 1969).

PROPER TIMES FOR THERMAL INFRARED OVERFLIGHTS

In planning for a thermal infrared overflight, consideration must be given to the time of day for obtaining the optimum results. For example, daytime sensing of surface radiance within the 3- to 5-μm wavelength region contains a component of reflected solar radiation. This mixed response represents a potential source of error in determining the intensity of thermal infrared radiation emitted by ground objects. For example, the 3- to 4-μm region may contain approximately equal amounts of reflected and emitted infrared radiation. To reduce the influence of the reflected component, spectral bandpass filters are commonly employed on daytime missions to change the short wavelength boundary of the 3- to 5-μm window to about 4 μm. The 8- to 14-μm band can be used for surveys during the day without regard to reflected infrared because solar reflection largely ceases at a wavelength of about 4.5 μm.

For many applications, it is preferable to collect thermal imagery at night to minimize differential solar heating and shadowing. The predawn period is preferred if one is interested in recording the true emittance properties of objects—a time when radiant temperatures are the most stable (Figure 7.7). However, the greatest scene contrast during the night will normally occur in the early evening. Cloud shadows and winds are less likely to be a problem for nighttime imaging, but early-morning fog must be considered for predawn missions.

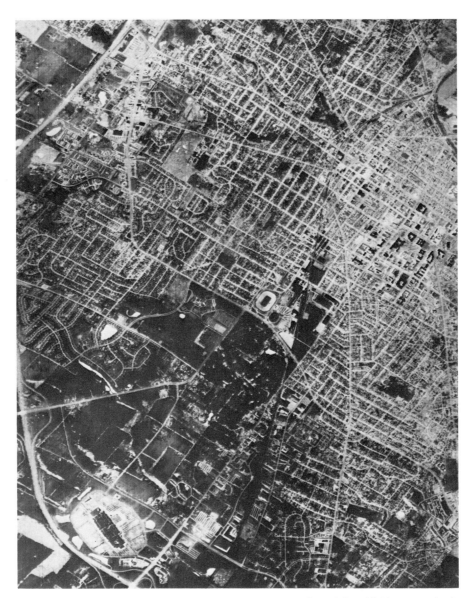

Figure 7.7. Predawn thermal infrared image (8.5 to 12.5 μm) of Ann Arbor, Michigan, acquired on 9 May 1979. Air temperature at ground level was 19 °C, and the sky was clear. Aircraft altitude was 2,700 m above ground level. (Courtesy George England, Daedalus Enterprises, Inc.)

Daytime applications include topographic and linear-feature detections (e.g., fault and fracture traces) and the monitoring of moisture stress in vegetation (when transpiration is in progress). Overflights are usually in the afternoon when radiant temperatures are highest, a condition yielding maximum image contrast. The optimum time of day is waived when there is need to monitor dynamic phenomena or processes (e.g., volcanic eruptions, forest fires, tidal currents, and discharges of thermal effluents).

Because of differential heating and cooling effects, there are two periods in the diurnal cycle when an object's heat emission coincides with the background. If a thermal infrared image is generated during these periods, the object and the background would be rendered in the same tone on the recorded film, thus obscuring the object. These two periods of thermal *crossover* occur shortly after dawn and shortly before sunset (Figure 7.8). If at all possible, thermal infrared missions are scheduled for times other than the crossover periods.

METEOROLOGICAL CONDITIONS

The following meteorological conditions can have pronounced effects on the quality of thermal infrared imagery (U.S. Department of the Army 1966, Stingelin 1969).

1. In addition to its buffeting of aircraft, wind tends to smear or streak

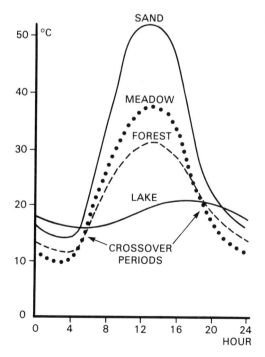

Figure 7.8. Diurnal variation in temperature of four kinds of surface cover. (Adapted from Fagerlund et al. 1970.)

thermal imagery; the degree of smearing increases with increasing wind velocity. For this reason, airborne surveys should never be carried out under strong wind.

2. After rain or snow, general terrain lacks sufficient thermal contrast to yield meaningful data. Only hot targets, such as fires or heated man-made objects, will generally stand out under such conditions.

3. Fog and clouds below an aircraft drastically attenuate the thermal infrared energy available for detection, making it nearly impossible to obtain usable data. Haze and smoke, however, do not constitute a serious problem.

4. The shadowed areas from high-altitude clouds are cool compared to the background. Because less solar energy is available, materials that normally heat and cool at different rates may have had time to approach temperature equilibrium. Cloud density and the type of material in the shadowed area influence the quality of data received from that area.

5. In areas exhibiting topographic variability, the sinking and collection of cold air in the low-lying areas can account for a lack of thermal detail. This can be an especially serious problem for predawn data imaging.

All else remaining equal, the best thermal infrared imagery is acquired under clear skies with no wind.

INTERPRETATION OF THERMAL INFRARED IMAGES

It must be remembered that the information recorded on infrared images is based on thermal radiation characteristics of surfaces rather than on light-reflective (photographic) responses. The amount of thermal infrared radiation emitted is proportional to the fourth power of an object's temperature and directly proportional to its emissivity (Equation 7.3). Unless these factors are understood, the unique advantages of thermal infrared reconnaissance cannot be gained, and interpreters might decide that a thermal infrared image is nothing but an aerial photograph with degraded resolution.

The following descriptions of terrain features detectable on thermal infrared images are summarized from Sabins (1978), U.S. Department of the Army (1966), and the U.S. Departments of the Army, Navy, and Air Force (1967). Many of the tonal descriptions are depicted in image form in Figures 7.2, 7.7, and 7.9.

Water Versus Soil and Rock

Bodies of open water are generally cooler (darker tones) than soil and rock during the day, but at night their surface temperatures are reversed, with water being the warmest (lighter tones). This is primarily because convection does not operate to transfer heat energy in soil and rock. Consequently, heat is concentrated near their surfaces during the day, causing a higher

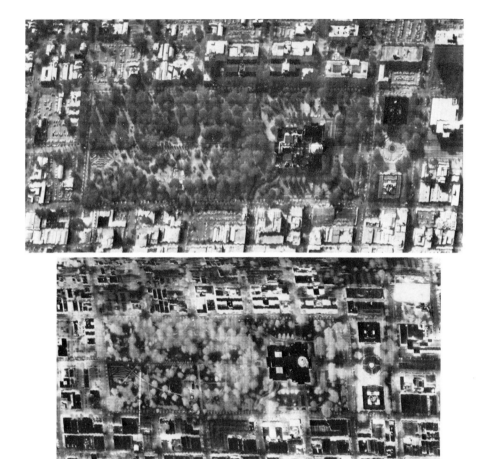

Figure 7.9.   Diurnal thermal infrared images (8 to 14 μm) of Capitol Mall, Sacramento, California. Image acquisition times were 11:25 A.M. (top) and 12:20 A.M. (bottom). These correlative images illustrate the diurnal thermal reversals that occur for several types of targets. For example, a small circular water fountain (right center) imaged black (cold) during the day but white (warm) in darkness. The same shift also occurred for various types of trees and ornamental shrubs, but the degree of tonal reversal was somewhat less intense (dark gray to light gray). An opposite tonal reversal (white to black) occurred for grass areas and most of the rooftops. Note that building and tree shadows are present only in the day image. (Courtesy George England, Daedalus Enterprises, Inc.)

temperature. During the night cooling period, heat is radiated to the atmosphere and is not replenished by convection currents in these solids, causing surface temperatures to be lower than those for water bodies.

If the time of data collection is not known, the thermal signatures of any water bodies are a reliable index: the image was generated at night if water bodies have lighter image tones than adjacent terrain; if water bodies are depicted in darker tones than the adjacent terrain, the image was made during the day.

Vegetation

Green deciduous trees normally appear cooler (darker tones) than their surroundings during daylight hours and warmer (lighter tones) at night. Transpiration is at its maximum during the day, and this process lowers the leaf temperature, causing the foliage to have a cool signature. This type of vegetation appears warm on nighttime images because of the high water content of the leaves and by convective warming by the air in conjunction with night inversions of air temperature (i.e., air temperature at crown height is warmer than at ground level). Because evergreen trees experience less diurnal temperature variation than deciduous trees do, gray-level variations are usually less extreme.

Grass and other low-lying vegetation are warmest during the day but rapidly approach local air temperature after sunset. On a calm night, the air next to the ground is apt to be cooler than a few metres aloft, and consequently, low-lying vegetation will image in darker tones than deciduous or needle-leaf trees. Less vigorous or dead foliage maintains a higher temperature (lighter tones) than healthy vegetation because of a lack of transpiration.

Damp Ground

All else remaining equal, damp ground is cooler (darker tones) than dry ground, during both day and night because of the cooling effect caused by the evaporation of absorbed water.

Pavement

Materials such as concrete, asphalt, and packed dirt appear relatively warm (light tones) both day and night. They have considerable surface-to-volume ratios and continually absorb large amounts of solar radiation during the day. Because of their relatively high thermal capacities, these materials radiate strongly for many hours after sunset. Packed earth appears in the darkest tones of the three materials on nighttime imagery because it loses its heat at the highest rate.

Metal Surfaces

Bare metal surfaces appear in dark tones on both day and night images because of their cold radiant temperatures. Their shiny surfaces have much lower emissivities than other substances normally found in aerial reconnaissance and, consequently, they emit much less thermal radiation.

High-temperature Sources

Thermal infrared radiation from targets such as forest fires is relatively unaffected by time of day. The emitted radiation from these targets remains fairly constant, appearing hot (light tones) at all times.

Ghosts

The ghost impressions of certain objects may appear, particularly on nighttime thermal infrared images, when the object that produced a temperature differential has been removed. For example, airplanes or automobiles that have been parked on asphalt for several hours before sunset (shading the asphalt) and then are removed leave ghost impressions that are detectable for many hours.

◼ SOME USES OF THERMAL INFRARED IMAGES

In agriculture, thermal infrared images have been used in identification of crop species and soil types, in detection of crop diseases, in animal censuses, and in determination of the relative moisture content of various soils. Experiments have indicated that some plant foliage, especially the leaves of many trees, appears to be similar to blackbody emitters in the wavelength region of 3.7 to 5.5 μm. As a result, leaf temperatures may be remotely measured, or their relative temperatures inferred. Such knowledge can be useful for determining various aspects of plant health, age, and relative water supply or degree of irrigation. In addition, sensor systems that image large areas offer the hope of early detection of thermal damage or frost damage to fruit groves.

In the field of geology, thermal infrared imagery has been used for (1) mapping joints and faults that have a high moisture content, (2) discrimination and delineation of rock types (bare rock must be exposed), (3) surveillance of active volcanoes, (4) mapping the surface expressions of geothermal activity, (5) detection of caves in karst terrain, and (6) mapping underground coal-mine fires. Multispectral sensing in the 8- to 14-μm region offers potential for detecting emissivity variations that relate to important compositional information about certain rocks.

Infrared images can be used to extract a considerable amount of information from surface water bodies. Hot effluents that result in water pollution when discharged into streams or lakes are easily detected because they usually have higher temperatures than the receiving water (Plate 8). Thermal infrared images have also been used to detect circulation patterns and zones of mixing in water bodies. Under certain conditions it is possible to locate areas where there is groundwater discharge into an ocean or estuary. Critically needed freshwater sources have been discovered along the coast of Hawaii by detailed analysis of thermal infrared imagery.

Infrared imagery from the 3- to 5-μm wavelength region is ideally suited to the detection and mapping of forest fires because of high surface temperatures. The perimeter and relative intensity of fires, along with the location of separated spot fires, are discernible in daylight or darkness when normal vision from the air is obscured by smoke.

▨ FOREST FIRE DETECTION SYSTEM

The function of a forest fire detection system is to locate fires before they become large enough to cause significant damage. The general performance requirements for an airborne thermal infrared fire surveillance system have been outlined by Madden (1973). Such a system must:

1. Detect a small, latent-stage forest fire in the presence of background temperature extremes.
2. Present information in such a way that a photo interpreter can accurately locate the fire.
3. Patrol large areas.
4. Locate small spot fires adjacent to a large fire.
5. Image large fires in such a way that fire perimeters, including smoldering edges and flaming fronts, can be accurately established.
6. Locate small, hot fires within a large, burned area during mop-up operations.
7. Make near–real-time, high-quality imagery of the area traversed for navigation, for in-flight interpretation of fire location, and for interpretation at the fire camp of a large fire's progress.

The foregoing criteria indicate a need for fire detection equipment that quickly detects and locates small, latent-stage fires while surveying large forested areas. One such system has been operated on a routine basis since 1971 by the U.S. Forest Service (Figure 7.10). The *bispectral forest fire detection system* uses two detectors sensitive to the 3- to 4-μm and 8.5- to 11-μm wavelength regions. The real-time correlation by algebraic subtraction of the two bands renders a 10:1 improvement in the target-to-background signal over 3- to 4-μm monospectral equipment. The system is capable of detecting 0.09 m^2, 600 °C targets against backgrounds ranging from 0 to 50 °C at altitudes from 5,000 m above the terrain. A unique feature of the equipment is the target-discriminator module (TDM), which prints event markers on the side of the image to indicate hot targets too small to print on the actual image itself. A Doppler radar and navigation computer are used to permit the accurate flying of predetermined tracks (Hirsch et al. 1971, Heller and Ulliman 1983). An image produced by this system is shown in Figure 7.11.

▨ SCANNER IMAGE DISTORTIONS

Scanner images often bear strong resemblances to conventional aerial photographs, but unless corrected they have an inherent geometric distortion due to the nature of line scanning. Because the scanner mirror sweeps an angle on either side of vertical, the ground resolution cell is larger at the ends of a scan line than along the nadir line. The scanner mirror rotates at a constant angular rate, but the image data are recorded at a constant linear rate. This dictates that each ground resolution cell is recorded as an equal area (i.e., as

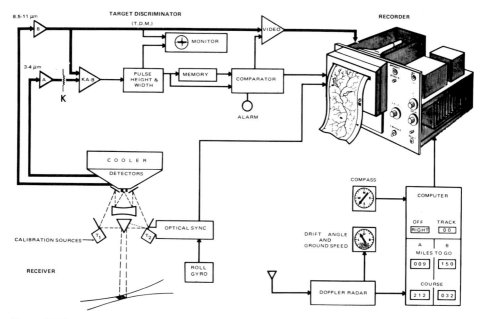

Figure 7.10. Diagrammetic representation of the bispectral forest fire detection system. (Courtesy Northern Forest Fire Laboratory, U.S. Forest Service.)

the look angle increases, larger and larger ground areas are compressed into equal image areas). This effect is called *scale compression*, and it gives ground features the appearance of being wrapped around a cylinder.

A *panoramic image* incorporates scale compression (Figure 7.9). This type of distortion can be associated with direct film recording, but its effects can be removed by a special correction program when data on magnetic tape are recorded onto film. A *rectilinear image* is produced by this process (Figure 7.4).

Scale varies with distance from the nadir line on a panoramic image. Therefore, precise measurements are not possible, making the imagery more suitable for identification than for purely mensurational purposes. The effective focal length of the scanner can be combined with flight altitude to yield approximate image scale along the nadir line only. For rectilinear images, the effective focal length can be combined with flight altitude to yield approximate scale in both the along- and across-track dimensions. Formulas for determining the scale of a conventional photograph may be used to determine the scale of scanner images if the effective focal length is substituted for the focal length of the camera lens.

Distortions from aircraft motion are roll, pitch, yaw, and drift. Some scanner systems have gyro stabilization to eliminate the effects of aircraft roll on the imagery. The effect of uncompensated aircraft roll on the imagery is a displacement of objects to the right or left of the center line. Pitch and yaw

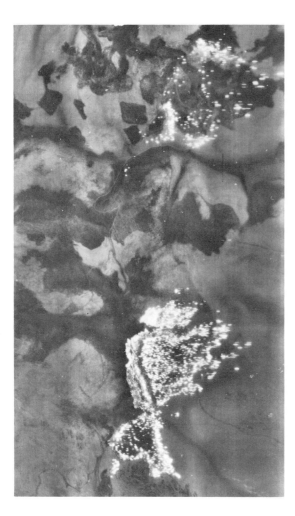

Figure 7.11. Night thermal infrared image of a wildfire produced by the bispectral forest fire detection system. See Figure 7-10. (Courtesy Northern Forest Fire Laboratory, U.S. Forest Service.)

compress or elongate images. This compression and elongation may vary laterally across the film so that wedging takes place, as in the case of yaw. These distortions are not as noticeable or as frequently encountered as those caused by roll, however.

If a crosswind is blowing at the time the imagery is made, the aircraft heading and aircraft track may not coincide. Because of this, all points except those at the nadir are skewed in the direction of the aircraft crab. Any turns of the aircraft during the imagery run will cause straight roads parallel to the flight track to appear curved, and straight roads that cross the flight path at oblique angles may appear to be S shaped.

PUSHBROOM SCANNER

The pushbroom scanner is a new-generation sensing system that forms images without moving optics (e.g., scanning mirror) and offers high spatial and spectral resolution. A pushbroom scanner employs numerous and very small (13 by 13 μm) solid-state detectors (charge coupled devices, or CCDs). The detector elements are closely packed in a one-dimensional linear array orthogonal to the flight path. There is typically one detector array for each spectral band, and a single array may contain more than 1,000 individual detector elements. Each array is located in the focal plane of the instrument's imaging lens so that the entire line of a ground scene in the across-track direction is focused on the array at one time (Figure 7.12).

Pushbroom scanning describes the technique of using the forward motion of a platform to "sweep" a linear array of detectors across a ground scene being imaged. Electronic sampling of the detectors in the across-track dimension provides the orthogonal "scan" component to form an image, and the platform motion along its flight or orbital path produces successive lines of the image— the along-track dimension. The detector array is electronically sampled at the appropriate rate to ensure that contiguous image lines are produced (Thompson 1979).

ADVANTAGES OF A PUSHBROOM SENSOR

Some of the advantages that a pushbroom sensor offers over an optical-mechanical scanner are as follows:

1. Improved radiometric sensitivity due to the longer detector dwell time on each ground resolution cell; this leads to a high signal/noise ratio (i.e., effectively less noise).

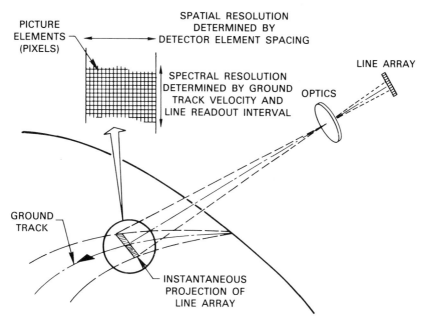

Figure 7.12. Schematic showing the general characteristics of a pushbroom imaging sensor (Short 1982).

2. Greater reliability and longer operating life due to the elimination of complex mechanical components.

3. High geometric accuracy in the across-track direction because of the fixed geometry of the detector arrays; this simplifies image reconstruction and processing tasks.

4. Lighter weight and lower power requirements; this makes it especially well suited for small satellites and airplanes.

A current disadvantage of pushbroom technology is that available CCD detectors cannot operate at wavelengths longer than about 1.1 μm.

CURRENT AND FUTURE PUSHBROOM SYSTEMS

Currently, the only operational airborne pushbroom scanner in existence is the Multispectral Electro-optical Imaging Scanner (MEIS), developed by MacDonald Dettwiler and Associates for the Canada Centre for Remote Sensing. MEIS is designed with eight independent optical channels and uses CCD linear arrays each with 1,728 elements. Five of the channels cover the 0.39- and 1.1-μm spectrum range with provision for the three additional channels to extend the wavelength range when suitable CCDs become available. The sensor has a real-time processing capability to provide geometric and radiometric corrections and interchannel registration (McColl et al. 1983). A multispectral image produced by the MEIS system is shown in Plate 7.

Pushbroom sensor technology was first space tested on the NASA Space Shuttle flight STS-7 in 1983. The sensor, the Modular Optoelectronic Multispectral Scanner (MOMS), was developed by the Space Division of MBB (Germany) for the German Ministry for Research and Technology (BMFT). The flight constituted a preoperational experiment to test the sensor in space. The sensor produced high-resolution (20 m) monochromatic images of selected ground areas.

A pushbroom sensor will be tested in space by the French Système Probatoire d'Observation de la Terre (SPOT-1) satellite, which was scheduled for launch in 1985. SPOT-1 will carry two high-resolution visible (HRV) pushbroom sensors, each having multispectral and panchromatic capabilities. In the multispectral mode, the spectral sensitivities are: 0.50 to 0.59 μm (green); 0.61 to 0.68 μm (red); and 0.79 to 0.89 μm (near-infrared). Image resolution will be 20 m. In the panchromatic mode, the spectral sensitivity is 0.51 to 0.7 μm, and image resolution will be 10 m. Details of the SPOT satellite mission are given by Chevrel et al. (1981) and Begni (1982).

RADAR PRINCIPLES

The term *radar* is an acronym of the phrase *radio detection and ranging*. Radar is a remote-sensing device that is active (i.e., it provides its own illumination energy). It transmits pulses of microwave energy and then receives reflections of the signal from a target. The reflected component is called the *echo* or *backscatter*. By providing its own illumination, radar operates entirely independent of sunlight, and equally effective missions can be conducted by day or night. In addition, the angle and direction of microwave illumination for imaging radars can be controlled to enhance features of special interest.

Radar systems operate in the microwave portion of the electromagnetic spectrum, where wavelengths range from a few millimetres to more than a metre. Radars are *monochromatic-type sensors* because they use microwave energy of single wavelengths as does a laser. Table 7.3 lists wavelength subdivisions of the microwave spectrum, letter codes, and the single wavelengths that have been used for imaging radars; the random letter designations are a carryover from the military when radar development was classified. Long-wavelength radars (e.g., L-band) are unhindered by clouds or precipitation and offer potential for penetrating unconsolidated surface materials, such as dry sand.

DEVELOPMENT OF SIDE-LOOKING IMAGING RADARS

Most people are familiar with *plan position indicator* (PPI), or the type of radar used for weather forecasting, navigation, and air traffic control. PPI, developed during World War II, was used extensively for detecting and tracking airplanes and ships and for navigating in darkness (e.g., night bombing missions). However, it was discovered that certain low-resolution type surfaces (e.g., land-water, urban-rural) could be differentiated on the sweeping circular display when the microwave beam from the rotating antenna of an airborne PPI was directed toward the terrain.

TABLE 7.3. Bands Composing the Microwave Spectrum

Letter Code		Wavelength Range (cm)	Common Wavelengths for Imaging Radars (cm)
P		133.0–77.0	
L		77.0–19.0	25.0 and 23.5
S		19.0– 7.7	
C		7.7– 4.8	6.0
X		4.8– 2.7	3.2 and 3.0
K		2.7– 0.8	
	Ku	2.4– 1.7	
	K	1.7– 1.1	
	Ka	1.1– 0.8	0.86[a]
Q		0.8– 0.6	
V		0.6– 0.5	

[a]Operations ceased in 1973.

Based in large measure on this finding, *side-looking airborne radar* (SLAR), or simply *side-looking radar* (SLR), was developed after the war specifically as a high-resolution, wide-swath imaging system. The side-look concept was adopted by the military so that extensive areas behind enemy lines could be safely imaged from an aircraft, a special capability known as "long-range standoff." The military began using SLARs in the 1950s, and certain systems and associated images were declassified for civilian uses beginning in the mid-1960s.

There are two types of SLAR: *real-aperture* (antenna) radar (RAR), also known as brute-force radar, and *synthetic-aperture*, or coherent, radar (SAR). The primary difference between the two systems is in their resolving power. SAR, the newest system, was specifically developed to achieve high, constant resolution from great distances, including orbital altitudes. To date, SARs have successfully operated from two NASA spacecraft—Seasat and the Space Shuttle.

DEFINITION OF TERMS FOR SLAR

Before proceeding to the operation of an imaging radar system, it is appropriate to first discuss the terminology and characteristics of SLAR operations. As shown in Figure 7.13, an airplane or spacecraft moves at some velocity and at some altitude in an *azimuth* or *along-track direction*. Through a fixed antenna, pulses of microwave energy are propagated outward in a perpendicular plane at the speed of light in the *range, look*, or *across-track direction. Slant range* is the line-of-sight distance measured from the antenna to the terrain target, while *ground range* is the horizontal distance measured along the surface from the *ground track* or *nadir line* to the target. The area closest to ground track where a radar pulse intercepts the terrain is the *near range*, and the area of pulse termination farthest from ground track is the *far range*.

The angle measured between a horizontal plane relative to the earth's surface and the radar beam defines the *depression angle* (i.e., the angle of illumination). Far range and near range represent the minimum and maximum depression angles, respectively, over the entire *image swath*. The angle measured from a vertical plane to the radar beam is the *look angle* off ground track. The depression angle and look angle are complementary angles.

The *incidence angle* is the angle measured between the beam and the normal to the local surface. Unlike the look angle and depression angle, which are fixed, the incidence angle varies in accordance with the slope of the terrain. The look angle and incidence angle are equal only in the special case where the terrain is level (Ford 1980).

REAL-APERTURE RADAR

In the simplest terms, a RAR system consists of: (1) a transmitter, (2) a receiver, (3) a TR (transmit-receive) switch or duplexer, (4) an antenna that serves in both transmission and reception, (5) a cathode-ray tube (CRT)

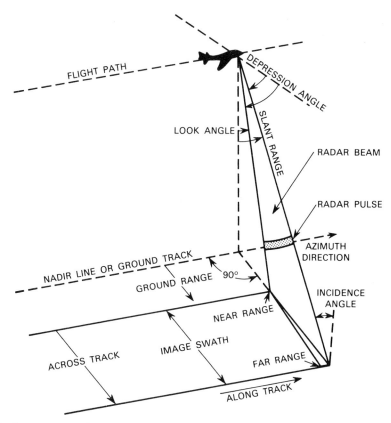

Figure 7.13. Geometry characteristics of side-looking airborne radar. Shown is the common single-look SLAR configuration. A few systems are dual-look, wherein two antennas simultaneously image to the left and right of the nadir line.

display, and (6) a photographic recording device (Figure 7.14). During operation, the following processes take place:

1. The transmitter generates a short burst or pulse of polarized microwave energy at a discrete wavelength, which is propagated in a vertical fan-shaped beam by the directional antenna; propagation is perpendicular to the ground track. (The polarization parameter is discussed in a later section.)

2. As the pulse strikes a narrow strip of the terrain, a portion of it is reflected back to the aircraft, where it is intercepted by the same antenna and sent to a sensitive radio receiver. The receiver converts the detected pulse into an amplified video (electrical) signal.

3. Because the same antenna is used for both transmitting and receiving, the TR switch disconnects the transmitter following pulse propagation and connects the receiver to the antenna for reception of the return echo. This alternating process is continuously repeated (on the order of 1,000 to 2,000 times per second) as the aircraft advances along the flight path. With this forward motion, the radar beams are moved to new positions, enabling

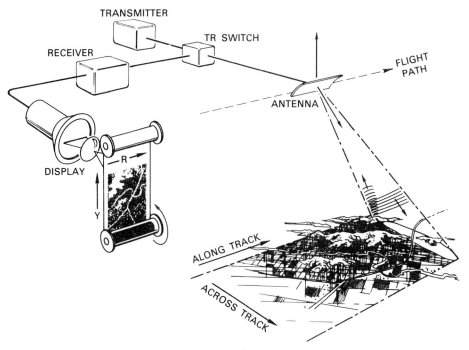

Figure 7.14.   Representation of a real-aperture radar (RAR) system. (Courtesy Goodyear Aerospace Corp.)

succeeding pulses to intercept adjacent strips of terrain ("scanning" function).

4. The receiver produces a fluctuating video signal for each returned pulse. Its amplitude is directly proportional to the intensity of the backscatter received at any instant.

5. The fluctuating signal proportionally modulates the intensity of a moving spot of light (a small electron beam) on a CRT display. The fluctuating light is focused on the surface of a photographic film and swept across the film; a single line is traced for each returned pulse. Ultimately, the individual pulse echoes are recorded side by side as the film is advanced, forming a two-dimensional radar image. The film advances at a rate proportional to the aircraft ground speed. When processed, the film exhibits tonal densities that are a measure of the backscatter intensity returned from the target scene; in positive form, strong returns equate to light tones while weak returns are portrayed in dark tones (Figure 7.15). Radar return energy varies in response to a complex combination of ground and radar system properties (discussed in a later section).

6. Based upon the sweep velocity or acceleration of the CRT's electron beam, the image display can be either slant range or ground range for the across-track ordinate. If the sweep rate is linear, the horizontal separation

of targets in near range will be compressed, resulting in a *slant-range image* (Figure 7.15). However, by applying a hyperbolic (nonlinear) waveform to the CRT's circuitry, the sweep rate can be reduced in near range relative to far range. As a result, a *ground-range image* portrays targets from level terrain in their relative ground positions.

RADAR RESOLUTION VERSUS RADAR DETECTION

Radar resolution is defined as the minimum ground separation between two targets of equal reflectivity that will enable them to appear individually in a processed radar image. Radar detection is a measure of the smallest object that can be discerned on an image as a result of its ability to reflect microwave energy. Consequently, it is often possible to detect targets much smaller than the resolution distance (e.g., vehicles and power lines) because of their high reflectivities. SLAR has two different resolutions that are independently determined by the radar system: range resolution (perpendicular to ground track) and azimuth resolution (parallel to ground track).

RANGE RESOLUTION

Range, or across-track, resolution is determined by the length of the radar pulse. For a radar system to discern two targets that have equal reflectivity and are close together, all parts of their reflected signals must be received at the antenna at different times or they will appear as one large object on an image.

In Figure 7.16 it is seen that objects separated by a slant-range distance equal to or less than $\tau/2$, where τ is the slant-range pulse length, will produce reflections that arrive at the antenna as one continuous pulse, dictating that they be imaged as one large object (targets A, B, C). If the slant-range separation is greater than $\tau/2$, the pulses from targets C and D will not overlap, and their signals will be recorded separately. Thus, *slant-range resolution* (R_{sr}), measured in the across-track dimension, is equal to one-half the transmitted pulse length (Barr 1968). Pulse length is measured in microseconds (10^6 sec) and is converted from time to distance by multiplying by the speed of light (3×10^8 m/sec); pulse distance is measured in slant range.

To convert R_{sr} to *ground-range resolution* (R_{gr}), the solution is:

$$R_{gr} = \frac{\tau}{2\cos\beta} \qquad\qquad \textbf{Equation 7.6}$$

where: τ = Pulse length as distance
β = Antenna depression angle

It is noted from the foregoing equation that (1) ground-range resolution improves as the distance from the ground track increases (i.e., across-track

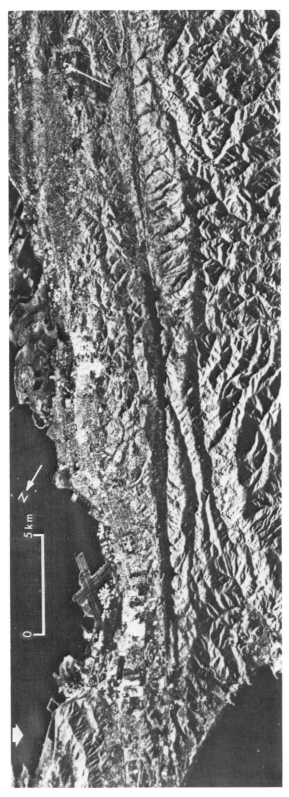

Figure 7.15. Westinghouse Corp. Ka-band (0.86-cm wavelength) RAR image of the San Francisco Peninsula. The San Andreas fault system is clearly depicted along the length of the image at midrange. San Francisco International Airport is on the left, and the Stanford Linear Accelerator building is on the right just above (east of) the San Andreas fault. Look direction is indicated by the arrow. Image compression in near range is due to slant-range presentation. (Courtesy U.S. Geological Survey.)

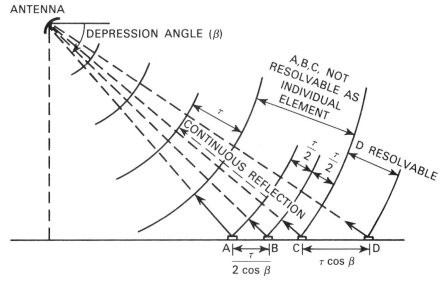

Figure 7.16. Range or across-track resolution for a side-looking airborne radar system (Barr 1968).

resolution is better in far range than in near range because β is smaller) and (2) resolution can be improved by shortening the pulse length. However, a point will be reached when a drastically shortened pulse will not contain sufficient energy for its echoes to be detected by the receiver. A method of overcoming this limitation is to employ a long, frequency-modulated pulse and a receiver designed to act on the modulation to effect a shortening of the pulse through electronic compression. It is the short "effective" length that then determines range resolution. High-resolution systems using this technique are known as *chirp radars* (Raytheon Company 1969).

AZIMUTH RESOLUTION

Azimuth or along-track resolution is determined by the width of the terrain strip illuminated by a radar pulse, which is a function of beamwidth. In Figure 7.17 it is shown that the beamwidth increases with range. Thus, two objects at C and D (at the same range) are in the beam simultaneously, and their echoes will be received at the same time. Consequently, they will appear as one extended object on an image. Two objects at A and B are separated by a distance greater than the beamwidth; their returns will be received and recorded separately. Thus, to separate two targets in the along-track direction, it is necessary that their separation on the ground be greater than the width of the radar beam.

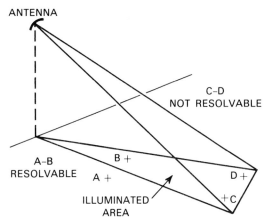

Figure 7.17. Azimuth or along-track resolution for a side-looking airborne radar system (Barr 1968).

The equation for determining azimuth resolution (R_a) is:

$$R_a = \frac{0.7 \lambda \, Rs}{Da}$$

Equation 7.7

where: λ = Operating wavelength
Rs = Slant range to the target
Da = Length of antenna

The relationships expressed in Equation 7.7 show that (1) azimuth resolution decreases in proportion to increasing range (i.e., resolution is best in near range, where the width of the beam is narrowest) and (2) a long antenna or a short operating wavelength will improve azimuth resolution. Both of the latter two parameters enable the radar beam to be focused into a narrower angle; beam spreading is inversely proportional to antenna length and directly proportional to wavelength.

There are several ways to obtain improved azimuth resolution with conventional RARs: a long antenna, a short operating wavelength, or a close-in range interval. However, the practical limit of antenna length for aircraft stability is about 5 m, and the all-weather capability of radar is effectively reduced when the wavelength is decreased below about 3 cm. Because of these limitations, RARs are best suited for low-level, short-range operations (LaPrade 1976).

SYNTHETIC-APERTURE RADAR

SARs have been developed in recent years to overcome the restrictions imposed by brute-force systems. SARs use sophisticated signal storage and processing techniques to produce an effective narrow beamwidth without the use of a long physical antenna or a short operating wavelength.

SAR employs a relatively short, real antenna that transmits a relatively wide beam of microwave energy (Figure 7.18). The effect of an extremely long antenna is synthesized by using the forward motion of the platform to carry the real antenna to successive positions along the flight path. These successive positions are treated electronically as though each was an individual element of the same antenna. The synthetic antenna's length is directly proportional to range—as range increases, antenna length increases. This produces a synthetic beam with constant width in the azimuth direction, regardless of range (Figure 7.18). Consequently, azimuth resolution remains constant throughout the range interval.

The theoretical limit of azimuth resolution for SAR is equal to one-half the real antenna length (L/2). However, azimuth resolution is usually made equal to the range resolution element by special "focusing" techniques.

Synthetic antennas reach staggering sizes because length is determined by the time the sensor is receiving echoes from a terrain feature. For example, a 1- or 2-m-long aircraft-mounted antenna can produce a synthetic antenna 600-m long, and an 11-m real antenna can be synthesized to an effective length of about 15 km from an orbital platform.

In operation, the short SAR antenna transmits phase-coherent pulses at regular intervals along the flight line. The echoes from each terrain feature are recorded as *phase histories* on photographic film (called the data or signal film) for optical processing or on high-density digital tape (HDDT) for digital processing. A phase history contains a record of Doppler frequency changes and amplitude modulations of a target as it passed through the beam of the moving antenna.

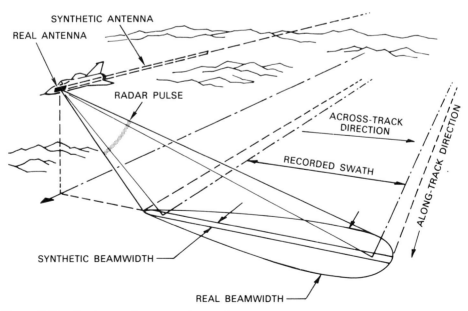

Figure 7.18. Fundamental concept of a synthetic-aperture radar system. (Courtesy Goodyear Aerospace Corp.)

SAR OPTICAL CORRELATION

To produce interpretable information, the phase histories on the data film must be processed by an optical correlator. By using a coherent light source (laser), the data film is illuminated and, with the aid of a range-imaging optical system, the target phase histories are focused onto a second piece of film, where location, size, and intensity characteristics are preserved with high fidelity. This becomes the original negative-image film. The laser light is analogous to the radar energy, and the data film is analogous to the synthetic antenna. The optical correlation process is illustrated in Figure 7.19.

As a method for recording more distinct radar signal levels, the Goodyear Aerospace Corporation has employed color film as an option to present the final image (Peterson 1976). In this method a monochromatic laser beam (one wavelength within either the red, green, or blue spectrum) is transmitted through the data film onto a color image film. In practice, only two of the three emulsion layers are used in a single correlation. Because of the slight overlap in the film's spectral sensitivities, saturation of one of the dye layers will be followed on increasing exposure by activation of the second layer.

If the film is exposed at a laser wavelength of 0.59 μm, a low-level exposure produces shades of red because of the excitation of the cyan dye layer, while added exposure causes the magenta dye layer to be exposed, adding green. The addition of green to red results in a color shift to yellow. This emulsion combination produces a red-yellow radar image (Plate 8).

SAR DIGITAL CORRELATION

For digital correlation, the transformation from raw to interpretable data is performed mathematically by using special-purpose high-speed computers. Unlike optical correlation, digital correlation produces no intermediate signal film. The signal data, stored on HDDTs, are processed with appropriate

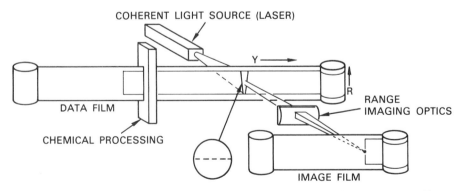

Figure 7.19. Optical correlator system for synthetic-aperture radar data processing. (Courtesy Goodyear Aerospace Corp.)

software and placed on computer-compatible tapes (CCTs). The CCT data incorporate radiometric and geometric corrections. Photographic images are then made from the CCTs with film-writing equipment (see Chapter 15). Digital correlation is time consuming and expensive, but the output is amenable to quantitative analysis, and unwanted artifacts contributed by the hardware and film processing of optical correlation are eliminated.

▓ SAR RESOLUTION

SAR systems are capable of producing high-resolution and constant-resolution images, making them ideally suited for high-level, long-range applications. Civilian SARs are capable of producing images of 3-m resolution (range and azimuth) from aircraft altitudes (Figure 7.20) and images of 25-m resolution from earth-orbiting satellites (Figure 7.21).

▓ PROCESSING IN NEAR REAL TIME

Certain radar systems (e.g., the MacDonald Dettwiler and Associates' Integrated Radar Imaging System, or IRIS) can (1) produce in-flight images (paper or film transparencies), (2) transmit images to ground stations for analysis in near real time, and (3) store the raw signal data on HDDTs for high-precision ground processing after the mission (Figure 7.22). In-flight images are especially useful for environmental surveillance (e.g., oil-spill monitoring, flood monitoring, and sea-ice reconnaissance) and for correcting or adjusting system variables during the mission (e.g., aircraft drift, aircraft ground speed, and depression angle).

A data link system for the near-real-time display of radar images will be an important component of Radarsat, an imaging microwave satellite planned for launch by Canada in 1990. It will carry a C-band (6-cm wavelength) SAR with 25- to 30-m resolution. For prime users, scaled and annotated images will be processed within 4 hr of overflight.

▓ POLARIZATION OF MICROWAVE ENERGY

Modern radar imaging systems transmit microwave energy (electrical field) that is vibrating in either a horizontally (H) or vertically (V) polarized plane. On striking the terrain, the polarized pulse interacts with the surface and is depolarized (rotated) to varying degrees. Depolarization of the return signal is caused by several terrain parameters, including surface roughness and object geometry. When depolarized, the pulse vibrates in several planes, but in most circumstances it returns to the antenna in the same polarized plane that it was transmitted in and is so recorded. This results in a *parallel-polarized* or *like-polarized image:* an HH image (horizontal transmit, hori-

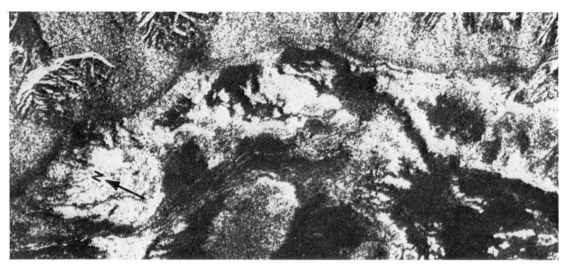

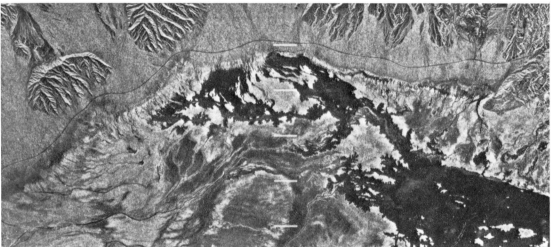

Figure 7.20.   X-band (3-cm wavelength) SAR images showing a portion of Death Valley, California, acquired by the U.S. Strategic Air Command (Goodyear Aerospace system). Top image has 15-m resolution (range and azimuth); bottom image has 3-m resolution (range and azimuth). Light bars on bottom image are electronically produced range marks to indicate increments of distance. Scale is about 1:70,000. (Courtesy U.S. Geological Survey.)

zontal receive) or a VV image (vertical transmit, vertical receive). The most common SLAR design is HH, and all images used in this chapter are HH presentations unless otherwise specified.

Some radar systems are equipped with a second antenna element that simultaneously receives the cross-polarized component of the depolarized return signal; the cross-polarized component vibrates at right angles to the polarization of the transmitted pulse. This results in a *cross-polarized image*: an HV image (horizontal transmit, vertical receive) or a VH image (vertical transmit, horizontal receive).

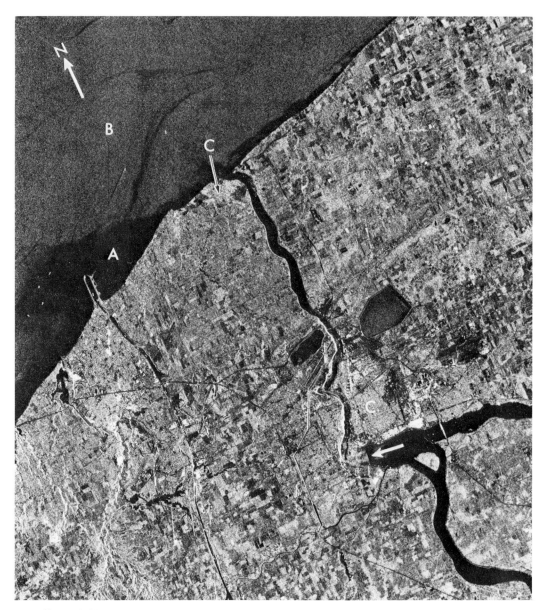

Figure 7.21.   Seasat SAR image (L-band, 23.5-cm wavelength) of Lake Ontario and Niagara Falls (arrow). Image textures include (A) smooth—calm water, (B) grainy—rough water, and (C) speckled—urban area. Digitally processed with 25-m range and azimuth resolution by MacDonald Dettwiler and Associates, Ltd. Scale is about 1:250,000. (Courtesy David Okerson, MacDonald Dettwiler and Associates, Ltd.)

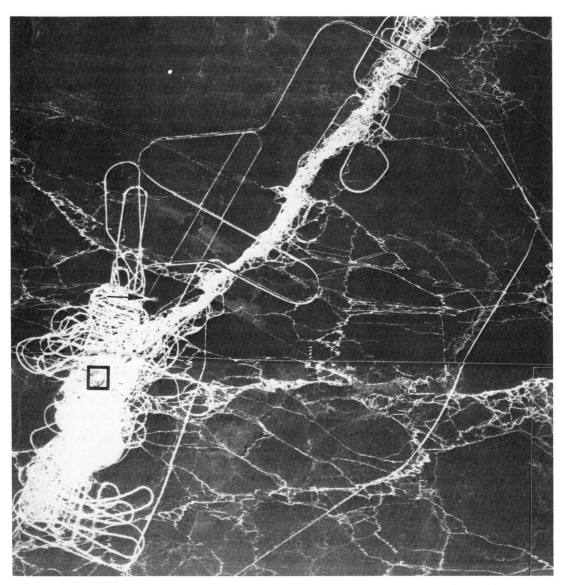

Figure 7.22.   X-band (3-cm wavelength) SAR image of new ice in the Beaufort Sea. The curvilinear features are tracks of an icebreaker (marked by an arrow) engaged in breaking a path in the ice for a drill ship (within square). New ice is rather smooth and is imaged as a weak return. The tracks are made of blocks of jagged rough ice and produce strong return signals. The image was generated by a real-time digital processor onboard the aircraft and linked by radio directly to the drill ship and the icebreaker so that the operation could be easily coordinated. (Courtesy R. Keith Raney, Canada Centre for Remote Sensing.)

A radar system containing two antenna elements allows for the simultaneous film recording of return echoes from the identical ground area in like and cross polarizations. This results in two image-pair scenarios: HH-HV and VV-VH. The former configuration has been employed most frequently (Figure 7.23). This type of SLAR is called a dual polarization or multipolarity radar.

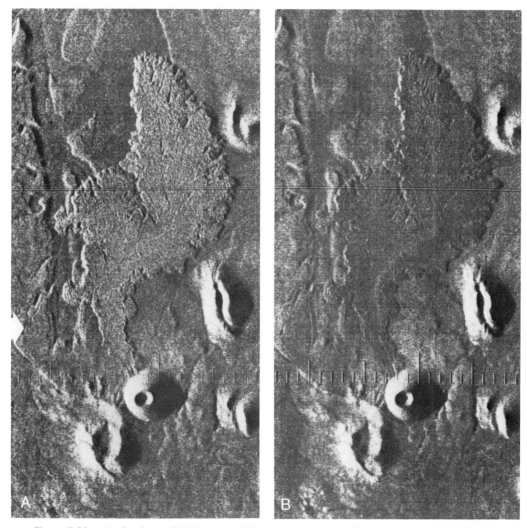

Figure 7.23.   Dual-polarized RAR images of SP Mountain and lava flow, Arizona, generated by the Westinghouse Corp. Ka-band (0.86-cm wavelength) SLAR system: (A) parallel-polarized image—HH, (B) cross-polarized image—HV. The lava flow is significantly brighter on the HH image because the flow's basaltic andesite blocks form natural corner reflectors. This geometric configuration caused minimal rotation of the horizontally polarized incident wave. Look direction (east) is indicated by the arrow. Light bars on the images are electronically produced range marks to indicate increments of distance. Scale is about 1:80,000. (Courtesy Gerald G. Schaber, U.S. Geological Survey.)

MULTICHANNEL RADAR

A state-of-the-art extension of single-wavelength, dual-polarization radar is a multispectral, multipolarity (multichannel) SAR. The first operational multichannel system was developed by the Environmental Research Institute of Michigan (ERIM). The ERIM radar can produce four simultaneous images at two wavelengths and two polarizations.

Figure 7.24 shows a set of four images generated by the ERIM system for a mixed forest-agricultural area; the multichannels are X-band HH, X-band HV, L-band HH, and L-band HV. As noted by Jackson (1980), multichannel SAR appears to provide potential advantages over single-wavelength, single-polarity SAR similar to the advantages of multispectral over single-channel sensing in the visible and infrared spectral regions.

RADAR SHADOWS

Because radar illuminates the terrain along the line of sight (i.e., *unidirectional illumination*), protruding topographic features can prevent the beam from striking their backslopes (slopes facing away from the radar

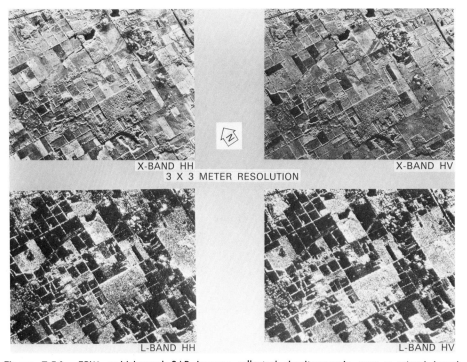

Figure 7.24. ERIM multichannel SAR images collected simultaneously over a mixed forest-agricultural area near Saginaw, Michigan. (Courtesy Eric S. Kasischke, Radar Division, Environmental Research Institute of Michigan.)

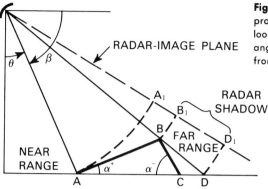

Figure 7.25. Radar shadow of surface BCD projected as B_1D_1 on radar image; shown are look angle θ, depression angle β, foreslope angle a^+, and backslope angle a^-. (Adapted from Ford et al. 1980.)

beam). These no-return areas represent radar shadows, and they will appear black on a positive image because no backscatter is returned to the sensor from their surfaces.

Figure 7.25 illustrates a mountain illuminated by a radar pulse. Part of the pulse is reflected from the foreslope (slope facing the radar beam) surface AB; the remainder of the pulse continues along a line of sight and intercepts the terrain at D. Consequently, the surface BCD is not illuminated, and it will appear as a black void on the resulting image.

Slopes are in shadow when the backslope angle is larger (steeper) than the depression angle ($a^- > \beta$). A backslope is just illuminated or grazed by the radar beam when $a^- = \beta$, and the backslope is fully illuminated when $a^- < \beta$ (Simonett and Davis 1983).

Note in Figure 7.25 that a radar shadow can fall only in the range direction, or away from the antenna. When shadows are discernible in a radar image, the azimuth-shadow concept always makes it possible to identify the near- and far-range portions.

The parameters that determine the size of radar shadows are the antenna depression angle, the relative relief of the terrain, and the slant range to the target:

1. Radar shadow length is inversely proportional to depression angle; the smaller the depression angle, the longer the shadow.
2. At a given depression angle and at a common range, the highest obstruction will produce the longest shadow.
3. Shadow lengths of terrain features of equal height and slope become proportionally longer as range increases because radar illumination becomes more oblique in far range.

Because the SLAR's relatively low angle of illumination produces a highlighting and shadowing effect, topographic features with a strike oblique or parallel to the beam front are often enhanced (Figure 7.26). The juxtaposition of a strong return (light tone) from a foreslope and little or no return from the backslope results in an image that has a pseudostereoscopic or three-dimensional appearance.

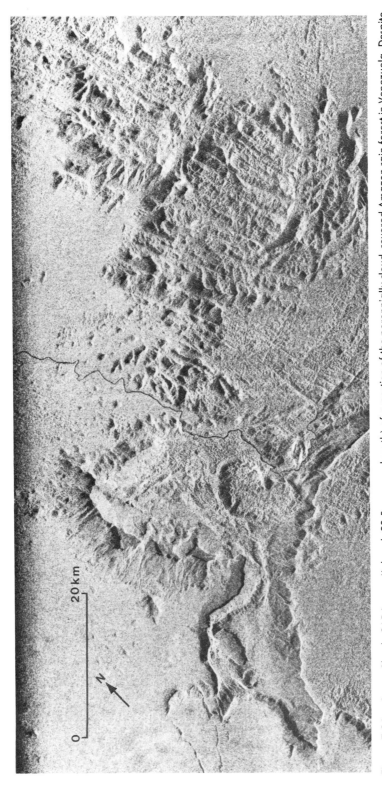

Figure 7.26. Space Shuttle SAR image (L-band, 23.5-cm wavelength) of a portion of the perennially cloud-covered Amazon rain forest in Venezuela. Despite the heavy vegetation, the topography is well displayed because terrain locally modulated the backscatter to produce light foreslopes and dark backslopes (Ford et al. 1983). Resolution is about 40 m. Topographic expression is best seen by rotating the book 180° (i.e., with the shadows falling toward the viewer). (Courtesy John P. Ford, Jet Propulsion Laboratory.)

Under certain conditions, the heights of features above the datum plane can be ascertained from their radar shadows (LaPrade and Leonardo 1969). The relative elevations of features producing the shadows are derived from shadow lengths plus a knowledge of the image scale and the type of across-track geometry (slant-range or ground-range format).

RADAR FORESHORTENING AND LAYOVER

Variable topographic relief in a scene causes geometric effects that result in uncorrectable distortions of a radar image. The most important of these are *foreshortening* and *layover*. The time a foreslope is illuminated (determined by the depression angle) determines the slope length on a radar image. This effect is called radar foreshortening, and it results in the compression of foreslopes relative to backslopes (Figure 7.27).

Layover is an extreme case of foreshortening that occurs when the look angle is smaller than the foreslope angle ($\theta < a^+$). In this situation, the radar pulse will intercept the top of an object before it strikes the base, and hence the echo from the summit will be received first, since radar is a range-measuring device. This concept is illustrated in Figure 7.28. Note that the ordering of surface elements on the projected image plane is the reverse of the ground ordering (Ford et al. 1980, Pravdo et al. 1983, Simonett and Davis 1983). In an actual image, a topographic feature appears to be laid over on its side toward near range (Figure 7.29).

RELIEF DISPLACEMENT

SLAR images differ from vertical photographs in terms of relief displacement in both X and Y directions because radar is a distance or range-measuring sensor and a camera is an angle-measuring device. In the across-track direction, topographic features are displayed toward the nadir line in a radar image, whereas displacement is away from the nadir point in a vertical photograph. Because of the SLAR's side-look operation, there is no topographic displacement in the along-track direction.

RADAR STEREO

Because SLAR produces displacements as a function of relief in the range direction, the distortions can yield radar parallax and thus a visual stereoscopic model. SLAR images showing the same ground area can be viewed with either conventional lens or mirror stereoscopes by using (1) adjacent overlapping images, (2) images obtained from different altitudes but presented at the same scale, or (3) images obtained from opposite look directions (Figure 7.30).

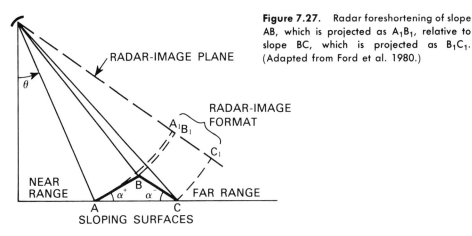

Figure 7.27. Radar foreshortening of slope AB, which is projected as A_1B_1, relative to slope BC, which is projected as B_1C_1. (Adapted from Ford et al. 1980.)

The first two configurations yield "same-side" stereo, while the third configuration produces "opposite-side" stereo. The latter coverage is the least desirable because shadows fall in opposite directions. A red-yellow SAR stereopair ("same-side") is presented in Plate 8.

RADAR AREA COVERAGE

A large-area view in a small format is a prime capability of an imaging radar system. An aircraft-operated, single-antenna SLAR can produce in excess of 20,000 km² of terrain coverage in an hour by illuminating continuous or overlapping swaths. Individual image swath widths can exceed 50 km.

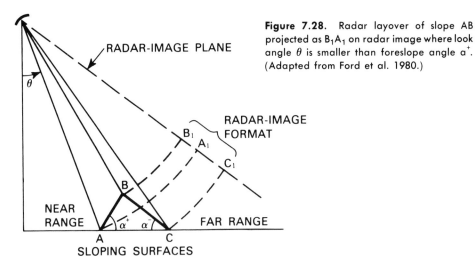

Figure 7.28. Radar layover of slope AB projected as B_1A_1 on radar image where look angle θ is smaller than foreslope angle a^+. (Adapted from Ford et al. 1980.)

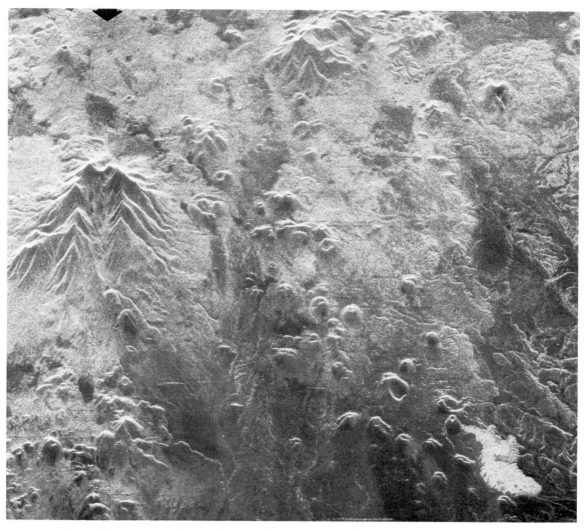

Figure 7.29.   Seasat SAR image (L-band, 23.5-cm wavelength) of the San Francisco Volcanic Field, Arizona, acquired on 19 July 1978. Note the layover of major topographic features. This effect occurs on Seasat images whenever a foreslope as seen by the radar exceeds about 20°. Look direction (approximately northeast) is indicated by the arrow. Scale is about 1:250,000. (Courtesy U.S. Geological Survey.)

From an orbital altitude, the NASA Space Shuttle SAR imaged approximately 10 million km² of the earth's surface in 8 hr during its 1981 mission.

SLAR images are usually acquired at regional scales (e.g., 1:250,000 to 1:500,000), but the negatives, particularly those generated by SAR, can be enlarged to scales as large as 1:50,000 or 1:25,000 without significant loss of detail. Mosaics are often compiled with overlapping image strips printed at scales of 1:100,000 or 1:250,000.

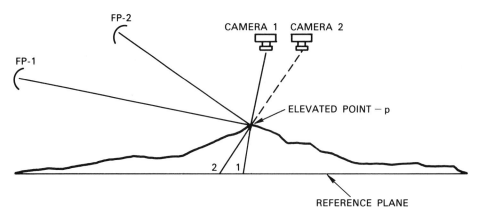

Figure 7.30. Relationship between "same-side" radar stereo and conventional photographic stereo. Note that the elevated point is displaced in the radar-image reference plane made from flight path 1 (FP-1) by an amount equal to that of the photograph of camera 1; the same also holds true for radar flight path 2 (FP-2) and camera 2. Thus, the same stereo model is developed (Graham 1976). (Courtesy Goodyear Aerospace Corp.)

RADAR MOSAICS

High-quality radar mosaics incorporate images having shadows falling in the same direction (i.e., images obtained with the same aircraft heading). Image strips are also acquired with about 60 percent overlap. For SAR mosaics only far-range portions of the images are used in the compilation process to minimize the effects of layover (Figure 7.31). RAR mosaics normally incorporate near-range portions of the image strips to avoid azimuth resolution decay in far range (Figure 7.32). Ground-range images greatly simplify the construction of a radar mosaic.

RADAR RETURN STRENGTH AND IMAGE TONE

The strength of radar return and, hence, image tone are primarily influenced by the following ground and radar system properties:

Ground Properties

Surface slope (macroscale relief)
Surface roughness (microscale relief)
Complex dielectric constant
Feature orientation

Radar System Properties

Operating wavelength
Antenna depression angle

Polarization
Antenna look direction

How these properties individually and in combination influence radar return intensity is discussed in the following section.

SURFACE SLOPE

The combination of antenna depression angle of the incident radar pulse with surface slope results in local angles of incidence that significantly affect the direction of backscatter. The slope of topographic or macrorelief features

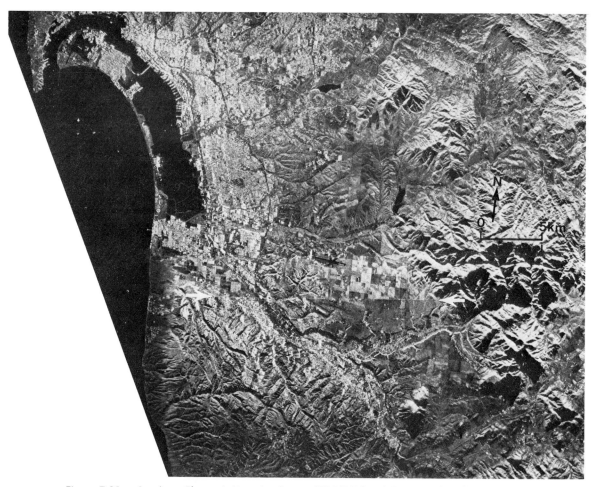

Figure 7.31.   Goodyear Electronic Mapping System (GEMS) X-band (3-cm wavelength) SAR mosaic of the San Diego, California, region. The radar images were obtained through partial cloud cover at an altitude of 12 km. Resolution in range and azimuth is approximately 15 m. A portion of the U.S.–Mexico border is discernible (as land-use differences) between the arrows. (Courtesy Goodyear Aerospace Corp. and Aero Service Division of Western Geophysical of America.)

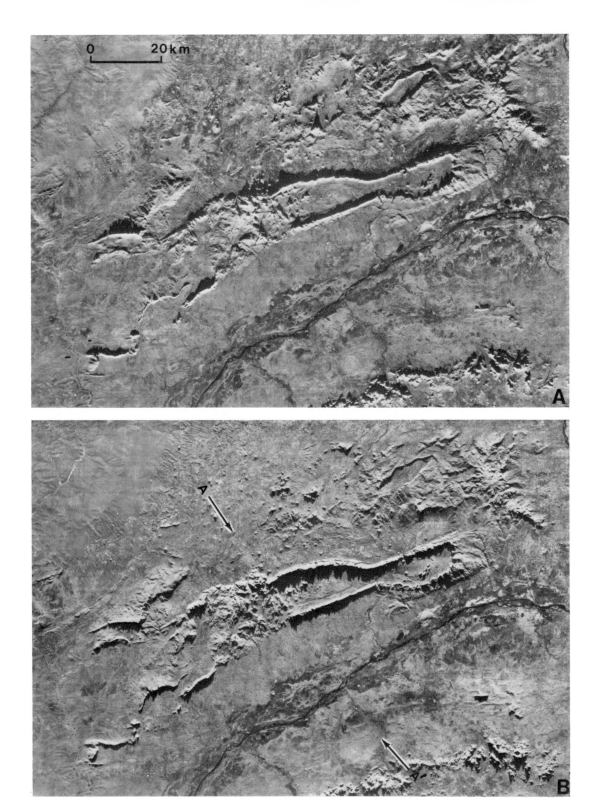

Figure 7.32. Motorola X-band (3.2-cm wavelength) RAR mosaics (opposite looks) reduced from original scale of 1:250,000. Shown is an 18,500-km² area in east-central Nigeria: (A) north look, (B) south look, and (A-A') trace of major fault, which is not apparent on north-look mosaic. The prominent structure is an anticline in Cretaceous sandstone. (Courtesy Ron Gelnett, MARS Associates, Inc.)

is responsible for strong echoes when they are oriented at an angle toward the radar system. Independent of wavelength, maximum reflection occurs when the incident radar wavefront is perpendicular to the local slope, a condition known as *normal incidence*. With normal incidence, the reflection and incidence paths are the same; thus, much of the energy is returned directly to the receiver. In this situation, the slope effect can completely obliterate any information relating to the microrelief of the surface (e.g., vegetation cover), a condition known as *foreslope brightening*. This translates into a bright and often saturated image tone (Bare and Dellwig 1978).

Conversely, a slope oriented away from the antenna produces weaker returns and appears darker on an image. A shadow "no-return" results when a slope is tilted away from the antenna at a great enough angle (Figure 7.26).

SURFACE ROUGHNESS

One of the most important considerations in determining radar return intensity is the interrelationship between the roughness of an object's surface (microrelief) and a radar system's wavelength and depression angle. Unlike topographic or macroscale roughness, which is measured in metres, surface roughness or microscale relief is measured in centimetres (i.e., in wavelength-sized units). This type of roughness is represented by small textural features such as leaves, twigs, cobbles, and pebbles. Although there is no absolute measure, the average vertical dimension of microrelief is a statistical approximation of a material's surface roughness. Methods for collecting and statistically analyzing information about the roughness of surfaces without vegetation are described by Schaber et al. (1980).

Two major categories of radar reflection can take place according to surface roughness—specular and diffuse. As illustrated in Figure 7.33, a "radar-

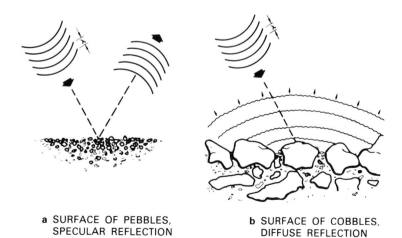

a SURFACE OF PEBBLES, SPECULAR REFLECTION

b SURFACE OF COBBLES, DIFFUSE REFLECTION

Figure 7.33.   Specular and diffuse radar reflection. Note that pebbles are "smooth" compared to wavelength (λ) and the cobbles are "rough" compared to wavelength. (Courtesy Goodyear Aerospace Corp.)

smooth" surface reflects the incident pulse in a single direction away from the antenna. In accordance with *Snell's Law*, the pulse will be reflected at an angle equal to and at a direction opposite that at which it strikes the surface (i.e., the *Fresnel-reflection direction*). This process is called *specular reflection*, and the surface is said to be a *specular* or *mirror reflector*. Terrain features that are specular reflectors include playas, pavement surfaces, and calm bodies of water. They are responsible for no or very low returns (dark image tones), except in the case of normal incidence (Figure 7.34).

A "radar-rough" surface (e.g., boulders, jagged sea ice, certain types of vegetation) is composed of numerous small facets that scatter the energy of an incident pulse in many different directions, with some portion of the pulse being reflected back toward the antenna (Figure 7.33). When many of the facets are perpendicular or nearly so to the direction of pulse propagation, regardless of incidence angle relative to the datum plane, a large proportion of the signal will be reflected back toward the antenna. This process is called *diffuse reflection*, and the surface is referred to as a *diffuse reflector* or *Lambertian surface* (Bare and Dellwig 1978). Such surfaces are responsible for bright image tones; until saturation of the system occurs, the rougher the surface, the brighter the tone (Figure 7.34).

Maximum surface roughness is represented by an *isotropic scatterer*, which is responsible for an extremely strong echo, virtually independent of depression angle. Its microrelief is several times greater than the operating wavelength. Isotropic scatterers include certain forms of vegetation, boulder fields, and rough-surfaced sea ice. In Figure 7.34, the silty rock salt (rough facies) unit represents an isotropic scattering surface.

A given surface, however, may be rough for some wavelengths and smooth for others, or for the same wavelength, a surface may be either smooth or rough for different depression angles (Figure 7.24). The relationship of wavelength and depression angle to surface roughness can be described by the *Rayleigh criterion*, which considers a surface to be smooth if:

$$h < \frac{\lambda}{8 \sin \beta} \qquad \textbf{Equation 7.8}$$

where: h = Average vertical height of microrelief
λ = Operating wavelength
β = Antenna depression angle

By solving for h, the theoretical boundary or breakpoint between radar-smooth and radar-rough surfaces is defined for a given wavelength and depression angle. Accordingly, surfaces with a value of h less than the calculated value should produce dark image tones, and surfaces with a value of h greater than the calculated value should be responsible for bright image tones. Observe from Equation 7.8 that (1) at any depression angle, a given surface becomes rougher as wavelength decreases, and (2) independent of wavelength, a given surface becomes smoother as depression angle decreases (i.e., as range increases).

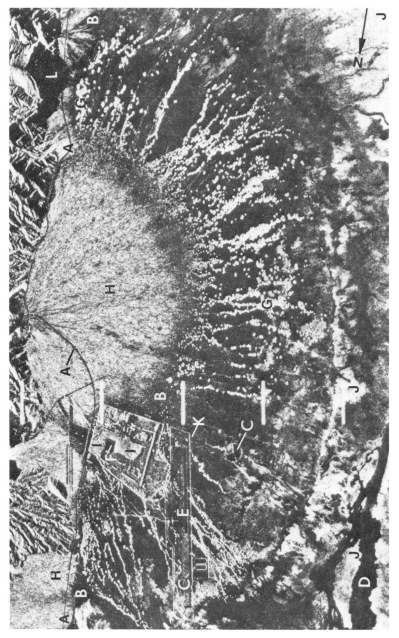

Figure 7.34. X-band (3-cm wavelength) SAR image of the Furnace Creek Ranch area, Death Valley, California (acquired by the U.S. Strategic Air Command, Goodyear Aerospace system). Variations in tone are due to differences in surface roughness relative to wavelength. Specular targets include: (A) paved highway, (B) sand zone, (C) calm water, (D) dry floodplain deposits, (E) paved runway, and (F) short grass. Diffuse targets include: (G) honey mesquite shrubs, (H) subangular to subrounded cobbles and boulders, (I) date palm grove, and (J) jagged pinnacles of silty rock salt. A metal fence is shown at K and a radar shadow at L. Resolution in range and azimuth is about 3 m. Light bars on the image are electronically produced range marks to indicate increments of distance. Scale is about 1:40,000. (Courtesy U.S. Geological Survey.)

There are in nature, however, many surfaces that are in between radar rough and radar smooth. Peake and Oliver (1971) modified the Rayleigh criterion to define the upper and lower values of h for a surface of intermediate roughness. The *smooth criterion* (h_s) considers a surface to be radar smooth if:

$$h_s < \frac{\lambda}{25 \sin \beta}$$ **Equation 7.9**

The *rough criterion* (h_r) considers a surface to be radar rough if:

$$h_r > \frac{\lambda}{4.4 \sin \beta}$$ **Equation 7.10**

Surfaces with a roughness falling between the two calculated boundaries (h_s and h_r) will produce an intermediate radar return and hence gray image signatures (Schaber et al. 1976, Sabins, 1980).

Specular features, however, can be responsible for strong returns if their smooth surfaces are configured to form corner reflectors. When oriented perpendicular to the radar beam, a major part of the incident energy is returned to the antenna regardless of wavelength and depression angle. This is called the *cardinal-point effect.* Corner reflectors are a common occurrence in an urban environment where vertical walls intersect the horizontal ground. Consequently, when illuminated from the proper azimuth, man-made structures usually stand out from their surroundings on radar images (Figure 7.35).

COMPLEX DIELECTRIC CONSTANT

The complex dielectric constant (ϵ) is dependent on the electrical properties of a material and is a measure of a material's ability to conduct or reflect microwave energy; as ϵ increases, reflectivity increases, whereas conductivity or penetration decreases. Generally, the dielectric constant of most naturally occurring materials, when dry, ranges from about 3 to 8 at radar wavelengths. Because of this small range, radar generally is considered to be insensitive to the electrical properties of a surface material in the absence of water.

When moist, however, a material's effective dielectric constant may approach 80 (i.e., to the dielectric of liquid water in the same wavelength region). Thus, ground targets produce significantly stronger returns when they are damp (Figure 7.36). The dielectric of a terrain material increases in an approximate linear relationship to increasing moisture content.

For free water and ice, the dielectric constant is not of primary relevance in determining backscatter intensity. Rather, the controlling property is the physical state of their surfaces; calm water and smooth ice are specular reflectors, and rough water and rough ice are diffuse reflectors (Figures 7.37 and 7.38).

Metallic structures such as bridges, ships, oil platforms, fences, railroad tracks, power lines and towers, act as antennas, strongly reflecting the incident energy (Elachi 1982). Such objects often appear as white targets,

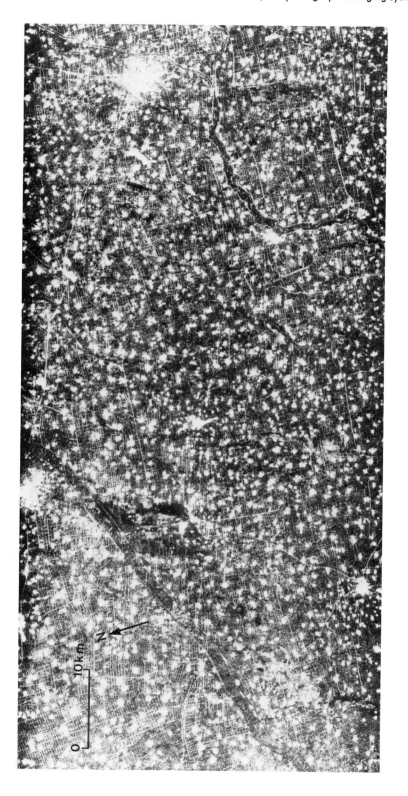

Figure 7.35. Space Shuttle SAR image (L-band, 23.5-cm wavelength) of Hebei-Shandong, People's Republic of China. The multitude of bright spots are small villages (density of about one per km²). The bright spots coalesce into several large cities. (Courtesy John P. Ford, Jet Propulsion Laboratory.)

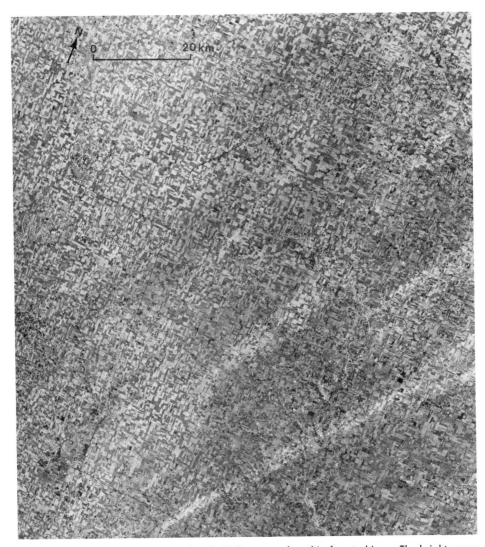

Figure 7.36. Seasat SAR image (L-band, 23.5-cm wavelength) of central Iowa. The bright areas result from the increased moisture content of soil and vegetation caused by rain occurring 10 to 12 hr before the image was recorded. (Courtesy John P. Ford, Jet Propulsion Laboratory.)

"blooming" to a size on the image greater than would be indicated by their physical sizes (Bare and Dellwig 1978). Echo strength from metal objects can be further intensified by corner reflector configurations (Figure 7.39).

POLARIZATION

Polarization is a fundamental system parameter that can influence backscatter strength. Important considerations are the polarization vector of the incident signal and the depolarizing effects of the terrain. Radar image tone can be affected by the following polarization-terrain interactions.

Given the polarization pairs (HH-HV) and (VV-VH), the like-polarized components (HH, VV) will be dominated by single reflection or direct scattering from the surface (i.e., *surface scattering*). The cross-polarized returns (HV, VH) will be determined by multiple reflection from within the complex surface of the medium (i.e., *volume scattering*), which depolarizes the impinging pulse (Figure 7.24). Surfaces that are radar rough cause depolarization—generally, as surface roughness increases, depolarization increases. Volume scattering commonly occurs with vegetation, for example, because of its structure (i.e., the leaves, branches, and trunks act in concert to reflect the energy along multiple paths). All else remaining equal, the following statements apply:

1. The brighter the tone on an HH or VV image, the greater the contribution from surface scattering.

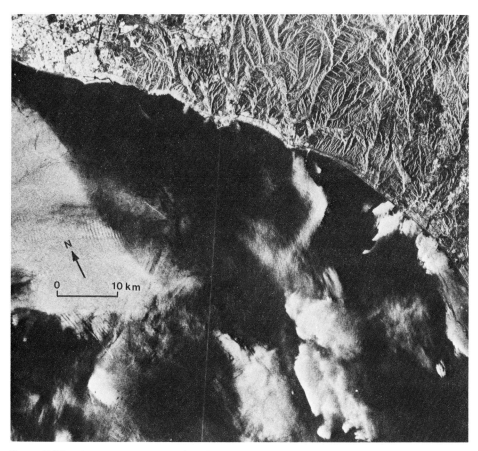

Figure 7.37. Seasat SAR image (L-band, 23.5-cm wavelength) of the southern California coast. Although the image appears to show clouds over the Pacific Ocean, the radar "sees" through the atmosphere and records only reflections received from the surface. The light and dark areas on the ocean surface represent differences in roughness caused by local winds. (Courtesy John P. Ford, Jet Propulsion Laboratory.)

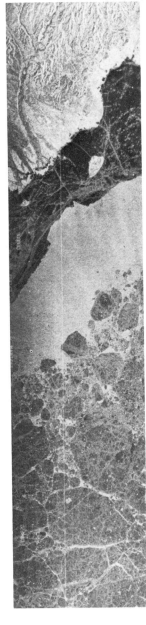

Figure 7.38. Seasat SAR image ((L-band, 23.5-cm wavelength) showing a portion of the Beaufort Sea ice pack west of Banks Island, Canada (right). The region is northeast of Alaska and some 800 km inside the Arctic Circle. The image, obtained as the satellite overflew the area at 1:55 A.M. 11 July 1978, contains a wealth of ice formation. The dark zone adjacent to Banks Island is an area of shore-fast ice composed primarily of relatively smooth first-year sea ice, 0.9 to 1.8 m thick. Rough pressure ridges are seen within the shore-fast zone, and west of this zone is an area of open water, called a shore lead. At the western edge of the lead is a marginal ice zone composed of a mixture of open water and rounded, multi-year ice floes, typically 3 to 4.6 m thick, and some first-year ice. Farther west is the main polar pack, made up of large floes as much as 19 km in diameter, surrounded by new leads. A random pattern of pressure ridges is visible within the floes. The very bright areas within the floes indicate intensive surface roughness, called rubble fields. (Courtesy Jet Propulsion Laboratory.)

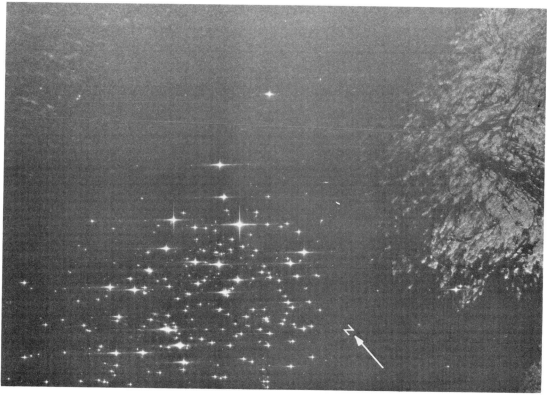

Figure 7.39. Space Shuttle SAR image (L-band, 23.5-cm wavelength) of a portion of the Arabian Sea showing bright-point targets (wellhead towers, oil platforms, and ships) in the Rugg az Zaqqum Oil Field. The star-shaped patterns result from corner reflections from metal surfaces when the orientation angle is about 90°. Medium tones in the right portion of the image indicate rough water surfaces (Ford et al. 1983). Scale is about 1:500,000. (Courtesy Mohamed A. Tarabzouni, Saudi Arabian National Center for Science and Technology.

2. The brighter the tone on an HV or VH image, the greater the contribution from volume scattering. Because the cross-polarized return is usually weaker than the like-polarized return, the power gain of the cross-polarized receiver is often increased. Therefore, care must be exercised when comparing gray tones of a like- and cross-polarized image pair.

Daily et al. (1978) and LaPrade (1974) have summarized additional polarization effects:

1. Corner reflectors produce extremely strong backscatter with minimal rotation of the incident polarization. Hence, such targets are bright on HH and VV images and dark on HV and VH images (Figure 7.23).
2. Regarding surface dielectric constant changes, HH images are the least sensitive, and HV and VV images are the most sensitive.
3. A spherical target (e.g., gravel) does not depolarize unless it is densely

packed, giving appreciable multiple scattering; nonspherical gravel always depolarizes.

RADAR PENETRATION—ATMOSPHERIC AND SURFACE

When dealing with imaging radar, two types of penetration must be considered—atmospheric and surface. Atmospheric attenuation effects on radar signals are most pronounced for the shortest wavelengths. X-band radar will penetrate haze, dust, fog, clouds, and all but the most severe thunderstorms (Figure 7.40). Ka-band radar (no longer operational) has some cloud penetration capability, but microwave energy at this wavelength is reflected by precipitation and thick cloud formations. L-band radars are "all-weather" because they can operate through any atmospheric condition, including heavy precipitation. Echoes returned from atmospheric components have bright signatures on a positive radar image.

X-, C-, and L-band radars are especially effective in wet tropical environments that are perennially cloud covered. In numerous tropical countries, radar images have provided the first cloud-free views of vast uncharted regions (Figure 7.26). With the dual advantage of atmospheric penetration and active illumination, radar is also an exceptional sensor for applications in the high latitudes—areas characterized by weak solar illumination and adverse weather conditions (Figures 7.22 and 7.38).

The depth of microwave penetration into a surface is strongly dependent on

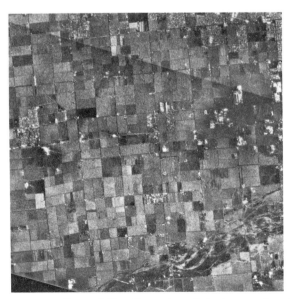 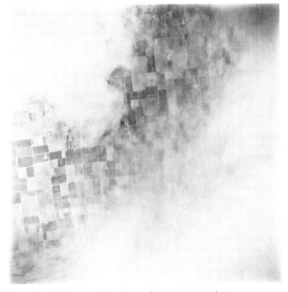

Figure 7.40. Comparison of air photograph and X-band radar image for atmospheric penetration differences. (Courtesy Goodyear Aerospace Corp.)

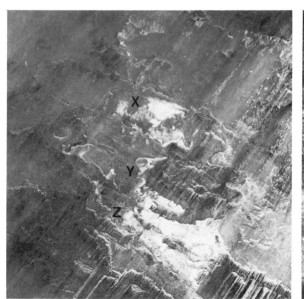
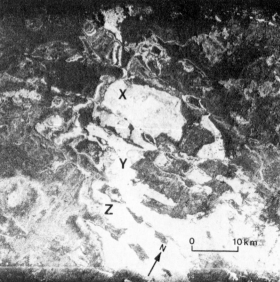

Figure 7.41. Landsat Multispectral Scanner image (0.8–1.1 μm), left, and Space Shuttle SAR image (L-band, 23.5-cm wavelength) of the southern part of the Limestone Plateau in Egypt. The plateau's surface at X, Y, and Z is covered by a veneer of unconsolidated sediment (dark on Landsat image); light areas on the Landsat image represent Paleocene to Eocene limestone bedrock. The SAR signals penetrated the unconsolidated sediment, producing "bright" responses from buried bedrock, including localities X, Y, and Z. At locality X, the bedrock was found to be covered by about 1.1 m of drift sand and fine-pebble alluvium. (Courtesy Gerald G. Schaber, U.S. Geological Survey.)

operating wavelength and the complex dielectric constant: as wavelength increases, penetration increases; as ϵ increases, penetration decreases and reflectivity increases. With appreciable moisture content (determining effective ϵ), penetration depth is practically negligible at all wavelengths used in imaging radars.

A recent discovery has shown that (1) the L-band signals from the Space Shuttle's imaging radar (SIR-A) penetrated the extremely dry sand deposits of the eastern Sahara of Egypt and Sudan (McCauley et al. 1982) and (2) Seasat's L-band signals penetrated as much as 2 m of alluvium in the Mojave Desert of California to reveal buried igneous dikes (Blom et al. 1984). In the eastern Sahara, SIR-A's signals penetrated sand sheets, dunes, and drift sand to reveal previously unknown buried valleys, geologic structures, and possible Stone Age occupation sites. Field studies in Egypt verify radar signal penetration of at least 2 m (Figure 7.41).

As described by Blom et al. (1984), theoretical studies indicate that for microwave penetration to occur (1) the grain size of the cover material must be less than about one-tenth of the radar wavelength, (2) the moisture level in the surface material must be less than about 1 percent, and (3) the cover material thickness should not exceed a few metres. In addition, the subsurface targets must have a scattering contrast that makes them observable on the images (i.e., the surface material must be radar smooth and the subsurface feature must be radar rough). Given these conditions, about 10 percent of the earth's land surface is amenable to penetration investigations (Jet Propulsion Laboratory 1983).

There is also evidence that soft new snow can be penetrated to some depth, permitting reflection from objects buried in it. For example, Cannon (1980) was able to identify a lava flow (Seward Peninsula, Alaska) blanketed by about 1 m of dry snow on X-band RAR imagery. Penetration apparently does not occur with crusted snow, which behaves as a specular reflector, directing the energy away from the antenna (Rydstrom et al. 1979).

Radar energy is not likely to be able to penetrate a closed forest canopy, because leaf sizes are usually on the same order of magnitude as radar wavelengths and because of the moisture content of the leaves. Both factors make leaves fairly efficient backscatter surfaces (Figure 7.42). On radar images where a dense canopy tends to be at a uniform height above the ground, the treetop surface will closely follow the ground contours, creating the impression of the topographic slope below (Short 1982) (Figure 7.26).

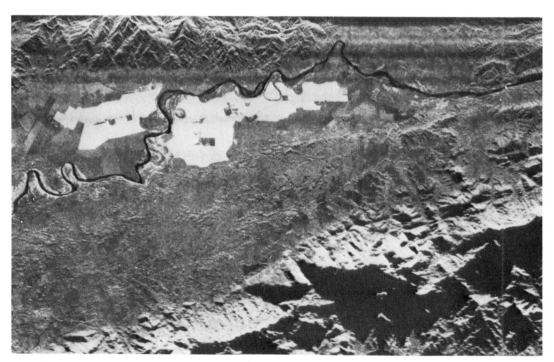

Figure 7.42. Motorola X-band (3.2-cm wavelength) RAR image of banana plantations along the Motagua River, Guatemala. The banana plantations are characterized by an exceptionally high return signal. The sharp boundaries between the low plains and adjacent mountains, both north and south of the river, are faults. Scale is about 1:250,000. (Courtesy Ron Gelnett, MARS Associates, Inc.)

ANTENNA LOOK DIRECTION AND FEATURE ORIENTATION

Antenna look direction with respect to the orientation of landscape features being illuminated by pulses of microwave energy (i.e., the *orientation angle*) can be a major factor in determining the intensity of backscatter and the quality of the resulting positive image. The orientation angle has limits of 0° to 90°.

Images of multiple look directions, if available, can increase data content appreciably. For example, Gelnett (1978) states that four orthogonal looks are necessary to obtain the maximum amount of data available from radar imagery:

Four orthogonal looks = 100 percent data content
Two opposite looks   = 90 percent data content
Two orthogonal looks   = 80 percent data content
One look   = 70 percent data content

Figure 7.43 illustrates two orthogonal looks of a highly fractured and faulted landscape in Nigeria. Note how some fracture sets are more apparent in one look than in the other. Although the increase in data content is shown in this example, the reader must understand that (1) it required flying the survey area twice, effectively doubling the cost of the data-collection and data-reduction costs of the survey, and (2) the data lost to radar shadows in one direction were not recovered in the second orthogonal look (Gelnett 1978). Recovery of data lost in radar shadow areas is possible, however, with opposite-look images (Figure 7.32).

Bryan (1979) found that different orientation angles formed between cultural targets and antenna look direction could produce dramatic differences in image gray tone. For example, large areas within the Los Angeles region were found to be portrayed in significantly darker tones on L-band SAR images than adjacent areas having similar land cover. The most pronounced tonal change for common targets occurred when the orientation angle between the antenna look direction and the trend of the streets and the accompanying walls of structures was less than about 10° or 15°. Consequently, Bryan acknowledges that an a priori knowledge of this orientation is necessary to insure accurate interpretation of radar images. This consideration is especially important for satellite systems because they have fixed azimuth angles that may not be optimal with respect to feature orientations. With aircraft radars, flight lines may be changed to compensate for the orientation of features that are of particular importance.

RADAR IMAGE INTERPRETATION

Although a radar image initially may appear similar to an aerial photograph with a low sun angle, remember that the photograph is a record of terrain reflectance averaged over a relatively broad band of wavelengths in

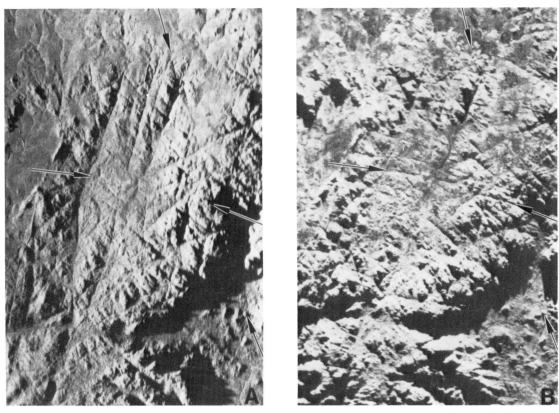

Figure 7.43. Motorola X-band (3.2-cm wavelength) RAR images incorporating orthogonal look directions of the same area in Nigeria—(A) east look, (B) south look. Compare fractures indicated by arrows on both images. Flight altitudes and depression angles are the same for both images. Scale is about 1:250,000. (Courtesy Ron Gelnett, MARS Associates, Inc.)

the visible and near-infrared spectrum, whereas the radar image displays the microwave reflectivity characteristics of terrain objects at only a single wavelength. Consequently, objects that appear identical in a photograph may appear completely different in a radar image. That the objects do appear different is the reason the information available from the radar sensor is unique (Figure 7.44).

Another fundamental difference between SLAR imagery and aerial photography is based on the relative position of the sensor and illumination source with respect to the terrain being imaged. Shadows are presented on photographs as a function of both camera position and sun position. Conversely, because radar provides its own illumination, shadows are always created downrange from both positive and negative terrain features. Radar illumination, unlike solar illumination, is not uniform across the terrain because there is a progressive change in the depression angle from near to far range. Thus, for identical terrain features, there is a progressive increase in the extent of shadowing at increased ground-range distances (Parry 1973).

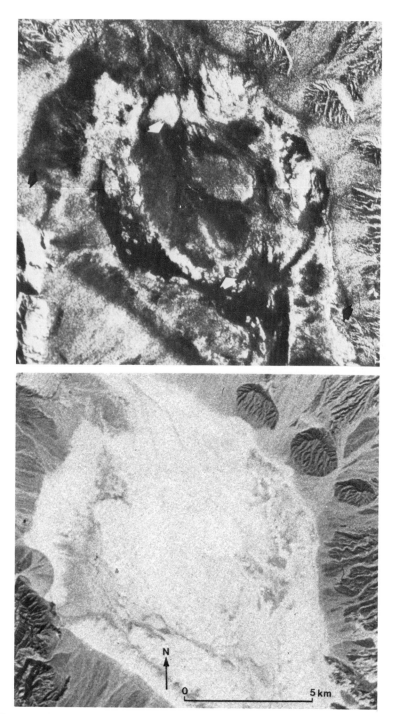

Figure 7.44. X-band (3-cm wavelength) SAR image (top) acquired by the U.S. Strategic Air Command (Goodyear Aerospace system) and Skylab photograph (bottom) enlarged from a normal color emulsion (0.4–0.7 μm) of Cottonball Basin, Death Valley, California. Analysis of the radar image revealed the existence of two suspect fault traces in evaporite deposits that are less than 2,000 years old (between arrows). The traces are well defined on the image because the radar system was able to differentiate surface roughness variations at the centimetre scale. The features are not recognizable on the photograph because tonal variations are primarily a record of spectral reflectivity differences that are related to changes in surface chemistry and not to small-scale changes in surface roughness (Berlin et al. 1980).

With a proper understanding of SLAR operation and the controls of radar scattering from landscape features, the interpretive techniques that have been developed for airphoto analysis are applicable to the interpretation of radar images (i.e., tone, shadow, texture, size, shape, pattern, and location). These interpretive techniques are discussed in the following section.

The tone of a radar image (1) is a qualitative measure of microwave backscatter strength and (2) is a product of many ground and radar system parameters. The radar return for each ground resolution cell is encoded on photographic film in tones of gray ranging from black to white; the stronger the return, the brighter the tone until saturation occurs. Radar echoes are described as being strong, moderate, weak, or "no return." Table 7.4 summarizes general surface states and a qualitative description of associated echo strengths and image tones.

Strong-intensity returns (light image tones) are typically indicative of prominent cultural and topographic features and isotropic scatterers. In general, cultivated fields and most terrain surfaces behave as scatterers and are responsible for diffuse reflection of varying intensity. The features can appear in a considerable number of gray tones. Weak or no returns are commonly associated with calm hydrographic features, smooth-surfaced ice, certain types of depositional landforms, and paved surfaces; these targets are denoted by dark image tones.

Radar shadows represent no energy returns and are depicted by black voids. Shadows are very important in radar image interpretation because they indicate the presence of positive and negative terrain. Radar shadows can substantially aid in the interpretation of topographic relief, relative rock resistance (and hence general lithology), and geologic structure (Raytheon Company 1969). As with aerial photographs, most interpreters orient a radar image so that the shadows fall toward them (i.e., near range at top). If this is not done, there is apt to be *topography inversion*, or a *pseudoscopic view*, whereby hills appear as valleys and valleys appear as hills (Figure 7.45).

The spatial distribution and frequency of tone changes for assemblages of individual surface elements represent image texture. While the average areal or regional tone of a segment of a radar image indicates the capability of the corresponding feature to reflect microwave energy, image texture is a qualitative measure of reflection variability within that particular unit (i.e., the micro-variability of reflecting surfaces). Image texture can be categorized as being smooth, grainy, or speckled in order of increasing coarseness.

Uniformity of tone, that is, a smooth image texture, is usually diagnostic of a homogeneous surface. Grainy and speckled textures are commonly associated with radar-rough surfaces because they are responsible for varying degrees of diffuse reflection over a short horizontal distance (e.g., local brightness variance caused by vegetation density differences). Smooth, grainy, and speckled image textures are illustrated in Figure 7.21.

Image texture is also influenced by the wavelength and resolution of the radar system, by the original image scale, and by the amount of image enlargement. The actual appearance of texture becomes coarser with enlargement. If enlarged too much, however, a texture unrelated to terrain conditions will be introduced because of the effect of the film's photographic grain (Barr 1968, Parry 1973).

Differentiating natural and cultural targets on radar imagery is usually possible because many cultural features have regular geometric shapes. Even though natural features usually have irregular shapes, many can be identified by their perimeter shapes alone (e.g., alluvial fans, lava flows, cinder cones, hydrologic features, and folded strata). The shapes of radar shadows enable the interpreter to infer information about the height, shape, size, and spatial form of terrain features.

As with aerial photographs, the more the dimensions of an object exceed resolution cell size, the more accurate its shape and size are defined on a radar image. However, metal objects often "bloom" to a size on the image greater than would be indicated by their actual sizes (Bare and Dellwig 1978). For RAR images, objects that appear as discrete items in the near range may appear as a combined (and thus enlarged) feature in the far range because of the decay in azimuth resolution.

Pattern refers to the spatial arrangement of objects within a scene. Analogous to shape, patterns observable in radar images are more accurately depicted when the objects involved exceed the resolution cell size. The scene context of an object can assist in its identification. For example, bright targets in water at a port may be deduced to be ships even if their shapes and sizes are grossly distorted. Correspondingly, objects spanning rivers may logically be assumed to be bridges, regardless of their size and shape depictions in a radar image (Bare and Dellwig 1978).

EARTH-RESOURCES SATELLITES

Several NASA manned spaceflights (e.g., Gemini, Apollo, and Skylab) have provided photography of the earth as part of their mission objectives. However, most remotely sensed data obtained from earth orbit has been through the deployment of unmanned satellites. Except for certain military reconnaissance spacecraft, the sensor systems carried by unmanned satellites are of a nonphotographic type.

The United States, although virtually alone in providing satellite-acquired earth-resources observational data in the 1970s, will be joined by a number of countries beginning in the mid-1980s. Their remote-sensing satellite systems will offer a potentially valuable complement to those of the United States. Planned programs call for additional spectral bands and spectral ranges, improvements in spatial resolution and times of coverage beyond those available by the U.S. program (Data Management Subcommittee 1982). Descriptions of future international remote-sensing satellite programs are found in Doyle (1982) and User Service Section (1982b). The remainder of this chapter is devoted to a discussion of five U.S. environmental satellite programs: Landsat, Heat Capacity Mapping Mission, Nimbus 7 (Coastal Zone Color Scanner), Seasat, and Space Shuttle.

TABLE 7.4. Surface States and Representative SLAR Tonal Ranges[a]

Surface State	Reflection Characteristics	Tonal Range
	Topographic	
Level terrain	Specular reflection if smooth; weak to no return	Dark tones to black
Foreslope	Relatively strong return; maximum return with normal incidence	Medium to light tones
Backslope	Relatively weak return at grazing incidence; no return when slope is not illuminated (radar shadow)	Medium to dark tones
		Black
	Geologic	
Smooth surfaces (see Equations 7.8 to 7.10)	Specular reflection when terrain is relatively flat; weak to no return	Dark tones to black
Rough surfaces (see Equations 7.8 to 7.10)	Diffuse reflection; moderate to strong returns	Medium to light tones
Smooth and rough surfaces	Reflection influenced by topographic slope	Lighter tones produced by foreslope effect
	Reflection influenced by moisture content (influence of the dielectric constant of water, if water does not produce a smooth surface)	Lighter tones produced by increasing moisture content
Natural corner reflectors produced in bedrock	Maximum return with proper orientation angle	Very light tones
	Hydrographic and Sea Ice	
Smooth water and ice surfaces	Specular reflection; weak to no return	Dark tones to black

Rough water and ice surfaces	Diffuse reflection; moderate to strong returns	Medium to light tones
Vegetation		
Dense woodland	Diffuse reflection; moderate to strong returns; return strength dependent on variables such as density, deciduous versus coniferous, absence or presence of water	Medium to light tones
Grassy areas	Specular and diffuse reflection; moderate to weak returns; return strength dependent on variables such as microrelief, presence or absence of water, and wavelength	Medium to dark tones
Agricultural crops	Variable strong to weak returns; return strength dependent on variables such as density, microrelief, presence or absence of water, and wavelength	Light to dark tones
Vegetation (general)	Reflection influenced by topographic slope	Lighter tones produced by foreslope effect
	Reflection influenced by moisture content (influence of the dielectric constant of water)	Lighter tones produced by increasing moisture content
Cultural Targets		
Streets, highways, runways Railroads, ships, bridges, transmission lines, and other metal objects	Specular reflection; weak or no return Maximum return with proper orientation angle	Dark tones to black Very light tones
Corner reflectors produced by vertical walls intersecting horizontal ground plane	Maximum return with proper orientation angle	Very light tones

[a] Adapted from Barr (1968).

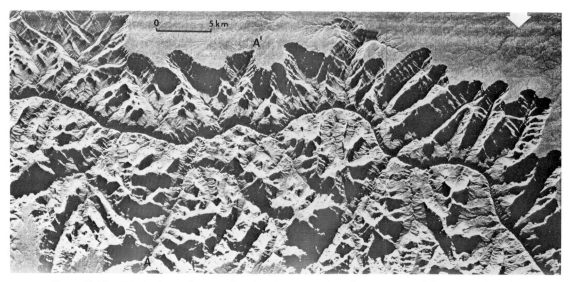

Figure 7.45.   Westinghouse Corp. Ka-band (0.86-cm wavelength) RAR image of the eastern Grand Canyon, Arizona. Note the excellent enhancement of lineaments created by radar shadowing. The Bright Angel fault is clearly discernible (A-A'). Look direction (approximately north) is indicated by the arrow. The effect of topography inversion for this scene can be demonstrated by rotating the book 180° (i.e., so the shadows fall away from the viewer). (Courtesy Gerald G. Schaber, U.S. Geological Survey.)

LANDSAT PROGRAM

Landsat (*land sat*ellite) represents the first spacecraft program designed specifically for collecting multispectral radiance data from a vertical perspective at a moderate resolution for monitoring and managing natural resources. Until 13 January 1975 the Landsat program was known as the Earth Resources Technology Satellite (ERTS) program. In 1982 NASA transferred the operation and management of the Landsat system to the National Oceanic and Atmospheric Administration (NOAA). To date five Landsats that have been launched (Table 7.5) have acquired more than 1.5 million images, systematically and repetitively covering most of the earth. Scientists representing government agencies, research institutes, petroleum

TABLE 7.5. Landsat Periods of Operation		
Landsat	Launch	Deactivation
-1	23 July 1972	6 January 1978
-2	22 January 1975	27 July 1983
-3	5 March 1978	7 September 1983
-4	16 July 1982	——
-5	1 March 1984	——

and mining companies, and educational institutions from more than 100 countries have used Landsat images for a variety of earth-resources survey and monitoring programs.

Landsats-1, -2, and -3 far exceeded their expected lifespans of one year (Table 7.5). Although it was planned that Landsat-4 would have a three-year mission life, serious power problems have affected its performance, and it has been placed in a "reduced-mission mode" by NASA. Because Landsat-4 could fail at any time, its backup, Landsat-5, was placed in orbit in March 1984, more than one year ahead of schedule. Landsat-5 is used for routine data collection, while Landsat-4 is used for special acquisitions. However, at the first signs of further failure, Landsat-4 will be placed in a lower "parking" orbit where it potentially can be retrieved for repairs during a future Space Shuttle mission. The U.S. government has not determined the nature and scope of the Landsat program after Landsat-5.

LANDSAT ORBITAL CHARACTERISTICS

Landsats-1, -2, and -3 orbit the earth in repetitive, near-polar, sun-synchronous paths at a nominal altitude of 917 km over the equator. The orbital plane is inclined 99° (measured clockwise from the equator). Each spacecraft circles the earth in 103 min, or 14 times per day, and every daylight (imaging) pass is from north to south. After 18 days, or 252 passes, the satellite returns to the same position (i.e., orbit 252 falls directly on orbit 1). Thus, based upon one operating satellite, the earth is imaged, from 82° N latitude to 82° S latitude, at 18-day intervals.

A sun-synchronous orbit ensures repeatable sun-illumination conditions, enabling a Landsat spacecraft to pass over the same area at about the same local time every 18 days. For example, the daylight crossing at the equator is at about 9:40 A.M. local time.

The orbits of Landsats-4 and -5 are also near-polar and sun-synchronous, but the nominal altitude of each spacecraft is 705 km at the equator. The lower orbit produces an earth-coverage cycle of 16 days per satellite (excluding the polar regions). The lower orbit is necessary to achieve an improved ground resolution for the primary sensor (Thematic Mapper) carried on Landsats-4 and -5. The following discussion summarizes the characteristics of the Landsat sensors.

MULTISPECTRAL SCANNER (MSS)

An earth-viewing sensor carried by all five Landsats is the Multispectral Scanner (MSS), which synchronously collects reflected radiation in four discrete spectral bands ranging from 0.5 to 1.1 μm (Table 7.6). From Table 7.6 one will note that a new numbering system is used to designate the four bands of the Landsat-4 and -5 MSS. What are known as bands 4, 5, 6, and 7 for the

Landsats-1, -2, and -3[a]	Landsats-4, -5	Wavelength Range (μm)	Spectral Region[b]
Band 4	Band 1	0.5–0.6	Green
Band 5	Band 2	0.6–0.7	Red
Band 6	Band 3	0.7–0.8	Reflected infrared
Band 7	Band 4	0.8–1.1	Reflected infrared

TABLE 7.6. Characteristics of the Landsat Multispectral Scanner

[a] The Multispectral Scanner on Landsat-3 contained a thermal infrared band but it never became operational.
[b] The spectral bands were selected primarily for anticipated agricultural studies.

first three Landsat MSS sensors are known, respectively, as Landsat-4 and -5 MSS bands 1, 2, 3, and 4; the spectral coverage of the instrument, however, remains unchanged. The MSS was the primary or lead sensor on Landsats-1, -2, and -3.

The MSS sensor incorporates six detectors per band at the focal plane, and with each oscillation of its primary or scanning mirror, six lines of ground data are collected for each band. The mirror scans the earth in a 185-km swath perpendicular to the orbital path. These MSS characteristics are illustrated in Figure 7.46.

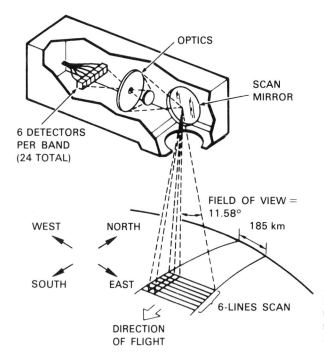

Figure 7.46. Schematic representation of the Landsat Multispectral Scanner. (Adapted from Short 1982.)

A geometrically corrected MSS image measures 185 km across track by 170 km along track, and ground resolution is approximately 80 m. An image deviates from a rectangle by the distance the earth rotated beneath the satellite during the 25 sec the data were being acquired from the top to the bottom of a nominal MSS scene. Thus, the area imaged incorporates rotational skew and is represented as a parallelogram (Figure 7.47).

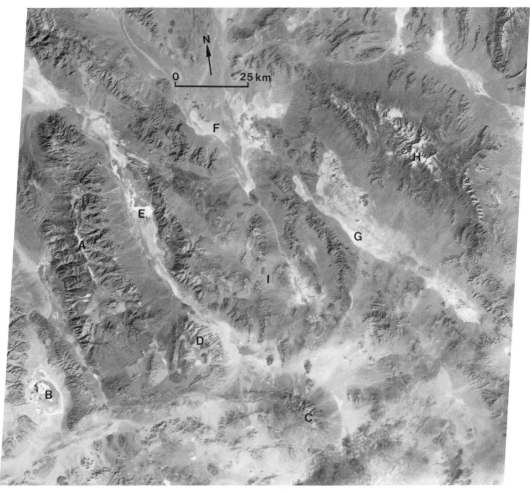

Figure 7.47.   Landsat-4 band 2 (0.6–0.7 μm) Multispectral Scanner image of a portion of the Basin and Range Province in California and Nevada acquired 17 November 1982. Annotations include: (A) Panamint Range, (B) Searles Lake, (C) Avawatz Mountains, (D) Owshead Mountains, (E) Death Valley, (F) Amargosa Valley, (G) Pahrump Valley, and (H) Spring Mountains. (Courtesy EROS Data Center, U.S. Geological Survey.)

▓ RETURN BEAM VIDICON CAMERA

Landsats-1 and -2 carried a multispectral Return Beam Vidicon (RBV) camera system, consisting of three bore-sighted vidicon tube cameras that collected reflectance data in three spectral bands (0.475–0.575 μm, 0.58–0.68 μm, and 0.69–0.83 μm). However, electrical problems, experienced within weeks after the launch of Landsat-1, curtailed operation of the RBV system. The RBV unit was not activated on Landsat-2, largely because of the success of the MSS sensor.

On Landsat-3, a panchromatic RBV system served as a successful high-resolution mapping device. The unit consisted of two vidicon tube cameras that viewed 98-by-98-km ground scenes with 16-km overlap and 13-m sidelap. The side-by-side mounted cameras operated alternately, enabling four "sub-scene" images to closely approximate the same ground coverage of a single MSS image. The two RBVs had a single broadband sensitivity of 0.505–0.75 μm, and ground resolution was approximately 30 m.

An RBV subscene image of the Grand Canyon is shown in Figure 7.48. Note that, unlike an MSS image, the field of view is not skewed. This is because an image is "frozen" on the vidicon plate during shuttering.

▓ THEMATIC MAPPER

The primary sensor carried by Landsats-4 and -5 is the Thematic Mapper (TM), which is a second-generation earth-observation scanner. Although relying heavily on the technology of the MSS, the TM incorporates improved spatial resolution, additional spectral bands, greater radiometric accuracy, and improved geometric fidelity over its MSS predecessor. TM is designed to collect radiance data simultaneously with the MSS instrument; each sensor scans a swath 185 km wide.

The Thematic Mapper collects radiance data in seven discrete spectral bands ranging from 0.45 to 12.5 μm. Except for band 7 (2.08–2.35 μm), the bands were specifically selected for vegetation analysis; band 7 was proposed for geological applications. Band designations, spectral ranges, and principal applications are presented in Table 7.7. Ground resolution for the TM bands is 30 m, except for the 10.4- to 12.5-μm thermal infrared band which has a resolution element of 120 m. Three TM images are presented in Figure 7.49; these images were generated simultaneously with the MSS image shown in Figure 7.47 (compare for resolution differences).

Nighttime thermal images (band 6) can be acquired by the TM because of its thermal infrared sensitivity (Figure 7.50). The earth-emitted data are collected during nighttime, south-to-north passes.

The TM scans in both directions normal to the ground track (i.e., *bidirectional scanning*). A 16-element detector array is used for each of the 30-m resolution bands, while four detectors are used for the thermal infrared band. Therefore, 16 scan lines are generated for bands 1–5 and 7 and 4 for band 6 during each sweep of the mirror.

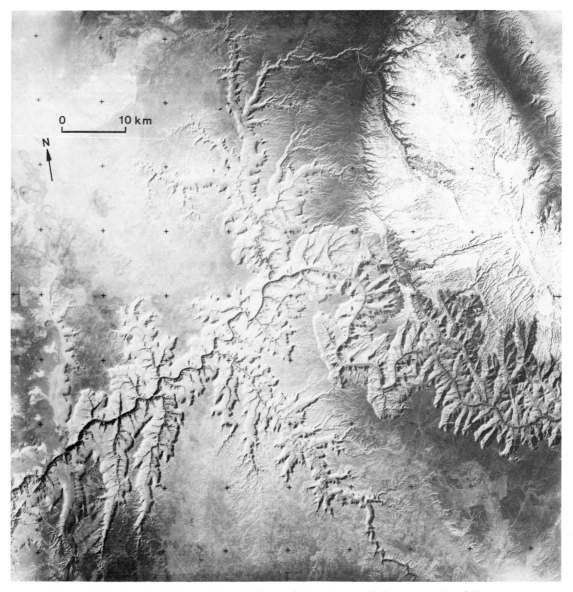

Figure 7.48. Landsat-3 Return Beam Vidicon subscene image of the eastern Grand Canyon, Arizona, acquired 22 March 1981. Approximately 15 cm of snow covered the ground on the North Rim. The crosses are reseau marks (etched on the camera's vidicon surface) used to correct image geometry. Compare with Figure 7.45. (Courtesy EROS Data Center, U.S. Geological Survey.)

LANDSAT MSS AND TM COLOR-COMPOSITE IMAGES

Any three black-and-white MSS or TM positive film transparencies can be combined into a color-composite image. This is normally done by the following photographic technique. Three film positives are punch-registered with a

TABLE 7.7. Characteristics of the Landsat-4 and -5 Thematic Mapper

Band Number	Wavelength Range (μm)	Spectral Region	Application
1	0.45– 0.52	Blue	Designed for water body penetration, making it useful for coastal water mapping; also useful for differentiation of soil from vegetation, and deciduous from coniferous flora
2	0.52– 0.60	Green	Designed to measure visible green reflectance peak of vegetation for vigor assessment
3	0.63– 0.69	Red	A chlorophyll absorption band important for vegetation discrimination
4	0.76– 0.90	Reflected infrared	Useful for determining biomass content and for delineation of water bodies
5	1.55– 1.75	Reflected infrared	Indicative of vegetation moisture content and soil moisture; also useful for differentiation of snow from clouds
6	10.40–12.50	Thermal infrared	For use in vegetation stress analysis, soil moisture discrimination, and general thermal mapping
7	2.08– 2.35	Reflected infrared	Potential for discriminating rock types and for hydrothermal mapping

Adapted from User Services Section (1982b).

sheet of unexposed color-transparent film. Each transparency is then contact printed onto the color film by using blue, green, and red filtered light. The usual MSS band-filter combination is as follows: band 4 projected through blue filtered light, band 5 projected through green filtered light, and band 7 projected through red filtered light (Plates 9, 11, and 12). For Landsats-4 and -5, MSS bands 1, 2, and 4 would be color coded in identical fashion. Such composites resemble conventional infrared color photography but at a diminished resolution.

For TM images, an infrared color-composite image is produced by projecting TM bands 2, 3, and 4 through blue, green, and red filtered light, respectively. A natural color image can be made by projecting TM bands 1, 2, and 3 through blue, green, and red filtered light, respectively. Other three-band combinations can be color coded to enhance features of special interest. Four different TM color-composite images are shown in Plate 10.

LANDSAT RECEPTION STATIONS AND DATA-DISTRIBUTION CENTERS

Image data from Landsat sensors are transmitted at microwave frequencies to ground receiving stations and recorded on magnetic (video) tape. In addition to those in the United States, ground stations are located in the following countries: Argentina, Australia, Brazil, Canada, India, Indonesia,

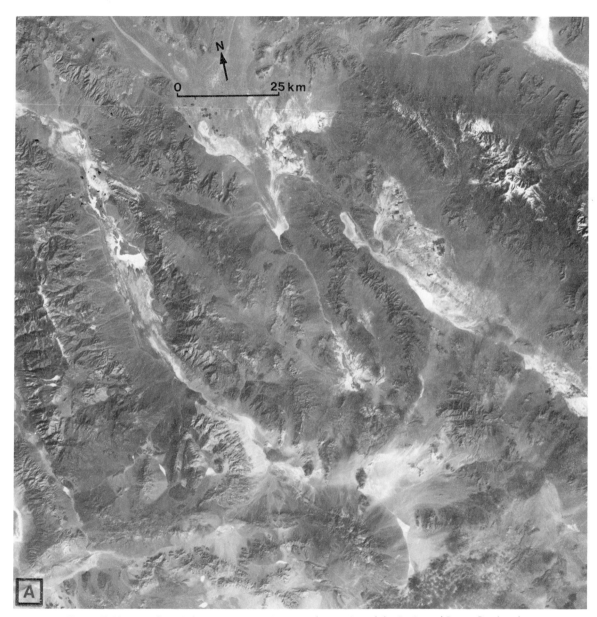

Figure 7.49. Landsat-4 Thematic Mapper images of a portion of the Basin and Range Province in California and Nevada acquired 17 November 1982. (A) band 3—0.63–0.68 μm; (B) band 5—1.55–1.75 μm; and (C) band 6—10.40–12.50 μm. Compare with Figure 7.47 and Plate 10. (Courtesy EROS Data Center, U.S. Geological Survey.)

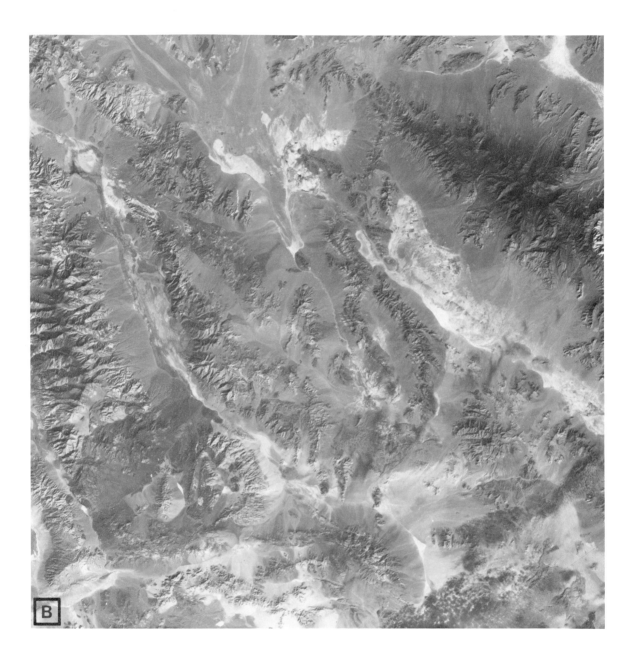

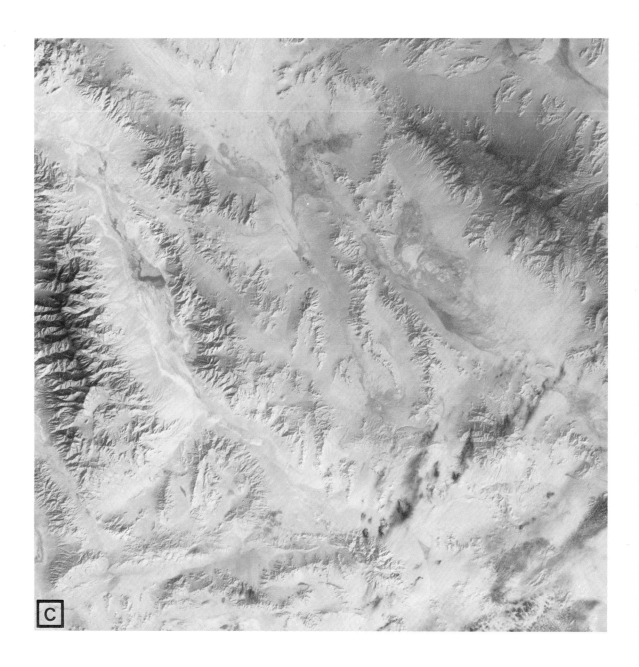

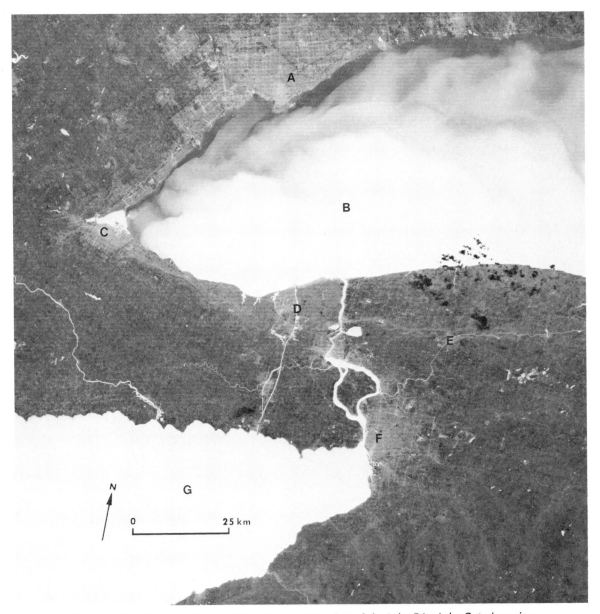

Figure 7.50.   Nighttime thermal infrared image (band 6) of the Lake Erie–Lake Ontario region acquired 22 August 1982 by the Landsat-4 Thematic Mapper at approximately 2:00 A.M. Annotations include: (A) Toronto, (B) Lake Ontario, (C) Hamilton, (D) Welland Canal, (E) Erie Canal, (F) Buffalo, and (G) Lake Erie. Rivers, canals, and lakes are light toned, being warmer than the surrounding land. Lake Erie is uniformly warm, whereas the water in Lake Ontario shows lateral thermal stratification. Water in a bay at Hamilton is quite warm, owing in part to effluents from nearby mills. Note the street patterns evident in Toronto and Buffalo and the cold cloud tops along the south shore of Lake Ontario (Short and Stuart 1982). Compare with Figure 7.21. (Courtesy EROS Data Center, U.S. Geological Survey.)

Italy, Japan, People's Republic of China, Republic of South Africa, Sweden, Thailand, and Upper Volta. Several of the foreign stations are being upgraded with TM ground data-handling equipment. Each station's field of view covers a radius of about 2,700 km (somewhat less for Landsats-4 and -5 because of their lower orbit).

Video tapes of Landsat data undergo a process of annotation, correction (geometric and radiometric), and conversion to film and digital products. Landsat images incorporate gray-scale wedges and an annotation block that contains a variety of information (e.g., date of image acquisition, geographic coordinates, sun angle, sun azimuth, type and band of sensor, and frame identification number). International ground stations handle both data processing and data distribution.

In the United States, the NASA Data Processing Facility at the Goddard Space Flight Center in Greenbelt, Maryland, produces Landsat data (in digital form) which are transferred to the EROS Data Center (EDC), the facility in the United States solely responsible for disseminating Landsat data to the public. There, the data are further processed, when warranted, and recorded on high-resolution film, computer-compatible tapes (CCTs), or floppy disks (currently MSS data only). The digital products (CCTs and floppies) enable the data to be subjected to special computer processing routines (see Chapter 15).

Color and black-and-white prints are available from EDC at standard scales of 1:1,000,000; 1:500,000; and 1:250,000. Film negatives and positives of MSS and TM data are normally produced at a scale of 1:1,000,000 and at a scale of 1:500,000 for Landsat-3 RBV images. Inquiries covering Landsat products may be directed to Landsat Customer Services Section, EROS Data Center, Sioux Falls, SD 57198.

HEAT CAPACITY MAPPING MISSION (HCMM) SATELLITE

The Heat Capacity Mapping Mission (HCMM) was an experimental space project sponsored by NASA. HCMM was designed to investigate the feasibility of using day and night thermal infrared data for discriminating different surface materials and different states (e.g., the degree of soil moisture) from earth orbit. The satellite carried a two-channel scanner called the *Heat Capacity Mapping Radiometer* (HCMR). The "visible" channel had a sensitivity of 0.5–1.1 μm, and the sensitivity of the thermal infrared channel was 10.5–12.5 μm. Ground resolution at nadir was 500 m for the visible channel and 600 m for the thermal channel. The scanner's angular field of view (swath width) was 700 km. Simultaneously acquired images, covering the southwestern United States and northern Mexico, are shown in Figures 7.51 and 7.52.

The HCMM satellite was launched 26 April 1978 and placed in a 97.6° orbit at an altitude of 620 km. HCMM flight operations were ended 30 September 1980 because of battery deterioration. Although HCMM was intended to last only a year, it worked for about 29 months.

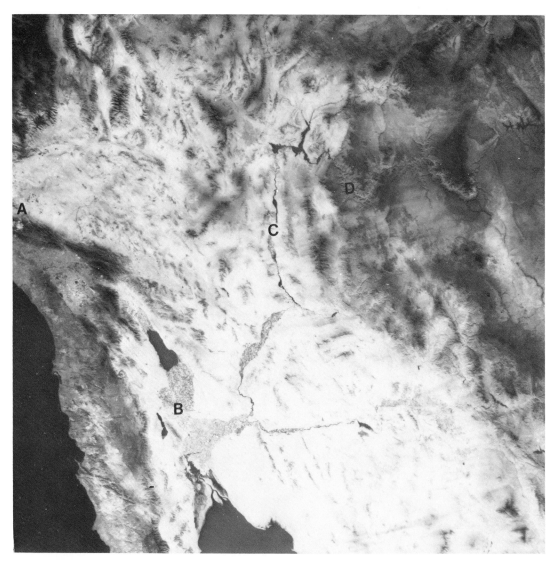

Figure 7.51.   Heat Capacity Mapping Radiometer (HCMR) thermal infrared image (10.5–12.5 μm) of the southwestern United States and northern Mexico acquired 24 October 1979. The scene measures about 700 by 700 km (equivalent to approximately 16 Landsat MSS images). Annotations include: (A) San Andreas fault, (B) U.S.–Mexico border, (C) Colorado River, and (D) Grand Canyon. The east-trending dark streaks are interpreted as wind-oriented condensation (Short and Stuart 1982). Compare with Figure 7.52. (Courtesy U.S. Geological Survey.)

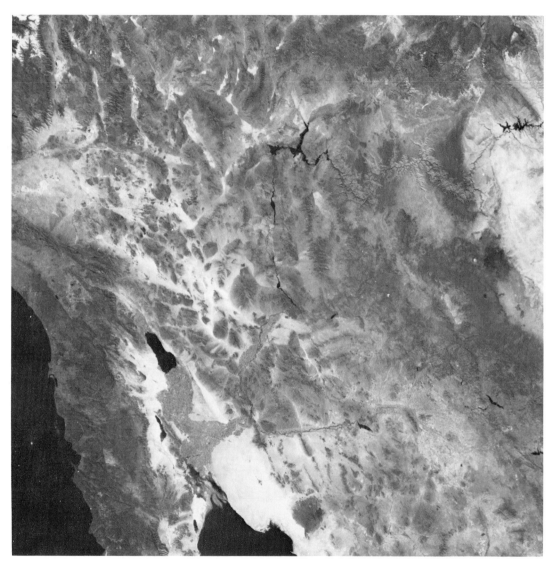

Figure 7.52.   Heat Capacity Mapping Radiometer (HCMR) "visible" image (0.5–1.1 μm) of the southwestern United States and northern Mexico, acquired 24 October 1979. Compare with Figure 7.51. (Courtesy U.S. Geological Survey.)

Because of HCMM's orbital characteristics, day and night coverage was possible for the midlatitudes (16-day return cycle for both day and night orbits). For example at 40° N latitude, coverage occurred at about 1:30 P.M. and 2:30 A.M. local time. These are appropriate times for observing the maximum and minimum temperatures of the diurnal cycle. The day-night radiant-temperature data also can be used with the daytime visible data to estimate the thermal inertia of cover materials.

Because HCMM was an experimental mission, it was not designed to obtain global coverage. Carrying no tape recorder, it was able to obtain data only when it was within range of certain ground receiving stations. Image coverage, however, is available for extensive areas of North America, western Europe, northern Africa, and eastern Australia (about 38,000 standard-image products). Data in image and CCT formats, user's guides, and associated catalogs are available from the National Space Science Data Center, World Data Center-A, Code 601, NASA Goddard Space Flight Center, Greenbelt, MD 20771.

NIMBUS-7 COASTAL ZONE COLOR SCANNER

The Nimbus-7 satellite, launched October 1978, is equipped with nine sensors. Eight systems are designed for atmospheric measurements; the ninth sensor, the Coastal Zone Color Scanner (CZCS), is of particular importance to earth-resources specialists because it collects radiance data from the ocean environment. Nimbus-7 is in a sun-synchronous, near-polar, 955-km orbit; its repeat cycle is six days.

The six-channel CZCS has (1) four high-sensitivity bands, each 0.02 μm wide, and centered at 0.44 μm (blue), 0.52 μm (blue-green), 0.55 μm (green), and 0.67 μm (red); (2) a lower sensitivity near-infrared band (0.7–0.8 μm); and (3) a thermal infrared channel (10.5–12.5 μm) (Table 7.8). Image resolution is 800 m, and the image swath width is 1,800 km.

TABLE 7.8. Characteristics of the Coastal Zone Color Scanner

Channel	Wavelength Range (μm)	Measurements
1	0.43– 0.45	Chlorophyll absorption
2	0.51– 0.53	Chlorophyll absorption
3	0.54– 0.56	Gelbstoffe (yellow substance)
4	0.66– 0.68	Chlorophyll concentration
5	0.70– 0.80	Surface vegetation
6	10.50–12.50	Surface temperature

Adapted from Southworth (1983).

The four visible channels each provide different spectral views of subtle water patterns. When the images are color composited, estimates can be made of phytoplankton concentrations (basic food available to fisheries) and inorganic suspended matter such as silt. The thermal infrared channel, operating only intermittently, is used for assessing surface temperatures. The near-infrared channel is used to detect surface vegetation and as a water detector for subsequent processing of the other bands (Gower 1983). Simultaneously collected CZCS images for the coastal area of Bangladesh are shown in Figure 7.53.

Inquiries regarding CZCS image and CCT data can be made to the Environmental Satellite Data and Information Service, National Climatic Center, Satellite Data Services Division, World Weather Building, Room 100, Washington, DC 20233.

▨ SEASAT OCEAN-MONITORING SATELLITE

Launched by NASA 26 June 1978, Seasat (*sea satellite*), the first experimental ocean-monitoring satellite, operated until 9 October 1978, when a massive short circuit in the power system prematurely ended its anticipated year-long mission. Seasat carried five sensors in a near-polar, 108° inclination orbit at a nominal altitude of 800 km; about 14 earth orbits were completed each day.

The instrument payload consisted of a visible-infrared radiometer and four microwave sensors—radar altimeter, radar scatterometer, scanning multi-frequency microwave radiometer, and a SAR imaging system. These five complementary sensors collected a massive amount of information on surface winds (speed and direction), wave heights and lengths, currents, water temperatures, ice conditions, and coastal storm activity.

The Seasat SAR operated over water and land, providing the first orbital radar images of both surfaces (Figures 7.21, 7.29, 7.36, 7.37, and 7.38). However, because the imaging radar system was designed primarily to observe ocean surfaces, a steep or large depression angle was required; consequently, layover occurs in land images where terrain foreslopes exceeded the complement of the depression angle (17° for near range and 23° for far range). Despite this limitation, a variety of terrestrial information can be interpreted from Seasat radar images. Major characteristics of the Seasat SAR are listed in Table 7.9.

Only five ground stations were equipped to receive Seasat SAR data—Goldstone, California; Fairbanks, Alaska; Merritt Island, Florida; Shoe Cove, Newfoundland; and Oakhanger, England. Consequently, image coverage is limited to North America, parts of the Caribbean and Central America, and parts of western Europe. Inquiries pertaining to Seasat radar image coverage and costs can be made to the Environmental Satellite Data and Information Service (same address as for CZCS data).

Standard products for optically and digitally correlated Seasat data

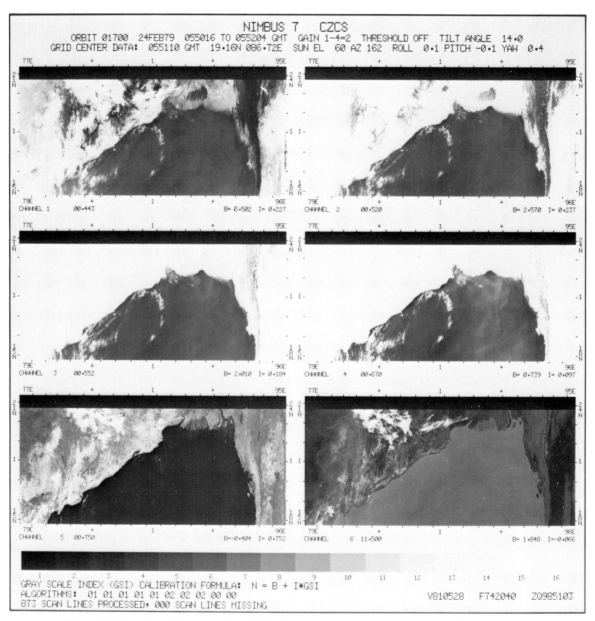

Figure 7.53. Nimbus-7 Coastal Zone Color Scanner (CZCS) images of the Bangladesh coastal region. Each image measures 700 × 1,636 km. Refer to Table 7.8 for wavelength boundaries of each channel. (Courtesy C. J. Robinove and C. Scott Southworth, U.S. Geological Survey.)

TABLE 7.9. Seasat Imaging Radar Characteristics

Antenna type	Synthetic aperture
Antenna depression angles (full scene)	
Near range	73°
Far range	67°
Radar wavelength	23.5 cm (L-band)
Polarization	Horizontal transmit, horizontal receive (H-H)
Range and azimuth resolution	
Optically correlated	40 m
Digitally correlated	25 m
Swath width	100 km

include 1:500,000-scale paper prints, duplicate negatives, and positive transparencies. Digitally processed scenes are also available on 9-track CCTs.

SPACE SHUTTLE

The NASA Space Shuttle is a new manned spacecraft system that can be used (1) as an orbital laboratory for highly specialized scientific experiments, (2) as a platform for remote-sensing observations, and (3) as a vehicle from which to launch or retrieve earth-orbiting satellites. Unlike previous spacecraft, the shuttle vehicle is reusable for round-trip flights into space. Shuttle missions will usually last from 3 to 30 days.

In November 1981 Space Shuttle *Columbia* carried its first payload of scientific experiments into earth orbit. One component of this payload was the Shuttle Imaging Radar (SIR-A) system. It performed flawlessly and imaged a land-water area of about 10 million km^2 between 41° N latitude and 36° S latitude; parts of all continents except Antarctica were imaged. The sensor was in operation for 8 hr.

SIR-A possessed many of the characteristics of the SAR system that operated on Seasat in 1978. The principal difference between the two radars was that SIR-A incorporated a much smaller depression angle (40° versus 66° at center of ground swath). In areas of high relief, the 40° depression angle greatly reduced layover effects that characterized Seasat land images. Significant characteristics of the SIR-A sensor are summarized in Table 7.10.

SIR-A acquired images of a wide range of different surfaces (Figures 7.26, 7.35, 7.39, and 7.41). The images, like those from Seasat, are currently finding application in a number of earth-science disciplines. Optically processed SIR-A images in film or print forms (1:500,000 scale) are available from the National Space Science Data Center (same address as for HCMM data).

TABLE 7.10. Shuttle Imaging Radar Characteristics

Antenna type	Synthetic aperture
Antenna depression angle (full scene)	
Near range	43°
Far range	37°
Radar wavelength	23.5 cm (L-band)
Polarization	Horizontal transmit, horizontal receive (HH)
Range and azimuth resolution	40 m
Swath width	50 km
Nominal altitude of Space Shuttle	259 km

PROBLEMS

1. Obtain comparative photographic, thermal infrared, and SLAR imagery of a test area in your region. Beginning with what you regard as the lowest-quality imagery, delineate principal hydrographic features, prominent man-made structures, landforms, vegetative types, agricultural areas, and so on. Then prepare a brief written report of your findings.

2. Obtain comparative earth-satellite imagery and conventional optical imagery of a local area. Beginning with the satellite imagery, attempt to classify the dominant terrain features, agricultural patterns, and vegetation types. Repeat the process with aerial photography. Then prepare transparent overlays from each set of imagery for a graphical comparison of results. Verify results by ground checks wherever feasible.

References

Bare, J. E. and L. F. Dellwig. 1978. *Shuttle experimental radar for geological exploration.* University of Kansas, Lawrence, RSL Technical Report 364-1, 84 pp., illus.

Barr, D. J. 1968. *Use of side-looking airborne radar (SLAR) imagery for engineering soils studies.* U.S. Army Engineer Topographic Laboratories, Fort Belvoir, Va., Technical Report 46-TR, 156 pp., illus.

Begni, G. 1982. Selection of the optimum spectral bands for the SPOT satellite. *Photogrammetric Engineering and Remote Sensing* 48:1613–1620, illus.

Berlin, G. L. and G. G. Schaber. 1971. Geology and radar mosaics. *Journal of Geological Education* 19:212–217, illus.

Berlin, G. L., G. G. Schaber, and K. C. Horstman. 1980. Possible fault detection in Cottonball Basin, California: An application of radar remote sensing. *Remote Sensing of Environment* 10:33–42, illus.

Berlin, G. L., G. G. Schaber, R. C. Kozak, and P. Chavez, Jr. 1982. Cliff and slope topography of part of the Grand Canyon, Arizona, as characterized on a Seasat radar image. *Remote Sensing of Environment* 12:81–85, illus.

Blom, Ronald G., Robert E. Crippen, and Charles Elachi. 1984. Detection of subsurface features in Seasat radar images of Means Valley, Mojave Desert, California. *Geology* 12:346–349, illus.

Bryan, M. Leonard. 1979. The effect of radar azimuth angle on cultural data. *Photogrammetric Engineering and Remote Sensing* 45:1097–1107, illus.

Buettner, K. J. K. and C. D. Kern. 1965. Determination of infrared sensitivities of terrestrial surfaces. *Journal of Geophysical Research* 70:1329–1337, illus.

Cannon, P. Jan. 1980. Applications of radar imagery to arctic and subarctic problems. In *Radar geology: an assessment.* Jet Propulsion Laboratory, Pasadena, Calif., JPL Publication 80-61, pp. 265–274, illus.

Chevrel, Michele, Michel Courtois, and Gilbert Weill. 1981. The SPOT satellite remote sensing mission. *Photogrammetric Engineering and Remote Sensing* 47:1163–1171, illus.

Daily, M., C. Elachi, T. Farr, W. Stromberg, S. Williams, and G. Schaber. 1978. *Application of multispectral radar and Landsat imagery to geologic mapping in Death Valley.* Jet Propulsion Laboratory, Pasadena, Calif., JPL Publication 78-19, 47 pp., illus.

Data Management Subcommittee. 1982. *Recommendations concerning satellite-acquired resource data.* The Geosat Committee, Inc., San Francisco, 23 pp.

Doyle, Frederick J. 1982. *Status of satellite remote sensing programs.* U.S. Geological Survey, Reston, Va., Open-File Report 82-237, 21 pp., illus.

Dunning, C. E. and Fred E. Nicodemus. 1965. Targets. In *Handbook of military infrared technology.* Government Printing Office, Washington D.C., pp. 57–94.

Elachi, Charles. 1982. Radar images of the earth from space. *Scientific American* 247:54–61, illus.

Fagerlund, E., B. Kleman, L. Sellin, and H. Svensson. 1970. Physical studies of nature by thermal mapping. *Earth-Science Reviews* 6:169–180, illus.

Ford, J. P. 1980. Analysis of Seasat orbital radar imagery for geologic mapping in the Appalachian Valley and Ridge Province, Tennessee-Kentucky, Virginia. In *Radar geology: an assessment.* Jet Propulsion Laboratory, Pasadena, Calif., JPL Publication 80-61, pp. 75–111, illus.

Ford, J. P., R. G. Blom, M. L. Bryan, M. I. Daily, T. H. Dixon, C. Elachi, and E. C. Xenos. 1980. *Seasat views North America, the Caribbean, and western Europe with imaging radar.* Jet Propulsion Laboratory, Pasadena, Calif., JPL Publication 80-67, 139 pp., illus.

Ford, J. P., J. B. Cimino, and C. Elachi. 1983. *Space Shuttle Columbia views the world with imaging radar: The SIR-A experiment.* Jet Propulsion Laboratory, Pasadena, Calif., JPL Publication 82-95, 177 pp., illus.

Gelnett, R. H. 1978. Importance of look direction and depression angles in geologic applications of SLAR. MARS Associates, Inc., Phoenix, Arizona, Technical Report TR-04823, 15 pp., illus.

Gelnett, R. H., L. F. Dellwig, and J. E. Bare. 1978. Increased visibility from the invisible: a comparison of radar and Landsat in tropical environments. In *Twelfth International Symposium on Remote Sensing of Environment.* Environmental Research Institute of Michigan, Ann Arbor, Mich., pp. 2205–2216, illus.

Gower, J. F. 1983. Coastal Zone Colour Scanner (CZCS), new spectral data for water. *Remote Sensing in Canada* 11:10.

Graham, L. C. 1976. Earth resources radar stereo considerations. Goodyear Aerospace Corporation, Litchfield Park, Ariz., 13 pp., illus.

Heller, Robert C. and Joseph J. Ulliman (editors). 1983. Forest resource assessments.

In *Manual of remote sensing*, 2nd ed. American Society of Photogrammetry, Falls Church, Va., pp. 2229–2324, illus.

Hirsh, S. N., R. F. Kruckeberg, and F. H. Madden. 1971. The bispectral forest fire detection system. In *Proceedings, seventh international symposium on remote sensing of environment*. Environmental Research Institute of Michigan, Ann Arbor, Mich., pp. 2253–2272, illus.

Jackson, P. L. 1980. Multichannel SAR in geologic interpretation: an appraisal. In *Radar geology: an assessment*. Jet Propulsion Laboratory, Pasadena, Calif., JPL Publication 80-61, pp. 233–250, illus.

Jensen, Homer, L. C. Graham, Leonard J. Porcello, and Emmett N. Leith. 1977. Side-looking airborne radar. *Scientific American* 237:84–95, illus.

Jet Propulsion Laboratory. 1983. *Shuttle imaging radar-C (SIR-C)*. Pasadena, Calif., JPL Publication 83-47, 12 pp., illus.

Kahle, Anne B. and Alexander F. H. Goetz. 1983. Mineralogic information from a new airborne thermal infrared multispectral scanner. *Science* 222:24–27, illus.

Kozak, R. C., G. L. Berlin, and P. S. Chavez, Jr. 1981. Seasat radar image of the Phoenix, Arizona, region. *International Journal of Remote Sensing* 2:295–298, illus.

Landgrebe, D. A. 1974. Machine processing of remotely sensed data. In ERTS image interpretation workshop syllabus. U.S. Geological Survey, Sioux Falls, S.Dak., Open-File Report 75-196, sec. XIV, pp. 1–36, illus.

LaPrade, G. L. 1974. Radar polarization effects for imaging radars. Goodyear Aerospace Corporation, Litchfield Park, Ariz., 20 pp., illus.

———. 1976. Basic concepts of synthetic-aperture, side-looking radar. Goodyear Aerospace Corporation, Litchfield Park, Ariz., 8 pp., illus.

LaPrade, G. L. and E. S. Leonardo. 1969. Elevations from radar imagery. *Photogrammetric Engineering* 35:366–377, illus.

Lillesand, Thomas M. and Ralph W. Kiefer. 1979. *Remote sensing and image interpretation*. John Wiley and Sons, New York, 612 pp., illus.

Madden, Forrest H. 1973. *Performance requirements for airborne infrared forest fire surveillance equipment*. U.S. Forest Service, Intermountain Forest and Range Experiment Station, Research Note INT-167, 7 pp., illus.

McCauley, J. F., G. G. Schaber, C. S. Breed, M. J. Grolier, C. V. Haynes, B. Issawi, C. Elachi, and R. Blom. 1982. Subsurface valleys and geoarcheology of the eastern Sahara revealed by shuttle radar. *Science* 218:1004–1019, illus.

McColl, W. D., R. A. Neville, and S. M. Till. 1983. Multi-detector electro-optical imaging scanner MEIS-II. Paper presented at the Eighth Canadian Symposium on Remote Sensing, Montreal.

Moore, R. K. 1966. *Radar as a sensor*. University of Kansas, Lawrence, Report 61-7, 55 pp., illus.

Parry, J. T. 1973. *The role of AN/APS-94D X-band SLAR in terrain analysis*. Defense Research Board of Canada, Ottawa, Ont., 128 pp., illus.

Peake, W. H. and T. L. Oliver. 1971. *The response of terrestrial surfaces at microwave frequencies*. Ohio State University Electroscience Laboratory, Columbus, Report APAL-TR-70-301, 255 pp., illus.

Peterson, R. K. 1976. *Wide dynamic range color radar imagery*. Goodyear Aerospace Corporation, Litchfield Park, Ariz., 23 pp., illus.

Pravdo, S. H., B. Huneycutt, B. M. Holt, and D. N. Held. 1983. *Seasat synthetic-aperture radar data user's manual*. Jet Propulsion Laboratory, Pasadena, Calif., JPL Publication 82-90, 108 pp., illus.

Raytheon Co. 1969. *Training course on data reduction of radar topographic imagery.* National Technical Information Service, Springfield, Va., 6 chapters, illus.

Rinker, J. N. 1975. *Remote sensing notes-infrared thermal.* EROS Data Center, U.S. Geological Survey, Sioux Falls, S.Dak., 13 pp., illus.

Rydstrom, H. O., G. L. LaPrade, E. S. Leonardo, and L. F. Dellwig. 1979. *Radar imagery interpretation adaptable to planetary investigations.* Goodyear Aerospace Corporation, Litchfield Park, Ariz., 228 pp., illus.

Sabins, Floyd F., Jr. 1978. *Remote sensing, principles and interpretation.* W. H. Freeman and Co., San Francisco, 426 pp., illus.

———. 1980. Seasat radar image of San Andreas fault, California. *American Association of Petroleum Geologists Bulletin* 64:619–628, illus.

Schaber, G. G., G. L. Berlin, and W. E. Brown, Jr. 1976. Variations in surface roughness within Death Valley, California: geologic evaluation of 25-cm wavelength radar images. *Geological Society of America Bulletin* 87:29–41, illus.

Schaber, G. G., G. L. Berlin, and R. J. Pike. 1980. Terrain analysis procedures for modeling radar backscatter. In *Radar geology: an assessment.* Jet Propulsion Laboratory, Pasadena, Calif., JPL Publication 80-61, pp. 168–199, illus.

Short, Nicholas M. 1982. *The Landsat tutorial workbook.* Government Printing Office, Washington, D.C., NASA Reference Publication 1078, 553 pp., illus.

Short, Nicholas M., and Locke M. Stuart, Jr. 1982. *The Heat Capacity Mapping Mission (HCMM) anthology.* Government Printing Office, Washington, D.C., NASA Special Paper 465, 264 pp., illus.

Simonett, David S. and Robert E. Davis. 1983. Image analysis—active microwave. In *Manual of remote sensing,* 2nd ed. American Society of Photogrammetry, Falls Church, Va., pp. 1125–1181, illus.

Southworth, C. Scott. 1983. *Index of earth resources observation systems.* U.S. Geological Survey, Reston, Va., pamphlet, illus.

Stingelin, Ronald W. 1969. Operational airborne thermal imaging studies. *Geophysics* 34:760–771, illus.

Thompson, Leslie L. 1979. Remote sensing using solid-state array technology. *Photogrammetric Engineering and Remote Sensing* 45:47–55, illus.

U.S. Department of the Army. 1966. Surveillance system, infrared AN/UAS-4A. U.S. Department of the Army, Washington, D.C., 7 chapters plus appendix, illus.

U.S. Departments of the Army, Navy, and Air Force. 1977. *Image interpretation handbook.* Government Printing Office, Washington, D.C., Vol. 1, 7 chapters plus appendix, illus.

User Services Section. 1982a. Landsat-4. *Landsat Data Users Notes* 23:1–12, illus.

———. 1982b. International land satellite programs. *Landsat Data Users Notes* 24:4–6.

▨ Chapter 8

Geographic Information Systems and Land-Use–Land-Cover Mapping

▨ PLANNING PHASES

The process of environmental and natural-resources planning and management may be arbitrarily divided into four chronological phases:

1. *Awareness and organization:* The recognition that a problem exists and that detailed studies based on specific objectives will be required for successful planning.
2. *Inventory and data handling:* The collecting, collating, analyzing, and reporting of information on land and natural resources and associated socioeconomic conditions.
3. *Decision making:* Consideration of alternatives, evaluation of impacts of proposed actions, and resolution of conflicts.
4. *Action:* Converting plans to action.

This chapter is largely devoted to the second phase, that is, to the role computerized geographic information systems (GIS) can play in inventory and data handling activities and land use and land cover—an important and necessary element in all comprehensive geographic information systems.

▓ OVERVIEW OF GEOGRAPHIC INFORMATION SYSTEMS

Planning organizations need vast amounts of accurate and timely information on physical resources and related socioeconomic factors to help guide their management and planning decisions. This ideally requires the organization and storage of what is known and the provision for rapid information retrieval in forms acceptable to an array of users. Over the past several years, a number of different computer-based systems have been developed to help meet this need.

A GIS is designed to accept, organize, statistically analyze, and display diverse types of spatial information that are digitally referenced to a common coordinate system of a particular projection and scale (Figure 8.1). Each variable is archived in a computer-compatible digital format as a geographically referenced layer or plane called a *data base*. Data bases can represent many different kinds of areal information; representative examples include terrain descriptors, soil and lithology types, climate, land use, land cover, population density, land ownership, and digital image radiance data. When digitally registered to each other, the data sets of n layers compose the GIS *data bank* related to a given problem (Figure 8.2).

If each data set is visualized as an independent overlay for a given base map, then two or more data observations can be analyzed for a single location—a technique known as *overlay* or *composite analysis*. The computer search for

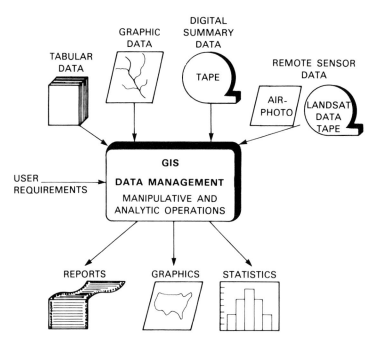

Figure 8.1. Schematic diagram showing a generalized geographic information system (GIS) for data management (Short 1982).

such formatted data is analogous to that of passing a needle through each registered map overlay (Figure 8.2).

From the foregoing discussion, it is apparent that a geographic information system has a dual data-handling responsibility (i.e., it must handle both *positional* or *map data* as well as *attribute* or *descriptive data*). Map data are explicit locational identifiers (i.e., Cartesian coordinates) associated with the spatial entities of points, lines, and areas or polygons (Figure 8.3). Attributes can represent both qualitative data (e.g., soil type) and quantitative data (e.g., soil texture, soil salinity, soil porosity) keyed to each spatial entity.

GEOGRAPHIC INFORMATION SYSTEM CAPABILITIES

A state-of-the-art GIS should be capable of the following:

1. Accepting data inputs in one or more formats (e.g., analog map and overlay information, tabulations, digital-image data)
2. Storing and maintaining information with the necessary spatial relationships

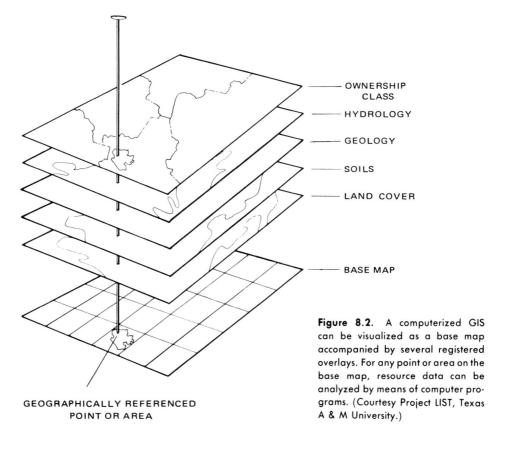

OWNERSHIP CLASS

HYDROLOGY

GEOLOGY

SOILS

LAND COVER

BASE MAP

GEOGRAPHICALLY REFERENCED
POINT OR AREA

Figure 8.2. A computerized GIS can be visualized as a base map accompanied by several registered overlays. For any point or area on the base map, resource data can be analyzed by means of computer programs. (Courtesy Project LIST, Texas A & M University.)

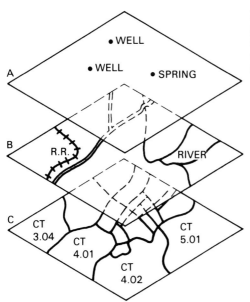

Figure 8.3. Schematic representation of geographic phenomena: (A) point phenomena, (B) linear phenomena, and (C) polygon, or area, phenomena, in this case census tracts. (Adapted from Greenlee 1979.)

3. Manipulating data (search and retrieval, computations, etc.) in a timely manner
4. Some level of modeling that takes into account data interrelationships and cause-and-effect responses of the appropriate factors
5. Presenting data outputs in a variety of ways (e.g., tabulations, video displays, and computer-generated maps)

An ideal GIS would be designed to serve diverse users; furthermore, it would be capable of continuously being updated as new data became available. In view of the great amount of information it may use, it is not surprising that a GIS relies heavily on high-speed digital computers, a comprehensive and powerful program or software package, and a variety of peripheral input-output devices (Figure 8.4).

ELEMENTS OF A DIGITAL GEOGRAPHIC INFORMATION SYSTEM

A GIS is built around a framework of five basic technical elements: (1) encoding, (2) data input, (3) data management, (4) manipulative operations, and (5) output products (Figure 8.5). Unless otherwise specified, the following discussion of these elements is largely summarized from the works of Greenlee (1979), Short (1982), and Marble et al. (1983).

Encoding

Two position indexing systems can be used to encode spatial entities that are portrayed as points, lines, or polygons—(1) *grid-cell* or *raster coding* and (2) *polygon* or *vector coding*. Grid-cell coding is conceptually a matrix system superimposed over the geography such that the attribute information can be collected by a systematic array of grid squares or cells. Normally, the information category most dominant for each cell is encoded (Figure 8.6). Because cell size largely determines class accuracy, two methods have emerged to assist in preserving data integrity: (1) decreasing cell size or (2) listing the relative amounts of each data type falling within a cell. Grid cells are functionally identical to the picture elements or pixels that compose a digital image (see Chapter 15).

With polygon coding, the perimeter of each areal unit containing the desired attribute data is digitally encoded and stored. One type of polygon indexing is *topological coding*, whereby arcs are formed by connecting nodes, and polygons are formed by connecting arcs (Figure 8.7). Polygon coding more accurately defines boundaries and requires less computer storage space than does the grid-coding structure.

Data Input

Analog information (e.g., hard-copy map data) is converted to digital domain by the digitization process for GIS input. Methods of data capture are by *manual* or *hand-tracing digitizing* (e.g., tablet or table digitizers) and *automatic digitizing* (e.g., drum or laser-beam scanners). An integral part of

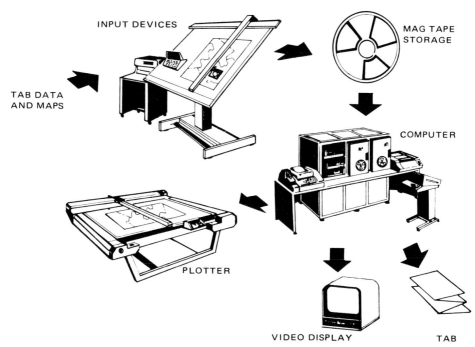

Figure 8.4. Schematic representation of a GIS. In addition to commercial GISs, most digital image processing systems (IPS) can be modified to store and manipulate geographically encoded data (see Chapter 15). (Courtesy Project LIST, Texas A & M University.)

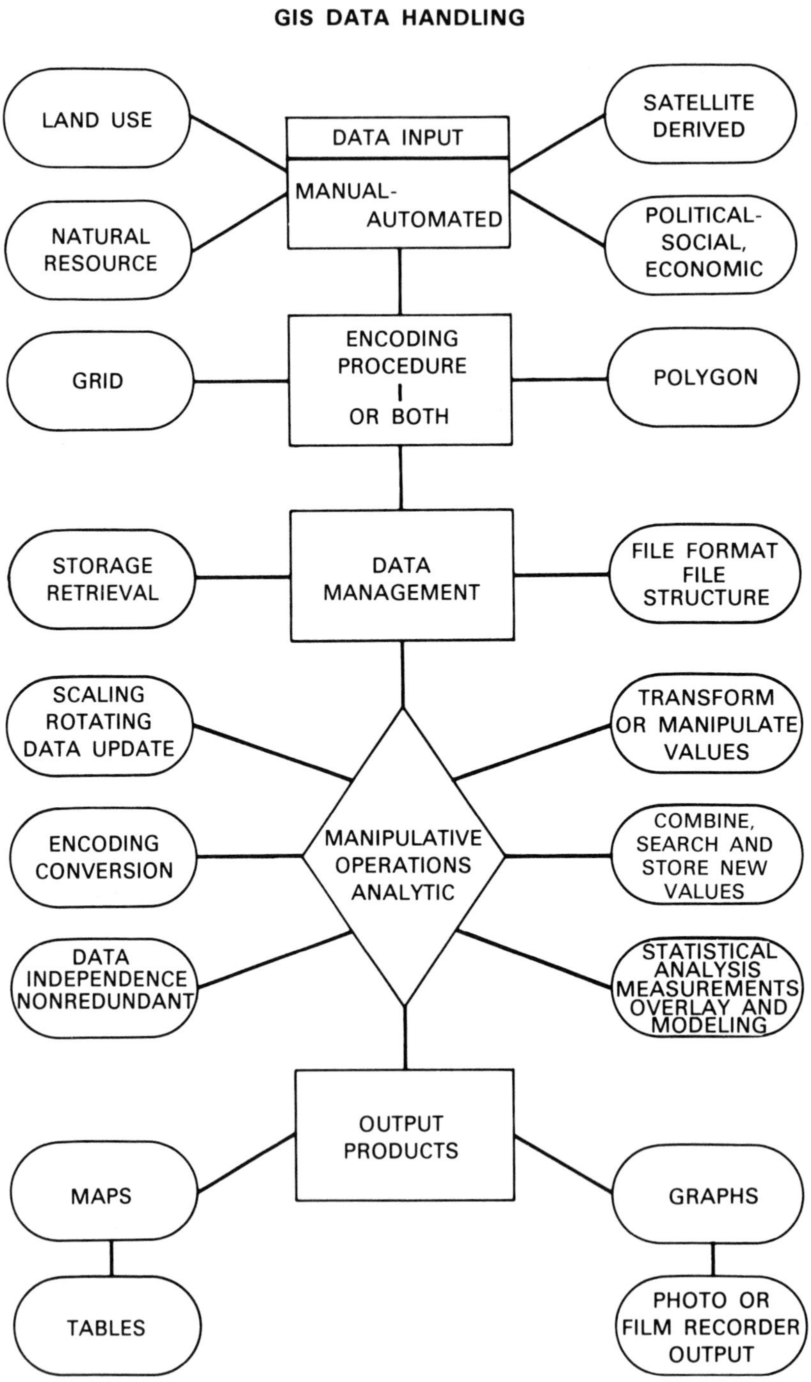

Figure 8.5. Flow diagram of steps in a typical GIS (Short 1982).

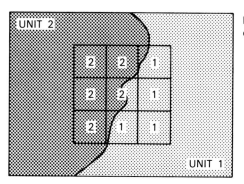

Figure 8.6. Grid-cell coding. (Adapted from Greenlee 1979.)

both methods is a connected display system that enables an operator to edit the data for erroneous values and to recapture omissions. Data already in digital form (e.g., satellite images) usually have to be reformatted and scaled to match the geometry of the GIS reference map projection.

Data Management

Because of the large volume and variety of data, plus the wide range of potential applications, data management is extremely important for the successful and efficient operation of a GIS. The management system consists of a series of computer programs to perform all data entry, storage, retrieval, and maintenance tasks.

Manipulative Operations

GISs are capable of performing two kinds of automated analysis: (1) *surface analysis* and (2) *overlay analysis*. Surface analysis applies to intravariable relationships that exist within one data plane. For example, soil categories can be grouped together, analyzed, and labeled according to agricultural value (McFarland 1982). Area measurements could also be made for both the

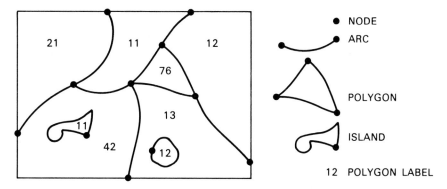

Figure 8.7. Topological elements of a polygon map (Mitchell et al. 1977).

original and interpretive data bases. Most surface analysis produces new variables that can be applied to other surface or overlay analysis procedures.

A GIS is capable of performing automated overlay analysis that applies to intervariable relationships created by overlaying or stacking two or more data planes. Thus, location is held constant and several variables are simultaneously evaluated. Because raster formatting spatially prearranges data, vector-formatted information is often converted to a grid-cell structure for overlay analysis processing to improve data-handling efficiency.

One of the most common uses of overlay analysis is to derive statistical data and special maps describing shared characteristics. For example, given the data bases of land use and land cover and of topographic slope, one could ascertain how many hectares of agricultural land exceed a particular slope. An interpretive map could also be produced to show where these conditions were met. This new data set could be integrated with other data bases (e.g., soil type, land ownership) for additional analysis (McFarland 1982).

Quantitative interpretation by overlay analysis is accomplished by establishing a numerical index for each qualitative variable. For example, with vegetation type, soil type, and topography data bases, an interpretation of erosional properties could be calculated by using quantitative indices for these three variables as they relate to erosion potential (Figure 8.8). Overlay analysis also allows data variables to be weighted according to their relative importance. In the previous example, topography may be determined to be more important than either vegetation type or soil type in determining erosion potential.

By using quantitative interpretation and weighting techniques, data bank variables can be used with two types of prediction models. For example, *evaluative models* can be developed to assess environmental characteristics (e.g., wildlife habitat, forest fire potential, groundwater contamination, accessibility to transportation systems), and *allocative models* can be developed to indicate areas best suited for specific land uses (e.g., urban development, transportation routing, irrigated agriculture development).

Johnson and Loveland (1980) developed a GIS allocative model to evaluate several types of geobased data for determining land irrigation suitabilities in the Stanfield, Oregon, area. The variables of existing land cover, soil characteristics, and topographic slope (Figures 8.9, 8.10, and 8.11) were used to create a composite irrigability map that defined the physical capability of the land to support irrigation development (Figure 8.12). Two additional variables, horizontal and vertical distance from water (Figures 8.13 and 8.14), were then evaluated in terms of development costs to determine their effect on the location of irrigation development (pumping costs increase as distance from water increases, and the greater the pump lift the greater the cost of providing water). The land-factor irrigability map (Figure 8.12) was then digitally merged with the distance-from-water data (economic factors) to modify irrigability potential (Figure 8.15). This revised analysis predicted the actual location of irrigation development.

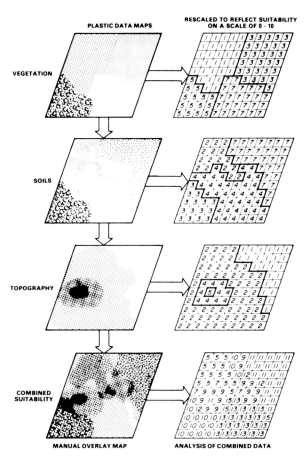

Figure 8.8. Overlay analysis using a grid model (Short 1982).

PLASTIC DATA MAPS

RESCALED TO REFLECT SUITABILITY ON A SCALE OF 0 - 10

VEGETATION

SOILS

TOPOGRAPHY

COMBINED SUITABILITY

MANUAL OVERLAY MAP   ANALYSIS OF COMBINED DATA

DATA VARIABLE COMBINATION

GRID MODEL

Output Products

A GIS can retrieve and display data in graphic or tabular forms, or both. Most systems are capable of producing hard-copy charts, scatter diagrams, tables, and maps in various forms and sizes. In addition, all systems have a TV monitor on which graphic or tabular information for segments of a data base or multiple data bases can be displayed (Figure 8.4). This represents *interactive analysis* because the retrieval and display of data are in near real time (see Chapter 15).

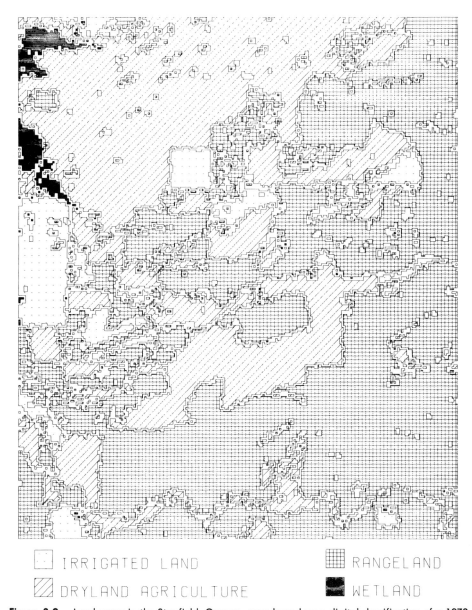

Figure 8.9. Land cover in the Stanfield, Oregon, area based on a digital classification of a 1972 Landsat Multispectral Scanner (MSS) image. The assumption of the classification scheme is that both dryland agriculture and rangeland constitute potentially irrigable land areas, whereas wetlands are not considered capable of irrigation development. (Courtesy Thomas R. Loveland, Technicolor Government Services, EROS Data Center.)

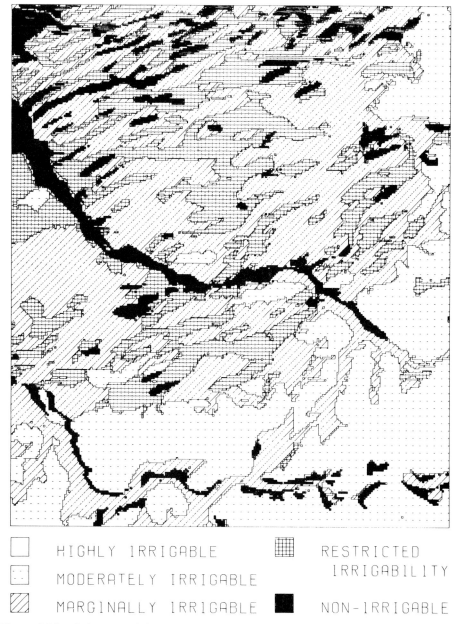

Figure 8.10. Soil potential for irrigation based on an evaluation of soil characteristics (e.g., thickness, texture, salinity). (Courtesy Thomas R. Loveland, Technicolor Government Services, EROS Data Center.)

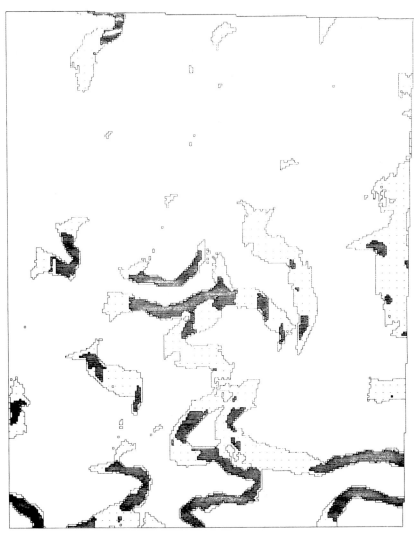

0-6   PERCENT SLOPE

7-12 PERCENT SLOPE

EXCEEDS 12 PERCENT SLOPE

Figure 8.11.   Percent slope calculated from digital terrain data: slopes greater than 12 percent—unirrigable by any present irrigation system; 7–12 percent slope—irrigable by center-pivot irrigation systems; and 0–6 percent slope—irrigable by most conventional irrigation methods. (Courtesy Thomas R. Loveland, Technicolor Government Services, EROS Data Center.)

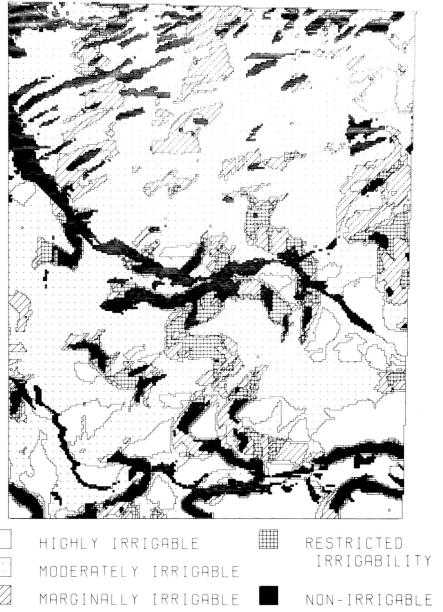

	HIGHLY IRRIGABLE	⊞	RESTRICTED IRRIGABILITY
	MODERATELY IRRIGABLE		
▨	MARGINALLY IRRIGABLE	■	NON-IRRIGABLE

Figure 8.12. Composite irrigability based on land cover, soil characteristics, and percent slope. (Courtesy Thomas R. Loveland, Technicolor Government Services, EROS Data Center.)

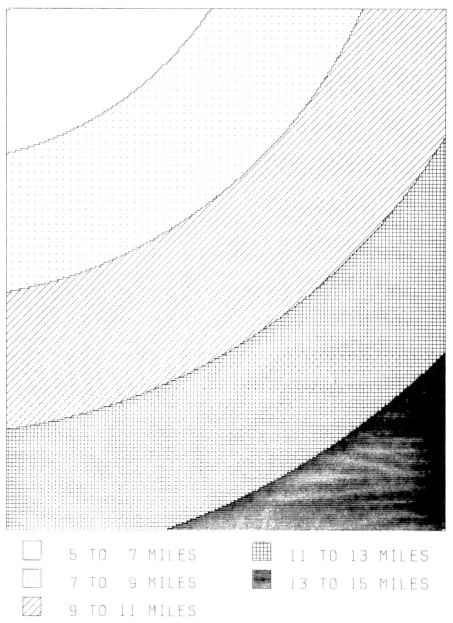

Figure 8.13.   Horizontal distance from water. (Courtesy Thomas R. Loveland, Technicolor Government Services, EROS Data Center.)

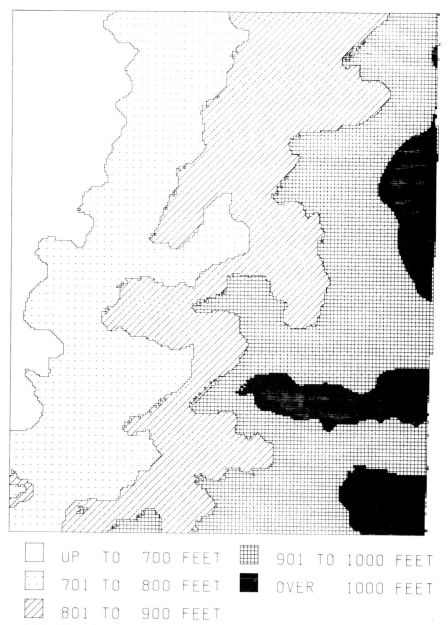

UP   TO   700 FEET   901 TO 1000 FEET

701 TO   800 FEET   OVER   1000 FEET

801 TO   900 FEET

Figure 8.14.   Vertical distance from water. (Courtesy Thomas R. Loveland, Technicolor Government Services, EROS Data Center.)

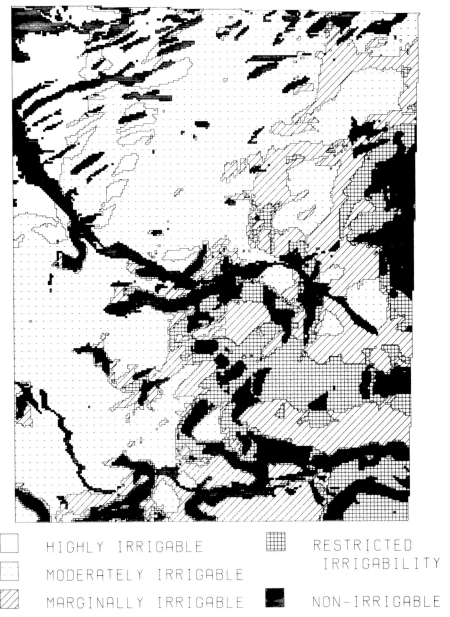

Figure 8.15. Composite irrigability including economic considerations (distance from water). Compare with Figure 8.12. (Courtesy Thomas R. Loveland, Technicolor Government Services, EROS Data Center.)

LAND USE AND LAND COVER DEFINED

Although the terms *land use* and *land cover* have been used interchangeably, it is important to remember that the two expressions are not necessarily synonymous. Land use encompasses several different aspects of man's relationship to the environment (e.g., activity, ownership, land quality). By comparison, land cover is represented by the natural and artificial compositions covering the earth's surface at a certain location. For example, the land cover for a given area might be classified as deciduous forest when the land use is that of a wildlife refuge or mining operation (Figure 8.16). The distinction between the two terms is particularly important when such information is interpreted from aerial photographs and electro-optical images.

CLASSIFICATION SYSTEMS

Classification systems for describing *land use* and *land cover* have been the subject of extensive research and symposia in North America and Europe for more than three decades. During the last decade, the major emphasis has been on the development of classification schemes that incorporate information

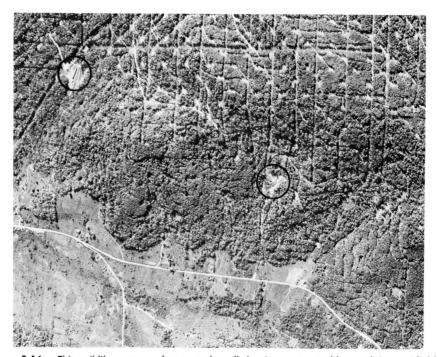

Figure 8.16.   This quiltlike pattern of trees and small clearings connected by roads is an oil field in McKean County, Pennsylvania. Two pumping stations are encircled. The difference between older and newer drillings is shown by the regrowth of vegetation. Scale is 1:20,000. (Courtesy U.S. Department of Agriculture.)

derived from remotely sensed data. Although no system will probably ever be developed that is universally acceptable, several classification schemes are being used at the national, regional, and local levels (Jensen et al. 1983).

The expandable system devised by the U.S. Geological Survey (USGS) (Anderson et al. 1976) represents a national classification scheme that has achieved widespread acceptance and is being used in a number of operational mapping programs. With two levels of detail, it can be used with remotely sensed data at various resolutions and scales. It has also served as a framework for more detailed regional and local classification systems because it is sufficiently inclusive (Table 8.1). Much of the remainder of the chapter is devoted to that national system, herein referred to as the USGS system.

FEATURES OF THE USGS SYSTEM

The USGS hierarchical system (i.e., ordered classes) incorporates the features of several existing classification systems that are amenable to data derived from remote sensors, including imagery and photography from satellites and high-altitude aircraft. The system attempts to meet the need for current overview assessments of land use and land cover on a basis that is uniform in categorization at the first and second levels of detail. It is intentionally left open-ended so that various levels of government, for example, may have flexibility in developing more detailed classifications at the third and fourth levels. Such an approach permits various agencies to meet their particular needs for land-resource management and planning and at the same time remain compatible with the national system (Table 8.1). For detailed descriptions of the 9 level I and 37 level II categories, the reader is referred to Anderson et al. (1976).

The types of land-use and land-cover categorization developed in the USGS classification system can be related to systems for classification of land capability, vulnerability to certain management practices, potential for any particular activity, or land value, either intrinsic or speculative. The functions that lands fill will usually be associated with certain types of cover. Thus, the image interpreter attempts to identify land-cover patterns and shapes as a means of deriving information about land use (Figure 8.17).

CLASSIFICATION CRITERIA

According to the USGS, a land-use–land-cover classification system that can effectively employ orbital and high-altitude remote-sensor data should meet the following criteria:

1. Interpretation accuracy in the identification of land-use and land-cover categories from remote-sensor data should be 85 percent or greater.
2. The accuracy of interpretation for the several categories should be about equal.

TABLE 8.1. Land-Use and Land-Cover Classification System for Use With Remote-Sensor Data[a]	
Level I (and Map Color)	**Level II**
1 Urban or built-up land (red)	11 Residential
	12 Commercial and services
	13 Industrial
	14 Transportation, communications, and utilities
	15 Industrial and commercial complexes
	16 Mixed urban or built-up land
	17 Other urban or built-up land
2 Agricultural land (light brown)	21 Cropland and pasture
	22 Orchards, groves, vineyards, nurseries, and ornamental horticultural areas
	23 Confined feeding operations
	24 Other agricultural land
3 Rangeland (light orange)	31 Herbaceous rangeland
	32 Shrub and brush rangeland
	33 Mixed rangeland
4 Forest land (green)	41 Deciduous forest land
	42 Evergreen forest land
	43 Mixed forest land
5 Water (dark blue)	51 Streams and canals
	52 Lakes
	53 Reservoirs
	54 Bays and estuaries
6 Wetland (light blue)	61 Forest wetland
	62 Nonforested wetland
7 Barren land (gray)..................	71 Dry salt flats
	72 Beaches
	73 Sandy areas other than beaches
	74 Bare, exposed rock
	75 Strip mines, quarries, and gravel pits
	76 Transitional areas
	77 Mixed barren land
8 Tundra (green-gray)	81 Shrub and brush tundra
	82 Herbaceous tundra
	83 Bare ground tundra
	84 Wet tundra
	85 Mixed tundra
9 Perennial snow or ice (white)	91 Perennial snowfields
	92 Glaciers

[a]Level I is based primarily on surface cover; level II is derived from both cover and use. Color codes are based on recommendations of the International Geographical Union.

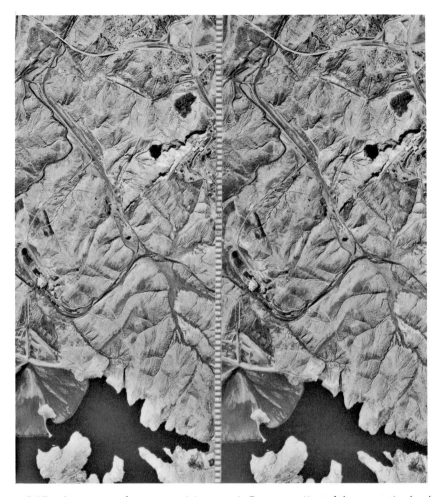

Figure 8.17. Stereogram of a copper-mining area in Tennessee. Most of the vegetation has been killed by smelter fumes. (Courtesy Tennessee Valley Authority.)

3. Repeatable or repetitive results should be obtainable from one interpreter to another and from one time of sensing to another.
4. The classification system should be applicable over extensive areas.
5. The categorization should permit vegetation and other types of land cover to be used as surrogates for activity.
6. The classification system should be suitable for use with remote-sensor data obtained at different times of the year.
7. Effective use of subcategories that can be obtained from ground surveys or from the use of larger-scale or enhanced remote-sensor data should be possible.
8. Aggregation of categories must be possible.

9. Comparison with future land-use data should be possible.
10. Multiple uses of land should be recognized when possible.

For land-use and land-cover data needed for planning and management, accuracy of interpretation at the generalized first and second levels is satisfactory when the interpreter makes the correct interpretation 85 to 90 percent of the time. Except for urban and built-up areas, this can often be achieved with satellite imagery. For regulation of land use or for tax assessment, for example, greater accuracy may be required. And greater accuracy will normally imply higher cost.

The problem of classifying *multiple uses* occurring on a single parcel of land is not easily solved. Multiple uses may occur simultaneously, as in the instance of agricultural land or forest land being used for recreational activities, hunting, or camping. Uses may also occur alternately, as would be the case with a major reservoir that provided flood control during spring runoff and generated power during summer peak-demand periods. All of these activities would not be detected on a single aerial image; thus the selected categorization may be necessarily based on the dominant or apparent use on the date of the sensor image (Figure 8.18).

Vertical arrangements of land uses above or below terrain surfaces produce added complexities for image interpreters. Mineral deposits under croplands or forests, electrical transmission lines crossing pastures, garages underground or on roofs of buildings, and subways beneath urban areas all exemplify situations which must be resolved by individual users and compilers of land-use data.

▨ MINIMUM AREAS AND IMAGE RESOLUTION

The minimum area that can be classified as to land use and land cover depends on (1) the scale and resolution of the original sensor image or data source, (2) the scale of data compilation or image interpretation, and (3) the final scale of the land-use information or map. It is difficult to delineate and symbolize any map area smaller than 0.25 to 0.5 cm on a side. Actual ground area represented by such parcels depends on the scale of the map.

A wide variety of remote-sensing systems and imagery can be used for the different levels of land-use and land-cover classifications. Each sensor provides a degree of image resolution that is dependent upon flight altitude and effective focal length (or scale). For example, assuming a focal length of 15 cm, the flight altitudes and image scales in Table 8.2 would be appropriate when manual (nonautomated) interpretation is anticipated.

The foregoing recommendations are approximate guidelines and not absolutes. With future technological advances, such tabulations will need to be revised. In fact, the entire classification system may undergo a complete metamorphosis as greater dependence is placed on automatic data analysis and automatic image interpretation.

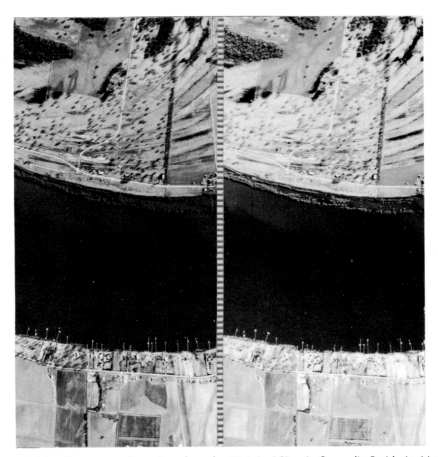

Figure 8.18.   Stereogram of a section along the Mississippi River in Concordia Parish, Louisiana. Land use is predominantly agricultural, but the housing and boat docks along one shoreline would likely be classed as urban-residential or urban-recreational. Scale is about 1:24,000. (Courtesy U.S. Geological Survey.)

TABLE 8.2. Appropriate Flight Altitudes and Image Scales for Manual Interpretation of Land Use and Land Cover		
Classification Level	Sensor Platform or Altitudes	Approximate Range of Image Scales
I	Earth satellites	1:500,000 to 1:3,000,000
II	9,000–12,000 m	1:60,000 to 1:80,000
III	3,000–9,000 m	1:20,000 to 1:60,000
IV	1,200–3,000 m	1:8,000 to 1:20,000

■ EXPANDED CLASSIFICATIONS

One of the primary virtues of a hierarchical classification system is that it is structured for developing categories at more detailed levels. This feature also permits subsequent aggregation or disaggregation of land units without difficulty.

The USGS system is aimed at complete standardization at levels I and II only. Users of the system are encouraged to develop their own subcategories for levels III and IV. Table 8.3 shows how residential land might be subdivided in a level III classification.

This particular breakdown of residential land employs criteria of capacity, type, and permanency of residence as the discriminating factors among classes. Criteria applied to other situations could include density of dwellings, tenancy, age of construction. Such a level III categorization would require use of supplemental information, that is, data not wholly discernible from remote-sensor imagery alone.

A level III land-use and land-cover classification system has been developed for two types of applications in Connecticut (Table 8.4). Once the entire state is mapped at this level, the resulting land-use and land-cover data will be correlated with water-use and evapotranspiration coefficients to produce information (1) for the Connecticut Water Use Information System and (2) for developing water-balance models for the state's drainage basins (National Mapping Division 1982). The primary source materials for the level III interpretations are 1:80,000-scale and 1:12,000-scale black-and-white aerial photographs.

Regarding additional applications at higher levels of land-use and land-cover detail, Berlin and Mitchell (1975) developed a level III classification scheme for use in identifying the man-made causes of groundwater pollution. Baker (1981) developed and tested a level III land-use and land-cover classification system for the management of the North Carolina barrier islands (National Mapping Division 1982).

TABLE 8.3. Example of Subdivisions in a Level III Land-Use–Land-Cover Classification

Level I	Level II	Level III
1 Urban or built-up land	11 Residential	111 Single-family units
		112 Multifamily units
		113 Group quarters
		114 Residential hotels
		115 Mobile-home parks
		116 Transient lodgings
		117 Other

TABLE 8.4. Proposed Connecticut Land-Use and Land-Cover Classification System

Level I	Level II	Level III
1 Urban or built-up land	11 Residential	111 Rural
		112 Low density
		113 Medium density
		114 High density
	12 Commercial and services	121 Low impervious cover
		122 Medium impervious cover
		123 Medium impervious cover, mostly buildings
		124 High impervious cover
		125 High impervious cover, mostly buildings
	13 Industrial	131 Electric-power generating stations
		132 Other industrial
	14 Transportation, communications, and utilities	141 Limited access highways
		142 Railway facilities
		143 Airports
		144 Port facilities
		145 Oil and gas storage facilities
		146 Water treatment facilities
		147 Sewage treatment facilities
		148 Waste disposal sites
		149 Other transportation, communications, and utilities
	17 Other urban or built-up land	171 Golf courses
		172 Other urban or built-up land
2 Agricultural land	21 Cropland and pasture	210 Cropland and pasture
	22 Orchards, groves, vineyards, nurseries, and ornamental horticultural areas	221 Orchards
		222 Greenhouses
		223 Other groves, vineyards, nurseries, and ornamental horticultural areas
	23 Confined feeding operations	231 Dairy confined feeding operations
		232 Poultry confined feeding operations
		233 Other confined feeding operations
	24 Other agricultural land	240 Other agricultural land

TABLE 8.4/*continued*

Level I	Level II	Level III
3 Rangeland	32 Shrub and brush rangeland	321 Eastern brushland
4 Forest land	41 Deciduous forest land	411 Deciduous, 10–50 percent crown cover
		412 Deciduous, greater than 50 percent crown cover
	42 Evergreen forest land	421 Evergreen, 10–50 percent crown cover
		422 Evergreen, greater than 50 percent crown cover
	43 Mixed forest land	431 Mixed, 10–50 percent crown cover
		432 Mixed, greater than 50 percent crown cover
5 Water	51 Streams and canals	510 Streams and canals
	52 Lakes	520 Lakes
	53 Reservoirs	530 Reservoirs
	54 Bays and estuaries	540 Bays and estuaries
6 Wetland	61 Forested wetland	611 Deciduous forested wetland
		612 Evergreen forested wetland
		613 Mixed forested wetland
	62 Nonforested wetland	621 Freshwater nonforested wetland
		622 Brackish and saltwater nonforested wetland
7 Barren land	72 Beaches	720 Beaches
	73 Sandy areas other than beaches	730 Sandy areas other than beaches
	75 Strip mines, quarries, and gravel pits	751 Sand and gravel pits
		752 Other strip mines and quarries
	76 Transitional areas	760 Transitional areas

Courtesy Richard E. Witmer, U.S. Geological Survey.

■ USGS MAPPING AND DATA COMPILATION PROGRAM

Since 1974 the USGS has been engaged in a mapping and data-compilation program to provide nationwide land-use–land-cover and associated polygon maps at scales of 1:250,000 or 1:100,000 and area statistical data. The associated maps portray certain types of natural and administrative areas that can be graphically and statistically compared to the land-use and land-cover information. The maps presently provided by the USGS program consist of the following:

1. Land use and land cover
2. Political units (state and county boundaries)
3. Hydrographic units (watershed boundaries corresponding to USGS-defined drainage basins)
4. Census county subdivisions (boundaries for census tracts within Standard Metropolitan Statistical Areas and for minor civil divisions outside of those areas)
5. Federal land ownership (inventory of ownership for 28 agencies)
6. State land ownership (optional, data provided by cooperating state)

The land-use–land-cover maps are compiled to show level II categories of the USGS classification system (Table 8.1). A primary source material for land-use–land-cover compilation is 1:58,000-scale infrared color photography produced by the National High-Altitude Photography Program (see Chapter 5). Compilation specifications (e.g., minimum sizes of mapping units, minimum densities of appropriate objects, and line weight for delineating polygons) are documented by Loelkes (1977). The specifications ensure the replicability and coherence of the data sets derived from using the USGS classification system (Witmer 1978).

As part of the USGS compilation program, the land-use–land-cover maps and associated maps are digitized, and the resultant digital data bases are handled by a computerized GIS—the *Geographic Information Retrieval and Analysis System* or GIRAS (Mitchell et al. 1977). GIRAS has the capability to input, manipulate, analyze, and output the digital spatial data. The general system flow of GIRAS is presented in Figure 8.19. Digital data-base tapes and a variety of graphical and statistical products can be produced by GIRAS.

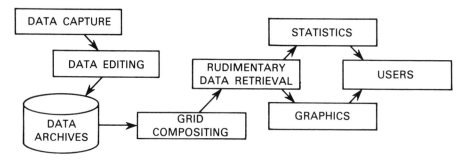

Figure 8.19.   General system flow of GIRAS (Mitchell et al. 1977).

Kleckner (1981) describes several current capabilities of GIRAS:

> One ability is to plot and replicate the land use and land cover and associated map data originally compiled from remotely sensed data. The entire map, selected map parts, or a combination of two or more whole maps or map parts can be plotted using high speed computer-driven plotters. This makes possible the ready comparison of the distribution patterns of different categories. The user can also plot out selected categories of land use and land cover. Changes in map scale and projection can also be accomplished, facilitating the overlay of maps in GIRAS with other maps such as soil maps.
>
> Another application of the GIRAS is computer-assisted cartography leading to the actual color printing of land use and land cover maps. Many manual techniques are involved in preparing a map for lithographic printing. The USGS is now exploring ways to eliminate many of these manual techniques by using digital data and computer techniques.
>
> Another capability involves calculating the area of land use and land cover types within specified units such as counties, census county subdivisions, and drainage basins. Land use and land cover statistical data can then be compared to other data sets.

Additional information on the status of the USGS mapping and data-compilation program and the availability of current data may be obtained from the Office of Geographic Research, National Mapping Division, 521 National Center, U.S. Geological Survey, Reston, VA 22092.

LAND-USE CHANGES

In an analysis of the economic development of any area, land use provides one of the more valuable indicators of rural, urban, and industrial growth. Sequential aerial imagery makes it feasible for a trained interpreter to evaluate land-use patterns at two or more distinct times (Figure 8.20). Comparative coverage in the form of conventional photography is available for many sections of the United States and Canada; some of these exposures date back to the early 1920s. Since 1972, satellite imagery has been obtained at periodic intervals.

Land-use–land-cover classifications at levels I and II are usually adaptable for evaluation of past changes in land use. Problems arise when more detailed breakdowns are desired, because reliable ground checks cannot be made for the older sets of imagery; such verifications may require extensive supplementary surveys, including personal interviews with local residents.

SIGNIFICANCE OF LAND-USE PATTERNS

The varieties of tones, patterns, and spatial arrangements depicted on photographs and images reflect the combined works of nature and the cultural patterns of humankind. Human activities in settling, cultivating, mining, and exploiting various land resources have left characteristic marks upon the

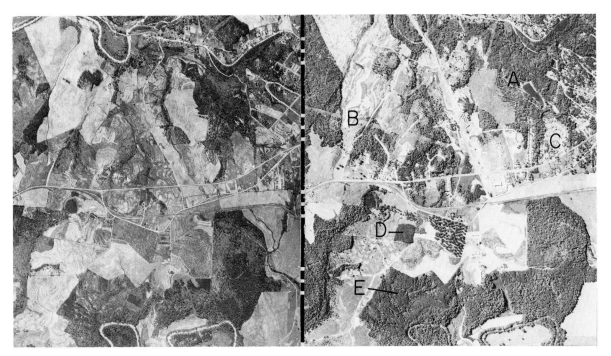

Figure 8.20. Rural area photographed before and after an interval of 16 years. Among changes evident on the right exposure are: (A) a new pond; (B) a cleared right-of-way; (C) a new residential area; (D) a pine plantation; and (E) reversion of an abandoned field to forest land. Scale is about 1:24,000. (Courtesy U.S. Department of Agriculture.)

earth's surface. Many of the telltale markings are unattractive, undesirable, or completely out of phase with the concept of natural resources conservation. Still, much can be learned from studies of these indelible footprints, for certain land-use patterns are repeated wherever humankind vies with natural forces in shaping the environment.

In the early days on the American frontier, travel was usually by wagon road or along navigable streams; hence, the first settlements were found along these natural highways. The advent of systematic land surveys and the development of railroad networks resulted in new settlement patterns and methods of land exploitation. After rural populations migrated to expanding cities, transportation systems became dominated by private automobiles, multilane highway networks, and commercial aircraft. When these kinds of changes are recorded, remotely sensed data become historical documents of considerable value. Examples of changing land-use patterns owing to residential growth are shown in Figures 8.21 and 8.22.

PROBLEMS

1. Investigate the status of a land-resource information system in your region. Prepare a written report or classroom presentation on the capabilities of the system and the user groups that it is designed to serve.

2. Develop and test a set of level III and level IV classifications for at least two of the major categories of land in your region. Use these detailed classifications to prepare a land-use and land-cover map, as outlined in problem 3.

3. Obtain the most recent aerial imagery and topographic quadrangle map available for a local area that can be checked from the ground. Then:
   a. Prepare a radial line plot to adjust the image scale to the scale of the base map (see Chapter 6).
   b. Delineate the effective area of each image frame.
   c. Interpret each frame of imagery and delineate current land-use and land-cover classes. Be sure to include the expanded classes developed in problem 2.

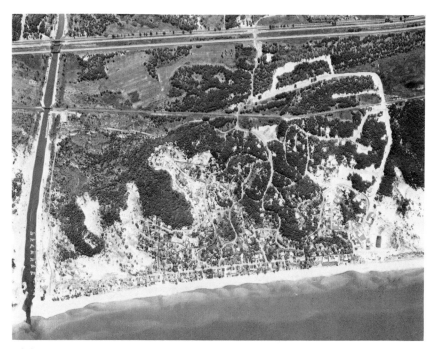

Figure 8.21. Active sand dunes along the Lake Michigan shore in Porter County, Indiana. Much of the stabilizing native vegetation has been removed to make room for expanding residential property. Scale is 1:20,000. (Courtesy U.S. Department of Agriculture.)

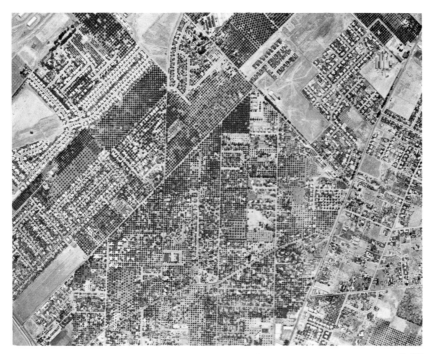

Figure 8.22.   Encroachment of residential property on orchards in Contra Costa County, California. Scale is 1:20,000. (Courtesy U.S. Department of Agriculture.)

Many interpreters have found the following sequence of interpretation to be best for minimizing errors:

1. Waterways and shorelines
2. Rights-of-way
3. Urban and built-up land
4. Forest land
5. Agricultural land
6. Rangeland
7. Barren land
8. Other categories

The exact sequence, of course, will depend on the predominant features and land-use classes actually present in a given locality.

d. Ground check as many image classifications as possible, and make necessary corrections on each frame.

e. Construct a planimetric map (in overlay form) at the exact scale of the topographic base map. Show major transportation routes and drainage features on the overlay.

f. Use a sketchmaster or another device to transfer the land-use–land-cover delineations from the image frames to the planimetric overlay.

g. Determine the area of each major classification (level I or level II). Present in tabular form on a separate sheet.

h. Color the level I categories according to the system proposed in Table 8.1.

i. Ink the final overlay and add the appropriate title and legend. Check the final overlay for errors and omissions by referring to the map correction sheet that follows.

MAP CORRECTION SHEET

Name _____

ITEM		POINTS MAXIMUM	POINTS AWARDED

MAP BORDER AND BOUNDARY

Border too wide	Border not straight		
Border too narrow	Border not uniform width		
Border margin incorrect	Paper incorrect size		
Trim lines not erased		(10)	_____

TITLE

Letters too small	Words misspelled		
Letters too large	Words not spaced evenly		
Lettering faulty	Abbreviations incorrect		
Title incomplete	Date missing		
Title misproportioned		(15)	_____

LEGEND: CLASSIFICATIONS AND SYMBOLS

Symbols incorrect	Words improperly spaced		
Symbol(s) omitted	Lettering faulty		
Symbols improperly aligned	Type blocks faulty		
Words misspelled	Wording poor	(20)	_____

THE MAP PROPER

Instructions not followed	Roads located incorrectly		
Property boundary wrong	Roads variable in width		
Streams incorrectly drawn	Roads too wide or too narrow		
Type lines improperly drawn	Roads poorly drawn		
Minimum areas incorrect	Lettering faulty		
Interpretation incorrect	Lettering misoriented		
Coloring too light	Colors not uniform		
Coloring too heavy	Symbols incorrect		
Wrong colors used	Areas unclassified		
Features not identified			
Omissions _____		(30)	_____

MISCELLANEOUS FEATURES

North arrow _____   Declination _____

Graphic scale _____   Signature _____

Drawn from _____

Photographs taken (date) _____   (15) _____

GENERAL APPEARANCE

Pencil lines not erased	Map soiled, torn, wrinkled
Ink smeared, erasures present	Wrong kind of paper used

Remarks _____

_____   (10) _____

TOTAL (100) _____

References

Adeniyi, Peter O. 1980. Land-use change analysis using sequential aerial photography and computer techniques. *Photogrammetric Engineering and Remote Sensing* 46:1447–1464, illus.

Anderson, James R., Ernest E. Hardy, John T. Roach, and Richard E. Witmer. 1976. *A land-use and land-cover classification system for use with remote sensor data.* U.S. Geological Survey, Reston, Va. Professional Paper 964, 28 pp., illus.

Avery, T. E. 1974. A statewide land information system. Texas Assembly on Land Use, College Station, 9 pp.

———. 1965. Measuring land-use changes on USDA photographs. *Photogrammetric Engineering* 31:620–624, illus.

Baker, R. D., J. DeSteiguer, D. Grand, and M. Newton. 1979. Land-use/land-cover mapping from aerial photographs. *Photogrammetric Engineering and Remote Sensing* 45:661–668, illus.

Baker, Simon. 1981. A level III land use and land cover classification of the North Carolina barrier island system. East Carolina University, Greenville, 11 pp.

Berlin, G. L. and W. B. Mitchell. 1975. Level III land-use demonstration categories for identifying manmade causes of ground-water pollution. In *Norfolk and environs: A land-use perspective.* U.S. Geological Survey, Reston, Va., pp. A7–A10.

Campbell, James B. 1983. *Mapping the land: aerial imagery for land use information.* Association of American Geographers, Washington, D.C., 96 pp., illus.

Gautam, N. C. 1976. Aerial photo-interpretation techniques for classifying urban land use. *Photogrammetric Engineering and Remote Sensing* 42:815–822, illus.

Greenlee, David D. 1980. *Application of spatial analysis techniques to remotely sensed images and ancillary geocoded data.* U.S. Geological Survey, Sioux Falls, S. Dak., 20 pp., illus.

———. 1979. *Reference notes: spatial analysis concepts.* U.S. Geological Survey, Sioux Falls, S. Dak., 43 pp., illus.

Jensen, J. R., M. L. Bryan, S. Z. Friedman, F. M. Henderson, R. K. Holz, D. Lindgren, D. L. Toll, R. A. Welch, and J. R. Wray. 1983. Urban/suburban land use analysis. In *Manual of remote sensing.* 2nd ed. American Society of Photogrammetry, Falls Church, Va., pp. 1571–1666, illus.

Johnson, Gary E. and Thomas R. Loveland. 1980. The Columbia River and tributaries irrigation withdrawals analysis project: Feasibility analysis and future plans. In *Symposium, identifying irrigated lands using remote sensing techniques.* Missouri River Basin Commission, Omaha, Neb., pp. 37–47, illus.

Kleckner, Richard L. 1982. Classification systems for natural resource management. In *Proceedings Pecora VII symposium—Remote sensing: an input to geographic information systems in the 1980's.* American Society of Photogrammetry, Falls Church, Va., pp. 65–70.

———. 1981. A national program of land use and land cover mapping and data compilation. In *Planning future land uses.* ASA, CSSA, SSSA, Madison, Wis., pp. 7–13, illus.

Lins, Harry F., Jr. 1976. Land-use mapping from Skylab-S-190B photography. *Photogrammetric Engineering and Remote Sensing* 42:301–307, illus.

Loelkes, George L., Jr. 1977. *Specifications for land use and land cover and associated maps.* U.S. Geological Survey, Reston, Va. Open File Report 77-555, 51 pp., illus.

Marble, D. F., D. J. Peuquet, A. R. Boyle, N. Bryant, H. W. Calkins, T. Johnson, and A. Zobrist. 1983. Geographic information systems and remote sensing. In

Manual of remote sensing. 2nd ed. American Society of Photogrammetry, Falls Church, Va., pp. 923–958, illus.

McFarland, William D. 1982. Geographic data bases for natural resources. In *Remote Sensing for resources management.* Soil Conservation Society of America, Ankeny, Iowa, pp. 41–50, illus.

Marchner, F. J. 1959. *Land use and its patterns in the United States.* Government Printing Office, Washington, D.C. U.S. Department of Agriculture Handbook 153, 277 pp., illus.

Mitchell, William B., Stephen C. Guptill, K. Eric Anderson, Robin G. Fegas, and Cheryl A. Hallam. 1977. *GIRAS: A geographic information retrieval and analysis system for handling land use and land cover data.* U.S. Geological Survey, Reston, Va. Professional Paper 1059, 16 pp., illus.

National Mapping Division. 1982. *Research, investigations, and technical developments, national mapping program.* U.S. Geological Survey, Reston, Va. Open File Report 82-236, 85 pp., illus.

Nunnally, Nelson R. and Richard E. Witmer. 1970. Remote sensing for land-use studies. *Photogrammetric Engineering* 36:449–453.

Pauludan, C. T. 1976. Land use surveys based on remote sensing from high altitudes. *Geographica Helvetica* 31:17–24, illus.

Schneider, Sigfrid and Erich Strunk. 1972. *Deutschland neu entdeckt.* Von Hase and Koehler Verlag, Mainz, West Germany, 96 sections, illus.

Short, Nicholas M. 1982. *The Landsat tutorial workbook.* Government Printing Office, Washington, D.C. NASA Reference Publication 1078, 553 pp., illus.

Wiedel, Joseph W. and Richard Kleckner. 1974. *Using remote sensor data for land use mapping and inventory: A user guide.* U.S. Geological Survey, Reston, Va. Interagency Report USGS-253, 12 sections, illus.

Witmer, Richard E. 1978. U.S. Geological Survey land-use and land cover classification system. *Journal of Forestry* 76:661–666, illus.

▧ Chapter 9

Prehistoric and Historic Archeology

▧ A NEW PERSPECTIVE

Remote-sensor imagery is a vital tool of archeologists, historical geographers, and others who are concerned with the discovery, evaluation, and preservation of prehistoric and historic sites. Although many such sites are still being discovered by accident (e.g., during surveys for a new highway alignment), aerial imagery provides a systematic means of searching out features that may have gone unnoticed for centuries (Figure 9.1). Furthermore, the remote-sensor imagery itself constitutes historical data; once acquired, it becomes an historical document of conditions that existed at a certain time and place.

In arid climates, the detection and delineation of archeological sites may be fairly simple, especially where vegetation is sparse or absent. By contrast, detection may be extremely difficult in high-rainfall regions such as tropical forests. Potential sites may not only be obscured by vegetation, but their ground scale alone may render them virtually invisible to terrestrial observers. The greater range and vertical perspective afforded by aerial imagery thus provides a new dimension in the search for and delineation of archeological sites. Even when such sites are not clearly discernible, probable locales for detailed ground exploration may be predicted by image analysis of environmental and microenvironmental zones.

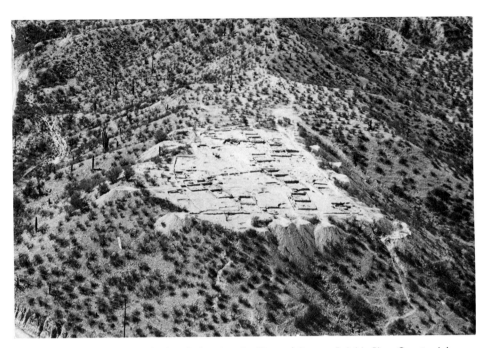

Figure 9.1.   Oblique view of Indian habitation site (Second Canyon Ruin) in Pima County, Arizona. The village covers an area of about 150 by 300 m; the ruin was first discovered in 1969. Excavation revealed that the site was occupied during two different periods by Hohokam and Salado Indians (circa A.D. 700 to 1000 and A.D. 1250 to 1350). (Courtesy Arizona Department of Transportation and the Arizona State Museum.)

Site detection may be accomplished by visual aerial reconnaissance or by use of various remote sensors such as aerial cameras, thermal infrared scanners, and side-looking airborne radar. This chapter describes techniques that might be used with any type of imagery, but emphasis is placed on conventional photography because of its superiority in terms of scale and resolution (Figure 9.2).

EARLY DEVELOPMENTS

Aerial reconnaissance and photographic interpretation have been tools of the archeologist for many years, and entire books have been devoted to the chronology of site discoveries from the air (Deuel 1969). Several early findings were based on visual sightings of unusual ground markings by World War I pilots in the Near East. Such discoveries were later followed up with extensive airphoto coverage, and much of the pioneering work in photoarcheology was conducted in Europe, the Mediterranean region, and North Africa (Figure 9.3).

A contribution of special interest to historical geographers was the work of John Bradford, an English archeologist who was interested in reconstructing the rural landscape of the Romans. He found that aerial photography revealed the Roman system of dividing conquered territory into squares of 20 by 20 actus (710 by 710 m). In many instances, the land subdivisions were still intact. Small-scale vertical airphotos made it possible to see more of the landscape in a single view and from a different perspective, thus revealing patterns of fields in areas where they had been previously unrecognized.

In 1922 the Englishman O. G. S. Crawford demonstrated the utility of patterns of various ground markings to delineate probable sites in the United Kingdom. His successes are exemplified by the fact that he discovered more Celtic, Roman, and "henge" sites in one year than had previously been found during 100 years of ground reconnaissance. This work firmly established aerial techniques for archeological exploration in England.

In southern Peru mysterious markings in the desert soil had been observed over a period of many years. The markings are scattered over an area of about 16 by 64 km and were formed by the piling up of varnished pebbles of the desert floor, which caused the lighter-colored soils underneath to be exposed. From aerial photographs, archeologists were able to discern patterns from the markings. Rectangles, trapezoids, and centers from which lines radiated were observed, as were giant effigies of birds and spiders. Due to the great size of the figures, their identities could not be determined from the ground. It is believed that the markings were made by Nazca Indians, but the significance of the figures has not been fully explained.

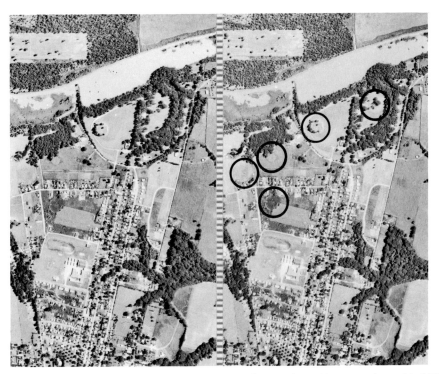

Figure 9.2. Marksville prehistoric Indian site in Avoyelles Parish, Louisiana, as pictured in 1968. Circled are some of the known and probable mound sites dating from the Burial Mound I and II periods (1000 B.C. to A.D. 700). Scale is about 1:20,000. (Courtesy U.S. Department of Agriculture.)

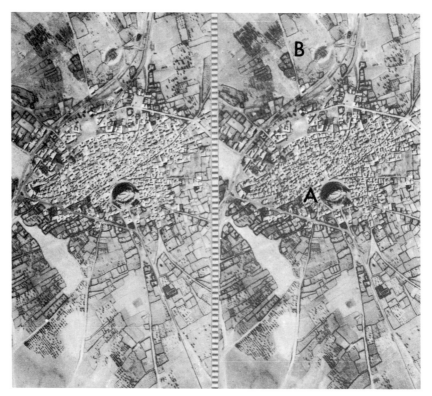

Figure 9.3. Ancient Roman ruins in North Africa. The coliseum at A dominates the contemporary mud and brick Arab homes and also serves as a focal point for roads that radiate outward from the village. This is a prime example of the influence of a past culture on a more recent settlement pattern; the present village has retained many of the spatial features of a typical Roman city. Much of the original coliseum structure has remained intact. Just outside the village, at B, is evidence of an abandoned amphitheater, with trees growing on the floor of the ancient structure. (Courtesy Henry Svehlak, from the Frank Beatty airphoto collection of North Africa.)

In spite of the foregoing examples of notable successes during the 1920s and 1930s, photoarcheological techniques were still somewhat limited during this period. This restraint was at least partially due to shortages in trained professional personnel and the reluctant acceptance of a new methodology by individuals and institutions that were in a position to support and use the results of significant discoveries. It is, therefore, not surprising that many early site discoveries were made by amateur archeologists, pilots, and aerial observers.

NORTH AMERICAN EXPLORATIONS

Early aerial explorations in North America include coverage of the Cahokia Indian mounds in western Illinois and both visual reconnaissance and photographic flights by Charles and Anne Lindbergh over the American

Southwest and the Yucatán peninsula of Mexico (Figure 9.4). Early flights over tropical areas produced only limited success because of insufficient advance planning and dense, masking ground cover. Nevertheless, a few important sites were located, and the attendant publicity generated induced several foundations and universities to send archeological expeditions into Mexico and South America. Since 1934, most of the site discoveries in these regions have been made through aerial reconnaissance or photographic interpretation.

The following listing, though quite incomplete, provides *examples of sites* in the United States that have been discovered, delineated, or mapped through aerial techniques:

1922—Mapping of Cahokia Indian mounds in Illinois
1930—Lindbergh flights over pueblo ruins of Chaco Canyon, New Mexico
1932—Photographic evidence of effigy sites (giant Indian intaglios) on bluffs above the Colorado River near Blythe, California, and delineation of Hohokam Indian irrigation canals in southern Arizona

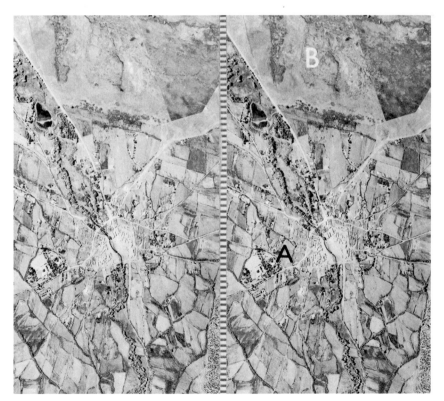

Figure 9.4.   Large Indian pueblo village (A) near Taos, New Mexico, as photographed in 1962. The remains of an abandoned habitation site can be seen at B. Scale is about 1:20,000. (Courtesy U.S. Department of Agriculture.)

1948—Mapping of Zuni and Hopi Indian pueblos in Arizona and New Mexico

1953—Detailed site mapping of concentric banks of earthworks (part of mound complex) near Poverty Point, Louisiana

1959—Discovery of village sites in the Alaskan tundra

1965—Discovery and delineation of fortified village sites along the Missouri River in South Dakota

1969—Discovery of prehistoric Indian agricultural plots (with thermal infrared images) in northern Arizona

1970—Discovery and mapping of ancient roadways and Indian pueblos in the vicinity of Chaco Canyon, New Mexico

In spite of technological advances, the applications of aerial archeology have been limited in the United States until the past few years. This may be a reflection of our greater interest in the present than in our ancestry, but there are probably other reasons also. Among these are (1) the relatively short period of established human settlement, (2) the feeling that many, if not most, sites have already been described, and (3) the attitude that more impressive sites are likely to be found outside United States boundaries. Whether these are valid generalizations is yet to be determined (Figures 9.5 and 9.6).

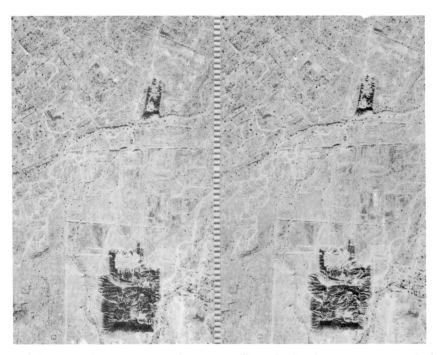

Figure 9.5. Ruins of pre-Inca pyramid, ancient walls, and related structures in Peru. Scale is approximately 1:6,000.

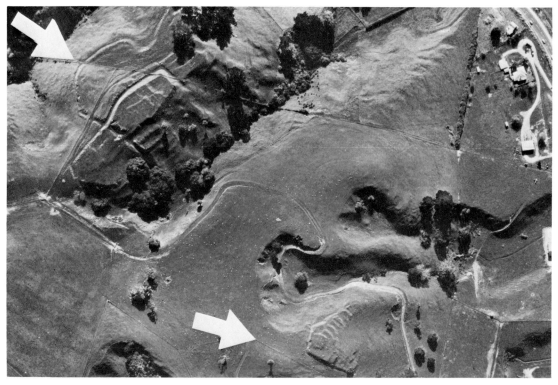

Figure 9.6.   Remnants of Maori fortifications can be seen at the upper left and lower center of this vertical view taken near Maketu, New Zealand. Maketu was once the headquarters of the Arawa tribe; the ancestors of this tribe arrived from Hawaiki about A.D. 1350. (Courtesy New Zealand Aerial Mapping, Ltd.)

▨ SITE DETECTION PRINCIPLES

The archeologist who relies on ground reconnaissance for the detection of archeological sites is limited to sites that are (1) small enough to be comprehended on the ground from visible remains, (2) accessible within practical and economical limits, (3) still visible in spite of modern-day cultivation and construction, and (4) recognizable, even though the erosional effects of nature may have been operating over a long time.

Fortunately, aerial discovery techniques are not as severely limited by the foregoing conditions. Remains of past landscapes that are too large to be comprehended from the ground, or which may have been incorporated into the present landscape and thus have gone unrecognized, are often detectable on some form of aerial imagery. And the advantage of a greater range and vertical perspective, as depicted on an aerial view, helps our understanding of the patterns of things that are seen but not understood on the ground (Figures 9.7 and 9.8).

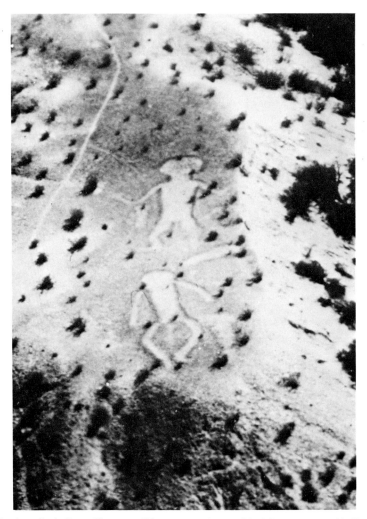

Figure 9.7. Intaglio Indian effigy, possibly representing mythical figures, on a bluff above the Colorado River near Needles, California. (Bureau of Reclamation, photograph by Heilman.)

For example, subtle suggestions of buried landscapes are sometimes revealed on conventional aerial photographs by shadow patterns, variations in soil coloration, or differences in the height, density, or color of the plants that grow above the buried features. Moreover, because some remote sensors operate outside the visible portion of the electromagnetic spectrum, they provide the archeologist with another eye into the past. For example, thermal infrared images may denote potential sites if buried or faintly expressed surface features of archeological significance emit detectable amounts of thermal energy.

▨ SHADOW MARKS

Shadow marks are site indicators produced by the sun's rays falling obliquely on minor terrain configurations or irregularities. Such surface irregularities may have been caused by soil accumulations on the ground, by mounds of earth that resulted from older structures, or by buried remains of archeological value. Old earthworks, unnoticed banks and ditches, and other characteristics of previous landscapes may sometimes be discernible from shadow marks on aerial photographs—even though such features are virtually invisible to a ground observer (Figure 9.9).

Shadow marks denote variations in surface relief through contrasting tones of shadows, normal photographic tones, and highlighted areas. Because an oblique sun angle is ordinarily required for good shadow marks to be produced, photographic flights should be planned for early mornings or late afternoons. The lower the relief, the more oblique the sun angle must be for

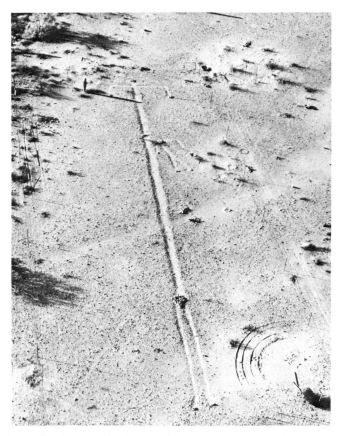

Figure 9.8.   Giant effigy figure in the desert, on the present Gila River Indian Reservation, Arizona. (Courtesy Arizona State Museum.)

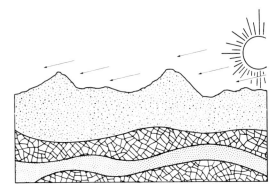

Figure 9.9. Profile of terrain model (top) showing the formation of shadow marks as a result of a low sun angle. The lower sketch represents the same terrain as seen in a vertical view.

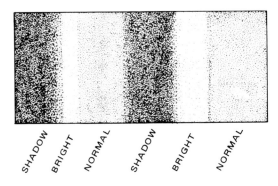

SHADOW   BRIGHT   NORMAL   SHADOW   BRIGHT   NORMAL

details to be discerned. Detection of very faint relief may also be aided by the presence of a light snow cover on the terrain.

The direction of the sun's rays and the altitude of the sun at the time of photography are important in that they produce diagnostic shadow marks. When the sun's rays are parallel to a bank or ditch, the tone on the photograph may be perfectly uniform and nonrevealing. For the best contrast between light and shadow, the sun's rays should form an angle as close as possible to 90° with suspected linear relief features. In planning exploratory flights, it may therefore be necessary to photograph an area at different times of day or during different seasons. For oblique photography, the diagnostic effectiveness of shadows is improved when the camera tends to face into a low sun.

Additional problems in obtaining good shadow marks are caused by shadows of obscuring objects, such as hills, trees, and buildings. The masking of minor shadow marks by vegetation may be somewhat alleviated with dormant-season photography (i.e., photography when deciduous plants are leafless). In all instances, clear air and a minimum of atmospheric haze provide the best results (Figure 9.10).

Shadow marks have proven especially valuable for revealing old field systems in England. During the Celtic era, it was the practice to define ownership boundaries with ditches. A ditch was dug along the boundary by the two landowners, and a ridge of earth was thrown up on both sides.

Remnants of these double hedgebanks, with a ditch in between, are often revealed by shadow marks.

Large earthworks of low relief may also be revealed from marks. It was this technique that led to the delineation of an extensive Indian village site on a presently cultivated floodplain at Poverty Point, Louisiana. The site contains the remains of six concentric banks and ditches, each one more than 1 km in diameter. Cultivation and erosion had reduced the broad, low banks to a height of about 1.2 m, and they remained unrecognized for many years because of the sheer size of the earthworks (Figure 9.11).

SOIL MARKS

Soil marks are variations in the natural color, texture, and moisture of the soil; these variations may result from man-made ditches and depressions, excavations, or earth fills. In many instances, the soil profile has been so severely disturbed that the original subsoil has become the present surface soil. The contrasts in photographic tones may be striking and quite definitive,

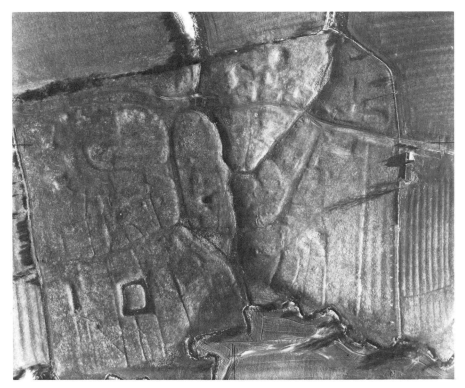

Figure 9.10. Shadow marks outlining an ancient medieval village site in England. (Cambridge University Collection, copyright reserved.)

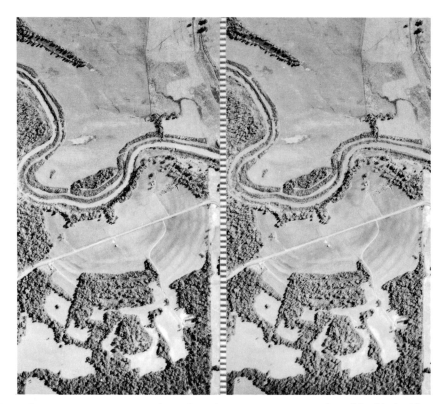

Figure 9.11.   Poverty Point, an Indian village habitation site in West Carroll Parish, Louisiana, as pictured in 1969. Dating from the close of the Late Archaic Period, the principal remains consist of a concentric octagonal figure about 1,200 m across and composed of six rows of earth ridges. Site construction and occupation are estimated at circa 800 to 600 B.C. Scale is about 1:20,000. (Courtesy U.S. Department of Agriculture.)

even though such marks are rarely apparent to ground observers. Soil marks may permit the archeologist to distinguish layers of past human occupation and to detect architectural patterns, ditches, canals, or other human alterations of previous landscapes. Natural features such as abandoned streambeds may also be delineated from soil marks (Figure 9.12).

The type of subsoil present is an important factor in the production of soil marks. Light-colored subsoils in combination with dark surface soils provide excellent marks; for example, where a chalky subsoil contrasts strongly with a brownish surface soil, outstanding soil marks are rendered. In some regions of western Europe, definitive soil marks are closely associated with the distribution of loess; conversely, limestone subsoils appear to be poor for forming soil marks. The mark-producing capability of several soil types in West Germany has been summarized by Martin (1971).

Soil marks are most easily detected after the first plowing of a field that has gone uncultivated for a long time. Weathering tends to emphasize soil marks in fields that have been plowed and left fallow for several years. Soil marks may reappear annually upon plowing and gradually become less distinct. Eventually, as the surface soil becomes nearly uniform, the marks may disappear. Tractors that plow as deep as 40 to 50 cm can destroy soil marks that have persisted for hundreds, or even thousands, of years. Harrowing, drilling, and ridging practices are particularly destructive to soil marks.

The best time for photographing soil marks is soon after plowing and following a heavy rainfall. At such times, distinctive marks may be produced by the differential drying rates of contrasting soil types or soil mixtures. When *moisture variations* constitute a major diagnostic factor, infrared films are preferred. However, where *soil color differences* are significant, panchromatic emulsions may be equally suitable or even superior for delineating soil marks (Figure 9.13).

Although many significant discoveries revealed by soil marks have been in the more arid regions, important discoveries also have occurred in humid areas. In certain sections of England, such as the Fen Basin and chalk regions, soil marks have revealed numerous remains of previous landscapes. And similar markings have also served to outline buried ditches enclosing ancient Roman fields.

CROP OR PLANT MARKS

Cultivated crops and native plants (e.g., grasses) may reveal the existence of buried landscapes by variations in their color, density, or height. These variations, which may indicate differences in plant-root penetration, can result from the remains of such features as ditches, pits, or buried wall

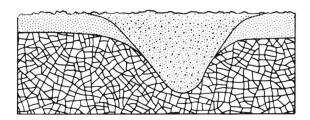

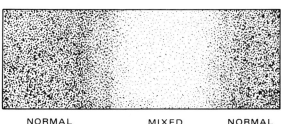

NORMAL	MIXED	NORMAL
SOIL	TOPSOIL	SOIL
COLOR	& SUBSOIL	COLOR

Figure 9.12. Profile of terrain model (top) showing the formation of soil marks. The lower sketch represents the same terrain as seen in a vertical view.

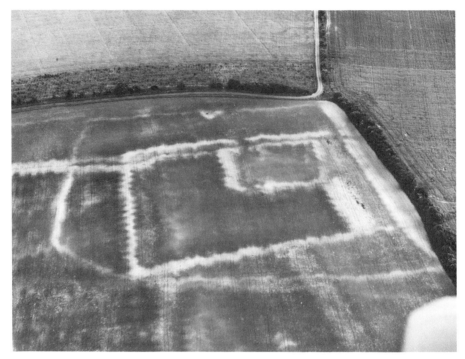

Figure 9.13. Oblique view of distinctive soil marks in an English field. (Cambridge University Collection, copyright reserved.)

fragments. Plant marks may reappear year after year, even though the causal buried remains may lie well below all cultivation levels. And they may continue to show up long after all traces of soil marks have vanished.

Crop or plant marks may be classed as either positive or negative. Positive marks result where growth is stimulated by filled-in ditches, whereas negative marks (inhibited growth) can result from buried foundations and walls. Positive marks are the more common type. They are affected by the width and depth of the original excavation in the subsoil and are most pronounced when the excavation was large and deep. The minimum width of excavation required for the production of a plant mark is perhaps about 1 m. However, a plant or crop mark will seldom be as wide as the ditch or other feature beneath it.

For positive plant marks to be produced, the subsoil must be well drained. Thus, during dry periods, plants growing in deeper soil will be the only ones to flourish. Marks may not be present in areas with loose subsoils, because the roots of crops may extend as far down in undisturbed subsoils as in the loose silt of old excavations. The best subsoils for crop or plant marks are compact gravels, chalk, or silt. Limestone and sandy subsoils, along with loose gravels and clays, are generally unsuitable. Negative marks are usually independent of the subsoil, because buried foundations, walls, and roads almost always have an adverse effect on the crops growing above them (Figures 9.14 and 9.15).

In the production of crop marks, the type of plant cover is almost as important as the surface geology. Cereal crops are the best medium by which buried remains are revealed, but clover, sugar beets, and grass also give good results. In very dry weather, almost any type of vegetation may produce distinctive tonal signs; crop marks appear gradually, with the contrast and amount of detail steadily increasing. During periods of wet weather, color differences quickly vanish, but variations in plant height and density tend to remain. Also, wet-season plant marks may be visible for a longer period, because crops such as grains ripen more slowly and are harvested later.

Marks that result from plant *density* differences are best recorded on *vertical* photographs, whereas *oblique* views may be superior for detection of faint marks based on plant *color* or *height* differences. The oblique photographs are best obtained in midmorning or midafternoon during the drier summer months, the time most suitable for detection of faint tonal differences and minor plant height variations.

Crop or plant marks have revealed evidence of past Roman landscapes in Great Britain. Numerous Roman military remains such as camps, forts, battlefields, and roads have been discovered by plant marks as registered on aerial photographs.

SITE PREDICTION

Although aerial photographs have long been used by archeologists for site discovery, applications for site *prediction* are less publicized. As an example, panchromatic photographs in central New Mexico have revealed the location of ancient beach terraces in an area where some of the earliest American inhabitants hunted large game animals. Photo interpretation resulted in the delineation of a large "peninsula" where such game might have been easily trapped; this delineation thereby restricted the ground search to a specific area. Surface explorations subsequently revealed several sites that are believed to be the remains of hunting camps dating back 9,000 or more years.

As another example, the ability of infrared color film to register vigorous plant growth in distinctive shades of red may be of assistance in the definition of shallow subsurface water in arid regions. Such areas may have formerly been sites of surface springs and favored locations for habitation and villages.

SITE EVALUATIONS

For known historic or prehistoric sites, and particularly important for those that have not been excavated, aerial imagery can help determine the spatial extent, orientation, and significance of ancient structures (Figures 9.16, 9.17, and 9.18). From evaluations of aerial imagery it may be possible for

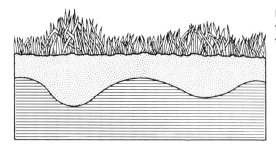

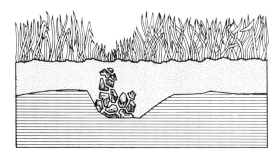

Figure 9.14. Diagrammetric representation of positive crop marks (top) and negative crop marks.

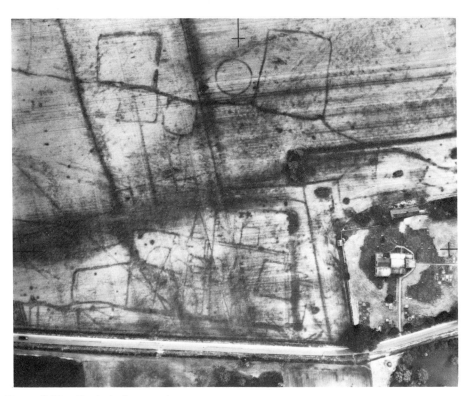

Figure 9.15. Vertical photograph of crop marks in a field in southern England. (Cambridge University Collection, copyright reserved.)

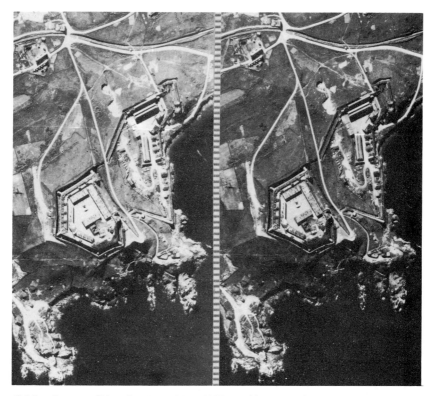

Figure 9.16.   Fortress of Napoleonic era (circa 1800) at Alderney, a channel island off the Normandy Coast of France. This 1945 view also depicts more recent coastal defenses, since the fortifications were renovated and employed by the German Army during World War II. (Courtesy Alberta Center for Remote Sensing.)

archeologists to draw inferences about past cultures, environmental zones, and the levels of technology that prevailed at a given time and place.

The concept of spatial extent is exemplified by such findings as giant Indian pictographs or clusters of earth mounds that were sometimes built as ceremonial burial grounds, effigy sites, or religious temples. Large earthworks of low relief (e.g., the concentric banks of Poverty Point, Louisiana) may be incomprehensible without the perspective afforded by an aerial view.

Where exploratory flights reveal only minor indications of habitation sites, it may be feasible to make inferences about other features or structures that are not discernible but which could have been logically associated with such sites. For instance, the discovery of an ancient Indian ball court (Figure 9.19) might lead an archeologist directly to an entire buried village.

For those features whose spatial extent is already known, aerial imagery and precise photogrammetric maps can be valuable in assessment of the significance, orientation, or original purpose of unusual structures. Stonehenge (Figure 9.20) and the Big Horn medicine wheel (Figure 9.21) are somewhat analogous structures of this type; both apparently functioned as early astronomical observatories.

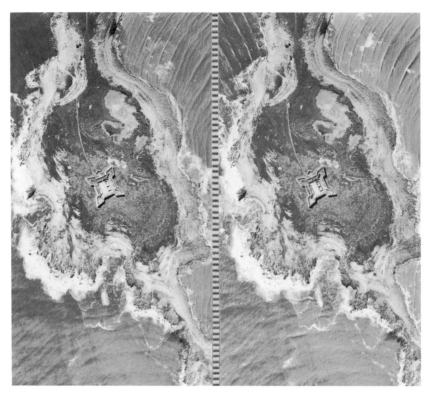

Figure 9.17. Fort Prince of Wales at the mouth of the Churchill River, Hudson Bay, Canada. The massive stone fortification was completed in 1772, some 40 years after construction was initiated. Scale is 1:15,840. (Courtesy Manitoba Center for Remote Sensing.)

The Big Horn medicine wheel reveals an especially interesting case study that has been documented by Eddy (1974). Constructed around A.D. 1700 at an altitude of nearly 3,000 m, it was first discovered by whites in the late 1800s. At that time, the local Indians interviewed were aware that the wheel existed, but none appeared to know its precise location or purpose. Because Indians tended to equate the word *medicine* with magic or the supernatural, the medicine wheel was long assumed to have served a religious or ceremonial function. It remained for astronomer Eddy, who worked with detailed photographs and field maps, to explain the orientation, solstitial alignments, and related functions of this primitive outdoor observatory.

PHOTOGRAMMETRIC SITE MAPPING

In many instances, remote-sensing procedures are more efficient than traditional methods for estimating excavation costs, site mapping, and making detailed studies of large structures and relationships. Photogrammetric mapping, a standard technique of engineers for many years, is now employed in the preparation of archeological site plans (Figures 9.22 and 9.23).

Applications of data derived through photogrammetry are readily apparent. Precisely compiled site maps are invaluable for ruin reconstruction and stabilization. Areas of structural weakness are more easily recognized, and the volume of materials to be removed during excavation or restoration can be quickly estimated. The site maps and aerial photographs themselves provide a permanent record of the site, its dimensions, and its spatial characteristics. Finally, when photogrammetric data are computer digitized, automated plotters can quickly reproduce site plans or other graphic information in the form of precision-drafted maps, overlays, or TV monitor displays.

SEQUENTIAL PHOTOGRAPHY

The step-by-step excavation or restoration of an historical site can be recorded by means of sequential photography. Such imagery may be obtained through conventional aerial techniques or through the use of ground-controlled camera platforms such as tripods, bipods, or captive balloons.

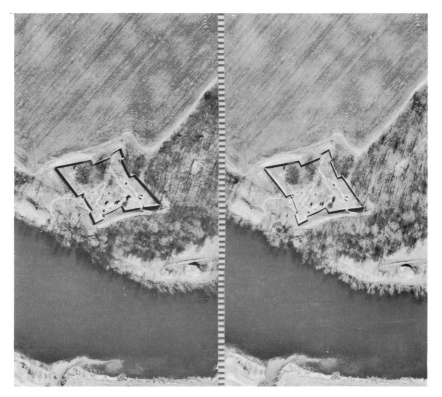

Figure 9.18. Fort Loudoun, a partially restored log palisade on the Little Tennessee River near Vonore, Tennessee, as seen in 1965. Completed in 1757, the fort was built to protect England's claims in the South and was the first British settlement in what is now Tennessee. It was surrendered in 1760 as a result of a siege by Cherokee Indians. Scale is about 1:4,800. (Courtesy Tennessee Valley Authority.)

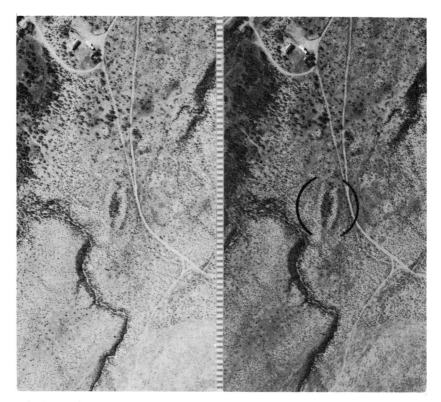

Figure 9.19. Prehistoric Indian ball court (unexcavated) in Pima County, Arizona. The estimated time of use by the Hohokam Indians (Santa Cruz–Scaton phases) was A.D. 800 to 1000. Scale is approximately 1:6,000. (Courtesy Arizona Department of Transportation.)

For smaller sites and "spot" excavations, the ground-based tripod or bipod platform works well. Regular hand cameras or aerial cameras that use 70-mm film can be rigged to provide vertical photographs—either as single exposures or in stereoscopic pairs. When the selected cameras are manually operated, the photographer must have access to the camera platform to advance and change the film and possibly to cock and release the shutter. Therefore, such setups prove most efficient when the height of the camera above the site is less than 10 m.

For larger sites and where the camera must be suspended 10 to 300 m above ground, tethered balloons can be used in conjunction with remotely controlled cameras for sequential photography. The design and suspension of several camera mounts for use with tethered balloons has been outlined by Whittlesey (1970). Sequential exposures obtained at various levels of excavation provide permanent records for the study of previous landscapes at successive periods of occupation. Used in this context, such imagery would effectively serve as "time-lapse" photography of past cultures.

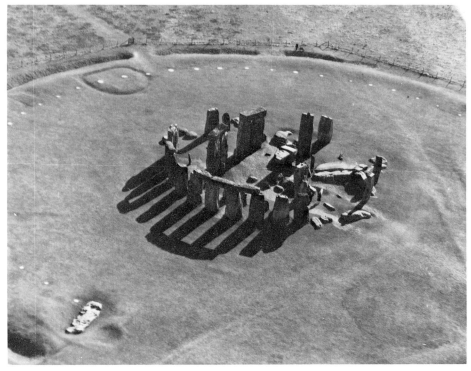

Figure 9.20. Stonehenge, an ancient megalithic monument on the Salisbury Plain, Wiltshire, England. Solstitial alignments indicate that the circular feature was constructed as an astronomical observatory. (Cambridge University Collection, copyright reserved.)

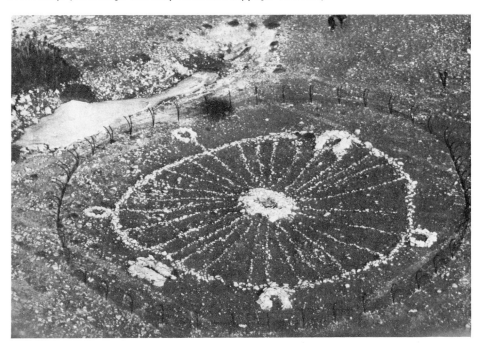

Figure 9.21. Oblique view of the Big Horn medicine wheel in northern Wyoming. Diameter is about 25 m. Built about A.D. 1700, the rock feature is believed to have served as a primitive astronomical observatory. (Courtesy Roger M. Williams, district ranger, U.S. Forest Service.)

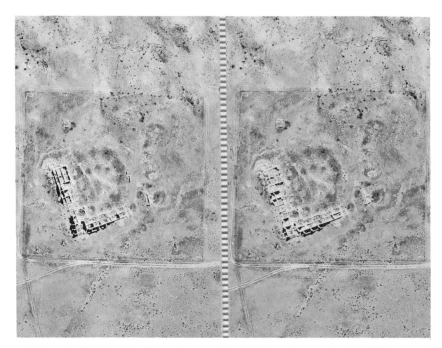

Figure 9.22.   Pueblo Pintado, Chaco Canyon, New Mexico, photographed in 1973 at a scale of 1:3,000. The top of the photograph faces east. Several similar Anasazi pueblo sites, dating from about A.D. 900 to 1150, are situated in this part of northwestern New Mexico. (Courtesy Koogle and Pouls Engineering and the Chaco Center, National Park Service and University of New Mexico.)

OBTAINING AERIAL IMAGERY

Numerous trials of photographic and nonphotographic sensors have been conducted in attempts to determine their suitability for archeological exploration. Because the major objective of each investigator tends to differ, however, a listing of rigid specifications cannot be set forth. On the other hand, there *are* general recommendations that can be made regarding imagery of ancient sites; those made here will refer to conventional photography unless otherwise stated.

As a general rule, vertical photographs are preferred for reconnaissance flights and for the detailed photogrammetric mapping of known sites. Oblique photographs may be specified for detection of crop or plant marks, and they also provide important records during site excavation or restoration (Figure 9.24).

For the detection and evaluation of most archeological sites, dry seasons of the year are preferred over wet periods, because the loss or retention of moisture by various soils provides more striking tonal contrasts during dry seasons. Density and condition of covering vegetation are additional seasonal factors for consideration. Growing-season photography is required for the detection and evaluation of crop or plant marks, for example.

Reconnaissance flights over humid regions are likely to be more successful when masking deciduous plants are leafless. And soil marks are most readily discernible after plowing but before the establishment of an agricultural crop. In summary, the photographic season must be selected on the basis of specific project objectives; there is no single period of the year that is best for all forms of archeological exploration.

TIME OF DAY

This specification is largely governed by the desired sun angle on the date of photography. For any given latitude and day of the year, the sun's declination can be determined in advance from a solar ephemeris or from special charts available from aerial film manufacturers.

The detection of shadow marks, as noted previously, may require a very low sun angle. When shadow marks are the objective, early morning or late afternoon photography may be required, especially at the lower latitudes. For

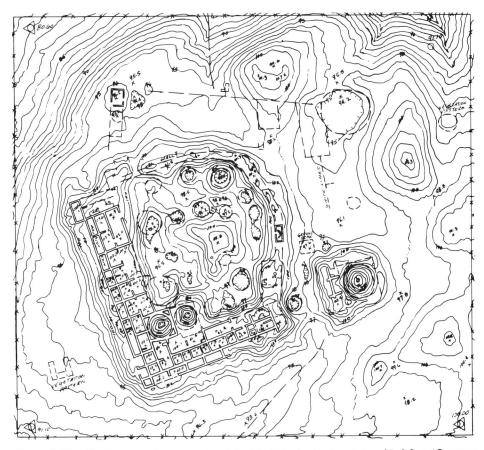

Figure 9.23. Planimetry and topography of Pueblo Pintado. Contour interval is 0.3 m. (Courtesy Koogle and Pouls Engineering and the Chaco Center, National Park Service and University of New Mexico.)

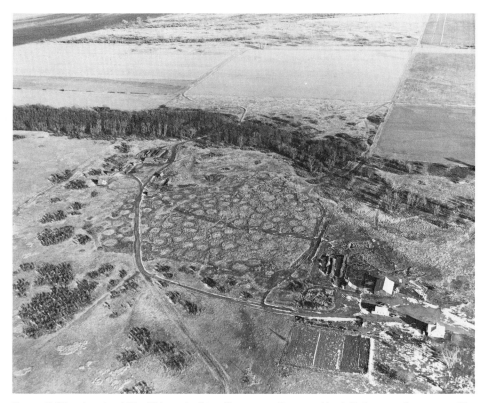

Figure 9.24. Locale of Big Hidatsa Indian village near Stanton, North Dakota, as it appeared in 1967. The circular depressions mark the sites of earth lodges that were located within a stockade. The village was occupied when Lewis and Clark explored the Missouri River (1804–1806) and continued in use until about 1845. (Courtesy North Dakota Highway Department.)

most vertical reconnaissance photography, however, a high sun angle is desired, for it minimizes shadows and provides maximum illumination of terrain features. Adequate sunlight is especially important for producing correctly balanced color photographs.

During midday photographic flights at the lower latitudes, precautions should be taken (especially with wide-angle camera lenses) to avoid hotspots on the exposures. Such hotspots, or sunspots, result from the absence of shadows (light halation), and they may destroy the exposure detail on a portion of each photographic frame. Because hotspots occur near a prolongation of a line from the sun through the exposure station (camera lens), their occurrence can be predicted—and avoided—by careful planning and timing of flights.

PHOTOGRAPHIC SCALE

In a consideration of photographic scale, we must distinguish between reconnaissance flights covering large regions and detailed photography of known or excavated sites. In the first instance, scales of 1:10,000 to 1:20,000 have been successfully employed in several countries, though on the basis of research reports, scales in the range of 1:3,000 to 1:10,000 appear to be preferred. The potential of very small-scale imagery transmitted from earth-orbiting satellites has not been fully evaluated from the archeological viewpoint, but certain linear features such as ancient roadways and extinct stream channels have been discerned on such imagery.

For photographing known, exposed, or excavated sites, various investigations have used photographic scales of from 1:500 to 1:5,000. Here, the scale specified is governed by the physical extent of the site and the degree of detail required. Extremely large scales are usually limited to sites being excavated or photogrammetrically mapped (e.g., burial mounds, fortifications, small villages, or pueblos).

TYPE OF FILM

Early archeological investigations used panchromatic, or black-and-white, photography—probably because this was the least expensive and most common type of coverage available. Panchromatic exposures made with a minus-blue filter are still considered quite useful and may be regarded as fairly standard for preliminary reconnaissance flights.

A number of investigators have reported tests that were conducted to compare color or infrared color exposures with black-and-white photography, but such comparisons have proven inconclusive because of differences in timing, scale, weather, or other factors. There *does* seem to be general agreement that color exposures are superior to black-and-white photographs, even when that superiority is limited to a saving of interpretation time. And infrared color photography is especially favored for mapping of subsurface details, such as buried foundations, walls, and other covered features. It may also be surmised that color or infrared color exposures are superior for detection of soil marks and certain classes of crop or plant marks.

It is somewhat surprising that only a few experiments using infrared black-and-white emulsions have been reported. Because this film is useful for revealing buried pipelines (through soil marks), it should be more fully evaluated for other applications (Figure 9.25). There is a need for the continued investigation of multispectral imagery and for comparison of film diapositives versus paper prints for detailed interpretation.

THERMAL INFRARED IMAGERY

While there are several potentially useful nonphotographic remote sensors available to the archeologist, imagery from thermal infrared scanners has received the most attention. Radar and ultraviolet sensors have been used in other scientific disciplines, but the thermal infrared portion of the electromagnetic spectrum appears to have a greater potential for archeological reconnaissance. No matter what types of nonphotographic sensors are

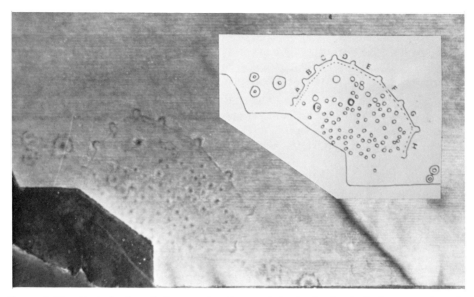

Figure 9.25. Vertical infrared photograph (1965) and sketch of a fortified village site along the Missouri River, 35 km south of Pierre, South Dakota.

The solid outer line on the sketch map marks the location of the moat; the dashed inner line represents the location of the palisade. The smaller circles indicate locations of older houses that were occupied at the time when the moat and palisade were actively defended. The larger, double circles show locations of more recent Indian earth lodges. Residual traces of these features can be seen in the photograph.

The presence and spacing of bastions, along with other evidence, indicate that the fortifications were built about A.D. 1200 to 1400. Scale is approximately 1:10,000. (Courtesy Carl H. Strandberg.)

employed, the resulting imagery commonly supplements rather than replaces conventional aerial photography.

Thermal infrared imagery is useful because a buried or faintly visible feature may absorb or emit thermal energy in an amount that differs from that of the surrounding terrain, thus providing a spectral "signature" (i.e., tonal contrast) that may reveal a potential archeological site. As an example, interpretation of thermal infrared imagery by Berlin et al. (1977) and Schaber and Gumerman (1969) led to the discovery of several prehistoric agricultural plots in northern Arizona. The thermal characteristics of these plots, located in an area of volcanic ash deposits, provided differential heat emissions that produced a definitive pattern on the imagery (i.e., a pattern of alternating ridge and swale features) that was not easily identified on simultaneously acquired panchromatic photographs (Figure 9.26).

▨ PROBLEMS

1. There are important areas of prehistoric and historic interest in most parts of the world. Attempt to locate some of these sites on available maps and aerial photographs. Summarize your findings in a brief report.

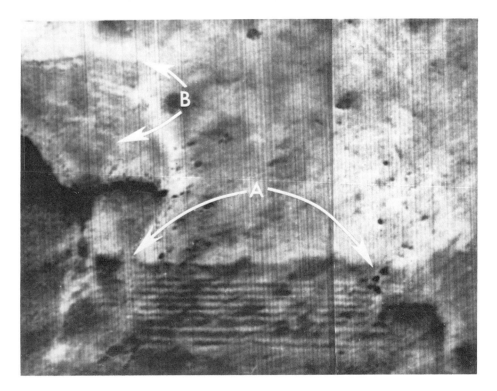

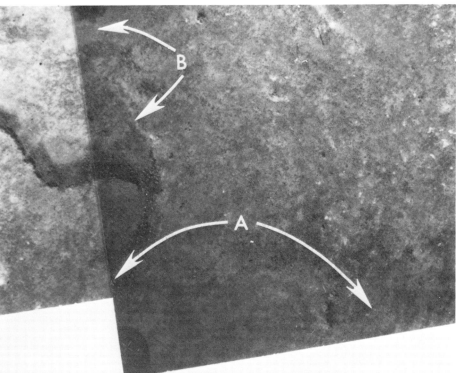

Figure 9.26. Simultaneously acquired thermal infrared image (8–14 µm), top, and panchromatic photography (0.5–0.7 µm) of two prehistoric Sinagua agricultural plots (A and B) in northern Arizona. The areas of agricultural activity are essentially undetectable on the photography. The plot at A measures approximately 67 m by 265 m. The recovery of pot shards of known age indicates that the farming activity occurred between A.D. 1065 and 1250 (Berlin et al. 1977).

2. Where would be the most *probable* areas in your region for the discovery of new sites? Why? Describe and illustrate (with photographs or sketches) the most important "find" in your locality during the past 50 years.

3. Locate a site that is currently being excavated or restored. Take your own low-altitude aerial photographs of the site or establish a ground-based camera station to obtain sequential photography as work progresses.

4. Attempt to locate shadow, soil, or crop marks on existing photography of your county or region. Explain, where possible, the origins of such marks (e.g., buried pipelines, filled-in canals).

5. Devise a single- or dual-camera setup to obtain (a) oblique stereoscopic photography or (b) vertical stereoscopic coverage from a ground-based tripod, a tethered balloon, or another type of platform.

References

Berlin, G. L., J. R. Ambler, R. H. Hevly, and G. G. Schaber. 1977. Identification of a Sinagua agricultural field by aerial thermography, soil chemistry, pollen/plant analysis, and archaeology. *American Antiquity*. 42:588–600, illus.

Bradford, John. 1957. *Ancient landscapes*. G. Bell and Sons, London, 297 pp., illus.

Carbonnell, Maurice. 1974. Historic center conservation. *Photogrammetric Engineering* 40:1059–1070, illus.

Crawford, O. G. S. 1953. *Archeology in the field*. Praeger, New York, 280 pp., illus.

de Leon, Porifirio García. 1974. Recuperacion de datos y la fotografía aérea. XLI Congreso Internacional de Americanistas, Simposio de arqueología, Mexico City, 41 pp., illus.

Deuel, Leo. 1969. *Flights into yesterday*. St. Martin's Press, New York, 332 pp., illus.

Eddy, John A. 1974. Astronomical alignment of the Big Horn medicine wheel. *Science* 184:1035–1043, illus.

Gumerman, George J., and Thomas R. Lyons. 1971. Archeological methodology and remote sensing. *Science* 172:126–132, illus.

Gumerman, George J., and James A. Neely. 1972. An archeological survey of the Tehucan Valley, Mexico: A test of color infrared photography. *American Antiquity* 37:520–527, illus.

Lyons, Thomas R., B. G. Pouls, and R. K. Hitchcock. 1972. The Kin Bineola irrigation study: an experiment in the use of aerial remote sensing techniques in archeology. Proceedings of the Third Annual Conference on Remote Sensing in Arid Lands, University of Arizona, Tucson, pp. 266–283, illus.

Magnusson, Magnus. 1972. *Introducing archeology*. The Bodley Head, London, 127 pp., illus.

Martin, Anne-Marie. 1971. Archeological sites—Soils and climate. *Photogrammetric Engineering* 37:353–357, illus.

St. Joseph, J. K. S. (ed.). 1966. *The uses of air photography*. John Baker Publishers, London, 166 pp., illus.

Schaber, Gerald G., and George J. Gumerman. 1969. Infrared scanning images: an archeological application. *Science* 164:712–713, illus.

Strandberg, Carl H. 1967. Photoarchaeology. *Photogrammetric Engineering*. 33:1152–1157, illus.

Stuart, George E., and Gene S. Stuart. 1969. *Discovering man's past in the Americas.* National Geographic Society, Washington, D.C., 212 pp., illus.

Vorbeck, Eduard, and Lothar Beckel. 1973. *Carnutum: rom an der Donau.* Otto Müller Verlag, Salzburg, 114 pp., illus.

Whittlesey, Julian H. 1970. Tethered balloon for archeological photos. *Photogrammetric Engineering* 36:181–186, illus.

Willey, Gordon R. 1966. *An introduction to American archeology*, Vol. 1: North and Middle America. Prentice-Hall, Englewood Cliffs, N.J., 530 pp., illus.

Chapter 10

Agriculture and Soils

WORLD FOOD PROBLEMS

The earth's agricultural base is vast, encompassing about 4 billion ha of arable land, pasture, and rangelands. Annual (as opposed to perennial) crops occupy 95 percent of the cultivated lands. The principal crops grown are summarized in Table 10.1. It can be seen that grains and oilseeds are planted on 80 percent of the total cultivated area. Major types of farming in the United States are shown in Figure 10.1.

The principal objectives of modern agriculture are to cultivate the soil for increasing crop yields while protecting the land from erosion or misuse. One of the truly critical problems facing the world today is that of increasing agricultural production to feed a continually expanding population; it has been estimated that two-thirds of the world's people have diets that are nutritionally deficient. By the year 2000 it is projected that the amount of arable land per capita will be only about 0.2 ha, as compared with about 0.5 ha in 1950.

Increases in crop yields will not solve the basic problem of unrestricted population growth. However, there is a definite need for international cooperation in the planning and administration of world agricultural programs. An important requirement for developing nations is a periodic agricultural census and inventory. Such information permits the monitoring of current production and the prediction of crop yields, so that serious food

TABLE 10.1. Generalized Breakdown of World Crops in Major Producing Countries	
Agricultural Crop	Percentage of Total Cultivated Area
Grains, including wheat, rice, corn, millet, sorghum, barley, oats, rye	73
Oilseeds, including soybean, peanut, sunflower	7
Roots and tubers, including potatoes, yams, cassava	5
Pulses, including peas, beans, lentils	4
Fibers, including cotton, flax, jute	4
Fruits and vegetables	3½
Sugarcane and sugar beets	2
Other crops (e.g., coffee, tea, tobacco)	1½
Total	100[a]

[a]Total approximate due to rounding of values.
From U.S. National Research Council and U.S. Department of Agriculture.

shortages or distribution problems can be recognized in time and corrective action can be taken. And because some areas of the world have untapped agricultural resources, current inventories can assist in the search for unused but potentially arable lands.

THE ROLE OF REMOTE SENSING

Because of the size, remoteness, diversity, variability, and vulnerability of the world's crops, accurate information on production during and following the crop season is limited to the crops grown in the more advanced countries. Even for these, the need for increased accuracy, timeliness, and detail of crop information is continually growing.

One promising means of meeting the current and future needs for crop information is remote sensing. Conventional, medium-scale aerial photographs have been used for decades in some regions for identification of major crops and monitoring of crop-area allotments. The use of more sophisticated techniques (e.g., high-altitude color photography, multispectral scanning, earth-satellite imagery) offers the potential of macroscopic agricultural surveys on a synoptic basis, along with detailed observations of selected croplands.

Remote sensing applied to a global program of assessment of unused but potentially arable land resources can hasten the attainment of a better balance between food requirements and food production for the world. Surveys of agricultural land from space altitudes permit the identification of present use of the land and show population-settlement patterns and transportation networks. Such surveys also permit the identification of land characteristics, such as major soil types, drainage, and topographical relief patterns, as a basis for evaluating the best potential use of the land. The following listing includes some of the more common applications of remote sensors in agricultural surveys:

Assessment of potentially arable lands
Classification of agricultural lands
Identification and distribution of crops cultivated
Crop areas and predicted crop yields
Periodic changes in crops or farming patterns
Detection of crop damage
Evaluation of plant diseases and plant vigor
Surveys and mapping of agricultural soils
Analysis of terrain and soil-forming processes
Evaluation of wind and water erosion

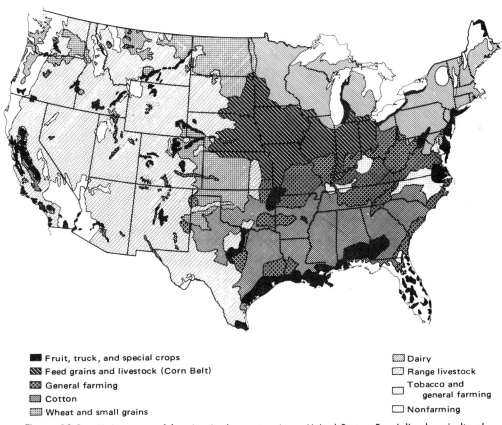

■ Fruit, truck, and special crops
▨ Feed grains and livestock (Corn Belt)
▩ General farming
▦ Cotton
▤ Wheat and small grains

▧ Dairy
▨ Range livestock
☐ Tobacco and general farming
☐ Nonfarming

Figure 10.1. Major types of farming in the conterminous United States. Specialized agricultural production areas are largely an indication of the effects of climate, soil type, and site. Proximity to markets is also a contributing factor in the location of fruit, vegetable, and dairy industries. (Courtesy U.S. Department of Agriculture.)

▓ LAND AND CROP CLASSIFICATIONS

The first step in the classification of agricultural land is that of learning to recognize broad categories that are easily separable on conventional photographs (Figure 10.2). In many regions of the world, the following six categories can be identified: seasonal row crops; continuous-cover crops; improved pasturelands; fallow or abandoned fields, including unimproved grazing lands; orchards; and vineyards. It is also usually possible to differentiate between irrigated and dry farming areas.

The next step is to compile a listing of all crops that occur in each type within the land area of interest; this can be accomplished with the assistance of local agricultural scientists. Farming practices in a given region are fairly stable, and completely foreign crops are rarely introduced on a large-scale basis. Therefore, crop identification procedures can be developed with little concern that familiar crops will suddenly be replaced by entirely new plant species.

Once a crop listing has been made, it is recommended that the interpreter learn to identify each *on the ground*. Ground identifications should be recorded directly on a set of current aerial photographs for reference purposes. For the nonagriculturalist, it will also be helpful to obtain ground or aerial oblique photography of each crop at periodic intervals during the planting, growing,

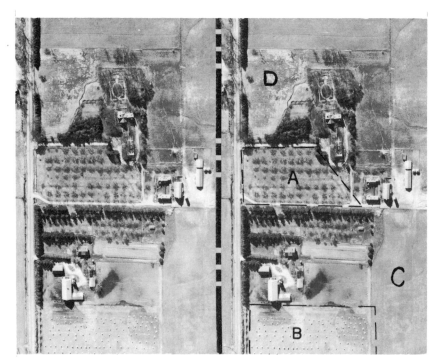

Figure 10.2. Agricultural land classes easily recognized on this Wisconsin farm include (A) an orchard; (B) shocks of grain; (C) field used for annual row crops; and (D) pasture. Scale is about 1:7,200.

and harvesting seasons. Some interpreters will then wish to prepare selective photographic "keys" based on the combined vertical and oblique views of each crop.

CROP CALENDARS

An intimate knowledge of the progressive development of each crop is essential if one is to make reliable identifications on aerial imagery at different times. This type of data can be summarized in the form of a *crop calendar*, that is, a detailed listing of the specific crops grown in an area, along with rotational cycles. The calendar determines which crops must be identified and the times of the year when they are visible and subject to discrimination. It may also be important to document the months during which a field changes from bare soil to crop A and then to crop B or back to bare soil.

Crop calendars can be used in conjunction with existing aerial photography to determine (1) whether there is a *single date* when certain crops can be distinguished from other crops or (2) what *combinations of dates* during the growing season will provide maximum crop discrimination. In many instances, unique spectral signatures will exist at one stage during the season, so that several individual crops can be separated. If a single date cannot be specified for a given kind of imagery, sequential photo coverage may be required. In this approach, crops are discriminated on the basis of changing patterns (e.g., bare soil to continuous-cover crop to bare soil) at particular dates throughout the year.

Table 10.2 describes monthly growth cycles for three major crops in the midwestern United States. It can be seen that one does not have to discriminate these crops when all have green foliage. For example, fields where winter wheat is to be sown are bare in September at a time when corn is tall and yellow. A similar state of affairs will occur at different times in different latitudes. Thus, the differences in planting, maturity, and harvesting dates for various crops can aid in their identification on aerial imagery.

SINGLE-DATE IMAGERY

The reliability of crop identification on single-date photography can be improved by observance of the following rules:

1. Schedule aerial coverage during the month when the most important crops are distinctly separable.
2. When a given crop exhibits no unique spectral signature during the growing season, obtain aerial coverage during the time when the fewest other similar crops are present.
3. Use the critical bare-soil months, or optimum crop discrimination periods, to predict the occurrence of the next crop in the rotational cycle.

TABLE 10.2. Crop Calendar for Three Major Crops in Ohio, Indiana, and Illinois

Month	Winter Wheat	Corn	Soybeans
January	Frozen or snow ——————————————————————→		
	Vegetation brown	Plowed, pasture or corn stalks	Plowed or stubble
February	Frozen or snow ——————————————————————→		
	Vegetation brown	Plowed, pasture or corn stalks	Plowed or stubble
March	Ground with vegetation brown	Plowed, pasture or corn stalks	Plowed or stubble
April	Becoming green to short green	Plowed, pasture or disked stalks	Plowed or stubble
May	Green, medium to tall	Planting, May 5 to June 20	Planting, May 10 to June 30
June	Yellow, harvest, June 20 to August 5	Short, green	Planting
July	Harvest or stubble	Green, ground covered	Dark ground, short green in rows
August	August 5—stubble or plowed	Green, full height	Green, ground essentially covered
September	Planting, September 10 to November 1	Drying starts, green to dry	Drying starts, harvest September 10 to November 1
October	Planting, dark soil and short green in drill rows	Harvest, September 25 to December 5	Harvest
November	Dark soil and short green in drill rows	Harvest or corn stubble	Plowed or stubble
December	Frozen or snow ——————————————————————→		
	Vegetation green to brown	Corn stubble, some field cut for silo filling	Plowed or stubble

From National Aeronautics and Space Administration and U.S. Department of Agriculture.

Where interpretation is based solely on conventional panchromatic photography, crop identification is extremely difficult (Figure 10.3). During early phases of the growing season, spring-planted crops are almost identical in tone and general appearance. After harvesting begins in late summer, crop differentiation is again difficult, especially for small grains. In a study of crop identification in northern Illinois, the optimum conditions for recognition of crops on panchromatic photographs were found to occur between July 15 and July 30 (Goodman 1959). During this brief period, cultivated crops, including alfalfa, wheat, corn, barley, oats, and soybeans, were identified.

Photographic tone and texture are the most important factors to be considered in recognition of individual crops on black-and-white prints. Local variations in farm practices, methods of plowing, and harvesting techniques have proved to be of limited value in the identification process. Tones may range from nearly black, in the case of oats and alfalfa fields, to almost white, as exhibited by stands of ripe wheat. Corn and soybeans are intermediate in tone.

After corn and soybeans have begun to mature, they may be separated on the basis of texture and differences in height. The mottled texture (light and dark spots) seen on many photographs of agricultural land is usually due to differences in soil moisture. The drier portions of fields, that is, higher elevations, tend to show up in light tones on panchromatic prints.

Irrigated or flooded crops such as rice are easily recognized by the presence of low, wavy terraces that show up as irregular lines on panchromatic film (Figure 10.4). Pasturelands can be detected by the presence of stock ponds or well-trodden lanes leading to and from barns or across roads that bisect fenced lands. Detailed studies of farmsteads and ranches on large-scale prints may also reveal the presence of dairy barns, horse stables, tent-shaped hog houses, and similar structures for animals (Figure 10.5).

Color and infrared color films, along with multispectral scanner imagery, appear to offer the greatest reliability for single-date crop discrimination. Limited studies employing radar imagery indicate that crops such as corn and

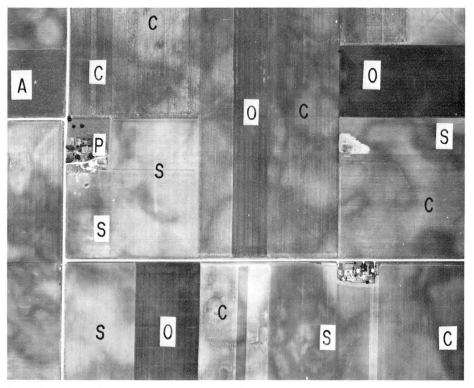

Figure 10.3.   Panchromatic photograph taken July 15 in McLean County, Illinois. Crops shown are alfalfa (A), corn (C), oats (O), pasture (P), and soybeans (S). Scale is about 1:7,200. (Courtesy University of Illinois.)

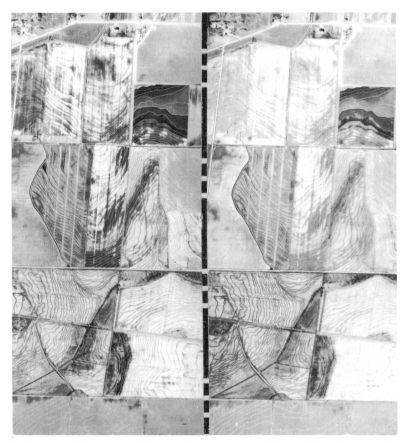

Figure 10.4.   Rice cultivation near Pine Bluff, Arkansas. Scale is 1:24,000. (Courtesy U.S. Department of Agriculture.)

sugar beets are easily separated. However, where several similar crops (e.g., grains) occur in the same area, the accuracy of identification from single-date imagery will rarely exceed 55 to 65 percent.

MULTIDATE IMAGERY

Optimum conditions for crop identification are found when imagery is available in more than one spectral band and on more than one date during the crop's rotational cycle. Under such circumstances, crop identification accuracy can exceed 80 percent.

As an example, a group of skilled interpreters were asked to classify 125 fields in the Mesa, Arizona, area into seven crop categories (Figure 10.6). Overall accuracy of identification on high-altitude, multidate, infrared color photography was 81 percent (Lauer 1971). Multidate photography has also been employed for a semioperational inventory of wheat, barley, and alfalfa on approximately 200,000 ha of cropland in Maricopa County, Arizona. Accuracy achieved by three skilled interpreters using 1:120,000-scale multidate color photography approached 90 percent for the entire county.

CROP AREA AND YIELD ESTIMATES

Information on crop areas and crop yields and forecasts during the growing season are of vital interest to agriculture. Techniques of area measurement are discussed in Chapter 4. It is worthy of mention that one of the principal reasons for the existence of the Agricultural Stabilization and Conservation Service in the U.S. Department of Agriculture is that agency's responsibility for monitoring crop areas.

Maintaining up-to-date checks of each farmer's annual planting allotment would be virtually impossible today without some form of aerial recon-

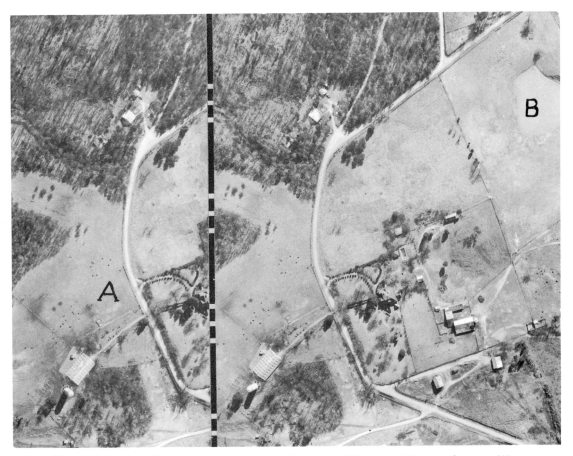

Figure 10.5. Cattle farm in eastern Tennessee. Cattle are visible grazing in improved pasture (A); note also the large stock pond (B). Scale is about 1:5,000.

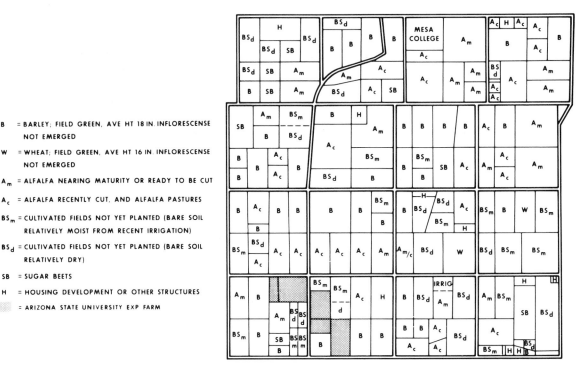

Figure 10.6. Agricultural test site showing ground identifications of irrigated crop types near Mesa, Arizona. Most of the crops (depicted in mid-March) were alfalfa and barley; several of the bare fields were planted to cotton about one month later. Land area is approximately 42 km^2. (Courtesy National Aeronautics and Space Administration.)

B   = BARLEY; FIELD GREEN, AVE HT 18 IN. INFLORESCENSE
       NOT EMERGED

W   = WHEAT; FIELD GREEN, AVE HT 16 IN. INFLORESCENCE
       NOT EMERGED

A$_m$ = ALFALFA NEARING MATURITY OR READY TO BE CUT

A$_c$ = ALFALFA RECENTLY CUT, AND ALFALFA PASTURES

BS$_m$ = CULTIVATED FIELDS NOT YET PLANTED (BARE SOIL
       RELATIVELY MOIST FROM RECENT IRRIGATION)

BS$_d$ = CULTIVATED FIELDS NOT YET PLANTED (BARE SOIL
       RELATIVELY DRY)

SB   = SUGAR BEETS

H   = HOUSING DEVELOPMENT OR OTHER STRUCTURES

░   = ARIZONA STATE UNIVERSITY EXP FARM

naissance. Accordingly, almost all sizable agricultural areas of the conterminous United States are rephotographed for the Agricultural Stabilization and Conservation Service at scheduled intervals of about three to seven years. Photographic enlargements, rectified to an exact scale by ground checks, are used to determine each owner's field area planted to price-supported crops such as cotton, wheat, peanuts, and tobacco. Although a few citizens have professed to resent this "spy method" of crop monitoring, it remains the most efficient technique for the detection of overplanted areas and the maintenance of equitable allotments for a majority of the nation's farmers.

Predictions of crop yield are derived from the product of field area and sample-based estimates of yield per unit area. Random ground samples are best measured as each field nears maturity, so that yield differences due to density, vigor, or disease incidence are taken into account. Where fields appear to be of uniform health and density on aerial photographs, a minimum of ground plots will be required. For certain types of cropland (e.g., orchards and vineyards), it *may* be feasible to estimate yields solely from high-quality color imagery.

▓ ORCHARDS AND VINEYARDS

As a rule, orchards are characterized by uniformly spaced rows of trees that give the appearance of a grid pattern. Orchards planted on level terrain (as are pecan and citrus orchards) are usually laid out in squares so that the same spacing exists between rows as between individual trees in the same row. On rolling to hilly terrain, tree rows may follow old cultivation terraces or land contours (as in peach and apple orchards). On the latter type, the sinuous lines of trees, when viewed on small-scale photographs, tend somewhat to resemble fingerprints.

For most orchards, the key identification characteristics are row spacing, crown size, crown shape, total height, and type of pruning employed (often visible in shadow patterns on large-scale photographs). Whether the plants are deciduous or evergreen is also of assistance for some localities.

Vineyards present a uniformly linear pattern on aerial photographs. Because of the localization of grape cultivation and the wider spacing between individual rows, vineyards are not likely to be confused with corn or other row crops of similar height and texture. Grapes are grown locally over much of the eastern United States, but the largest production area is found in north-central California.

▓ SEASONAL CHANGES IN FARM PATTERNS

Photographic comparisons of the same area taken during the four seasons show pronounced differences in the tones of soils, vegetation, and erosional features. Seasonal contrasts are particularly significant in midlatitude regions that have humid temperate climates. Where such areas are under intensive cultivation, changes can be detected not only in vegetation and soil moisture but also in the outlines of the fields themselves. These periodic changes, as depicted on panchromatic photography, may be summarized as follows:

Spring. Field patterns are sharp and distinct due to differences in the state of tillage and crop development. Mottled textures due to differences in soil moisture content are very distinct. High topographic positions, even those only a few centimetres above adjacent lower sites, tend to photograph in light tones. Low topographic positions photograph dark because of large local variations in soil moisture. Recently cultivated fields exhibit very light photo tones, which imply good internal soil drainage.

Summer. Photographs are dominated by dark tones of mature growing crops and heavily foliaged trees. Soil moisture content is normally low; therefore, bare soil tends to photograph light gray. Field patterns are somewhat subdued because of the predominance of green vegetation.

Autumn. Field patterns are relatively distinct because of various stages of crop development and harvesting. Differences in tone resulting from variations in soil moisture content are subdued.

Winter. Photographic tones are drab and dull, with some field patterns indistinct. Mottling due to variations in soil moisture is practically non-existent, and bare ground tends to photograph in dark tones because soil moisture content is uniformly high. A low angle of illumination causes sharp shadow patterns in wooded areas, producing a distinctive form of flecked texture. Gullies are usually more pronounced in winter than in summer, because the low winter sun casts denser shadows and dormant, leafless vegetation does not mask the surface.

Sequential photographic coverage on an annual cycle provides a basis for detection of complete changes in land use, for example, losses of agricultural lands due to highway construction, strip-mining, urbanization, and other factors. While such losses are not easily arrested, their adverse effect may be reduced by the selective allocation of less productive lands to some of these nonagricultural uses. Earth-satellite imagery holds great promise for making such evaluations periodically.

Large-scale aerial photographs can also be useful for livestock surveys, including counts by kind of animal, distribution of animals, and grazing preferences (Figure 10.7).

DAMAGE DETECTION

Locating and mapping natural disasters present problems for those in agricultural resources management. Among the major causes of damage to agricultural production are wind and water erosion, floods, fires, insects, and diseases. Knowledge of the extent and degree of damage is especially critical for those who must implement disaster relief. And, later on, crop losses must be assessed and provisions made for crop salvage or restoration.

During floods or extreme droughts, aerial coverage may indicate areas from which people and livestock should be rescued or relocated. In some instances, crop losses may be discernible directly from photography, along with damage to farm buildings, fences, corrals, and roads. The weather accompanying some natural disasters (e.g., hurricanes) may prohibit aerial photography until the weather has changed.

PLANT DISEASE DETECTION

Losses due to floods, windstorms, or droughts are minor compared to those resulting from plant diseases. Damage may begin when the crop is planted, continue throughout its growing period, and persist after harvest, when products are transported and placed in storage. Unless diseases are prevented or controlled, there can be no sustained improvement in crop production.

The economic gain from early disease detection is that of effectively increasing agricultural productivity. To employ fungicides or herbicides effectively, the agriculturalist must have sufficient advance warning of disease incidence, severity, and rate of spread. This need for immediate

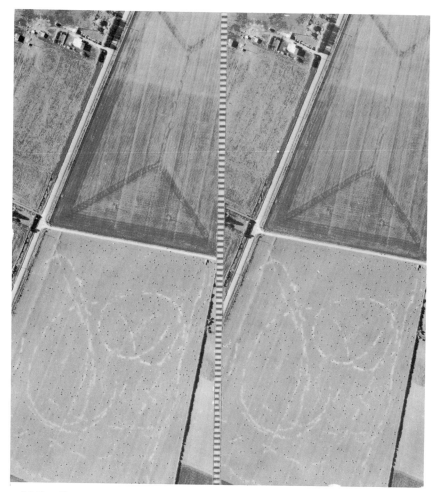

Figure 10.7. Sheep grazing in an improved pasture at South Canterbury, South Island, New Zealand. Scale is about 1:2,800. (Courtesy New Zealand Aerial Mapping, Ltd.)

diagnosis and control has resulted in numerous research studies aimed at previsual detection of losses in plant vigor.

Most successful experiments in the detection of plant vigor losses have used infrared color photography. The reason for this appears to be that many diseases result in a decreased reflectance of plant foliage in the near-infrared portion of the spectrum. The explanation of this phenomenon, as detailed by the National Academy of Sciences (1970), is as follows:

> The spongy mesophyll tissue of a healthy leaf, which is turgid, distended by water, and full of air spaces, is a very efficient reflector of any radiant energy and therefore of the near-infrared wavelengths. These pass the intervening palisade parenchyma tissue (which absorbs blue and red and reflects green from the visible). When its water relations are disturbed and the plant starts to

lose vigor, the mesophyll collapses, and as a result there may be great loss in the reflectance of near-infrared energy from the leaves almost immediately after the damaging agent has struck a plant. Furthermore, this change may occur long before there is any detectable change in reflectance from the visible part of the spectrum, since no change has yet occurred in the quantity or quality of chlorophyll in the palisade parenchyma cells. To detect this change photographically, a film sensitive to these near-infrared wavelengths is used.

Plant diseases that are apparently susceptible to detection through infrared photography include stem rusts of wheat and oats, potato blight, leaf spot of sugar beets, bacterial blight of field beans, and "young tree decline" of citrus trees. As a general rule, aerial photography has proven most successful when image scales were 1:8,000 and larger.

SOIL SURVEYS

Soil surveys constitute essential information for sustained agricultural production. For all practical purposes, soil characteristics determine the type of crop that can be grown and the production potential of that crop. As outlined by the National Academy of Sciences (1970):

> Information on soils is particularly important in an area in which new land is being brought into production. In many areas, pressing agricultural development has taken place without the essential data on soils needed for assessing the potential for successful development. There are many examples of failures in draining or irrigating land not suitable for drainage and irrigation. In other situations, land suitable for forest was cleared, put into agricultural production, and then found to be too erodible for crop production.

Until recently, soil surveyors have relied on conventional panchromatic photography, in conjunction with large amounts of fieldwork, to delineate soil boundaries. However, more promising and reliable results are now being obtained with color photography and multispectral scanner imagery (Figure 10.8). Photo scales of 1:6,000 or larger are usually preferred, and aerial flights are ideally scheduled soon after agricultural fields have been plowed.

SOIL-FORMING PROCESSES

Terrain elements are the features, attributes, and materials that make up a landscape. The more important factors to be considered in the evolution of landscapes and associated soils are topography, drainage patterns, local erosion, natural vegetation, and the works of humans. Topography is the result of the interaction of erosional and depositional agents, the nature of the rocks and soils, the structure of the earth's crust, and the climatic regime. The topographic surface is, in effect, a synthesis of all environmental elements into a single expression. As such, it plays an important role in soil surveys, because it provides a key for deducing the soil-forming processes at work in a given region (Figure 10.9).

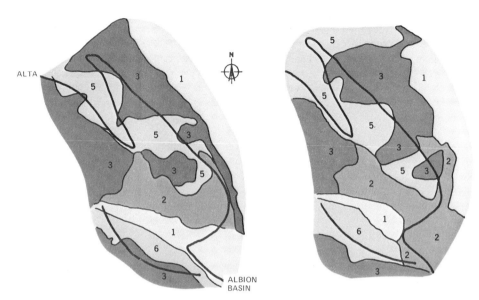

Figure 10.8.   Soil survey maps prepared by Soil Conservation Service techniques (left) and by automated classification from multispectral scanner data (right). This portion of the Little Cottonwood Canyon (Utah) measures about 1 by 1.5 km. Classifications are (1) rockland and shallow soils, (2) deep gravelly and cobbly soils and rockland, (3) deep gravelly and cobbly soils, (5) deep gravelly and cobbly soils with dark surfaces and clayey subsoils, (6) deep gravelly and cobbly soils in park areas. (Courtesy Earth Information Services, McDonnell-Douglas Corp.)

A number of attempts have been made to classify drainage patterns into specific regional groupings. When this can be done, much can be inferred with regard to soil type, geologic structure, amount and intensity of local precipitation, and land tenure history. However, stream patterns are almost infinitely variable, and the various types often grade into one another so that no single pattern appears to predominate. In some instances, a large drainage system may display several subtypes of drainage simultaneously. For example, the gross drainage pattern of a region may be dendritic, while associated lesser stream patterns may be pinnate. This situation is quite common in areas of deep loess deposits.

WIND EROSION

Features produced by wind and water erosion are important aids in photo interpretation because they are diagnostic of surface soil textures, soil profiles, and soil moisture. Specific implications of each type are discussed in the following paragraphs.

Evidences of wind erosion include blowouts, which are smoothly rounded and irregularly shaped depressions; sand streaks, which are light-toned but poorly defined parallel streaks; and sand blotches, which are light-toned and poorly defined patches. Evaluation of such features depends on a knowledge of prevailing wind direction, wind velocity, and the general climatic regime.

Figure 10.9. Soil-forming processes are based on the type of parent material, landform, drainage pattern, and local erosion (next three pages). (Courtesy Purdue University and U.S. Department of Commerce.)

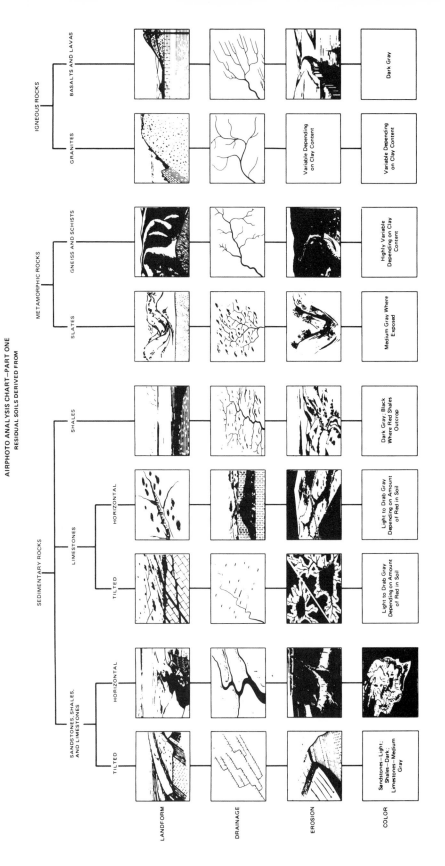

AIRPHOTO ANALYSIS CHART—PART ONE
RESIDUAL SOILS DERIVED FROM

AIRPHOTO ANALYSIS CHART—PART TWO

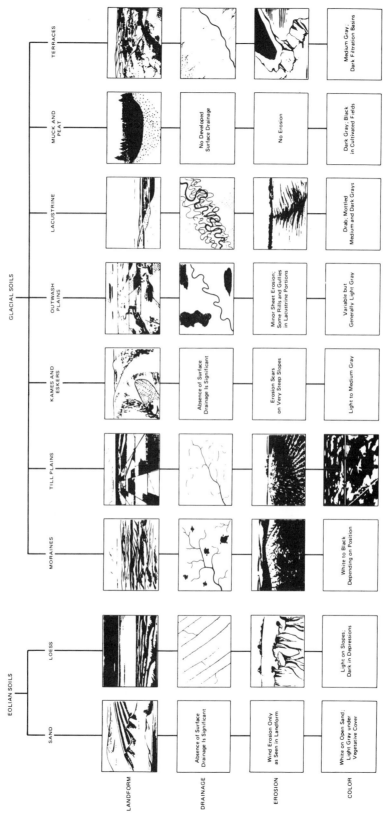

EOLIAN SOILS

SAND

LOESS

GLACIAL SOILS

MORAINES

TILL PLAINS

KAMES AND ESKERS

OUTWASH PLAINS

LACUSTRINE

MUCK AND PEAT

TERRACES

LANDFORM

DRAINAGE

Absence of Surface Drainage Is Significant

Absence of Surface Drainage Is Significant

No Developed Surface Drainage

EROSION

Wind Erosion Only as Seen in Landform

Erosion Scars on Very Steep Slopes

Minor Sheet Erosion; Some Rills and Gullies in Lacustrine Portions

No Erosion

COLOR

White on Open Sand; Light Gray under Vegetative Cover

Light on Slopes; Dark in Depressions

White to Black Depending on Position

Light to Medium Gray

Variable but Generally Light Gray

Drab, Mottled Medium and Dark Grays

Dark Gray, Black in Cultivated Fields

Medium Gray; Dark Filtration Basins

continued

Figure 10.9/ *continued*

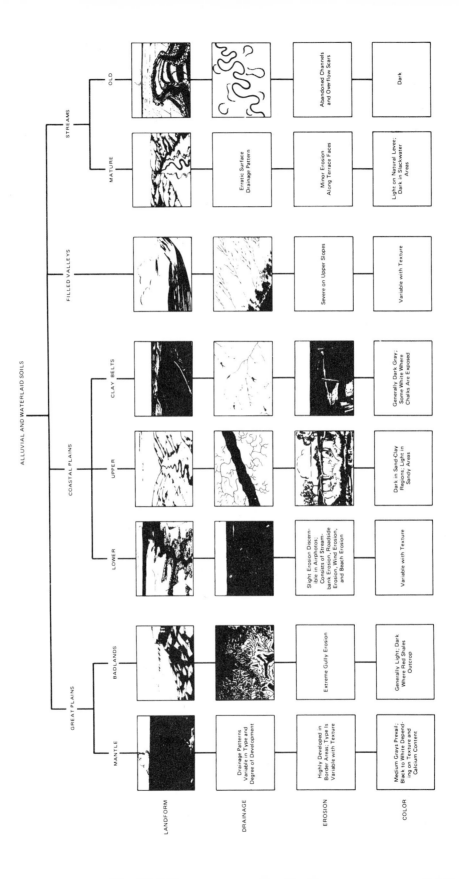

AIRPHOTO ANALYSIS CHART—PART THREE

ALLUVIAL AND WATERLAID SOILS

Climate is important because it provides some indication of probable soil moisture. Any surface unprotected by vegetation and not continuously moist may be eroded by the wind. Both local and regional topographic configurations should be kept in mind during the evaluation of eolian action, because mountains, hills, or other features may channel air movements in such a way that erosion is severe in one locality and insignificant in another.

Plowed fields, beaches, alluvial fans, and floodplains are examples of surfaces especially susceptible to wind erosion (Figure 10.10). In general, the finer the grain size, the greater the distance surface material is transported. As a result, a blowout with evidence of immediate deposition downwind implies relatively coarse-grained material, whereas a blowout without such evidence implies fine-grained material.

Many small erosional forms resulting from wind action are difficult to identify on airphotos. As a rule only the larger blowouts are readily picked out. Evidence of deposition is more easily detected, because resulting dunes or sheets present distinctive shapes or light-toned streaks and blotches. These are of considerable significance in regional land-use studies. In any given locality, wind-deposited materials tend to be of uniform size, resulting in homogeneous soils. This, in turn, implies that agricultural conditions in any one locality will be approximately uniform, provided slope, vegetation, and moisture conditions are similar.

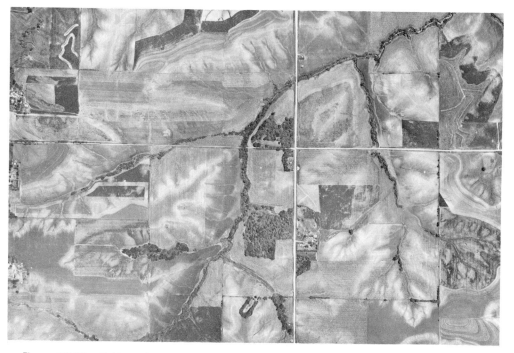

Figure 10.10.   Cultivated portion of a dissected loess plain in Harrison County, Iowa. The fine-grained eolian soils, deposited from glacial outwash areas to the north, are easily eroded by wind and water. Corn is the leading crop in this rolling plains area, with livestock providing the bulk of the farm income. Scale is about 1:20,000. (Courtesy U.S. Department of Agriculture.)

▨ WATER EROSION

Moving water is the major active agent in the development of the earth's surface configuration. Despite its awesome power in the form of floods and tidal waves, moving water is delicately responsive to variations in environment, and modest changes in the material being eroded or the climatic regime can profoundly modify the surface expressions produced. Therefore, the landscape patterns produced through the action of moving water are of great importance to the photo interpreter (Figure 10.11). In addition, the interpreter should have a basic knowledge of the interrelations between climate, surface materials, surface configuration, and vegetation (Figure 10.12). The relative importance of various factors influencing runoff varies according to specific environmental conditions that occur in a given area. Surface runoff is governed by the following general considerations:

1. The amount and intensity of rainfall determine the degree of runoff. A heavy rainfall of short duration may produce more runoff than the same amount over a longer period of time.

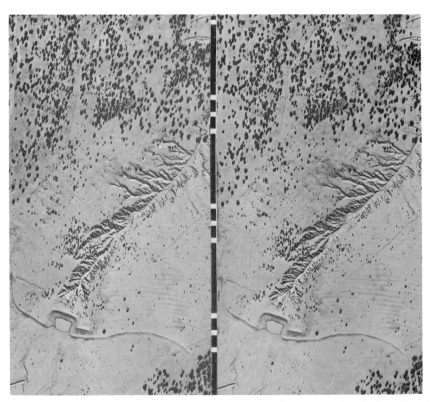

Figure 10.11. Dendritic drainage pattern formed in soft sediment near the Rio Grande in New Mexico. Scale is about 1:6,000. (Courtesy Abrams Aerial Survey Corp.)

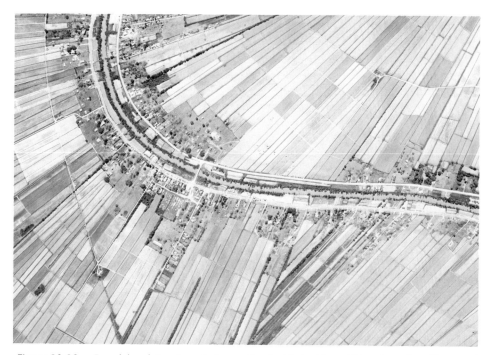

Figure 10.12. French longlot patterns in Assumption Parish, Louisiana. This pattern, found in several European countries, was brought over by early colonists, who depended on river transportation; each landowner thus had river frontage. Roads and dwellings are concentrated on artificial levees on either side of the river. The principal crops grown here are sugarcane, cotton, and rice. (Courtesy U.S. Department of Agriculture.)

2. The amount of runoff is dependent upon the moisture in the soil before rainfall. A given rainfall on wet soil will produce more runoff than the same rainfall on dry soil. A proportion of the incident water will be stored by the dry soil, whereas the wet soil has less available storage capacity.
3. A noncohesive soil is eroded more readily than a cohesive soil.
4. The greater the permeability of a soil the less the surface runoff.
5. In general, the greater the density of vegetation the less the runoff for a given quantity of incident water.
6. The steeper the slope the greater the surface runoff.

▓ PROBLEMS

1. Devise a crop calendar for the major crop types in your region. Obtain assistance, if necessary, from local agricultural agents or your state agricultural extension service.

2. Obtain aerial imagery of a local agricultural area on two or more dates during the growing season. Use your crop calendar, along with supple-

mentary information on cultivation practices, to identify as many crop types as feasible. Then check your identifications by ground visits to the fields classified. Tabulate as follows:

Photo Date:	Interpretation Date:		Ground Check Date:	
Field Number	Photo Evaluation		Ground Identification	
	Crop Type	Field Area	Crop Type	Field Area
1				
2				
3				
4				
5				
n				

Number of fields correctly identified _____

Percentage of fields correctly identified _____

Area of fields correctly identified _____

Percentage of total area correctly identified _____

Percentage of correct identifications for various crop types:

Crop A	Crop B	Crop C	Crop D	Crop E	Crop F

3. If feasible, investigate the use of infrared color photography for the detection of crop diseases in your locality. Prepare a written and illustrated report (or a slide presentation) on your findings.

References

Condit, H. R. 1970. The spectral reflectance of American soils. *Photogrammetric Engineering* 36:955–966, illus.

Edwards, G. J., T. Schehl, and E. P. DuCharme. 1975. Multispectral sensing of citrus young tree decline. *Photogrammetric Engineering* 41:653–657, illus.

Gerbermann, A. H., H. W. Gausman, and C. L. Wiegand. 1971. Color and color IR films for soil identification. *Photogrammetric Engineering* 37:359–364, illus.

Goodman, Marjorie Smith. 1964. Criteria for the identification of types of farming on aerial photographs. *Photogrammetric Engineering* 30:984–990, illus.

———. 1959. A technique for the identification of farm crops on aerial photographs. *Photogrammetric Engineering* 25:131–137, illus.

Hay, Claire M. 1974. Agricultural techniques with orbital and high-altitude imagery. *Photogrammetric Engineering* 40:1283–1293, illus.

Lauer, D. T. 1971. Testing multiband and multidate photography for crop identification. *Proceedings of the international workshop on earth resource survey systems.* Government Printing Office, Washington, D.C., pp. 33–45, illus.

Maurer, Hans. 1974. Quantification of textures: textural parameters and their significance for classifying agricultural crop types from colour aerial photographs. *Photogrammetria* 30:21–40, illus.

Meyer, M. P., and L. Calpouzos. 1968. Detection of crop diseases. *Photogrammetric Engineering* 34:554–557, illus.

National Academy of Sciences. 1970. *Remote sensing, with special reference to agriculture and forestry.* Agricultural Board, National Research Council, Washington, D.C. 424 pp., illus.

Parry, J. T., W. R. Cowan, and J. A. Heginbottom. 1969. Soil studies using aerial photographs. *Photogrammetric Engineering* 35:44–56, illus.

Philpotts, L. E., and V. R. Wallen. 1969. IR color for crop disease identification. *Photogrammetric Engineering* 35:1116–1125, illus.

Steiner, Dieter. 1970. Time dimension for crop surveys from space. *Photogrammetric Engineering* 36:187–194, illus.

■ Chapter 11

Forestry Applications

■ AERIAL PHOTOGRAPHY IN LAND MANAGEMENT

Foresters and range managers use aerial photographs for preparing forest-type maps, locating access roads and property boundaries, determining bearings and distances, and measuring areas. Skilled interpreters may also be adept at recognizing individual plant species and at appraising fire, insect, or disease damage by means of special photography. In addition to these applications, aerial photographs have proved valuable in range and wildlife habitat management, in outdoor recreation surveys, and in estimations of the volumes of standing trees.

In this chapter, emphasis is placed on the recognition and classification of vegetative types, identification of plant species on large-scale imagery, forest inventory techniques, and detection of plant vigor. Although photo interpretation can make the land manager's job easier, there are limitations that must be recognized. Accurate measurements of such items as tree diameter or quantity of forage are possible only on the ground. Aerial photographs are therefore used to complement, improve, or reduce fieldwork rather than take its place.

■ THE DISTRIBUTION OF VEGETATION

The occurrence and distribution of native vegetative cover in a given locality are governed by such elements as (1) annual or seasonal rainfall, (2) latitude, (3) elevation above sea level, (4) length of the growing season, (5) solar radiation and temperature regimes, (6) soil type and drainage conditions, (7) topographic aspect and slope, (8) prevailing winds, (9) salt spray, and (10) air pollutants. Within any given climatic zone, the *distribution* of available moisture can be as critical as the total amount. Temperature *extremes* are also controlling factors, because such extremes influence evaporation-transpiration ratios in various plant communities.

In some parts of temperate North America, notably the American Southwest, land elevation and precipitation are the two principal factors that determine the distribution of vegetative types. The controlling nature of these two elements in Arizona, for example, is illustrated in Table 11.1. This stratification is quite general, and local variations occur because of differences in soils, slope, and aspect.

A sound knowledge of plant ecology and the factors controlling the natural evolution of plant communities are of inestimable value to interpreters of vegetative features. Armed with such background information, one may often *predict* the kinds of native vegetation that will be encountered under specified environmental conditions.

THE CLASSIFICATION OF VEGETATION

The simplest classification method is one that merely discriminates vegetated from nonvegetated lands, followed by a subdivision of plant associations into productive or nonproductive sites. As an alternative, vegetated areas might be classed as one of the following basic ecological formations: desert scrub, grassland, chaparral, woodland, forest, or tundra. Such primary stratifications can sometimes be made from earth-satellite imagery.

Major problems one encounters in devising any rational classification system are (1) defining vegetative types so that the classes are mutually exclusive and (2) making allowance for the handling of transition zones, that

TABLE 11.1. Influences of Land Elevation and Precipitation on Vegetative Cover (Arizona)		
Vegetation Zone or Cover Type	Range of Land Elevation (Metres)	Range of Annual Precipitation (Millimetres)
Sonoran desert	450–1,200	75–380
Chaparral	1,050–1,500	300–430
Pinyon and juniper	1,350–2,250	380–480
Ponderosa pine	1,800–2,550	500–660
Aspen and Douglas-fir	2,400–2,850	580–740
Spruce and fir	2,550–3,450	680–890
Timberline	3,450–3,600	700+

is, areas where one plant community gradually changes to a different cover type. Wherever possible, it is desirable to adopt a standardized, hierarchical classification system that will be applicable across diverse geographic and political boundaries (see Chapter 8).

As an example of one type of classification approach, the following system has been proposed by the Food and Agriculture Organization of the United Nations (Lanly 1973). It is designed for an area classification of existing land use that could be employed for varied forest inventory projects, particularly those in tropical countries. The first step is the separation of land and water areas, followed by a breakdown of the total land area into these categories:

Forest Area

1. Natural forests
   a. Broad-leaved, excluding mangroves
   b. Coniferous
   c. Mixed broad-leaved and coniferous
   d. Pure bamboo
   e. Mangrove
   f. Coastal and riverine palms
   g. Temporarily unstocked
2. Man-made forests (items a through g above as applicable)

Other Wooded Area

1. Savanna: open woodlands
2. Heath: stunted and scrub forest
3. Trees in lines: windbreaks and shelterbelts
4. Other areas

Nonforest Area

1. Agricultural land
   a. Crops and improved pastures
   b. Plantations
2. Other lands
   a. Barren
   b. Natural rangelands and grasslands
   c. Swamp
   d. Heath, tundra
   e. Urban, industrial and communication
   f. Other areas

As with any classification system, the foregoing types must be clearly defined in rigorous terms. Otherwise, the most elemental discriminations (e.g., what *is* forest land?) can result in inconsistent image interpretations.

IDENTIFYING COVER TYPES

As outlined earlier, interpreters of vegetation should be well versed in plant ecology and the various factors that influence the distribution of native trees, shrubs, forbs, and grasses. Field experience in the region of interest is also a prime requisite, because many cover types must be deduced or inferred from associated factors instead of being recognized directly from their photographic images.

The inferential approach to cover-type identification becomes more and more important as image scales and resolution qualities are reduced. Range managers may rely exclusively on this technique where they must evaluate the grazing potential for lands obscured by dense forest canopies.

The degree to which cover types and plant species can be recognized depends on the quality, scale, and season of photography, the type of film used, and the interpreter's background and ability. The shape, texture, and tone (color) of plant foliage as seen on vertical photographs can also be influenced by stand age or topographic site. Furthermore, such images may be distorted by time of day, sun angle, atmospheric haze, clouds, or inconsistent processing of negatives and prints. In spite of insistence on rigid specifications, it is often impossible to obtain uniform imagery of extensive landholdings. Nevertheless, experienced interpreters *can* reliably distinguish cover types in diverse vegetative regions when photographic flights are carefully planned to minimize the foregoing limitations.

The first step in cover-type recognition is to determine which types should and should not be expected in a given locality. It will also be helpful for the interpreter to become familiar with the most common plant and environmental associations of those types most likely to be found. Much of this kind of information can be derived from generalized cover-type maps (Figure 11.1 and Table 11.2) and by ground or aircraft checks of the project area in advance of photo interpretation. And for limited regions, vegetative photo interpretation keys will be available.

The chief diagnostic features the interpreter uses in recognizing vegetative cover types are photographic texture (smoothness or coarseness of images), tonal contrast or color, relative sizes of crown images at a given photo scale, and topographic location or site. Most of these characteristics constitute rather weak clues when observed singly, but together they may comprise the final link in the chain of "identification by elimination." Several important cover types occurring in the United States and Canada are illustrated in Figures 11.2 through 11.7.

IDENTIFYING INDIVIDUAL SPECIES

The recognition of an individual species on aerial imagery is most easily accomplished when that species occurs naturally in pure, even-aged stands. Under such circumstances, the cover type and the plant species are synony-

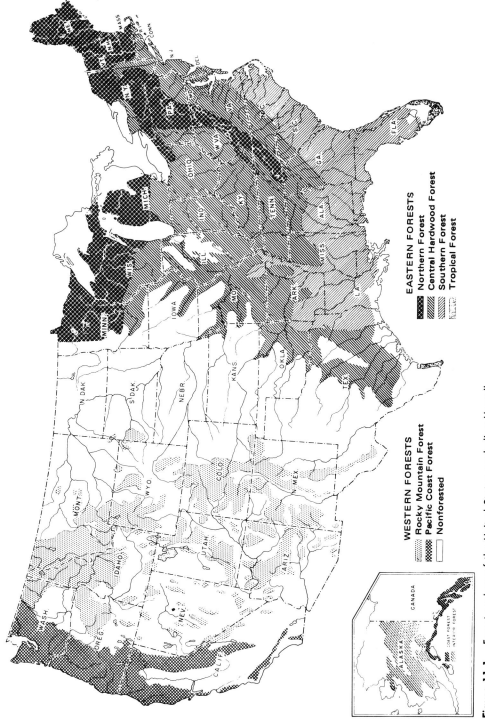

Figure 11.1. Forest regions of the United States, excluding Hawaii.

TABLE 11.2. Principal Trees of the Forest Regions of the United States[a]

Rocky Mountain Forest

Northern Portion (Northern Idaho and Western Montana)
Lodgepole pine
Douglas-fir
Western larch
Engelmann spruce
Ponderosa pine
Western white pine
Western redcedar
Grand and alpine firs
Western and mountain hemlocks
Whitebark pine
Balsam poplar

Eastern Oregon, Central Idaho, and Eastern Washington
Ponderosa pine
Douglas-fir
Lodgepole pine
Western larch
Engelmann spruce
Western redcedar
Western hemlock
White, grand, and alpine firs
Western white pine
Oaks and junipers (in Oregon)
Lodgepole pine
Douglas-fir
Ponderosa pine
Engelmann spruce
Alpine fir

Central Montana, Wyoming, and South Dakota
Limber pine
Aspen and cottonwoods
Rocky Mountain juniper
White spruce

Central Portion (Colorado, Utah, and Nevada)
Lodgepole pine
Engelmann and blue spruces
Alpine and white firs
Douglas-fir
Ponderosa pine
Aspen and cottonwoods
Pinyons
Rocky Mountain and Utah junipers
Bristlecone and limber pines
Mountain-mahogany

Southern Portion (New Mexico and Arizona)
Ponderosa pine
Douglas-fir
White, alpine, and corkbark firs
Engelmann and blue spruces
Pinyons
One-seed, alligator, and Rocky Mountain junipers
Aspen and cottonwoods
Limber, Mexican white, and Arizona pines
Oaks, walnut, sycamore, alder, boxelder
Arizona cypress

Pacific Coast Forest

Northern Portion (Western Washington and Western Oregon)
Douglas-fir
Western hemlock
Grand, noble, and Pacific silver firs
Western redcedar
Sitka and Engelmann spruces
Western white pine
Port Orford cedar and Alaska cedar
Western and alpine larches
Lodgepole pine
Mountain hemlock
Oaks, ashes, maples, birches, alders, cottonwoods, madrone

Southern Portion (California)
Ponderosa and Jeffrey pines
Sugar pine
Redwood and giant sequoia
White, red, grand, and Shasta red firs
California incense-cedar
Douglas-fir
Lodgepole pine
Knobcone and Digger pines
Bigcone spruce
Monterey and Gowen cypresses
Sierra and California junipers
Singleleaf pinyon
Oaks, buckeye, California laurel, alder, madrone

Southern Forest

Pine Lands
Shortleaf, loblolly, longleaf, slash, and sand pines
Southern red, black, post, laurel, cherrybark, and willow oaks
Sweetgum
Winged, American, and cedar elms
Black, red, sand, and pignut hickories
Eastern and southern redcedars
Basswoods

Alluvial Bottoms and Swamps
Sweetgum and tupelos
Water, laurel, live, overcup, Texas, and swamp white oaks
Southern cypress
Pecan, water and swamp hickories
Beech
River birch
Ashes

Alluvial Bottoms and Swamps
Red and silver maples
Cottonwoods and willows
Sycamore
Hackberry
Honeylocust
Holly
Redbay and sweetbay
Southern magnolia
Pond and spruce pines
Atlantic white-cedar

Central Hardwood Forest

Northern Portion
White, black, northern red, scarlet, bur, chestnut, and chinquapin oaks
Shagbark, mockernut, pignut, and butternut hickories
White, blue, green, and red ashes
American, rock, and slippery elms
Red, sugar, and silver maples
Beech
Pitch, shortleaf, and Virginia pines
Yellow-poplar
Sycamore
Chestnut
Black walnut
Cottonwoods
Hackberry
Black cherry
Basswoods
Ohio buckeye
Eastern redcedar

Southern Portion
White, post, southern red, blackjack, Shumard, chestnut, swamp chestnut, and pin oaks
Sweetgum and tupelos
Mockernut, pignut, southern shagbark, and shellbark hickories
Shortleaf and Virginia ("scrub") pines
White, blue, and red ashes
Yellow-poplar
Black locust
Elms
Sycamore
Black walnut
Silver and red maples
Beech
Dogwood
Persimmon
Cottonwoods and willows
Eastern redcedar
Osage-orange

Texas Portion
Post, southern red, and blackjack oaks
Eastern redcedar, Ashe juniper

Florida and Texas Forest—Tropical

Mangrove, false mangrove
Royal and thatch palms; palmettos
Florida yew
Wild figs
Seagrapes ("pigeon plum")
Blolly
Bahama lysiloma ("wild tamarind")
Wild-dilly
Gumbo-limbo
Poisontree
Inkwood
Button-mangrove
False-mastic ("wild olive")
Fishpoison-tree ("Jamaica dogwood")

Northern Forest

Northern Portion
Red, black, and white spruces
Balsam fir
Eastern white, red ("Norway"), jack, and pitch pines
Hemlock
Sugar and red maples
Beech
Northern red, white, black, and scarlet oaks
Yellow, paper, sweet, and gray birches
Quaking and bigtooth aspens
Basswoods
Black cherry
American, rock, and slippery elms
White and black ashes
Shagbark and pignut hickories
Butternut
Northern white-cedar
Tamarack

Southern Portion (Appalachian Region)
White, northern red, chestnut, black, and scarlet oaks
Chestnut
Hemlock
Eastern white, shortleaf, pitch, and Virginia ("scrub") pines
Sweet, yellow, and river birches
Basswood
Sugar and red maples
Beech
Red spruce
Fraser fir
Yellow-poplar
Cucumber magnolia
Black walnut and butternut
Black cherry
Pignut, mockernut, and red hickories
Black locust
Tupelos ("black gums")
Buckeye

Alaska—Forest

Coast Forest
Western hemlock (important)
Sitka spruce (important)
Western redcedar
Alaska cedar
Mountain hemlock
Lodgepole pine
Black cottonwood
Red and Sitka alders
Willows

Interior Forest
White (important) and black spruces
Alaska paper (important) and Kenai birches
Black cottonwood
Balsam poplar
Aspen
Willows
Tamarack

[a] The order indicates the relative importance or abundance of the trees.

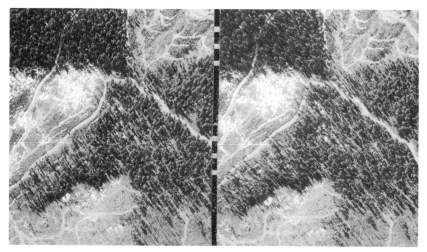

Figure 11.2.   Panchromatic stereogram of a recently logged stand of Douglas-fir in Lewis County, Washington. Scale is about 1:6,000. (Courtesy Northern Pacific Railroad.)

mous. Therefore, reliable delineations *may* be made from medium-scale imagery. As a rule, however, individual plants can be identified only on large-scale photography. The listing in Table 11.3, based on a synopsis of several research reports, illustrates the relationship between image scales and expected levels of plant recognition.

Photographic identification of individual plants requires that interpreters become familiar with a large number of species *on the ground*. For example, there are more than a thousand species of woody plants that occur naturally in the United States; professional foresters and range managers rarely know more than a third of this number. In Australia there are more than 800 species of eucalyptus trees; many of these species are difficult to separate even when they are within arm's reach.

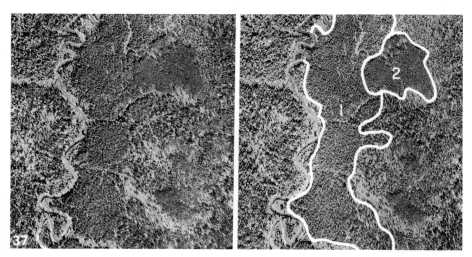

Figure 11.3.   Summer panchromatic stereogram of (1) balsam fir and (2) black spruce in Ontario. Scale is about 1:15,840. (Courtesy V. Zsilinszky, Ontario Department of Lands and Forests.)

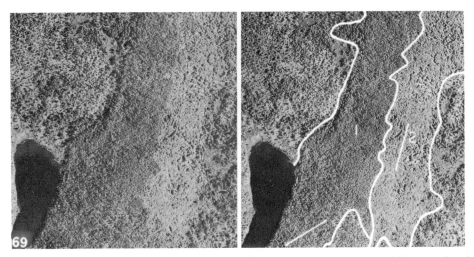

Figure 11.4. Summer panchromatic stereogram of (1) aspen and white birch and (2) young beech stand in Ontario. Scale is about 1:15,840. (Courtesy V. Zsilinszky, Ontario Department of Lands and Forests.)

SPECIES IDENTIFICATION CHARACTERISTICS

As a minimum, the interpreter should be familiar with the branching characteristics, crown shapes, and spatial distribution patterns of important species in the locality. Mature trees in sparsely stocked stands can often be recognized by the configuration of their crown shadows falling on level ground (Figure 11.8). A familiarity with tree crowns as seen from above (Figure 11.9) can be of invaluable assistance when large-scale imagery is being interpreted.

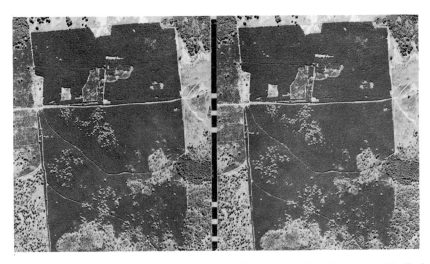

Figure 11.5. Summer panchromatic stereogram of red pine plantation (dark crowns) in the lower peninsula of Michigan. Scale is about 1:20,000. (Courtesy Abrams Aerial Survey Corp.)

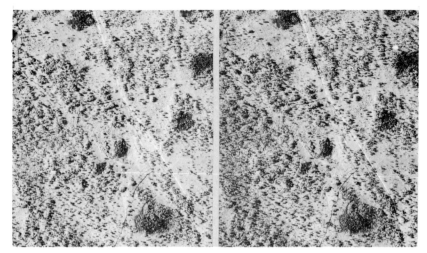

Figure 11.6. Autumn modified infrared stereogram of longleaf and slash pines (light-toned crowns) in the Georgia coastal plain. The dark, water-filled depressions are "ponds" of southern cypress. Scale is about 1:15,840.

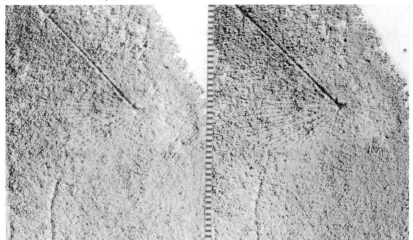

Figure 11.7. Panchromatic stereogram of a cable-logged area near Springfield, Louisiana. Principal cover types pictured are bottomland hardwoods and cypress–tupelo gum. Scale is about 1:6,000.

TABLE 11.3. Levels of Plant Recognition to be Expected at Selected Image Scales

Type of Imagery or Scale	General Level of Plant Discrimination
Earth-satellite imagery	Separation of extensive masses of evergreen versus deciduous forests
1:25,000–1:100,000	Recognition of broad vegetative types, largely by inferential processes
1:10,000–1:25,000	Direct identification of major cover types and species occurring in pure stands
1:2,500–1:10,000	Identification of individual trees and large shrubs
1:500–1:2,500	Identification of individual range plants and grassland types

Species identification can usually be aided by the use of conventional color or infrared color photography. In a study of Rocky Mountain rangelands, infrared color photography at scales of 1:800 to 1:1,500 proved superior to conventional color for the identification of shrubs (Driscoll and Coleman 1974). One experiment showed that 7 of 11 shrub species could be identified 83 percent of the time; the diagnostic image characteristics employed by interpreters were as follows:

1. Plant height
   a. ≥ 1.5 m
   b. ≤ 1.5 m
2. Shadow
   a. Distinct
   b. Indistinct
3. Crown margin
   a. Smooth
   b. Wavy
   c. Irregular
   d. Broken

4. Crown shape
   a. Indistinct
   b. Round
   c. Oblong
5. Foliage pattern
   a. Continuous
   b. Clumpy
   c. Irregular

6. Texture
   a. Fine
   b. Medium
   c. Coarse
   d. Stippled
   e. Mottled
   f. Hazy
7. Color: Numerically coded according to standardized color charts

Because range plants progress through distinctive growth stages each year, the date of photography is of utmost importance for the identification of various species. Most studies have indicated that the time of near-maximum foliage development is the best time of year for detection of the kind and amount of forage through remote sensing.

KEYS FOR SPECIES RECOGNITION

Photo interpretation keys are useful aids in the recognition of plant species, especially when such keys are illustrated with high-quality stereograms. Vegetation keys for U.S. and Canadian species are most easily constructed for northern and western forests where conifers predominate. In these regions, there are relatively few species to be considered and crown patterns are fairly distinctive for each important group.

A sample elimination key for identification of northern conifers is reproduced with Figure 11.13. In its original form, this tree species key was supplemented by descriptive materials and several illustrations. Selected examples of other tree species that may be identified on panchromatic stereograms are shown in Figures 11.10 through 11.13. A forest-type map based on a classification scheme developed by the Society of American Foresters is presented in Figure 11.14.

TREE VOLUME ESTIMATES

Where large-scale, stereoscopic photo coverage is available, it may be feasible to make direct estimates of individual tree volumes, by species or species groups. Sample-strip coverage obtained with 70-mm format cameras

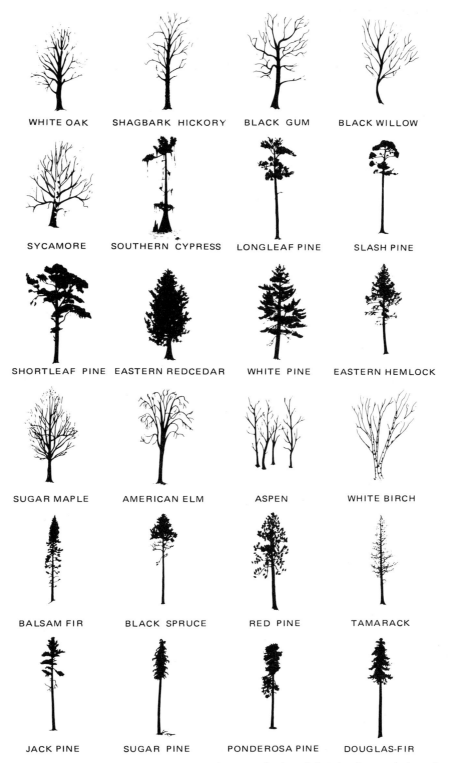

Figure 11.8. Silhouettes of 24 forest trees. When tree shadows fall on level ground, they often permit identification of individual species.

CONIFERS		HARDWOODS	
Light tip to center of bole with fine texture		Small light spots in crown	
Layered branches		Small clumps	
Wheel spokes		Small clumps with occasional long columnar branches (in young trees)	
Columnar branches			
Layered triangular-shaped branches		Limbs show	
Small clumps		Large masses of foliage divide crown (large older trees)	
Small light spots in crown			
Small starlike top		Fine texture	
Dark spot in center of small clumps		Fine columnar branches	
Fine texture with scraggly long branches			

Figure 11.9. Sketches of overhead views of tree crowns for several boreal species. (Courtesy U.S. Forest Service Remote Sensing Project, Berkeley, California.)

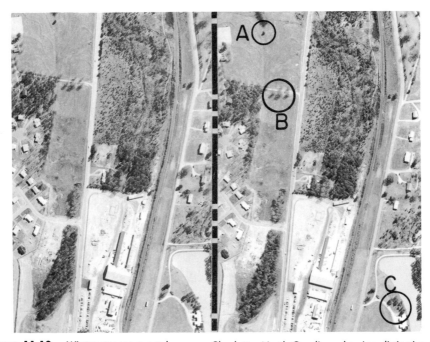

Figure 11.10. Winter stereogram taken near Charlotte, North Carolina, showing distinctive tree shadows of eastern redcedar (A), oaks devoid of foliage (B), and shortleaf pines (C). Compare with drawings in Figure 11.8. Scale is about 1:15,840.

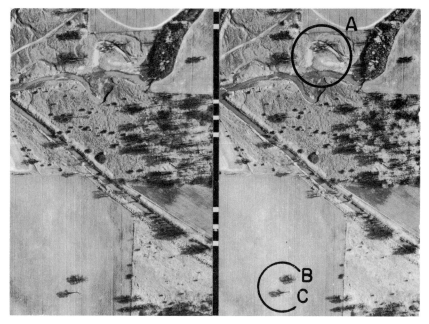

Figure 11.11. Winter stereogram taken near Grandville, Michigan, picturing distinctive tree shadows of American elm (A, C) and oak (B). Compare with drawings in Figure 11.8. Scale is about 1:6,000.

is often specified, at scales ranging from 1:1,000 to 1:5,000 (Figure 11.15). The determination of the *exact* negative scale is ideally accomplished by employment of a radar altimeter in the photographic aircraft.

Panchromatic film has been used successfully for individual tree evaluations in northern boreal forests; in several photographic experiments, the fall season (i.e., after deciduous trees are leafless but before snowfall) has been specified. This timing is regarded as ideal for species recognition. In other

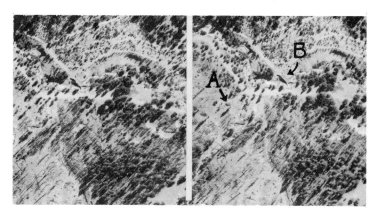

Figure 11.12. Stereogram from the Plumas National Forest in California, illustrating the shadow pattern of a sugar pine (A). Compare with drawing in Figure 11.8. At B is an abandoned bridge with roadway approaches washed out by severe erosion. Scale is about 1:5,000.

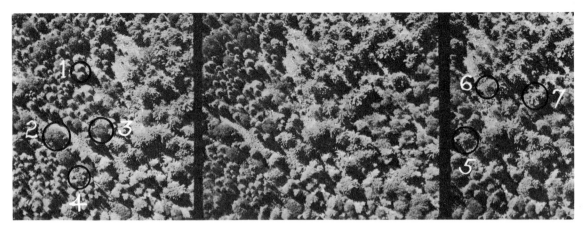

Figure 11.13. Stereo-triplet on 70-mm panchromatic film from the Superior National Forest in Minnesota. Species encircled are: (1) balsam fir, (2) quaking aspen, (3) paper birch, (4) red maple, (5) white spruce, (6) red pine, and (7) white pine. Scale is about 1:1,584. (Courtesy U.S. Forest Service Remote Sensing Project, Berkeley, California.)

KEY TO THE NORTHERN CONIFERS[a]	
1. Crowns small, or if large, then definitely cone-shaped	
2. Crown broadly conical, usually rounded tip, branches not prominent	Cedar
2. Crowns have a pointed top, or coarse branching, or both	
Crowns narrow, often cylindrical, trees frequently grow in swamps	Swamp-type black spruce
Crowns conical, deciduous, very light toned in fall, usually associated with black spruce	Tamarack
Crowns narrowly conical, very symmetrical, top pointed, branches less prominent than in white spruce	Balsam fir
Crowns narrowly conical, top often appears obtuse on photograph (except northern white spruce), branches more prominent than in balsam fir	White spruce, black spruce (except swamp type)
Crowns irregular, with pointed top, has thinner foliage and smoother texture than spruce and balsam fir	Jack pine
1. Crowns large and spreading, not narrowly conical, top often not well defined.	
3. Crowns very dense, irregular or broadly conical	
4. Individual branches very prominent, crown usually irregular	White pine
4. Individual branches rarely very prominent, crown usually conical	Eastern hemlock
3. Crowns open, oval (circular in plan view)	Red pine

[a]From Canada Department of Forestry.

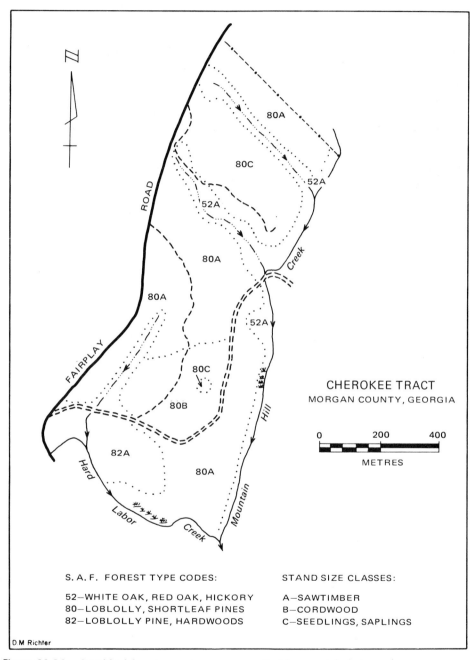

Figure 11.14. Simplified forest cover-type map compiled from aerial photographs.

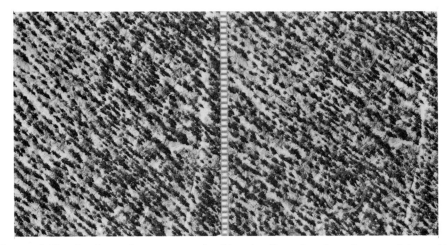

Figure 11.15. Panchromatic stereogram of a thinned radiata pine plantation near Rotorua, New Zealand. Tree counts, heights, and crown measurements can be made on such photographs. Scale is about 1:3,000. (Courtesy New Zealand Forest Service and New Zealand Aerial Mapping, Ltd.)

regions, of course, different film-season combinations may be preferred. Regardless of the film emulsion specified, the use of positive transparencies will generally yield more reliable *measurements* than the interpretation of photographic prints.

A common approach to volume determination is to substitute photographic measures of crown diameter (or crown area) and total tree height for the usual field tallies of stem diameter at breast height (dbh) and merchantable height, respectively (Figure 11.16). Regression equations are then developed for each species or species group for use in volume estimation. For example, the generalized linear equation, $\hat{Y} = a + bX$, may be employed if a "combined variable" (the product of crown and height measurements) is substituted as a value of X. Thus the general equation becomes:

$$\hat{Y} = a + b(cd^2 h), \text{ or } \hat{Y} = a + b(cah) \qquad \textbf{Equation 11.1}$$

where: $\hat{Y}$ = Tree volume, determined from a subsample of ground measurements to establish the regression coefficients a and b
    cd = Tree crown diameter
    ca = Tree crown area
    h = Total tree height

Other, more sophisticated regression models may prove superior to the foregoing equation form.

CROWN DIAMETERS OR AREAS

The value of crown measurements in equations predicting tree volume depends on the relationship that exists between crown dimensions and corresponding stem diameters or basal areas. High correlations of these variables often can be established for even-aged conifers that have not been subjected to undue suppression or stand competition; the relationship is usually linear for trees in the middle diameter or age classes.

The photographic determination of crown diameter is simply a linear measure, but measurements can be difficult because of the small sizes of tree images, the effects of crown shadows, and noncircular crowns (Figure 11.17). Various linear scales, magnifiers, and "crown wedges" are available for photographic measurements. Careful interpreters can measure to within ± 0.1 mm, so accuracy is dependent on image scale, film resolution, and the ability of the interpreter.

Measurements of crown area offer an alternative to crown diameter evaluations. Area determinations can be made with finely graduated dot grids or can be calculated from stereoplotter coordinates of points along the crown perimeters. As more sophisticated interpretation equipment becomes available, crown areas may entirely supplant crown diameters in tree volume equations.

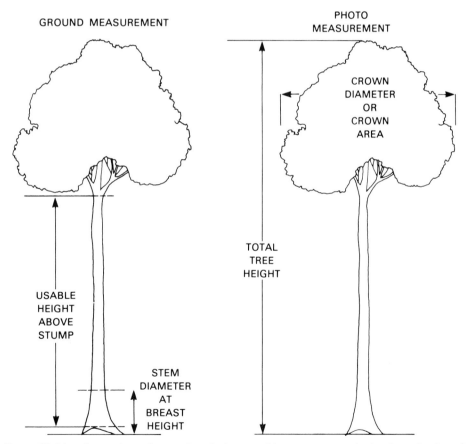

Figure 11.16. Comparison of ground and photographic measurements in the determination of individual tree volumes.

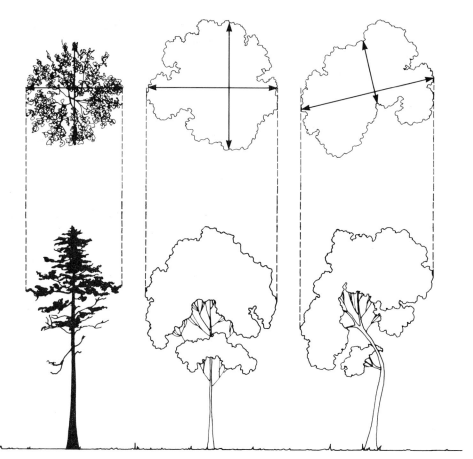

Figure 11.17.   The shapes of tree crowns as seen from above can make the measurement of crown diameter difficult.

▦ TREE VOLUME TABLES

Aerial tree volume tables are often compiled from volume prediction equations based on crown and height measurements. However, because more interpretation time is required for the measurement of heights than crowns, several single-entry volume tables (based on crown diameter or crown area alone) have been proposed. The approach is valid where tree heights are fairly uniform within specified crown classes. Table 11.4 was formulated from existing tarif tables by the following steps:

1. A tree volume equation was produced from optical dendrometer measurements of 58 standing trees; on the basis of this data, a tarif access table was derived.
2. An existing tarif table was selected for the area from which sample trees were drawn.

3. A crown diameter–stem diameter relationship, based on 600 tree measurements, was established for the sample area.
4. The crown diameter–stem diameter relationship was used to convert the selected tarif table to a single-entry aerial volume table based solely on crown diameter.

Although Table 11.4 is applicable only to a limited area in northern Arizona, the *method* of constructing the single-entry table may be useful in other areas where crown and stem diameters are closely correlated.

STAND VOLUME TABLES

Where only small-scale aerial photographs are available to interpreters, emphasis is on measurement of *stand variables* rather than individual tree variables. Aerial stand volume tables are multiple-entry tables that are usually based on assessments of two or three photographic characteristics of the dominant-codominant crown canopy—average stand height, average crown diameter (or crown area), and percentage of crown closure. These tables may be derived by multiple regression analysis; photographic measurements of the independent variables are made by several skilled interpreters, and a volume prediction equation is developed.

CROWN CLOSURE

Crown closure, also referred to as *crown cover* and *canopy closure*, is defined by photo interpreters as the percentage of a forest area occupied by the vertical projections of tree crowns. The concept is primarily applied to even-

TABLE 11.4. Tree Volume Table for Young-Growth Ponderosa Pine	
Crown Diameter (Metres)	Merchantable Volume, (Cubic Metres, to a 10-cm Top Diameter)
2.5	0.0453
3.0	0.0821
3.5	0.1246
4.0	0.1813
4.5	0.2492
5.0	0.3086
5.5	0.3823
6.0	0.4673
6.5	0.5523
7.0	0.6457
7.5	0.7562
8.0	0.8638
8.5	0.9771

Adapted from Hitchcock (1974).

aged stands or to the dominant-codominant canopy level of uneven-aged stands. In this context, the maximum value possible is 100 percent.

In theory, crown closure contributes to the prediction of stand volume, because such estimates are approximate indicators of stand density (e.g., the number of stems per hectare). Because basal areas and numbers of trees cannot be determined directly from small-scale photography, crown closure is sometimes substituted for these variables in volume prediction equations. Photographic estimates of crown closure are normally used, because reliable ground evaluations are much more difficult to obtain (Figures 11.18 and 11.19).

At photo scales of 1:15,000 and smaller, estimates of crown closure are usually made by ocular judgment, and stands are grouped into 10 percent classes. Ocular estimates are easiest in stands of low density; they become progressively more difficult as closure percentages increase. Minor stand openings are difficult to see on small-scale photographs, and they are often shrouded by tree shadows. These factors can lead to overestimates of crown closure, particularly in dense stands. And, if ocular estimates are erratic, the variable of crown closure may contribute very little to the prediction of stand volume.

With high-resolution photographs at scales of 1:5,000 to 1:15,000, it may be feasible to derive crown closure estimates with the aid of finely subdivided dot grids. Here, the proportion of the total number of dots that falls on tree crowns provides the estimate of crown closure. This estimation technique has the virtue of producing a reasonable degree of consistency among various photo interpreters; it is therefore recommended wherever applicable.

A modification of the foregoing technique involves the copying of aerial imagery onto 35-mm slides or microfilm. The images are then enlarged by conventional projection or by use of a microfilm reader, and dot counts and crown closure estimates can be made.

ESTIMATING STAND VOLUMES

Once an appropriate aerial volume table has been selected (or constructed), there are several procedures that can be employed in the derivation of stand volumes. One approach is as follows:

1. Outline tract boundaries on the photographs, using the effective area of every other print in each flight line. This assures stereoscopic coverage of the area on a minimum number of photographs and avoids duplication of measurements by the interpreter.
2. Delineate important cover types. Except where type lines define stands of relatively uniform density and total height, they should be further broken down into homogeneous units so that measures of height, crown closure, and crown diameter will apply to the entire unit. Generally, it is unnecessary to recognize stands smaller than 2 to 5 ha.
3. Determine the area of each condition class with dot grids or a planimeter. This determination can sometimes be made on contact prints.

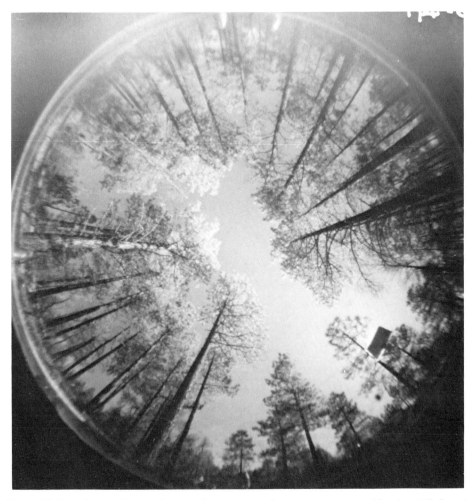

Figure 11.18.   A ground view of crown closure as seen by a canopy camera. (Courtesy U.S. Forest Service.)

4. By stereoscopic examination, measure the variables for entry into the aerial volume table. From the table, obtain the average volume per hectare for each condition class.
5. Multiply volumes per hectare from the table by condition class areas to determine gross volume for each class.
6. Add class volumes for the total gross volume on the tract.

VOLUME ADJUSTMENT FROM FIELD CHECKS

Aerial volume tables and volume prediction equations are not generally reliable enough for purely photographic estimates, and some allowance must be made for differences between gross volume estimates and actual net

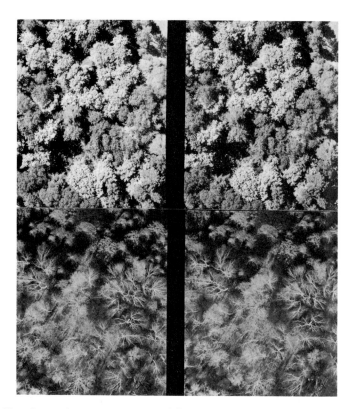

Figure 11.19.   Crown closure estimates are difficult when foliage and shadows obscure canopy openings (above) or when deciduous trees are leafless (below). Scale is about 1:1,000. (Courtesy Canada Department of Forestry.)

volumes on the ground. Therefore, a portion of the stands (or condition classes) that are interpreted should be checked in the field. If field volumes average 60 m³/ha as compared with 80 m³/ha for the photo estimates, the adjustment ratio would be 60/80, or 0.75. When the field checks are representative of the total area interpreted, the ratio can be applied to photo volume estimates to yield adjusted net volume. It is desirable to compute such ratios by forest types, because deciduous, broad-leaved trees are likely to require larger adjustments than conifers.

   The accuracy of aerial volume estimates depends not only upon the volume tables used, but also on the ability of interpreters who make the essential photographic assessments. Because subjective photo estimates often vary widely among individuals, it is advisable to have two or more interpreters assess each of the essential variables.

PHOTO STRATIFICATION FOR GROUND CRUISING

A photo-controlled ground cruise combines the features of aerial and ground estimating, offering a means of obtaining timber volumes with maximum efficiency. Photographs are used for area determination, for allocation of field sample units by forest type and stand size classes, and for designing of the pattern of fieldwork. Tree volumes, growth, cull percentages, form class, and other data are obtained on the ground by conventional methods. A photo-controlled cruise may increase the efficiency and reduce the total cost of an inventory on tracts as small as 50 ha.

The approach to an inventory of this kind is largely dependent on the types of strata recognized and the method of allocating field sample units. The total number of field plots to be measured is determined by cost considerations or by the statistical precision required. Once the number has been determined, the individual sample units are commonly distributed among various photo classifications by the technique of stratified random sampling.

If type boundaries have been accurately delineated and stands are homogeneous within the recognized classes, field plots can sometimes be taken along routes of easy travel without much bias being introduced. Usually, however, some kind of coordinate system is designated as a sampling frame; then a random selection of sample units is made within each stratum. Field measurements are taken by conventional procedures. Cumulative tally sheets or point-sampling may be employed to speed up the tree tally. After the volume per hectare for each stratum has been determined by field sampling, the values are multiplied by the appropriate stand areas. The result is the total volume on the tract, by cover types.

SPECIAL USES OF PHOTOGRAPHIC COVERAGE

Foresters and range managers have long used aerial photographs in various activities related to the prevention and control of wildfires. The potential fire danger in a given locality can be predicted by the intensive analysis of seasonal changes in plant cover. These "forest fuels" are readily mapped by special photographic flights timed at known periods of critical fire danger.

Presuppression activities include aerial photo searches for reliable sources of water during expected drought. Advance photographic coverage also provides information on existing fire lines and makes it feasible to lay out new lines and access routes before the occurrence of wildfires. Woodlands subject to heavy use by campers, hunters, and fishermen can be regularly monitored by means of up-to-date aerial photographs. The detection of wildfires by thermal infrared imagery techniques has been previously outlined in Chapter 7.

Special-purpose photography may also be used to advantage by foresters in estimation of timber volumes removed during harvesting operations or in assessment of logging and wind damage to residual stands of timber. In Figure 11.20, for example, individual stumps may be counted and merchantable logs that were removed may be estimated by measurement of photo distances between paired stumps and undisturbed treetops. The shadows reveal that stumps were cut rather high—probably an indication of the predominance of swell-butted bottomland hardwood species. The stand was rather heavily cut and subsequent flooding of the river flat will probably result in severe soil erosion. An example of wind damage to a timber stand is shown in Figure 11.21.

INVENTORIES OF FLOATING ROUNDWOOD

Cut roundwood being rafted down rivers, towed in booms, or stored in ponds can be inventoried with fair accuracy from large-scale aerial photographs. One technique for counting floating pulpwood sticks is based on a tally of individual bolts on sample "plots" that are randomly located in storage areas. The wood-storage perimeters are then delineated, and areas are determined with a dot grid or planimeter to provide expansion factors for the plot estimates. Photographic resolution and image size are major factors affecting the accuracy of such pulpwood stick counts.

Photography flown especially for inventories of floating roundwood should be taken when water areas are calm and when floating timber is spread out in a single layer. Where roundwood is piled high in several layers or covered by snow and ice, reliable counts are virtually impossible. The extremes in seasonal photographic coverage of floating roundwood are illustrated in Figures 11.22 and 11.23.

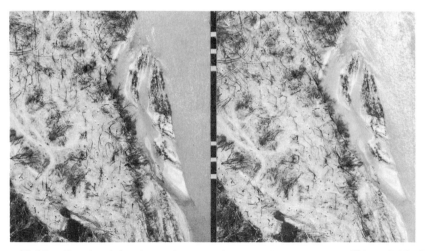

Figure 11.20.   Site of a timber-harvesting operation near Newcomerstown, Ohio. Individual tree stumps and residual tops are discernible. It is also evident that the river flat has been subjected to periodic flooding in the past. Scale is about 1:3,000. (Courtesy Abrams Aerial Survey Corp.)

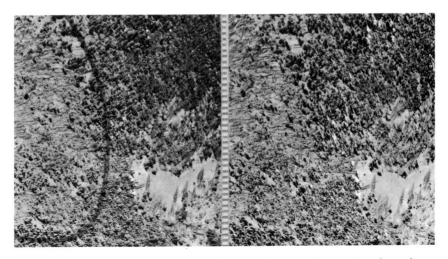

Figure 11.21. Timber blow-down on the Kaibab National Forest, in Arizona. Most downed trees are ponderosa pines. Scale is about 1:5,000. (Courtesy U.S. Forest Service.)

DETECTING PLANT VIGOR AND STRESS

Stress symptoms in vegetation result from a loss of vigor, which indicates an abnormal growing condition. Among the causal agents for loss of plant vigor are diseases, insects, soil moisture deficiencies, soil salinity, decreases in soil fertility, air pollutants, and so on. Because the symptoms of plant stress tend to be similar regardless of the causal agent, the agent itself usually must be determined by ground examination.

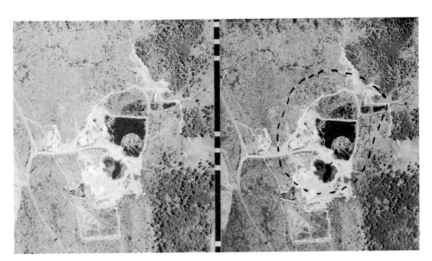

Figure 11.22. Sawmill storage pond for logs in Lewis County, Washington. Average log length and a reliable log count can be determined from such photography. Scale is about 1:6,000. (Courtesy Northern Pacific Railroad.)

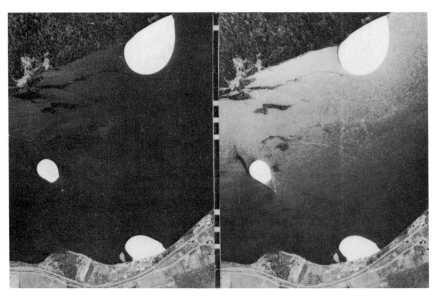

Figure 11.23.   Storage of floating roundwood along river banks in Aroostook County, Maine. A boom of wood is also being towed across the river. The mantle of snow and ice on the wood prohibits a reliable inventory. Scale is about 1:20,000. (Courtesy U.S. Department of Agriculture.)

The primary role of remote sensing research is (1) to find the best combination of films, filters, and image scales for detection of damaged plants and (2) to ascertain whether plants under stress can be detected *before* visual symptoms of decline are apparent (i.e., previsual detection). The most notable successes in previsual detection have been with infrared-sensitive films.

When plant foliage suddenly changes over extensive areas, conventional color or infrared color films provide an effective sensor at scales of 1:4,000 to 1:8,000. Skilled interpreters can then delineate the afflicted trees or shrubs, so that control or salvage operations can be planned. Losses from epidemics can also be quickly determined. However, this technique is limited, because the vegetation that has become visually detectable is already dying or dead. Control measures that can *save* such vegetation may thus be dependent on much earlier (previsual) detection—an achievement that has met with some success with black-and-white infrared and infrared color films.

An attempt to generalize some of the research findings in plant stress detection resulted in the compilation of Table 11.5. It should be emphasized that this tabulation merely provides a few *examples* of reported research and that the results are necessarily condensed and generalized. For a more complete summary, readers are referred to the references at the end of the chapter. An excellent guidebook to forest damage assessment has been prepared by Murtha (1972).

TABLE 11.5. Selected Examples of Plant Stress Detection

Causal Agent	Primary Species Affected	Imagery and Scale	Results or Detection Accuracy	Reporting Scientists
Balsam woolly aphid	Abies amabilis	Infrared color; 1:1,000	83% accuracy	Murtha and Harris
Black Hills beetle	Pinus ponderosa	Conventional color and infrared color; 1:7,920 and smaller	80%–90% accuracy at 1:7,920 scale	Heller
Pine butterfly	Pinus ponderosa	Infrared color; 1:127.000	70% of area, as compared to visual ground survey	Ciesla
Douglas-fir beetle	Pseudotsuga menziesii	Conventional color and pan; 1:5,000–1:10,000	High accuracy; no numerical results	Wear, Pope, and Orr
Smog (air pollution)	Pinus ponderosa and Pinus jeffreyi	Conventional color; 1:8,000	80%–90% accuracy	Wert, Miller, and Larsh
SO₂ fumes	Most forest vegetation and some shrubs	600–700 nm; satellite imagery	Delineation of damage zones	Murtha
Dutch elm disease	Ulmus americana	Infrared color; 1:8,000	90%–100% accuracy	Meyer and French

LAND CAPABILITY FOR OUTDOOR RECREATION

Existing techniques are readily available for the physical inventory of recreational sites; the real problem is that of establishing inventory criteria, that is, standards of what should be considered a recreational resource. The approach used for the Canada Land Inventory is quoted here.[1]

Seven classes of land are differentiated on the basis of the intensity of outdoor recreational use, or the quantity of outdoor recreation, which may be generated and sustained per unit area of land per annum, under perfect market conditions.

"Quantity" may be measured by visitor days, a visitor day being any reasonable portion of a twenty-four-hour period during which an individual person uses a unit of land for recreation.

"Perfect market conditions" implies uniform demand and accessibility for all areas, which means that location relative to population centres and to present access do not affect the classification.

Intensive and dispersed activities are recognized. Intensive activities are those in which relatively large numbers of people may be accommodated per unit area, while dispersed activities are those which normally require a relatively larger area per person.

Some important factors concerning the classification are:

1. The purpose of the inventory is to provide a reliable assessment of the quality, quantity and distribution of the natural recreation resources within the settled parts of Canada.
2. The inventory is of an essentially reconnaissance nature, based on interpretation of aerial photographs, field checks, and available records, and the maps should be interpreted accordingly.
3. The inventory classification is designed in accordance with present popular preferences in nonurban outdoor recreation. Urban areas (generally over 1,000 population with permanent urban character), as well as some nonurban industrial areas, are not classified.
4. Land is ranked according to its natural capability under existing conditions, whether in natural or modified state; but no assumptions are made concerning its capability given further major artificial modifications.
5. Sound recreation land management and development practices are assumed for all areas in practical relation to the natural capability of each area.
6. Water bodies are not directly classified. Their recreational values accrue to the adjoining shoreland or land unit.
7. Opportunities for recreation afforded by the presence in an area of wildlife and sport fish are indicated in instances where reliable information was available, but the ranking does not reflect the biological productivity of the area. Wildlife capability is indicated in a companion series of maps.

---

1. Canada Land Inventory Report No. 6, *Land Capability Classification for Outdoor Recreation*, Lands Directorate of the Department of the Environment, Ottawa, Canada, 1970.

RECREATIONAL SURVEYS

The objective of a recreational survey is to locate potential sites and transfer these areas to a base map of suitable scale. With up-to-date photographs in the hands of skilled interpreters, a preliminary recreational survey can be accomplished with a minimum of fieldwork.

Most types of photographic films are suitable, although color emulsions are generally preferred. Exposures should be planned during the dormant season when deciduous trees are leafless or during the season when the greatest numbers of people would be likely to use potential features. Photographic scales of 1:5,000 to 1:12,000 have been successfully employed; if large regions must be covered by a preliminary survey, the smallest scale that can be reliably interpreted should be chosen to avoid the handling and stereoscopic study of excessive numbers of exposures (Figure 11.24).

The photo interpretation phase will require the identification and delineation of such features as:

Natural vegetation	Existing structures
Land-use patterns	Historical features
Scenic terrain features	Access roads
Water resources	Paths or trails
Beaches and inlets	Soils and drainage
Potential docks or ramps	Topography

The more promising potential sites are then checked on the ground for verification of the interpreter's assessments of current land use, present ownership, site availability, and potentially undesirable features (e.g., polluted water, excessive noise, industrial fumes, or lack of suitable access).

After the elimination of those areas that are unavailable or undesirable, a final report is prepared, summarizing and ranking the recreational potential of each site recommended. The report should be accompanied by both ground and aerial photographs that have been annotated to emphasize salient features, needed improvements, and possible trouble spots.

PROBLEMS

1. Obtain the most recent aerial imagery available suitable for preparing a local cover-type map. Be sure that a planimetric or topographic base map is also available for the project area. Then:

   a. Prepare a radial line plot to adjust the image scale to the scale of the base map (see Chapter 6).

   b. Delineate the effective area of each image frame, or mark effective areas on alternate overlapping photographs if overlaps are sufficient.

   c. Interpret each frame of imagery and delineate major forest and range cover types. Minimum areas recognized should be approximately 1 cm^2, depending on image and base-map scales. The cover-type

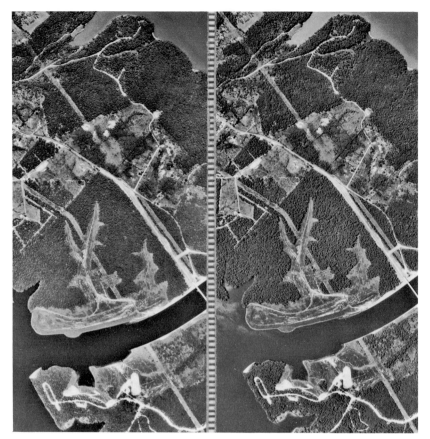

Figure 11.24.   Land-between-the-lakes area (Kentucky) where recreational facilities are highly developed. Scale is about 1:24,000. (Courtesy Tennessee Valley Authority.)

classifications used should be based on systems recommended by national mapping agencies or scientific organizations. Tree height or crown classes should also be recognized within each major cover-type group.

d. Ground check as many classifications as possible, and make corrections on each annotated frame.

e. Construct a planimetric (transparent) overlay at the exact scale of the base map. Show major drainages and transportation routes by use of standard mapping symbols.

f. Use a sketchmaster or another device to transfer the cover-type delineations from the annotated imagery to the planimetric overlay.

g. Ink the final overlay, and add the appropriate title, legend, and graphic scale. Check for errors and omissions by reference to the map correction sheet at the end of Chapter 8.

h. Color the major cover types according to a standardized system, or follow type-coding recommendations of your instructor.

2. Determine the land area of each major cover type shown on your finished overlay. Present in tabular form on a separate sheet, along with detailed definitions of each cover type.

3. Obtain 75 to 100 photographic measurements of crown area and total height for a coniferous species. Determine ground volumes of the same trees and attempt to fit a regression equation to the data by the method of least squares. Then use the equation for volume prediction in similar, adjacent stands.

4. Examine aerial photographs of an entire county at a local government agency or state highway department. Devise a set of inventory criteria and then locate at least three new potential recreational sites. Visit the sites on the ground and assess their relative potential, availability, and access. Explain your method of selection and site evaluation in an illustrated report.

References

Aldred, A. H., and J. K. Hall. 1975. Application of large-scale photography to a forest inventory. *Forestry Chronicle* 51(1):1–7, illus.

Aldred, A. H., and L. Sayn-Wittgenstein. 1972. *Tree diameters and volumes from large-scale aerial photographs.* Canadian Forest Service, Ottawa. Information Report FMR-X-40, 39 pp., illus.

Aldrich, Robert C. 1971. Space photos for land use and forestry. *Photogrammetric Engineering* 37:389–401, illus.

Avery, T. E., and H. E. Burkhart. 1983. *Forest Measurements.* 3rd ed. McGraw-Hill Book Co., New York. 339 pp., illus.

——, and James Canning. 1973. Tree measurements on large-scale aerial photographs. *New Zealand Journal of Forestry* 18(2):252–264, illus.

——, and M. P. Meyer. 1959. *Volume tables for aerial timber estimating in northern Minnesota.* U.S. Forest Service, Lake States Forest Experiment Station. Station Paper 78, 21 pp., illus.

Bonner, G. M. 1968. A comparison of photo and ground measurements of canopy density. *Forestry Chronicle* 44(3):12–16, illus.

Brown, Harry E., and David P. Worley. 1965. The canopy camera in forestry. *Journal of Forestry* 63:674–680, illus.

Carneggie, David M. 1968. *Analysis of remote sensing data for range resource management.* Annual progress report, Forestry Remote Sensing Laboratory, Berkeley, Calif. 62 pp., illus.

Ciesla, W. M. 1974. Forest insect damage from high-altitude color-IR photos. *Photogrammetric Engineering* 40:683–689, illus.

Driscoll, R. S., and M. D. Coleman. 1974. Color for shrubs. *Photogrammetric Engineering* 40:451–459, illus.

Hegg, Karl M. 1966. *A photo identification guide for the land and forest types of interior Alaska.* Northern Forest Experiment Station, Juneau, Alaska. 55 pp., illus.

Heller, Robert C. 1971. Detection and characterization of stress symptoms in forest vegetation. *Proceedings of the International Workshop on Earth Resource Survey Systems.* Government Printing Office, Washington, D.C., pp. 109–150, illus.

Heller, Robert C., G. E. Doverspike, and R. C. Aldrich. 1964. *Identification of tree species on large-scale panchromatic and color aerial photographs.* Government Printing Office, Washington, D.C. U.S. Department of Agriculture, Agriculture Handbook 261, 17 pp., illus.

Hitchcock, Harry C., III. 1974. Constructing an aerial volume table from existing tarif tables. *Journal of Forestry* 72:148–149, illus.

Johnson, E. W., and L. R. Sellman. 1974. *Forest cover photo-interpretation key for the Piedmont habitat region in Alabama.* Forestry Department Series 6, Auburn University, Auburn, Ala. 51 pp., illus.

Kippen, F. W., and L. Sayn-Wittgenstein. 1964. *Tree measurements on large-scale, vertical 70-mm air photographs.* Forest Research Branch, Canada Department of Forestry. Publication 1053, 16 pp., illus.

Lanly, J. P. 1973. *Manual of forest inventory, with special reference to mixed tropical forests.* Food and Agriculture Organization of the United Nations, Rome. 200 pp., illus.

Meyer, M. P., and D. W. French. 1967. Detection of diseased trees. *Photogrammetric Engineering* 33:1035–1040, illus.

Murtha, P. A. 1973. ERTS records SO_2 fume damage to forests, Wawa, Ontario. *Forestry Chronicle* 49(6):251–252, illus.

——. 1972. *A guide to air photo interpretation of forest damage in Canada.* Canadian Forestry Service, Ottawa. Publication 1292, 63 pp., illus.

——, and J. W. E. Harris. 1970. Air photo interpretation for balsam woolly aphid damage. *Journal of Remote Sensing* 1(5):3–5, illus.

Myers, B. J. 1974. *The application of color aerial photography to forestry: a literature review.* Forestry and Timber Bureau, Commonwealth of Australia, Canberra. Australian Department of Agriculture, Leaflet 124, 20 pp., illus.

Nielsen, U. 1971. *Tree and stand measurements from aerial photographs: an annotated bibliography.* Canadian Forestry Service, Ottawa. Information Report FMR-X-29, 111 pp.

Null, William S. 1969. Photographic interpretation of canopy density—a different approach. *Journal of Forestry* 67:175–177, illus.

Society of American Foresters. 1964. *Forest cover types of North America, exclusive of Mexico.* Committee on Forest Types, Washington, D.C. 67 pp., illus.

Stellingwerf, D. A. 1969. *Kodak Ektachrome infrared AERO film for forestry purposes.* International Training Centre, Enschede, Netherlands. 17 pp., illus.

Wear, J. F., R. B. Pope, and P. W. Orr. 1966. *Aerial photographic techniques for estimating damage by insects in western forests.* U.S. Forest Service, Pacific Northwest Forest and Range Experiment Station. 79 pp., illus.

Wert, S. L., P. R. Miller, and R. N. Larsh. 1970. Color photos detect smog injury to forest trees. *Journal of Forestry* 68:536–539, illus.

Zsilinszky, Victor G. 1966. *Photographic interpretation of tree species in Ontario.* 2nd ed. Ontario Department of Lands and Forests, Toronto. 86 pp., illus.

■ Chapter 12

Landforms and Physiographic Features

■ APPLICATIONS OF PHOTOGEOLOGY

The use of aerial photographs to obtain both qualitative and quantitative geologic information is referred to as *photogeology*. Geologists commonly use photographs for structural mapping, fuel and mineral exploration, and general engineering surveys. Geologic interpretation is based on the fundamental recognition elements of photographic tone, color, texture, pattern, relationships of associated features, shape, and size. Although oblique photographs are often of value to the photogeologist, most detailed analyses make use of vertical photography.

The quantity of geologic information that can be obtained from aerial photographs depends on terrain, climatic environment, and stage of the geomorphic cycle. Because features are more readily recognized where strong differences exist in the erosional resistance of adjacent rocks, sedimentary terrain may be expected to yield the greatest amount of information from aerial photographs. Metamorphic terrain may yield the least information, because metamorphic processes tend to destroy differences that may have existed in the unmetamorphosed rocks.

In petroleum exploration aerial photographs provide a wealth of information with regard to potential structural traps. Folds may be interpreted from a study of strike and dip of bedding or from stream patterns. Anomalous stream characteristics, such as deflections, may suggest subsurface structures. The variety of photographic criteria that suggests faults permits aerial photographs to be of particular use in ore-deposit and earthquake studies. Analysis of soil patterns yields information regarding permeability of the surficial materials that are a concern of the engineering geologist (Ray 1960).

Although detailed analyses of geomorphology, stratigraphy, and structural geology require professional training in geology, skilled interpreters may develop a high degree of proficiency in recognition of broad lithologic units and identification of distinctive landforms or surface features (Figure 12.1). Thus, the objective of this chapter is to provide the nongeologist with a simple introduction to the study of landforms and physiographic features through aerial photography.

LITHOLOGIC UNITS

It is usually valuable for the interpreter to be able to classify rock with respect to its general geologic type, that is, whether the rock was formed directly from a molten mass (igneous), by the deposition of rock grains transported by water or wind (sedimentary), or by the action of heat or pressure on previously existing rock (metamorphic). Landforms composed of these rock classes often show up with striking clarity on aerial photographs; in many instances, key physiographic signatures will reveal their lithologic composition to the practiced interpreter.

Igneous surface materials that may be directly recognized or identified by inference include granite, basalt, lava flows, volcanic glass (obsidian), and pumice. In the case of sedimentary materials, it may be possible for the interpreter to recognize gypsum sand, quartz sand, sandstone, dolomite, and limestone deposits. Gneiss is the principal metamorphic rock that is commonly observed, although the presence of such rocks as marble may be detected in open quarries. Simple inferences regarding surficial deposits can be of considerable economic importance to the engineering geologist in search of materials such as sand or gravel for construction projects (Figure 12.2).

The climate and stage of erosion are important influences on rock appearance. Because the climate controls the amount of moisture in a region, it directly influences soil formation, the depth of weathering, the amount of vegetative cover, and the rate of erosion. The stage of erosion reflects the extent to which the earth's surfaces have been dissected and weathered. Among early, middle, and late stages of erosion, the early and middle stages are the times of greatest topographic relief. As a rule, erosional patterns are more easily interpreted in arid regions, where vegetative cover is sparse or absent.

STRIKE AND DIP DETERMINATIONS

Patterns of fractures, faults, and dikes, usually discernible on aerial photographs, are important in mineralogical exploration. Inclined beds of sedimentary rock may also reveal structural anomalies that indicate possible

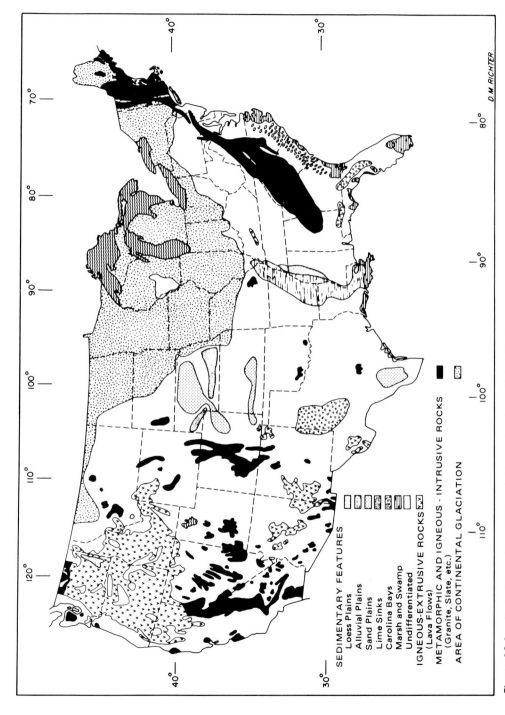

Figure 12.1.   Distinctive surface features in the conterminous United States.

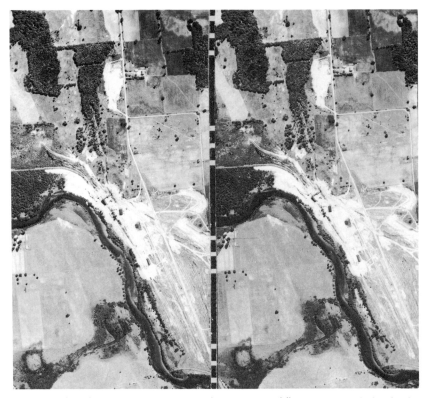

Figure 12.2.   A knowledge of the depositional characteristics of flowing streams led to the discovery of this sand deposit along a Michigan river. Scale is about 1:20,000.

mineral deposits. On high-quality photographs of the proper scale, it is possible to obtain quantitative information on tilted sedimentary beds by direct measurements of dip (the angle of a geologic surface with respect to the horizontal) and strike (the bearing of the line of intersection of an inclined geologic surface with the horizontal). Stated in another way, dip is the *angle* in which the inclined bed disappears beneath the ground, and strike is the *true compass bearing* of a line along the edge of the exposed dipping bed (Figure 12.3).

In some instances, the direction of the dip angle is also required for a complete description of the plane of contact between rock bodies. As stated by Dort (1964), "Dip is the angle and direction down which a mine would be excavated in order to follow a layer of coal. The strike is the direction along which that layer of coal would be exposed across a flat field."

When bedding surfaces coincide with topographic surfaces, the dip angle can be determined by measurement of the height difference between two points, one directly downslope from the other. Such height differences can be derived from measurements of stereoscopic parallax as described in Chapter

3. After the horizontal distance between the same two points is determined, the dip angle can be computed by this trigonometric relationship:

$$\frac{\text{Vertical distance}}{\text{Horizontal distance}} = \text{Tangent of dip angle} \qquad \textbf{Equation 12.1}$$

If relief in an area is low, the horizontal distance may be scaled directly from a single photograph without significant error in computation of the dip. However, when relief is moderate or high, a correction for the relief displacement of the upper point with respect to the lower point should be made. In the unique circumstance where the strike is radial from a photograph center, or the surface on which the dip to be measured is near a photograph center, there is little or no relief displacement in the dip direction, and no correction in scaling the horizontal distance need be made (Ray 1960).

The strike line generally can be determined with a protractor by inspection of the stereoscopic model and notation of two points of equal altitude on a bed. Where dips are low, however, tilt in the photographs will affect the direction of strike. The lower the dip, the greater the effect on the change in azimuth of the strike line.

ANALYSIS OF DRAINAGE PATTERNS

As was pointed out in Chapter 10, the type of drainage pattern prevailing on a given landform surface is often indicative of the kind of soil, parent material, and underlying lithologic structure. The absence of an integrated drainage system also provides information of significance. For example, the lack of a well-defined drainage network might indicate the presence of porous rock, such as basaltic lava, where surface water percolates downward to the water table through cracks and cavities. In other instances, soluble rocks such as

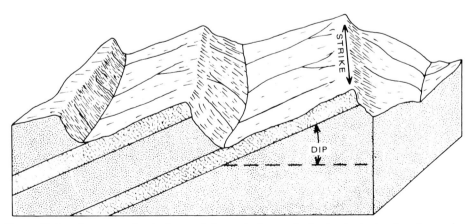

Figure 12.3.   Illustration of strike line and dip angle for gently dipping beds of sedimentary rocks.

limestone may absorb runoff through sinkholes and underground solution channels. And there are minor watersheds, such as dikes and drumlins, that may be too small to collect enough water for the establishment of a drainage pattern. Generally speaking, however, large landforms develop some detectable drainage system that may approximate one of the types pictured in Figure 12.4.

The *dendritic*, or treelike, pattern is a well-integrated pattern formed by the tributaries of a main stream as it branches and rebranches freely in all directions. This type of pattern implies that the area was originally flat and is composed of relatively uniform materials. Flat-lying beds of sedimentary rocks tend to develop dendritic drainage, as do areas of glacial till, tidal marshes, and localized areas in sandy coastal plains. The difference in texture (density) of a dendritic pattern may aid in identification of the surficial material; granitic areas, for example, exhibit a fine-textured dendritic pattern with repetitious curving tributaries outlining circular, domelike hills. The tributaries, as a result of steep slopes in granite hills, join each other at right angles. They appear pincerlike on photographs.

The *trellis* pattern, which resembles a vine trellis, is characteristic of folded or dipping rocks. The trellis pattern is developed over tilted sedimentary beds, and it results from rocks originally folded in parallel waves and then dissected. *Parallel* patterns consist of streams flowing side by side in the direction of the regional slope. The greater the slope, the more nearly parallel the drainage and the straighter the flow. Local areas of lava flows often have parallel drainage, even though the regional pattern may be radial. Alluvial fans may also exhibit parallel drainage, but the pattern may be locally influenced by faults. And coastal plains, because of their slope toward the sea, develop parallel drainage over broad regions.

Rectangular patterns, characterized by abrupt bends in streams, develop where a treelike drainage pattern prevails over a broad region but the pattern is locally influenced by faults, joints, or folds. Metamorphic rock surfaces, particularly those composed of schist and slate, commonly have rectangular drainage. Slate possesses a particularly fine-textured system. Its drainage pattern is extremely angular and has easily recognizable short gullies that are locally parallel.

Radial and *centripetal* patterns are characteristic of domes or depressions. For example, the sides of a dome or volcano might have a radial drainage system, while the pattern inside a volcanic cone or a dry lakebed (playa) might be centripetal, that is, converging toward the center of the depression. Granitic dome drainage channels may follow a circular path around the base of the dome when it is surrounded by tilted beds. These channels form an *annular* pattern, which is a modified form of radial drainage.

No system of landform grouping or lithologic classification is perfectly suited for photogeologic study. Any given photograph is likely to show two or more rock types, drainage patterns, structures, or depositional features. Therefore, it should be recognized that the classification scheme which follows is somewhat arbitrary and that other methods of grouping may also be appropriate.

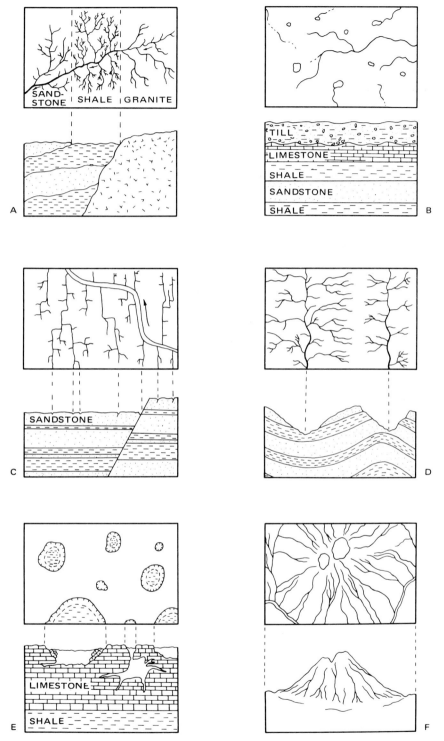

Figure 12.4. Drainage patterns and associated profiles for several types of landforms. Drainage types are: (A) dendritic, (B) deranged, (C) angular-rectangular, (D) trellis, (E) sinkhole, and (F) radial-annular. (Drawn by Douglas E. Grant.)

Flat-lying sedimentary rocks
Tilted sedimentary rocks
Igneous rocks
Metamorphic rocks
Fluvial landforms

Beach ridges and tidal flats
Glacial landscapes
Eolian features
Miscellaneous landscapes

FLAT-LYING SEDIMENTARY ROCKS

Sedimentary rocks are the most widely distributed surface materials in the world; as a result, they compose the principal lithologic features seen on aerial photographs. Sedimentary rocks are originally deposited as horizontal beds, but they may later become tilted or inclined as a result of folding and faulting. As used in this section, the term *flat-lying beds* refers to those sedimentary deposits that are tilted no more than a few degrees. Sedimentary rocks are of three basic types: sandstone, limestone, and shale. Such materials were formed from water-deposited materials associated with lakes or oceans. Almost all igneous or metamorphic landforms are in contact with one or more kinds of sedimentary rock (Figure 12.5).

Sand grains originally deposited along shorelines and later cemented together have resulted in sandstone beds up to 10 m thick in some parts of the world. Sandstone is a weather-resistant but porous material; as a consequence, the rock is a prime source of water in arid regions. The characteristic drainage pattern is dendritic to rectangular, depending on the presence of faults, fractures, and joints. Sandstone boundaries adjacent to lowland areas typically exhibit sharp, vertical cliffs because of the jointed but resistant qualities of the beds. When sandstone borders other sedimentary formations, the contact is commonly linear, because the more weather-resistant sandstone becomes a cap rock. Sandstone deposits, if not varnished, commonly photograph in light tones on panchromatic photographs because of the development of a thin mantle of sand and silt (Figure 12.6).

Shale is formed from the alternating deposition and compaction of waterborne silts and clays. Shale is an impervious rock, but it is weak and easily eroded. Drainage patterns are typically dendritic, and stream courses are meandering. In humid regions, rounded hills are characteristic of shale deposits, and photographic tones are mottled because of variations in moisture and the presence of organic material. Shale topography in arid regions exhibits minutely dissected hills with steep slopes, light photographic tones, and streams that usually are well entrenched in valley floors. Shale is commonly found as horizontal layers interbedded with sandstone or limestone (Figure 12.7). Such formations result in a stair-stepped topography that appears banded because of differences in vegetative growth.

Limestone is a sedimentary rock formed by the consolidation of calcareous shells of marine animals or by the chemical precipitation of calcium carbonate from seawater. Limestone plains are easily recognized by their concentrations of circular sinkholes that result from underground solution in stream

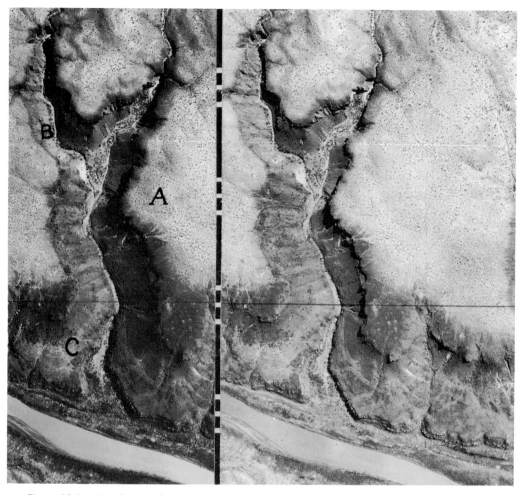

Figure 12.5.   Basaltic lava flow (darkest tones) overlying gently dipping beds of sedimentary rock in New Mexico. Note semidesert vegetation (A), joint-controlled rectangular drainage (B), and sedimentary beds in contact with lava cap rock (C). Scale is about 1:6,000.

channels. Where beds of limestone are inclined, sinkholes are somewhat elliptical in shape and may be exposed along bedding planes. Small amounts of water pass through these sinkholes, and, as solution takes place, an underground drainage system is developed. These underground channels are connected by vertical channels that show up as circular depressions on the surface (Figure 12.8). Limestone areas are generally light toned on photographs, except where sinkholes are filled with water. In well-developed limestone topography, there is little or no local surface drainage pattern, and few major streams are found.

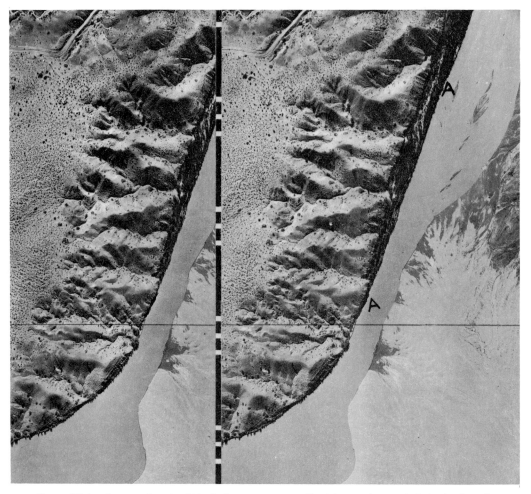

Figure 12.6.   Rectangular-dendritic drainage pattern on flat-lying sandstone-shale beds along the Rio Grande in New Mexico. The sharp cliffs and unusually straight river channel (A) suggest that the shoreline is structurally controlled. Scale is about 1:6,000.

TILTED SEDIMENTARY ROCKS

Horizontally deposited beds of sedimentary rock may become tilted or deformed through the development of faults and folds (Figure 12.9). Tilted strata, especially when composed of two or more rock types, show up as a series of nearly parallel continuous or broken ridges that may be either closely spaced or separated by valleys. Ridges may be of any height, and they are likely to exhibit a steeper slope on one side than on the other (Figure 12.10). In terms of weathering and erosion, sandstone appears as sharp ridges, shale is typified by well-dissected valleys, and limestone topography, in humid regions, has rounded hills and numerous sinkholes. Drainage systems usually form a trellis pattern, and large streams occur mainly in areas of shale deposits.

Alternating anticlines and synclines, along with the parallel banding of rocks, are the chief identifying features of inclined, interbedded sedimentary rocks (Figure 12.11). In humid climates, massive ridges indicate cap rocks of resistant sandstone; steep sides of ridges are usually covered by forest vegetation (Figure 12.12). As a rule, ridges are more rounded in humid climates. In arid regions, ridge lines have sharper crests, and vegetative cover is confined to stream valleys or sandstone-limestone outcrops.

The contact zone between tilted sedimentary rocks and flat-lying beds takes the form of a transition area where dip angles vary from steep to gentle. By contrast, sedimentary contacts with igneous intrusions or faults are denoted by distinct, linear boundaries.

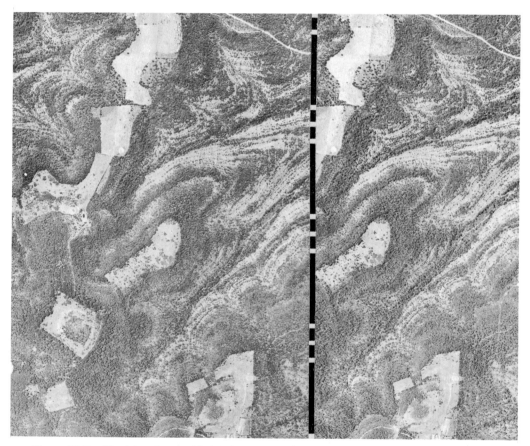

Figure 12.7. Flat-lying, interbedded sedimentary rocks in Baxter County, Arkansas. Dark bands supporting heavier vegetation are sandstone; lighter-toned bands are mainly shale or limestone deposits. Surface drainage is not well developed, and few gullies are found. The cap rock is principally sandstone. Scale is about 1:20,000.

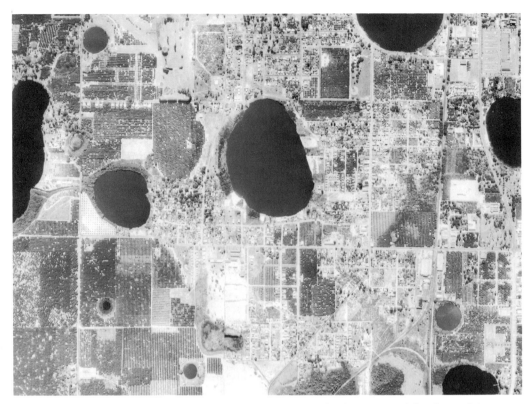

Figure 12.8. Rolling upland limestone ridge in Polk County, Florida. Numerous lakes (lime sinks) are found in this humid, subtropical karst region, which is planted in citrus orchards. Scale is about 1:20,000.

With flat-lying sedimentary rocks, stratigraphic thicknesses of exposed beds can be determined directly by measurements of stereoscopic parallax. If beds are inclined, however, the angle of dip must first be determined and then corrections must be made for relief displacement and for the effect of dip on the stratigraphic thickness (Figure 12.13).

Remote sensing finds its greatest application in structural geology, that is, the expression and configuration of geologic features shaped by deformation. Folded sedimentary beds are the most important structural features from an economic viewpoint. Many of the largest oil-producing areas are associated with folded sections of sandstone, limestone, and shale.

Relative ages of rocks can be determined from folding. Where the folded strata have been sufficiently eroded to produce their characteristic patterns, the age sequence of anticlines and domes is oldest-to-youngest, from the center outwards.

Faults and joints are fractures in rock. The presence of tectonic forces causes strain, stress, and even failure of affected rocks. Faults are planes along which movement has taken place (Figure 12.14). Joints are usually smaller than faults, with no movement accompanying them. Faults can occur singly but are commonly found in large numbers as fracture belts or fault systems. They can be tens of kilometres wide and hundreds of kilometres long. The analysis of such systems on aerial imagery provides a quick and effective means of evaluating the extent and effects of displacement.

Table 12.1 provides a comparison of common sedimentary and igneous rocks for purposes of photographic interpretation.

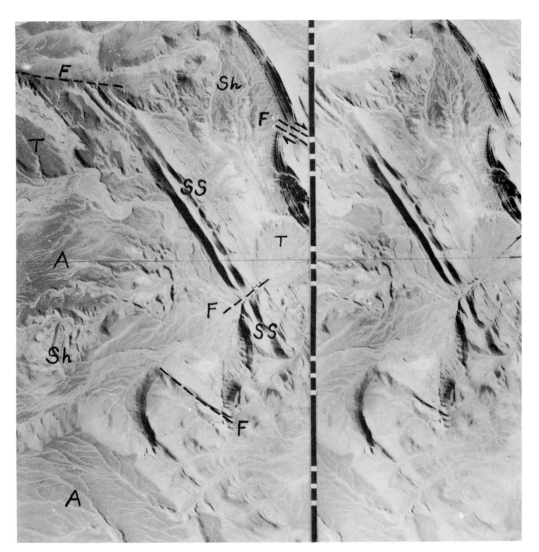

Figure 12.9.   Inclined sedimentary rocks and fault zones in the northern Sahara. Clearly discernible are sandstone *hogbacks* (SS), shale deposits (Sh), fault zones, (F), alluvial fans (A), and terraces of granular deposits (T). Scale is about 1:40,000. (Courtesy U.S. Air Force.)

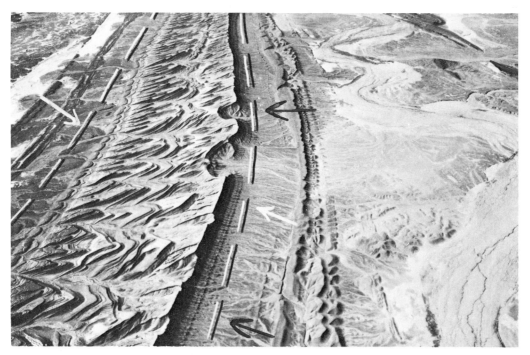

Figure 12.10. Oblique view of gently dipping beds of sandstone and shales in the Atlas Mountains of Mauritania, North Africa. Shale valleys are eroded and partially covered with alluvium. (Courtesy U.S. Air Force.)

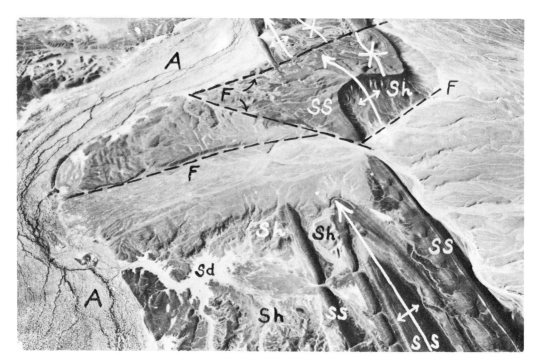

Figure 12.11. Oblique view of faulted anticline in North Africa. Note dark sandstone ridges (SS), shale with dendritic drainage (Sh), fault zones (F), alluvium (A), and sand (Sd). (Courtesy U.S. Air Force.)

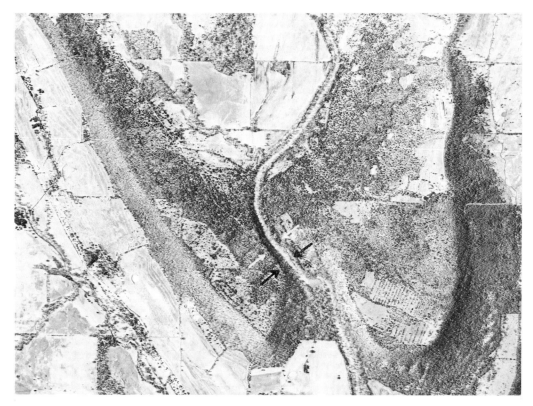

Figure 12.12.   Escarpment face of a plunging syncline in a humid region (Logan County, Arkansas). Arrows indicate a water gap eroded through the relatively soft sediments by Petit Jean Creek. Scale is about 1:20,000.

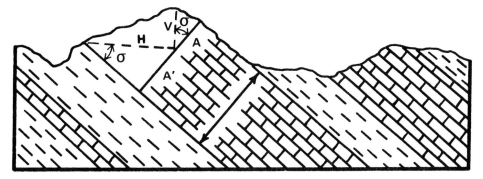

Figure 12.13.   Relationship of measurements needed for calculation of the thickness of dipping beds.

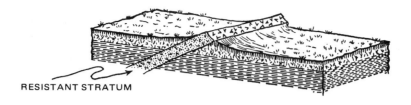

RESISTANT STRATUM

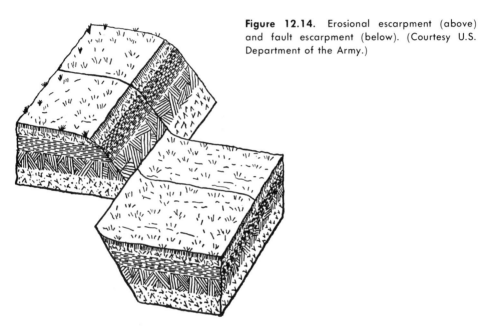

Figure 12.14. Erosional escarpment (above) and fault escarpment (below). (Courtesy U.S. Department of the Army.)

IGNEOUS ROCKS

Igneous rocks are classed as being either intrusive or extrusive. Intrusive rocks are formed by molten materials that are slowly cooled and solidified within the earth's crust. These rocks, such as granite, diorite, and gabbro, may later be exposed by erosion of overlain surface materials and often appear as large domes or as narrow belts (Figure 12.15)

Extrusive rocks are formed by the quick cooling and solidification of molten matter after it breaks through the earth's crust. This molten matter may flow over the surface, or it may be explosively ejected as fragments. Common types of extrusive rocks are basalt, rhyolite, andesite, and obsidian. Ejected fragments occur as volcanic ash or volcanic breccia.

Granite is one of the most frequently encountered intrusive rocks. Granitic surfaces, except for impermeable domes or jointed areas, have well-developed dendritic drainage patterns. Photographic tones are light, and the absence of stratification prevents confusion of granite with sedimentary rocks.

TABLE 12.1. Rock Type Comparison Chart

Sedimentary Rocks	Climate	Landforms	Drainage Pattern	Photo Tone	Suitability as Construction Material
Sandstone and conglomerate	Arid	High relief, bold cliffs, massive, angular	Dendritic, angular, trellis	Light	Excellent
	Humid	High relief, massive, rounded	Dendritic, trellis	Light to medium	Crushed rock, fill, riprap
Limestone	Arid	High relief, angular	Dendritic, trellis, angular	Light	Excellent
	Humid	Intermediate to low relief, rounded	Internal, dendritic, trellis	Light to medium	Crushed rock, cement
Shale	Arid	Low relief, slopes and valleys, angular dissection	Dendritic, parallel	Medium to dark	Poor
	Humid	Low relief, valleys smooth and rounded	Dendritic, parallel	Medium to dark	Poor
Igneous rocks					
Intrusive	Arid	Massive outcrops, bald domes	Dendritic, angular, annular, radial	Light, uniform	Excellent building stone and fill
	Humid	Rounded outcrops, subdued topography	Dendritic, angular, radial	Light, uniform	
Extrusive	Arid	Inclined flows, flat-topped plateaus, cliffs	Dendritic, parallel	Dark	Excellent crushed rock and fill
	Humid	Subdued and undulating topography	Dendritic	Dark	

From U.S. Army Engineer School, Ft. Belvoir, Virginia.

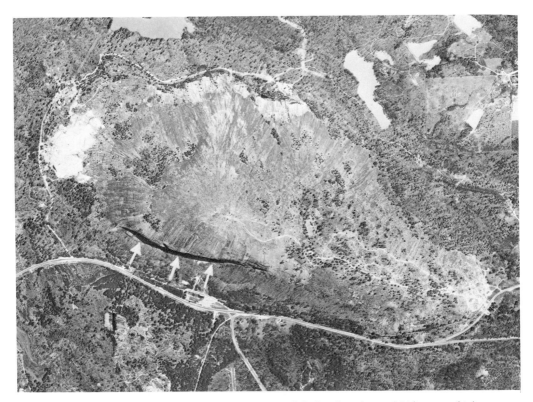

Figure 12.15.   Stone Mountain, Georgia, a granite exfoliation dome located 24 km east of Atlanta. The monadnock is about 11 km in circumference and rises 360 m above an ancient peneplain. Arrows indicate the location of a Civil War carving on steepest side. Scale is about 1:20,000.

The most widely distributed extrusive rock is basaltic lava, which is emitted from volcanic cones or fissures and flows over the adjacent surfaces as it cools and solidifies (Figure 12.16). A basaltic lava landform was illustrated earlier by Figure 12.5; topography may be flat or hilly, and minor surface irregularities are common. Canyon wall slopes are nearly vertical when breached by rivers, and both stratification and columnar jointing may be encountered. If a lava flow ends at an escarpment face or along a body of water, a distinct outline with serrated or ragged edges denotes the cliff boundary.

On panchromatic aerial photographs, basaltic lava appears in very dark tones; regional drainage patterns are likely to be of the parallel type because of slopes developed during original flows. In areas of predominantly igneous rock, basaltic lava may form resistant dikes or sills that are easily traced on aerial photographs (Figure 12.17).

METAMORPHIC ROCKS

When diastrophic forces of extreme heat and pressure alter the chemical and structural composition of igneous or sedimentary rocks, the resultant materials are known as metamorphic rocks. Among the more common metamorphic rocks are gneiss, schist, and slate.

Gneiss has a chemical composition similar, but not identical, to that of granite. Component minerals have a laminated arrangement that produces a banded appearance in the rock. Drainage patterns are angularly dendritic as a result of fractures, foliation, and possibly glaciation. Gneiss formations characteristically exhibit highly dissected hills that may occur as roughly parallel ridges (Figure 12.18).

Schist is a laminated rock largely composed of quartz, mica, and horn-

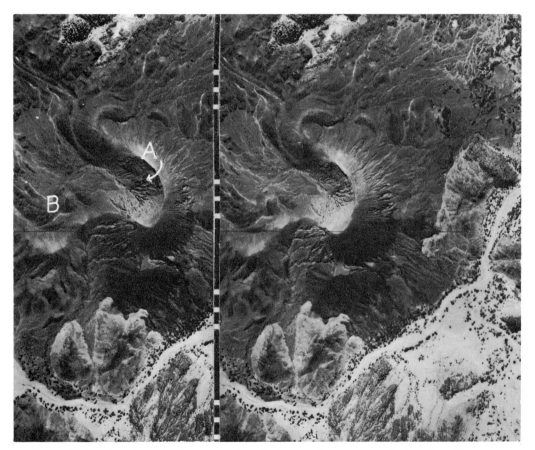

Figure 12.16. Inactive volcanic cone (A) breached by a subsequent basaltic lava flow (B). Note radial drainage pattern on side of cone. The location is Africa. (Courtesy U.S. Air Force.)

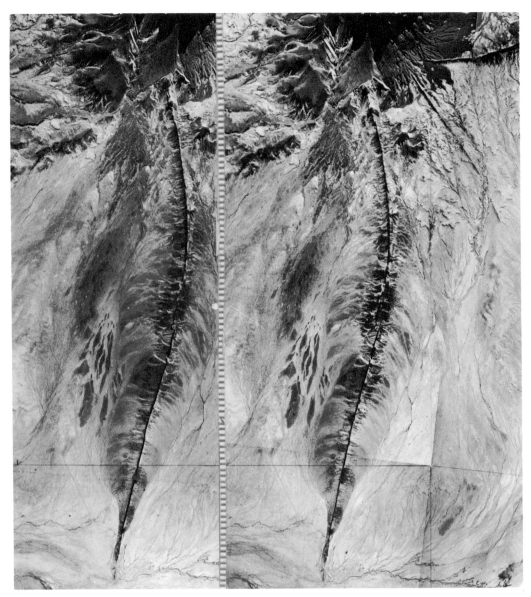

Figure 12.17. Large dike of basaltic lava radiating from Shiprock, an ancient volcanic structure in San Juan County, New Mexico. Scale is about 1:20,000. (Courtesy U.S. Department of Agriculture.)

blende. In arid regions, these rock surfaces are likely to be weathered into jagged outcrops (Figure 12.19). Covering soils may obscure the laminated structure in humid areas, but underlying schist formations may be revealed by a structurally controlled, rectangular drainage pattern. Parallel gullying is common on these easily eroded soils.

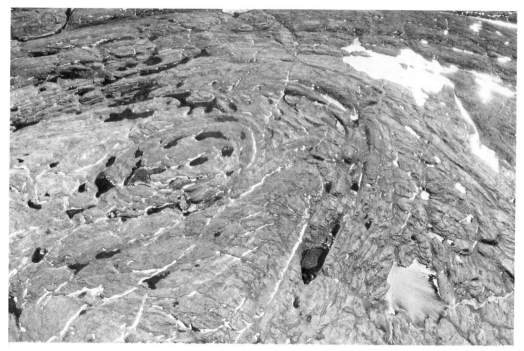

Figure 12.18. Oblique view of glaciated gneiss in Canada. Angular drainage, angular water boundaries, and parallel ridges serve to differentiate this metamorphic rock from granite.

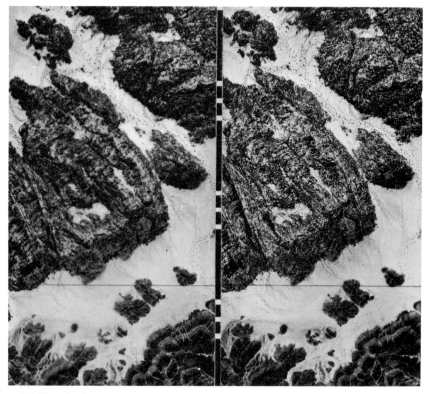

Figure 12.19. Dark-toned, laminated pattern of schists in Saudi Arabia. The sharp and rugged appearance results from alternating layers of hard and soft materials that are tilted upward, jointed, and weathered. Scale is about 1:40,000. (Courtesy U.S. Air Force.)

Slate is formed from metamorphosed shale. Topography is typically rugged in all climates, and the drainage pattern is rectangular and more highly developed than in shale or schist soils. Slate tends to photograph in a light gray tone on panchromatic film.

▓ FLUVIAL LANDFORMS

As defined here, fluvial landforms refer to those features shaped by stream erosion and deposition. Included are floodplains, filled valleys, alluvial fans, and deltas.

Earlier illustrations have depicted portions of the Mississippi alluvial valley. Meander floodplains are formed by streams subject to periodic flooding. During overflow periods, stream deposits on adjacent surfaces result in the formation of a broad plain of low relief. Such floodplains are characterized by channel scars, oxbow lakes, meander scrolls, slip-off slopes, and cut banks. This plain is composed of fine materials. Streams flow in single channels during flood stages, but at low water they may flow in braided channels (Figure 12.20).

Covered plains are constructed by floods that build up deposits and form natural levees, slack-water deposits, and backswamps. The deposited material is generally fine grained and thick. The covered plains may form over a meander plain because of a change in the flooding characteristics of the parent river.

Alluvial fans are formed by the action of running water when the velocity of a loaded stream flowing from a canyon is reduced and the coarser part of the stream load is deposited on a plain or valley floor. This action results in a sloping, fan-shaped deposit. The head of the fan is at the mouth of the highland stream, and its borders spread out into surrounding flat zones. In arid and semiarid areas, the texture of fan materials is predominantly coarse because of rapid weathering and torrential flooding. Dry channels are common (Figure 12.21).

Filled valleys are found in arid and semiarid regions in intermountain lowlands that have accumulated materials washed down from the mountains. They can be identified by their light tones, braided stream channels, lack of vegetation, and sharp topographic contrast to surrounding peaks.

Deltas are formed when flowing streams enter calm bodies of water such as lakes or oceans. Reduced stream velocity results in buildups of sediments at the mouth of the river (Figure 12.22). The arc-shaped (triangular) delta is most commonly observed. The delta of the Nile River is a prime example of this type. Stream channels may shift over the sand and silt surface, extending a delta seaward in all directions.

One of the outstanding characteristics of deltas is their level surface. Differences in elevation caused by stream channels, natural levees, lakes, and backswamps are minor when the extent of the delta is considered. Slight slopes may occur in very small deltas or in delta fans that are composed of coarse materials.

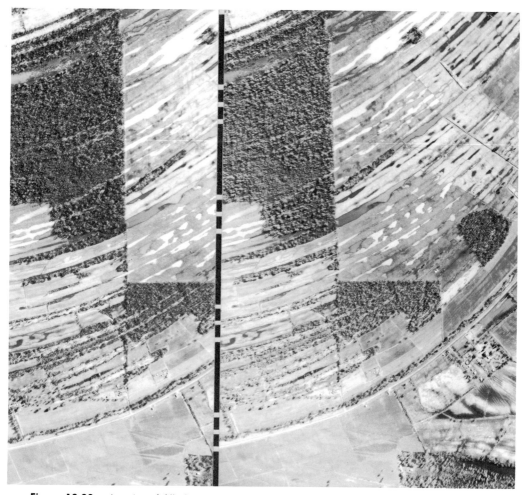

Figure 12.20.   A series of filled-in river meander scars in Concordia Parish, Louisiana. This is a common pattern in floodplains such as that of Mississippi. Scale is about 1:22,000.

BEACH RIDGES AND TIDAL FLATS

Beach ridges are formed when the level of a lake or an ocean is constant and wave action sorts and transports granular deposits of material. If the water level is slowly lowered, or if wave action is climatic, a series of ridges may develop. These ridges are usually found along the present-day shoreline but may be far inland if the water level or land surface changes drastically.

The outline of beach ridges is roughly rectangular and nearly parallels the shoreline. The boundary is smoothly curving to straight on the seaward side and less distinct or irregular to the landward side (Figure 12.23).

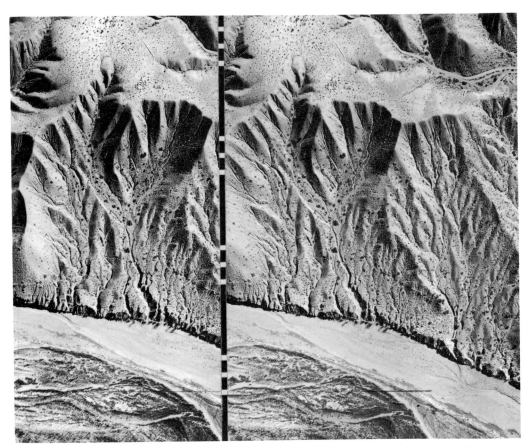

Figure 12.21. Dissected alluvial fan with parallel drainage and filled valley floor in New Mexico. Dry streambed has braided channel characteristics. Scale is about 1:6,000.

Tidal flats are formed along coastlines that are protected from wave action by sandbars, barrier beaches, or offshore islands (Figure 12.24). Lagoons or bays thus enclosed are filled with sediments and organic matter when streams empty into them. As a consequence, marshes subject to tidal fluctuations are formed. Tidal flats have an imperceptible amount of relief, and they become partially submerged at high tide. Mud flats are almost devoid of vegetation, but marshes may support dense growths of low marsh grass. Figure 5.9 illustrates the intricate drainage pattern characteristic of tidal marsh flats. Beach ridges are also clearly pictured on this photo index sheet.

GLACIAL LANDSCAPES

The extent of continental glaciation in the United States was shown by Figure 12.1. Continental glaciers did not cover Alaska, but there were many local mountain (alpine) glaciers there. Glaciers exerted great pressure on the land they overrode, profoundly modifying the landscape. Transported boulders, soil, disintegrated rock, and fresh rock were distributed throughout the glacial mass, especially in the bases of glaciers. As the ice masses melted, *glacial drift* was deposited over the landscape, thereby mantling it with debris.

Glacial drift is an all-inclusive term applied to soil or rock mixtures moved by ice or glacial meltwaters. This drift may or may not be water-sorted. Unsorted mixtures are called glacial till and are composed of a heterogeneous mixture of particle sizes. Water-sorted materials are called stratified drift and are composed of layered sands and gravels.

There are two distinct types of glaciation—mountain and continental. Certain landforms, such as till plains, lakebeds, and drumlins, are almost

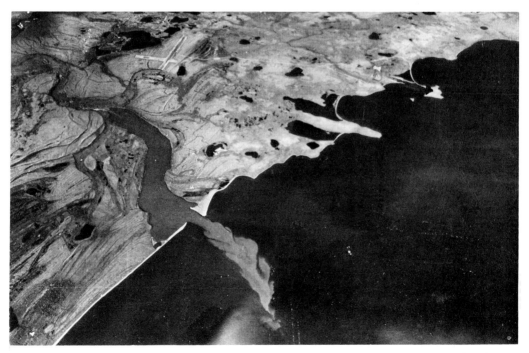

Figure 12.22.   Oblique view of a delta forming at Iliamna Lake, Alaska. Note the barrier beach across part of the mouth of the river. (Courtesy U.S. Air Force.)

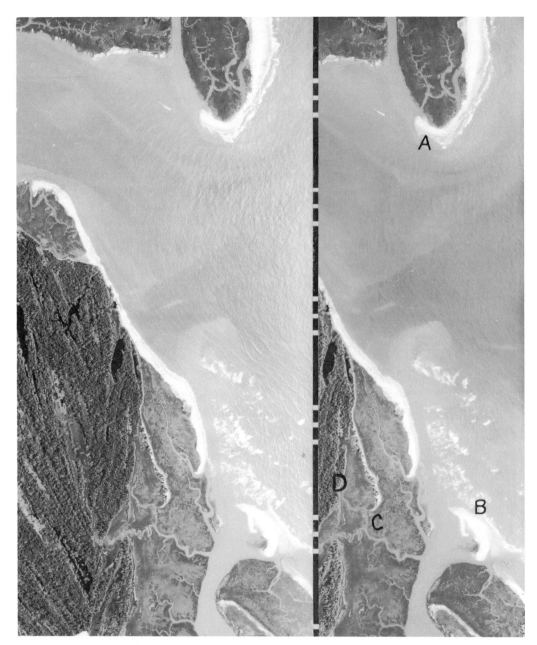

Figure 12.23.   Littoral features near Beaufort, South Carolina, include (A) a sand spit or hook, in a formative stage, (B) a barrier beach, (C) a tidal flat, and (D) beach ridges. Scale is about 1:20,000.

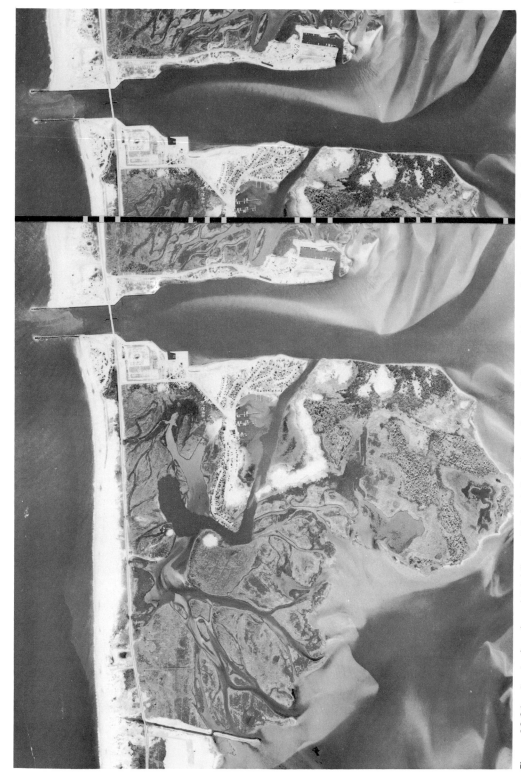

Figure 12.24. Barrier beach and tidal flat at Rehoboth Bay, Sussex County, Delaware. Note sand deposits in ship channel. Scale is about 1:20,000.

exclusively due to continental glaciation. Erosional features such as cirques, horns, and large U-shaped valleys are exclusively due to mountain glaciers (Figure 12.25). Three selected glacial features—*eskers*, *till plains*, and *drumlins*—are briefly discussed here.

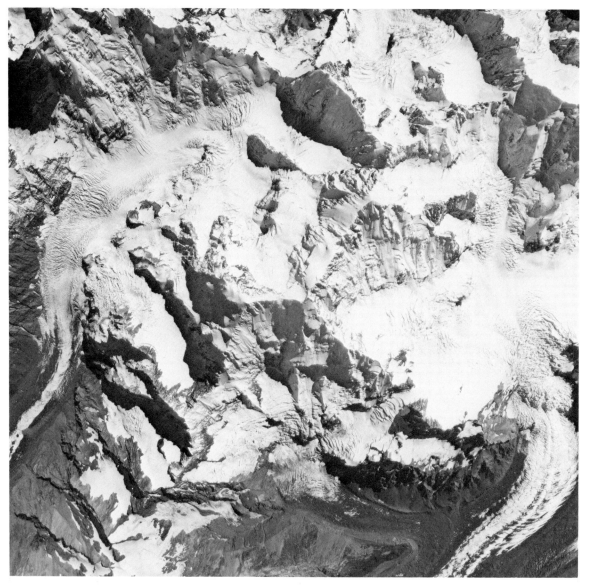

Figure 12.25. Glacial landscape in the vicinity of Mount Cook, South Island, New Zealand. Scale is about 1:63,000. (Courtesy New Zealand Department of Lands and Survey.)

Eskers are narrow, serpentine ridges of sand and gravel that were formed by glacial meltwater streams flowing in tunnels within or under immobile ice, by streams flowing on glacial surfaces, or by deposits in crevasses of glacial ice. They are distinctive and easily recognized on aerial photographs (Figure 12.26).

Till plains are composed of sorted and unsorted glacial materials; the mixture was deposited over the original land surface during a uniform retreat movement of glaciers. The till may be a thin veneer insufficient to obliterate the influence of the bedrock, or it may be thick enough to completely cover the bedrock. Layers of well-sorted sands and gravels may be found in deep vertical cuts of till.

Young till plains have an undulating surface that appears in mottled tones on panchromatic photographs (Figure 12.27). Other characteristics are field

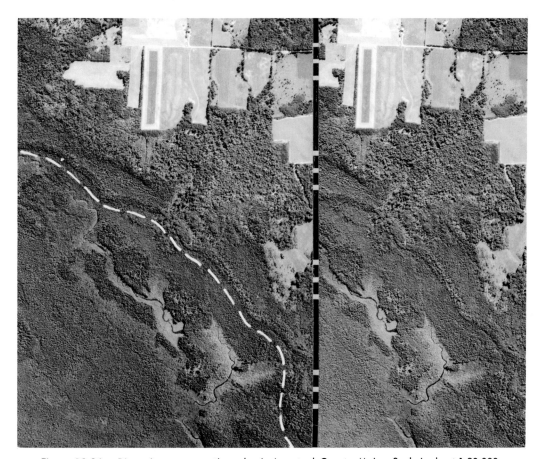

Figure 12.26.   Discontinuous serpentine esker in Aroostook County, Maine. Scale is about 1:20,000.

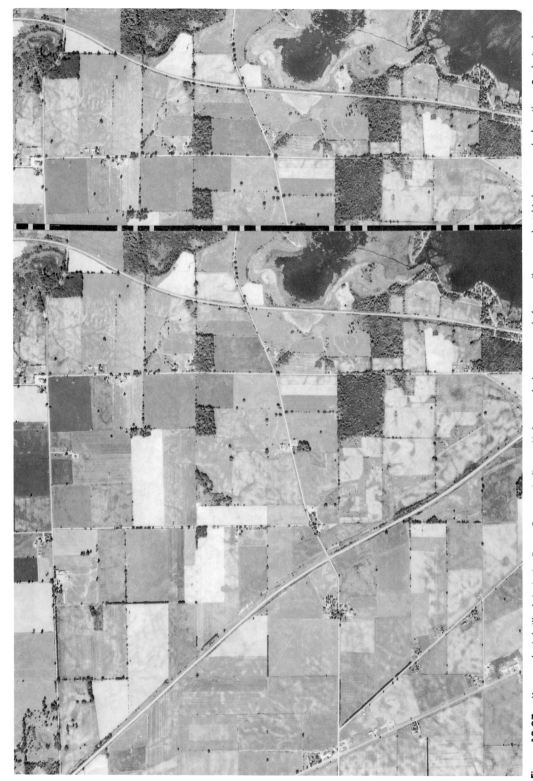

Figure 12.27. Young glacial till plain in La Porte County, Indiana. Light, mottled tones result from soil removal at higher ground elevations. Scale is about 1:20,000.

and road patterns that form nearly perfect rectangles. Old till plains have a level land surface and a well-developed dendritic drainage system. These areas show a lack of morainic topography and little or no tonal mottling on aerial photographs.

Drumlins are elliptical ridges 15 to 45 m high, 150 to 300 m wide, and up to 2 km long. They are composed of glacial till and are oriented with their long axes parallel to the direction of glacial movement. Drumlins taper in one direction; the head end usually points northward, and it is steeper and broader than the tail end (Figure 12.28). Generally, there is no drainage development on drumlins. However, there may be a few small gullies and mud-flow scars on the steepest slopes. Cultivated fields on drumlins are parallel to the long axis, and orchards are sometimes planted on these formations. If drumlin side slopes are steep, the formation may be densely timbered or in pasture.

EOLIAN FEATURES

Wind-deposited materials are commonly classified as either sand dunes or loess deposits. Sand dunes, most often found near shorelines or in desert areas, are formed by wind movement of granular material; the deposits are built up along obstructions in low-lying areas or behind the protective cover of rocks and bushes. The three main types of dunes are *barchan, longitudinal,* and *transverse.*

Barchan dunes, the most common, are crescent-shaped and are the basic unit for most dunes. They occur most frequently in inland areas where winds are strong and sand supply is meager. Barchan dunes with well-developed forms are not common. The horns of distinct barchan dunes point downwind. Longitudinal dunes are ridges which extend downwind from an obstruction. Their length is in line with the direction of the prevailing wind. Transverse dunes are formed by gentle winds blowing over areas of abundant sands. These dunes are scalloped ridges perpendicular to the direction of the wind, and they tend to migrate forward (Figure 12.29).

Dunes are mostly composed of quartz sand, though gypsum dunes occur in a few regions. Photographic tones are very light, except when dunes are covered by vegetation. Little or no surface drainage is apparent, because dunes are very porous.

Loess is a windborne deposit of silt normally found to the leeward side of deserts and glaciated regions. Windlaid silts that form loess deposits may be suspended in the air as dust and deposited on surfaces far from the silt origin. Deposits of loess may present a rolling or, when adjacent to streams, a highly dissected topography. If the loess mantle is thin, subdued features of the underlying landform will be dominant. Loess deposits provide good soils for agriculture (Figure 12.30).

Vertical bluffs and steep-sided, U-shaped gullies are the prime criteria for identification of loess deposits on aerial photographs. On a regional basis, the prevailing drainage pattern is dendritic (Figure 12.31). The boundary of loess is insignificant because a wide transitional zone usually exists between loess

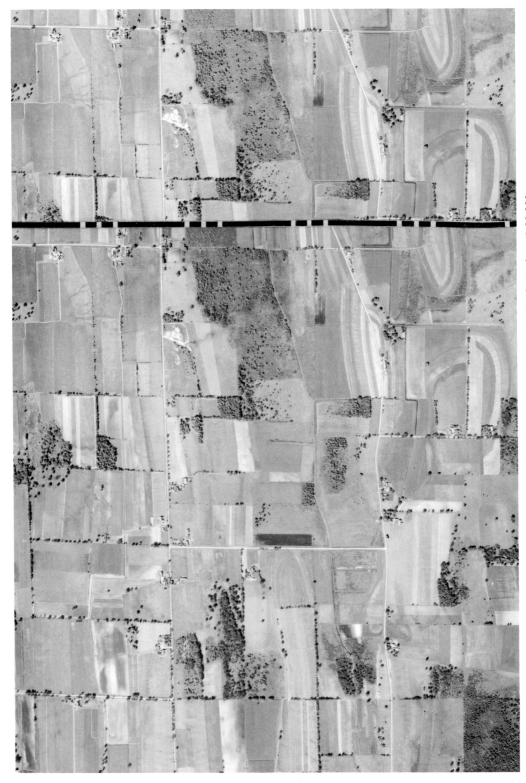

Figure 12.28. The effect of drumlins on agricultural patterns in Jefferson County, Wisconsin. Scale is about 1:20,000.

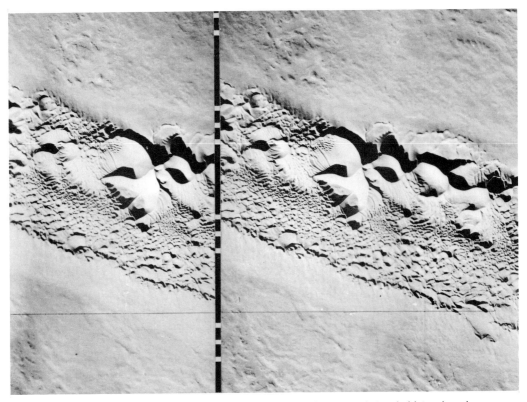

Figure 12.29. Transverse sand dunes in Algeria. The dunes are being held in place by an escarpment. Scale is about 1:40,000. (Courtesy U.S. Air Force.)

deposits and adjacent landforms. When these deposits are bounded by streams or floodplains, they form steep cliffs that follow the general outline of valleys.

▨ MISCELLANEOUS LANDSCAPES

Unusual landscapes, such as Mount Capulin in New Mexico (Figure 2.8) and Meteor Crater in Arizona (Figure 3.5), have been illustrated in earlier chapters. Pictured in this section are the Carolina bays (Figure 12.32) and part of a salt dome (Figure 12.33).

The Carolina bays are shallow, elliptical depressions of unknown origin that occur at low elevations in a belt of the Atlantic Coastal Plain from New Jersey to Georgia. The greatest concentrations of bays are located in North Carolina and South Carolina; it is estimated that the total number of these oval swamps may exceed 1 million. Locally, the bays may be referred to as "pocosins," an Indian term denoting a swamp on a hill, that is, having no external drainage system.

Most of the bays are shallow basins with poor internal drainage; local relief is normally less than 2 m. All are oriented northwest-southeast, and low, sandy rims are commonly found around the deeper southeasterly edges. These

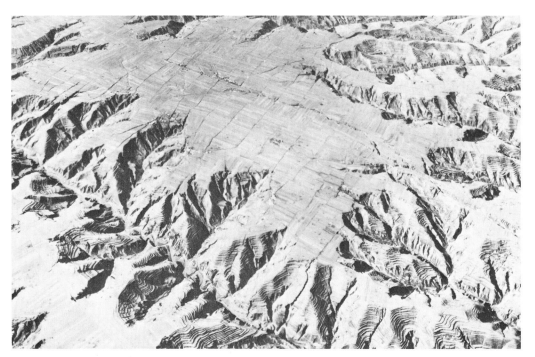

Figure 12.30.   Oblique view of a heavily eroded loess deposit near the Ching-Ho River in China. The U-shaped gullies are terraced and intensively cultivated. (Courtesy U.S. Air Force.)

characteristics have led to speculation that the bays were originally formed by intensive showers of meteorites from the northwest or by shock waves formed just ahead of meteorites that burned up as they entered the earth's atmosphere.

Most geomorphologists discount the theory of meteoritic origin, however. It is more commonly believed that the bays were originally formed by a series of complex, interacting processes involving underground solution and surface subsidence as found in limestone sink areas. The sinkholes may have been later elongated and rimmed with sand by wave action during interglacial periods. In some instances, the sandy rims may be the result of eolian processes. Regardless of origin, the Carolina bays constitute a unique and dominating feature of the Atlantic Coastal Plain.

In certain parts of the world, salt concentrated in closed-off basins reaches such high levels that it is precipitated along with other chemicals found in seawater. These deposits can attain large proportions, and they assume the shape of irregular subsurface patches along coastlines of emergence. Salt deposits are covered by impermeable clays or shales, which prevent solution by rain and seawater. In some cases, structural processes result in the formation of *salt plugs*; when these plugs appear near the surface, a domelike landform may be observed.

Radial drainage patterns are characteristic of salt domes. Various anomalies in stream patterns as seen on aerial photographs have led to the discovery of deep-seated salt domes along the Gulf Coast of the United States.

NONPHOTOGRAPHIC IMAGERY

Certain structural geologic features may be more readily recognized on side-looking airborne radar (SLAR) images than on conventional aerial photographs. Low relief and subdued features are accentuated when viewed from the proper direction (Figure 7.44). Runs over the same area in significantly different directions (more than 45° from each other) show that images taken in one direction may highlight features that are not emphasized on images taken in the other direction. Optimum direction is determined by the features that need to be delineated (Figures 7.32, 7.43, and 12.34).

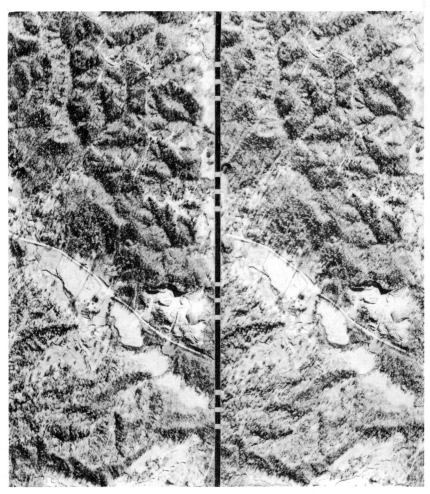

Figure 12.31. Eroded loess bluffs near Natchez, Mississippi. Loess deposits border the Mississippi River on the east from Natchez to Wisconsin. The source of these fine-textured deposits was alluvial material of glacial origin. In many places, the bluffs rise 60 m above adjacent alluvial plains. Scale is about 1:22,000.

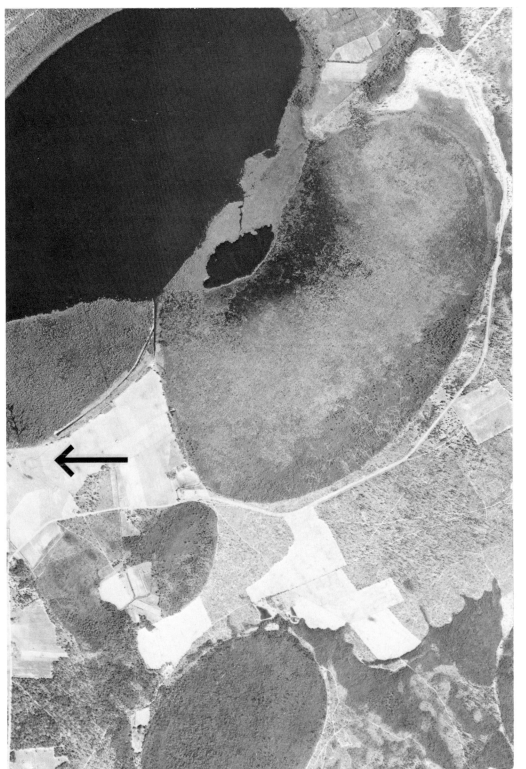

Figure 12.32. Intersecting Carolina bays in Cumberland County, North Carolina. Such depressions are oriented northwest-southeast. They are usually deeper at the southeast end, and sandy rims occur along southeastern edges. Arrow indicates north direction. Scale is about 1:20,000.

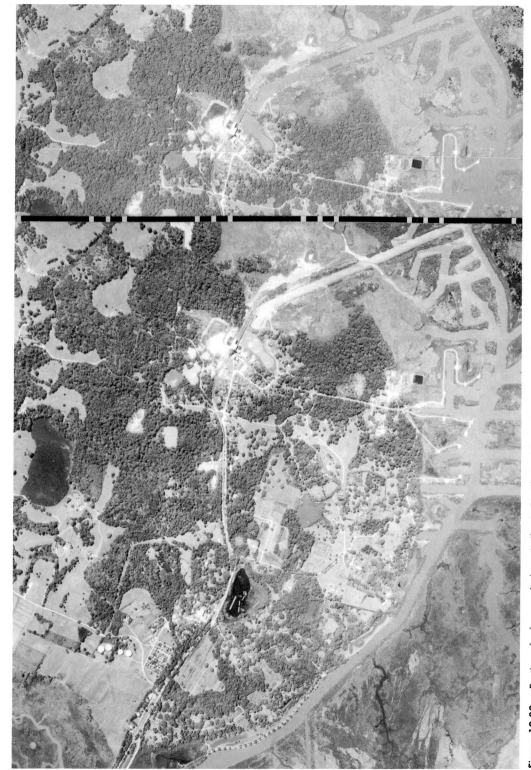

Figure 12.33. Portion of a large salt dome in Iberia Parish, Louisiana. A processing plant may be seen near the center of the stereoscopic view. Scale is about 1:20,000.

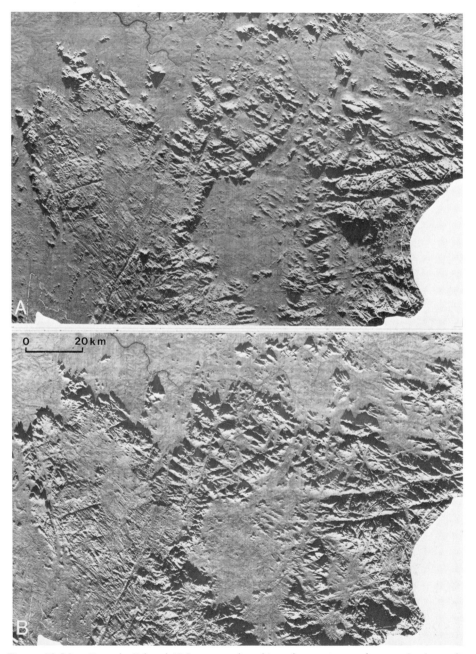

Figure 12.34. Motorola X-band (3.2-cm wavelength) real-aperature radar mosaics (opposite looks) reduced from original scale of 1:250,000. Shown is an 18,500-km² area in southeastern Nigeria: (A) north look, (B) south look. Note that some geologic features are more readily visible in one look than the other. (Courtesy Ron Gelnett, MARS Associates, Inc.)

A major contribution of satellite imagery to geology is its capability of detecting new linear features of the earth's surface. Lineaments ranging in length from hundreds of kilometres to less than a kilometre are being disclosed. In some areas of the world, poorly mapped in the past, the numbers of hitherto undetected lineaments have increased two to five times. Even in well-mapped regions, new satellite-based maps are far more detailed than previous ones. This improvement in detection of linear features is of great importance in the refinement of models for tectonic deformation and in setting forth new "targets" to be explored for minerals whose emplacements were fracture controlled (Figure 12.35).

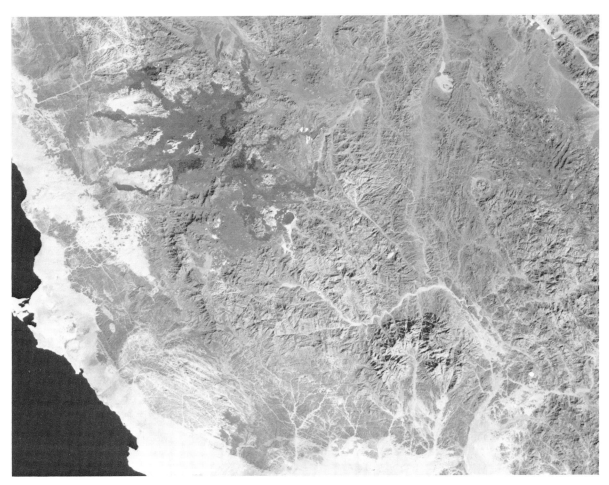

Figure 12.35. Landsat-1 Multispectral Scanner (MSS) image (subscene) of the mountainous zone, the Hijaz, bordering the Red Sea in Saudi Arabia. Spectral sensitivity is 0.8–1.1 μm. Scale is about 1:1,000,000. (Courtesy Lynda Sowers, U.S. Geological Survey.)

▓ GEOLOGIC MAPS AND SYMBOLS

A geologic map shows the horizontal positions (planimetric detail) of rock units as they crop out at the earth's surface. The rock units are usually called formations, and their limits are arbitrarily selected for mapping (Figure 12.36). Boundaries between rock units are called contacts, and the traces of contacts when shown on maps are called contact lines. The areas of formational outcrop may be shown in various colors or by some ruled pattern; the colors or patterns are generally overprinted on a topographic base map. A geologic map without topographic contours is called a contact map.

Geologic maps (in color) are issued by the U.S. Geological Survey and by most state geological agencies. On such maps, the various rock units may be identified by a series of commonly accepted symbols (Figure 12.37). Most maps will also include a detailed legend which describes the meaning of each symbol and "stacks" the geologic units up in correct age sequence, with the oldest on the bottom of the stack.

Common symbols used for structural maps are shown in Figure 12.38.

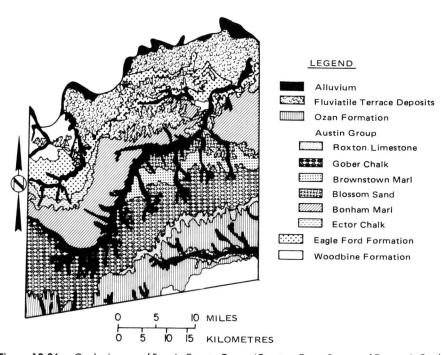

Figure 12.36.   Geologic map of Fannin County, Texas. (Courtesy Texas Bureau of Economic Geology and Purdue University.)

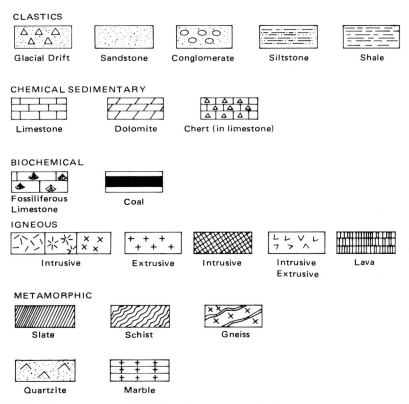

Figure 12.37.   Some common symbols for rock types on geologic maps.

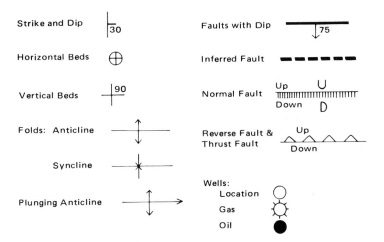

Figure 12.38.   Some common symbols for structural features on geologic maps.

PROBLEMS

1. Study a set of aerial photographs and corresponding topographic maps for a portion of your own county. Complete the following form as a means of summarizing the physiography and surface geology:

   a. Principal landforms _____

   _____

   b. Stream drainage patterns (primary and secondary) _____

   _____

   _____

   c. Stream drainage texture _____

   _____

   d. Major vegetative cover types _____

   _____

   e. Photo tones of major outcrops or surficial deposits _____

   _____

   _____

   _____

   f. Climate and annual precipitation _____

   _____

   g. General rock types present _____

   _____

   h. Specific rock types present _____

   _____

2. Obtain a stereoscopic pair of aerial photographs showing dipping beds of sedimentary rocks in an arid region. Determine the strike and dip of the most prominent beds and (if feasible) measure the thickness of the upper beds.

3. Prepare a simple photo overlay for a local area to show surficial rock types by standard geologic symbols.

4. Prepare a simple structural map (in overlay form) for a set of photographs supplied by your instructor. Indicate the axes of major folds, fault lines, escarpments, joints, and other structural features by standard geologic symbols. Describe the principal drainage pattern of the area and its relation to the structural development.

References

Bascom, Willard. 1960. *Beaches. Scientific American* reprint, W. H. Freeman and Co., San Francisco. 12 pp., illus.

Denny, Charles S., et al. 1968. *A descriptive catalog of selected aerial photographs of geologic features in the United States.* U.S. Geological Survey, Reston, Va. Professional Paper 590, 79 pp., illus.

Dort, Wakefield. 1964. *Laboratory studies in physical geology.* 2nd ed. Burgess Publishing Co., Minneapolis. 226 pp., illus.

Gimbarzevsky, Philip. 1966. Land inventory interpretation. *Programmetric Engineering* 32:967–976, illus.

Hamblin, W. K. 1975. *The earth's dynamic systems.* Burgess Publishing Co., Minneapolis. 578 pp., illus.

———, and J. D. Howard. 1975. *Exercises in physical geology.* 4th ed. Burgess Publishing Co., Minneapolis. 233 pp., illus.

Kiefer, Ralph W. 1967. Landform features in the United States. *Photogrammetric Engineering* 33:174–182, illus.

Lattman, L. H., and R. G. Ray. 1965. *Aerial photographs in field geology.* Holt, Rinehart and Winston, New York. 221 pp., illus.

Ray, Richard G. 1960. *Aerial photographs in geologic interpretation and mapping.* U.S. Geological Survey, Reston, Va. Professional Paper 373, 230 pp., illus.

Reeves, Robert G. 1969. Structural geologic interpretations from radar imagery. *Geological Society of America Bulletin* 80:2159–2164, illus.

Shelton, John S. 1966. *Geology illustrated.* W. H. Freeman and Co., San Francisco. 434 pp., illus.

U.S. Department of the Army. 1968. *Rock types.* U.S. Army Engineer School, Ft. Belvoir, Va. 44 pp., illus.

———. 1967. *Granular and fine-grain material.* U.S. Army Engineer School, Ft. Belvoir, Va. 53 pp., illus.

U.S. Department of Commerce. 1960. *The identification of rock types.* Government Printing Office, Washington, D.C. 17 pp., illus.

U.S. Naval Photographic Interpretation Center. 1956. *Military geology.* Government Printing Office, Washington, D.C. 174 pp., illus.

von Bandat, Horst F. 1962. *Aerogeology.* Gulf Publishing Co., Houston. 350 pp., illus.

Wanless, Harold R. 1965. *Aerial stereo photographs.* Hubbard Scientific Co., Northbrook, Ill. 92 pp., illus.

Warren, Charles R., et al. 1969. *A descriptive catalog of selected aerial photographs of geologic features outside the United States.* U.S. Geological Survey, Reston, Va. Professional Paper 591, 23 pp., illus.

Way, Douglas S. 1973. *Terrain analysis: a guide to site selection using aerial photographic interpretation.* Dowden, Hutchinson, and Ross, Stroudsburg, Penn. 392 pp., illus.

Chapter 13

Engineering Applications and Mining Patterns

■ SURVEYS FOR CONSTRUCTION MATERIALS

Today almost all major highways, railroads, airfields, canals, and pipelines are planned and constructed on the basis of information derived through aerial surveys. Construction engineers rely on photogrammetric techniques to evaluate alternative locations for levees, dams, and hydroelectric structures, to conduct water pollution and stream siltation studies, to search for construction materials such as sand or gravel, and to measure stockpiles of raw materials (Figure 13.1).

Although construction materials such as aggregate and compacted fill are usually regarded as low-cost resources, their presence or absence can significantly affect urban and industrial activity. Most contractors depend on local sources for construction materials, and considerable funds may be expended in searching for economical deposits of aggregate and fill.

With regard to granular materials, their location and type depends on the geology and physiography of an area, both of which can be assessed from aerial photography. It is possible to tell whether a deposit is sand or gravel, and it may also be possible to determine the presence and types of overburden. In short, the aerial photograph provides a reliable means of locating and determining the areal extent of granular deposits.

In a materials survey, it is often desirable to make a comparative analysis of two or more potential construction sites; this analysis can be largely accom-

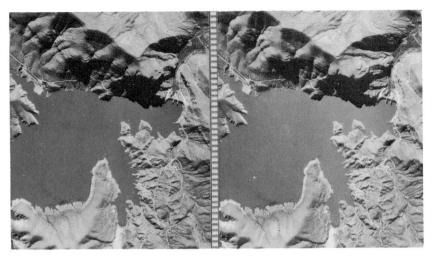

Figure 13.1.   Dam on San Carlos Lake, Arizona. Construction materials are not easily obtained for most sites in mountainous terrain. Scale is about 1:42,000.

plished through photographic interpretation. While it may not be possible to predict the suitability of materials for cement or concrete, it *is* possible to identify a given deposit as sand or gravel and to determine whether a large deposit is to be expected.

Photographic specifications for materials surveys vary from one region to another. Black-and-white exposures at a scale of 1:15,000 to 1:25,000 are often suitable in arid environments, but infrared color is the preferred sensor in most other regions.

▨ HIGHWAY LOCATION STUDIES

In spite of global problems of overpopulation, there are still many regions of the world that are almost undeveloped. Before such areas can be made suitable for exploitation, economic development, and human habitation, highways, railroads, and other access routes must be developed and maintained. In addition, new or enlarged transportation arteries are being designed and built each year in advanced countries, and photogrammetric surveys are playing an increasingly important role in these projects (Figure 13.2).

Although there are notable differences, photographic interpretation techniques used in route location studies are similar to those employed for other engineering projects. The scientific evaluation of alternative routes requires studies of rather large areas, with emphasis on the analysis of surface soils, drainage characteristics, and searches for aggregate materials. It is, therefore, advantageous to have such projects staffed by engineers with geological training or by engineering geologists with a working knowledge of soils.

The uses of aerial photographs for the development of a new highway or railroad route may be conveniently organized into three distinct stages or phases, namely, (1) reconnaissance surveys and regional exploration, (2)

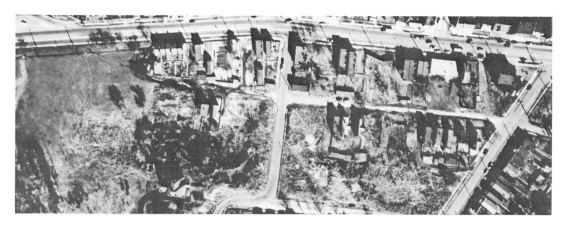

"P & P" SHEETS ARE WIDELY USED IN CONNECTION WITH PIPELINE LOCATION, HIGHWAY DESIGN, TRANSMISSION LINES, MICROWAVE TOWER LOCATION, AND MANY OTHER ENGINEERING PROBLEMS. THE SCALE AND THE ORDER OF VERTICAL ACCURACY ARE INDIVIDUALLY DESIGNED TO MEET THE REQUIREMENTS OF THE SPECIFIC PROJECT.

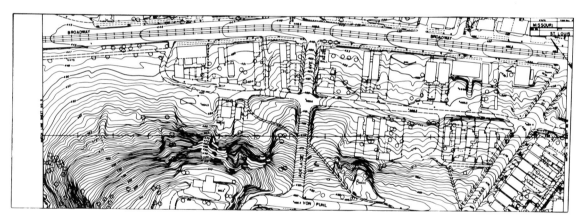

THIS PLAN SHEET, WITH 1-FT (0.3 m) CONTOURS, COVERS THE SAME AREA AS THE AERIAL PHOTOGRAPH SHOWN ABOVE.

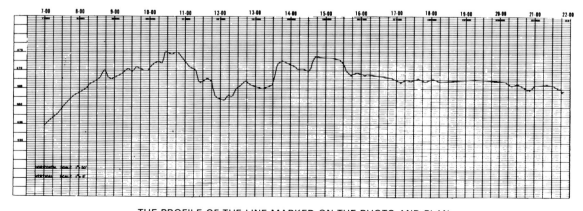

THE PROFILE OF THE LINE MARKED ON THE PHOTO AND PLAN.

Figure 13.2. Example of a plan-and-profile sheet compiled for an engineering survey. (Courtesy Jack Ammann Photogrammetric Engineers, Inc.)

preconstruction studies and comparisons of feasible routes, and (3) intensive study of the best route. Each phase refines the route location to a higher degree than the preceding stage. The basic task in location is the fitting of the road or railroad structure to the natural features of an area in a manner that will be most economical in construction and operation. This demands that natural features be effectively assessed, and aerial photographs provide an efficient means of meeting this objective. Natural features to be evaluated in a location study are topography, drainage, property values, soils and geology, borrow sources, vegetation, and special trouble areas. Imposed upon this information about the natural features of the area is the engineer's competence in determining the length, grade, and alignment of the route and the type of structures needed.

The principal physiographic features that determine the location and cost of a new transportation route are these:

1. Steepness and irregularity of the terrain
2. Soil composition, depth, and moisture content
3. Prevailing drainage characteristics
4. Limiting features, such as mountain passes, sites available for bridges or tunnels, box canyons, and large cemeteries
5. Availability of granular construction materials near the proposed corridor

THE RECONNAISSANCE SURVEY

The primary objective of a reconnaissance survey is to choose several corridors that appear to be technically feasible routes. An area having a width of 30 to 50 percent of the distance between terminals is studied on available maps and aerial photographs. If recent stereoscopic coverage of a suitable scale is not available, special photographic flights may be required. Depending on local topographic relief and intensity of land use, photographic scales may range from 1:10,000 to 1:50,000. It is desirable to use the smallest scale practical, because fewer stereoscopic setups are needed to encompass a given corridor area—with commensurate savings in time and money.

Where topographic maps have not been previously compiled for an area, the land surface may be evaluated solely through stereoscopic study of photographs. Spot elevations can be obtained by parallax measurements, followed by form-line sketches of terrain. Form lines on individual contact prints may then be transferred to photo index sheets for a composite view of the various corridors in terms of drainage, broad soil groupings, land-use patterns, and rough comparisons of property values.

COMPARISONS OF FEASIBLE ROUTES

In this second stage, the small-scale photographs used for reconnaissance may be unsuitable, because the principal corridors should be covered by recent mapping photography that will produce contour intervals of 2 or 3 m.

Print scales may range from about 1:2,500 in heavily populated urban areas to about 1:12,000 in rural areas where land use is less intensive and right-of-way costs are likely to be lower.

From this large-scale photography, topographic maps are prepared of each corridor; single-strip maps at a scale of 1:2,500 to 1:5,000 have often proved suitable in the United States. Such maps are commonly tied to existing horizontal and vertical control for refinement and reliability in evaluation of alternate routes; whenever possible, state systems of plane coordinates are used in plotting of the base maps. Preconstruction studies of alternative routes also require a close scrutiny of soil types, aggregate materials sources, vegetation obstacles such as muskeg or large timber reserves, and engineering problems such as hard rock cuts, tunnels, or landslides.

Plan-and-profile sheets are plotted, and proposed highway cross sections are computed at stations established along each feasible route. Every route location is examined with regard to drainage, intersections, right-of-way costs, and road-user benefits; this procedure narrows the choice of locations to perhaps two or three alignments. These remaining alignments are then replotted to show traffic lanes, along with the profiles and grades of primary intersections. Positions and sizes of culverts are determined, and the extent of channel work is shown. Preliminary design work on large structures (e.g., bridges) may also be initiated.

For final cost comparisons, grading contours of the highway-to-be, based on the recommended grade, are superimposed on the map. Amounts of cut and fill are determined by the planimetering of areas of horizontal sections (defined by each grading contour and the original ground contour) and multiplication of those results by the contour interval. This method gives a graphic picture of the finished highway from which work limits, lengths of structures, and extent of seeding, as well as right-of-way and grading, are determined.

SURVEY OF THE BEST ROUTE

In the third phase, the photo interpretation task involves a more detailed study of drainage, soils, geology, and property values for the selected construction route. Large-scale photography of the chosen corridor is used in the preparation of topographic strip maps 0.1 to 1 km wide along the path of the proposed highway. Map scales and contour intervals required in this engineering stage range from about 1:500 with 0.5-m intervals to 1:5,000 with 3-m intervals. The highway centerline is located on the strip maps and then staked out on the ground for preliminary grading. This sets the stage for actual road construction to begin (Figure 13.3).

Through the combination of aerial photographs and reliable strip maps, the construction engineer can be confident that all feasible routes have been given due consideration. Such assurances were acquired only via tedious and time-consuming ground survey methods before the adoption of photogrammetric surveys by highway designers and engineers.

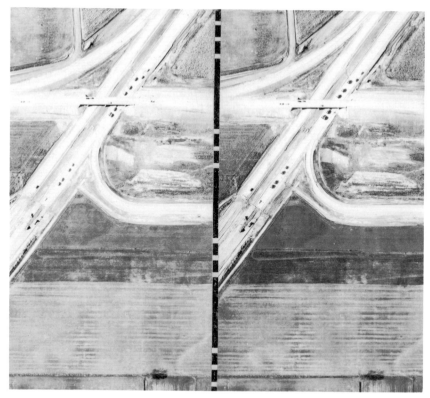

Figure 13.3.   Construction of a divided, limited-access highway in Michigan. Several loaded dump trucks and some grading equipment are discernible. Note that bridges or overpasses are usually completed before road surfacing. Scale is about 1:6,000.

BRIDGE CONSTRUCTION

Bridges for highways and railroads assume a wide variety of shapes and designs in accordance with cost considerations, type and intensity of traffic, load limits, availability of local construction materials, and considerations of minimum spans or clearances for underpassing automobiles, trains, or ships. A vertical stereogram of parallel highway and railroad bridges is shown in Figure 13.4.

In regions of steep topography, bridging costs may constitute the largest single expenditure for new railroad or highway routes. Once they are constructed and in service, the replacement or modification of heavily traversed spans becomes a major engineering problem. As indicated earlier, bridges are normally completed first in the construction of new transportation arteries. The logic of this established procedure is illustrated by the construction of limited-access highways through populated regions; overpasses must be built at an early stage to avoid interference with existing traffic on intersecting roads and to permit uninhibited work on the new right-of-way.

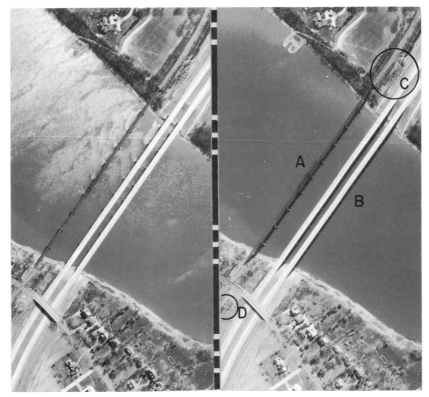

Figure 13.4.   Steel truss-frame railroad bridge (A) and dual-lane concrete highway bridge (B) at Toledo, Ohio. Note that supporting piers for all three spans are aligned to allow easy passage of small craft underneath. Power transmission towers are circled on opposite river banks (C, D). Scale is about 1:7,920.

When new highway bypasses are planned through urban or industrial areas, existing spans or trestles may require modification because of insufficient clearances. Figure 13.5 provides an apt example. Stereoscopic study of this photograph reveals that the old railroad trestle is supported by very closely spaced piers that will not permit the passage of automobile traffic underneath. Thus, the construction of the new roadway requires that a wide-span railroad trestle be built to replace the older structure.

HYDROELECTRIC DAMS AND RESERVOIRS

The distribution of hydroelectric facilities in the conterminous United States is governed largely by topography and amount of rainfall. The greatest waterpower potential is to be found in mountainous regions where stream gradients are high and precipitation is heavy (Figure 13.6). In dry climates, especially where stream gradients are low, hydroelectric capacities are

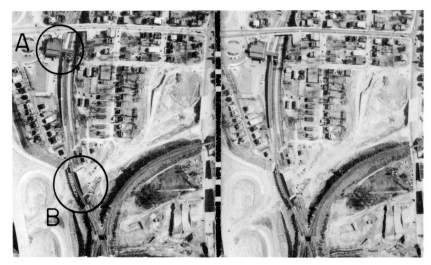

Figure 13.5.   Railroad passenger station (A) and construction of a highway overpass for trains (B). Note planned extension of new highway through residential area. Scale is about 1:7,920.

minimal; in fact, the impoundment of sufficient water supplies for human consumption is often a matter of grave concern to inhabitants (Figure 13.7). To assist the beginning interpreter in recognizing the components of hydro-electric installations, the basic nomenclature of a low-pressure dam is presented in Figure 13.8.

In many instances, human and industrial needs for clean water are most critical in regions where ground and surface water sources are inadequate. California, with its rapidly expanding economy and population, is a case in point. Several large cities, notably Los Angeles, receive much of their water via aqueducts from sources hundreds of kilometres away. Still, the basic problem of obtaining increasing quantities of unpolluted water for persons residing in arid regions remains largely unsolved.

To increase supplies of surface water, reservoirs have been constructed near cities by the impoundment of rivers and streams. Unfortunately, watershed conservation practices have often lagged far behind engineering construction, with the consequence that hastily conceived reservoirs often have a short life expectancy because of rapid sedimentation. As a general rule, large reservoirs should not be constructed unless administrative controls over the entire watershed can be exercised; only in this way can vegetative cover be maintained properly for the interception of precipitation, reduction of surface erosion, and minimization of sedimentation. Aerial photography obtained at regularly scheduled times offers an efficient means of monitoring water levels and checking periodic fluctuations in reservoirs (Figure 13.9). Panchromatic photographs usually provide good information on siltation levels, while shorelines and small tributaries are more distinctive on black-and-white infrared or infrared color exposures.

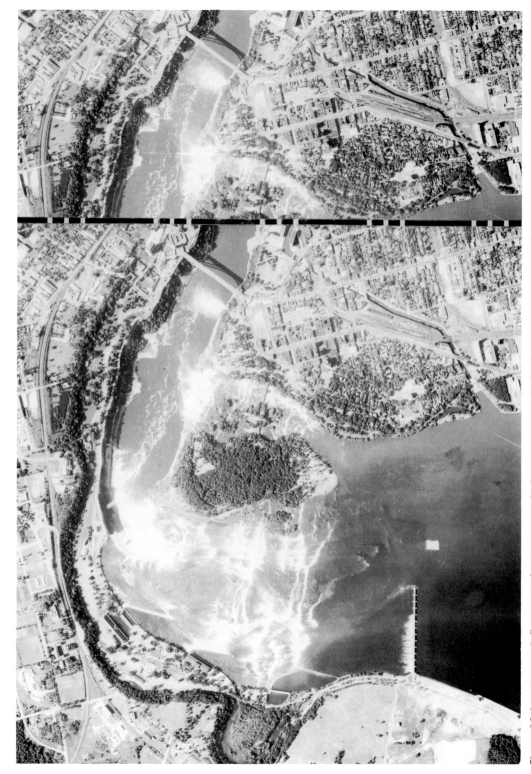

Figure 13.6. Niagara Falls, New York. Waterpower facilities are intensively developed in this region. Scale is about 1:20,000.

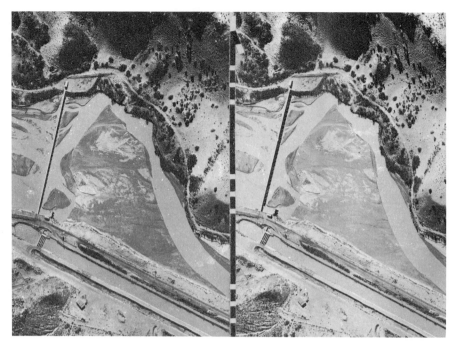

Figure 13.7. Low-pressure dam on the Rio Grande in New Mexico. In this dry area, stream gradients are low, precipitation is meager, and occasional flash floods result in severe soil erosion. The problem of siltation behind the dam is evident here. Scale is about 1:6,000. (Courtesy Abrams Aerial Survey Corp.)

AERIAL DETECTION OF WATER POLLUTION

Water pollution studies are concerned with the changing characteristics of water that render it unfit or undesirable for human consumption, aquatic life, and industrial use. Among the principal sources of water pollution are sewage and oxygen-consuming wastes, industrial by-products dumped into streams and lakes, radioactive substances, and agricultural pesticides. Increases in the temperature of water as a result of its use for industrial cooling may also be regarded as a form of pollution if the aquatic environment is endangered as a result (Figure 13.10).

Aerial photographs provide a means of detecting and assessing the extent of some forms of water pollution. Although infrared color films and image-producing thermal sensors are often desirable for making detailed lake and stream surveys, some types of water pollutants can be discerned on panchromatic film exposed through a minus-blue filter. Under most circumstances, stream pollutants enter bodies of water from man-made "point sources" or from diffused sources that may be either natural or man-made. Point sources such as sewage outfalls are often identifiable on aerial photographs because of sharp tonal contrasts between concentrated effluents and the receiving waters (Figures 13.11 and 13.12).

Organic and inorganic industrial effluents include vegetable processing wastes, pulp and paper residues, sulfuric acid, metallic salts, and petrochemical wastes. Because industrial effluents are commonly discharged into streams and estuaries through piped outlets, the concentrated pollution trouble spots are easily seen on aerial photographs. In the vicinity of seacoasts, these wastes may be responsible for huge areas of foul-smelling water that extend into the ocean for several kilometres. Oil slicks and petroleum effluents, which are not easily dissipated, are extremely detrimental to waterfowl (Figure 13.13).

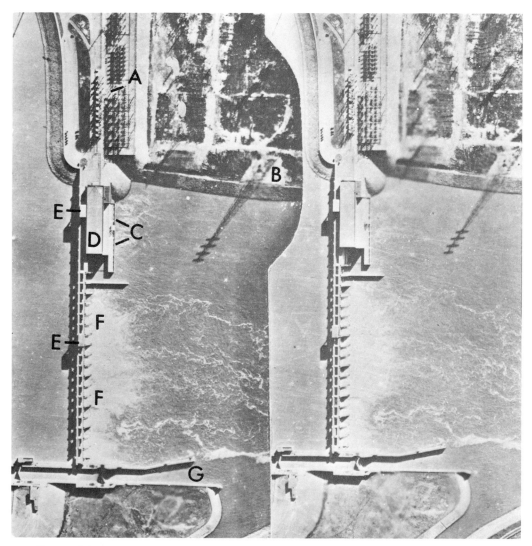

Figure 13.8. Features easily recognized in this stereogram of a low-pressure dam include: (A) the transformer and switching yard, (B) the transmission tower, (C) tail races, (D) the generator hall, (E) traveling gate cranes, (F) the dam gates, and (G) a lock for ships. (Courtesy U.S. Air Force.)

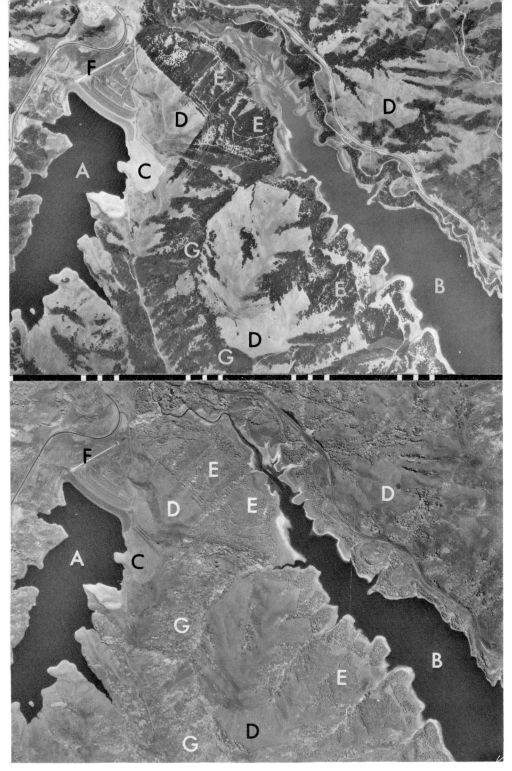

Figure 13.9. Panchromatic (above) and infrared (below) photographs of the Briones (A) and San Pablo (B) reservoirs in Contra Costa County, California. The Briones reservoir has a new earth dam and a low degree of sedimentation; the San Pablo reservoir has a much higher degree of sedimentation. Also discernible are: (C) exposed soil, (D) annual grasslands, (E) Monterey pine, (F) spillway, and (G) mixed hardwoods. Scale is about 1:33,500. (Courtesy U.S. Forest Service Remote Sensing Project, Berkeley, California.)

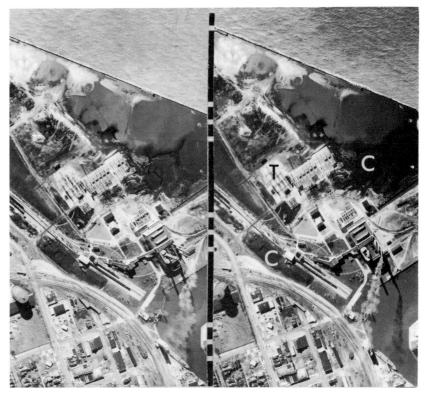

Figure 13.10.   Thermal electric power plant along the shore of Lake Michigan. Piles of coal (C) and the transformer unit (T) are easily picked out. Such plants use large amounts of water for cooling. The water used for cooling is returned to the lake at a temperature higher than it possessed when it was removed. Scale is about 1:15,840.

A large amount of remote-sensing research has been devoted to studies of water *quality.* As a rule, emphasis has been on those kinds of pollutants that result in gross changes in the physical appearance or temperature of water as registered by a particular sensor. The source and areal extent of water pollutants may thus be readily ascertained, but measurements of such values as chemical concentrations and exact water temperatures must still be obtained by field sampling.

Color or infrared color films at scales of 1:5,000 to 1:10,000 are often recommended for studies of water quality. Conventional color appears to be preferred for detection of turbidity, sedimentation, and sewage outfalls, whereas infrared color is recommended for evaluations of thermal pollution. There are indications that nonphotographic sensors such as multispectral and thermal scanners may prove ideal for monitoring water quality. For example, oil slicks are clearly registered on thermal scanner imagery in the 8 to 14 μm band of the electromagnetic spectrum when there is a temperature difference between the oil film and the adjacent water.

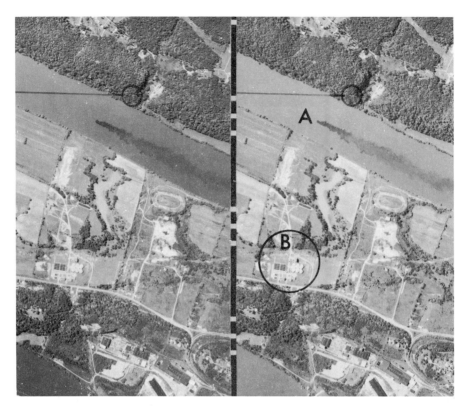

Figure 13.11. A sewage outfall below the surface of the Tennessee River produced the dark pollution pattern (A) on this photograph taken near Chattanooga; the sewage treatment plant is encircled (B). The dark coloration of the effluent is an indication of low levels of dissolved oxygen, a situation detrimental to fish and other aquatic life. Scale is about 1:20,000. (Courtesy U.S. Department of Agriculture.)

SURVEYS OF COASTAL WETLANDS

Coastal zones include shorelines and beaches, tidal areas, marshes, and associated wetlands. Because many large United States cities and about one-third of the population are concentrated near wetlands, there has been a severe deterioration of fragile coastal environments. The belated realization of the economic and esthetic value of coastal areas has finally led to programs of wetlands management and rejuvenation; remote sensing therefore has a role in the inventorying and periodic monitoring of such environments.

Both color and infrared color photography, at scales of 1:10,000 to 1:20,000, have proven valuable for such tasks as:

1. Monitoring coastal erosion and vegetative destruction
2. Evaluating changes in sedimentation of streams and estuaries
3. Detecting water pollution and the deterioration of shellfish, sports fish, and wildlife habitats

4. Documenting cultural and environmental changes due to dredging, land filling, land clearing, waste disposal, construction, and other activities

One method of monitoring beach erosion is based on a network of inland ground control points that can be located on photographs taken at annual or semiannual intervals. Ground distances between these permanent control points and selected points along the coastline (at a specified tide stage) are measured so changes over the years can be detected. Conventional color photography is preferred, where available, because of its superior water-penetration qualities.

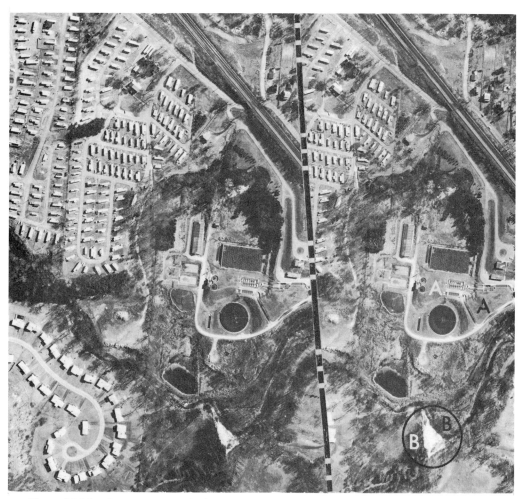

Figure 13.12. Sewage treatment plant (A) and eventual discharge of effluent into stream (B) in Monroe County, New York. The desirability of the new residential area (lower left) is probably questionable on certain days when wind currents are unfavorable. Scale is about 1:6,000.

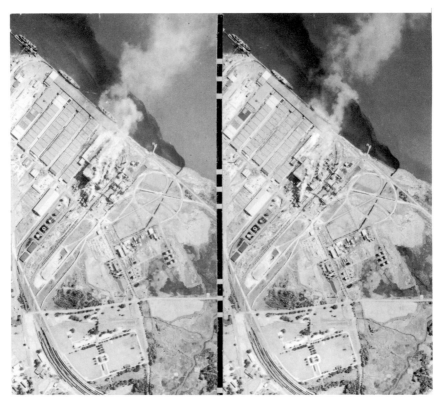

Figure 13.13. Discharge of petrochemical wastes into a large river near the Charleston, South Carolina, naval shipyard. Scale is about 1:20,000.

Periodic inventories and mapping of wetlands areas are preferably accomplished with infrared color photography. As a minimum, such inventories commonly require (1) the determination of the mean high-water line so that riparian rights can be established, (2) the location of upper wetlands boundaries, and (3) the detailed mapping of vegetation (major cover types) down to a minimum area of 2 to 4 ha. In several coastal states, more detailed inventories have been completed, and wetlands are scheduled for remapping at periodic intervals.

DISASTER SURVEYS

Certain aspects of fires and pestilence have been discussed in earlier chapters; here, essential surveys following such catastrophes as floods and earthquakes are given consideration. Although the prospects of major floods can often be predicted with a high degree of reliability, this fact has not served as a deterrent to the human occupation of floodplains and low-lying coastal areas. Similarly, settlements in known earthquake zones (e.g., along the San

Andreas fault) continue to expand in total disregard of past and future dangers. It is certain that there *will* be major calamities, and remote sensing can be of assistance following severe disasters.

An initial problem is that of obtaining aerial coverage as soon as possible following a catastrophe—and possibly at regular intervals for weeks afterwards. Where weather conditions prohibit immediate photographic surveys, SLAR imagery may be initially specified and used to advantage.

Some of the major items that may be evaluated through analysis of large-scale (1:4,000 to 1:8,000) aerial imagery include:

1. Drinking water supplies, the condition of utilities such as electrical and gas service systems, availability of heating or cooking fuels, and the condition of telephone and communications systems
2. Damages to critical structures, such as hospitals, food warehouses, residential housing, water purification plants, sewage disposal facilities, and food-processing industries
3. Evacuation routes, such as railroads, highways, and airfields
4. General support and logistical planning for relief teams moving into affected areas
5. Soil and terrain damage, including the location and distribution of geologic faults and fractures
6. Reconstruction planning

SURFACE MINING PATTERNS

Periodic inventories of mine-disturbed lands are needed for the monitoring of environmental damage and for the planning or assessment of reclamation efforts. Most surface and some underground mining operations exhibit characteristic patterns or signatures that permit their identification on medium-scale photography.

Several examples of mining operations are pictured in Figures 13.14–13.21; minerals involved are sulfur, phosphates, bauxite, lead and zinc, copper, gold, coal, and petroleum. These stereograms are on panchromatic film, although it will be obvious to the reader that color films are preferred wherever available.

Almost all domestic sulfur is mined from deposits in Texas and Louisiana. Sulfur may be found in nearly pure form as crystals and powders, or it may occur in combination with metals, for example, iron sulfide or pyrite. Most of the industrial production in the United States is consumed in the form of sulfuric acid. Phosphates are mined in the southeastern and western states; more than three-fourths of the total production is used for commercial fertilizers. The distinctive pattern of open-pit phosphate mines is easily recognized on aerial photographs.

Bauxite mining in the United States is concentrated in central Arkansas, although commercial deposits are also exploited in Alabama, Georgia, and Virginia. Imports of bauxite (aluminum ore) largely come from Jamaica and

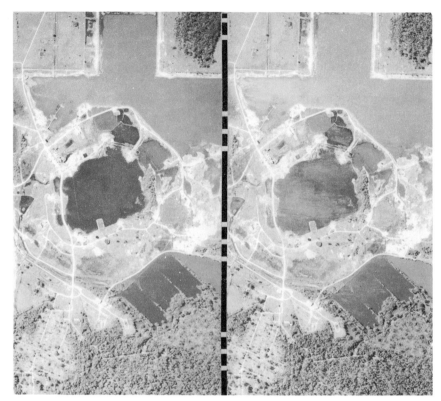

Figure 13.14.   Mining of sulfur in Calcasieu Parish, Louisiana. Deposits are underground here, so the surface features remain relatively undisturbed around the structural dome. Scale is about 1:20,000. (Courtesy U.S. Department of Agriculture.)

South America. The deposits in this country occur near the surface, so open-pit mining is common; resulting photographic patterns are somewhat similar to those produced by the extraction of sand, gravel, and limestone.

Lead and zinc ores are found in a number of states, but U.S. deposits are rapidly becoming depleted. Copper is in short supply, and much of the country's consumption of this important metal has been imported in the past. Gold may be found in underground deposits in association with quartz or combined with copper, silver, lead, or zinc. It also occurs in gravel deposits near the surface and may be placer-mined as free gold by means of dredges and hydraulic devices that wash through large quantities of coarse, granular materials.

Deep, underground deposits of coal are tapped by vertical shafts or by horizontal extraction through bedding exposures in side hills. Flat-lying coal deposits nearer the surface are strip-mined; vegetation is cleared and the bedrock is fractured by systematic blasting. Then the overburden is removed by large draglines, and power shovels scoop the uncovered coal into trucks. The resulting landscape is often a series of elongated piles of waste material (overburden) that is methodically placed in previously dug trenches as the stripping progresses.

Reclamation of strip-mined lands and reestablishment of vegetative cover are difficult and costly undertakings. Coal resources are widely distributed throughout the United States, and the locations of steel plants are normally governed by the proximity of coal, limestone, and iron ore deposits. Baltimore, Birmingham, Cleveland, Detroit, and Pittsburgh are among the larger steel-manufacturing centers.

Petroleum exploration may produce a variety of surface patterns as seen on vertical aerial photographs; two such variations are illustrated in this volume. In forested regions, a patchwork mosaic of small clearings connected by a grid system of access roads is a common indicator. Shadows of drilling rigs, oil

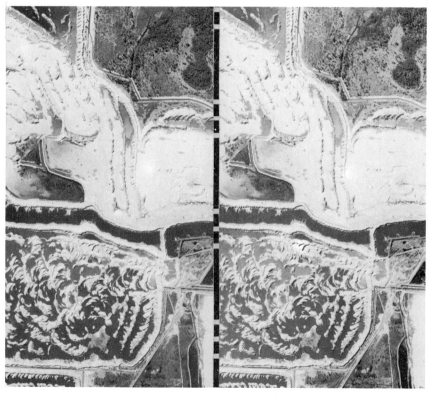

Figure 13.15.   Open-pit phosphate mine in Polk County, Florida. Unless drastic land reclamation measures are taken here, these scars will blot the landscape for years. Scale is about 1:20,000. (Courtesy U.S. Department of Agriculture.)

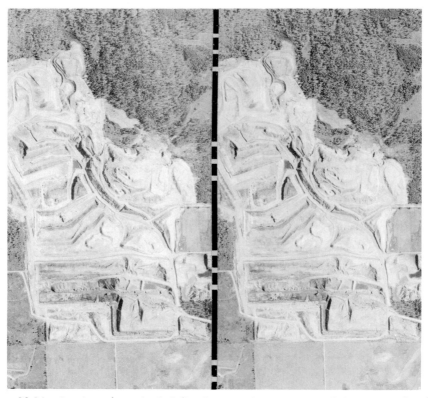

Figure 13.16. Bauxite surface mine in Saline County, Arkansas. Note the light tones produced by aluminum ore. Scale is about 1:20,000. (Courtesy U.S. Department of Agriculture.)

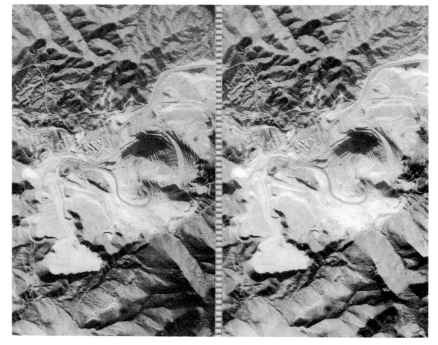

Figure 13.17. Open-pit copper mining in the vicinity of Miami, Arizona. Scale is about 1:42,000.

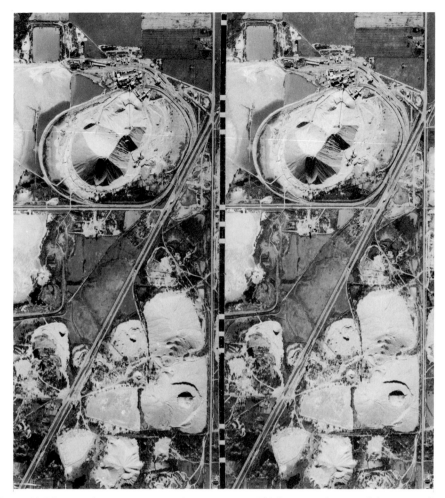

Figure 13.18.   Lead-zinc extraction in Ottawa County, Oklahoma. Underground deposits are being brought to the smelter shown at the top of the photograph. Scale is about 1:20,000. (Courtesy U.S. Department of Agriculture.)

derricks, and pumping stations aid in identification. As successful wells are brought into production, small, dark-toned sludge ponds may be seen, along with oil storage tanks. The leading oil-producing fields in the United States are found in the midcontinent region, which includes such states as Kansas, Oklahoma, Texas, and Louisiana.

STOCKPILE INVENTORIES

Huge stockpiles of raw materials such as coal, limestone, mineral ores, fertilizers, and pulpwood chips must be periodically measured for inventory and cost accounting. In earlier days, such inventories were accomplished by

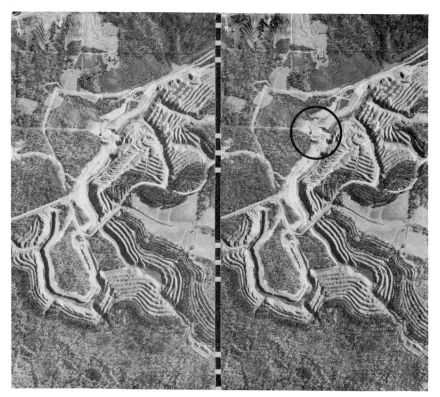

Figure 13.19.   Strip-mining of coal in Walker County, Alabama. A power shovel working a seam of coal is encircled. Scale is about 1:20,000. (Courtesy U.S. Department of Agriculture.)

laborious plane-table surveys or ground cross-sectioning; today, cubic volumes of materials 25 m or more in height and covering 20 ha may be determined accurately and efficiently by photogrammetric methods.

In the photographic approach, piles are contoured at 0.5-m intervals on the slopes and a 25-cm auxiliary contour on the tops. This is accomplished photogrammetrically by stereoscopic plotting of the contours of each pile from large-scale aerial photographs (e.g., about 1:400). After contouring, the area of each contoured layer or slice is determined by planimetry and the cubic volume is computed.

When weight conversions per cubic metre or per cubic yard are known, volumes of piles may be converted to weight values (Table 13.1). Corrections should be made for variations in density for different piles of the same materials, because settling or compression will result in significant changes in volume-weight ratios. In summary, the photogrammetric method of stockpile inventory has these advantages:

1. It is more accurate, economical, and convenient.

2. Inventories can be set for one date, because all pictures can be obtained in one day.
3. Ground control need be established only once.
4. The method provides a permanent record of the size of the pile at the time the picture was taken, and volume can be checked at any future time if any question arises as to the accuracy of the record.
5. No bulldozing or pile dressing is required, whereas these operations are usually necessary in the cross-section method.

PROBLEMS

1. Plan and conduct an engineering materials survey for granular materials in your locality. Use existing aerial photographs, soils maps, geologic maps, and topographic quadrangle sheets as aids. Prepare a written report on your findings.

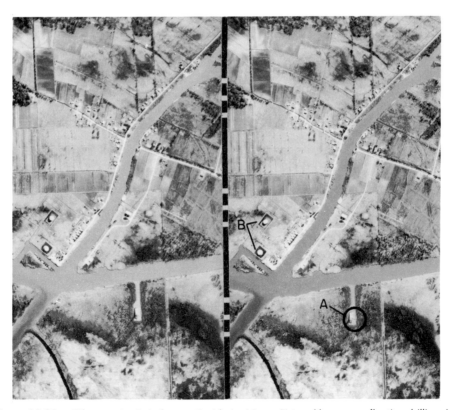

Figure 13.20.   Oil extraction in Lafayette Parish, Louisiana. Pictured here are a floating drilling rig (A) and oil storage tanks (B). In areas where canals are common, drilling equipment is easily hauled by barge from one location to another. Scale is about 1:20,000. (Courtesy U.S. Department of Agriculture.)

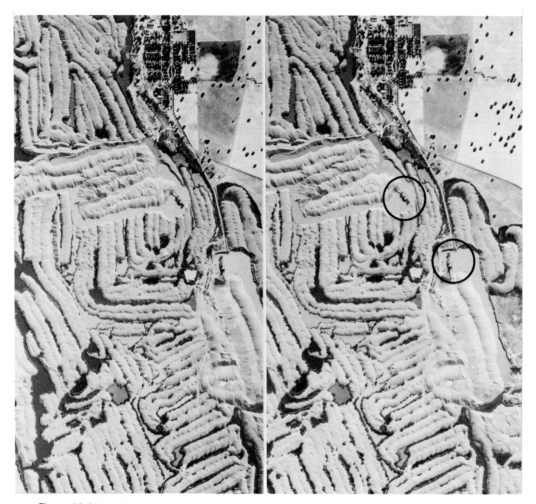

Figure 13.21.   Placer-mining of gold in Yuba County, California. Dredges may be seen in the circled areas. Scale is about 1:20,000. (Courtesy U.S. Department of Agriculture.)

2. Plan and conduct an aerial survey (based on visual reconnaissance or photographs) of the prominent sewage outfalls in your county. How many municipalities (if any) discharge untreated sewage into lakes and streams? Are there ordinances that prohibit such practices? Investigate.

3. Are there rivers in your county subject to flooding at periodic intervals? Consult with local planners or construction engineers to verify your

TABLE 13.1. Approximate Weights of Materials in Metric and English Units[°]

Material	Weight (Kilograms per Cubic Metre)	Weight (Pounds per Cubic Yard)
Cement, Portland, loose	1,506	2,538
Concrete, 1:2:4 mixture		
Trap rock	2,385	4,020
Gravel	2,341	3,945
Limestone	2,308	3,890
Sandstone	2,237	3,770
Cinder	1,697	2,860
Clay, dry, loose	1,009	1,700
Clay, damp, plastic	1,691	2,850
Clay and gravel, dry	1,602	2,700
Earth, dry, loose	1,172	1,975
Earth, moist, loose	1,252	2,110
Earth, moist, packed	1,537	2,590
Earth, mud, flowing	1,730	2,916
Earth, mud, packed	1,839	3,100
Garbage	400–801	675–1,350
Riprap, limestone	1,543–1,955	2,600–3,295
Riprap, sandstone	1,442	2,430
Riprap, shale	1,679	2,830
Rubbish, including ashes	128	216
Sand and gravel, dry, loose	1,442–1,679	2,430–2,830
Sand and gravel, dry, packed	1,602–1,922	2,700–3,240
Sand and gravel, wet	2,017	3,400
Snow, fresh-fallen	80–193	135–325
Snow, wet	240–320	405–540
Coal, anthracite, natural	1,554	2,620
Coal, bituminous, natural	1,347	2,270
Coal, lignite, natural	1,252	2,110
Coal, anthracite, piled	753–930	1,270–1,567
Coal, bituminous, piled	641–866	1,080–1,460

[°]English weights from International Harvester Company. Metric values were obtained by use of a multiplying factor of 0.5933.

findings. From a study of aerial photographs, can you suggest measures that would minimize the damage from future floods?

4. Make a complete aerial inventory of all active surface mines (including gravel and borrow pits) in your county. Classify by type of material extracted, areal extent, and potential impact on surrounding land values. Are steps being taken to restore landscapes after mines are worked out? Summarize your findings in a written, illustrated report.

References

Anderson, R. R., and F. J. Wobber. 1973. Wetlands mapping in New Jersey. *Photogrammetric Engineering* 39:353–358, illus.

Dumbleton, M. J., and G. West. 1970. *Air photograph interpretation for road engineers in Britain*. Reed Research Laboratory, Crowthorne, Berkshire, England. 25 pp., illus.

Garofalo, Donald, and F. J. Wobber. 1974. Solid waste and remote sensing. *Photogrammetric Engineering* 40:45–59, illus.

Klooster, S. A., and J. P. Scherz. 1974. Water quality by photographic analysis. *Photogrammetric Engineering* 40:927–935, illus.

Massa, William S. 1958. Inventory of large coal piles. *Photogrammetric Engineering* 24:77–81.

Piech, K. R., and J. F. Walker. 1972. Outfall inventory using airphoto interpretation. *Photogrammetric Engineering* 38:907–914, illus.

Stafford, D. B., and J. Langfelder. 1971. Air photo survey of coastal erosion. *Photogrammetric Engineering* 37:565–575, illus.

Strandberg, Carl H. 1967. *Aerial discovery manual*. John Wiley and Sons, New York, 249 pp., illus.

Waelti, Hans. 1970. Forest road planning. *Photogrammetric Engineering* 36:246–252, illus.

Wobber, F. J. 1971. Imaging techniques for oil pollution survey purposes. *Photographic Applications in Science, Technology and Medicine* 6(4):16–23, illus.

Chapter 14

Urban-Industrial Patterns

■ THE AIRPHOTO APPROACH TO URBAN PLANNING

Urban planning may be defined as the orderly regulation of the physical facilities of a city to meet the changing economic and social needs of a community, including the development of plans for future industrial expansion. Although city managers have long relied upon large-scale maps for zoning and urban renewal projects, the widespread use of photo interpretation techniques by municipal organizations represents a comparatively recent trend. It is now recognized, however, that properly timed aerial photography offers a unique and efficient means of studying such critical municipal factors as population growth, transportation networks, real estate assessment, and recreational needs. Aerial photographs provide the administrator with a complete perspective view of the city and its environs. As a result, the administrator is better equipped to analyze socioeconomic patterns, residential distributions, industrial requirements, and the need for extension of public utilities and services.

The intense competition for space among residential, industrial, recreational, agricultural, and transportation interests presents a continual series of problems to the urban planner. Whenever any portion of a city's limited environment is allocated to one of these interests, careful consideration must be given to the probable impact of that allocation on each of the other competing interests and on the residents of the area.

Sequential aerial photography is now available for many cities in the United States and Canada (Figure 14.1). Through the study of comparative photographs taken at intervals of several years, it is possible to determine the effects of major decisions made by previous municipal managers during the growth of a city. Accordingly, an excellent file of case histories is made available to incumbent urban planners who wish to capitalize on both the good and bad decisions of their predecessors.

A SYSTEMATIC GUIDE TO URBAN ANALYSIS

A series of 11 topical guides designed to aid geographers in the systematic study of aerial photographs has been prepared by Stone (1964). These guides are postulated on the theory that photo interpretation is largely a deductive rather than an inductive process and, therefore, analyses should proceed from the known parts of a topic to the unknown. If interpretation activities are organized for working from general patterns toward specific identifications or inferences, stereoscopic study will begin with the smallest scale of photography and end with prints of the largest scale available. A topical outline for the interpretation of urban features is presented here. In using prepared guides of this type, the interpreter must realize that positive identifications are rarely possible for all urban patterns; thus, listings of uncertain areas should be accompanied by several possible identifications based on the concept of associated features.

1. Outline built-up areas having urban characteristics.
2. Mark the major land and water transportation routes passing through the city (Figure 14.2).
3. Mark the principal commercial airports (Figure 14.3).
4. For the built-up area, outline subareas to show types of water bodies, drainage systems, terrain configuration, and natural vegetation.
5. Divide the built-up area into subareas based on differences in street patterns.
6. Outline the older and newer parts of the city.
7. Identify the principal transportation routes within the city.
8. Mark the minor land and water transportation routes passing through the city.
9. Circle the places where there is a change in the type of transportation (Figure 14.4).
10. Outline the primary commercial subareas in the central business district and in the suburbs.
11. Outline principal industrial subareas, including municipal utilities.
12. Outline subareas of warehouses and open storage.
13. Mark the recreational areas.
14. Mark the cemeteries.

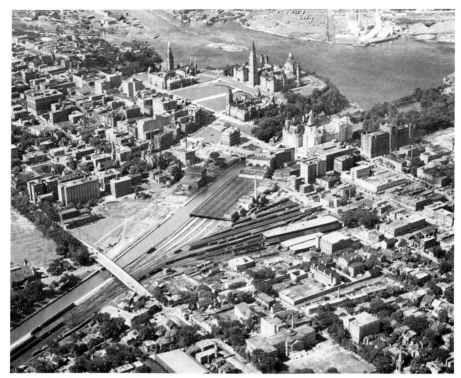

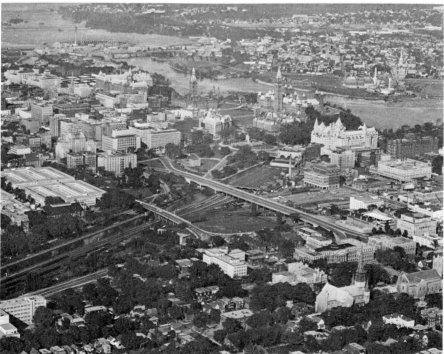

Figure 14.1. Oblique views of downtown Ottawa, Canada, in 1928 (top) and in 1964. Parliament buildings are near top center of each photograph. (Courtesy Surveys and Mapping Branch, Canada Department of Energy, Mines, and Resources.)

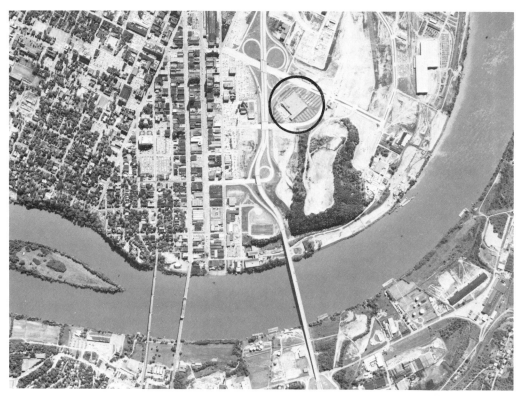

Figure 14.2. Interstate highway bypassing the central business district of Chattanooga, Tennessee. Although some added parking areas are evident between the highway interchanges and the downtown section, shopping centers, such as the one circled, pose an economic threat to downtown merchants. This type of problem confronts many cities. Scale is about 1:20,000.

15. Outline sections of the residential subareas by differing characteristics of the residences and lots and their relative locations to other functional subareas.
16. Mark the principal administrative and government buildings.
17. Mark the secondary commercial centers.
18. Mark the isolated industrial plants.
19. Mark the probable locations of light industrial establishments.

Information accumulated for a given urban area becomes the basis for more detailed studies. For example, in planning for future expansion of public facilities, correlations might be established between information on population density, number of automobiles per dwelling unit, or water use per capita and such planning multiplier factors as roadway capacity or area of recreational land per thousand persons.

▓ PARKING AND TRANSPORTATION STUDIES

Special photographic flights made during peak traffic periods are ideal for discovering bottlenecks in automobile flow patterns. Similarly, coverage of congested business districts can quickly reveal diurnal parking patterns and the locations of districts having shortages or surpluses of parking spaces during each hour of the day. Law enforcement officers have also found sequential, low-altitude photographs to be of assistance in pinpointing areas where cars are habitually parked in restricted zones.

Individually painted parking spaces can be easily discerned and counted at photographic scales of 1:6,000; at larger scales, the size and type of vehicle can also be assessed (Figure 14.5). In a few cities, aerial surveys of parking facilities have revealed that there is sufficient unused space in vacant backyards and alleys within the business district to make available more than double the existing parking capacity. Photographs also revealed that traffic would be able to reach parking lots behind shops if only a few new access streets were opened to handle the traffic flow. In other urban areas, aerial

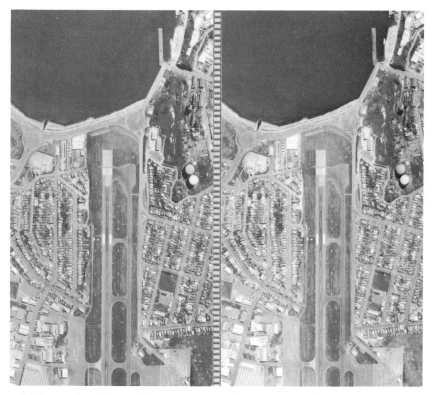

Figure 14.3. Portion of the municipal airport at Wellington, New Zealand. Scale is about 1:20,000. (Courtesy New Zealand Department of Lands and Survey.)

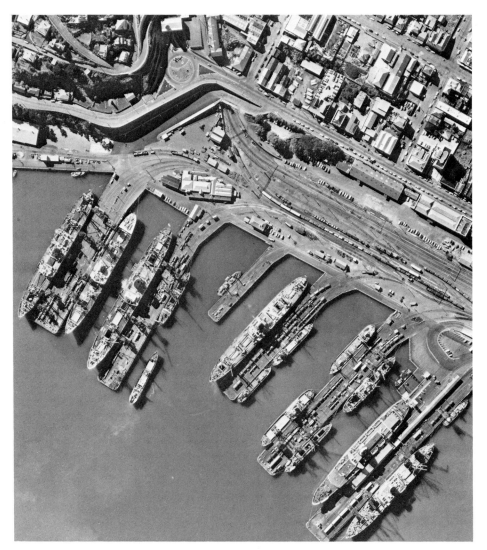

Figure 14.4.   Lyttleton Harbor, near Christchurch, New Zealand. Such areas constitute a focal point for water, rail, and auto transportation. (Courtesy New Zealand Department of Lands and Survey.)

photographs have indicated that more parking facilities than were originally allotted will have to be provided; additional spaces are often needed to supply legal parking for vehicles that previously used loading zones and other nonallocated spaces.

When the time interval between successive, overlapping aerial exposures is known, speeds of vehicles imaged on adjacent prints can be computed (Figure 14.6). Such information can be of considerable utility in the analysis of traffic flows during rush hour. For some European countries, close-range terrestrial photographs made with stereometric cameras provide permanent pictorial records of traffic accidents. The precision of photogrammetric determinations of such items as tire marks, vehicle positions, and collision damage has been firmly established, so that photographic evaluations are commonly admissible as court evidence. The photogrammetric technique provides more reliable measurements than ground taping of distances, and the accident scene can be reexamined from files of four or five carefully oriented stereopairs. Furthermore, the stereometric process shortens the investigation time at the accident scene, with the result that roadways can be cleared for regular traffic with a minimum of delay.

PATTERNS OF RESIDENTIAL DEVELOPMENT

Many urban planners believe that the only answer to the control of haphazard urban sprawl is a rigidly administered property zoning system. Certainly there are valid arguments favoring the orderly regulation of

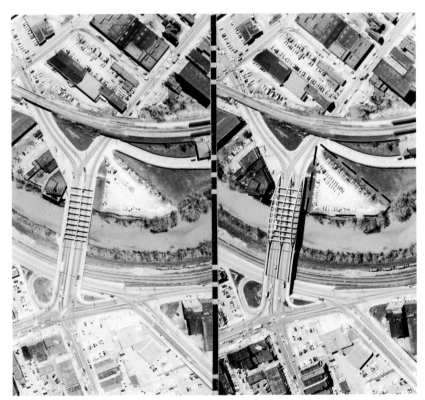

Figure 14.5. Large-scale view of parking lots in Youngstown, Ohio, at about 11 A.M. Note concentrations of vehicles in some lots and surplus spaces in others. Buses, trucks, and compact cars can be distinguished from standard-sized automobiles. Scale is about 1:3,960.

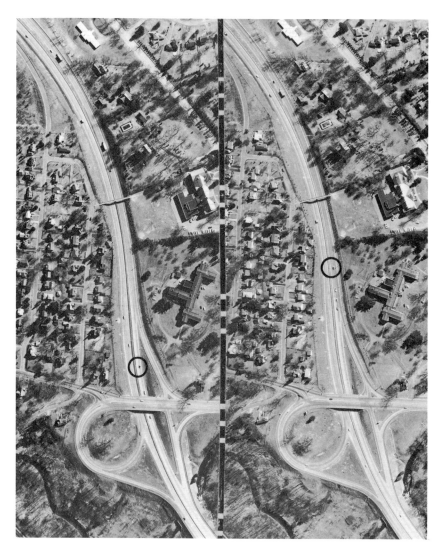

Figure 14.6. The speed of the circled vehicle may be computed from a knowledge of the time interval between photo exposures. What would be the auto's rate of speed if the exposure interval were 12 seconds? Scale is about 1:6,000.

community development; otherwise smoky industrial plants may force down property values in exclusive suburbs, and taverns might be constructed adjacent to school buildings.

The suburbanite who wishes to reside in an area free from polluted air, speeding automobiles, and supersonic aircraft may be hard-pressed to find solace in today's metropolis. Nevertheless, interpreters of urban features have found that residential property is one of the key indicators of a family's socioeconomic status and that a person's address often reveals much more about an individual than just where he or she lives. One might, for example, reflect upon the social or economic status associated with a residence on San Francisco's Nob Hill around 1900. Residence location has meaning not only in terms of real estate cost or rental, but also in terms of occupation, educational level, income class, nationality group, cultural attributes, and even religious preferences.

Even though the typical single-family dwelling in America has grown larger and more luxurious, the high cost of scarcity of building sites results in more and more houses being built on smaller parcels of real estate. The confining atmosphere and unimaginative landscaping that results are painfully illustrated by Figures 14.7 and 14.8.

INDICATORS OF HOUSING QUALITY

Information is required periodically on residential housing quality for evaluation and mapping of neighborhoods that need remedial action and for allocation of housing improvement funds. Among the factors obtainable from

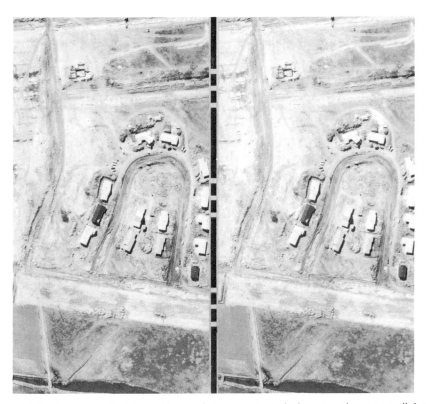

Figure 14.7. Large ranch-style residences being constructed close together on small lots in Milwaukee, Wisconsin. As is commonly seen in new subdivisions, sod, topsoil, and trees have been scraped away to make for more efficient materials handlings. The monotony of this scoured landscape will remain for years to come. Scale is about 1:4,800.

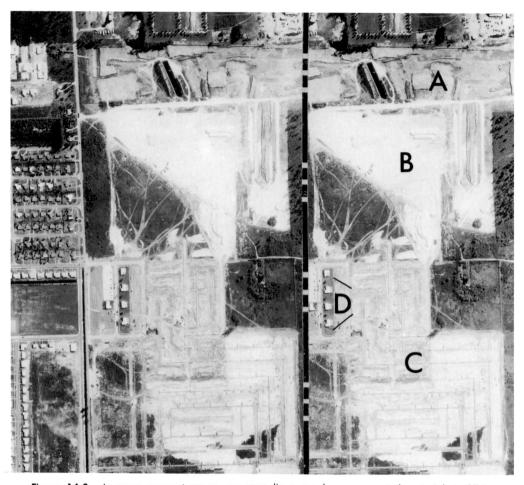

Figure 14.8. In many seacoast areas, one may dig a canal, use excavated materials to fill in lowlands, and create a subdivision with waterfront residences. Here in Dade County, Florida, excavated sand (A) is transported to adjacent development areas (B, C). In anticipation of advance residential sales, four model homes are already open to customers (D). The final result will seemingly appear somewhat similar to the mill-town arrangement at the extreme left edge of the picture. Scale is about 1:10,000.

remote-sensor data, the following appear to be positively correlated with housing quality:

1. Availability of on-street parking
2. Freedom from loading and parking hazards
3. Ample street width
4. Freedom from traffic hazards
5. Minimal amount of refuse
6. Moderate street grades
7. Easy access to buildings

Most evaluations of such diagnostic characteristics have used conventional large-scale (1:5,000 to 1:10,000) aerial photography. However, one interesting application of thermal infrared scanners may be cited: the heat loss from homes and office buildings with poor insulation can be readily distinguished on infrared imagery.

In areas of high population density, it has also proven possible to estimate the *number* of dwelling units from infrared color photography at a scale of 1:20,000. From such estimates, additional inferences can be made about population density and the total population of selected urban areas.

URBAN RECREATIONAL PLANNING

The failure of many large cities to make early provision for parks, golf courses, and other outdoor recreational facilities has resulted in tremendous pressures on existing lands as populations have increased. Notable examples of foresight by city planners would include such urban oases as Central Park in Manhattan, Rock Creek Park in Washington, D.C., and City Park in New Orleans. In many other heavily populated regions, however, carefully maintained havens of grass and trees may be sorely inadequate or wholly lacking.

When open areas are not reserved for public use at an early stage in a city's growth, rising real estate values may effectively block the establishment of large municipal parks and athletic facilities at a later date. As a result, private country clubs, concentrated tourist attractions, or spectator sports may offer the only alternatives to local residents (Figures 14.9–14.12).

Surveys of population pressures on existing recreational areas and inventories of potential recreational sites are often aided by intensive study of large-scale aerial photographs. Diagnostic factors that are commonly evaluated to indicate areas of high recreational potential include the following:

1. Population factors, such as building density, existing recreational opportunities, kind and direction of urban expansion
2. Current land use, including factors that might limit or prohibit recreational development (e.g., undesirable industries nearby)
3. Characteristics of potential water-based recreational sites (e.g., size, shape, shoreline configuration, depth, water quality)
4. Existing and potential roads for access to new sites and for use by hikers, skiers, or horseback riders
5. Character and appeal of vegetation on potential sites

LEGAL APPLICATIONS OF REMOTE SENSING

Following is a partial listing of the types of legal problems for which remote-sensor imagery might play a vital part:

1. Discovery and assessment of taxable property
2. Establishment of boundary lines in ownership disputes

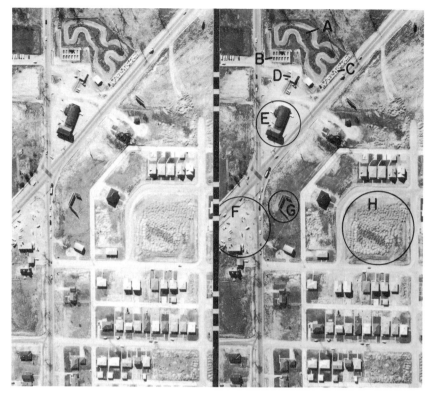

Figure 14.9. Recreational and related service facilities near a residential development in Milwaukee, Wisconsin. Items designated are: (A) a go-cart track, (B) trampoline pits, (C) miniature golf, (D) a drive-in restaurant, (E) a roller rink or dance hall, (F) a gas station, and (G) billboards. The dumped fill material (H) possibly came from basements excavated for new houses. Note that lots in the lower part of the picture are so narrow that many homes are of the "shotgun" design, with no space for driveways. Scale is about 1:5,000.

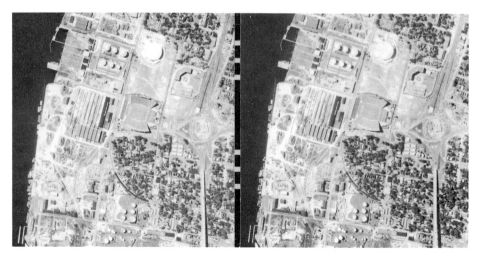

Figure 14.10. Stadium in Jacksonville, Florida, where the annual Gator Bowl football game is held (near the center of photograph). Scale is about 1:16,000.

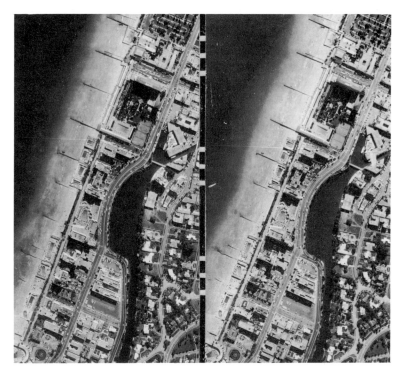

Figure 14.11. Hotels along Miami Beach, Florida, represent intensively developed recreational facilities for tourists. Scale is about 1:10,000.

3. Appraisal of lands to be condemned under states' rights of eminent domain
4. Discovery and evaluation of the illegal deposition of fill dirt or waste materials on private property
5. Auto, railway, and airline accidents
6. Inventory of damages from fires, hurricanes, floods, and other disasters
7. Evaluation of vegetation killed by noxious fumes from industrial point sources
8. Timber trespass

The discovery and assessment of taxable property (e.g., improvements to single-family residences) may be cited as an application of remote-sensing techniques. Recent improvements shown on property records can be checked against "apparent" improvements as determined from the interpretation of large-scale aerial photographs; discrepancies are then cross-checked against building permit files. Irregularities that cannot be reconciled are subsequently scheduled for ground check or appraisal. The kinds of improvements most easily found on aerial photographs are additions to existing residences, new garages, swimming pools, apartment buildings, and commercial blacktop areas.

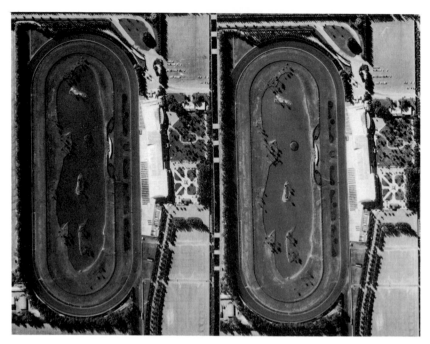

Figure 14.12.   Horse racing, one of America's leading spectator sports, attracts many thousands to Hialeah Park in Miami, Florida, each year. Palm trees and a central lake add to the esthetic value of the location. Scale is about 1:10,000.

RECOGNITION OF INDUSTRIAL FEATURES

The general classification or specific identification of certain industrial features is of vital concern to photo interpreters engaged in urban planning, control of water and air pollution, or military target analysis. In a few instances, unique structures or rooftop signs can make the task exceedingly simple (Figures 14.13 and 14.14). In other cases, however, the correct categorization may require sound knowledge of industrial components, a high degree of deductive reasoning, and one or more photo interpretation keys. The more one knows about industrial processing methods, the more success one will have in recognizing those same activities on vertical aerial photographs.

As pointed out by Chisnell and Cole (1958), each type of industrial complex has a unique sequence of raw materials, buildings, equipment, end products, and waste that typify the industry. Many of these components can be seen directly on aerial photographs; others (those that are obscured or are inside structures) must be detected by inference from the images of minor associated components. By studying the distinctive shapes, patterns, or tones of raw materials, for example, one may frequently deduce the kinds of processes or equipment that are hidden from view. Arrangements of chimneys, stacks, boilers, tanks, conveyors, and overhead cranes may also provide essential identification clues. And, finally, the finished product can occasionally be seen as it emerges from an assembly line or is stored in open yards awaiting shipment.

A number of photo interpretation guides for use in identification of general classes of industries have been compiled by or for various military agencies. One of these selective keys (Figure 14.15) is based on general industrial categorizations of extraction, processing, and fabrication. If industries are imaged on photographs at a scale of about 1:20,000 or larger, it has been shown that relatively unskilled interpreters can use such a key to categorize various industries, even though a specific identification may not be possible. Because industrial components tend to exhibit common images irrespective of geographic location, this key is applicable in many parts of the world.

To use the various recognition features to categorize an industry from its image components, follow the procedure recommended here:

1. Decide whether it is an extraction, processing, or fabrication industry.
2. If it is a processing industry, decide whether it is chemical, heat, or mechanical processing—in that order.
3. If it is a fabrication industry, decide whether it is light or heavy fabrication.

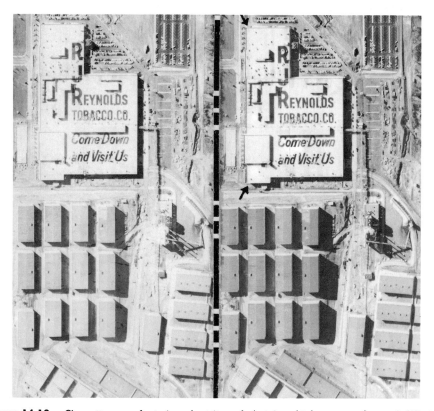

Figure 14.13. Cigarette-manufacturing plant (top of photo) and tobacco warehouses in Winston-Salem, North Carolina. Scale is about 1:7,920.

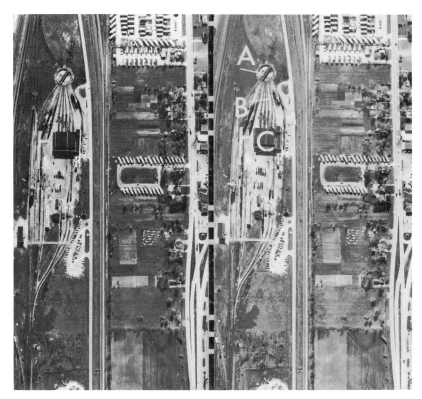

Figure 14.14. If one can recognize a railroad turntable (A) and locomotives (B), then it can be deduced that the engines are being shunted into a repair or maintenance shop (C). This heavy fabrication industry is located at New Haven, Indiana. Scale is about 1:7,920.

EXAMPLES OF INDUSTRIAL CATEGORIES

Extraction industries, typified by oil drilling, rock quarries, gravel pits, and mining operations, are among the easiest types of industries to classify. They may be recognized by the presence of excavations, ponds, mine shafts, and earth-moving equipment; buildings are usually small and often of temporary construction. Frequently, such operations appear to be rather disorganized as viewed on aerial photographs, even though extracted materials are mechanically handled by conveyors or stored in ponds, tanks, or bins. In some cases, the interpreter must exercise special care in distinguishing waste piles from usable materials. The surface mining patterns that were illustrated in Chapter 13 provide appropriate examples of the extraction industries.

Processing industries are divided into three subclasses: mechanical, chemical, and heat processing. Mechanical processing industries are those that size, sort, separate, or change the physical form or appearance of raw materials. Industries that are typical of this category are sawmills, grain mills, and ore concentration plants; utilities in the same grouping would include hydroelectric plants and water purification and sewage disposal installations. Several of these types of industries were also illustrated in Chapter 13.

Chemical processing industries are those that employ chemicals to separate, treat, or rearrange the constituents of raw materials. Among representative chemical processing industries are those for sulfuric acid pro-

---

INDUSTRIAL CLASSIFICATION KEY

Extraction industries are characterized by these features: excavations, mine headframes, ponds, and derricks; piles of waste; bulk materials stored in piles, ponds, or tanks; handling equipment (e.g., conveyors, pipelines, bulldozers, cranes, power shovels, or mine cars); buildings that are few and small.

Processing industries are characterized by these features: facilities for storage of large quantities of bulk materials in piles, ponds, silos, tanks, hoppers, and bunkers; facilities for handling of bulk materials (e.g., conveyors, pipelines, cranes, and mobile equipment); large outdoor processing equipment (e.g., blast furnaces, cooling towers, kilns, and chemical-processing towers; provision for large quantities of heat or power as evidenced by boiler houses); oil tanks, coal piles, large chimneys or many smokestacks, or transformer yards; large or complex buildings; piles or ponds of waste. Three types of processing industries may be recognized:
1. Mechanical processing is typified by few pipelines or closed tanks, little fuel in evidence, few stacks, and no kilns.
2. Chemical processing is typified by many closed or tall tanks, gasholders, pipelines, and much large, outdoor processing equipment.
3. Heat processing is typified by few pipelines or tanks, large chimneys or many stacks, large quantities of fuel, and kilns.

Fabrication industries are characterized by these features: few facilities for storing or handling bulk materials; a minimum of outdoor equipment except for cranes; little or no waste; buildings may be large or small and of almost any structural design.
1. Heavy fabrication plants are typified by heavy steel-frame, one-story buildings, storage yards with heavy lifting equipment, and rail lines entering buildings.
2. Light fabrication plants are typified by light steel-frame or wood-frame buildings and wall-bearing, multistory structures, lack of heavy lifting equipment, and little open storage of raw materials.

Figure 14.15. Sample classification key for use in identifying general classes of industries. (From Thomas C. Chisnell and Gordon E. Cole, 1958, Industrial Components—A Photo Interpretation Key on Industry, *Photogrammetric Engineering* 24:590–602. Copyright 1958 by the American Society of Photogrammetry. Reprinted with permission.)

duction, aluminum production, petroleum refining, wood pressure treatment, and by-products coke production (Figures 14.16–14.18).

Heat processing industries use heat to refine, divide, or reshape raw materials or to produce energy from raw materials. Large quantities of fuel are required, waste piles are common, and blast furnaces or kilns are often in evidence. Thermal electric power production is included in this category, along with cement production, clay products manufacturing, iron production, and copper smelting (Figures 14.19–14.21).

Fabrication industries are those that use the output of processing plants to form or assemble finished products. Although a majority of all industries are of the fabrication type, they are the most difficult to identify specifically because most of the activities are hidden from view by well-constructed buildings and enclosures. There is little outdoor equipment in evidence except for large cranes; bulk materials, waste piles, and storage ponds are usually

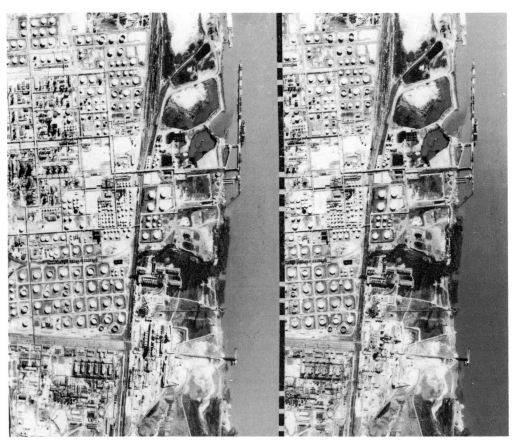

Figure 14.16.   Petroleum refinery along the Mississippi River at Baton Rouge, Louisiana. Although this chemical processing industry is pictured at a scale of about 1:25,000, it is a sufficiently distinctive complex to be categorized by use of the industrial classification key.

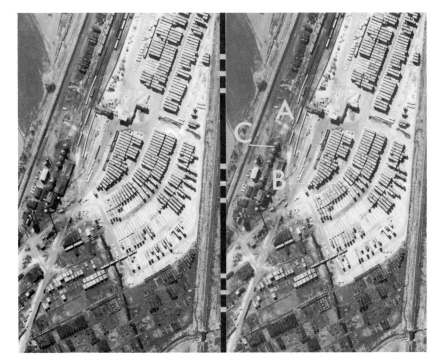

Figure 14.17. This chemical processing plant near Milwaukee, Wisconsin, is engaged in the preservative treatment of wood materials with creosote. Both untreated stacks of wood (light tones) and treated materials (dark tones) are visible in the storage yard. Tram cars of untreated materials (A) may be seen lined up for movement into the pressure cylinder (B). Liquid preservatives are stored in cylindrical tanks (C). Scale is about 1:4,800.

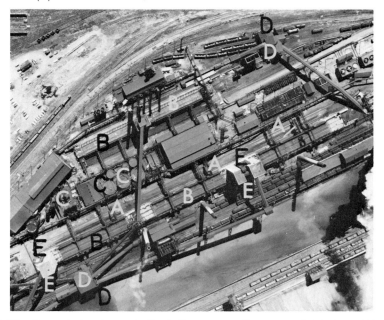

Figure 14.18. By-products coke production in Youngstown. Components labeled are: (A) pushing rams to move coke from ovens into quenching cars, (B) long coke ovens, (C) tank storage of tars and other coal by-products, (D) buildings where coal is washed, and (E) towers where coal is fed into coke ovens. Scale is about 1:3,960. Although this would usually be classed as a chemical processing industry, heat processes are also in evidence at installations such as this.

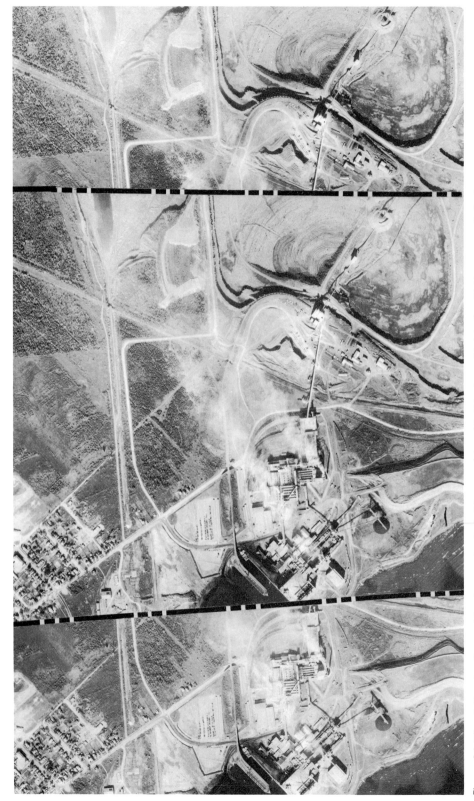

Figure 14.19. Both extraction and heat processing industries are pictured in this stereo-triplet of a Michigan cement plant.

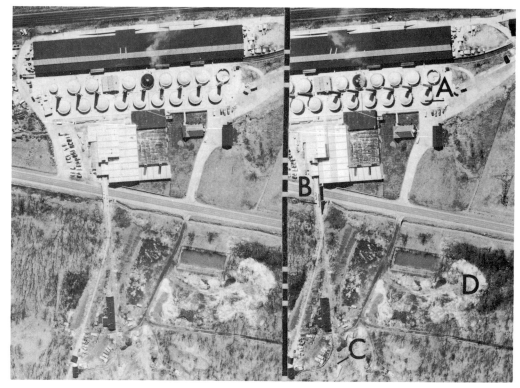

Figure 14.20. Clay products constitute the output of this heat processing industry at Newcomerstown, Ohio. Key components include: (A) clay kilns, (B) tram cars of raw materials, (C) a hillside tunnel to a clay mine, and (D) waste materials. Scale is about 1:3,000. (Courtesy Abrams Aerial Survey Corp.)

absent. Heavy fabrication industries include structural steel production, shipbuilding, and the manufacture or repair of railroad cars and locomotives (Figure 14.22). Typical of the light fabrication industries are aircraft assembly, canning and meatpacking, small-boat construction, and the manufacture of plastics products (Figures 14.23 and 14.24).

Most interpreters find that the best way to identify an industrial complex is by looking for components that are key recognition features of the classification in which the industry falls. While one or two components may not provide a specific identification, associations with other features will usually provide the missing link in the recognition chain. Knowledge of the photographic scale and the exact geographic locale of photography are additional factors that are of primary importance in recognition of industries. When available, current sets of county maps, topographic quadrangle sheets, stereogram files of representative industries, and a recent commercial atlas are valuable reference aids to photo interpreters.

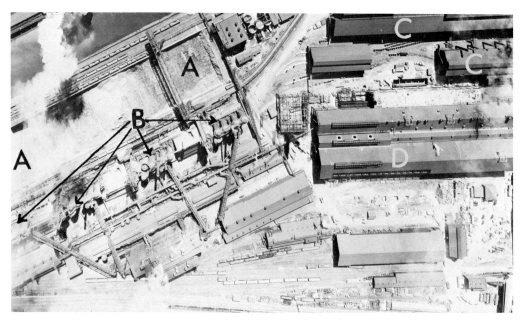

Figure 14.21. Heat processing industry at Youngstown, Ohio. Designated here are: (A) limestone and iron-ore storage bins, (B) blast furnaces that use coke, iron ore, and limestone to produce pig iron, (C) buildings housing open-hearth furnaces, and (D) iron-rolling mills. Scale is about 1:3,960.

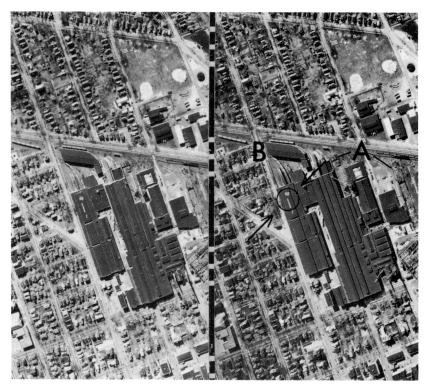

Figure 14.22. Pullman railroad cars are manufactured at this heavy fabrication plant in Michigan City, Indiana. Visible are storage yards with overhead cranes (A) and rail lines entering the building (B). Painted on the roof is the name of the city and its longitude and latitude. Scale is about 1:15,840.

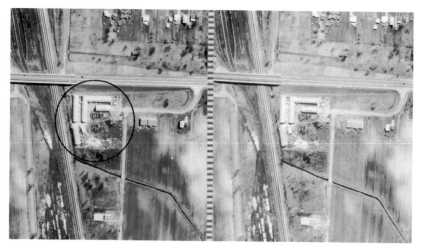

Figure 14.23.   Small-boat factory near Toledo, Ohio. Scale is about 1:7,920.

▨ CAPACITIES OF STORAGE TANKS

The capacity of any cylindrical storage tank can be determined from measurements of its inside diameter (d) and height (h). These values are merely substituted into the formula for the volume of a cylinder:

$$\text{Volume} = \frac{\pi d^2}{4}(h), \text{ or } 0.7854d^2(h) \qquad \textbf{Equation 14.1}$$

When cylinder diameters and heights are measured in metres, volumes will be derived in cubic metres. Where the dimensions are in feet, volumes will be in cubic feet. Depending on whether stored materials are in solid or liquid form, cubic volumes may be subsequently converted to weight values or to other measurement units (see Table 13.1 and tables on the inside back cover).

▨ PROBLEMS

1. Make a systematic urban analysis of a nearby metropolitan area by following the interpretation guidelines described in this chapter. Then, based on your analysis, attempt to formulate answers to these types of questions:

   a. Has recent economic growth been mainly in the central business district or in outlying areas?

   b. In which principal *direction* has growth proceeded? Is the direction due largely to topography, available surface transportation routes, water routes, or other factors? List, in order of importance.

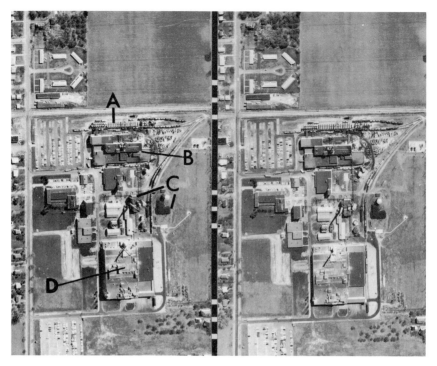

Figure 14.24.   This plastics plant in Toledo, Ohio, apparently combines both chemical processing and light fabrication activities. Identified are: (A) liquid chemical storage tanks, (B) a chemical processing building, (C) a power plant and coal piles, and (D) a multistory fabrication building. Scale is about 1:7,920.

      c. Has the central business district been rejuvenated with new office buildings, parks, civic centers, or a stadium? Locate such developments on your photographs, and explain how they have affected downtown parking and access to key areas of the city.

2. Assume that you have a high-altitude photograph (or photo mosaic) of a city that is unknown to you. Attempt to list no more than five to ten diagnostic features that you consider to be unique or key identification elements, for example:
    a. The predominant pattern of land subdivision or street layout
    b. Presence of coastal shorelines, bays, major rivers, canals, or lakes, along with their shapes and orientations
    c. Location and configuration of major commercial and military airports
    d. Presence of city parks, golf courses, athletic fields, institutional campuses, and fairgrounds
    e. Location and configuration of major highways and railways
    f. Location and general types of major industries
    g. An estimate of the population

When your list of key features is completed, rank them in order of presumed importance. Then attempt to list all those cities that (to your knowledge) have the critical attributes. If an identification has not been made at this point, consult an atlas for the final determination. Could you now devise a simple photo identification key for the largest 20 cities in your state or country?

3. Using photographs supplied by your instructor, classify at least ten different industrial sites by using the key provided in this chapter.

4. Determine the cubic capacities of several storage tanks (or similar structures) from photographic measurements. Check your results by ground measurements, and explain reasons for differences.

References

Chisnell, Thomas C., and Gordon E. Cole. 1958. Industrial components—a photo interpretation key on industry. *Photogrammetric Engineering* 24:590–602, illus.

Davis, Jeanne M. 1966. *Uses of airphotos for rural and urban planning.* Government Printing Office, Washington, D.C. U.S. Department of Agriculture, Agriculture Handbook 315, 40 pp., illus.

Horton, Frank E. 1971. The application of remote sensing techniques to urban data acquisition. *Proceedings of the International Workshop on Earth Resources Survey Systems.* Government Printing Office, Washington, D.C., pp. 213–223.

Lindgren, David T. 1971. Dwelling unit estimation with color-IR photos. *Photogrammetric Engineering* 37:373–377, illus.

Lindsay, John J. 1969. Locating potential outdoor recreation areas from aerial photographs. *Journal of Forestry* 67:33–35.

Rex, R. L. 1963. *Evaluation and conclusions of assessing and improvement control by aerial assessment and interpretation methods: a case history.* Sidewell Studio, Chicago. 15 pp., illus.

Richter, Dennis M. 1969. Sequential urban change. *Photogrammetric Engineering* 35:764–770, illus.

Stone, Kirk H. 1964. A guide to the interpretation and analysis of aerial photos. *Annals of the Association of American Geographers* 54:318–328.

Wolf, Alfred L. 1967. *Aerial photography as a legal tool.* Reprint of Eastman Kodak Co., Rochester, N.Y. 4 pp., illus.

Wray, James R. 1971. Census cities project and atlas of urban and regional change. *Proceedings of the International Workshop on Earth Resources Survey Systems.* Government Printing Office, Washington, D.C., pp. 243–259, illus.

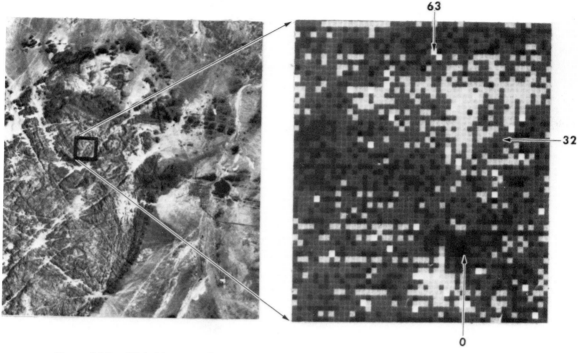

Figure 15.1.   Digital image, enlarged subscene showing pixel matrix, and three digital numbers representing high, intermediate, and low radiance amplitudes.

The median of the DN distribution is identified from the cumulative percent column (i.e., the DN closest to 50 percent). The percent symbols within the histogram represent a cumulative percent curve (Figure 15.3). The DN distribution in Figure 15.3 appears to be bell-shaped (trending toward a Gaussian or normal distribution).

Quantitative measures (computer calculated) for the distribution in Figure 15.3 are: mean, 30.0; median, 30.0; standard deviation, 10.9; and skew, 0.00. Agreement of the mean and median indicates a normality, and zero skewness categorizes the distribution as symmetrical.

INTERACTIVE AND BATCH PROCESSING

There are two computer-based methods for processing digital image data—interactive and batch. With interactive processing, an operator-analyst has direct control over the computer while a job is running; the system must be responsive to the analyst's input messages. This enables an analyst to review intermediate or final processing results as black-and-white or color images on a TV monitor as they are created. The major disadvantage of this method of operation is that the processing is usually performed on relatively small digital arrays to assure completion in a reasonable time.

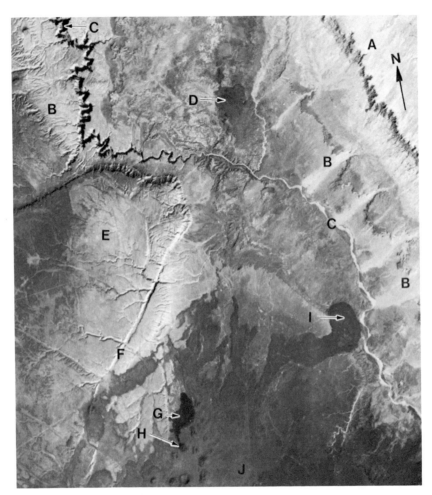

Figure 15.2. Landsat-1 MSS band 7 digital subscene image for a volcanic and sedimentary region in northern Arizona obtained on 29 October 1973. The image contains approximately 610,000 picture elements. Scale is 1:500,000. Annotated features include: (A) Moenkopi Plateau, (B) Painted Desert, (C) Little Colorado River, (D) Shadow Mountain, (E) Coconino Plateau, (F) Mesa Butte fault zone, (G) SP Flow, (H) SP Mountain, (I) Black Point Flow, and (J) San Francisco Plateau. (Courtesy U.S. Geological Survey.)

With batch processing, a set of instructions for an image-processing task must be prepared in total before the job is submitted to the computer. The job is then run with the user having no further access to it. Processing results are normally available shortly after a job has been submitted, but the work can take hours, or even days, when there are many jobs to run. Moreover, because there is no human-computer interaction during a computing job, some procedures can take many iterations before a satisfactory result is achieved.

Even with these shortcomings, batch processing is extremely useful if large volumes of data must be handled efficiently. For example, once an analyst has developed an optimum processing routine on a representative data sample, the routine can be developed into a batch-processing operation on large digital arrays and on additional images without further analyst participation. Therefore, the most versatile image-processing system is one of a *hybrid* or *complementary configuration,* incorporating both interactive and batch-processing capabilities.

DN	%	Cumulative %	Frequency
1	2.095	2.09	12901
2	0.109	2.20	672
3	0.095	2.30	583
4	0.077	2.38	476
5	0.025	2.40	156
6	0.226	2.63	1392
7	0.118	2.75	725
8	0.349	3.09	2148
9	0.578	3.67	3558
10	0.750	4.42	4618
11	0.408	4.83	2514
12	0.648	5.48	3992
13	0.616	6.09	3796
14	0.846	6.94	5208
15	0.478	7.42	2945
16	2.333	9.75	14369
17	2.353	12.10	14487
18	1.285	13.39	7913
19	3.089	16.48	19020
20	1.614	18.09	9939
21	4.214	22.31	25950
22	0.856	23.16	5269
23	5.166	28.33	31810
24	3.377	31.70	20798
25	1.763	33.47	10854
26	4.869	38.34	29986
27	1.032	39.37	6355
28	4.791	44.16	29501
29	1.011	45.17	6226
30	6.213	51.38	38260
31	4.210	55.59	25926
32	2.113	57.71	13012
33	4.047	61.75	24923
34	2.073	63.83	12768
35	4.002	67.83	24642
36	2.893	70.72	17817
37	3.953	74.68	24341
38	3.628	78.30	22339
39	2.418	80.72	14893
40	2.505	83.23	15426
41	3.032	86.26	18673
42	1.156	87.41	7117
43	2.027	89.44	12481
44	0.921	90.36	5670
45	2.568	92.93	15813
46	1.549	94.48	9539
47	0.722	95.20	4449
48	1.239	96.44	7630
49	0.520	96.96	3201
50	0.385	97.35	2373
51	0.738	98.08	4544
52	0.740	98.82	4556
53	0.162	98.99	1000
54	0.285	99.27	1756
55	0.110	99.38	677
56	0.183	99.56	1125
57	0.061	99.62	376
58	0.132	99.76	814
59	0.084	99.84	517
60	0.013	99.85	78
61	0.049	99.90	301
62	0.012	99.91	72
63	0.086	100.00	530

Figure 15.3. Histogram of DN values for the Landsat-1 MSS band 7 image shown in Figure 15.2. (Courtesy U.S. Geological Survey.)

IMAGE-PROCESSING SYSTEMS

Many different image-processing systems (hardware and software) are available on the commercial market. Prices range from about $5,000 to $50,000 for *microcomputer-based systems* having a limited level of capability, to more than $700,000 for state-of-the-art *minicomputer-based systems*. A directory of suppliers of image-processing systems is available from the User Services Section of the EROS Data Center.

Most interactive systems have a built-in expansion and modification capability based upon modular construction or the building-block concept. This type of architecture enables (1) a system to be expanded from a single-user to a multi-user configuration and (2) state-of-the-art hardware and software to be incorporated into the existing system to increase capacity or keep pace with expanding requirements.

SOFTWARE

The software or program package is an essential element of an image-processing system, and a system with comprehensive capabilities may contain several hundred routines. Software packages are usually expandable, enabling existing programs to be modified or special routines to be added by the user. If there are no in-house programmers to accomplish this, most suppliers of image-processing systems provide a custom programming service. Programs can also be purchased from commercial software suppliers or from the Computer Software Management and Information Center (COSMIC), a federally funded facility at the University of Georgia that sells computer programs developed under government sponsorship. A list of software suppliers (batch and interactive) is available from the EROS Data Center, User Services Section.

Many systems make use of a software interactive menu or functions directory. This mode of operation allows an analyst to select appropriate image processing and display options from lists presented on a display monitor. Beyond menus, many systems use interactive prompts, which are of particular value to users who have no programming knowledge because they lead the person step by step through each required routine; this feature is sometimes termed "user friendly." Some companies supply menus in several languages, including English, French, and Spanish. Also, some interactive systems are *hardwired* (i.e., programs wired permanently into the computer's circuitry), enabling a number of common operations to be executed on input digital data by simply depressing function keys.

MINICOMPUTER-BASED IMAGE-PROCESSING SYSTEMS

A generalized hardware configuration of a minicomputer-based image-processing system is shown in Figure 15.4. Specific characteristics and functions of its principal components are described in the following paragraphs.

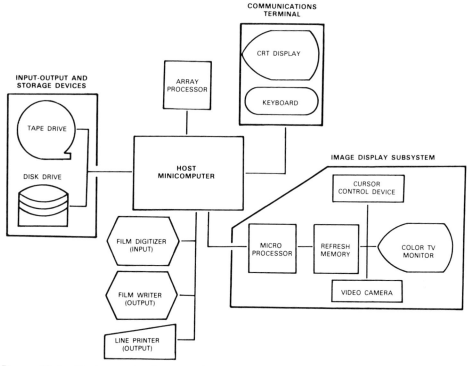

Figure 15.4. Single-user hardware configuration of a minicomputer-based image-processing system capable of processing digital data in both batch and interactive modes.

MINICOMPUTER AND ARRAY PROCESSOR

The heart of an interactive image-processing system is the host minicomputer, which performs software analyses, controls all input-output, and supervises the operation of the entire system. Minicomputers used for image processing are typically configured with from 256 kilobytes (Kb) to 2 megabytes (Mb) of main or internal memory.

For certain operations, significant savings in processing throughout can be realized if an array processor is interfaced to the host computer. The array processor is capable of performing several time-consuming operations simultaneously or in parallel (e.g., arithmetic computations, address indexing, memory fetches, storing) at very high speeds rather than serially or sequentially as is the case with a standard computer's central processing unit (CPU). For a given task, an array processor may be 100 times faster than the host CPU. Once tasks for the array processor are assigned by the host computer, it can proceed to perform other processing tasks.

COMMUNICATIONS TERMINAL

The communications terminal or operator console is composed of a cathode-ray tube (CRT) monitor and a typewriterlike keyboard. It is through the communications terminal that an analyst interacts directly with the computer. For the hardware configuration shown in Figure 15.4, the communications terminal is used both as the system-operation station (including batch-processing job setups) and the analyst station for the image-display subsystem. The CRT monitor enables various types of information to be presented to the analyst during a processing session; these include input-output messages, statistical information and graphical presentations for a given image, program menus, and queries regarding erroneous or incomplete user commands. An interactive system can be configured with several terminals if there are to be multiple users.

DATA STORAGE

The magnetic disk and associated disk drive are direct-access devices for the storage of image data and software. For interactive systems, memory capacities generally range from 20 to 200 Mb per disk. Large interactive units usually use separate disks to store two types of data: (1) the system disk contains the operating system and applications software, and (2) multiple-image storage disks are used as an extension of the host computer's main memory to store on-line digital images as they are manipulated by the applications programs. Smaller systems usually use a single disk for system and image storage.

The most widely used medium for the external, or off-line, storage of digital image information is magnetic tape. A magnetic-tape drive is used (1) to load images stored on tape to the direct-access storage disk unit for processing and (2) for writing image data onto tape after processing. Three tape drive configurations are presently available for minicomputers:

1. *Single density:* 315, 630, or 2460 bits/cm (800, 1600, or 6250 bits/in)
2. *Dual density:* 315/630 or 630/2460 bits/cm
3. *Triple density:* 315/630/2460 bits/cm

All images kept on-line for processing are stored on disk rather than tape because data access and readback from disk are much faster than from tape.

IMAGE-DISPLAY SUBSYSTEM

The image-display subsystem consists of a microprocessor, refresh memory, color TV monitor, and a cursor-control device. In large-scale systems, the microprocessor is capable of internally performing certain image processing operations on digital data loaded by the host CPU. The microprocessor in less sophisticated systems may perform only control operations for the image-display subsystem. The microprocessor can be controlled by the analyst from the communications terminal and architecturally is a peripheral device to the host minicomputer.

Refresh-memory channels are used to store multiple images and graphics or graphic overlays (e.g., alphanumeric image annotations, map information, polygonal masks, histograms of image-related statistical information) that are to be displayed on the TV screen. The memory media are usually random-access memory (RAM) semiconductor silicon chips that each hold millions of electronic circuits. Data stored in refresh memory can be extracted many times per second and displayed on the TV monitor. The amount of refresh memory available on existing interactive systems varies between 3 and 16 image planes or channels and 1 to 16 graphics planes. Normal pixel depths for each image plane range from 4 to 8 bits. The depth is usually a single bit for a graphics plane.

Two common video output configurations are these: (1) any three refresh-image channels can be used simultaneously to produce blue, green, and red refresh-image signals for a color-composite display on the screen, and (2) each refresh-memory plane can be used to produce individual video signals for either black-and-white or pseudocolor displays. *Pseudocolor* is a processing technique that arbitrarily assigns color to image brightness; it can provide dramatic improvements in image contrast because small changes in intensity can be transformed to abrupt changes in color (Lyons 1977). Because the video signals are refreshed up to 60 times per second, a stable, flicker-free image can be produced on the TV screen.

The color TV monitor is the principal device enabling the analyst to view images in near real time rather than waiting for the results to be "written" on film and developed. Common display resolutions are 256 by 256 pixels, 512 by 512 pixels (the industry standard), and 1,024 by 1,024 pixels. These pixel resolutions dictate that the display of an entire scene (e.g., MSS or TM) requires sampling or subsetting (i.e., using every *nth* line and sample). Sampling is sometimes termed *overview*, and although there is a considerable loss in resolution, it does permit the analyst to visually select image subareas for detailed analyses at full or improved pixel resolution.

A cursor is an electronic targeting device that defines pixel coordinates. It can be positioned on any pixel in the displayed image by some type of control (e.g., joystick, trackball, or a special stylus called a light pen). The cursor can be displayed on the TV screen in various shapes, but common forms are crosshairs, arrows, and rectangles. To enhance the detectability of the cursor against the image background, many vendors offer features such as cursor blinking, color cursors, and variable-intensity cursors. This enables an analyst, for example, to position a cursor over individual pixels to access intensity data and select control points for geometric corrections (fixed cursor) or to outline image subareas for special processing (window cursor) (LaPado et al. 1978).

HARDCOPY OUTPUT DEVICES

There are various types of output devices for producing hardcopy records of image-processing results. The most common nonphotographic unit is a line printer which records letters, numbers, and a range of symbols on computer printout paper. All information displayed on the operator's CRT (e.g., programs, statistical information and DN histograms for a given image) can be printed. The unit may also be used to (1) print spatial arrays of DNs enabling an analyst to see exact DN values at given pixel locations, and (2) generate gray-scale images by overprinting. With the latter output, gray-level approximations are formed by repetitive printing of different characters per pixel location. Because a single printout page can accommodate only 1,250 to 7,200 pixels, data for small image subareas are commonly printed at full or slightly compressed resolution. More recently, matrix printers have been introduced that produce dot graphics that are superior to character over-printing and allow for more pixels to be placed on each page.

The most desirable form of hardcopy is some type of film product. The simplest procedure is to photograph the TV screen with a detached 35- or 70-mm camera. However, because these off-the-screen photographs incorporate *barrel*, or *curvature*, distortion, they are best suited for quick-look documentation purposes. Distortion-free color and black-and-white hardcopy can, however, be obtained by a photographic system that intercepts video signals traveling from the refresh-image channels to the color TV monitor. With the Polaroid Videoprint system, a videoprocessor converts video signals into images on a flat-faced CRT (eliminates barrel distortion); an internal camera system is then used to photograph the raster display. The system is capable of producing negatives, Polaroid prints, or 35-mm color transparencies.

High-resolution hardcopy images suitable for interpretation and mapping can be produced by a film writer or plotter. With the Optronics International's rotating-drum film writer, film copy is provided by attaching unexposed film (commonly 25.4 cm by 25.4 cm) to the outside of a rotating drum and allowing a light source to sequentially expose the film pixel by pixel in proportion to the DN values that are being read from refresh memory, disk, or magnetic tape. There are 256 gray-scale modulation levels for 8-bit data (Barrett 1978). Common pixel resolutions for remote sensing vary from 25 to 200 μm at 25-μm steps. A film writer is especially well suited to generating images with a dense matrix of values because more than 350 million pixels can be recorded on a single piece of 25.4 cm by 25.4 cm film.

Optronics International offers models that can use both black-and-white and color films or panchromatic film only. For the panchromatic medium, images can be produced as negatives or positive transparencies (inter-negatives). Three film positives that have been punch-registered to a piece of unexposed color-transparent film can be used to produce a color-composite image by contact printing each transparency onto the color film using blue, green, and red filtered light (Condit and Chavez 1979).

Because many remotely sensed images are recorded directly on film (aerial photographs, thermal infrared, and radar images), state-of-the-art inter-active systems are normally configured with some type of film digitizer (e.g., drum scanner, flatbed scanner, TV-video digitizer). A film digitizer scans color or monochrome films and converts film density variations into digital numbers for computer processing, a process known as *digitization*. An Optronics International's drum scanner can digitize an image to 256 DN levels at selectable sampling rasters or spot sizes as small as 12.5 μm by 12.5 μm. For a color product, the film is scanned sequentially through blue, green, and red filtered light to extract density data from each of the film's three dye layers.

MICROCOMPUTER-BASED IMAGE-PROCESSING SYSTEMS

The recent revolution in microprocessor technology has led to the production of relatively inexpensive microcomputer-based image-processing systems. Microcomputer hardware-software systems can vary in price from about $18,500 for the Remote Image Processing System by Spectral Data Corporation to as inexpensive as $3,500 for Apple Computer-based systems.[1]

Primarily because of limited CPU speeds, a micro-system can process and display only relatively small digital data sets. Even with this limitation, however, micro-systems are adequate for many research endeavors, and they are rapidly becoming important teaching tools in many academic institutions and government agencies.

Because of data-set size limitations, DNs can be stored on floppy disks rather than larger-capacity CCTs. There are two ways to get floppies with image data: (1) floppy disks containing Landsat MSS subscenes can be purchased from the EROS Data Center, or (2) a microcomputer can be interfaced to a larger computer having tape drives; in this configuration, subscenes from a CCT can be downloaded to the microcomputer for reformatting and disk storage.

REMOTE IMAGE PROCESSING SYSTEM

The Remote Image Processing System (RIPS) is an outgrowth of an EROS Data Center (EDC) project aimed at demonstrating the feasibility of using micro-systems in support of Department of Interior remote-sensing projects. EROS Data Center assembled several RIPS prototypes in the early 1980s, and Spectral Data Corporation began selling the commercial equivalent of RIPS in 1983.

The minimum RIPS configuration consists of a central processing unit with 64 Kb of core memory, two 20-cm (8-in.) floppy disk drives with 2.4 Mb of auxiliary storage, a communications terminal, a color TV monitor, a joystick, and a software package containing several applications programs (Figure 15.5). RIPS is capable of storing and processing three single-image planes measuring 256 by 240 pixels at a 4-bit depth for color-composite displays

1. Prices quoted in this chapter are in 1983 dollars; they are intended for comparative purposes only and are subject to change without notice. Potential purchasers of image-processing equipment should therefore consult current catalogs and price listings.

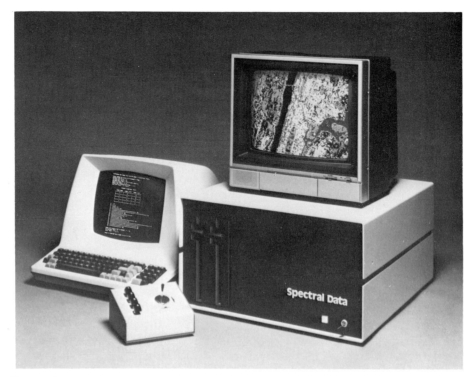

Figure 15.5. Microcomputer-based image-processing system. (Courtesy Edward Yost, Spectral Data Corporation.)

(blue, green, red) and one 256-by-240-pixel image plane at an 8-bit depth for black-and-white operations. Optional peripherals include a TV-video digitizer, color printer, and a telephone modem that can link RIPS to a larger mainframe computer to handle Landsat CCT subscene transfers.

Several options are available for RIPS software expansion:

1. Optional programs can be purchased from Spectral Data Corporation.
2. Special-purpose software can be written by RIPS owners because RIPS has a program development capability.
3. Routines written by EDC scientists and operational on Spectral Data's RIPS can be purchased from the EROS Data Center for a copying fee (software written to floppy disks).

APPLE PERSONAL IMAGE PROCESSING SYSTEM

The Apple Personal Image Processing System (APPLEPIPS), developed by the Telesys Group, is one of the software packages available for the Apple II Computer. APPLEPIPS includes algorithms for image algebra (DN averaging, differencing, multiplying, two-band ratioing), density slicing, contrast and edge enhancement, and classification schemes. The largest APPLEPIPS display resolution is 140 by 96 pixels, and display capabilities are limited to only single-band images in either 6 or 16 colors (Welch et al. 1983). The APPLEPIPS software is available for about $1,000.

The basic hardware components for an Apple-based system are an Apple II Computer with 48 Kb core memory, one or two minifloppy disk drives, a standard color TV, which serves as the system's monitor and image-display screen, and a downloader modem (total hardware price is about $2,500). Other applications software is available from COSMIC and several commercial suppliers (contact EROS Data Center, User Services Section).

◼ EROS DATA CENTER DIGITAL PRODUCTS

The EROS Data Center provides Landsat digital image data to the public on CCTs and floppy disks. CCTs were developed for use with large-scale image-processing systems and floppy disks with the more recently introduced micro-systems.

The standard nine-track CCT is available at packing densities of 630 and 2460 bits/cm (1600 and 6250 bits/in.); storage capacities are 45 and 180 Mb, respectively. Factors such as sensor type, tape density, and scene coverage determine the number of CCTs needed for a particular study (Table 15.4).

Landsat MSS digital data became available on 20-cm (8-in.), 77-track floppy disks in late 1982. The ground area represented on a floppy is significantly smaller than that contained on a CCT: 256 lines by 240 samples (61,440 pixels) for *system-corrected data* and 226 lines by 226 samples (51,076 pixels) for *precision-corrected data*. The latter product has stringent ground-control requirements and can be geographically referenced to a U.S. Geological Survey 7.5-minute (1:24,000) quadrangle. The system-corrected product has a lower geometric accuracy. Subscenes must be identified on a special grid that is overlayed on a 1:1,000,000-scale image of the full MSS scene from which the product is to be derived. It is anticipated that TM data will eventually become available on floppy disks.

TABLE 15.4. Landsat CCT Products, EROS Data Center

Sensor—Coverage	Tape Density (bits/cm)	(bits/in.)	Number of Tapes
MSS CCT, 4 bands	630	1600	1
(full scene)	2460	6250	1
RBV, 1 band	630	1600	4
(full scene)	2460	6250	4
RBV, 1 band	630	1600	1
(quarter scene)	2460	6250	1
TM, 7 bands	630	1600	7
(full scene)	2460	6250	4

▨ IMAGE RESTORATION

Image restoration or *preprocessing* is concerned with correcting a degraded (i.e., distorted, noisy) digital image to its intended form. Image correction (clean-up) is one of the most important stages of digital processing, because many enhancement and classification operations will emphasize image imperfections to such an extent that useful information can be obscured (Condit and Chavez 1979). For this reason, preprocessing usually precedes other types of image processing.

A series of computer algorithms have been developed to recognize and remove several types of errors and distracting effects from digital images. They include:

1. Geometric distortions
2. Noise patterns
3. Variations in solar illumination angle
4. Atmospheric haze

All of the algorithms are applicable to multispectral images (e.g., Landsat MSS), but a digitized radar image might need to be subjected to only the first two correction routines. An image that has undergone the appropriate preprocessing is called a *data base*.

▨ GEOMETRIC CORRECTION

Numerous systematic and nonsystematic geometric distortions are inherent in raw digital images. Because systematic distortions are constant over time, they are predictable, and geometric transformations are relatively simple to design and inexpensive to run. The purpose of these transformations is to correct pixel locational errors, thereby placing ground features in their correct positions throughout the image.

▨ SKEW

Skew is one type of systematic distortion associated with the Landsat system. Skew distortion is introduced as a result of the earth's rotation and the satellite's orbital movements as an image is being acquired by the MSS. Each MSS scene is *deskewed* by an algorithm that shifts scan lines by a calculated number of pixels—a number dependent on the estimated latitude for the scan line being processed with respect to the starting line of the image (Rohde et al. 1978). For example, at 40° N latitude the right-hand shift between the top and bottom lines of a frame is 122 pixels (Moik 1980). Skew correction produces the familiar parallelogram shape of a full MSS scene (Figure 7.47).

▩ NONSYSTEMATIC DISTORTIONS

Altitude and attitude variations (roll, pitch, yaw) and topographic elevation differences are responsible for nonsystematic (random) distortions in a digital image. The correction process depends on the scene and makes use of well-distributed ground control points that are identifiable in both the distorted image and a reference map or control base (e.g., highway intersections, airport runways, and other landmarks). Each ground control point is identified by line-sample (image) and latitude-longitude (map) coordinates. These values are then used to establish the geometric transformations required to match the image to the map. The reference coordinate system for correcting Landsat MSS images can be based on several map projections (e.g., Hotline Oblique Mercator, Universal Transverse Mercator, and Polar Stereographic) (Figure 6.2).

▩ RESAMPLING

Because the new locations of transformed pixels will rarely coincide with the locations of input or source pixels, DNs for the transformed pixels must be interpolated from the neighborhood surrounding the source pixel. This process is called resampling, and three algorithms can be used (U.S. Geological Survey 1983, Moik 1980) (Figure 15.6). They are as follows:

1. **Nearest-neighbor resampling:** DN equal to that of the nearest input pixel is assigned to the output pixel. Because the true location may be off-set by as much as 1/2 pixel in the output matrix, linear features in particular will have a blocky, steplike appearance. Computational requirements are relatively low because only one input value is required to determine a resampled value.
2. **Bilinear interpolation:** Output DNs are determined by taking a proximity-weighted average of input DNs from the four nearest pixels. There will be a loss in image resolution because of the smoothing or blurring

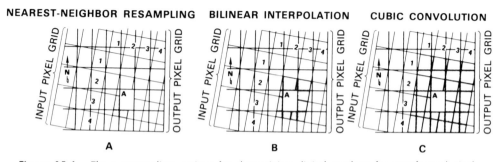

Figure 15.6.   Three resampling options for determining digital numbers for transformed pixels (Short 1982).

caused by DN averaging. Three to four times more computation time is required than with the nearest-neighbor technique.

3. **Cubic convolution:** Output DNs are assigned on the basis of a weighted average of input DNs from 16 surrounding pixels. This resampling approach has virtually replaced bilinear interpolation because its blurring effect is much less noticeable on a processed image. Cubic convolution requires the most computation (it takes 10 to 12 times longer to run than the nearest-neighbor technique).

NOISE CORRECTION

The sensing and recording process can introduce electronic noise to an image—noise that is independent of the information transmitted from the scene. Both *random* and *periodic noise* may be found in a digital image. Periodic noise masks radiance data, in essence producing "two-component" DNs (i.e., some combination of valid and nonvalid data). Random noise represents only nonvalid image data. An example of periodic noise is six-line banding (six-line scanner noise), commonly associated with uncorrected Landsat MSS images. Two types of random noise are bit errors (speckle or spike noise) and line drops.

SIX-LINE BANDING

The MSS system uses a six-detector array for each of the four spectral bands, enabling six ground lines to be imaged simultaneously during each sweep of the mirror (Figure 7.46). However, because the detectors have slightly different output responses, the resulting raw images often exhibit a striping effect that can reduce (1) the accuracy of image classification statistics because some DNs are contaminated with a noise component or (2) the aesthetic appearance of an image (Figure 15.7, Plate 9A). Several *destriping* methods have been devised to remove or suppress this noise pattern. For example, the EROS Data Center uses a two-pass, "through-the-image" operation; the following description of the EROS technique is from Rohde et al. (1978).

In the first pass, DN data for each detector are normalized with the relationship:

$$DN_{o(j,s)} = DN_{I(j,s)} \left(\frac{S_A}{S_I}\right) + M_A - M_I \left(\frac{S_A}{S_I}\right) \qquad \textbf{Equation 15.1}$$

where: $DN_{o(j,s)}$ = Digital number of output pixel at line j, sample s
  $DN_{I(j,s)}$ = Digital number of input pixel at line j, sample s
  S_A = Standard deviation of entire scene
  S_I = Standard deviation of individual detector (I = 1 to 6)
  M_A = Mean DN value of entire scene
  M_I = Mean DN value of individual detector

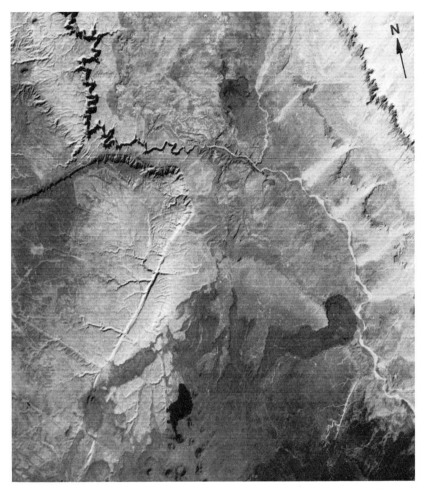

Figure 15.7.   Unprocessed Landsat-1 MSS band 7 subscene image for a volcanic and sedimentary region in northern Arizona obtained 29 October 1973. Scale is 1:500,000. This image incorporates six-line banding and several lines of dropped data. Compare with computer-corrected image shown in Figure 15.2. (Courtesy U.S. Geological Survey.)

If local statistics differ markedly from those derived from the total scene, the one-pass algorithm may not be totally effective. A second-pass algorithm is then used to perform a local averaging (smoothing) adjustment to remove the residual striping from the affected subregions. With the second pass, the digital data are processed in six-line groups. The first line of each group is selected as a "good data," or reference line (DNs will remain unchanged), and each succeeding line is processed to be similar to the line above. A local average along line I ($LOCAV_I$) of 75 pixels in each direction from the pixel being processed in a line is compared to the corresponding local average from the preceding line, I − 1 ($LOCAV_I^{-1}$). If this difference is less than a predetermined threshold value, the pixel's digital number is modified by the difference:

$$DN_{o(j,s)} = DN_{I(j,s)} - D \qquad \text{Equation 15.2}$$

where: $DN_{o(j,s)}$ = Digital number of output pixel at line j, sample s
$DN_{I(j,s)}$ = Digital number of input pixel at line j, sample s
D = $LOCAV_I - LOCAV_I^{-1}$

The 75-pixel window is moved at one-pixel increments through the image from left to right and from top to bottom. The visual effect of destriping is shown in Figure 15.2.

BIT ERRORS AND LINE DROPS

Bit errors are represented by isolated spikes (each of one pixel) of high or low DNs that deviate significantly from values of surrounding pixels, and horizontal lines of anomalous DN values represent line drops (Figure 15.7). Rather than adjusting DN values as with six-line banding, restorations for bit and line noise use artificial data, and the improvement is, therefore, "cosmetic."

Bit errors can be removed from a digital image by comparing each pixel value with its neighbors; if the difference exceeds a certain threshold value, the pixel is considered a noise point and the aberrant value is replaced by the average of neighboring pixel values (Moik 1980). Commonly used neighborhoods or windows have dimensions of 3 by 3 pixels or 5 by 5 pixels.

Lost lines of data can be replaced (1) by average values calculated from the line immediately above and the line immediately below the lost line, or (2) by DNs from the preceding line. Line replacement by the averaging method for an MSS image is shown in Figure 15.2 (compare with Figure 15.7).

SUN-ANGLE CORRECTION

If images (e.g., Landsat MSS) generated during different times of the year are to be used for mosaics or compared for change detection, the seasonal effects of variations in solar illumination angle should be normalized. Corrections can be made by dividing DNs for each pixel by the cosine of the illumination angle. Scene brightness for each image, regardless of season, is normalized to a solar-illumination angle of 90°. Because the function assumes a smooth, flat surface, topographic shadows are retained.

CORRECTION FOR ATMOSPHERIC SCATTERING

Whenever multispectral images are generated from the visible and near-infrared spectral regions, they are affected unequally by atmospheric scattering. Because scattering is inversely proportional to wavelength, the images representing the shorter wavelength regions are affected the most. Regarding the MSS system on Landsats-1, -2, -3, band 4 (0.5–0.6 μm) will have the highest component of scattered light and band 7 (0.8–1.1 μm) the lowest component (MSS bands 1 and 4 on Landsats-4 and -5).

The scattering process contributes radiance from the atmosphere (haze), which reduces scene contrast; water vapor is the major controlling parameter. A black-and-white image so affected will have a washed-out or fogged appearance. For many uncorrected MSS color-composite images (e.g., bands 4, 5, 7), the effect of scattering is manifested by an overall bluish cast caused by the dominance of haze in band 4.

A common haze correction technique uses histograms of MSS images that contain deep water bodies, topographic shadows, or cloud shadows (Chavez 1975). The method assumes band 7 is essentially free of haze, and thus deep water or shadow pixels are black. A histogram of band 7 will therefore contain 0 DNs, or at most, DN 1 values, but the histograms for the other three bands will not. Rather, the bars for these histograms are displaced to the right (the shorter the wavelength, the larger the displacement), and at some DN level there is an abrupt increase in DN pixel frequencies. The general lack of DNs below this level is attributed to the scattering component. Therefore, the DN where the abrupt increase occurs is assumed to be the haze component. This value is subtracted from all pixel values in that band, thus producing a haze removal correction at a first-order approximation.

Histograms showing the distribution of MSS DNs before adjustment for atmospheric scattering for an area in northern Arizona are presented in Figure 15.8. Haze DN values for this scene are as follows: band 4 = 12, band 5 = 7, band 6 = 4, and band 7 = 0.

Because atmospheric scattering depends on wavelength and varies with time, obtaining haze-free radiance values is especially important for spectral ratio analysis and normalizing multitemporal images. If data-base images are to be used only for visual interpretations, atmospheric correction is not needed because bias subtraction is accomplished when the DN data are enhanced for contrast (Schowengerdt 1983). The above techniques are discussed in the following sections of this chapter.

IMAGE ENHANCEMENT

The goal of image enhancement is to improve the detectability of objects or patterns in a digital image for visual interpretation. However, because certain enhanced images do not resemble their original forms, the user must understand changes caused by the processing if interpretation is to be correct. Enhancement can be divided into the following categories:

1. Contrast stretching
2. Spatial filtering
3. Edge enhancement
4. Directional first differencing

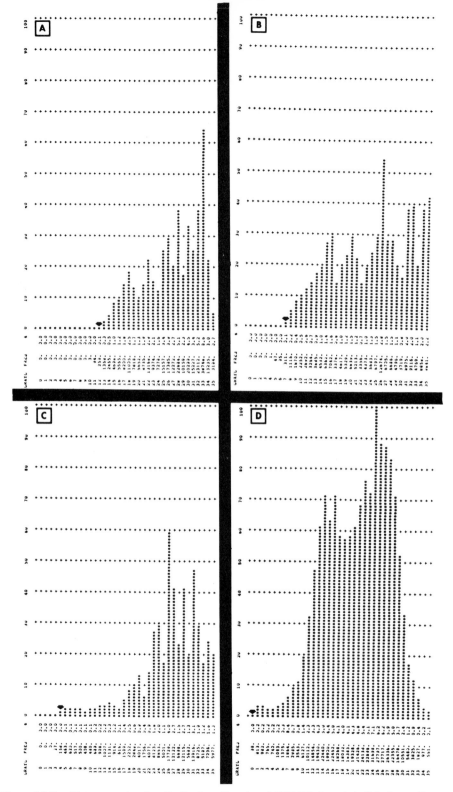

Figure 15.8. Histograms showing distribution of Landsat-1 MSS DNs (bands 4–7) before adjustment for atmospheric scattering. DNs represent radiance values for a volcanic and sedimentary landscape in northern Arizona (see Figure 15.7). Haze DN values (arrows) are as follows: band 4 = 12, band 5 = 7, band 6 = 4, and band 7 = 0. (Courtesy U.S. Geological Survey.)

5. Multispectral band ratioing
6. Simulated natural color
7. Linear data transformations

These operations are applied to digital image data after the appropriate preprocessing steps have been completed.

CONTRAST STRETCHING

Contrast stretching is designed to accentuate the contrast between features of interest in a digital image. It is accomplished by redistributing a range of input digital numbers to fill a larger output scale. The redistribution can be linear *(uniform expansion)* or nonlinear *(nonuniform expansion)*. Several types of contrast stretches can be applied to data bases; which will be the most effective is determined by the range and variation of the original DNs and the nature of the investigation.

LINEAR STRETCHES

Increasing the contrast in a single digital image, while preserving original radiance relationships, can be accomplished by a linear stretch. Linear contrast enhancement is done by assigning new DNs to each pixel with the linear relationship:

$$DN_{o(j,s)} = \left(\frac{DN_{I(j,s)} - MIN}{MAX - MIN}\right)255 \qquad \textbf{Equation 15.3}$$

where: $DN_{o(j,s)}$ = Output digital number at line j, sample s
$DN_{I(j,s)}$ = Original digital number of input image at line j, sample s
MIN = Minimum DN parameter in input image (user selected)
MAX = Maximum DN parameter in input image (user selected)

All pixels with DN values equal to or less than MIN are reassigned the value 0, and pixels with DNs equal to or greater than MAX are reassigned the value 255. All DNs between MIN and MAX have a multiplier applied to them that linearly expands the range of DNs between 0 and 255. This increases the difference between DNs of image features, and as this increases, the contrast between these features also increases (Rohde et al. 1978).

The simplest linear stretch is one that expands 6- and 7-bit data to an 8-bit scale (Figure 15.9A). DN input-output parameters for computer entry can be written as shown in Table 15.5. Both transformations would increase image contrast because gray-level or DN separations have been expanded by factors of two (7-bit) and four (6-bit) as illustrated in Table 15.6.

The contrast between features can be further increased if the lower and upper tails of a frequency distribution are truncated, or trimmed, before enhancement, a process known as *histogram trimming*. Truncation allows a

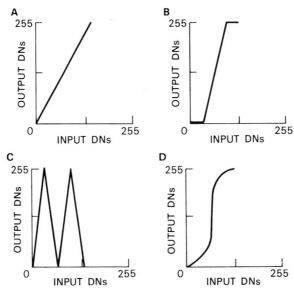

Figure 15.9.   Basic types of contrast stretches: (A) linear without saturation, (B) linear with saturation, (C) sinusoidal or "sine," and (D) nonlinear. Note that input DNs are in a 7-bit format and output DNs are in an 8-bit format.

narrower range of input DNs to undergo expansion to the full 0–255 scale (Figure 15.9B). This type of linear stretch is especially applicable to a Gaussian distribution because a relatively few DN pixel counts occupy the tails. However, it is advantageous at times to select the truncation parameters by trial and error on an interactive image analysis system to insure that there is not a significant loss of meaningful information (Rohde et al. 1978, Short 1982).

Plate 9B shows a portion of a Landsat-1 MSS 4, 5, 7 data-base color-composite image that incorporates this type of linear contrast enhancement. The MIN/MAX values for each band were determined by interactive analysis. The stretch parameters are listed in Table 15.7.

Although the image data for Plate 9B were preprocessed by the histogram correction algorithm to remove atmospheric haze effects, the lower DN

TABLE 15.5. Expanding 6- and 7-Bit Data to an 8-Bit Scale by Linear Stretches

7- to 8-Bit Expansion			6- to 8-Bit Expansion		
Input DN		Output DN	Input DN		Output DN
0	(goes to)	0	0	(goes to)	0
127		255	63		255
255[a]		255[a]	255[a]		255[a]

[a]"255 (goes to) 255" statement is used to terminate the stretch algorithm.

TABLE 15.6. Expansion of 6- and 7-Bit Data to an 8-Bit Scale With Resultant DN Separations

	DN Sequence						
7-Bit DNs:	0	1	2	3	4	5	6
to							
8-Bit DNs:	0	2	4	6	8	10	12
6-Bit DNs:	0	1	2	3	4	5	6
to							
8-Bit DNs:	0	4	8	12	16	20	24

truncation parameter for this type of linear stretch produces, in essence, a subtraction bias that will correct for atmospheric haze. For this reason, the histogram correction algorithm for haze removal can often be omitted in the preprocessing stage if the images are to be used for color composites (e.g., MSS bands 4, 5, 7).

AREA-SPECIFIC STRETCH

The area-specific stretch (linear form) is used to enhance a portion of an image that is of interest to the analyst. For example, if a data-base image contained both land and water surfaces, an area-specific stretch could enhance subtle patterns in the water. Most of the land information would likely be lost because its DNs would lie outside the DN range of water. Likewise, a second area-specific stretch could be implemented on the same data to enhance only the land patterns.

Figure 15.10 shows two Landsat-1 MSS band 4 images incorporating area-specific stretches for bottom reflectance enhancement for water and surface reflectance enhancement for land. The stretch parameters are given in Table 15.8.

TABLE 15.7. Linear Stretches on MSS Bands 4, 5, and 7 Using Histogram Trimming[a]

Band 4		Band 5		Band 7	
Input DN	Output DN	Input DN	Output DN	Input DN	Output DN
0	0	0	0	0	0
3	0	7	0	5	0
67	255	111	255	57	255
255	255	255	255	255	255

[a]Color-composite image incorporating these stretches is presented on Plate 9B.

TABLE 15.8. Area-Specific Stretches on a Landsat-1 MSS Band 4 Image for Bottom Reflectance and Surface Reflectance

Bottom Reflectance (Water)[a]		Surface Reflectance (Land)[a]	
Input DN	Output DN	Input DN	Output DN
0	0	0	0
45	255	45	0
255	255	90	255
		255	255

[a]Images incorporating these stretches are presented in Figure 15.10.

SINUSOIDAL STRETCH

A sinusoidal, or "sine," stretch is designed to enhance subtle differences within "homogeneous" units such as a forest stand, volcanic field, or dune field. The stretch parameters are usually determined from the form of the DN distribution (histogram interpretation). The distribution is divided into several intervals or ranges and each of these is expanded over the output range. Through trial and error it has been found that an image will not become overly "busy" if there are six or fewer intervals and each interval is 15 to 20 DNs wide. Range boundaries are established where there are breaks or diminutions in the DN distribution.

Because several different input DNs can be mapped to one output DN, sinusoidal stretches are usually applied to three multispectral images that are to be color combined. This reduces the possibility that two different features will have the identical color output. The reason this stretch is called sinusoidal is that when input and output DN stretch parameters are plotted against each other, a sinusoidal curve is formed (Chavez et al. 1977a) (Figure 15.9C).

A Landsat-1 MSS 4, 5, 7 color-composite image incorporating sinusoidal stretches is shown in Plate 9C. Note that when compared to a conventional MSS 4, 5, 7 color-composite image (Plate 9B), there is little or no correlation in color for the same ground features. Note also that the sinusoidal-stretched image shows details within volcanic areas and surficial deposits that are not discernible in the conventional infrared color image. The sinusoidal stretch parameters for the image shown in Plate 9C are listed in Table 15.9.

NONLINEAR STRETCHES

Nonlinear stretches have flexible parameters that are controlled by DN pixel frequencies and the shape of the original distribution (Figure 15.9D). Two types are the *uniform distribution stretch* and the *Gaussian stretch*. With the uniform distribution stretch, original DNs are redistributed on the basis of their frequency of occurrence; the greatest contrast enhancement occurs within the range with the most original DNs. The Gaussian stretch forces a skewed frequency distribution of input data to a normal or nonskewed distribution. This stretch is useful if distributions are skewed in such a way that features could become abnormally light or dark when stretched linearly. The Gaussian stretch prevents saturation while enhancing overall scene contrast (USGS 1983).

COMPARISON OF LINEAR- AND GAUSSIAN-STRETCHED RBV IMAGES

The effects of linear and Gaussian stretches on a Landsat-3 Return Beam Vidicon (RBV) image of the eastern Grand Canyon are illustrated in Figure 15.11. Because the original 7-bit digital data represent a positive skewness frequency distribution (steep slope for low DN tail, shallow slope for high DN tail), the linear stretch expands the distribution but does not alter its shape. Hence, the enhanced image lacks contrast in the dark-toned areas. However, the Gaussian stretch expands the low DN tail preferentially so the output distribution resembles a normal curve. This has the effect of preferentially increasing contrast in the darker areas. This nonlinear adjustment is made possible by forcing the input median DN to the output median DN or 127 for an 8-bit scale (see Table 15.10).

From the Gaussian stretch parameters (Table 15.10), it can be seen that the first 50 percent of the input data lie between DNs 0 and 50, or 51 levels, and these are being redistributed over 128 levels (0 to 127). Therefore, the separation or spacing between DNs in the output will vary between 2 and 3 (average separation of 2.5 DN). However, 77 DNs are included in the second 50 percent, and, consequently, the DN separation for this part of the distribution will vary between 2 and 1 (average separation of 1.7 DN).

SPATIAL FILTERING

Filtering a digital image in the spatial domain is designed to enhance different scales of tonal or DN "roughness" (i.e., different *spatial frequencies*). Unlike enhancement by contrast stretching, spatial filtering depends not only

TABLE 15.9. Sinusoidal Stretches on MSS Bands 4, 5, and 7[a]

Band 4		Band 5		Band 7	
Input DN	Output DN	Input DN	Output DN	Input DN	Output DN
0	0	0	0	0	0
18	255	19	255	15	255
35	0	40	0	29	0
56	255	63	255	44	255
72	0	79	0	63	0
255	255	102	255	255	255
		255	255		

[a]Color-composite image incorporating these stretches is presented in Plate 9C.

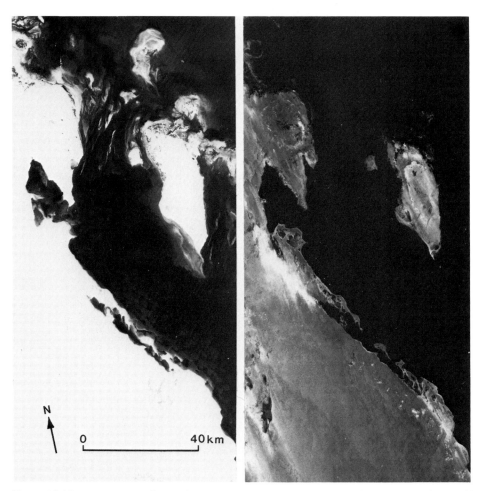

Figure 15.10   Two versions of a Landsat-1 MSS band 4 subscene image of the western Arabian Gulf region obtained 4 September 1972. Each image incorporates a different area-specific stretch to enhance bottom reflectance patterns of the Arabian Gulf (left) and reflectance patterns of the land surface in Saudi Arabia and Bahrain. Many of the light-toned features in the gulf are coral reefs. Band 4 was selected to highlight bottom features because its wavelengths (0.5–0.6 μm) penetrate water to a maximum depth of about 20 m. Band 5 (0.6–0.7 μm) penetrates only about 2 m; bands 6 and 7 (0.7–0.8 and 0.8–1.1 μm, respectively) do not penetrate water. (Courtesy Pat S. Chavez, Jr., U.S. Geological Survey.)

upon the value of the pixel being processed, but also on the pixel values surrounding it (i.e., its *neighborhood*). In this regard, spatial filtering is an *area operation*, while contrast stretching is a *point operation*. Spatial filters are used to either emphasize or de-emphasize abrupt changes in pixel DNs, thereby altering an image's textural appearance (Lillesand and Kiefer 1979).

A digital image contains both low- and high-frequency spatial information; their sum constitutes the original image. The *low-frequency component* (LFC) represents gradual DN changes over a relatively large number of pixels (i.e.,

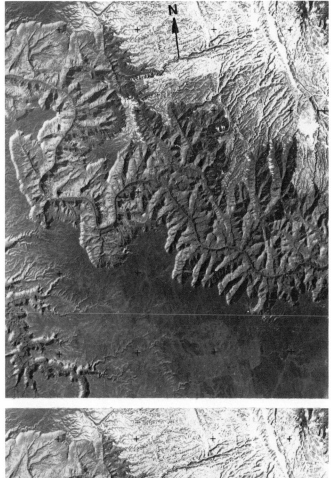

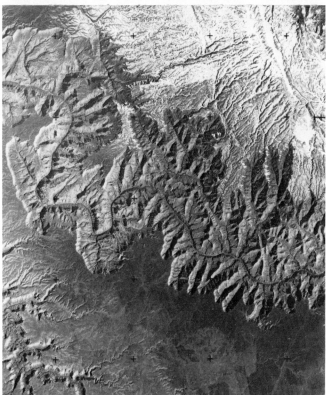

Figure 15.11. Landsat-3 RBV subscene image of the eastern Grand Canyon, Arizona, incorporating a standard linear contrast stretch (top) and a Gaussian contrast stretch. Scale is about 1:500,000. Acquisition date: 22 March 1981. (Courtesy Pat S. Chavez, Jr., U.S. Geological Survey.)

TABLE 15.10. Gaussian and Linear Stretches for a Landsat RBV Image Having a Positive Skewness[a]

Gaussian Stretch		Linear Stretch	
Input DN	Output DN	Input DN	Output DN
0	0	0	0
50 (median) 127		127	255
127	255	255	255
255	255		

[a]Images incorporating these stretches are presented in Figure 15.11.

low tonal variance). The LFC, therefore, defines the "smooth" areas of an image (e.g., forest cover, lava field, or water). The *high-frequency component* (HFC) represents rapid DN changes over a short space (i.e., large tonal variance). The HFC defines the "rough" areas or the details of an image (e.g., slope attitude contrasts, lithologic contacts, drainage networks, lineaments, and cultural linear features).

Algorithms that perform spatial-frequency enhancement are called filters because they pass or emphasize certain spatial frequencies and suppress others. Spatial filters that pass high frequencies, emphasizing the details of an image, are called *high-pass filters* (HPF). Conversely, *low-pass filters* (LPF) produce image smoothing by suppressing the high spatial frequencies.

The spatial filter is simply a subarray (*box* or *window*) of N by M pixels that is moved through the larger image array. The filter is usually of an odd-integer dimension along each side so that a central pixel exists for DN reassignment based upon surrounding pixel values. Filter shapes can be square or rectangular. Square filters (e.g., 31 lines by 31 samples) have uniform weights, ensuring that enhancement is equal in all image directions *(uniform-weight filters)*. Rectangular filters provide maximum enhancement to features trending perpendicular to the long axis of the filter *(directional filters)*. Two common forms of directional filters are the *horizontal-line filter* (e.g., 1 line by 31 samples) and the *vertical-line filter* (e.g., 31 lines by 1 sample). Care must be exercised in interpreting directionally filtered images because the filtering operation may produce artificial linear features that must be distinguished from actual features.

LOW-PASS SPATIAL FILTERING

The low-pass spatial filter is implemented by calculating a local DN average of an N-by-M digital array or window centered around the pixel being processed. The DN average of the filter box (A) is considered to be the low-frequency component:

$$\mathrm{LFC}_{(j,s)} = \mathrm{S}_{(j,s)} \Big/ \mathrm{N}_{(j,s)} = \mathrm{A} \qquad\qquad \textbf{Equation 15.4}$$

where: $\text{LFC}_{(j,s)}$ = Low-frequency component at line j, sample s
   $S_{(j,s)}$ = Sum of valid DNs in the filter box centered at line j, sample s
   $N_{(j,s)}$ = Number of pixels with a valid DN value in the filter box centered at line j, sample s

(Note: invalid data could include cloud and shadow information.)

Thus, the output digital number (DN_o) centered at line j, sample s, is equal to the local DN average computed from N by M pixels (A) and centered at line j, sample s:

$$\text{DN}_{o(j,s)} = A_{(j,s)} \qquad\qquad \textbf{Equation 15.5}$$

For a 3-by-3-pixel box, for example, the central pixel's original value would be replaced by the DN average of 9 pixels if there was a deviation (Figure 15.12).

The LPF moves in 1-pixel increments from left-to-right and from top-to-bottom until all pixel values in the original image have been replaced with window averages. So that the edge pixels of an image can be center points in the filter box, internal pixels are unfolded vertically, horizontally, and diagonally along the sides of the image (Figure 15.13). For image output, the LPF DNs are usually subjected to a contrast stretch operation to expand the data distribution.

The low-pass algorithm reduces deviations from the local average, and thus produces image smoothing or blurring; as filter size increases, smoothing increases. Because of the blurring effect, low-pass filtering is useful for reducing certain noise patterns (e.g., bit errors or salt-and-pepper noise) and for smoothing blocky image data before visual interpretation or numerical analysis (Figure 15.14). Filter sizes to accomplish this are usually 3 by 3 or 5 by 5 pixels.

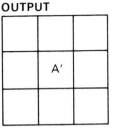

PIXEL	DN
A	42
B	38
C	41
D	40
E	37
F	44
G	38
H	42
I	38

$A' = (A + B + C \ldots + I)/9$
$A' = 360/9$
$A' = 40$

Figure 15.12.   Concept of low-pass spatial filtering for a 3-by-3-pixel window. Note that the low-frequency component (A') is equal to the window's DN average.

PIXEL	DN
A	42
E	37
A	42
C	41
B	38
C	41
A	42
E	37
A	42

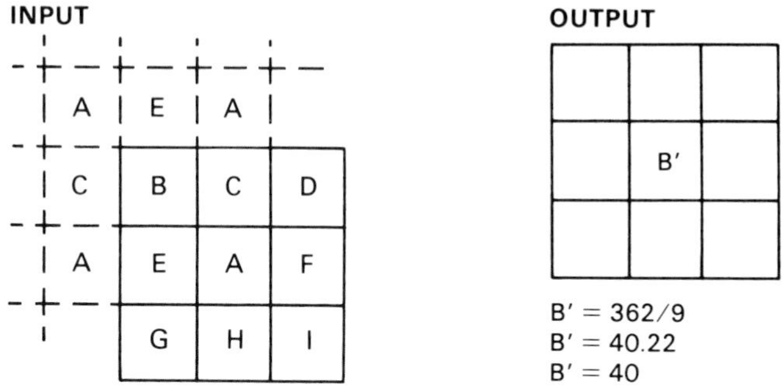

INPUT

```
- + - + - + - + -
  |  A  |  E  |  A  |
- + -
  |  C     B    C    D
- + -
  |  A     E    A    F
- + -
  |       G    H    I
```

OUTPUT

```
┌─────┬─────┬─────┐
│     │     │     │
├─────┼─────┼─────┤
│     │     │ B'  │
├─────┼─────┼─────┤
│     │     │     │
└─────┴─────┴─────┘
```

B' = 362/9
B' = 40.22
B' = 40

Figure 15.13   Concept of unfolding image pixels to position B as the central point for a 3-by-3-pixel low-pass filter operation.

HIGH-PASS SPATIAL FILTERING

From an earlier discussion, it will be remembered that the sum of the LFC and HFC equals the original image. Therefore, the high-frequency component of a digital image can be determined by the following relationship:

$$DN_{o(j,s)} = DN_{I(j,s)} - A_{(j,s)} + K \qquad \textbf{Equation 15.6}$$

where: $DN_{o(j,s)}$ = Output digital number at line j, sample s
$DN_{I(j,s)}$ = Original digital number of input image at line j, sample s
A   = Local DN average computed from N by M pixels and centered at line j, sample s
K   = Constant to keep all values positive; default = 127

Because the subtraction process in Equation 15.6 can produce either positive or negative integers, a constant (K) is added to keep all values positive and centered between 0 and 255; this output is then assigned to the central pixel. The constant used is normally the median of the output data range (e.g., 127 for 8-bit data). A linear contrast stretch is then applied to the output DNs to increase scene contrast. The visual effect of Equation 15.6 is illustrated in Figure 15.15.

High-pass filtered images (e.g., from the Landsat MSS and RBV sensors) are normally used for identifying and mapping structural geologic features, including faults, fractures, and monoclines, that are characterized by different spatial frequency ranges. In general, a high-pass filter enhances features that are less than half the size of the window being used, while de-emphasizing features that are more than half the window size. For this reason, filters with different sized windows are used to highlight small-, inter-mediate-, and large-scale structures; filter sizes to accomplish this could be 11 by 11 pixels, 51 by 51 pixels, and 101 by 101 pixels, respectively (Figure 15.16).

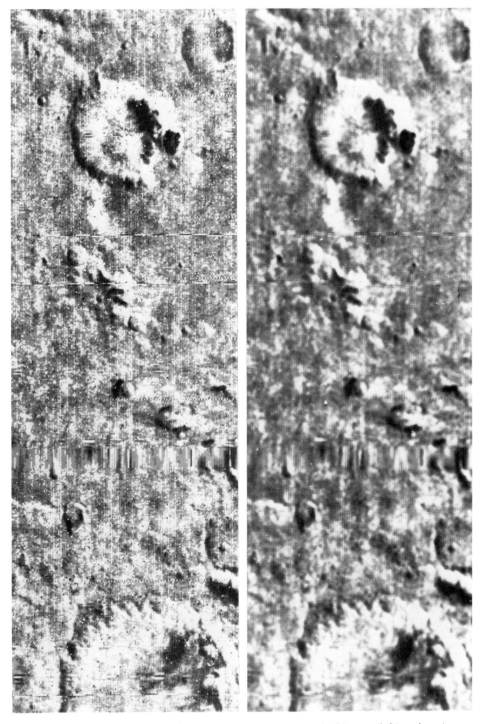

Figure 15.14.   Mars-Mariner 9 subscene images: contrast-stretched image (left) and an image produced by a 3-by-3-pixel low-pass filter (Condit and Chavez 1979).

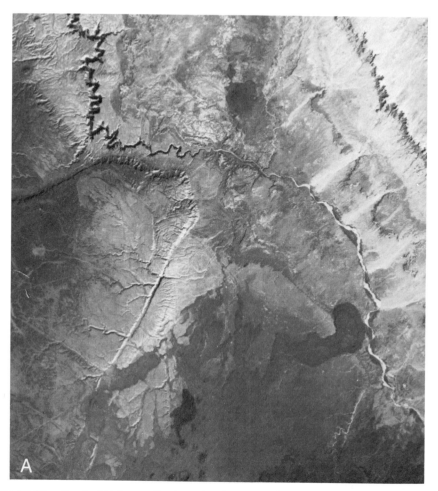

Figure 15.15. Result of high-pass filtering a Landsat-1 MSS band 5 subscene image of northern Arizona: (A) original data-base image, (B) 31-by-31-pixel LPF image, and (C) 31-by-31-pixel HPF image. Essentially, the HPF image is the original image minus the LPF image (image C = image A – image B). The images have been contrast stretched to emphasize their differences. See Figure 15.2 for feature identifications. (Courtesy U.S. Geological Survey.)

Three-band, color-composite images can be produced when black-and-white filtered images are available for multiple bands (e.g., Landsat MSS bands 4, 5, and 7). Compositing is done so that potential enhancement differences from three separate HPF images can be incorporated into a single, false-color image (Plate 9D).

EDGE ENHANCEMENT

The edge enhancement algorithm is designed to enhance rapid changes in DN levels from one pixel to the next. These very abrupt changes represent high spatial frequencies called edges. An edge can be a *boundary* separating

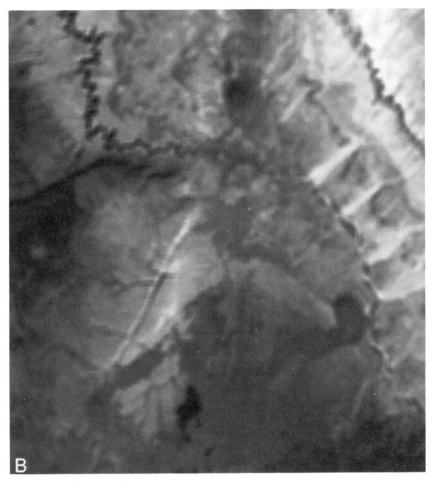

Figure 15.15/*continued*

two different features or a *line* that differs from the features on both its sides. Edge enhancement has the effect of producing a "sharper" image because the high-frequency information is strengthened by high-pass filtering.

Edge enhancement corrects the Modulation Transfer Function (MTF) response of a digital imaging system (e.g., Landsat MSS and TM sensors). Because an imaging system samples a continuous function at discrete intervals, high-frequency information cannot be recorded with the same precision as the lower-frequency data. Thus, spatial frequencies representing fine detail or edge information are suppressed. Edge enhancement, to a first-order approximation, corrects the MTF response by emphasizing the higher spatial frequencies (i.e., high frequencies are recorded with the same precision as low frequencies) (Chavez and Bauer 1982).

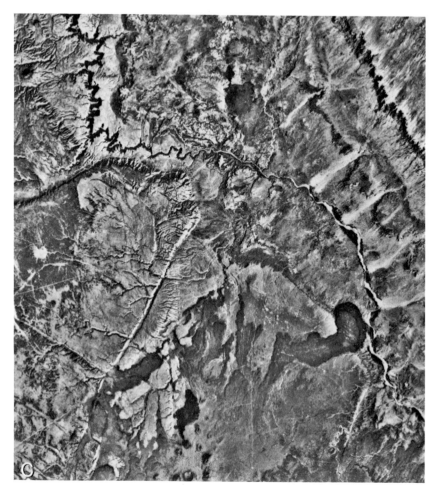

Figure 15.15/*continued*

Basically, the enhancement of edges in a digital image is accomplished as follows:

1. Generate an HPF image using a 3-by-3-pixel to 9-by-9-pixel window; the output is the edge component.
2. Add the original data-base image back into the HPF image; the output is edge enhanced.
3. Increase scene contrast in the edge-enhanced output by applying a linear stretch.

An image produced in this manner contains both radiometric or low-frequency information and exaggerated local contrast or high-frequency information (Figure 15.17).

The edge enhancement algorithm can be expressed with the relationship:

$$DN_{o(j,s)} = K(1 - X) + DN_{I(j,s)}(1 + X) - A_{(j,s)} \qquad \textbf{Equation 15.7}$$

where: $DN_{o(j,s)}$ = Output digital number at line j, sample s
  K = Constant to keep all values positive; default = 127 (median of output range for 8-bit data)
  X = Fraction of input digital number (DN_I) to be added back to the high-frequency component

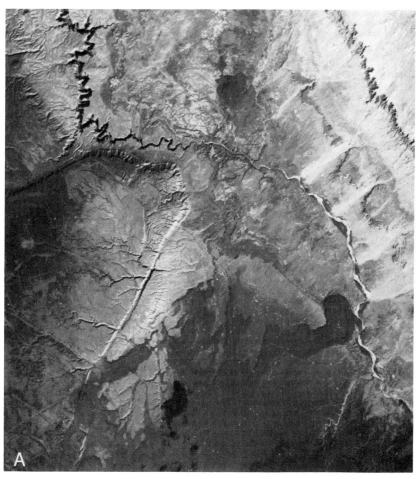

Figure 15.16. High-pass filtering a Landsat-1 MSS band 5 subscene image of northern Arizona: (A) original data-base image, (B) 11-by-11-pixel HPF image, (C) 51-by-51-pixel HPF image, and (D) 101-by-101-pixel HPF image. Note that as the window size is increased, fewer low-frequency components are removed from the original image and more high-frequency components are retained. See Figure 15.2 for feature identifications. (Courtesy U.S. Geological Survey.)

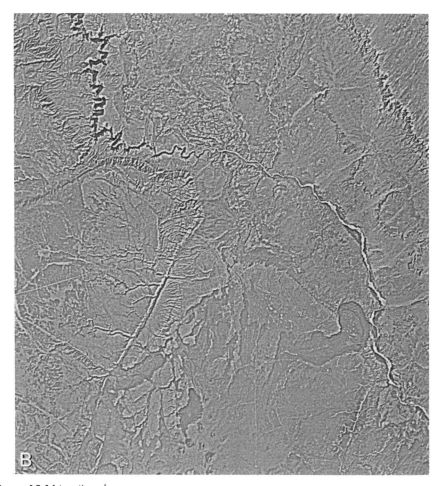

Figure 15.16/*continued*

$$A_{(j,s)} = \text{Local DN average computed from } N \text{ by } M \text{ pixels and centered at line } j, \text{ sample } s$$

Note that if 100 percent of the original image data are added back to the HPF output (i.e., X = 1 or 100 percent add-back), Equation 15.7 reduces to:

$$127(1-1) + DN_{I(j,s)}(1+1) - A_{(j,s)}$$
$$0 + DN_{I(j,s)}(2) - A_{(j,s)} \qquad \textbf{Equation 15.8}$$
$$DN_{o(j,s)} = 2DN_{I(j,s)} - A_{(j,s)}$$

From Equation 15.8 it can be seen that pixel DNs that are larger than the local average become still larger after edge enhancement, and DNs less than

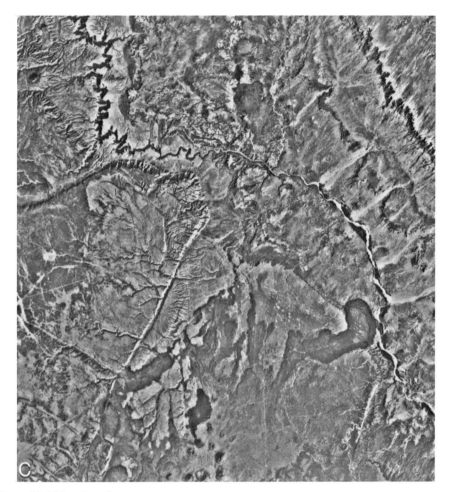

Figure 15.16/*continued*

the local average become smaller. This relationship can be illustrated as follows:

Line number	480	481
Sample number	612	613
DN_I	44	42
A	42	44
DN_o	46	40

If an edge occurred between samples 612 and 613, note that the DN_I difference is 2, but the DN_o difference is 6. This type of DN adjustment would exaggerate the local contrast (Rohde et al. 1978).

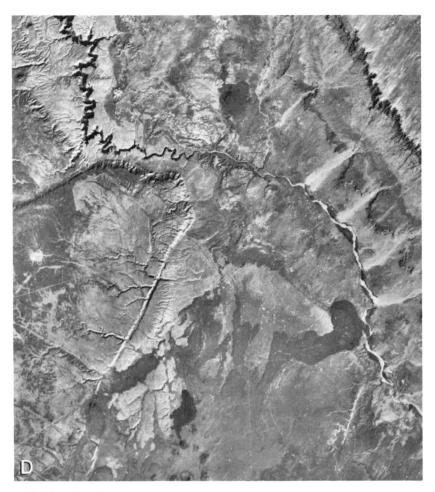

Figure 15.16/*continued*

Varying the X parameter in Equation 15.7 enables the analyst to control the amount of original image data that is added back to the high-frequency component. Such an option makes it possible to reduce the dynamic range between light and dark image areas in direct proportion to diminutions in X. This can permit greater recognizability of high-frequency objects because low-frequency albedo or brightness masking effects are reduced. For example, Berlin et al. (1982) evaluated MSS 4, 5, 7 infrared color edge-enhanced images with different "add-back" percentages and found that the one with 30 percent add-back was superior for highlighting small stands of phreatophytic vegetation in northern Saudi Arabia.

As was previously mentioned, filter dimensions for the edge enhancement algorithm, applicable to Landsat MSS data, can vary from 3 by 3 to 9 by 9 pixels. Filter size is dependent upon the "busyness" (i.e., number of edges) of the image being processed. Generally, the smallest filters are used for "rough" images, while the larger filters are best suited for use with "smooth" images (Figures 15.18 and 15.19). This is because an HPF enhances features that are less than half the size of the filter window and de-emphasizes features that are more than half the window size. Chavez and Bauer (1982) have developed a quantitative technique that automatically selects the optimum filter size for enhancing the edges in a particular digital image.

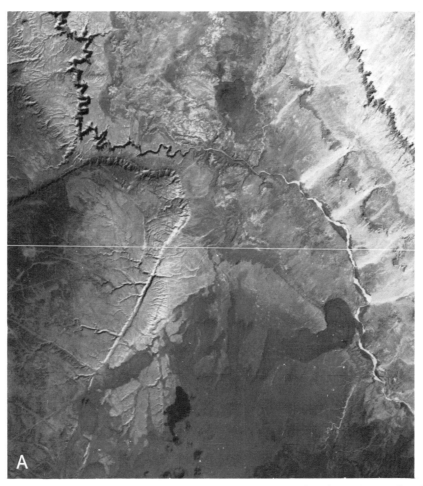

Figure 15.17.   Edge-enhanced processing for a Landsat-1 MSS band 5 subscene image of northern Arizona: (A) original data-base image, (B) 5-by-5-pixel HPF image, and (C) edge-enhanced image. The edge-enhanced image is the sum of the HPF and original images (image C = image A + image B). The images have been contrast stretched to emphasize their differences. See Figure 15.2 for feature identifications. (Courtesy U.S. Geological Survey.)

Figure 15.17/*continued*

Because of the asthestic improvements created by edge enhancement, multiple-band images are commonly subjected to this type of processing for color compositing. An edge-enhanced Landsat-1 MSS 4, 5, 7 infrared color image (3-by-3-pixel window) is presented in Plate 9E; a companion image without edge enhancement is shown in Plate 9B for comparison.

DIRECTIONAL FIRST DIFFERENCING

Analogous to edge enhancement by high-pass spatial filtering, the directional first-differencing algorithm, which approximates the first derivative, is designed to highlight the edge information in a digital image. First

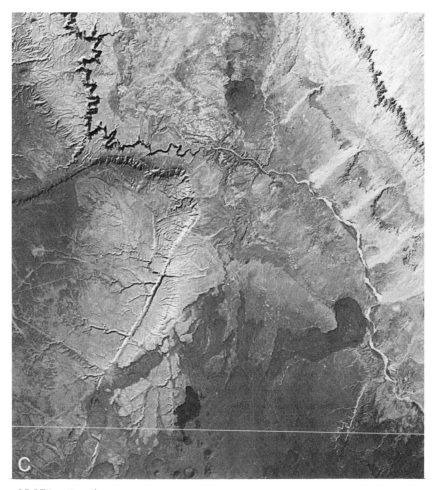

Figure 15.17/*continued*

differencing enhances edges on a pixel-to-pixel scale by simple DN sub-traction. The algorithm developed at the USGS's Image Processing Facility (IPF) produces the first difference of the image input in the horizontal, vertical, and diagonal directions (Chavez et al. 1977b). DN differences are computed at the pixel $X_{j,s}$ by the following equations:

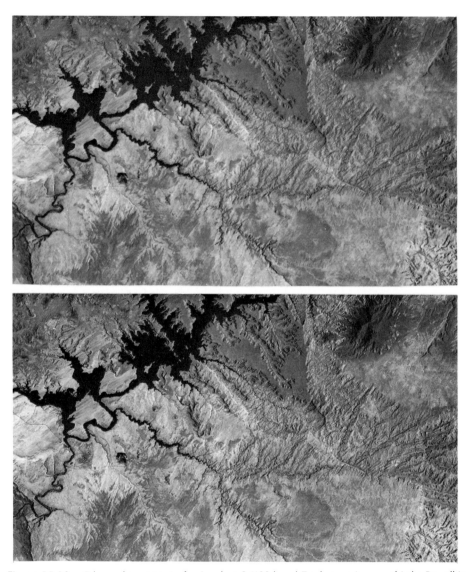

Figure 15.18.   Edge enhancement of a Landsat-2 MSS band 7 subscene image of Lake Powell in Arizona and Utah: original data-base image (top) and the edge-enhanced image with a 3-by-3-pixel window. Both images incorporate a linear contrast stretch. (Courtesy Pat S. Chavez, Jr., U.S. Geological Survey.)

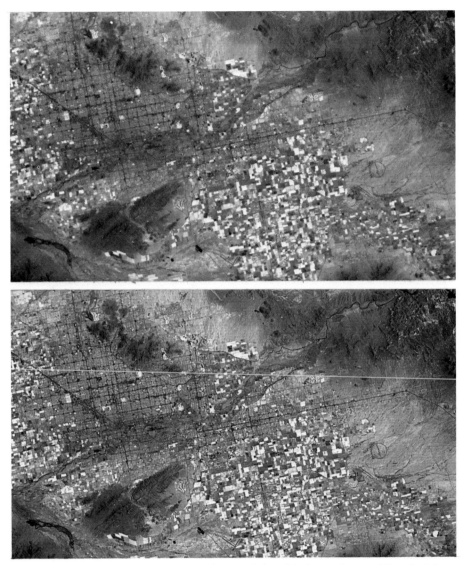

Figure 15.19.   Edge enhancement of a Landsat-2 MSS band 7 subscene image of Phoenix, Arizona, and environs: original data-base image (top) and the edge-enhanced image with a 7-by-7-pixel window. Both images incorporate a linear contrast stretch. (Courtesy Pat S. Chavez, Jr., U.S. Geological Survey.)

Horizontal: $DN_0 = DN_I(X_{j,s}) - DN_I(X_{j,s+1}) + K$ **Equation 15.9**

Vertical: $DN_0 - DN_I(X_{j,s}) - DN_I(X_{j+1,s}) + K$ **Equation 15.10**

Diagonal: $DN_0 = DN_I(X_{j,s}) - DN_I(X_{j+1,s+1}) + K$ **Equation 15.11**

where: DN_0 = Output digital number
    DN_I = Input digital number
    K   = Constant to keep all values positive; default = 127
    j = Line number
    s = Sample number

The subtraction output can be either negative or positive; consequently, a constant (K) is added to make all values positive and centered between 0 and 255. The IPF software uses the median of the output data range as K, or DN 127 for 8-bit data: 127 = 0 difference, 128 = +1 difference, 126 = −1 difference, and so on. Output DNs cluster around midrange because most pixel-to-pixel changes are relatively small.

For an image display, the first-difference DNs are contrast stretched to accentuate edge amplitudes. The MIN-MAX stretch limits are usually selected so as to be equidistant from midrange to ensure that an intermediate gray signature in the image indicates no DN difference between adjacent pixels. Three Landsat MSS band 5 first-difference images, along with a standard reference image, are shown in Figure 15.20.

Three directional algorithms are used because any edge trending in the same direction as the first-difference vector will be suppressed. Edge de-emphasis occurs because the differencing shows no pixel-to-pixel DN change as the subtraction process moves over the long axis of the edge; an edge would be detected only at its ends. Edges trending normal to the direction of the first difference are enhanced the most because of different DNs on adjacent sides of the edge. The preferential highlighting of edges is illustrated in Figure 15.20.

MULTISPECTRAL BAND RATIOING

The interband ratioing of multispectral images enhances subtle *spectral-reflectance* or color differences between surface materials that are often difficult to detect in standard images (i.e., single band images and color

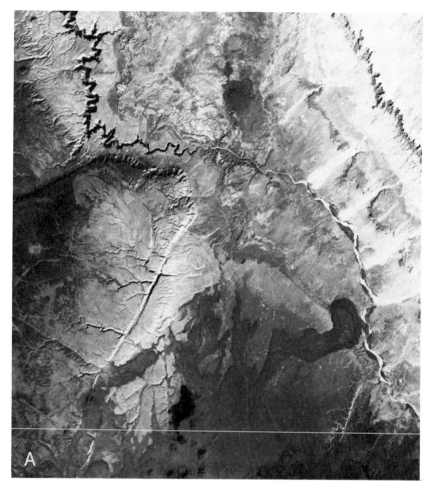

Figure 15.20.   Result of first differencing a Landsat-1 MSS band 5 subscene image of an area in northern Arizona: (A) original data-base image, (B) horizontal first-difference image, (C) vertical first-difference image, and (D) diagonal first-difference image. Note that edges in the first-difference images are dark toned when the subtraction process moves from light to dark areas in the input image and light toned when the subtraction process moves from dark to light areas in the input image. All images incorporate linear contrast stretches. See Figure 15.2 for feature identifications. (Courtesy U.S. Geological Survey.)

composites). Ratioing accentuates color differences while removing first-order brightness or albedo variations caused by topography (i.e., sunlit or shadowed slopes). Thus, interband ratioing effectively normalizes spectral data by removing brightness contrasts and emphasizing the color content of the data (Lyon 1977).

Ratioing is accomplished by dividing the data-base DNs in one spectral band by the data-base DNs in a second spectral band for each spatially

Figure 15.20/*continued*

registered pixel pair. The quotients are then converted to 8-bit integers using a multiplication factor (Figure 15.21). The ratio algorithm can be expressed in the form:

$$\mathrm{DN}_{o(j,s)} = \left(\frac{\mathrm{DN}X_{(j,s)}}{\mathrm{DN}Y_{(j,s)}}\right)\mathrm{K} \qquad \textbf{Equation 15.12}$$

where: $\mathrm{DN}_{o(j,s)}$ = Output digital number at line j, sample s
$\mathrm{DN}X_{(j,s)}$ = Input digital number of band X at line j, sample s
$\mathrm{DN}Y_{(j,s)}$ = Input digital number of band Y, at line j, sample s
K = Normalization factor for converting quotients to 8-bit integers; default = 100

Figure 15.20/*continued*

The output DN distribution is expanded by a contrast stretch before image construction. The DN redistribution is usually linear (i.e., uniform distribution) to preserve the original ratio relationships. The extreme tones in a ratio image represent the largest spectral-reflectivity differences.

Preprocessing for noise removal is most important because ratioing will enhance noise patterns. In addition, the atmospheric haze component must be removed before the ratioing of interband DNs. If the atmospheric scattering component is present, ratioing will produce incorrect values because haze is an additive component and dependent on wavelength (i.e., the unequal effects of haze are not cancelled by interband division, Equation 15.12). Topographic suppression does not occur when the haze component remains in the pre-ratioed data.

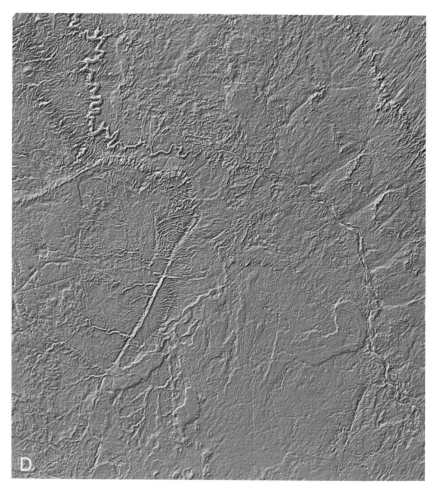

Figure 15.20/continued

The removal of illumination differences in a ratio image is illustrated in Figure 15.22. Note that a uniform material (unit A or unit B) has the same ratio value on both the sunlit and shadowed slopes. Thus, the material would be depicted in a common tone in the ratio image. The sensation of relief would therefore be removed because the image would show no brightness or albedo differences caused by topography.

Figure 15.22 also illustrates a potential disadvantage of spectral-band ratioing. Although two different materials may have different absolute values (units A and C), they can have identical ratio values (e.g., $16/20 = 0.8$ and $32/40 = 0.8$). Under these circumstances, there would be a potential loss of information because the units could not be distinguished on the basis of image

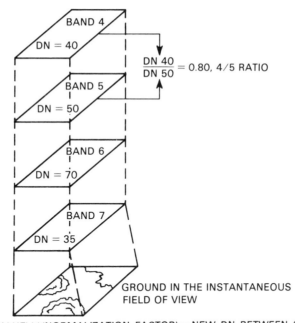

$$\frac{DN\ 40}{DN\ 50} = 0.80,\ 4/5\ RATIO$$

GROUND IN THE INSTANTANEOUS
FIELD OF VIEW

(RATIO VALUE) × (NORMALIZATION FACTOR) = NEW DN BETWEEN 0 AND 255

Figure 15.21. Concept of spectral band ratioing, in this case the four bands of the Landsat Multispectral Scanner (MSS). (Adapted from Taranik 1978.)

tone (perhaps by shape differences). The problem would be compounded if the units were contiguous because they would appear as a homogeneous material in the ratio image. These same units would probably be separable in standard band images.

RATIO COMBINATIONS

The number (n) of possible ratio combinations for a multispectral sensor with P bands is $n = P(P - 1)$. Thus, for the Landsat Multispectral Scanner's (MSS) four bands, there are 12 different ratio combinations—5/4, 6/4, 6/5, 7/4, 7/5, 7/6, and their six reciprocals (Table 7.6). For the Landsat Thematic Mapper (TM) (Table 7.7), there are 30 different ratio combinations (15 original, 15 reciprocal). Most ratio applications have been with MSS data because of their availability since 1972. Four Landsat-1 MSS bands for an area in northern Arizona (Figure 15.23) were digitally divided in pairs to produce the six ratio images shown in Figure 15.24.

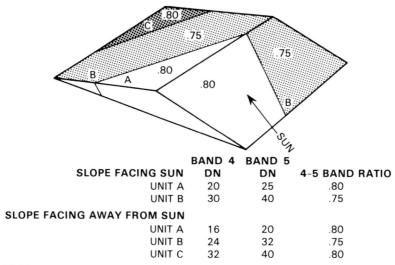

	BAND 4	BAND 5	
SLOPE FACING SUN	**DN**	**DN**	**4-5 BAND RATIO**
UNIT A	20	25	.80
UNIT B	30	40	.75
SLOPE FACING AWAY FROM SUN			
UNIT A	16	20	.80
UNIT B	24	32	.75
UNIT C	32	40	.80

Figure 15.22.   Concept of removing illumination differences by interband ratioing. (Adapted from Taranik 1978.)

▨ USES OF MSS RATIOS

The general utility of MSS ratios is described below; several of their uses are illustrated in Figure 15.24.

1. The 4/5, 4/7, 5/7, and 6/7 ratios are important for characterizing soil and rock units. Such an ordering would have vegetation depicted in dark signatures.
2. The 5/4 ratio is especially sensitive to the presence of iron oxide. In Figure 15.24A, the light image tones at sites 1 and 2 are associated with the Triassic Moenkopi Formation (reddish-brown mudstone, siltstone, and sandstone) and the Triassic Moenave Formation (reddish-orange sandstone and sandy siltstone), respectively. In a 4/5 image, these same units would be depicted in dark signatures.
3. The 6/4, 6/5, 7/4, and 7/5 ratios are useful for highlighting vegetation patterns because of the large differences in reflectance between the infrared bands (6 and 7) and visible bands (4 and 5). In Figure 15.24B the primary vegetation types are pinon-juniper (area 1) and tamarisk or salt cedar (area 2).
4. The 7/5 ratio is the most useful of the MSS ratios for assessing the relative greenness of vegetation (e.g., stressed plants versus unstressed) and for estimating biomass.
5. The 5/6 or 6/5 ratio is most often used for distinguishing general material types of soil and rock, vegetation, and water. The ratio, however, is not very useful for discrimination within any one material class. Observe in Figure 15.24C that the 6/5 ratio separates vegetation from soil

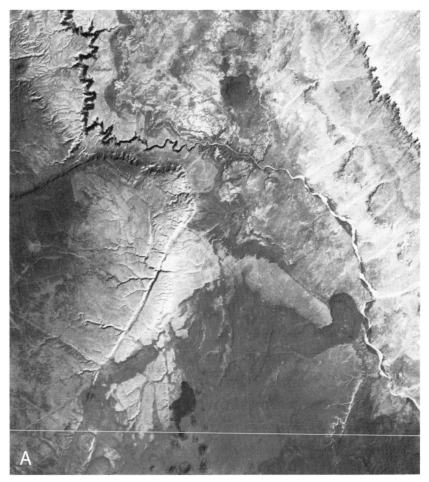

Figure 15.23. Contrast-stretched Landsat-1 MSS subscene images of an area in northern Arizona acquired 29 October 1973: (A) band 4, 0.5–0.6 μm; (B) band 5, 0.6–0.7 μm; (C) band 6, 0.7–0.8 μm; and (D) band 7, 0.8–1.1 μm. Compare with Figure 15.24. Note the redundancy of data in these images. See Figure 15.2 for feature identifications. (Courtesy U.S. Geological Survey.)

and rock, but that there is very little tonal variation within either material class. Chavez et al. (1977a) demonstrated how the 5/6 ratio, with the appropriate contrast stretch, would be used for producing thematic maps of soil and rock, vegetation, and water (Figure 15.25).

COLOR-COMPOSITE RATIO IMAGES

The ability to distinguish between different surface materials can be significantly increased by selectively combining three black-and-white ratio image sets into false-color composites (Plates 9F-G). The increase in dis-

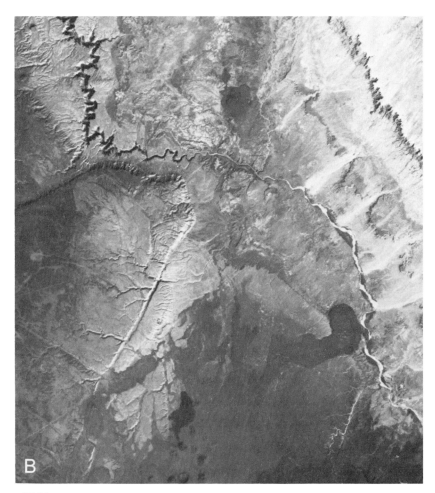

Figure 15.23/*continued*

crimination occurs for two primary reasons: (1) spectral-reflectivity information from three different ratio images is combined, and (2) the colors created by compositing permit a wider range of visual discriminations because of the eye's sensitivity to subtle hue changes (Blodget et al. 1978).

Selecting the three-ratio combination for color compositing that will allow for the optimum discrimination of material classes in a scene can be both difficult and time consuming because of the large number of possible combinations. For example, excluding reciprocals, 20 combinations can be made from the six MSS ratios, taken three at a time, and 455 different combinations are possible with the 15 nonthermal TM ratio images. To help overcome the selection problem, Chavez et al. (1982) devised a quantitative technique, called the Optimum Index Factor (OIF), that ranks all possible ratio combinations according to the amount of correlation and total variance

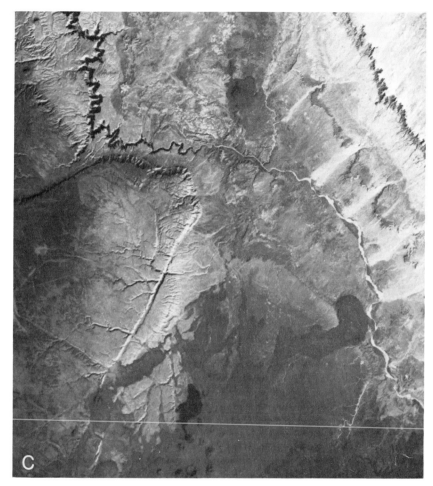

Figure 15.23/*continued*

present between the various ratios under consideration (e.g., six MSS ratios). The three-ratio combination with the highest ranking should contain the most information with the least amount of duplication.

False-color MSS ratio images have been used successfully in many geological investigations for lithology mapping and identifying alteration halos and mineralized areas. For example, the ratio combination 4/5, 5/6, 6/7 was used by Rowan et al. (1974) for discriminating rock types and detecting hydrothermally altered areas in south-central Nevada; by Blodget et al. (1978) for the discrimination of rock types in southwestern Saudi Arabia; and by Chavez et al. (1982) for identifying different rock types and surficial deposits in north-central Arizona. Spirakis and Condit (1975) used the ratio combination of 4/7, 6/4, 7/4 to detect uranium mineralization in the Cameron

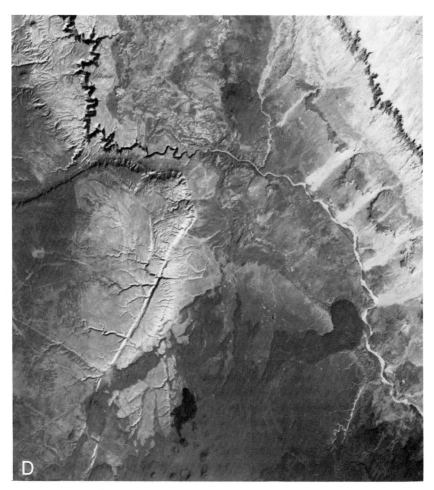

Figure 15.23/*continued*

District, Arizona. The ratio combination 4/5, 4/6, 6/7 was used by Raines et al. (1978) to identify facies related to uranium deposits in the Powder River Basin, Wyoming.

In some cases, albedo information lost in the ratioing process (e.g., units A and C in Figure 15.22) can be restored by color-combining a single spectral band image with two ratioed images. The resulting *hybrid-ratio* false-color image will enhance both albedo and spectral color differences (Chavez et al. 1977b). However, topographic detail is restored with the reintroduction of the albedo information (Plate 9H).

SIMULATED NATURAL COLOR

The USGS Image Processing Facility has developed a technique for producing a modified Landsat MSS image in which colors appear approximately as the human eye would perceive them from orbital altitudes, but in the

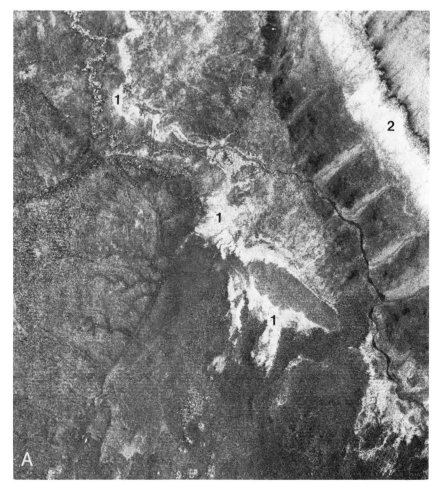

Figure 15.24. Contrast-stretched MSS ratio images of an area in northern Arizona: (A) 5/4 ratio, (B) 6/4 ratio, (C) 6/5 ratio, (D) 7/4 ratio, (E) 7/5 ratio, and (F) 7/6 ratio. Refer to text for explanation of numerical annotations. Note that the images are almost free of brightness contrasts caused by topographic slope. Compare with Figure 15.23. (Courtesy U.S. Geological Survey.)

absence of an intervening atmosphere (Plate 9I). The *simulated natural-color image* is devoid of atmospheric haze and accentuates subtle color differences. Essentially the procedure is to predict the blue part of the spectrum, which is not sensed by the MSS. The blue component is derived from the shape of the spectrum in the green, red, and near-infrared MSS data (Eliason et al. 1974).

A schematic diagram illustrating how simulated natural color is achieved is shown in Figure 15.26. The procedure can be summarized as follows:

1. The 5/6 ratio is used to identify pixels as belonging to the major surface categories of vegetation (ratio value equals 0.45 ± 0.2), soil and rock (ratio value equals 0.95 ± 0.25), and water (ratio value exceeds 1.45).

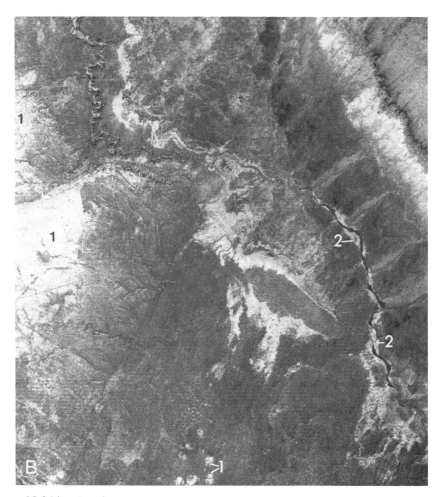

Figure 15.24/*continued*

2. Material-dependent algorithms are applied to the real MSS data (i.e., bands 4–7) to determine the digital numbers for the pixels in the new "blue band" or "band 3."
3. To produce a color-composite image, "band 3" is projected through blue light, band 4 through green light, and band 5 through red light (Plate 9I).

LINEAR DATA TRANSFORMATIONS

The individual bands of a multispectral data set are often observed to be highly correlated or redundant in their informational content, that is, they are visually and numerically similar (Figure 15.23). Two mathematical trans-

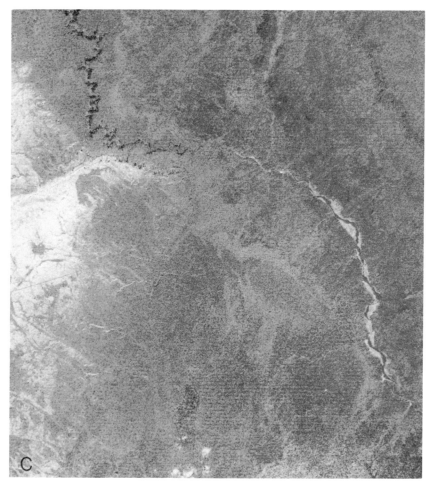

Figure 15.24/*continued*

formation techniques, *principal components analysis* (PCA) and *canonical analysis* (CA), are often used to minimize this spectral redundancy, while reducing or compressing the dimensionality of the data (i.e., fewer channels are needed to accurately describe the original data set).

The techniques are similar in that they both compute a set of new (transformed) variables called *components*, with each component largely independent of the others (uncorrelated). Geometrically, the components represent a set of mutually orthogonal and independent axes that are fitted to the original data such that the first new axis contains the highest percentage of the total variance or scatter in the data set, with each succeeding (lower-order) axis containing less variance (Figure 15.27).

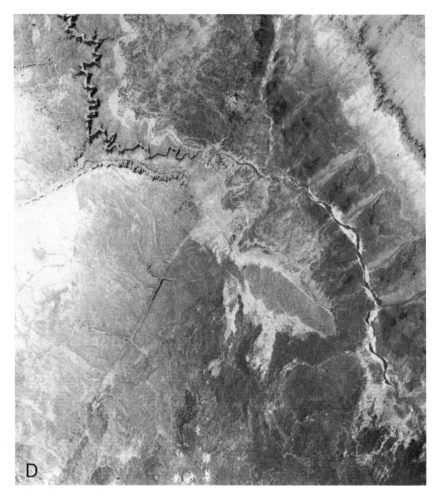

Figure 15.24/*continued*

PRINCIPAL COMPONENTS ANALYSIS

Principal components analysis can be applied to all or any subset of the channels composing a multispectral data set (e.g., n-group of single bands, n-group of ratios, combination of bands and ratios). The number of components produced will equal the number of channels being analyzed. Thus, there can be up to four and seven principal components for the Landsat MSS and TM sensors, respectively.

In a highly correlated MSS data set, for example, the largest percentage of the total scene variance will be included in the first principal component (PC1), with the lower-order components (PCs 2, 3, and 4) each containing a smaller percentage of the total variance. The lowest-order, or last component, tends to be dominated by undesirable noise. Thus, the first three principal

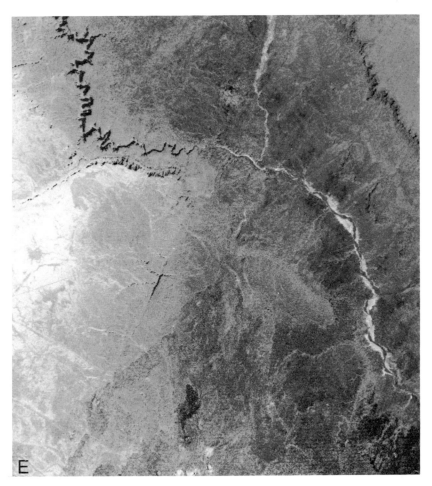

Figure 15.24/*continued*

components contain nearly all the effective information existing in the original four bands, and the last component can be neglected. In this situation, when the transformed pixel values are converted to film format for photographic displays, PCs 1, 2, and 3 can be analyzed as single black-and-white images or the three component images can be combined to form a color composite. In digital domain, the three components can be used as input to automatic image classification algorithms. The geologic applications of Landsat MSS principal component images are described by Blodget et al. (1978), Santisteban and Munoz (1978), and Williams (1983).

Figure 15.28 shows two Landsat-4 TM subscene images representing band 5 (1.55–1.75 μm) and band 7 (2.08–2.35 μm) and their corresponding principal component images (PC1 and PC2). Because the two input bands were so highly correlated, 98.4 percent of the total variance of the two input images was

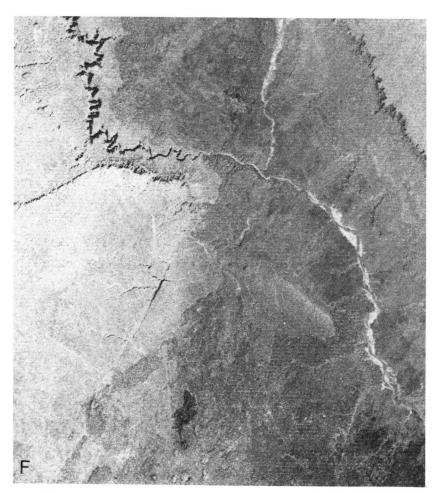

Figure 15.24/*continued*

contained in PC1. PC2 contained the remaining variance (1.6 percent), which included most of the noise but also zones of hydrothermal alteration associated with a porphyry copper deposit. This "selective" technique of using the most correlated image pairs for principal components analysis was developed by Chavez et al. (1982, 1984) to maximize the amount of information that would be contained in a single, three-component, color-composite image when using either six MSS ratios or seven TM bands as input variables.

CANONICAL ANALYSIS

Canonical analysis, also referred to as multiple-discriminant analysis, differs from principal components analysis in that it produces a series of data transformations based upon the unique spectral characteristics of a set of

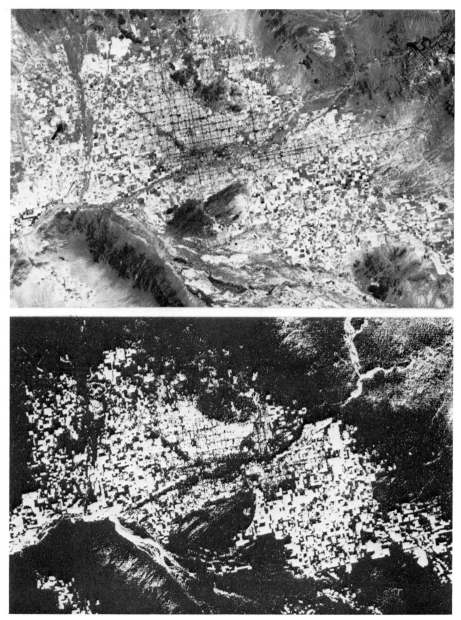

Figure 15.25.   Landsat-2 MSS band 7 subscene image of Phoenix, Arizona, generated 15 May 1974 (top) and a thematic map of vegetation produced from the MSS band 5/6 ratio. For the thematic map image, a contrast stretch was used to map the 5/6 "vegetation DNs" to 255 or white and the remainder to 0 DN or black. (Courtesy Pat S. Chavez, Jr., U.S. Geological Survey.)

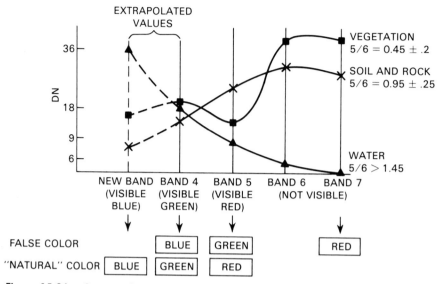

Figure 15.26. Concept of natural-color simulation for Landsat MSS data. (Adapted from Taranik 1978.)

user-defined land cover or feature categories established for a given data base and application. The main objective of canonical analysis is to increase the separability of categories defined with the data while minimizing the differences occurring within each category. The linear transformation is such that the maximum category separability is placed on the first rotated axis (first canonical component, or CC1) with the succeeding or lower-order axes

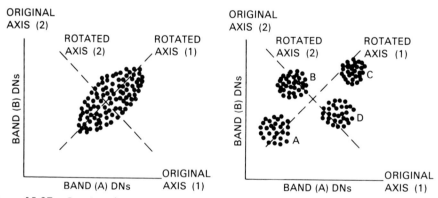

Figure 15.27. Rotation of axes in two-dimensional space for a hypothetical two-band data set by *principal components analysis* (left) and *canonical analysis* (right). The first rotated axis (first principal component, first canonical component) is positioned to account for the largest percentage of the total variance, with the second rotated axis (second principal component, second canonical component) containing the remaining variance. Principal components analysis uses DN information from the total scene, whereas canonical analysis uses the spectral characteristics of categories defined within the data to increase their separability (in this case, four material classes, A–D). (Adapted from Jensen and Waltz 1979.)

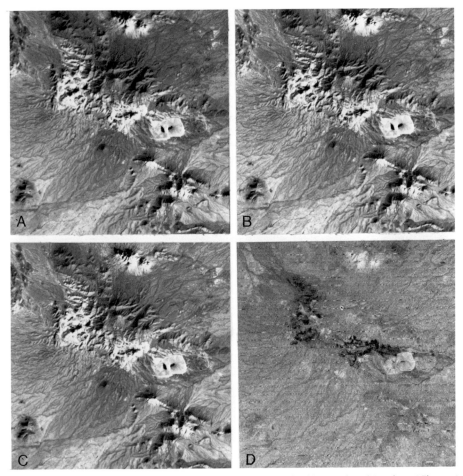

Figure 15.28. Results of principal components processing a highly correlated Landsat-4 Thematic Mapper (TM) band pair: (A) TM band 4 subscene image of the Silver Bell district, Arizona, (B) TM band 7 subscene image, (C) first principal component (PC1) image of TM bands 5 and 7, and (D) second principal component (PC2) image of TM bands 5 and 7. In image D, the dark signatures closely correspond to zones of hydrothermal alteration associated with a porphyry copper deposit. All images incorporate linear contrast stretches. (Courtesy Pat S. Chavez, Jr., U.S. Geological Survey.)

containing successively less category separability (Figure 15.27). Canonical analysis creates one less transformed component than the number of defined categories (Holm 1982).

Canonical analysis is most often used as a preprocessing step to image classification because of its potential (1) for improving classification accuracy by increasing the separability of categories defined within the data and (2) for improving computer processing efficiency by reducing data dimensionality. For example, Holm (1982) used canonical analysis to reduce a 12-band MSS data set (Landsat MSS bands 4–7 from three dates) to six transformed canonical channels or components without the loss of any cover-type information (50 percent reduction). Cover types included wheat, alfalfa, potatoes, corn, soybeans, rangeland, and water. The percent of cover-type separability for each of the six transformed canonical components is as follows: CC1, 47.21 percent; CC2, 27.43 percent; CC3, 14.61 percent; CC4, 4.90 percent; CC5, 4.67 percent; and CC6, 1.18 percent. Images of the six canonical components are shown in Figure 15.29, and a graphic representation of the cover-type separability for each channel is shown in Figure 15.30. Infrared color images and a "ground truth" map for the study area are presented in Plate 11.

▦ IMAGE CLASSIFICATION

Image enhancement improves the detectability of objects or patterns in a digital image for *visual interpretation*. Automated digital analysis or *image classification* is an information extraction process (*machine* or *automated interpretation*) that involves the application of pattern recognition theory to multispectral images. Simply stated, image classification analyzes the spectral properties of various surface features (e.g., crops) in a multiband image and sorts the spectral data into spectrally similar categories by the use of predefined, numerical decision rules (Holm 1982).

The general procedure for image classification follows five basic steps:

1. **Training class selection.** The initial step involves defining image properties (i.e., pixel DN values) that represent a group of information or training classes.
2. **Generation of statistical parameters.** Statistical algorithms are used to define the unique spectral characteristics *(spectral signatures)* of the training classes. Typical statistical parameters include class means, standard deviations, covariance matrices, and correlation matrices. The statistical descriptions are used to "train" the classification algorithm.
3. **Data classification.** The "trained" classification algorithm assigns each pixel composing the data set of interest to one of the training class categories.
4. **Evaluation and refinement.** An assessment is made of the classification accuracy. Returning to step 1 and repeating the process is required if the classification results are judged to be unacceptable. A common reason for classification refinement is the excessive spectral overlap between categories.
5. **Documentation.** Once a final classification is acceptable, the results are documented in the form of maps and tabular data summaries.

▦ CLASSIFICATION APPROACHES

Two primary approaches can be used for defining training classes: unsupervised and supervised (Figure 15.31). *Unsupervised classification* uses an automatic clustering algorithm that analyzes the "unknown" pixels in the

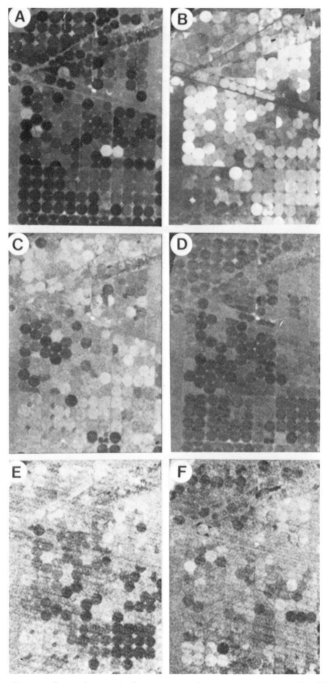

Figure 15.29. Six transformed canonical component images representing the Clarke, Oregon, region: (A) CC1, (B) CC2, (C) CC3, (D) CC4, (E) CC5, and (F) CC6. CC1 has the maximum separability between cover types, with succeeding components having progressively less cover-type separability. Compare with Plate 11. Average field size for the center-pivot irrigation system is 53 ha. (Courtesy Thomas M. Holm, Technicolor Government Services, Inc., EROS Data Center, Sioux Falls, S. Dak.)

Channel 1

Crop Types	1	2	3	4	5	6	7
1	*	–	–	–	–	–	–
2	–	*	*	–	–	–	–
3	–	*	*	–	–	–	–
4	–	–	–	*	–	–	–
5	–	–	–	–	*	–	–
6	–	–	–	–	–	*	*
7	–	–	–	–	–	*	*

Channel 2

Crop Types	1	2	3	4	5	6	7
1	*	–	–	–	–	–	–
2	–	*	–	–	–	–	–
3	–	–	*	–	*	–	–
4	–	–	–	*	–	–	–
5	–	–	*	–	*	–	–
6	–	–	–	–	–	*	–
7	–	–	–	–	–	–	*

Channel 3

Crop Types	1	2	3	4	5	6	7
1	*	–	–	–	–	–	–
2	–	*	–	–	–	–	–
3	–	–	*	–	–	–	–
4	–	–	–	*	–	–	*
5	–	–	–	–	*	–	–
6	–	–	–	–	–	*	–
7	–	–	–	*	–	–	*

Channel 4

Crop Types	1	2	3	4	5	6	7
1	*	–	–	–	–	–	–
2	–	*	–	–	–	*	*
3	–	–	*	–	–	–	–
4	–	–	–	*	*	–	–
5	–	–	–	*	*	–	–
6	–	*	–	–	–	*	*
7	–	*	–	–	–	*	*

Channel 5

Crop Types	1	2	3	4	5	6	7
1	*	*	–	–	*	*	–
2	*	*	–	–	*	*	–
3	–	–	*	–	–	–	–
4	–	–	–	*	–	–	–
5	*	*	–	–	*	*	–
6	*	*	–	–	*	*	–
7	–	–	–	–	–	–	*

Channel 6

Crop Types	1	2	3	4	5	6	7
1	*	*	–	–	*	–	–
2	*	*	–	–	*	–	–
3	–	–	*	*	–	*	–
4	–	–	*	*	–	*	–
5	–	*	–	–	*	–	–
6	–	–	*	*	–	*	–
7	–	–	–	–	–	–	*

All Channels

Crop Types	1	2	3	4	5	6	7
1	*	–	–	–	–	–	–
2	–	*	–	–	–	–	–
3	–	–	*	–	–	–	–
4	–	–	–	*	–	–	–
5	–	–	–	–	*	–	–
6	–	–	–	–	–	*	–
7	–	–	–	–	–	–	*

Legend

1	Wheat
2	Alfalfa
3	Potatoes
4	Corn
5	Soybeans
6	Rangeland
7	Water

–indicates cover types are separable
*indicates cover types are not separable

Figure 15.30. Graphic representation of cover-type separability for six separate canonical transformed components, or channels, and a summary of the separability of all six channels combined. Graph illustrates where there was some degree of confusion in determining cover-type separability. (Courtesy Thomas M. Holm, Technicolor Government Services, Inc., EROS Data Center, Sioux Falls, S. Dak.)

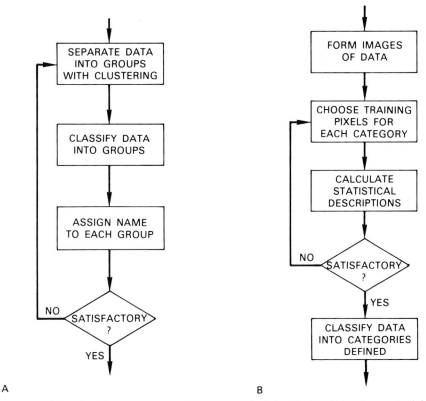

Figure 15.31.   Flow diagrams representing unsupervised classification (A) and supervised classification (B) (Short 1982).

data base and divides them into a number of *spectrally distinct classes* based upon their natural groupings (i.e., clusters) in n-spectral dimensions. The analyst specifies the number of spectral classes into which the data are to be grouped. The spectral classes defined by the clustering algorithm are then used to classify the entire data set. After the classification is completed, the analyst must identify the cover type represented by each spectral class, using various types of reference information (e.g., infrared color images and photographs, published maps, field reconnaissance data, etc.). Only then are cover-type labels assigned to the spectral classes (Figure 15.32). Generally, as the number of spectral classes increases, the ability to identify each class becomes more difficult. A flow diagram of unsupervised classification is shown in Figure 15.31.

With *supervised classification*, the analyst selects areas of known cover type in the image and specifies these to the computer as training areas. Statistical measures are generated for the training areas and input to the classifier, which then determines other areas in the image that have similar spectral characteristics (Figure 15.33). Supervised classification usually requires less

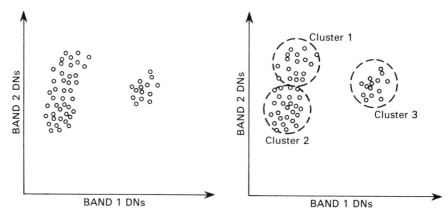

Figure 15.32. Concept of clustering a hypothetical two-band data set. *Top:* Two-dimensional plot of pixel DNs that the analyst wants grouped into three spectral classes. *Bottom:* Results of cluster analysis; the clustering algorithm automatically groups the data into three clusters or spectral classes. An image or map showing the spatial attributes of spectral classes would have to be compared to ground reference data to determine their true identity and value. (Adapted from Landgrebe 1974.)

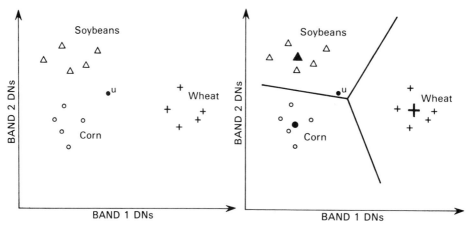

Figure 15.33. Concept of supervised classification for a hypothetical two-band data set. *Top:* Two-dimensional plot of pixel DNs representing three crop types and an unknown point *U*. *Bottom:* Result of minimum distance to means classification to determine which crop class point *U* is associated with. This particular supervised algorithm first determines the conditional centroid or center point of each class. Then the locus of points equidistant from the three centroids is plotted, resulting in three straight-line segments, or decision boundaries. In this example, point *U* would be associated with the soybean class as a result of its location with respect to the decision boundaries. (Adapted from Landgrebe 1974.)

computer time to execute than unsupervised classification because it relies on explicit analyst guidelines, and it does not require a clustering step. A flow diagram of supervised classification is shown in Figure 15.31.

CLASSIFICATION ACCURACIES

Image classification using Landsat MSS data has been the most successful for identifying various types of agricultural crops and natural vegetation. In general, geologic applications have met with less success, largely because lithologic units are rarely homogeneous, and they are commonly masked by various amounts of soil, vegetation, colluvium, and organic debris. Such factors make selection of representative training areas extremely difficult, especially in areas of rugged relief where spectral signatures are influenced by variations in illumination (Abrams 1980).

Improvements in classification accuracy can usually be realized by incorporating additional data sets into the classification algorithm. For example, when attempting to classify diverse crop types within a given area, a single Landsat MSS data set of four spectral dimensions may not have the necessary spectral contrasts for all crop types represented. However, by using several co-registered MSS digital images acquired on different dates in the growing season, it would be possible to track the phenologic changes of crop types and to incorporate these changes into the decision criteria for classification (Holm 1982). This process is called *multitemporal image classification.*

MULTITEMPORAL IMAGE CLASSIFICATION AND CANONICAL ANALYSIS

An example of classifying Landsat MSS digital images for crop-type discrimination using multitemporal data and canonical analysis has been presented by Holm (1982, 1983) for the Clarke, Oregon, region (Plate 11). Canonical analysis was used to transform a 12-band, three-date Landsat MSS data set into 6 transformed channels. A comparison of the classification based on the 6 canonical channels (minimum distance to mean classifier) and the 12 MSS channels (maximum likelihood classifier) showed no significant difference in terms of classification accuracy—75.8 and 75.9 percent, respectively. While accuracies were nearly identical, computer processing unit (CPU) time was 14,871 CPU seconds for the 12-band classification and 4,240 seconds for the canonical-based classification. The notable difference in time was due to the reduction in data dimensionality and the differences in the complexity of the classifiers used.

▨ DATA-SET MERGING

The digital merging or co-registration of different spectral and nonspectral data sets is becoming an increasingly important component of digital image processing because it allows for the simultaneous analysis (visual or machine aided) of many types of information for the same ground area. Merging is the spatial superposition of digital images taken at *different wavelengths*, at *different times*, or by *different sensors*, plus digital images representing *ancillary reference information* such that *congruent measurements* can be obtained for each corresponding pixel (Moik 1980). Data-set merging can be of benefit to both computer-based analysis, including multidimensional classification and change detection, plus visual interpretation, including stereoscopic and multisensor image analysis. Examples of these applications are discussed in a later section of this chapter.

▨ DATA-SET PREPARATION

To accomplish digital merging, every data set must be in the proper numerical and spatially ordered form. For analog images such as aerial photographs, a digitizer is used to convert density variations into a two-dimensional array of digital numbers. Nonimage spatial data, such as point and polygon observations, must be transformed from a vector to a raster or grid-cell structure (Figure 8.6). *Surface generation* (also referred to as *surface interpolation*) is a mathematical process for estimating values for every cell of a grid from a set of irregularly spaced point measurements. Essentially, surface interpolation fills in the gaps between data points based upon some distance weighing function. For computer manipulation and image representation, the data are rescaled from their original range of values to the dynamic range of the image-processing system, for example, 0–255 DN for an 8-bit scale (Figure 15.34). Data depicted as polygons (e.g., soil and lithology maps) do not require surface interpolation. Rather, each bounded area is assigned a constant value corresponding to a particular unit (Eliason et al. 1983).

Once the data sets are in digital form, it is then necessary to reformat and scale them to match the geometry of a common reference system. Registration can be accomplished by selecting one image as a reference and spatially manipulating the others to coincide with it (the "master-slave" technique) or by registering all of the images to a reference map.

▨ DIGITAL TERRAIN DATA

Topography information is often an important component in digital merging projects. Fortunately, digital elevation data are available for the entire United States. The CCTs provide elevations in a grid-cell format at

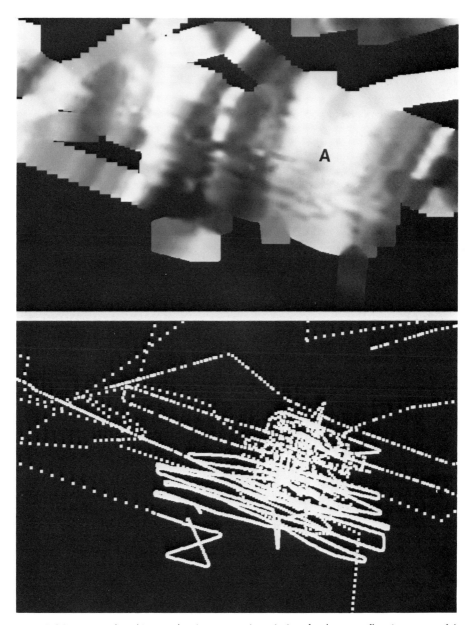

Figure 15.34. Interpolated image showing magnetic variations for the ocean floor in an area of the Mid-Atlantic Ridge (A). Image tone is related to the intensity of the magnetic field: light tones equal "high magnetics"; dark tones equal "low magnetics." The ship paths along which the original point data were collected are shown in the bottom image. Digital interpolation was used to fill in the gaps between the original points by a distance-weighing function. (Courtesy Pat S. Chavez, Jr., U.S. Geological Survey.)

three resolutions. Special computer algorithms have been developed to calculate other topographic parameters from the elevation data (e.g., slope, aspect or slope direction, and solar illumination angle) and to convert the data to standard image formats (Figure 15.35). Specific information regarding digital elevation data and ordering information can be obtained from the User Services Section, National Cartographic Information Center, U.S. Geological Survey, 507 National Center, Reston, VA 22092.

MULTIDIMENSIONAL IMAGE CLASSIFICATION

Improving the recognition accuracy in image classification can usually be achieved by combining multispectral image data with certain types of ancillary information, such as topographic information derived from digital tapes describing terrain. For example, Strahler et al. (1978) demonstrated that the accuracy in classifying forest-cover from Landsat MSS images could be improved 27 percent by incorporating elevation and aspect information into the classification algorithm. Inclusion of the topographic information made it possible for the classifier to differentiate between species with similar spectral characteristics but different habitats. This technique of combining multispectral and ancillary information into the classification algorithm is called *multidimensional image classification*.

CHANGE-DETECTION IMAGES

Temporal information for a given area can be extracted from co-registered images that were acquired at different times by *multitemporal* or *multidate processing*. The change detection can be seasonal (e.g., snow cover, flooding, agricultural practices, natural vegetation growth cycles) or permanent (e.g., urbanization, forest clear-cutting, surface mining).

A common form of multitemporal processing is band differencing. For example, after two Landsat MSS images have undergone clean-up and digital registration, the DNs of one image can be subtracted from those of the second image. The resulting DNs can be positive, negative, or zero (no change). For image output, a readjustment value (127 DN for 8-bit data) is added to all "differences" so that medium gray represents no change and dark and light tones represent negative and positive differences, respectively. Contrast stretching is commonly employed to further emphasize the differences (Figure 15.36). This type of image is referred to as a *temporal-difference image* because of the subtraction of the image for one date from that of another date.

Similar results can be obtained when the same bands from two different dates are ratioed. Unlike differencing, however, the division process removes first-order brightness variations caused by topography (Chavez et al. 1977a). An image produced by this process is called a *temporal-ratio image*.

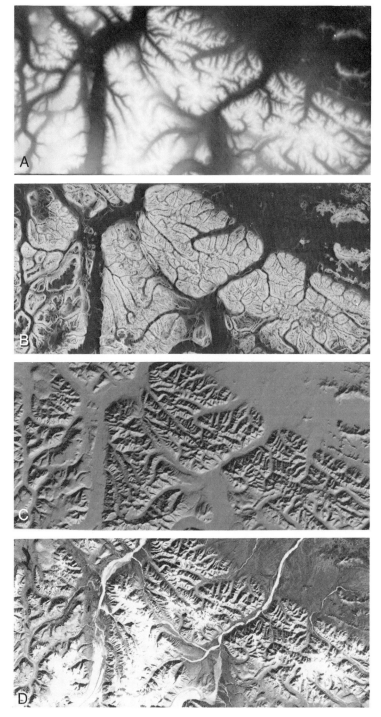

Figure 15.35. Computer-generated images derived from digital elevation data for a portion of the Nabesna quadrangle, Alaska, where tones are proportional to the ranges of the parameters. (A) Elevation image where black represents the lowest elevation and white the highest elevation. (B) Percent slope image where black represents level terrain and white the steepest terrain. (C) Shaded-relief image where black represents surfaces facing away from the illumination source and white represents surfaces facing the illumination source. A Landsat MSS band 5 image, acquired 18 September 1973 is included as a reference (D). (Courtesy Charles M. Trautwein, U.S. Geological Survey.)

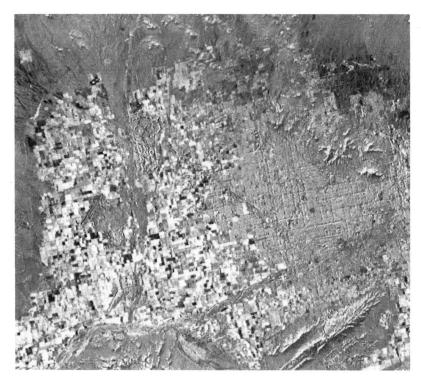

Figure 15.36.   Temporal-difference image of Phoenix, Arizona, and environs: the MSS band 7 image obtained 29 November 1974 subtracted from the 15 May 1974 image. Most of the changes are associated with seasonal vegetation because band 7 was used. Light signatures represent maximum responses in May and dark signatures represent maximum responses in November. (Courtesy Pat S. Chavez, Jr., U.S. Geological Survey.)

▨ MULTISENSOR IMAGE MERGING

The merging of images from different remote-sensing systems exploits the strengths or advantages of each system in a simultaneous image display. Within the past few years, the following multisensor images have been successfully combined in a variety of configurations:

1. Landsat RBV and MSS images
2. Landsat MSS and airborne multispectral, multipolarized radar images
3. Landsat MSS and Seasat radar images
4. Landsat MSS and SIR-A radar images
5. Seasat and SIR-A radar images

Plate 12 shows the results of combining a Landsat MSS infrared color-composite image (bands 4, 5, and 7) with a Landsat RBV image. The resulting high-resolution composite image was generated using a seven-step process (U.S. Geological Survey 1980):

1. Approximately 20 corresponding points were manually identified by line and sample coordinates on both the MSS and RBV images to establish a first-order (affine) transformation.
2. The transformation and bilinear interpolation were used to align the MSS data set with the RBV data set.
3. MSS bands 4, 5, and 7 were normalized by dividing each pixel in each band by the sum of the corresponding pixel values in all three bands. This, in effect, removes the brightness, or albedo information, from the MSS data while retaining the color, or spectral information.
4. The MSS data were scaled, using nearest-neighbor resampling, to the same grid and pixel size as the higher-resolution RBV data.
5. The brightness component was replaced in the MSS data at a finer resolution by multiplying each normalized MSS band by the RBV data.
6. Black-and-white positive transparencies were made for the new bands 4, 5, and 7.
7. The three black-and-white positive transparencies were made into the infrared color-composite image using standard photographic laboratory color-compositing techniques. The resulting composite incorporates the *spectral resolution* of the original MSS component and the *spatial resolution* of the RBV component; spatial resolution was improved approximately 2.6 times (MSS at 79 m and RBV at 30 m).

Chavez et al. (1983) successfully combined Landsat MSS and SIR-A images in various forms for geologic mapping of the Al Hisma Plateau of Saudi Arabia. They demonstrated that once the data sets were co-registered, three arithmetic transformations could be used to digitally combine the MSS and SIR-A data: (1) addition, (2) subtraction, and (3) ratioing (Figure 15.37). A correlation matrix then was used to identify the transformation that contained the most scene variance. Both the addition and ratioing transformations were selected by this process, and summed and ratioed color-composite images were generated for visual interpretation:

Summed Color-Composite Image
MSS 4 + SIR-A   (blue filtered light)
MSS 5 + SIR-A   (green filtered light)
MSS 7 + SIR-A   (red filtered light)

Ratioed Color-Composite Image
MSS 4 / SIR-A   (blue filtered light)
MSS 5 / SIR-A   (green filtered light)
MSS 7 / SIR-A   (red filtered light)

Both composite images proved useful for discriminating different lithologies and surficial deposits in the region because they incorporated both surface color information (MSS component) and surface texture information (SIR-A component) in simultaneous displays.

SYNTHETIC STEREOGRAPHIC LANDSAT MSS IMAGES

Stereoscopy is a powerful interpretation tool, but it has had only limited success with Landsat MSS images. This is because the images exhibit a weak stereoscopic effect and coverage is limited to small areas where there is overlap between orbital passes. However, by processing the images with digital terrain elevation data, a computer algorithm can introduce artificial parallax into a monoscopic image (single band or color composite) as a linear

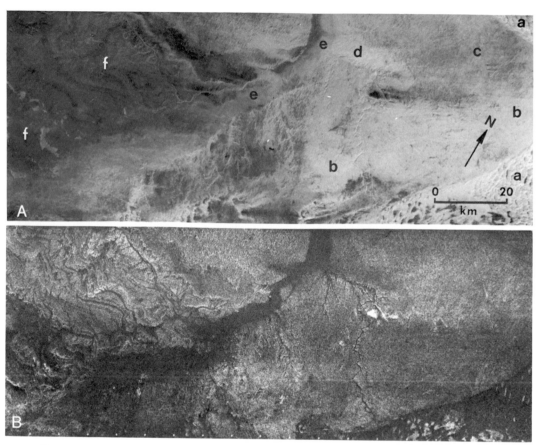

Figure 15.37. Digital merging of Landsat MSS band 7 and SIR-A images for the Al Hisma Plateau of Saudi Arabia. (A) Contrast-stretched MSS band 7 data-base image stenciled for common coverage with the SIR-A data-base image. (B) SIR-A image after digital registration to the MSS band 7 image. (C) Summed image produced by digitally adding the registered SIR-A image to the MSS band 7 image. (D) Differenced image produced by digitally subtracting the SIR-A image from the MSS band 7 image. (E) Ratioed image produced by dividing the MSS band 7 image with the SIR-A image. Annotations include: (a) An Nafud sand sea, (b) drift sand deposits, (c) exposed surface of the Tawil Sandstone, (d) sand dune field, (e) probable paleo channel of a now defunct trunk stream, (f) mesa and butte landscape of the Tabuk Formation (sandstone, shale, and siltstone). (Courtesy Pat S. Chavez, Jr., U.S. Geological Survey.)

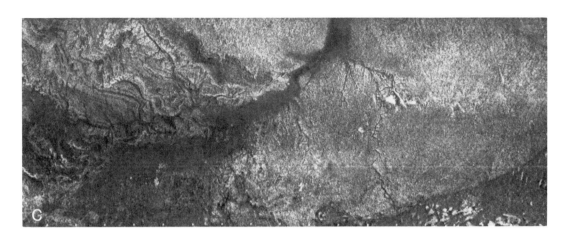

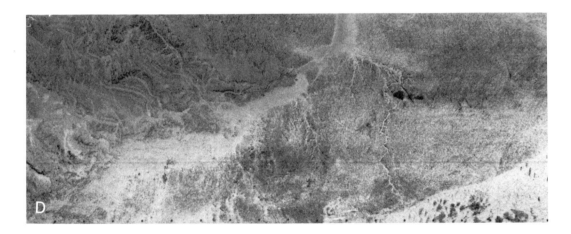

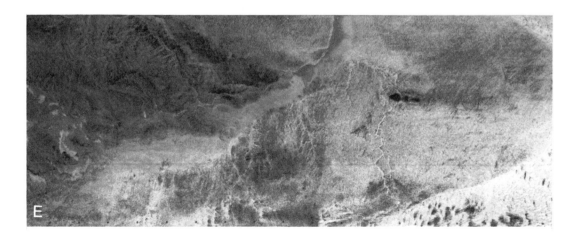

function of terrain height at each picture element (Batson et al. 1976) (Figure 15.38). A stereogram made from a single Landsat MSS band 7 image is shown in Figure 15.39.

Stereographic Landsat MSS images can also be generated by introducing relief displacement proportional to the magnitude of other data-set values, including residual aeromagnetic data, gravity data, and geochemical data (Figure 15.40). In fact, any continuous data set that is spatially related in X and Y directions and varies in the Z or vertical direction can be processed to create stereoscopic views showing the morphology of the data-set structure (Trautwein et al. 1982).

COMMERCIAL ENHANCEMENTS

In February 1979 the EROS Data Center began producing digitally enhanced Landsat MSS images with the EROS Digital Image Processing System (EDIPS). Standard EDIPS processing consists of four functions (Short 1982):

1. Radiometric correction of data to adjust for satellite and sensor anomalies (e.g., varying detector responses)
2. Geometrical correction and data resampling
3. Atmospheric haze removal

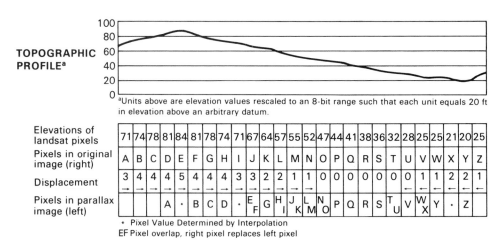

TOPOGRAPHIC PROFILE[a]

[a]Units above are elevation values rescaled to an 8-bit range such that each unit equals 20 ft in elevation above an arbitrary datum.

Elevations of landsat pixels	71	74	78	81	84	81	78	74	71	67	64	57	55	52	47	44	41	38	36	32	28	25	25	21	20	25
Pixels in original image (right)	A	B	C	D	E	F	G	H	I	J	K	L	M	N	O	P	Q	R	S	T	U	V	W	X	Y	Z
Displacement	3→	4→	4→	4→	5→	4→	4→	4→	3→	3→	2→	2→	1→	1→	0→	0→	0→	0→	0→	0→	0→	1←	1←	2←	2←	1←
Pixels in parallax image (left)				A	·	B	C	D	·	E/F	G	H/I	J/K	L/M	N/O	P	Q	R	S	T/U	V	W/X	Y	·	Z	

• Pixel Value Determined by Interpolation
EF Pixel overlap, right pixel replaces left pixel

Figure 15.38. Generation of artificial parallax for stereographic viewing. The topographic profile shows elevations along a single line of data in the digital topography data set as illustrated in the matrix below the profile. Elevation values can be related to Landsat MSS pixels in the same spatial position. By application of a stereographic generation equation, MSS pixels are shifted to create relief displacement that is proportional to the relief in the topographic profile. This results in a distorted image that when viewed stereoscopically with the original image produces a three-dimensional effect (Trautwein et al. 1982).

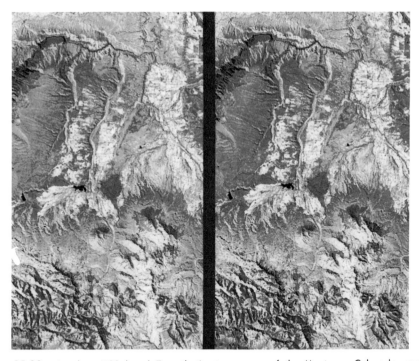

Figure 15.39. Landsat MSS band 7 synthetic stereogram of the Montrose, Colorado, region. Artificial stereoscopy was created from digital elevation data. The left-hand (distorted) image contains pixels that are shifted (proportional to elevation) to create relief displacement. (Courtesy Pat S. Chavez, Jr., U.S. Geological Survey.)

4. Display and analysis of the distribution of the DNs, leading to the mapping of image gray levels to preassigned film density levels via logarithmic tables

In addition, edge enhancement and user-defined contrast stretches can be performed by special request. EDIPS output includes film negatives and positives generated by laser beam recorders and CCTs. It is anticipated that EDIPS processing will be extended to TM images.

There are a number of companies and research organizations, primarily in North America and Europe, that offer comprehensive image-processing services. For MSS data, common enhancements include contrast stretching, edge enhancement, and band ratioing.

PROBLEMS

1. Discuss the advantages of an image-processing system that incorporates both interactive processing and batch processing.

2. Refer to Equation 15.3. If the minimum and maximum DN parameters

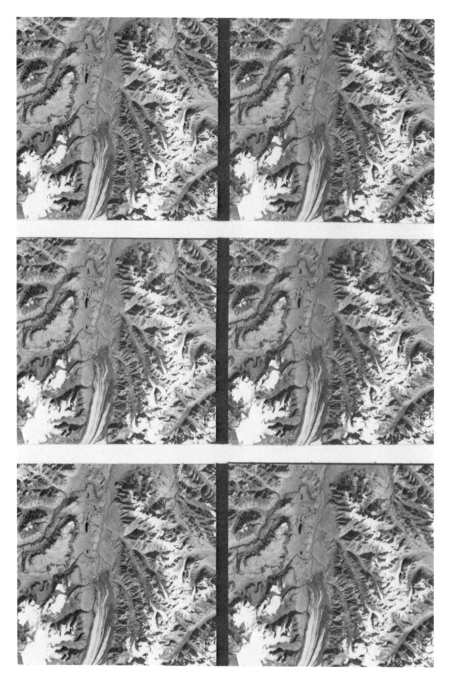

Figure 15.40.   Stereoscopically combined data sets for the Nabesna quadrangle region, Alaska. Parallax was digitally introduced into a Landsat MSS band 7 image as a function of residual aeromagnetic data (top stereogram), gravity data (middle stereogram), and geochemical copper data (bottom stereogram). (Courtesy Charles M. Trautwein, U.S. Geological Survey.)

are 16 and 106, what are the output (stretched) digital numbers when the original values are 42, 13, 94, and 111? Given the above minimum and maximum DN parameters, what type of contrast stretch is indicated?

3. Examine the DN histogram shown on page 457 and explain why a contrast stretch incorporating truncation might be appropriate. Also, devise an 8-bit sinusoidal stretch for the DN distribution shown based on histogram interpretation:

Sinusoidal Stretch Parameters

Input DN	Output DN
0	0
255	255

4. How does edge enhancement differ from high-pass spatial filtering?

5. Rank the following MSS ratios by their ability to highlight vegetation patterns. Justify your ranking heirarchy.

6/7 _____

7/5 _____

5/4 _____

6. What is the difference between image classification, multitemporal image classification, and multidimensional image classification?

References

Abrams, Michael J. 1980. Lithologic mapping. In *Remote sensing in geology.* John Wiley & Sons, New York, pp. 381–418, illus.

Barrett, Alan S. 1978. *An introduction to computer-assisted image processing and analysis.* Optronics International, Inc., Chelmsford, Mass., 13 pp., illus.

Batson, R. M., Kathleen Edwards, and E. M. Eliason. 1976. Synthetic stereo and Landsat pictures. *Photogrammetric Engineering and Remote Sensing* 42:1279–1284, illus.

Berlin, G. L., and P. S. Chavez, Jr. 1982. Structural evaluation of the eastern Grand Canyon region, Arizona, using Landsat-3 RBV/MSS standard and digitally enhanced images. In *Proceedings, international symposium on remote sensing of environment, second thematic conference.* Environmental Research Institute of Michigan, Ann Arbor, pp. 827–842, illus.

Berlin, G. L., P. S. Chavez, Jr., T. E. Grow, and L. A. Soderblom. 1976. Preliminary geologic analysis of southwest Jordan from computer enhanced Landsat-1 image data. In *Proceedings, 42nd annual meeting.* American Society of Photogrammetry, Falls Church, Va., pp. 545–564, illus.

Berlin, G. L., M. A. Tarabzouni, and Z. M. Munshi. 1982. Vegetation assessment of the northern Arabian Shield for ground-water exploration using edge-enhanced MSS images. In *Proceedings, 16th international symposium on remote sensing of environment.* Environmental Research Institute of Michigan, Ann Arbor, pp. 539–547, illus.

Blodget, H. W., F. J. Gunther, and M. H. Podwysocki. 1978. *Discrimination of rock classes and alteration products in southwestern Saudi Arabia with computer-enhanced Landsat data.* Government Printing Office, Washington, D.C. NASA Technical Paper 1327, 35 pp., illus.

Chavez, P. S., Jr. 1975. Atmospheric, solar, and MTF corrections for ERTS digital imagery. In *Proceedings, American Society of Photogrammetry.* American Society of Photogrammetry, Falls Church, Va., pp. 69–69a.

Chavez, P. S., Jr., and B. Bauer. 1982. An automatic optimum kernal-size selection technique for edge enhancement. *Remote Sensing of Environment* 12:23–38, illus.

Chavez, P. S., Jr., G. L. Berlin, and A. V. Acosta. 1977b. Computer processing of Landsat MSS digital data for linear enhancements. In *Proceedings, second annual William T. Pecora memorial symposium.* American Society of Photogrammetry, Falls Church, Va., pp. 235–250, illus.

Chavez, P. S., Jr., G. L. Berlin, and W. B. Mitchell. 1977a. Computer enhancement techniques of Landsat MSS digital images for land use/land cover assessments. In *Remote sensing of earth resources,* Vol. 6. University of Tennessee Space Institute, Tullahoma, pp. 259–275, illus.

Chavez, P. S., Jr., G. L. Berlin, and L. B. Sowers. 1982. Statistical method for selecting Landsat MSS ratios. *Journal of Applied Photographic Engineering* 8:23–30, illus.

Chavez, P. S., Jr., G. L. Berlin, and M. A. Tarabzouni. 1983. Discriminating lithologies and surficial deposits in the Al Hisma Plateau region of Saudi Arabia with digitally combined Landsat MSS and SIR-A images. In *Proceedings, national conference on resource management applications: energy and environment.* Center for Earth Resource Management Applications, Springfield, Va., vol. 4, pp. 22–34, illus.

Chavez, P. S., Jr., S. C. Guptill, and J. A. Bowell. 1984. Image processing techniques for Thematic Mapper data. In *Proceedings, 50th annual meeting.* American Society of Photogrammetry, Falls Church, Va., vol. 2, pp. 728–743, illus.

Condit, C. D. and P. S. Chavez, Jr. 1979. *Basic concepts of computerized digital image processing for geologists.* Government Printing Office, Washington, D.C. Geological Survey Bulletin 1462, 16 pp., illus.

Eliason, E. M., P. S. Chavez, Jr., and L. A. Soderblom. 1974. Simulated "true color" images for ERTS data. *Geology* 2:231–234, illus.

Eliason, P. T., T. J. Donovan, and P. S. Chavez, Jr. 1983. Integration of geologic, geochemical, and geophysical data of the Cement oil field, Oklahoma, using spatial array processing. *Geophysics* 48:1305–1317, illus.

Fleming, M. D., J. S. Berkebile, and R. M. Hoffer. 1975. Computer-aided analysis of Landsat-1 MSS data: a comparison of three approaches, including a "modified clustering" approach. Purdue University, West Lafayette, Ind., LARS Information Note 072475, 10 pp., illus.

Gillespie, Alan R. 1980. Digital techniques of image enhancement. In *Remote sensing in geology.* John Wiley & Sons, New York, pp. 139–226, illus.

Holm, T. M. 1982. Canonical analysis: *The use of transformed Landsat data for crop type discrimination.* U.S. Geological Survey, Sioux Falls, S. Dak., 72 pp., illus.

———. 1983. Canonical analysis of crop type discrimination. In *Proceedings, ninth international symposium on machine processing of remotely sensed data.* Purdue University, West Lafayette, Ind., p. 216.

Hutchinson, Charles F. 1982. Techniques for combining Landsat and ancillary data for digital classification improvement. *Photogrammetric Engineering and Remote Sensing* 48:123–130, illus.

Jensen, Susan K. and Frederick A. Waltz. 1979. Principal components analysis and canonical analysis in remote sensing. In *Proceedings, 45th annual meeting.* American Society of Photogrammetry, Falls Church, Va., pp. 337–348, illus.

Landgrebe, D. A. 1974. Machine processing of remotely sensed data. In *Syllabus, workshop on remote sensing and image interpretation.* U.S. Geological Survey, Sioux Falls, S. Dak., Open File Report 75-196, Section 14, pp. 1–36, illus.

LaPado, R., C. Reader, and L. Hubble. 1978. *Image processing displays: A report on commercially available state-of-the-art features.* ESL, Inc., Sunnyvale, Calif., 88 pp.

Lillesand, Thomas M. and Ralph W. Kiefer. 1979. *Remote sensing and image interpretation.* John Wiley & Sons, New York, 612 pp., illus.

Lyon, R. J. P. 1977. Mineral exploration applications of digitally processed Landsat imagery. In *Proceedings, first annual William T. Pecora memorial symposium.* Government Printing Office, Washington, D.C. Geological Survey Professional Paper 1015, pp. 271–292, illus.

Lyons, Esmond C., Jr. 1977. Digital image processing: An overview. *Computer* 10:10–24, illus.

Moik, Johannes G. 1980. *Digital processing of remotely sensed images.* Government Printing Office, Washington, D.C. NASA Special Paper 431, 330 pp., illus.

Raines, G. L., T. W. Offield, and E. S. Santos. 1978. Remote sensing and subsurface definition of facies and structure related to uranium deposits, Powder River Basin, Wyoming. *Economic Geology* 73:1706–1723, illus.

Rohde, W. G., J. K. Lo, and R. A. Pohl. 1978. EROS Data Center Landsat digital enhancement techniques and imagery availability. *Canadian Journal of Remote Sensing* 4:63–76, illus.

Rosenfeld, Azriel and Avinash C. Kak. 1982. *Digital picture processing.* 2nd ed. Academic Press, New York, 848 pp., illus.

Rowan, L. C., P. H. Wetlaufer, A. F. H. Goetz, F. C. Billingsley, and J. H. Stewart. 1974. *Discrimination of rock types and detection of hydrothermally altered areas in south-central Nevada by the use of computer-enhanced ERTS images.* Government Printing Office, Washington, D.C. Geological Survey Professional Paper 883, 35 pp., illus.

Sabins, Floyd F., Jr. 1978. *Remote sensing principles and interpretation.* W. H. Freeman & Co., San Francisco, 426 pp., illus.

Santisteban, A. and L. Munoz. 1978. Principal components of a multispectral image: Application to a geological problem. *IBM Journal of Research and Development* 22:444–454, illus.

Schowengerdt, Robert A. 1983. *Techniques for image processing and classification in remote sensing.* Academic Press, New York, 249 pp., illus.

Short, Nicholas M. 1982. *The Landsat tutorial workbook,* Government Printing Office, Washington, D.C. NASA Reference Publication 1078, 553 pp., illus.

Spirakis, C. S. and C. D. Condit. 1975. *Preliminary report of the use of Landsat-1 (ERTS-1) reflectance data in locating alteration zones associated with uranium mineralization near Cameron, Arizona.* U.S. Geological Survey, Reston, Va., Open File Report 75-416, 23 pp., illus.

Strahler, A. H., T. L. Logan, and N. A. Bryant. 1978. Improving forest cover classification accuracy from Landsat by introducing topographic information. In *Proceedings, 12th international symposium on remote sensing of environment.*

Environmental Research Institute of Michigan, Ann Arbor, pp. 727–742, illus.

Taranik, James V. 1978. *Principles of computer processing of Landsat data for geologic applications.* U.S. Geological Survey, Sioux Falls, S. Dak., Open File Report 78-117, 50 pp., illus.

Trautwein, Charles M., David D. Greenlee, and Donald G. Orr. 1982. *Digital data base application to porphyry copper mineralization in Alaska-case study summary.* U.S. Geological Survey, Sioux Falls, S. Dak., Open File Report 82-801, 14 pp., illus.

U.S. Geological Survey. 1980. Landsat-3 MSS-RBV false-color composite image of the San Francisco area. EROS Data Center, Sioux Falls, S. Dak.

———. 1983. *20th international remote sensing workshop, quantitative remote sensing.* EROS Data Center, Sioux Falls, S. Dak., 24 pp., illus.

Welch, Roy A., Thomas R. Jordan, and E. Lynn Usery. 1983. Microcomputers in the mapping sciences. *Computer Graphics World* 6:33–39, illus.

Williams, Richard S. 1983. Geological applications. In *Manual of remote sensing.* 2nd ed. American Society of Photogrammetry, Falls Church, Va., pp. 1667–1953, illus.

Glossary of Selected Photogrammetric and Remote-Sensing Terms

ACTIVE REMOTE SENSING Remote-sensing systems that provide their own radiation output (e.g., active radar).

ADDITIVE COLOR VIEWER Projector for black-and-white positive transparencies obtained from a multiband camera or multispectral scanner. Transparencies, in groups of three, are superimposed on a viewing screen by the use of blue, green, and red filtered light.

AERIAL PHOTOGRAPH, OBLIQUE A photograph taken with the camera axis directed between the horizontal and the vertical (1) *high oblique:* An oblique photograph in which the apparent horizon is shown. (2) *low oblique:* An oblique photograph in which the apparent horizon is not shown. (MRS)[1]

AERIAL PHOTOGRAPH, VERTICAL An aerial photograph made with the optical axis of the camera perpendicular to the ground and the film horizontal.

AIR BASE The imaginary line joining two aerial camera stations; specifically the length of such a line.

ALGORITHM (1) A fixed step-by-step procedure to accomplish a given result; usually a simplified procedure for solving a complex problem; also a full statement of a finite number of steps. (2) A computer-oriented procedure for resolving a problem. (MRS)

1. Many of the terms are taken from the *Manual of Photogrammetry* (4th edition) and the *Manual of Remote Sensing* (2nd edition) by permission of the American Society of Photogrammetry. These terms are identified, respectively, as MP and MRS.

ALTITUDE Height of a sensor platform above a datum, usually mean sea level.

ANAGLYPH A stereogram in which the two views are printed superimposed in complementary colors. A three-dimensional image is rendered when the stereogram is viewed through spectacles having filters of the same two colors (usually red and green).

ANCILLARY DATA In remote sensing, secondary data pertaining to the area or classes of interest, such as topographical, demographic, or climatological data. Ancillary data may be digitized and used in the analysis process in conjunction with the primary remote-sensing data. (MRS)

ANGLE OF COVERAGE The apex of the cone of rays passing through the front nodal point of a lens. *Normal-angle lens:* a lens having an angle of coverage up to 75°; *wide-angle lens:* a lens having an angle of coverage of 75° to 100°; *ultrawide-angle lens:* a lens having an angle of coverage greater than 100°. (MP)

APERTURE, RELATIVE The ratio of the equivalent focal length to the diameter of the entrance "pupil" of a photographic lens (e.g., f/4.5). Also called *f/number, f/stop, aperture stop, diaphragm stop, speed.* (MRS)

BAND (1) A selection of wavelengths. (2) Frequency band. (3) Absorption band. (4) A group of tracks on a magnetic drum. (5) A range of radar frequencies, such as X-band or L-band. (MRS)

BASE, FILM A thin, flexible, transparent sheet of stable plastic material. (MP)

BASE, PHOTO The distance between the principal points of two adjacent prints of a series of vertical aerial photographs. It is usually measured on one print after transferring the principal point of the other print. (MRS)

BATCH PROCESSING The method of data processing in which data and programs are entered into a computer which then carries out the entire operation with no further instructions. (MRS)

BLACKBODY Theoretical object that is both a perfect absorber and a perfect radiator or emitter; its emissivity is 1. All other bodies (*graybodies*) are less efficient absorbers and radiators, and their emissivities are always less than 1.

CAMERA A lightproof chamber or box in which the image of an exterior object is projected upon a sensitized plate or film, through an opening usually equipped with a *lens* or *lenses, shutter,* and *variable aperture. Aerial camera:* A camera specially designed for use in aircraft. (MP)

CAMERA, MULTIBAND A camera that exposes different areas of one film, or more than one film, through one lens and a beam splitter, or two or more lenses equipped with different filters, to provide two or more photographs in different spectral bands. (MRS)

CAMERA, PANORAMIC A camera with a very wide angle of view, up to horizon to horizon, usually by means of a moving (sweeping) lens. (MRS)

CAMERA STATION The point in space, in the air or on the ground, occupied by the camera lens at the moment of exposure. Also called the exposure station. In aerial photography the camera station is called the "air station." (MRS)

COLOR COMPOSITE A color picture produced by assigning a color to a particular spectral band. In Landsat, blue is ordinarily assigned to MSS band 4 (0.5–0.6 μm), green to band 5 (0.6–0.7 μm), and red to band 7 (0.8–1.1 μm), to form a picture closely approximating an infrared color photograph. (MRS)

COLOR FILM Photographic film composed of three emulsion layers sensitized to the three primary colors of the visible spectrum: blue, green, and red (0.4–0.7 μm). When properly exposed and processed, the color rendition closely approximates the original scene as viewed by the human eye. For this reason, the film goes by various names: *normal color, conventional color,* and *natural color.*

CONTACT PRINT A print made from a negative or a diapositive in direct contact with sensitized material. (MRS)

CONTRAST, SUBJECT The difference in light intensity between the brightest highlights and the deepest shadow.

CONTROL POINT A reference point precisely located on a photograph and on the ground; used in assembly of photographs for map compilation.

CROSSOVER, THERMAL Two periods in the diurnal cycle when an object's heat emission coincides with the background because of differential heating and cooling effects. The two periods occur shortly after dawn and shortly before sunset. If at all possible, thermal infrared missions are scheduled for time frames removed from crossover periods.

DATA-SET MERGING Computer routines that integrate multiple sets of data from the same location such that congruent measurements can be made. Representative types of information include geographical, geological, geophysical, geochemical, and multispectral radiance data.

DATA TRANSFORMATION Mathematical techniques used to minimize spectral redundancy in the informational content of multispectral images, while reducing or compressing the dimensionality of the data (*principal components analysis* and *canonical analysis*).

DENSITOMETER A device for measuring the density of an image. The instrument measures the magnitude of the light transmitted through the film. A *microdensitometer* is a special type of densitometer for determining densities in very small areas.

DEPTH OF FIELD The distance between the points nearest to and farthest from the camera that are in focus and acceptably "sharp."

DIAPOSITIVE A positive photographic print on a transparent medium, usually glass. Most commonly used in stereoplotting instruments.

DIGITAL COMPUTER A computer that is capable of executing and performing operations on data represented in digital or numerical form as opposed to an analog computer which accepts input data represented by voltage variations.

DIGITAL IMAGE A two-dimensional array of small areas called *picture elements* or *pixels* that correspond spatially to relatively small ground areas called *ground resolution cells.*

DIGITAL IMAGE PROCESSING   Computer operations applied to digital image data to execute functions such as restoration, enhancement, and classification.

DIGITIZATION   The process of converting film density variations into digital numbers (DNs) for computer processing.

DISTORTION   Any shift in the position of an image on a photograph which alters the perspective characteristics of the photograph. Causes of image distortion include lens aberration, differential shrinkage of film or paper, and motion of the film or camera. (MP)

DISPLACEMENT   Any shift in the position of an image on a photograph that does not alter the perspective characteristics of the photograph (i.e., shift due to tilt of the photograph, scale change in the photograph, and relief of the objects photographed). (MP)

DODGING   A process used while enlarging photographs by projection. Light that passes through certain parts of the negative is held back, and prevented from striking the sensitized paper. Manual dodging is done by holding a piece of opaque material between the enlarger lens and the easel. Electronic dodging is produced by feedback of signal voltage through the negative or positive to be printed to minimize density variations of produced materials. (MP)

DOT GRID   Film positive containing regularly spaced dots for determining areas; also called *dot planimeter*.

EFFECTIVE AREA OF AERIAL PHOTOGRAPH   That central part of the photograph delimited by the bisectors of overlaps with adjacent photographs. On a vertical photograph, all images within the effective area have less displacement than their corresponding images on adjacent photographs. (MP)

ELECTROMAGNETIC RADIATION (EMR)   Energy propagated through space or through material media in the form of an advancing disturbance in electric and magnetic fields existing in space or in the media. The term *radiation*, alone, is used commonly for this type of energy, although it actually has a broader meaning. Also called *electromagnetic energy*. (MP)

ELECTROMAGNETIC SPECTRUM   The ordered array of known electromagnetic radiations extending from the shortest cosmic rays, through gamma rays, X-rays, ultraviolet radiation, visible radiation, infrared radiation, and including microwave and all other wavelengths of radio energy. (MRS)

ELECTRO-OPTICAL SCANNER   A nonphotographic imaging system that, through a rotating or oscillating mirror, views a series of narrow ground strips at right angles to the line of flight. The forward motion of the sensor platform causes new ground strips to be covered by successive scan lines, thus building up a two-dimensional record of reflectance or emittance information.

EMISSIVITY   Ratio expression of the energy radiated from an object at a given temperature in relationship to the radiation emitted from a *blackbody* at the same temperature.

EMULSION (PHOTOGRAPHY) A suspension of a light-sensitive silver salt (especially silver chloride or silver bromide) in a colloidal medium (usually gelatin), which is used for coating photographic films, plates, and papers. (MP)

EXPOSURE The total quantity of light received per unit area on a sensitized plate or film. Also, the act of exposing a light-sensitive material to a light source.

FIDUCIAL MARKS Index marks (usually four), rigidly connected with the camera lens through the camera body, which form images on the negative. The intersection of lines drawn between opposite fiducial marks defines the *principal point* of the photograph.

FILTER Any material which, by absorption or reflection, selectively modifies the radiation transmitted through an optical system. (MRS)

FILTERING In analysis, the removal of certain spectral or spatial frequencies to highlight features in the remaining image. (MRS)

FOCAL LENGTH The distance measured along the optical axis from the optical center (near *nodal point*) of the lens to the plane of critical focus of a very distant object. (MRS)

FOCUS The point at which the rays from a point source of light reunite and cross after passing through a camera lens. In practice, the plane in which a sharp image of any scene is formed. (MRS)

GEOGRAPHIC INFORMATION SYSTEM Computer-based system that is designed to accept, organize, statistically analyze, and display diverse types of spatial information that are digitally referenced to a common coordinate system.

GLOSSY PRINT Print made on photographic paper having a shiny surface; usually more suitable for interpretation than a *matte print.*

GROUND DATA Supporting data collected on the ground, and information derived therefrom, as an aid to the interpretation of remotely recorded surveys, such as aerial imagery. Generally, this should be performed concurrently with the aerial surveys. Data regarding weather, soils, and vegetation types and conditions are typical. (MRS)

GROUND INFORMATION Information derived from *ground data* and *surveys* to support interpretation of remotely sensed data. (MRS)

GROUND RESOLUTION CELL The area on the terrain that is covered by the instantaneous field of view of a detector. The size of the ground resolution cell is determined by the altitude of the remote-sensing system and the instaneous field of view of the detector. (MRS)

GROUND TRUTH (JARGON) Term coined for data and information obtained on surface or subsurface features to aid in interpretation of remotely sensed data. *Ground data* and *ground information* are preferred terms. (MRS)

HOMOLOGOUS PHOTOGRAPHS Two or more overlapping photographs having different camera stations. (MP)

HOTSPOT (SUNSPOT)   The destruction of fine image detail on a portion of an aerial photograph. It is caused by the absence of shadows and by halation near the prolongation of a line from the sun through the exposure station.

IMAGE   The permanent record of the likeness of any natural or man-made features, objects, and activities. Images can be acquired directly on photographic materials using cameras, or indirectly if nonimaging types of sensors have been used in data collection. (MP)

IMAGE CLASSIFICATION   Quantitative decision rules that classify or identify objects or patterns on the basis of their multispectral radiance values; as such the normal output is analogous to an image map requiring no visual interpretation.

IMAGE ENHANCEMENT   Computer routines that improve the detectability of objects or patterns in a digital image for visual interpretation. Operations include contrast stretching, spatial filtering, edge enhancement, and ratioing.

IMAGE RESTORATION   Computer routines that correct a degraded digital image to its intended form. Also called *preprocessing* or *clean-up*.

IMAGERY   The products of image-forming instruments (analogous to *photography*). (MRS)

INFRARED BLACK-AND-WHITE FILM   Photographic film primarily sensitive to the spectral region between 0.4 and 0.9 μm. The film's infrared sensitivity is best described as "near infrared" because it utilizes only a narrow band (0.7 to 0.9 μm) of the total infrared spectrum.

INFRARED COLOR FILM   Photographic film composed of three emulsion layers sensitized to green, red, and near-infrared radiation (0.5 to 0.9 μm). A yellow filter is always placed over the camera lens to absorb blue light to which the three emulsion layers are also sensitive.

INFRARED SPECTRUM   Pertaining to energy in the 0.7- to 1,000-μm region of the electromagnetic spectrum; that portion of the electromagnetic spectrum situated between the visible and microwave regions.

INSTANTANEOUS FIELD OF VIEW (IFOV)   A term specifically denoting the narrow field of view designed into detectors, particularly scanning radiometer systems, so that, while as much as 120° may be under scan, only electromagnetic radiation from a small area is being recorded at any one instant. (MRS)

INTERACTIVE IMAGE PROCESSING   The use of an operator or analyst at a console that provides the means of assessing, preprocessing, feature extracting, classifying, identifying, and displaying the original imagery or the processed imagery for subjective evaluations and further interactions. (MRS)

INTERVALOMETER   A timing device for automatically operating the shutter of a camera at selected intervals. (MP)

INVERTED TOPOGRAPHY   A reversal of the normal stereoscopic effect, whereby valleys appear as mountains and mountains appear as valleys. It normally occurs when a photograph or image is oriented so that the shadows fall away from the interpreter. Also called *pseudoscopic view*.

LIGHT   Visible radiation (about 0.4–0.7 μm in wavelength) considered in terms of its luminous efficiency (i.e., evaluated in proportion to its ability to stimulate the sense of sight). (MRS)

MAPPING PHOTOGRAPHY   Aerial photography obtained by precisely calibrated *mapping cameras* and conforming to mapping specifications, as distinguished from aerial photography for other purposes. Also called *aerial cartographic photography, cartographic photography; charting photography; survey photography.* (MP)

MATTE PRINT   Print made on photographic paper having a dull (non-reflective) finish; more suitable for pencil or ink annotations than a *glossy print.*

MICROWAVE SPECTRUM   The portion of the electromagnetic spectrum between about 1 m and 1 mm in wavelength, bounded on the short wavelength side by the far infrared and on the long wavelength side by radio waves. (MRS)

MOSAIC, CONTROLLED   A mosaic that is laid to ground control and uses prints that have been rectified as shown to be necessary by the control. (MRS)

MOSAICKING   The assembling of photographs or other images whose edges are cut and matched to form a continuous photographic representation of a portion of the earth's surface. (MRS)

MULTIDIMENSIONAL IMAGE CLASSIFICATION   Process of combining multispectral image data with certain types of *ancillary information* (e.g., topographic information) to improve the accuracy of image classification algorithms.

MULTISPECTRAL REMOTE SENSING   Employment of one or more sensors to obtain simultaneous imagery from different portions (bands) of the electromagnetic spectrum.

MULTISPECTRAL SCANNER   An electro-optical sensor that is capable of operating simultaneously in the ultraviolet, visible, reflected infrared, and thermal infrared regions of the electromagnetic spectrum. The number of spectral channels or bands can range from fewer than 10 to more than 20.

MULTITEMPORAL IMAGE CLASSIFICATION   Process of combining multispectral images acquired on different dates to improve the accuracy of image classification algorithms.

NADIR   That point on the celestial sphere vertically below the observer, or 180° from the zenith. (2) That point on the ground vertically beneath the perspective of the camera lens. (MRS)

ORTHOPHOTOGRAPH   A photograph copy prepared from a perspective photograph, in which the displacements of images due to a tilt and relief have been removed.

PANCHROMATIC FILM (PAN FILM)   Photographic black-and-white film having approximately the same range of wavelength sensitivity as that of the human eye (0.4–0.7 μm).

PARALLAX The apparent displacement of the position of a body, with respect to a reference point or system, caused by a shift in the point of observation. (MP)

PARALLAX WEDGE A simplified *stereometer* for measuring object heights on stereoscopic pairs of photographs. It consists of two slightly converging rows of dots or graduated lines printed on a transparent templet that can be stereoscopically fused into a single row or line for making parallax measurements. (MP)

PASSIVE REMOTE SENSING Remote-sensing systems that are dependent upon natural sources of external energy such as solar radiation or thermal infrared emissions (e.g., electro-optical sensors).

PHOTOGRAMMETRY The art or science of obtaining reliable measurements by means of photography. (MRS)

PHOTOGRAPH A picture formed by the action of light on a base material coated with a sensitized solution that is chemically treated to fix the image points at the desired density. Usually now taken to mean the direct action of electromagnetic radiation on the sensitized material. Compare *image*. (MRS)

PHOTOGRAPHIC DAY One with good visibility, bright sunlight, and less than 10 percent cloud cover.

PHOTOGRAPHIC INTERPRETATION The act of examining photographic images to identify objects and judge their significance. *Photo interpretation*, and *image interpretation* are other widely used terms. (MRS)

PHOTOGRAPHIC INTERPRETATION KEY Reference material designed to facilitate the rapid, accurate identification of features from a study of their photographic images. The key usually consists of two parts: (a) image examples and (b) a word description.

PHOTOGRAPHY The art, science, and process of producing images on sensitized material through the action of light. The term *photography* is sometimes incorrectly used in place of *photographs;* however, the distinction between the process and the product is a valuable one and should be observed. (MP)

PIXEL (Derived from *picture element*.) A data element having both spatial and spectral aspects. The spatial variable defines the apparent size of the resolution cell (i.e., the area on the ground represented by the data values), and the spectral variable defines the intensity of the spectral response for that cell in a particular channel. (MRS)

PLANIMETER An instrument used to measure the area of any figure by passing a tracer around its boundaries and recording the area encompassed. (MP)

PROJECTIONS A systematic drawing of lines on a plane surface to represent the *parallels* of latitude and the *meridians* of longitude of the earth or a section of the earth. (MP)

PUSHBROOM SCANNER A new generation sensing system that forms images without moving optics (e.g., scanning mirror) and offers high spatial and spectral resolution. A pushbroom scanner employs numerous and very small solid-state detector elements that are closely packed in one-dimensional linear arrays orthogonal to the flight path. There is typically one array for each spectral band.

QUADRANGLE   A rectangular, or nearly so, area covered by a map or plat, usually bounded by given meridians of longitude and parallels of latitude. Sometimes shortened to *quad;* also called *quadrangle map.* (MP)

RADAR   (1) The principle of locating targets or objects by the measurement of reflections of radio-frequency energy from them. (2) A term applied to devices and systems that make use of this principle. Acronym for *radio detection and ranging.* (MP)

RADAR, IMAGING   An active remote-sensing device that transmits pulses of microwave energy and then receives reflections of the signal from a target. The reflected component is called the *echo* or *backscatter.*

RADAR DETECTION   A measure of the smallest object that can be discerned in a radar image as a result of its ability to reflect microwave energy.

RADAR RESOLUTION   The minimum ground separation between two targets of equal reflectivity that will enable them to appear individually in a processed radar image.

RADIOMETER   An instrument for quantitively measuring the intensity of electromagnetic radiation in some band of wavelengths in any part of the electromagnetic spectrum. Usually used with a modifier, such as an infrared radiometer or a microwave radiometer. (MRS)

RECTIFICATION, PHOTOGRAPH   The process of converting a tilted or oblique photograph to the plane of the vertical.

REMOTE SENSING   In the broadest sense, the measurement or acquisition of information of some property of an object or phenomenon, by a recording device that is not in physical contact with the object under study; for example, the use at a distance (as from an aircraft, spacecraft, or ship) of any device for gathering information pertinent to the environment, such as measurements of force fields, electromagnetic radiation, or acoustic energy. The technique employs such devices as cameras, lasers, and radio receivers, radar systems, sonar, seismographs, gravimeters, magnetometers, and scintillation counters. (MRS)

RESOLVING POWER   A mathematical expression of lens definition; usually stated as the maximum number of lines per millimetre that can be resolved (or seen as separate lines) in an image.

SCALE   The ratio of a distance on a photograph or map to its corresponding distance on the ground. The scale of a photograph varies from point to point because of displacements caused by tilt and relief, but is usually taken as f/H where f is the principal distance of the camera and H is the height of the camera above mean ground elevation. Scale may be expressed as a ratio, 1:24,000; a representative fraction, 1/24,000; or an equivalence, 1 in. = 2,000 ft (MP)

SEMIMATTE PRINT   A print intermediate in glossiness between a *glossy* and *matte* print.

SIGNATURE   The characteristics or patterns of physical features that permit objects to be recognized on aerial imagery. A category is said to have a signature only if the characteristic pattern is highly representative of all units of that category.

SOFTWARE   A set of computer programs, procedures, and possibly associated documentation concerned with the operation of a data-processing system. (MP)

SPECTRAL BAND   An interval in the electromagnetic spectrum defined by two wavelengths, frequencies, or wave numbers. (MRS)

STEREOMETER   A measuring device containing a micrometer movement by means of which the separation of two *index marks* can be changed to measure parallax difference on a stereoscopic pair of photographs. Also called *parallax bar*. (MP)

STEREOSCOPE   An optical instrument that deflects normally converging lines of sight so that each eye views a different photographic image, resulting in a three-dimensional effect. The instruments are of three general types: lens stereoscopes, mirror or reflecting stereoscopes, and zoom magnifying stereoscopes.

STEREOSCOPIC COVERAGE   Aerial photography acquired with sufficient overlap to permit complete stereoscopic analysis. Flights are planned so that photographs will overlap about 60 percent of their width in the line of flight and 20 to 30 percent between flight strips.

STEREOSCOPIC PLOTTING INSTRUMENT or STEREOSCOPIC PLOTTER   An instrument for plotting a map or obtaining spatial solutions by observation of stereoscopic models formed by stereopairs of photographs. (MP)

STEREOSCOPY   The science and art that deals with the use of *binocular vision* for observation of a pair of overlapping photographs or other perspective views, and with the methods by which such viewing is produced. (MP)

SYNTHETIC STEREO IMAGE   A stereo model made by digital processing of a single image. Topographic data are used in calculating the geometric distortion. (MRS)

TEMPERATURE or THERMAL RESOLUTION   The smallest distinguishable radiant temperature difference between an object and its background. The thermal resolution of state-of-the-art thermal infrared scanners is on the order of ± 0.1 °C.

TEMPLET (TEMPLATE)   A device used in radial triangulation to represent the aerial photograph; the templet is a record of radial directions taken from the photographs.

TEXTURE   In a photo image, the frequency of change and arrangement of tones. Some descriptive adjectives for textures are fine, medium, or coarse; and stippled or mottled. (MRS)

THERMAL INFRARED SCANNER   An electro-optical sensor that has an operational sensitivity to one or both of the thermal infrared "windows" (*broadband thermal infrared*) or to multiple channels in the 8- to 14-μm wavelength region *(multispectral thermal infrared)*.

TONE   Each distinguishable shade of gray from white to black on an image. (MRS)

TRANSPARENCY   A photographic print on a clear base, especially adaptable for viewing by transmitted light. Also, the light-transmitting capability of a material. (MP)

VERTICAL EXAGGERATION   An increase or decrease in the vertical dimension of the perceived stereo model when compared to its horizontal dimension ratio of the actual object. (MP)

VIDICON CAMERA   A nonphotographic system whereby a latent image is temporarily stored on a photoconductive faceplate and is scanned by an internal election beam. This process creates a series of electronic signals which, in a satellite, are telemetered to earth stations, where they are used to produce visible images on photographic film or on a television screen.

VIGNETTING FILTER   A filter that gradually decreases in density from the center toward the edges. It is used in photography or printing processes to produce a photograph of uniform density.

WINDOW   A band of the electromagnetic spectrum that offers maximum transmission and minimal attenuation through a particular medium with the use of a specific sensor. (MRS)

Index

Student Survey

Thomas Eugene Avery & Graydon Lennis Berlin
INTERPRETATION OF AERIAL PHOTOGRAPHS,
FOURTH EDITION

Students, send us your ideas!

The authors and the publisher want to know how well this book served you and what can be done to improve it for those who will use it in the future. By completing and returning this questionnaire, you can help us develop better textbooks. We value your opinion and want to hear your comments. Thank you.

Your name (optional) _____ School _____

Your mailing address _____

City _____ State _____ ZIP _____

Instructor's name (optional) _____ Course title _____

1. How does this book compare with other texts you have used? (Check one)
   ☐ Superior   ☐ Better than most   ☐ Comparable   ☐ Not as good as most

2. Circle those chapters you especially liked:
   Chapters: 1   2   3   4   5   6   7   8   9   10   11   12   13   14   15
   Comments:

3. Circle those chapters you think could be improved:
   Chapters: 1   2   3   4   5   6   7   8   9   10   11   12   13   14   15
   Comments:

4. Please rate the following (check one for each line):

	Excellent	Good	Average	Poor
Readability of text material	( )	( )	( )	( )
Logical organization	( )	( )	( )	( )
General layout and design	( )	( )	( )	( )
Up-to-date treatment of subject	( )	( )	( )	( )

Match with instructor's course organization ( ) ( ) ( ) ( )
Illustrations that clarify the text ( ) ( ) ( ) ( )
Selection of topics ( ) ( ) ( ) ( )
Explanation of difficult concepts ( ) ( ) ( ) ( )

5. List any chapters that your instructor did not assign. _____

_____

6. What additional topics did your instructor discuss that were not covered in the text?

_____

7. Did you buy this book new or used? □ New □ Used
Do you plan to keep the book or sell it? □ Keep it □ Sell it
Do you think your instructor should continue to assign this book? □ Yes □ No

8. After taking the course, are you interested in taking more courses in this field?
□ Yes □ No
Did you take this course to fulfill a requirement, or as an elective?
□ Required □ Elective

9. What is your major? _____
Your class rank? □ Freshman □ Sophomore □ Junior
□ Senior □ Other, specify:

10. GENERAL COMMENTS:

May we quote you in our advertising? □ Yes □ No

Please remove this page and mail to: Editorial Department
Burgess Publishing Company
7108 Ohms Lane
Minneapolis, MN 55435

THANK YOU!